Econometrics
Alchemy or Science?

To Bob and Rena,
who began this development

Econometrics
Alchemy or Science?

Essays in Econometric Methodology

David F. Hendry

BLACKWELL
Oxford UK & Cambridge USA

First Published 1993

Blackwell Publishers
108 Cowley Road
Oxford OX4 1JF
UK

238 Main Street
Suite 501
Cambridge, MA 02142
USA

British Library Cataloguing-in-Publication Data
A CIP catalogue record for this book is available from the British Library.

Library of Congress Cataloging-in-Publication Data
Hendry, David F.
   Econometrics: alchemy or science?   Essays in Econometric methodology/David F. Hendry.
      p.   cm.
   Includes bibliographical references and index.
   ISBN 1-55786-264-8
   1. Econometric models.   2. Econometrics.   I. Title.
   HB141.H46   1993
   330'.01'5195–dc20   91-27541   CIP

Typeset in 10 on 12 pt Times by Colset Pte. Ltd., Singapore
Printed in Great Britain by T.J. Press Ltd., Padstow, Cornwall

Contents

Preface

This is a collection of my main essays on econometric methodology from the period 1974–85 during which the approach developed into its present form, integrated by a commentary on the motivations, personalities and ideas central to its formalization. Sue Corbett of Blackwell Publishers initiated the idea of drawing together the main steps through which the methodology had evolved, since a developmental viewpoint can be clarifying. In particular, an important part of the explanation for why a given methodology takes its current form are the successes and failures of its earlier incarnations. As each study reproduced below was undertaken, new issues and problems were highlighted, stimulating further developments and leading me to discard aspects of previous approaches as inadequate. Indeed, that process has continued unabated, so the story is still progressing, outdating some of the themes and interpretations discussed herein, but fortunately not the historical sequence. The ideas discussed below are now sufficiently developed, interrelated and formalized to allow an integrated treatment, and the outcome is the present volume.

Five criteria were used to select the included papers from the 40 that I published during 1971–85: their importance in the evolution of the methodology; their role in the continuity of the exposition; their focus on methodology; the subject matter of their empirical application; and the accessibility or otherwise of the original publication to economists world-wide. The first and third criteria eliminated technical papers on econometric theory, estimation methods (other than the synthesis in chapter 13) and Monte Carlo techniques (except for the second half of chapter 7). Conversely, despite their being accessible, eight papers from international econometrics journals were included because of their central role and the needs of continuity. Given an overall length restriction, the fourth criterion induced the arbitrary choice of including studies of consumers' expenditure and money demand but excluding most of my empirical papers on housing and credit markets, despite the fact that the latter came high on the fifth criterion. The second and fifth criteria then led to the choice of most of the remaining chapters, except for the Postscript which extends the horizon to 1989.

The book is divided into four parts: Roots and Route Maps, Empirical Modelling

Strategies, Formalization, and Retrospect and Prospect. The preambles to each part and to each chapter sketch the points that I believe I was trying to make at the time, the lessons I learnt, the developments which were triggered in turn, and the crucial issues I completely missed! Since the chapters differ greatly in the mathematical, statistical and conceptual demands they make of the reader, the major departures in their ordering from the historical sequence arise from attempting to ensure a more even progression in difficulty. In practice, most of the methodological developments recorded below derived from confronting substantive empirical problems. Not only are theory and application inseparable below, each empirical study is itself the vehicle for the exposition and the analysis of the associated methodological advance or rethink. Often, precise formalization of the concepts, principles and procedures came later. Consequently, while chapters 2, 3, 6–12 and 18 concern specific empirical problems, they have a substantial theoretical component as well as analyses of practical problems like collinearity, seasonality, autocorrelation, simultaneity and parameter constancy. Throughout, attention is restricted to the analysis of economic time-series data, based on linear models (perhaps after suitable data transformation).

'Methodology' is construed in the wide sense of 'the study of methods' (see, for example the usage in chapter 2) and most of the book concerns specifics rather than grand themes. It seems self-contradictory to claim that there exists a single valid methodology for discovering hitherto unknown features of our world: until they are discovered, we cannot know what would have been the 'best' way of discovering them. This argument does not render methodology otiose: there may be no best way to drive a car, but steering with one's eyes closed is patently a bad way. Critical appraisal of currently used methods is feasible and can reveal serious flaws in them. Much of the book concerns doing so (destructive criticism) and then offering a less objectionable alternative (constructive criticism) which is evaluated in turn. Criticisms are based on theoretical economic and econometric analyses, empirical applications and Monte Carlo simulations, which interact to narrow down the range of legitimate (or perhaps 'best practice') methods. By pursuing such an approach to the study of economic time series, the book contributes to the steady progress of econometric methodology that we have witnessed in recent years. Finally, since half of the chapters were originally written as expositions of important technical developments, methodological advances or new concepts, most of which remain germane, the material should help in understanding recent debates about econometric methodology.

Acknowledgements

Writing this part of a book is a double pleasure: the thought that most of the hard work has been completed combines with the remembrances of the kindnesses and help accorded by so many at every stage in the book's creation, from my first strivings to understand econometrics, through the evolution of the various ideas described below, to the final collation of this collection.

Since ideas can be understood only in relation to pre-established knowledge, I owe an immense, if implicit, debt to earlier econometricians and statisticians: the references are partial acknowledgement of that debt. Peter Fisk and Bert Shaw steered me into economics; Derek Peare guided my first steps in econometrics; Denis Sargan and Jim Durbin respectively established my technical knowledge of econometrics and of time-series analysis; and Meghnad Desai, Bill Phillips and Denis Sargan taught me how to link econometrics and economic analysis in quantitative economics. I am greatly indebted to them all for their efforts, and to the London School of Economics for financing my graduate studies.

The individual chapters explicitly acknowledge the advice and intellectual and financial help which I received while writing each paper – except, of course, for the role of each of my co-authors! Co-authors kindly agreed to the publication of the many joint papers reprinted here, and helpfully commented on earlier drafts of preambles. I can record with pleasure not only the essential part they played in bringing their respective papers to fruition, but also their invaluable encouragement and assistance in helping to set straight the historical record and the analyses presented below: my grateful thanks to Gordon Anderson, James Davidson, Rob Engle, Neil Ericsson, Robin Harrison, Grayham Mizon, John Muellbauer, Adrian Neale, Adrian Pagan, Jean-François Richard, Denis Sargan, Aris Spanos, Frank Srba, Pravin Trivedi, Thomas von Ungern-Sternberg, Ken Wallis and Stephen Yeo.

I am also indebted to Julia Campos, David Cox, Søren Johansen and Robin Rowley for their helpful comments on the preambles.

Many wonderful colleagues have saved me from even more egregious mistakes than those I have undoubtedly made, and in addition to my co-authors and those just acknowledged, special thanks go to Chris Allsopp, Angus Deaton, Meghnad

Desai, John Flemming, Jean-Pierre Florens, Chris Gilbert, Terence Gorman, Clive Granger, Andrew Harvey, Svend Hylleberg, Bob Marshall, Mary Morgan, Knud Munk, Michel Mouchart, Steve Nickell, Timo Teräsvirta, Tom Rothenberg, Honor Stamler, Ross Starr and Hal White.

Throughout my career, I have been ably supported by a sequence of superb research officers, who greatly increased my productivity: I am indebted to Robin Harrison, Andy Tremayne, Frank Srba, Yock Chong, Neil Ericsson, Adrian Neale, Mike Clements and Jurgen Doornik. Of equal importance, I have been looked after by excellent secretaries who often managed to decipher handwriting its producer could not reread, and even corrected mathematical mistakes. My grateful thanks to Luba Mumford, Raija Thomson, Christine Wills, Jean Brotherhood and Maureen Baker. One of my largest debts in producing this book is to Jean Brotherhood whose lightning typing, tireless efforts and unbounded efficiency played a key role at every stage of the project. I am especially grateful to Jean for continuing to work on the book even after retiring (which I hope was not precipitated by the task!). Julia Campos, Steven Cook and Neil Ericsson kindly proof-read the text and Julia prepared the indices.

The unsung heroes are the many generations of students and seminar participants whose comments on, and reactions to, the evolving approach were a continuous and valuable stimulus to its improvement: my thanks to them all, with the hope that they might find the end product of use.

As the Preface notes, the book was the brainchild of Sue Corbett of Blackwell Publishers and I am delighted to record my thanks to her both for suggesting the project and for sustaining it through its initial stages. To Romesh Vaitilingam goes the credit for stimulating me to complete the book in a finite time.

I am grateful to the following companies, organizations and societies for their kind permission to reprint the papers herein: Cambridge University Press, The Econometric Society (*Econometrica*), *Economica*, *European Economic Review*, Federal Reserve Bank of Minneapolis, Gower Publishing Company Ltd, International Statistical Institute (*International Statistical Review*), *Journal of Econometrics*, London Business School, Elsevier Science Publishers B.V. (North-Holland), *Oxford Review of Economic Policy*, Oxford University Press, Royal Economic Society (*Economic Journal*), Scottish Economic Society (*Scottish Journal of Political Economy*), Society for Economic Analysis Ltd (*Review of Economic Studies*) and Tieto Ltd.

It is a pleasure to record my thanks to the many institutions who have supported my research over the years, especially the UK Social Science Research Council, now renamed the Economic and Social Research Council, for seventeen years of finance for research officers, travel and communication; the London School of Economics, where I was employed from 1969 to 1981; and Oxford University who still employ me. I am also grateful for shorter periods of support from Yale University, the University of California at Berkeley, the Australian National University, the Centre for Operations Research and Econometrics at the University of Louvain-la-Neuve, the University of California at San Diego and Duke University.

Finally, I owe a great debt to my wife Evelyn and daughter Vivien for their support and encouragement, both while I was struggling with the ideas embodied in the original papers and while writing the preambles.

Introduction

The collection begins with the paper after which it is named, since that chapter provides a gentle romp through many of the major topics and offers a guide to the main themes of the book. Moreover, it was written at about the half-way stage in time between my first rudimentary grapplings with model specification issues and my views as of 1990. Nevertheless, chapter 1 has a serious message: econometrics is potentially scientific precisely because alchemy is creatable, detectable and refutable. Although important technical difficulties about the properties of tests and of model selection procedures based on sequential testing await resolution, model evaluation is a legitimate activity independently of past and present controversies about the constructive uses of econometrics. That 'the three golden rules of econometrics are test, test and test' is a constant theme from my first research to my latest writings. The validity of a model is a property of the model in relation to the evidence and so cannot be affected by how that model is selected. If the model is valid, it will pass all of our tests at an appropriate significance level (usually dependent on the sample size, the number of tests and the data characteristics). If the model is invalid, we should be able to detect that by a sufficiently rigorous test procedure. In neither case, therefore, can validity be affected by how the model was found, designed or created. In practice, models are more or less adequate approximations rather than strictly valid or invalid, but the point remains that the adequacy of an empirical model is an intrinsic property which is not impugned by the method of construction. As we shall see, however, such an implication does not make the selection method irrelevant: in particular, some methods (e.g. guessing) have little chance of discovering adequate models. Much of the present volume concerns developing criteria for model adequacy and analysing alternative approaches to building empirical models, so 'methodology' is construed in the general sense ('with a small m' as Boland (1989) expresses it) and does not entail only the grand issues (as, for example, in Popper, 1968).

The alchemy practised in chapter 1 is to explain UK inflation 'better' by rainfall than by the stock of money. Since chapter 1 was written, an immense literature has evolved concerning the analysis of non-stationary data and nonsense regressions, and the converses of cointegration and error correction. These analyses help resolve when we can attach meaning to empirical regressions, so the associated concepts recur many times below.

The roots of the approach are taken up in chapters 2 and 3, which embody many of my later ideas in embryonic form. My first empirical modelling exercise was a small system of aggregate demand relationships in the UK, using estimators specifically developed to tackle the 'problems of autocorrelation and simultaneity'. Chapter 2 sought to apply the approaches in Sargan (1958) and (1964a) to small simultaneous systems, in order to discriminate between cases where (vector) residual autocorrelation arose from autoregressive errors or from mis-specification of the lag structure of the observed data series, and to ascertain the relative importance of dynamic mis-specification and simultaneity. Rather than simply asserting that residual autocorrelation reflected autoregressive errors and therefore applying a 'more sophisticated' estimation method to resolve that problem, tests were used to check whether the dynamics of the pre-specified model needed to be generalized. Therein lay three difficulties that I did not clearly perceive at the time of writing (1969), but which became increasingly obvious as my work on the approach proceeded.

1   In practice, the correct model was not known *a priori*, merely requiring estimation of its parameters. An awkward model selection problem generally confronted any empirical investigator and the conventional paradigm of assuming that the model was known in advance of examining the data was simply not appropriate.

2   It was not legitimate to use the outcomes of model specification tests for constructive revision of a model. If a model was incorrect, many test statistics might yield rejection outcomes and so it could not be appropriate in general to assume that, if any given null hypothesis was false, the postulated alternative must be true: both could be false, because the framework was incorrect.

3   Generalizing an initial simple model in the face of specification test rejections raised a host of problems, not least that of when to stop and what sense to make of earlier interpretations when a later test rejected.

At this stage, these were merely puzzles to me. Chapter 3 was written five years after chapter 2 and embodies (albeit in an inchoate form) a number of roots that have since proved dominant. The approach is more nearly that of simplifying an initial general system; an attempt is made to account for the performance of previous empirical models by testing them for mis-specifications predicted by the economic theory; and the underlying economic theory, which patched a static long run onto dynamic adjustment, delivered a model form which I later recognized as an error correction mechanism. Both chapters skirt around, but miss, Denis Sargan's later notion of common factors in lag polynomials (denoted COMFAC; see Sargan (1980a) and chapter 4), and the importance of data non-stationarities, issues which play an important part in what follows.

Part I is completed by chapter 4, again written about five years further on (1980), jointly with Adrian Pagan and Denis Sargan. Written with 'hindsight' relative to most of the other chapters herein, it is offered as a route map, sketching the major issues, models, concepts and techniques, and referring forwards to later chapters. All of part I is explicitly system oriented, but my empirical efforts had starkly revealed that few of the component equations were trustworthy, and so without any conscious decision my attention gradually became focused on single-equation models.

Part II, which describes the development of empirical modelling strategies, reflects that tendency. Throughout the late 1960s and early to mid-1970s, much of the research into time-series econometrics reflected an intense rivalry between a data-analytic viewpoint (closely related to Box and Jenkins, 1976) and economic-theory-driven econometric modelling. At the London School of Economics (LSE), from where most of the material in this book originated, the econometrics research group included (for substantial periods up to 1980) James Davidson, Meghnad Desai, James Durbin, Andrew Harvey, myself, Grayham Mizon, Denis Sargan, Pravin Trivedi and Kenneth Wallis. At the risk of simultaneous over-simplification and excessive generality, we emphasized the complementarity of the two approaches, and sought to synthesize the best elements in both. In setting the scene for part II, chapter 5 commences with an extract evaluating the 'time-series' approach to econometrics, which summarizes the main themes to follow. These include a critique of pure time-series methods, as well as brief discussions of non-stationarity, differencing and error correction models, the reinterpretation of residual auto-correlation (now using Denis Sargan's COMFAC idea), the explanation of competing models' findings and ways to reduce the proliferation of conflicting results, and the respective roles of criticism and construction.

COMFAC in single equations is discussed at greater length in chapters 6 and 7, written jointly with Grayham Mizon. These comprise two closely related papers investigating the important conceptual clarification of autoregressive errors as common-factor dynamics. However, the evidence seemed less favourable to its being a solution to model selection problems in practice. Chapter 8 (written with James Davidson, Frank Srba and Stephen Yeo) also considers many of the issues raised in chapter 5, especially the explanation of other models' results, and while it is substantively focused on modelling aggregate consumers' expenditure, it has a strong methodological slant: modelling strategies, parameter constancy, collinearity, seasonality and encompassing are investigated. Although the main product was an empirical equation which could claim some success (since known as DHSY from the acronym of its authors), its properties immediately prompted a progressive improvement, stimulated by Thomas von Ungern-Sternberg and reproduced as chapter 9. A third extension, to test whether DHSY could encompass the rational-expectations permanent-income model of Robert Hall (1978), appears as chapter 10 (again with James Davidson), which *en route* allowed both replication and testing of the earlier findings. The penultimate chapter of this volume provides a retro-spective evaluation of the empirical evidence on consumers' expenditure and the success of the chapter 8 model as of 1982, while doubling as a final exposition of the empirical methodology. This group of four papers is intended to illustrate the progressive nature of the research in practice. A recent review is provided in Hendry et al. (1990b).

The major area of application now switches from consumers' expenditure to transactions money demand, although historically that switch actually happened after chapter 8. Contemporaneously, a major change took place in the methodology. DHSY was written as a 'detective story'; investigators were viewed as acquiring evidence, forming conjectures, testing hypotheses and seeking to create a model which could account for the complete set of evidence confronting them, both successes and failures. Beyond rigorous testing and encompassing, the methodology was unstructured and almost anarchical in what stratagems were acceptable. This presented a gloomy prospect – did empirical researchers all need Sherlock Holmes's acumen, industry and creativity to make any useful contributions?

Two events set the scene for the later integrated approach. First, in the COMFAC approach, one must commence from the most general model considered admissible and then sequentially simplify it, testing at each step whether or not a given lagged set of variables corresponds to an autoregressive error. It is inherently 'general to specific' as in testing (say) the order of a data autoregression in Anderson (1971). Pravin Trivedi (1973) had applied the Anderson approach and Grayham Mizon also adopted this viewpoint in his 1977a paper on selecting dynamic models using ordered and nested sequences of tests. Nevertheless, I did not realize the generality of that idea and hence did not perceive its wide applicability beyond dynamic specification. DHSY had stumbled over the need to test against the general model but did not focus on its central role in a structured methodology. Incidentally, note that chapter 8 was first written in 1974–5 and was essentially completed before chapter 7 was begun, even though they appeared in the reverse order – which is why the later publication does not reflect the earlier one.

Second, Jean-François Richard at the Centre for Operations Research and Econometrics (CORE) (Louvain-la-Neuve, Belgium, where a group was investigating model reduction methods) realized that there were close parallels between the emerging LSE approach and that evolving at CORE. Richard's paper to the 1977 Econometric Society Meeting in Vienna1 (published as Richard, 1980) combined with the Sargan–Mizon viewpoint made me realize at last (probably after dozens of hours of discussion!) that the solution to most of my earlier puzzles lay in commencing empirical modelling from the general, not from the specific. Chapter 11 reflects this *gestalt* shift and opens up a far more positive prospect for empirical econometrics based on a structured and communicable approach. As Adrian Pagan notes in his 1987 survey, commencing from a general model is central to most of the major methodological approaches now extant in econometrics. Of course, generality is not a panacea to all econometric ills: no matter how general its initial specification in terms of dynamics, error structures, functional forms or evolving parameters, a relationship between inflation and rainfall must remain nonsense. Indeed, given the earlier argument that model validity is independent of the selection method, the issue about modelling strategy is really one of research efficiency, as will emerge below.

The initial objective in chapter 11 was to field-test the emerging methods in a new area and investigate their ability both to produce useful or improved models and to encompass previous findings. Chapter 11 also offers a critique of 'simple-to-general' modelling methods and contrasts the outcome with that achieved by working throughout within an initially general well-defined framework and seeking admissible simplifications which yield parsimonious, constant and encompassing equations. A test of this model on new data is also reproduced, extracted from chapter 17. Chapter 12 is a later evaluation and replication exercise based on an improved though closely similar specification developed at the Bank of England (see Trundle, 1982); but be warned, it provides a polemical conclusion to part II! Hendry and Ericsson (1991a, b) conclude this sequence and Baba et al. (1992) apply the approach to US data.

Part III turns to the formalization of the concepts and methods. First, chapter 13 explains why the topic of 'optimal estimation' hardly appears in the plot, despite being a necessary ingredient of empirical modelling. The answer is that the notion of an 'estimator-generating equation' (EGE) reduces the vast literature on estimating individual equations and linear simultaneous systems to a single relatively simple expression. The chapter shows how to derive the EGE from the 'score' (first derivative of the log-likelihood function) and then how to solve the EGE for all existing estimators (and many more). The issue of how to obtain and compute maximum likelihood estimators is also tackled in terms of the properties of numerical optimization algorithms. The original paper analysed the case of linear systems with vector autoregressive errors, but the relevant sections have been omitted here.

While it only surfaces explicitly in chapters 14 and 19, much of my time and effort have been devoted to making the methodology operational by writing suitable computer programs to implement new methods and approaches. The early 'software' was a collection of rather unfriendly mainframe batch programs whose primary virtue was simply that the tools were rendered usable. Since then, the approach has been implemented on personal computers (PCs) via PC-GIVE, an interactive menu-driven modelling program specifically developed to embody the methodology and technology discussed in this book in friendly software, to facilitate both teaching and research in time-series econometrics (see Hendry, 1986c). PC-GIVE builds upon the well-tested and accurate algorithms of the AUTOREG library (described in chapter 14, written with Frank Srba who also programmed many of the routines), but exploits the powerful graphics available on PCs to allow the most 'sophisticated' of econometrics to be easily used and readily understood.[2] The Postscript reproduces the Introduction to the PC-GIVE book.

As will be obvious from the affiliations of the co-authors, from the mid-1980s onwards the conceptual frameworks and approaches of two other institutions began to be assimilated into my views (and, in turn, their views were also modified). First, as noted above, the econometricians at CORE, comprising in particular Jean-Pierre Florens, Michel Mouchart and Jean-François Richard, had pursued a programme of research into the general notion of model reduction in a Bayesian framework (since synthesized in Florens et al., 1990). The merging of this research with the LSE approach not only offered a more structured methodology, it also induced a considerable advance in formalizing key modelling concepts such as exogeneity and encompassing, which play important roles below. Secondly, the econometrics group at the University of California at San Diego, including Robert Engle, Clive Granger and Halbert White, also focused on time-series econometrics and were advancing the analysis on several related fronts, especially in developing relevant tests, more robust procedures and the concept of cointegration.

Those generous – and vital! – institutions that fund research often complain about requests for overseas travel money, yet to the extent that the methodology advanced herein has lasting value, much of its worth would never have materialized for me without a regular three-way interchange between London (now Oxford), Louvain-la-Neuve (and later also Duke University) and the University of California, San Diego. As attested by the acknowledgements to many of my publications, criticisms from those of a related yet different perspective are essential in clarifying one's own thinking: a substantial proportion of the good ideas in this volume emerged during intensive discussions in the coffee lounges, common rooms, seminars and offices of CORE, LSE and UC San Diego.

The crucial, but highly contentious, topic of exogeneity which is analysed in chapter 15 (jointly with Rob Engle and Jean-François Richard) is a product of such interchanges and provides a formal account of the role of conditioning in the applied studies of part II. Three concepts of exogeneity (weak, strong and super) are advanced to sustain, conditional inference, conditional forecasting and conditional policy analysis respectively. The tentative formalization of many of the modelling concepts offered in chapter 16 (written with Jean-François Richard) likewise develops the CORE–LSE link and evolved through extensive discussions between myself and Jean-François while I enjoyed the generous hospitality which he and his family extended to me when I resided with them for the second half of 1979. The chapter investigates the constructs of innovations, invariance, encompassing and admissibility, relates these to exogeneity and progressive modelling strategies, and introduces the notion of designing models to satisfy certain criteria. An overview, again jointly with Jean-François, linking these statistical concepts to economic formulations, is provided in chapter 17, which also generalizes the estimator-generating formula to so-called 'incomplete' linear models. A sequence of six expository themes is proposed for interpreting time-series econometrics: models are derived as reductions from the process which actually generated the data, inducing parameter transformations (affecting their constancy, invariance and interpretation); conditioning and weak exogeneity are linked to contingent plans of economic agents; a typology of linear dynamic equations is advanced (described earlier in the chapter 4 route map and so not reproduced here); an EGE covers estimation theory for linear sub-systems; the efficient score describes diagnostic testing; and encompassing interrelates empirical models. Thus, almost the whole of part III reflects a synthesis of the LSE ideas with those developed at CORE. Perhaps the single most important link for me is that of general-to-specific modelling with the theory of reduction, from which a much clearer conception of modelling and model-related concepts emerges. As chapter 19 describes, the links with San Diego have in turn borne many valuable products since 1984.

The volume ends in part IV. Chapter 18 offers an exposition of the main ideas and concepts, using the application of consumers' expenditure behaviour in the United Kingdom to clarify their empirical content and implications. The Postscript summarizes the model class; the properties of specific linear models, including cointegration and error correction; model evaluation and the associated information taxonomy, leading onto sequential conditioning; exogeneity and invariance; constancy and recursivity; encompassing; and the theory of reduction as a basis for modelling. Test types, modelling strategies and system estimation are also briefly discussed. Extensions of the approach to system modelling are provided in Hendry et al. (1988) and Hendry and Mizon (1991). Granger (1990) conveniently draws together much of the general methodological debate, and Hendry et al. (1990a) extensively discuss their respective viewpoints.

As noted above, a short preamble precedes each chapter, noting its salient themes, links to earlier and later developments, lessons learnt or missed, some of the major influences and some of the personalities who swayed the development in fruitful directions. For coherence, and to avoid duplication, all references have been updated to published versions, in an author–date format, and are collected at the end of the volume.

I hope that chapter 1 is sufficiently self-contained and clearly written that it does not need a separate preamble!

Notes

1   Which was also the precursor to chapter 15; see below.
2   PC-GIVE is available from the Oxford Institute of Economics and Statistics: see Hendry (1989).

Part I
Roots and Route Maps

1

Econometrics – Alchemy or Science?

1 Alchemy and Science

While there are many distinguished precedents for public lectures at the School being discourses about subjects on which the speaker is an evident amateur, I do not intend to discuss at length either 'scientific method' or the general relationship between 'alchemy' and 'science'. No doubt my colleagues in the Philosophy and Scientific Method Department will be greatly relieved. Nevertheless, some background will be useful, especially to distinguish connotative from denotative aspects of 'alchemy' and 'science'.

Alchemy denotes the putative art of transmuting base metals into noble ones, a possibility implicit in Greek *theories* of matter; as such, alchemical *experiments* helped focus chemical effort and could be interpreted as embryonic systematic chemistry. In this sense, my question is simply a matter of timing – after all, the title does not juxtapose astrology and science!

The familiar connotations of alchemy are less happy, and are well represented by Ben Jonson's erudite comedy *The Alchemist* (1612) with its bogus and obscurantist 'puffer' (so-called from the phrenetic use of bellows in transmutation attempts) called Subtle. That the pejorative sense is now dominant may derive partly from the mystical associations of the quest for the 'Philosophers' Stone' and partly from 'recipes' for simulating gold using alloys of base metals; intended to deceive the public, such recipes may well have deceived many alchemists themselves. The relevance of these comments to the current state of econometrics will be apparent shortly.

Precisely what 'science' denotes is remarkably unclear, but the present mental associations of objectivity and progress ensure that simply using this prestigious

Reprinted from *Economica*, 47 (1980) 387–406. I am indebted to many colleagues for their help and advice in preparing this inaugural lecture but should like to thank in particular Mary Morgan, John Muellbauer, Frank Srba and Raija Thomson. The research was financed in part by Grant HR6727/1 from the Social Science Research Council to the Study in the History of Econometric Thought at the London School of Economics.

epithet confers an air of authority; to wit, the London School of Economics and Political Science – would anyone attend the London School of Economics and Political Alchemy? Parenthetically, the implication of authority is rather odd given that the fifteenth-century revival of science in western Europe was a reaction against argument by authority. In any case, the high reputation of the physical sciences may decline in the next decade should public expectations on environmental control remain unfulfilled; if there are many more nuclear accidents, we may yet be glad to be called 'political economists' rather than 'economic scientists'.

What is this thing called 'science'? (See the excellent text by Chalmers, 1976.) During an address under the shadows of Sir Karl Popper and the late Imre Lakatos, whose distinguished contributions have revolutionized our understanding of 'science', there is a distinct risk of yielding several hostages to fortune by trespassing on a debate that has flourished since Francis Bacon (see Popper, 1968, 1969; Lakatos, 1974). This danger notwithstanding, an adequate if condensed view is as follows.

Science is a public process. It uses systems of concepts called theories to help interpret and unify observation statements called data; in turn the data are used to check or 'test' the theories. Theory creation may be inductive, but demonstration and testing are deductive, although, in inexact subjects, testing will involve statistical inference. Theories that are at once simple, general and coherent are valued as they aid productive and precise scientific practice. In particular, restrictiveness increases the hazards of possible rejection and hence augments 'plausibility' if disconfirmation does not occur. Although objectivity and potential falsifiability against data are crucial to science, in practice observations are theory dependent, rejections can be rationalized (often leading to degenerate research programmes) and, even when evidence is highly unfavourable and reasonable alternative theories exist, views are usually changed only slowly: after all, we are discussing a *human* endeavour! As Baron Turgot expressed the matter in 1749: 'Suppositions which are arrived at on the basis of a small number of poorly understood facts yield to suppositions which are less absurd, although no more true' (Meek, 1973, p. 45). The history of natural science (e.g. Mason, 1977) provides many instances of ideas derided at conception which are taken as axiomatic later, and Kuhn (1970) has argued that science actually progresses through 'revolutionary' changes in basic theoretical frameworks brought about by cumulative failures to solve problems. Note that in this characterization experimentation may be a useful, but is not an essential, attribute.

Alchemy could well have remained 'scientific' – perhaps as a degenerate research programme or a rejected theory – but instead it seems to have turned to mysticism and away from objectivity. Stainslas de Rola (1973) argues that the unfortunate connotations of alchemy are undeserved since 'immature science' is a false interpretation of alchemy and 'true' alchemy is actually a secret art striving for the 'absolute'. Feel free to choose the intended meaning of 'alchemy' in my title!

2 Econometrics

Unfortunately, I must now try to explain what 'econometrics' comprises. Do not confuse the word with 'econo-mystics' or with 'economic-tricks', nor yet with 'icon-ometrics'. While we may indulge in all of these activities, they are not central to the discipline. Nor are econometricians primarily engaged in measuring the heights of economists.

A more accurate idea of the subject is provided in the constitution of the Econometric Society, founded in 1930, which defined its main objectives as 'the advancement of economic theory in its relation to statistics and mathematics' (*Econometrica*, 1933, p. 1). In this broad sense, econometrics commences an analysis of the relationships between economic variables (such as quantities and prices, incomes and expenditures, etc.) by abstracting the main phenomena of interest and stating theories thereof in mathematical form. The empirical usefulness of the resulting 'models' is evaluated using statistical information of supposed relevance, and econometrics in the narrow sense (used hereafter) concerns the interpretation and analysis of such data in the context of 'established' economic theory.

Thus, econometric theory is the study of the properties of data generation processes, techniques for analysing economic data, methods of estimating numerical magnitudes of parameters with unknown values and procedures for testing economic hypotheses; it plays an analogous role in primarily non-experimental disciplines to that of statistical theory in inexact experimental sciences (e.g. Blalock, 1961). As expressed by Wold (1969), 'Econometrics is seen as a vehicle for fundamental innovations in scientific method, above all, in the development of operative fore-casting procedures in non-experimental situations.' In Wold's view, econometrics needs to overcome both a lack of experimentation (which precludes reproducible knowledge) and the passivity of forecasts based on extrapolative methods.

Applied and empirical econometrics are sometimes regarded as separate 'engineer-ing' branches of the subject, literally involving the mere application of standard statistical methods to economic data. Since, to quote Frisch (1933), 'the mutual penetration of quantitative economic theory and statistical observation is the essence of econometrics', the greatest loss from our inability to experiment may be the artificial divisions it promotes between data collectors, data users, econometric theorists and mathematical economists.

The need for quantitative empirical knowledge to answer questions involving changes in economic variables has been adequately promulgated by Schumpeter (1933) and Phillips (1956) (the former argued that economics is really the most quantitative of *all* the sciences since economic quantities are made numerical by life itself whereas other subjects had to *invent* their measurement processes). For predicting the consequences of changes, forecasting likely future outcomes and controlling variables to attain objectives, econometric models play a central role in modern economics. Substantial resources have been devoted to empirical macro-econometric models which comprise hundreds or even thousands of statistically calibrated equations, each purporting to represent some autonomous facet of the behaviour of economic agents such as consumers and producers, the whole intended to describe accurately the overall evolution of the economy.

Despite its obvious potential, econometrics has not had an easy time from many who have made major contributions to the development of economics, beginning with Keynes's famous review in 1939 of Tinbergen's book, *Statistical Testing of Business-Cycle Theories*. In an oft-quoted passage in his Comment (1940, p. 156) Keynes accepts that Tinbergen's approach is objective but continues:

No one could be more frank, more painstaking, more free from subjective bias or *parti pris* than Professor Tinbergen. There is no one, therefore, so far as human qualities go, whom it would be safer to trust with black magic. That there is anyone I would trust with it at the present stage, or that this brand of *statistical alchemy* is ripe to become a branch of science, I am not yet persuaded. But Newton, Boyle and Locke all played with Alchemy. So let him continue.

(Keynes, 1940, p. 156; my italics)

It is interesting to record the following quotation from Geoffrey Keynes (1946): 'Newton was *not* the first of the Age of Reason. He was the last of the magicians . . . an unbridled addict [of alchemy] . . . [during] the very years when he was composing the *Principia*.' Oh that econometrics had such alchemists as Newton! Again the issue is one of timing since Maynard Keynes, despite his trenchant criticisms, does *not* liken econometrics to a theoryless reading of entrails as some seem to believe. (For a fuller discussion of Keynes's views on econometrics, see Patinkin, 1976). Notwithstanding Keynes's comments, Tinbergen was later joint recipient of the first Nobel Prize in *economics*.

An echo of this debate recurs in the early 1970s. For example, following a sharp critique of mathematical economics as having 'no links with concrete facts', Worswick (1972) suggests that some econometricians are not 'engaged in forging tools to arrange and measure actual facts, so much as making a marvellous array of *pretend-tools*' (my italics). In the same issue of the *Economic Journal*, Phelps Brown (1972) also concludes against econometrics, commenting that 'running regressions between time series is only likely to deceive'. Added to these innuendoes of 'alchemical' practices, Leontief (1971) has characterized econometrics as 'an attempt to compensate for the glaring weakness of the data base available to us by the widest possible use of more and more sophisticated statistical techniques'. To quote Hicks, 'the relevance of these methods [i.e. econometrics] to economics should not be taken for granted; . . . [Keynes] would not have been surprised to find that . . . econometrics is now in some disarray' (1979, p. xi). With the manifest breakdown in the early 1970s of the large empirical macroeconometric systems, outside scepticism does not bear mention.

Rather than abandon the study of econometrics or reply to those criticisms by quoting equally eminent authorities who hold more favourable views (e.g. Stone, 1951; Koopmans, 1957, 1979), I should like instead to demonstrate the scientific status of econometrics by first showing alchemy at work empirically. This will enable us to understand the sense in which the quoted criticisms are valid, and by explaining why various apparently alchemical results are obtained *en route* my approach will suggest constructive strategies for enhancing the role of scientific method in econometrics.

So let us practise alchemy!

3 Econometrics as Alchemy

Econometricians have found their Philosophers' Stone; it is called regression analysis and is used for transforming data into 'significant' results! Deception is easily practised from false recipes intended to simulate useful findings, and these are derogatively referred to by the profession as 'nonsense regressions' (although I could not find an equivalent of 'puffer', regressor already having another meaning).

Figure 1.1 presents (seasonally adjusted) quarterly time-series data for the United Kingdom over the period 1964(ii)–1975(ii) relating to the age-old and seemingly unresolved controversy concerning the effect of money (here personal sector M3) on prices (here the consumer price index); the variables, denoted M and P, are plotted on a logarithmic scale. Advance warning that 'alchemy' may be present could be gleaned from the letters to *The Times*, 4–6 April 1977, where Llewellyn and Witcomb establish a higher correlation between annual inflation and cases of dysentery in Scotland (one year earlier) than Mills obtained between inflation and the rate of change of excess money supply (two years before).

The plot of M against P in figure 1.2 seems to confirm their close relationship (the correlation is over 0.99). Regression estimates of the explanation of P by M yield the results in figure 1.3; the fit is impressive as M 'explains' 98 per cent of the variation of P and has a 'significant' coefficient (the quantities in parentheses are estimated standard errors).[1] The residuals are systematic rather than random, but this so-called 'nuisance' of autocorrelation (see chapter 6) can be 'eliminated' by suitably transforming the equation to introduce lagged values of the variables (i.e. the values of the variables in the previous period, denoted M_{t-1}, P_{t-1}): see

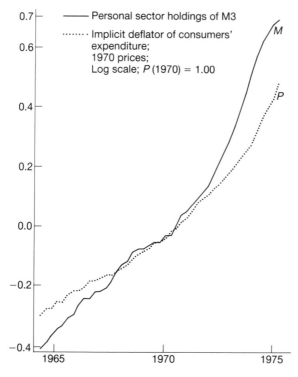

Figure 1.1 Quarterly time-series data for the United Kingdom over the period 1964(ii)–1975(ii).

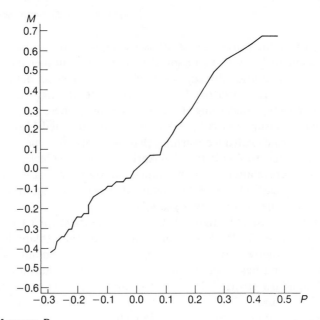

Figure 1.2 *M* versus *P*.

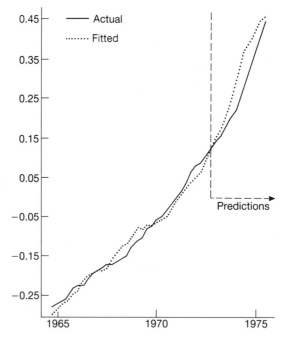

Figure 1.3 *P*, static equation

$$\hat{P} = -0.02 + 0.73M$$
$$\quad\ \ (0.003)\ (0.016)$$

$$R^2 = 0.984 \qquad s = 1.7 \qquad d = 0.3.$$

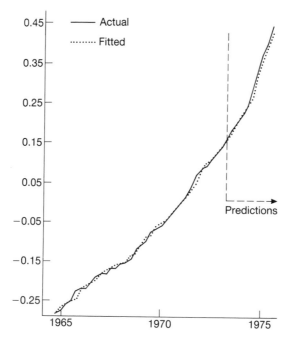

Figure 1.4 *P*, dynamic equation

$$\hat{P}_t = 0.02 + 0.995P_{t-1} - 0.00M_t + 0.02M_{t-1}$$
$$\quad\;\; (0.003)\;\;(0.057)\qquad (0.097)\;\;\;(0.094)$$

$$R^2 = 0.999 \qquad s = 0.5 \qquad d = 1.6.$$

figure 1.4. The squared correlation is now 0.9985 but the money variables no longer significantly influence *P* and a prediction test rejects the constancy of the parameters of the equation. Evidently, we can make money matter or not by appropriate specification of the model, and hence '(self?) deception' is easy by selecting whichever finding 'corroborates one's theory'.

A second example will clarify this issue. Hendry's theory of inflation is that a certain variable (of great interest in this country) is the 'real cause' of rising prices. I am 'certain' that the variable (denoted *C*) is exogenous, that causality is from *C* to *P only* and (so far as I am aware) that *C* is outside government control although data are readily available in government publications. Figure 1.5 shows the quarterly time series (seasonally *un*adjusted) and figure 1.6 the cross-plot of *P* against *C* (again in logs). There is evidently a close but non-linear relationship, and regression analysis assuming a quadratic equation yields the results in figure 1.7. As earlier, there is a 'good fit', the coefficients are 'significant', but autocorrelation remains and the equation predicts badly. However, assuming a first-order autoregressive error process[2] at last produces the results I anticipated (see figure 1.8); the fit is spectacular, the parameters are 'highly significant', there is no obvious residual autocorrelation (on an 'eyeball' test), and the predictive test does not reject the model. My theory performs decidedly better than the naive version of the monetary

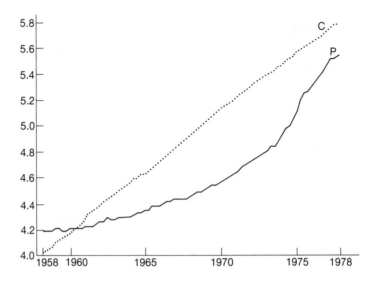

Figure 1.5 *P*, consumers' expenditure deflator; *C*, see text: log scale; $P(1970) = 100$.

one but, alas, the whole exercise is futile as well as deceitful since *C* is simply cumulative rainfall in the United Kingdom. It is meaningless to talk about 'confirming' theories when spurious results are so easily obtained.

Since correlation does not entail any direction of causation, perhaps the rapid inflation explains our wet weather? One must regret the omission of such an important theory from the otherwise excellent *History of the Theories of Rain* by Middleton (1965).

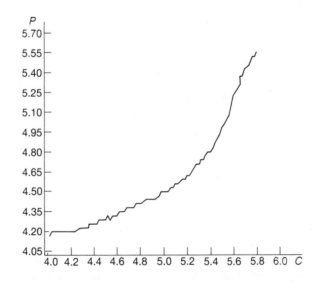

Figure 1.6 Cross-plot of *P* against *C*.

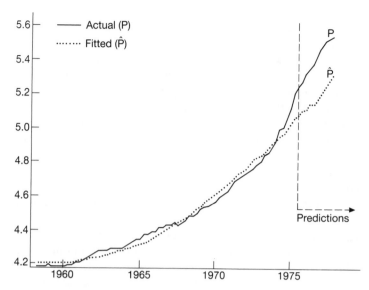

Figure 1.7 *P*, structural equation

$$\hat{P} = \underset{(0.55)}{10.9} - \underset{(0.23)}{3.2C} + \underset{(0.02)}{0.39C^2}$$

$$R^2 = 0.982 \qquad s = 3.6 \qquad d = 0.1.$$

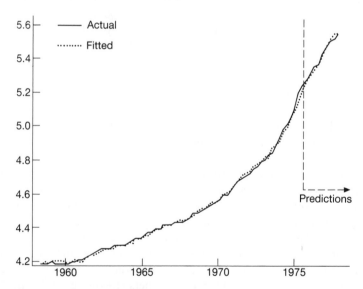

Figure 1.8 *P*, autoregressive equation

$$\hat{P}_t = \underset{(3.6)}{21.1} - \underset{(1.4)}{7.2C_t} + \underset{(0.13)}{0.78C_t^2} + \underset{(0.02)}{0.94\hat{U}_{t-1}}$$

$$R^2 = 0.998 \qquad s = 1.2$$

$$\chi_1^2 = 25 \qquad \chi_{11}^2 = 35 \qquad F(10, 65) = 1.1.$$

Doubtless, some equations extant in econometric folklore are little less spurious than those I have presented. Before you despair at this hopeless subject, the statistical problem just illustrated was analysed in one of its manifestations by Yule in 1926 and has been re-emphasized many times since (see in particular Granger and Newbold, 1974). The crucial factor for my argument is that *before* doing these regressions the relevant theory enabled me to *deduce* what would occur and hence to construct the desired examples on my first try – what could be more scientific? We understand this problem and have many tests for the validity of empirical models (those just quoted duly fail two such tests[3]). We even have theories that reveal that prediction need not be a powerful test of a model since false models can manifest parameter constancy (chapter 11).

Such understanding is well past the stage of alchemy even if some editors can be persuaded to publish on the basis of econometric fools' gold: *caveat emptor*, but do not denigrate the whole subject. That modern chemistry can explain alchemical results is a confirmation of its scientific status, not cast into doubt by any modern charlatans who might use chemical theory to simulate gold. The case for scientific econometrics rests instead on *best* practice empirical work such as Sargan (1964a) – a precursor of many useful developments in recent econometrics. My discussion also highlights that an essential requirement of any useful model in a *non-experimental* subject is that it can explain why previous *false* models provided their observed results (see chapter 8).

To conclude this section, it must be stressed that none of the evidence presented lends support to, or casts doubt on, any theory of aggregate price determination, nor is it asserted that 'nonsense' regressions of the type illustrated constitute the basis of the criticisms noted earlier, a point amplified below.

4 Econometrics' Problems

To quote Patinkin (1976), 'though not all of Keynes' criticisms were well taken . . . I find it somewhat depressing to see how many of them are, in practice, still of relevance today'. Forty years after Keynes wrote, his review should still be compulsory reading for all who seek to apply statistical methods to economic observations. Taken literally, Keynes comes close to asserting that no economic theory is ever testable, in which case, of course, economics itself ceases to be scientific – I doubt if Keynes intended this implication. However, his objections make an excellent list of what might be called 'problems of the linear regression model', namely (in modern parlance): using an incomplete set of determining factors (omitted variables bias); building models with unobservable variables (such as expectations), estimated from badly measured data based on index numbers (Keynes calls this the 'frightful inadequacy of most of the statistics'); obtaining 'spurious' correlations from the use of 'proxy' variables and simultaneity as well as (and I quote) the 'mine [Mr Yule] sprang under the contraptions of optimistic statisticians'; being unable to separate the distinct effects of multicollinear variables; assuming linear functional forms not knowing the appropriate dimensions of the regressors; mis-specifying the dynamic reactions and lag lengths; incorrectly pre-filtering the data; invalidly inferring 'causes' from correlations; predicting inaccurately (non-constant parameters); confusing statistical with economic 'significance' of results and failing to relate economic theory to econometrics. (I cannot resist quoting Keynes again – 'If the method cannot prove or disprove a qualitative theory and if it cannot give a quantitative guide to the future, is it worth while? For, assuredly, it is not a very lucid way of describing the past.') To Keynes's list of problems, I would add stochastic mis-specification, incorrect exogeneity assumptions (see Koopmans, 1950a; and chapter 15), inadequate sample sizes, aggregation, lack of structural identification and an inability to refer back uniquely from observed empirical results to any given initial theory.

That the subject is exceedingly complicated does not entail that it is hopeless. Considerable progress has been made on the technical aspects, such as studying the consequences of the various problems just listed, designing means of detecting these, developing methods that mitigate some of their ill effects or handle several complications at once, and analysing the properties of estimators when the sample size is small (see Sargan, 1976; Phillips, 1977; *inter alia*). Much of this technical work is essential background to understanding and correctly interpreting empirical findings and, although some work may have turned out to be otiose in retrospect, the ever-increasing level of technique is not a symptom of alchemy. To borrow Worswick's phrase, whether or not 'econometric escalation' is justifiable will depend on whether it facilitates clearer findings or camouflages tenuous evidence.

Empirical practice has tended to lag behind the theory 'frontier' with unfortunate consequences. Well before the oil crisis, critics suggested that macroeconometric systems were seriously mis-specified and hence would manifest predictive failure if changes in the process generating the data merely altered the *correlation* structure of the variables (see, for example, the discussion in Hickman, 1972). Many of the specification mistakes were obvious and relatively easy to correct, and doing so might have helped to prevent the models failing so badly just when they were most needed. Even so, that cataclysm and similar government-induced events are one of the few ways in which false models can be rejected – econometrics may be the sole beneficiary from government manipulation of the economy. Without wishing to look this particular gift-horse in the mouth, dare one suggest that controlled experiments could be more informative than inadvertent and uncontrolled ones?

At the micro-level, experimentation is occurring (for example on diurnal variation in energy consumption with changing tariff structures). Regrettably, experimental 'control' is proving elusive, especially for relativities and dynamical and inertial patterns of behaviour. Despite such difficulties, experimentation in economics merits far greater resources than the meagre financial ration currently allocated by our political masters allows. This is *not* a criticism of the Social Science Research Council (SSRC), which has played a major role in supporting econometric research in the United Kingdom from a very limited budget roughly equal to the interest on the annual grant to the Science Research Council. As Leontief (1971) expressed the matter, 'the scientists have their machines while the economists are still waiting for their data'. To mention one constructive step, the collection of panel data would be of very great assistance in testing economic theories at a disaggregated level.

Economic data are notoriously unreliable (see, for example, Morgenstern, 1950) and in an important sense econometrics is little more than an attempted solution to our acute shortage of decent data. Yet accurate observation is vital. To take one important example, a variable like 'real personal disposable income' is extremely difficult to 'measure' accurately and a constant price series of after-tax 'income' of the personal sector bears little relation to the economist's concept of 'income' (as defined, for example, by Hicks, 1939, ch. 14). Unfortunately, discrepancies in measuring income may have major policy implications. If income is measured using real rather than nominal interest rates to ensure that changes in real wealth are equal to real income less real expenditure, then the ratio of consumers' expenditure to adjusted income has not fallen particularly sharply, unlike the ratio of the unadjusted series (see chapter 9). Thus, the savings ratio 'properly measured' may not have risen at all. A non-obvious converse is that the government may not be in deficit. A recent Bank of England study (Taylor and Threadgold, 1979) has done the appropriate 'inflation accounting' at the macro-level, with dramatic results: if the implicit tax created by inflation eroding the real value of those financial assets that are public sector debt is added to government revenue, and subtracted from personal sector savings, then the government has frequently been in real surplus and the private sector in real deficit (see their table C).

One might anticipate that the massive nominal borrowing by the public sector, now apparently the main focus of government policy, has altered the 'national debt', and this expectation is quite correct – in a most surprising way. Certainly, the nominal level of the debt has increased rapidly, but as Reid (1977) has shown, the ratio of national debt to national income – which seems a sensible measure of real public indebtedness – was in 1975 similar to the value prevailing at the end of the *last* century and hence probably close to its *lowest* value since the Napoleonic wars!

An implication of these two statistics (namely, the real government surplus and the falling real debt ratio) is that the state of *net* government indebtedness to the rest of the economy must have been changing. Hibbert (1979) has kindly provided the orders of magnitude that he has recently calculated, and even with all the usual caveats about definitions and data accuracy the numbers are stunning. In 1957 the public sector was a net debtor to the tune of about 8 per cent of total net national wealth; by 1966 it has become a net creditor to a similar extent, and by 1975 the public sector owned 26 per cent of net national wealth. The statistics mesh consistently and reveal enormous and very rapid real changes behind the monetary veil. Such an outcome does not seem to have been an intended consequence of any postwar government policy. Yet a further implication of these data is that the recession manifest in the current high level of unemployment may be due in part to the implicit government surplus with the public sector borrowing requirement (PSBR) being a mere monetary epiphenomenon.

The facts in this last conjecture are fairly well established, although the interpretation and policy implications may not be unique. For my purposes, the conjecture need not even be correct since my point is that attempts to reduce the PSBR in the belief that it is a 'cause' of inflation rather than a 'consequence' of recession will impose major costs on society *if that belief is mistaken*. Would it not have been worthwhile to devote rather greater resources to researching the matter beforehand?

Yet our government has reduced the SSRC's budget – and in its calculations of 'average student costs' implicitly values the entire research output of the university sector at zero. However little the government might value our theories or empirical evidence, to base policy on hope or belief really is alchemy. Keynes, this time in his *General Theory* (1936, p. 383), provides the most apt quotation: 'Practical men, who believe themselves to be quite exempt from any intellectual influences, are actually the slaves of some defunct economists.' I hesitate to continue his quote – but he did then say 'Madmen in authority, who hear voices in the air, are distilling their frenzy from some academic scribbler of a few years back'. Hopefully, that will not be the fate of this lecture a few years hence.

Stretching somewhat my argument about the value of data, endless billions of dollars have been spent on space exploration by the US government just to collect a few observations of some lumps of rock and gas (with incidental kudos, 'technical spin-off' and tenuous 'defence' advantages). What government anywhere has spent one-thousandth as much in deliberately observing (experimentally or non-experimentally) or trying to understand an economic system of at least equal importance to our lives?

5 A Structure for Econometrics

Econometricians are the natural critics of economists' empirical findings, and although that is an easy way to make enemies, the counter-criticisms of econometrics noted earlier are not simply the revenge of the aggrieved. However, their valid basis is *not* econometric alchemy but a misallocation of resources. (This is not a new theme; for an earlier debate, see Orcutt (1952) and the following discussion.)

What should have become a relatively minor aspect of the subject, namely deriving methods for estimating the parameters of known models, has been accorded the centre of the stage as casual perusal of any current econometrics textbook will confirm. The rapid development of computer speeds and storage capacity should by now have relegated most of estimation theory to footnotes about numerical approximations and refocused attention on all of the issues surrounding methodology, inference, model formulation and equation selection (see Griliches, 1974; Mizon, 1977a; Leamer, 1978). We have responded as quickly as Diplodocus used to move on a frosty morning and should remember that the Saurischia once dominant are now extinct.

The economic system is the outcome of centuries of adaptive human behaviour; agents seem to optimize their 'state' given the environment, which adapts in response both socially and physically. Econometricians conceptualize this system as a complex non-linear, interdependent, multivariate, disequilibrium dynamical process dependent on agents' expectations and their adjustments, subject to random shocks, and involving many phenomena that are unobservable; relevant time-series data are inaccurate and exist for only short periods and for a few major variables; economic theories are highly simplified abstractions usually of a comparative statics form invoking many explicit *ceteris paribus* clauses (with yet others implicitly required), most of which are invalid in empirical applications – little wonder that our macroeconometric representations are less than perfect.

This conceptualization is the real basis for Keynes's critique, but instead of construing the issue as one of 'problems for the linear model', turn the matter on its head and begin with a characterization of the economy that does have the relevant properties. As elsewhere, it may pay to take an overview to be simplified if allowable rather than attempt to generalize a simple approach in many different directions simultaneously. A crude schematic structure for econometrics is as follows. To a first approximation, after suitably transforming the original variables (with all non-linearities allocated to identities), many data generation processes in economics can be conceived of as (see, *inter alia*, Richard, 1980)

$$y_t \,|\, z_t \sim \mathrm{N}(\mathit{\Pi} z_t, \mathit{\Omega}) \qquad (t = 1, \ldots, T) \tag{1.1}$$

where y_t is a vector of endogenous variables, z_t is a vector of all relevant past and present information (so that $\mathscr{E}(y_t \,|\, z_t) = \mathit{\Pi} z_t$ where $\mathscr{E}$ denotes the expectations operator) and $x_t \sim \mathrm{NI}(\mu, \Psi)$ denotes a variate that is normally and independently distributed, with a mean of μ and a covariance matrix of Ψ. The parameter matrix $(\mathit{\Pi}, \mathit{\Omega}) = P$ is taken as approximately constant by working in a sufficiently large (but assumed finite) dimensional parameter space. Normality is a convenient fiction which restricts attention to sample information in the first two moments of the data, and independence of successive observations is achieved by construction. For sufficiently large T, accurate data and knowledge of both the required data transformations and the composition of z_t, the enormous number of parameters in P could be estimated directly using the fact that (1.1) defines the likelihood function

$$\mathscr{L}(P; y_t \,|\, z_t). \tag{1.2}$$

An 'economic theory' corresponds to asserting that P depends on only a smaller number of parameters, denoted by the vector θ, and written as[4]

$$P = f(\theta) \qquad \theta \in \Theta \tag{1.3}$$

where Θ is the parameter space; if θ is identifiable (i.e. uniquely entailed by P) then all hypotheses like (1.3) can be tested using the principle due to Wald (1943).

In terms of my discussion of 'science', estimation of P hardly qualifies and is far from providing a simple theory. A major role of equation (1.3) is to limit the number of variables that have to be considered (which is a crude application of Occam's razor) but the real case against 'measurement without theory' has been powerfully presented by Koopmans (1949) in his well-known debate with Vining (1949a, b). Many of my present criticisms were noted by both parties to that debate. Accepting that we must work within the best available economic theory framework to contribute towards scientific knowledge, the econometric problem arises because the scale of the model and the paucity of the available observations preclude direct estimation of P (but see Sargent and Sims, 1977) and indeed of θ. Attention is thereby focused on submodels and hence on the weak exogeneity properties of the 'regressor' variables in the submodels. If $\mathscr{L}(\cdot)$ can be factorized in terms of both data and parameters such that

$$\mathscr{L}(\cdot) = \mathscr{L}_1(\theta_1; y_{1t} \,|\, y_{2t}, z_t)\,\mathscr{L}_2(\theta_2; y_{2t} \,|\, z_t) \tag{1.4}$$

where $(\theta_1, \theta_2) \in \Theta_1 \times \Theta_2$, so that any changes in either θ_i leaves the other unaffected (for a precise statement, see chapter 15) and θ_2 are 'nuisance parameters', then $\mathscr{L}_1(\cdot)$ can be analysed separately from $\mathscr{L}_2(\cdot)$ (Koopmans, 1950a). In such a case, y_2 is said to be weakly exogenous for θ_1 and y_{2t} can be taken as given when analysing the submodel that determines y_{1t}. One interesting implication is that variables about which agents form 'rational expectations' cannot be taken as weakly exogenous since, by hypothesis, θ_1 depends on θ_2 in such models.

Even assuming that no mistakes have been made in formulating $\mathscr{L}_1(\cdot)$ and that the dimensionality is tractable, it is still unlikely that detailed analysis of the likelihood function will be feasible and some summarization will prove essential (Edwards, 1972). Estimation theory concerns alternative rules of attaching numbers to θ_1 given the data, and this can be done in (infinitely) many ways which can have very different properties. Nevertheless, the entire topic can be resolved by noting that (for $L = \log_e \mathscr{L}$)

$$\frac{\partial L_1}{\partial \theta_1} = q_1(\theta_1) \tag{1.5}$$

is an estimator-generating equation in that other estimators can be interpreted as approximations to solving $q_1(\theta_1) = 0$ (see chapter 13, based on ideas considered by Durbin, 1988). Since computers have greatly alleviated the need to choose approximations that minimize the computational burden, we may as well solve for the most likely value of θ_1, i.e. $\hat{\theta}_1$ such that $q_1(\hat{\theta}_1) = 0$ and $(\partial q_1 / \partial \theta_1')_{\hat{\theta}_1}$ is negative definite (unless the likelihood function is such that the summarization in (1.5) will be misleading). Inference is also almost entirely dependent on $q(\cdot)$ (see, for example, Rao, 1973; Breusch and Pagan, 1980), and so we can proceed to other matters.

Additional problems which are less easily solved are, first, that at present $f(\theta)$ is based on an excessively idealized abstraction (which is more a guide to how the econometric model should look if the idealized state were to occur than a useful set of restrictions for imposing on data), and, second, that the structure and composition of z_t are unknown. Thus we have 'econometric modelling', that activity of matching an incorrect version of (1.3) to an inadequate representation of (1.1), using insufficient and inaccurate data. The resulting compromise can be awkward, or it can be a useful approximation which encompasses previous results, throws light on economic theory and is sufficiently constant for prediction, forecasting and perhaps even policy. Simply writing down an 'economic theory', manipulating it to a 'condensed form' (see Desai, 1981a) and 'calibrating' the resulting parameters[5] using a pseudo-sophisticated estimator based on poor data which the model does not adequately describe constitutes a recipe for disaster, not for simulating gold! Its only link with alchemy is self-deception.

As an illustration consider the transactions demand for money. In an equilibrium world with constant transactions technology and static expectations, agents are assumed to keep a constant ratio between nominal (real) money and nominal (real) income:

$$M/PY = K(\cdot). \tag{1.6}$$

Between such worlds, $K(\cdot)$ will be lower if interest rates r or inflation $\dot{p}$ are higher, yielding, for example,

$$M = K^*PYr^\alpha(1 + \dot{p})^\beta \qquad \alpha, \beta < 0. \tag{1.7}$$

In spite of the strong assumptions, (1.7) embodies a number of useful ideas (including independence from units of nominal variables) which it seems reasonable to require of an econometric model's solved equilibrium form. However, (1.7) is a demand schedule, not a behavioural plan, and it is not sensible to attempt direct estimation of α and β. Indeed, attempting to do so for M1 yields (see chapter 11)

$$\ln M_t = 7.6 + 0.18 \ln Y_t + 0.84 \ln P_t - 0.12 \ln r_t + 0.17\Delta \ln P_t \tag{1.8}$$
$$\quad\;\; (2.9)\;\,(0.30) \qquad (0.17) \qquad (0.02) \qquad (0.76)$$

$$T = 32 \qquad R^2 = 0.75 \qquad s = 0.019 \qquad d = 0.9 \qquad \chi^2(20) = 399$$

where T is the sample size. Such results are uninterpretable since d indicates significant autocorrelation (so that the quoted standard errors are badly downward biased) and the model is rejected by the $\chi^2(20)$ test for parameter constancy. The results hardly 'corroborate' the 'theory', and so we do not seem to find a relationship where one was anticipated on grounds of 'common sense' as much as 'economic theory'. Restricting the coefficients of Y and P to be unity increases s to 0.067 and lowers d to 0.45, and so that 'solution' can be rejected. Even neglecting the possibility that (1.8) is just another 'spurious regression', it is not possible to decide whether or not the 'theory' has been rejected since the model obviously does not adequately describe the disequilibrium data. Yet the dynamic equation eventually chosen as a reasonable model of the same data series had $s = 0.13$ and yielded the 'equilibrium' solution

$$\ln(M/PY) = \ln K^* - 0.38 \ln r - 3.67 \ln(1 + \dot{p}) \tag{1.9}$$
$$\qquad\qquad\quad (0.12) \qquad (1.98)$$

which is consistent with the hypothesized demand schedule. Moreover, the long-run homogeneity postulates could not be rejected, nor could parameter constancy (which also tested the weak exogeneity assumptions concerning P, Y and r) despite the obvious failure of (1.8).

My approach is admittedly *ad hoc*, since although 'optimization' is a sensible organizing principle for economic theory, derived models will be empirically useful only if the associated criteria functions adequately represent agents' decision problems (that is, their objectives, costs and constraints). Present formulations are not entirely satisfactory. Consequently, my own empirical 'research programme' has been to investigate modelling based on minimal assumptions about the intelligence of agents and the information available to them, with maximal reliance on data using 'economic theory' guidelines to restrict the class of model considered, as in the M1 example. Agents form contingent plans, but respond like servomechanisms to changes in weakly exogenous variables (see, for example, Phillips, 1954). The resulting feedback models mimic 'rational' behaviour for disequilibrium states around an otherwise constant steady-state growth path, and highlight features that seem worth incorporating in empirical time-series equations based on tighter theoretical specifications. The approach is complementary to both pure time-series analysis and theory-based quantitative economics, and has as its next stage the introduction of expectational and adaptive behaviour so that agents can learn to react rationally in non-steady-state worlds. Fortunately, others are also successfully tackling modelling from an economic theory viewpoint (see Nerlove, 1972) and, in particular, Muellbauer (1979) has derived interesting empirical equations from explicitly dynamic theories.

6 Is Econometrics Alchemy or Science?

The ease with which spurious results could be created suggested alchemy, but the scientific status of econometrics was illustrated by showing that such deceptions are testable. In our rapidly changing world, undetected fallacies quickly become positive instances of Goodhart's 'law' (1978) to the effect that all econometric models break down when used for policy.

It is difficult to provide a convincing case for the defence against Keynes's accusation almost 40 years ago that econometrics is statistical alchemy since many of his criticisms remain apposite. The characterization of science offered earlier did not exclude econometrics *a priori* simply because of its inability to conduct controlled experiments. But empirical substantiation of the claim to be a science does require the existence of credible evidence, namely findings that are acceptable independently of political beliefs or preconceptions about the structural form of the economy (for a related critique from a systems theorist, see Kalman, 1979). The turbulence of the 1970s has greatly facilitated the rejection of 'false' models, and although we are a long way from producing 'answers', striking progress has been achieved since Keynes wrote, albeit at the cost of making the subject highly technical and increasingly inaccessible to non-specialists (for an interesting exposition, see Bray, 1979).

The alternative claim has been made by Hicks (1979, p. xi) that 'as economics pushes on beyond "statics" it becomes less like science and more like history'. While this correctly highlights both the importance of the historical context and the fact that there is only one realization of any economic time series, it does not rule out a scientific approach to dynamic economics.

Econometricians may well tend to look too much where the light is and too little where the key might be found. Nevertheless, they are a positive help in trying to dispel the poor public image of economics (quantitative or otherwise) as a subject in which empty boxes are opened by assuming the existence of can-openers to reveal contents which any ten economists will interpret in 11 ways.

Whether or not econometrics will prove to be more analogous to alchemy than to science depends primarily on the spirit with which the subject is tackled. Obviously, I cannot speak for how others will choose to use econometrics, although I believe that at this School we have attempted to tackle the subject scientifically. Hopefully, my examples may persuade you that such is at least potentially feasible. Far more rapid progress could be made if all empirical studies would provide greatly improved test information to allow readers to judge plausibility correctly. The three golden rules of econometrics are test, test and test;[6] that all three rules are broken regularly in empirical applications is fortunately easily remedied. Rigorously tested models, which adequately described the available data, encompassed previous findings and were derived from well-based theories would greatly enhance any claim to be scientific.

The study of what little econometric light we have is far from being an easy option, especially as taught at this School; nevertheless, there can be few more exciting or intellectually rewarding subjects and I commend its study to you.

Notes

1 s and d respectively denote the equation standard error and the Durbin–Watson statistic. An estimated coefficient is conventionally called significant if the interval of plus and minus two standard errors does not include zero; in that case one can reject with approximately 95 per cent confidence the hypothesis that the coefficient is zero. Since both coefficients and their standard errors are estimated, and the numbers obtained depend on the method of estimation and the choice of model, 'significance' of coefficients can change radically with the equation specification, as indeed occurs below.

2 That is, where the residual in one period is proportional to the residual one period previously plus a random variable; i.e. $\hat{u}_t = \lambda \hat{u}_{t-1} + \hat{e}_t$, where $\hat{u}_t$ is the tth residual.

3 The two χ^2 values in figure 1.8 are a (likelihood ratio) test for a common factor (χ_1^2) and a 'Box–Pierce' test for residual autocorrelation (χ_{11}^2) respectively – see Pierce (1971), Breusch and Pagan (1980), Sargan (1980a) and chapter 7 – both of which 'reject' the model specification.

4 It may be useful to have a 'microeconomic foundation' for macroeconometrics but it is not essential and may be counterproductive: 'If it were necessary in the equations of hydrodynamics to specify the motion of every water molecule, a theory of ocean waves would be far beyond the means of 20th century science' (Wilson, 1979).

5 Or, to quote Hicks (1979, p. xi): 'decorated with least squares and confidence intervals'.

6 Notwithstanding the difficulties involved in calculating and controlling type I and II errors.

2

Stochastic Specification in an Aggregate Demand Model of the United Kingdom

Preamble

My first attempts at empirical macroeconometrics during 1969 were based on the following view of the 'conventional' approach to econometrics. Economic theorists had deduced how optimizing agents would behave in all aspects of economic life and hence what interdependencies should exist between observable variables; economic statisticians had designed and implemented measurement systems for national accounts so that the appropriate data series had been collected and collated; econometricians had estimated and tested empirical counterparts of the economists' theories on those data; but progress in econometric theory and computing had led to the development of more powerful estimators (namely, those I was going to use), the application of which to the already known economic structure would produce more efficient estimates of the parameters of interest – and hence better forecasts and policy. A major puzzle was why the assumptions of the econometric theory (e.g. those underlying the Gauss–Markov theorem) were not satisfied in data applications, but more sophisticated econometric estimators could be derived to take account of most 'problems'.

In my defence, I can only plead that my naivety dissipated very fast as I quickly realized that such an approach not only did not work, it could not work: after all, I knew some of the economic theorists – they were extremely clever, but they were not omniscient! And omniscience, or a close approximation thereto, was a necessary condition for such a methodology to work. I began at once to try and develop some improved approaches.

Many other researchers had also realized that the reigning emperor was at best scantily clad. Ed Leamer in his 1978 consolidation designated the above view as needing the Axiom of Correct Specification, so that the econometric model had to coincide with the actual economic mechanism except for an independent error. Clive Granger and Paul Newbold

Reprinted from *Econometrica*, 42, 3 (May 1974) 559–78. This is a substantially revised version of a paper presented to the Barcelona Meeting of the Econometric Society. The author gratefully acknowledges an immense debt to Denis Sargan for advice throughout the preparation of the paper and also wishes to thank Robin Harrison for valuable research assistance in developing the program library, and Pravin K. Trivedi, Kenneth F. Wallis and the Seminar Groups at Essex, Oxford and Warwick for useful comments on an earlier draft, while freeing them all of responsibility for any residual errors. The anonymous referees of *Econometrica* also helped to clarify the argument.

(1974) chastised many extant models as having 'nonsense equations', a follow-up to Yule (1926). And Charles Nelson (1972) demonstrated that simple extrapolative models often forecasted better than large-scale econometric systems. The present chapter was completed in 1969 before I was aware of many of the parallel critiques and developments (there were long publication delays even then!). Nevertheless, the points which were explicitly at the centre of the paper were as follows.

1   Dynamic and stochastic specification were inseparable – one could not expect to build useful models by arbitrarily asserting the former, and mechanistically patching the latter.
2   Simultaneity and dynamics also interacted closely and needed a joint treatment, albeit that time disaggregation reduced the role of the former and enhanced that of the latter.
3   Rigorous testing was essential ('we should know what problems are untreated, rather than just hope that they are absent') and had to be of interesting null hypotheses, using valid tests (not, for example, the Durbin–Watson statistic in dynamic models).
4   The likelihood function was central to estimation and inference (leading to chapter 13 below).
5   Serial correlation was an admissible simplification of the dynamics only if a test of the induced restrictions was insignificant. How to do this test was as yet only understood for first-order cases, following Sargan's seminal paper (1964a), but could be generalized to systems, revealing that cross-equation serial correlation could matter in practice.
6   Seasonality and dynamics also interacted, making model selection very complicated.
7   An operational emphasis was essential since econometric methods were useful only once they were embodied in a computer program, and as a consequence much of my effort went into writing and testing the software (the precursor to AUTOREG).

Some of the specific lessons which I learnt during the course of the study can also be seen.

(a)   Corroboration of theory-models is not enough to justify their adoption since the same data might also reject the model on a different test or corroborate a conflicting model (see Ericsson and Hendry (1989) for an extension).
(b)   Adopting the alternative hypothesis when a null is rejected is not only a *non sequitur*, it is frequently fairly disastrous in practice.
(c)   'Simple-to-general' modelling procedures have inherent flaws since a later rejection invalidates all earlier inferences.
(d)   To interpret *any* of the empirical evidence correctly, one needed to be able to account for *all* of the results.

While almost no work on Monte Carlo methods is included in this volume, I had undertaken a great deal of simulation analysis contemporaneously (see Hendry and Trivedi, 1972; Hendry, 1973; followed by Hendry and Harrison, 1974; Hendry, 1975a). In Monte Carlo methods, three important notions are transparent. First, the process generating the data, and the models fitted to those data, are distinct entities. Second, one knew the 'whole story' (i.e. the actual mechanism) and hence, except perhaps in very small samples, had no problem in understanding all of the evidence, even when mis-specified models were estimated. Third, 'simple-to-general' modelling strategies would not work well, especially compared with fitting the most general equation at the outset which in the limited context of Monte Carlo experiments would be tantamount to omniscience: since all the Monte Carlo studies used relatively simple data generation processes, it was easy to nest the actual data generation process in an estimable equation. However, 'real' data mechanisms were extremely complicated, and so the methodological implications of the third notion were not obvious to me at the time. The Monte Carlo analogy played and still plays an important background role in my thinking about modelling procedures, and by 1973 it was already altering my views and suggesting possible solutions to the problems I saw, as well as new critiques: if simple-to-general would not work when I knew the answer, why should it work when I did not?

However, I also missed some crucial lessons which were to recur later.

1   The paper contains no graphs: I never looked at the data! (although I did check its accuracy on printouts).
2   I simply assumed that all non-modelled variables would be 'exogenous' and hence would have appropriate statistical properties, although I doubt if I had a very clear idea about precisely what properties were needed (despite discussing whether or not to endogenize disposable income).
3   That the parameters of my theory-model might not be constant did not cross my mind despite the forecast test outcome – the real shock to my initial approach (sketched at the start of this Preamble) came when I tried to 'predict' the first two quarters of 1968 some time later and obtained values in the hundreds for my χ^2 forecast statistic with 12 degrees of freedom.[1]
4   The overall specification of the dynamic system (i.e. the so-called reduced form) followed from that of the structural model, so that the over-identification tests conducted were conditional on the untested validity of the unrestricted reduced form: I did not perceive that the entire order of the approach was inappropriate.

Thus, I was still conditioned in many ways to implicitly following the conventional road.

By the time this chapter appeared in print, the AUTOREG library (described in chapter 14) was well developed and quite widely used. Meghnad Desai pointed out one of the main methodological thrusts by referring to the library as a 'model destructor' since its vast array of tests usually could be relied on to detect some serious departure of a model's specification from its assumed properties. The need to test models destructively to ascertain their problems and weak points remains paramount and is a clear lesson of the following chapter.

However, the converse of rules or guidelines for model construction were prominent by their absence, making 1970–5 a difficult period for empirical researchers (some of whom virtually developed 'AUTOREG phobia' from fears about what it might do to lovingly constructed equations!). The need to develop a more constructive aspect was clear, and implicit in chapter 2 is an unsuccessful effort towards doing so by using test outcomes as 'constructive indicators of mis-specification in dynamic models', although that idea is countered by the caveat noted in (b) above. The evolution of a more coherent notion lay some time in the future, but the seeds of dissent were sown and several had taken root. Latent among these ideas was the glimmer that the procedures of empirical researchers were dependent on what their software allowed via easy calculations, which later emerges in chapter 8 as the notion that computer programs embody implicit methodologies, and in the final chapter as a program which had an explicit methodology.

Note

1   Actually, most of that failure was due to ignoring the reaction of consumers to a *pre-announced* tax change, so 'bad luck' mattered here – see the dummy variable for purchase tax in chapter 8. Still, it was a salutary lesson.

1 Introduction

Applied macroeconometric investigations have usually been directed at estimating the systematic or *deterministic* components of economic relationships, while paying minimal attention to the *stochastic* properties of the processes under study. Thus one can cite the common habit of assuming that errors are white noise; although this hypothesis is regularly (if not always validly) tested by the Durbin–Watson statistic, even when significant autocorrelation is indicated, it tends to be regarded as a nuisance (i.e. a problem to be removed) rather than as a factor to be integrated into the structural development of the model, or as information suggestive of the need to revise the dynamic specification.

One reason for this may be the (believed) difficulty of allowing for the joint existence of lagged endogenous regressors and autocorrelated disturbances in simultaneous systems of relationships. However, it is not yet clear which subset of these deserves most attention should it prove impossible to solve the complete estimation problem.[1] On the one hand, we know that mis-specification of the error structure in single dynamic equations can have serious effects on the validity of estimation and the accuracy of forecasts (see, for example, Malinvaud, 1966, ch. 14). Equally, the importance of an appropriate treatment of simultaneity has been amply demonstrated (see Johnston (1972, ch. 13) for a convenient summary), and in both cases the analytical asymptotic results have received subsequent experimental confirmation for small samples. Nevertheless, little is known about the relative importance of these two problems in empirical research or the degree of sensitivity of results to alternative estimator choices.

An important factor affecting this issue is the increasing availability of time-disaggregated data as this tends to enhance the role of 'recursive' formulations (simply construed as having all regressors predetermined) and hence both the value of and the need for methods which allow the estimation of high-order autocorrelation processes, but which ignore simultaneity (see Wallis, 1972a). Partially countering this, with short observation periods one must be prepared for cross-equation error *serial* covariances (and not just contemporaneous covariances), so that the development of models with non-diagonal matrices of autocorrelations becomes necessary (see Sargan, 1961; Hendry, 1971).

The estimates presented below are intended to assist in evaluating these problems. A dynamic model of aggregate demand in the United Kingdom is estimated by a variety of methods which depend on differing assumptions about simultaneity and autocorrelation to investigate the existence (or otherwise) of within- and/or between-equation error autocorrelations in a small empirical system which appears reasonably well specified on such conventional criteria as goodness of fit, simulation performance and forecast accuracy. The estimates can be interpreted as testing a number of specification assumptions that are normally maintained hypotheses, and the results suggest an important role for autocorrelation as a constructive indicator of mis-specification in dynamic models (compare Sargan, 1964a).

Indeed, despite its apparently satisfactory performance, the alternative estimators reveal a number of mis-specifications in the system under study. Appropriate computational methods have been developed for a wide range of autocorrelation processes, and it would seem that the instrumental variable class of estimators are not computationally expensive, yet can yield useful information. Systems methods are certainly feasible for the size of model used here, and so might be applicable to larger structures on a 'block recursive' basis (see Fisher, 1965), but they require considerably more computer time.

2 Methodology: Autocorrelation and Simultaneity

The formal structure of the model to be analysed[2] is

$$\sum_{i=0}^{n} B_i y_{t-i} + \sum_{j=0}^{k} C_j z_{t-j} = u_t \qquad (t = 1, \ldots, T) \tag{2.1}$$

where B_i and C_j are matrices of coefficients, $|B_0| \neq 0$, and y_t and z_t are $p \times 1$ and $q \times 1$ vectors of observations on the endogenous and exogenous variables at time t. The vector u_t is a $p \times 1$ vector of stochastic terms generated by

$$u_t = \sum_{i=1}^{m} R_i u_{t-i} + \varepsilon_t \tag{2.2}$$

where the R_i are $p \times p$ matrices of autoregressive coefficients and ε_t is NID$(0, \Sigma)$ with Σ positive definite and unrestricted. We assume there exists sufficient *a priori* information on the coefficients of the B_i and C_j to identify every parameter in (2.1) and (2.2) (see Sargan, 1961, 1972) and for stationarity we assume that all the roots of the polynomial matrices $\sum_{i=0}^{n} B_i L^i$ and $\sum_{i=0}^{m} R_i L^i$ lie outside the unit circle, where $L^\theta x_t = x_{t-\theta}$ and $R_0 \equiv I$.

Equation (2.2) defines an mth-order vector autoregressive process, the ith equation of which is (using $R_l = (r_{ijl})$)

$$u_{i,t} = \sum_{l=1}^{m} \sum_{j=1}^{p} r_{ijl} u_{j,t-l} + \varepsilon_{i,t} \qquad (i = 1, \ldots, p; \, t = 1, \ldots, T). \tag{2.3}$$

While consistent and asymptotically efficient estimates of (2.1) and (2.2) can be obtained by maximizing the required likelihood function, unless both m and p are small relative to the sample size, *unrestricted* estimation of (2.2) will not be possible or, if accomplished, will provide very imprecise coefficient estimates. Conversely, if invalid prior restrictions are imposed on (2.3), we shall obtain inconsistent estimates of the r_{ijl} and, when $n > 0$ (as will be assumed below), of the parameters of (2.1) also.[3] Thus, before opting for any particular compromise, it seems useful to consider the implications for estimator choice of alternative restrictions on the r_{ijl}.

One obvious possibility is $m = 0$ which reduces the analysis to two cases: (i) $p = 1$, whence (2.1) defines a single dynamic equation with predetermined regressors and white noise errors, so that ordinary least squares (OLS) estimation is legitimate; and (ii) $p > 1$ which defines a standard system of simultaneous equations, again with serially independent errors, and hence two-stage least squares (TSLS) or, if the entire system has been specified, full information maximum likelihood (FIML) are viable.

When $m > 0$ there are three situations to consider, soluble by generalizations of OLS, TSLS and FIML respectively:[4] (iii) if $p = 1$, (2.3) defines an mth-order scalar autoregressive process, estimable by the appropriate non-linear extension of least squares denoted autoregressive least squares (ALS) (see, for example, Malinvaud, 1966; Hendry and Trivedi, 1972); (iv) if $p > 1$ but all $r_{ijl} = 0$ for $i \neq j$ (i.e. there are no across-equation serial correlations), one can use the autoregressive generalization of the instrumental variable approach (AIV) proposed by Sargan (1959) (also see Sargan (1964a) and compare Fair (1970)); and (v) finally, when $p > 1$ and the R_i are non-diagonal, estimation can be accomplished by autoregressive full information maximum likelihood (AML) (see Sargan, 1961; Hendry, 1971).[5]

Below we apply all these estimators to the one body of data, and while this could be as misleading as data mining, the following justification is offered. Since (i)–(v) are special cases of the maintained hypothesis defined by (2.1) and (2.2), the methods locate optima in various subspaces of the complete parameter space and so should yield useful information about the stochastic structure of the model being used. This might, for example, indicate mis-specifications in the deterministic structure so that revision yields a system with white noise errors, estimable by (ii) (see, for example, the analysis of equations (2.4)–(2.7) below). Clearly, however, although the final set of estimates may not *directly* allow for autocorrelation, this is a completely different proposition from blindly assuming (ii) at the start of the study and never testing the assumption of serial independence. In effect, one would like to do an analysis of the residuals as in the classical regression model; because of the presence of lagged endogenous regressors, the autocorrelation properties of the residuals yield a biased picture of the spectrum of the errors; thus one adopts the reasonable alternative of estimating the parameters of the assumed error process.

Nevertheless, the results must be interpreted with care, since a 'significant' outcome of a test in (i), for example, may not be due to the failure of the particular hypothesis one wished to test, but may arise from the invalidity of some other assumption which at the time seemed safe to make but which later evidence leads one to doubt. Falsification of earlier premises is a familiar difficulty in empirical research, and the spirit of the following analysis is to interpret the results as an investigator would who had the same information as the reader at the stage each set of findings is presented rather than to adopt the omniscient position of 'knowing the whole story' at the start, as one might do in Monte Carlo work. This course seems preferable since one can never claim to know the 'true' structure in a science, and, indeed, the evidence from later results which leads one to question the initial estimates may itself be incorrect and hence be a poor basis for criticism.

3 Methodology: Autocorrelation and Dynamics

The determination of an appropriate lag structure in dynamic models is still mainly an empirical question often resolved by experimenting with a set of lagged regressors using OLS or TSLS. This could yield misleading results in view of the well-known lagged-dependent-variable-autocorrelated error bias, and so we adopt an approach which explicitly recognizes the interaction between the equation dynamics and the stochastic specification (see Sargan, 1964a). To illustrate this, consider (iii) with a model such that $m = n = p = 1$, and write the only equation in normalized form as

$$y_t = \beta y_{t-1} + \gamma' z_t + u_t \tag{2.4}$$

where the elements of z_t are predetermined. For simplicity, in this single-equation context, rewrite the appropriate specialization of (2.2) as

$$u_t = \rho_1 u_{t-1} + \varepsilon_t; \tag{2.5}$$

then transforming (2.4) to eliminate (2.5) yields

$$y_t = (\rho_1 + \beta) y_{t-1} - \rho_1 \beta y_{t-2} + \gamma' z_t - \rho_1 \gamma' z_{t-1} + \varepsilon_t \tag{2.6}$$

which we denote the restricted transformed equation (RTE). An alternative possibility is that (2.4) has a mis-specified dynamic structure (with the autocorrelation reflecting the omitted variables) and the correct relationship is a general linear one between y_t and $(y_{t-1}, y_{t-2}, z_t, z_{t-1})$. Deleting any redundant members of z_{t-1} (i.e. those which are linearly dependent on the elements of z_t such as a constant term), an estimable hypothesis is

$$y_t = a_0 y_{t-1} + a_1 y_{t-2} + a_2' z_t + a_3' z_{t-1}^* + v_t \tag{2.7}$$

where z_{t-1}^* is the set of non-redundant variables in z_{t-1}. Since (2.7) is equivalent to ignoring the autoregressive restriction in (2.6) and recombining regressors which occur more than once, it is denoted the unrestricted transformed equation (UTE). Equations (2.4) and (2.7) are estimable by OLS, and (2.6) by ALS, and on the basis of the residual sums of squares (S_1, S_2 and S_3 respectively) one can construct F and/or χ^2 tests based on the likelihood ratio principle to discriminate between the three alternatives.

First, one can test the significance of $\hat{\rho}_1$ in (2.6) either by using

$$T \log(S_1/S_3) \underset{A}{\sim} \chi^2_{(1)} \qquad \text{on} \qquad H_0: \rho_1 = 0 \tag{2.8}$$

or by the asymptotically equivalent t test on $\hat{\rho}_1$. Next the validity of the autoregressive restriction on (2.6) relative to (2.7) can be tested using

$$T \log(S_3/S_2) \underset{A}{\sim} \chi^2_{(N)} \tag{2.9}$$

where N is the number of restrictions imposed on (2.7) to obtain (2.6). Finally, we can test the significance of $\hat{a}_1$ and the $\hat{a}_{3i}$ in (2.7) either jointly by the standard F test on a set of additional regressors (which depends on $S_1/S_2 - 1$ and should be significant if both (2.8) and (2.9) are) or individually by t tests. Without enumerating all possible outcomes, if no test is significant one chooses (2.4) with white noise errors, whereas, if all are, (2.7) is selected, whence the entire procedure can be repeated with this as a new baseline. (Compare the 'identification' approach of Box and Jenkins, 1976.)

This analysis can easily be generalized to $n > 1$ and/or $m > 1$, though now, for example, one might also want to test 'composite' hypotheses[6] such as

$$u_t = \sum_{i=1}^{m} \rho_i u_{t-i} + \varepsilon_t \qquad (2.10)$$

against 'simple' ones such as

$$u_t = \rho_m u_{t-m} + \varepsilon_t \qquad (2.11)$$

to obtain a parsimonious representation of the autocorrelation. As discussed above, the further generalization to (iv) with $p > 1$ involves using instrumental variables rather than least squares, and if the equation is over-identified this allows an additional χ^2 specification test asymptotically equivalent to that proposed by Hood and Koopmans (1953) (see Basmann, 1960; Fisk, 1967). To maintain comparability between equations when using AIV, all the predetermined regressors in (2.7) are used as instruments when estimating (2.4) and (2.6), in addition to the set of over-identifying predetermined variables selected from the reduced form of (2.1). Finally, analogous generalizations are possible to (v) (see Hendry, 1971).

Since a large number of alternative estimators are used, to help control against 'spurious' results, the last two sample observations are retained for an asymptotically valid χ^2 test of post-sample parameter stability, applied to each final specification. Let f_t denote the vector of errors between the realized outcome and that 'predicted' by known values of all reduced form regressors, and let $\hat{\Omega}$ be a consistent estimate of the reduced form error variance matrix; then

$$\sum_{t=T+1}^{T+h} f_t' \, \hat{\Omega}^{-1} f_t \; \underset{A}{\approx} \; \chi^2_{ph} \qquad (2.12)$$

on the null hypothesis that all the parameters are stable and consistently estimated.[7]

4 An Aggregate Demand Model for the United Kingdom, 1957–1967

The system is intended to be a schematic representation of the demand sector of previous macro-models of the United Kingdom (see Ball and Burns, 1968; Hilton and Heathfield, 1970, especially the chapter by Byron; also compare Klein et al., 1961). We use quarterly seasonally unadjusted data series for the period 1957(i) to 1967(iv). To facilitate interestimator comparisons, only equations linear in both variables and parameters are considered, even though neither complication is insurmountable for most of the methods described below (see Eisenpress and Greenstadt (1966) and Klein (1969) for the former, and, for example, Wallis (1972a) and Williams (1972) for the latter).

The behavioural equations explain consumers' expenditure on durable goods (denoted by C_d) and all other goods and services (C_n), gross domestic fixed capital formation (I), inventory investment (I_v) and imports of goods and services (M). Gross domestic product (Y) is determined by the usual accounting identity, and the model is closed by an empirical relation to determine disposable income (Y_d). The majority of the specifications are conventional but naive; this is partly to minimize the computational burden and partly to focus attention on the stochastic processes.

Precise definitions of the variables are given in the Appendix and the exact specification of the system is indicated by the OLS estimates presented in table 2.1; dummy variables for a constant term and three seasonal shift factors are included in every equation but, to save space, estimates of these are not presented.

The specification of the individual equations requires little comment. Equation (i) is derived from a stock-adjustment expected (or permanent) income model, and includes a dummy variable N for the annual vehicle registration letter. In the United Kingdom since 1963, the last letter of vehicle registration plates represents the year of purchase and this has had a marked effect on the seasonal allocation of expenditure on cars; by switching the month in which new letters commenced, it was used as a policy instrument in 1967 to alter the seasonal pattern and so requires explicit inclusion in the equation given the decision to use a parametric representation of seasonality (compare Williams, 1972). Equation (ii) is simply a transformed permanent income equation, and (iii) and (iv) are derived from flexible accelerator–capital stock adjustment models. Equation (v) assumes linear price, income and stock building effects (lagged imports were not significant as a regressor) and (vi) is a transformed distributed lag relationship.[8]

It must be stressed that the present model only seems to be somewhat of a caricature because aggregate demand relationships have been intensively studied. The system is almost certainly mis-specified in a number of respects, which may well have generated the autocorrelation observed below,[9] but it would be incorrect to deduce that this vitiates the purpose of the exercise. In general we do not know how well specified our models are; one of the points of this paper is the importance of thoroughly testing as many assumptions as possible, revising the specification

Table 2.1 Ordinary least squares[a]

	R^2	s^{2b}	DW^c	$\chi^2_{(2)}{}^d$
(i) $\hat{C}_d = 0.10Y_d + 53N + 0.66C_{d1} - 0.25C_{d2}$ $\quad(0.03)^e \quad (15) \quad (0.14) \quad\quad (0.14)$	0.903	972	1.69	1.1
(ii) $\hat{C}_n = 0.10Y_d + 0.84C_{n1}$ $\quad\quad (0.06) \quad\; (0.09)$	0.994	926	2.64	3.7
(iii) $\hat{I} = 0.29\Delta Y + 0.29\Delta Y_1 + 0.64I_1 + 0.35I_2$ $\quad\quad (0.07) \quad\;\; (0.07) \quad\;\; (0.15) \quad (0.15)$	0.980	1000	1.95	0.5
(iv) $\hat{I}_v = 0.37\Delta Y + 0.50I_{v1} + 0.22I_{v2}$ $\quad\quad (0.09) \quad\;\; (0.14) \quad\;\; (0.14)$	0.732	1781	2.02	1.7
(v) $\hat{M} = 0.58I_v + 0.22Y_1 - 6.2P_m$ $\quad\quad (0.10) \quad (0.02) \quad\; (2.4)$	0.965	1235	1.69	4.5
(vi) $\hat{Y}_d = 0.42Y + 0.49Y_{d1}$ $\quad\quad (0.12) \quad (0.13)$	0.974	7298	1.81	0.4

[a] For definitions of symbols, see the appendix.
[b] s^2, equation error variance adjusted for degrees of freedom.
[c] DW, Durbin–Watson statistic.
[d] $\chi^2_{(2)}$, test of post-sample parameter stability.
[e] Standard errors are shown in parentheses below coefficients.

in the light of the information so obtained. The particular lag structure adopted for the model was chosen according to the analysis in section 3, but was tested only against the alternative of first-order autocorrelation.

5 Methods which Neglect Autocorrelation

5.1 Ordinary Least Squares

Table 2.1 presents these estimates (which of course also ignore simultaneity). The R^2 values are high, and every coefficient has the expected sign and a reasonable magnitude, although the long-run propensity to consume non-durables (0.64) is low, yielding an income elasticity at the mean of only 0.76. For durables (C_d) the corresponding elasticity is 1.86. The accelerator coefficients in (iii) and (iv) are rather large, suggesting an upward bias due to ignoring simultaneity through the GNP identity; the seasonal coefficients for I_v showed a sign pattern which was opposite to that for the other domestic expenditure series, suggesting a 'buffer stock' model. The income and price elasticities of demand for imports (evaluated using $(\partial M/\partial Z)/(\bar{Z}/\bar{M})$) are 0.90 and -0.41 respectively.

Given the method adopted for selecting the lag structure, it is perhaps not surprising that only one of the Durbin–Watson statistics indicates significant autocorrelation (on this, see section 6) but, except for (v), these are biased towards 2. Since none of the χ^2 tests of parameter stability is significant, the specification appears adequate, though some allowance for simultaneity seems desirable.

5.2 Two-stage Least Squares

The system comprises ten lagged endogenous and seven exogenous variables (the latter are N, P_m, GXT, a constant, and three seasonal dummies) which provides 17 possible instruments. Two selections were considered, namely using just the exogenous variables (plus a trend dummy), which yielded a number of coefficient estimates with 'wrong' signs, and using all the predetermined variables in the model, which yielded the set of results presented in table 2.2.[10]

All the coefficients of endogenous regressors (except in (iv)) are smaller than the corresponding values in table 2.1, as might be expected given the likely simultaneity biases affecting OLS (if the chosen instruments are more legitimate than the least squares regressors). Nevertheless, the estimates in three of the equations are unacceptable as their χ^2 test of specification is significant, although this result does not indicate what remedial action is required. Again, none of the parameter stability tests is significant, nor have the estimated error variances increased much, suggesting a flat likelihood surface.

5.3 Full Information Maximum Likelihood

The estimates recorded in table 2.3 are rather different from both previous sets: the short-run propensity in (ii) seems more sensible, although the long-run value

Table 2.2   Two-stage least squares

	$\chi^2_{(i)}$ [a]	NI	s^2	$\chi^2_{(2)}$
(i) $\hat{C}_d = 0.08Y_d + 54N + 0.69C_{d1} - 0.20C_{d2}$ $\quad\;\;(0.03)\quad(15)\quad(0.14)\quad\;\;(0.14)$	14.3	19	982	0.8
(ii) $\hat{C}_n = 0.04Y_d + 0.93C_{n1}$ $\quad\;\;\;(0.08)\quad\;\;(0.12)$	23.1^{*b}	18	957	3.2
(iii) $\hat{I} = 0.19\Delta Y + 0.24\Delta Y_1 + 0.69I_1 + 0.30I_2$ $\quad\;\;\;(0.11)\quad\;\;\;(0.08)\quad\;\;\;(0.16)\quad(0.16)$	20.1^{*}	19	1071	0.6
(iv) $\hat{I}_v = 0.42\Delta Y + 0.52I_{v1} + 0.20I_{v2}$ $\quad\;\;\;(0.13)\quad\;\;(0.15)\quad\;\;(0.14)$	13.1	18	1797	1.7
(v) $\hat{M} = 0.40I_v + 0.24Y_1 - 4.8P_m$ $\quad\;\;(0.14)\quad(0.03)\quad(2.6)$	7.4	19	1345	2.3
(vi) $\hat{Y}_d = 0.36Y + 0.56Y_{d1}$ $\quad\;\;\;(0.13)\quad(0.15)$	26.0^{*}	18	7361	0.4

[a] $\chi^2_{(i)}$ denotes a test of identification/specification with i degrees of freedom where $i = $ NI $-$ NR $- 4$ for NR regressors and NI instrumental variables used in estimation (e.g. $i = 11$ in (i)).
[b] The asterisk denotes significance at the 0.05 level.

remains low, and the accelerator effects are insignificant for both I and I_v, making these simply second-order autoregressions. This suggests that the apparently well-determined effects in OLS depend on simultaneity bias, especially as it is implausible to argue that fixed investment changes substantially in response to current sales movements. The sample correlations between the observations and the reduced form 'predictions' are high (the correlations between the simulated and realized paths are reasonable, being, for example, 0.94 for ΔY, which variable is indirectly derived) and the χ^2 tests for system parameter stability are insignificant, all the one-period-ahead forecasts (based on known values of predetermined variables) being within $\pm 2\omega$.

However, the likelihood ratio test of all the over-identifying restrictions yields a value of 150.9 for $\chi^2_{(60)}$, implying that some of the *a priori* restrictions are inconsistent with the sample information embodied in the unrestricted reduced form (URF). With only 39 observations but 17 regressors in the URF, the asymptotic justification for this statistic is very weak,[11] an interpretation supported by the value of 164.6 for the $\chi^2_{(12)}$ test of parameter stability applied to the URF forecasts which suggests a spurious goodness of fit over the sample period.

6 Methods Which Treat Autocorrelation but Neglect Simultaneity

6.1 Autoregressive Least Squares

An alternative cause of the changes between OLS and FIML in tables 2.1 and 2.3 might be that FIML is relatively more sensitive to mis-specification (see Cragg, 1968);

Table 2.3 Full information maximum likelihood

	$\omega^{2\,a}$	$v^{2\,b}$	CORR[c]
(i) $\hat{C}_d = 0.08Y_d + 58N + 0.68C_{d1} - 0.19C_{d2}$ $\quad\quad (0.02)\quad (12)\quad (0.11)\quad\quad (0.11)$	929	784	0.940
(ii) $\hat{C}_n = 0.15Y_d + 0.76C_{n1}$ $\quad\quad\; (0.07)\quad\; (0.10)$	835	804	0.997
(iii) $\hat{I} = -0.09\Delta Y + 0.09\Delta Y_1 + 0.76I_1 + 0.24I_2$ $\quad\quad\;\; (0.11)\quad\quad (0.09)\quad\quad (0.16)\quad (0.16)$	1231	1583	0.985
(iv) $\hat{I}_v = 0.09\Delta Y + 0.40I_{v1} + 0.33I_{v2}$ $\quad\quad\; (0.14)\quad\;\; (0.16)\quad\;\; (0.16)$	2249	1917	0.767
(v) $\hat{M} = 0.49I_v + 0.23Y_1 - 5.1P_m$ $\quad\quad\; (0.14)\quad (0.02)\quad\;\; (1.9)$	1921	1037	0.967
(vi) $\hat{Y}_d = 0.27Y + 0.67Y_{d1}$ $\quad\quad\; (0.11)\quad\;\; (0.12)$	7754	6513	0.984

One-period-ahead 'forecasts'

		C_d	C_n	I	I_v	M	Y_d	Y	ΔY	
1	Actual	520	4566	1486	5	1693	5507	6679	−96	
	Forecast	547	4555	1518	74	1697	5480	6787	12	$\chi^{2\;d}_{(6)} = 8.4$
2	Actual	537	4821	1546	−41	1665	5644	6856	177	
	Forecast	544	4757	1564	−49	1602	5614	6871	192	$\chi^{2\;d}_{(6)} = 11.1$

[a] Reduced form error variance, not adjusted for degrees of freedom.
[b] Structural form error variance, not adjusted for degrees of freedom.
[c] Correlation over the sample period between the 'dependent' variable and its value 'predicted' by the derived reduced form.
[d] System parameter stability test for one-period-ahead forecasts.

Table 2.4 Autoregressive least squares ($m = 1$)

	$\hat{\rho}_1$	SE$(\hat{\rho}_1)^a$	$\chi^{2\;b}_{(1)}$	$\chi^{2\;c}_{(i)}$	(i)	$\chi^2_{(2)}$	s^2	F$(j, l)^d$	(j, l)
(i)	0.41	(0.26)	2.2	1.1	2	1.1	950	0.8	3, 28
(ii)	−0.36	(0.17)	5.1*e	0.1	1	4.8	838	2.2	2, 31
(iii)	−0.01	(0.34)	0.0	0.0	1	0.4	1033	0.0	2, 29
(iv)	−0.01	(0.29)	0.0	1.5	1	1.6	1838	0.6	2, 30
(v)	0.13	(0.21)	0.5	1.5	3	3.2	1257	0.4	4, 28
(vi)	0.18	(0.28)	0.8	0.7	1	0.5	7379	0.6	2, 31

[a] Standard error of $\hat{\rho}_1$ (see, for example, (2.5)).
[b] Likelihood ratio test of $\rho_1 = 0$.
[c] Likelihood ratio test of the validity of the autoregressive restriction in (2.6) with i degrees of freedom.
[d] Test of

$$\begin{pmatrix} a_1 \\ a_3 \end{pmatrix} = 0$$

in (2.7) with (j, l) degrees of freedom.
[e] The asterisk denotes significance at the 0.05 level.

thus, as discussed in sections 1–3, we use ALS to check the dynamic formulation, and extend the analysis to allow for simultaneity in the next section. A value of $m = 4$ is chosen as a reasonable compromise between the sample size of 39 and the need to check for mis-specified seasonality (see, for example, Wallis, 1972a); thus error processes of the forms (2.5), (2.10) and (2.11) are estimated.

When $m = 1$, the point estimates are naturally very similar to those shown in table 2.1 (see section 3 above), and so table 2.4 just presents summary and test statistics. The dynamic specification appears to be locally acceptable as none of the χ^2 tests of (2.6) against (2.7) is significant, nor are any of the F tests on the joint significance of the additional regressors in (2.7) compared with (2.4). Thus the significant value of $\hat{\rho}_1$ in (ii) can be taken to represent autocorrelation and not an inappropriate lag structure. In fact the unrestricted transformed equation satisfies the autoregressive restriction almost exactly, the RTE and UTE being respectively[12]

$$\tilde{C}_n = 0.10Y_d + 0.49C_{n1} + 0.03Y_{d1} + 0.30C_{n2} \qquad S_2 = 26{,}820, \qquad (2.13)$$

$$\hat{C}_n = 0.10Y_d + 0.48C_{n1} + 0.02Y_{d1} + 0.32C_{n2} \qquad S_3 = 26{,}778. \qquad (2.14)$$

The formulation in terms of (2.4) and (2.5) is therefore preferable; it involves one fewer parameter, which effects a reduction in collinearity, without reducing the value of the likelihood function. Further, since (ii) is often derived from a transformed permanent income hypothesis, one might have postulated the equation

$$C_{nt} = b_1 \sum_{i=0}^{\infty} b_2^i Y_{dt-i} + \varepsilon_{2t} = b_1 Y_{dt} + b_2 C_{nt-1} + \varepsilon_{2t} - b_2 \varepsilon_{2t-1} \qquad (2.15)$$

which has an autocorrelation coefficient of $-b_2/(1 + b_2^2)$ (which would equal -0.49 if b_2 equalled 0.84, as in both OLS and ALS). There is simulation evidence

Table 2.5 Fourth-order autoregressive least squares

	$\chi^2_{(4)}$ [a]	$\chi^2_{(3)}$ [b]	s^2	$\chi^2_{(2)}$
(i) $\hat{C}_d = 0.07Y_d + 37N + 0.26C_{d1} - 0.66C_{d2} + \hat{u}_{1t}$ $\quad\;\;(0.04)\quad(12)\quad(0.11)\quad\;\;(0.12)$	8.2	6.5	933	4.9
$\hat{u}_{1t} = 0.43\hat{u}_{1,t-1} + 0.81\hat{u}_{1,t-2} + 0.02\hat{u}_{1,t-3} - 0.39\hat{u}_{1,t-4}$ $\quad\;\;(0.20)\qquad\;\;(0.24)\qquad\;\;(0.23)\qquad\;\;(0.20)$				
(ii) $\hat{C}_n = 0.11Y_d + 0.82C_{n1} + \hat{u}_{2t}$ $\quad\;\;\;(0.04)\quad\;\;(0.06)$	12.4[*c]	8.6[*]	665	7.9[*]
$\hat{u}_{2t} = 0.41\hat{u}_{2,t-1} - 0.33\hat{u}_{2,t-2} - 0.27\hat{u}_{2,t-3} + 0.17\hat{u}_{2,t-4}$ $\quad\;\;(0.18)\qquad\;\;(0.20)\qquad\;\;(0.20)\qquad\;\;(0.18)$				
(vi) $\hat{Y}_d = 0.58Y + 0.16Y_{d1} + \hat{u}_{6t}$ $\quad\;\;\;(0.15)\quad\;\;(0.26)$	10.3[*]	9.8[*]	6496	5.1
$\hat{u}_{6t} = 0.36\hat{u}_{6,t-1} - 0.02\hat{u}_{6,t-2} - 0.17\hat{u}_{6,t-3} + 0.52\hat{u}_{6,t-4}$ $\quad\;\;(0.27)\qquad\;\;(0.18)\qquad\;\;(0.19)\qquad\;\;(0.19)$				

[a] Likelihood ratio test of $\rho_i = 0(i = 1, \ldots, 4)$ in (2.10).
[b] Likelihood ratio test of the joint marginal significance of $\hat{\rho}_2$, $\hat{\rho}_3$ and $\hat{\rho}_4$ in (2.10).
[c] The asterisk denotes significance at the 0.05 level.

that, in samples of about 40, ALS estimates of ρ_1 are biased towards zero when ρ_1 is negative or is approximating a negative moving-average error (see Hendry and Trivedi, 1972); hence interpreting (2.5) as approximating the error on (2.15), one might judge these estimates as support for the standard permanent income model. Later results, however, suggest that this is an over-simplification.

Each equation can be estimated in a stepwise manner for $m = 2, 3$ and 4 for both of the processes (2.10) and (2.11) (which allows likelihood ratio tests on intermediate hypotheses); in table 2.5 we report the final set of results for (2.10) for the three equations which exhibit significant higher order autocorrelation.[13] The $\chi^2_{(4)}$ values for (iii), (iv) and (v) are 3.8, 1.4 and 0.1 respectively, providing no evidence of autocorrelation, and in every equation the roots of the estimated error processes lie outside the unit circle.

The $\chi^2_{(3)}$ statistic testing (2.10) against (2.5) indicates that autocorrelation of higher than first order is present for (ii) and (vi); clearly, therefore, the assumption of serial independence underlying 5.1 and 5.2 is untenable for these equations. Before concluding that one must therefore allow for such complex processes as are recorded in table 2.5, it seems worth investigating (2.11) and in particular testing (2.10) against (2.11). The relevant statistics for C_d, C_n and Y_d are presented in table 2.6; no significant changes materialize for I, I_v or M. Equations (ii) and (vi) have $\hat{\rho}_4$ values significantly different from zero on both t and $\chi^2_{(1)}$ tests, and rather unexpectedly, given the point estimates of the ρ_i (especially for (ii)), in no case is the likelihood ratio test of (2.11) against (2.10) significant. Thus such autocorrelation as is present in this model can be parsimoniously represented by (2.11). Indeed, the $\chi^2_{(2)}$ tests of parameter stability in table 2.5 are all considerably larger than those in table 2.6, suggesting that the former suffer from a degree of 'overfitting'.

Continuing the analysis discussed in section 3 but applied to four-period lags, we next test the appropriateness of autocorrelation as against dynamic misspecification, and the evidence (table 2.6, fourth and fifth columns) leads us to reject the hypothesis of appropriate dynamics for (i) and (ii), which implies that the autocorrelation is acting as a 'proxy' for the omitted lagged regressors. However, for (vi), an analysis similar to that of (2.13) and (2.14) favours the choice of the RTE. Now of course, all three reported F tests on the joint significance of the additional variables in the UTE reject the null hypothesis at the 0.05 level (as before, the corresponding F statistics for (iii)–(v) are insignificant).

Since these results relate to four-period lags, they could be interpreted alternatively

Table 2.6   Autoregressive least squares for a four-period lag.

	$\hat{\rho}_4$[a]	SE$(\hat{\rho}_4)$	$\chi^2_{(1)}$	$\chi^2_{(i)}$	(i)	$\chi^2_{(2)}$	s^2	F(j,l)	(j,l)	$\chi^2_{(3)}$[b]	s^2 of UTE
(i)	0.19	(0.21)	1.0	17.1[*c]	4	0.0	1013	3.0*	5, 23	7.2	740
(ii)	0.44	(0.17)	5.8*	12.8*	2	4.8	717	6.1*	3, 27	6.6	540
(vi)	0.41	(0.19)	5.9*	4.6	2	4.0	6588	3.0*	3, 27	4.4	6222

[a] As in table 2.4 but applying to (2.11) rather than (2.5).
[b] Likelihood ratio test of (2.10) against (2.11).
[c] The asterisk denotes significance at the 0.05 level.

as implying mis-specified seasonality. As noted above, a stable intercept-shift formulation cannot fully represent an evolving seasonal pattern, and this could induce fourth-order autocorrelation in the residuals. If we are willing to assume that such evolution is steady, it can be represented by a set of four seasonal dummies interactive with trend,[14] and the postulated model becomes

$$y_t = x_t' \lambda + \sum_{i=1}^{4} \alpha_i Q_{it} + \sum_{j=1}^{4} \delta_j (Q_{jt} t) + u_t \qquad (2.16)$$

where $x_t' = (y_{t-1} z_t')$ and the Q_{it} are the usual intercept-shift dummies. For hypotheses of the form (2.11), the preceding analysis was repeated on (2.16), and the essential results are recorded in table 2.7.

In (i), (ii) and (v), the $\hat{\delta}_j$ ($j = 1, \ldots, 4$) are significantly different from zero as a group, but this is not the case for (iii), (iv) and (vi), and so (compare table 2.6) the significance of $\hat{\rho}_4$ is neither necessary (v) nor sufficient (vi) for the significance of the $\hat{\delta}$s. In (i) and (v), however, the $\chi^2_{(2)}$ statistics reject the hypothesis of parameter stability, and so (2.16) is not an appropriate specification for these equations. A strong possibility is that the interactive dummies and the four-period lagged regressors are proxies; this can be tested by comparing their marginal joint significance in the UTE of (2.16) derived by assuming $u_t = \rho_4 u_{t-4} + \varepsilon_t$. Since the UTE includes both the $Q_{jt} t$ and (y_{t-4}, x_{t-4}') this is achieved by an F test on the partial significance of each set of regressors. Doing so, the hypothesis $\delta_j = 0$ ($j = 1, \ldots, 4$) is rejected only in equation (ii); conversely the regressors introduced by the transform are not significant in any equation.

Thus since $\hat{\rho}_4$ is not significant when estimating (2.16) for C_n, it seems reasonable to conclude that the fourth-order autocorrelation indicated seasonal mis-specification; indeed, $\hat{\rho}_1$ is also insignificant so that the interaction dummies have removed the autocorrelation completely for this equation. On the other hand, for C_d, the more appropriate formulation seems to involve four-period lagged regressors and level seasonal dummy variables. Finally, for Y_d the specification is not clear cut since if the $Q_{jt} t$ are *excluded* we observe fourth-order autocorrelation and cannot reject the autoregressive restriction in favour of omitted four-period

Table 2.7 Ordinary least squares and autoregressive least squares for $m = 4$

	Equation (2.16)			UTE of (2.16) $(m = 4)$			RTE of (2.16) $(m = 4)$					
	$F(4, j)^a$	j	$\chi^2_{(2)}$	$F\dagger(4, j)^{bc}$	j	$\chi^2_{(2)}$	$\hat{\rho}_4$	$SE(\hat{\rho}_4)$	$\chi^2_{(1)}$	$\chi^2_{(i)}$	i	$\chi^2_{(2)}$
(i)	2.9*	27	21.0*	2.4	19	13.9*	−0.11	0.22	0.4	16.4*	4	3.9*
(ii)	5.0*	29	5.3	5.2*	23	3.7	−0.07	0.20	0.2	1.1	2	4.6
(iii)	1.0	27	1.7	1.2	19	0.5	−0.39	0.23	4.9*	5.9	4	0.3
(iv)	1.2	28	5.8	2.1	21	6.9*	−0.31	0.24	2.6	5.9	3	5.3
(v)	5.9*	28	12.8*	2.7	21	4.1	−0.27	0.21	2.4	3.4	3	10.5*
(vi)	2.6	29	0.7	1.5	23	6.8*	0.03	0.22	0.02	5.2	2	0.8

[a]F test of the joint significance of the $\hat{\delta}_i$ in (2.16) with 4 and j degrees of freedom.
[b]F test of the joint significance of the $\hat{\delta}_i$ in the unrestricted transformed equation derived from (2.16) when allowing for fourth-order autocorrelation.
[c]Other notation as in tables 2.4 and 2.6.

lagged regressors, but if the interactive dummies are *included* they are insignificant as are both the four-period lag regressors and $\hat{\rho}_4$. Since the sample size after creating lags is now only 36, the inability to discriminate between such closely competing hypotheses is hardly surprising. The remaining equations stand as specified. Thus, detailed investigation of autocorrelation has revealed substantial misspecifications in dynamics and seasonality in the original structure, but this would obviously require further study should one desire to use some variant of this model for policy purposes.

7 A 'Limited Information' Treatment of Autocorrelation and Simultaneity

7.1 Autoregressive Instrumental Variable Approach

Since the discussion of section 6 ignores the endogeneity of some of the regressors, it is important to check whether the conclusions are altered when allowance is made for simultaneity. An analysis parallel to that of the previous section can be conducted, but using instrumental variables rather than least squares. As the ALS estimates have been adequately analysed we need only note that, when $m = 1$, the point estimates are close to those in table 2.2 (matching the similarity of OLS and ALS), the sole significant $\hat{\rho}_1$ again being in (ii) (with the same value as in table 2.4), and when $m = 4$ the results differ from those underlying table 2.6 in the way that the original OLS and TSLS estimates differed – namely, generally smaller coefficients for endogenous variables – but the values of $\hat{\rho}_4$ are almost identical.

For hypotheses of the form (2.10), the large number of lagged regressors rendered useless the choice of *all* predetermined variables as instruments and hence only the predetermined variables in the relevant UTE plus purely exogenous variables were used. Nevertheless, the results obtained were similar to those shown in table 2.5, the estimated autocorrelation coefficients and their standard errors being almost identical. Manifestly, therefore, one would have drawn equivalent conclusions to those obtained by ALS (though this might reflect an inappropriate choice or number of instruments). The computational costs of the two estimators are very similar, but the marginal cost of either set, given the other, is small assuming that one can commence each iterative algorithm at the point to which the other converged. Stress was placed on the former simply because the testing theory is better known, even though it depends on the invalid assumption that the regressors are predetermined.

8 Full Information Estimation of Vector Autocorrelation

In a study designed to understand the functioning of the economic system, an investigator would probably update his specification to incorporate the earlier results before proceeding to ascertain whether they were conditional on the assumption of zero across-equation autocorrelation. For comparability, the structural specification is being held constant here, and hence one must interpret the estimates in this section as more generalized checks for the forms of mis-specification discussed above but applied to the system as a whole.

When $m = 1$,

$$u_t = R_1 u_{t-1} + \varepsilon_t, \tag{2.17}$$

and transforming the system (2.1) to eliminate this autocorrelation yields

$$Ax_t - R_1 Ax_{t-1} = \varepsilon_t \tag{2.18}$$

where $A = (B_0, B_1, \ldots, B_n, C_0, \ldots, C_k)$ and $x_t' = (y_t', y_{t-1}', \ldots, y_{t-n}', z_t', \ldots, z_{t-k}')$ (which provides an alternative interpretation of the estimator as a generalization of FIML taking account of the non-linear between-parameter restrictions). For example, for $n = 2$ and $k = 0$ (as with the present model), we obtain the transformed structure

$$B_0 y_t + (B_1 - R_1 B_0) y_{t-1} + (B_2 - R_1 B_1) y_{t-2} - R_1 B_2 y_{t-3}$$

$$+ C_0 z_t - R_1 C_0 z_{t-1} = \varepsilon_t. \tag{2.19}$$

A significant value of R_1 will therefore augment the set of reduced form variables by (y_{t-3}, z_{t-1}), alter the weights in the lag distribution of $y = f(z)$ and, if off-diagonal elements are significant, introduce into an equation lagged values of variables which are in the system but which were not initially included in the structural formulation of that equation.

A vector generalization of the analysis in (2.4)–(2.7) could be applied to both the structural and the reduced form stochastic and dynamic specifications (see Hendry, 1971), but since the unrestricted reduced form of (2.19) involves 26 variables and the sample size is 39, this is hardly feasible, and so we concentrate on observing the effects on the structural parameters of estimating various specializations of (2.2).

For (2.17), the estimates are presented in table 2.8 and are very different from any of those discussed above. The hypothesis that $R_1 = 0$ is rejected on a likelihood ratio test ($\chi^2_{36} = 64.7$), four diagonal and three off-diagonal elements being larger than twice their standard errors.[15] This contrasts with the ALS and AIV results where only one equation exhibits significant first-order autocorrelation, and indicates the danger of relying on these estimators when R_1 is non-diagonal. In effect, what has transpired is a redistribution of 'explanatory power' from the equation dynamics to the error process; if one rearranges the estimates as in (2.19), retaining only those elements of $\hat{R}_1 \hat{A}$ which are greater than twice their standard errors for clarity, the resulting equations for C_d and I_v are, for example,[16]

$$\hat{C}_d = 0.17 Y_d + 45N - 35N_1 + 0.69C_{d1} - 0.07C_{d2} \tag{2.20}$$
$$\quad\;\; (0.03) \qquad (8) \quad\; (10)$$

and

$$\hat{I}_v = 0.18\Delta Y - 0.15\Delta Y_1 + 0.44C_{d1} - 19N_1 + 0.17I_{v1} + 0.27I_{v2}. \tag{2.21}$$
$$\quad\;\; (0.06) \qquad (0.06) \qquad (0.16) \qquad (8)$$

Thus (2.20) regenerates a relationship for C_d similar to that found earlier, while (2.21) reveals a slightly more complex accelerator than initially assumed, plus a

Table 2.8   Autoregressive maximum likelihood

	ω^2	v^2	CORR
(i) $\hat{C}_d = 0.17Y_d + 45N - 0.09C_{d1} - 0.13C_{d2} + \hat{u}_{1t}$ $\quad(0.04)\quad(8)\quad(0.13)\quad(0.11)$	835	729	0.946
(ii) $\hat{C}_n = 0.23Y_d + 0.66C_{n1} + \hat{u}_{2t}$ $\quad(0.07)\quad(0.09)$	611	458	0.998
(iii) $\hat{I} = 0.02\Delta Y + 0.10\Delta Y_1 + 0.32I_1 + 0.68I_2 + \hat{u}_{3t}$ $\quad(0.08)\quad(0.07)\quad(0.13)\quad(0.13)$	1251	1193	0.984
(iv) $\hat{I}_v = 0.18\Delta Y - 0.29I_{v1} + 0.04I_{v2} + \hat{u}_{4t}$ $\quad(0.07)\quad(0.18)\quad(0.15)$	1365	1067	0.866
(v) $\hat{M} = 0.99I_v + 0.24Y_1 - 4.0P_m + \hat{u}_{5t}$ $\quad(0.30)\quad(0.02)\quad(1.7)$	1685	1080	0.971
(vi) $\hat{Y}_d = 0.28Y + 0.64Y_{d1} + \hat{u}_{6t}$ $\quad(0.13)\quad(0.15)$	5966	4827	0.987

$$\hat{R}_1 = \begin{bmatrix} 0.78^* & -0.38 & -0.01 & -0.13 & 0.10 & 0.10 \\ 0.14 & -0.56^* & -0.18 & -0.01 & 0.42^* & -0.13 \\ 0.05 & 0.29 & 0.42^* & 0.09 & 0.11 & -0.06 \\ 0.44^* & 0.13 & 0.23 & 0.79^* & 0.33 & 0.02 \\ -0.29 & 0.18 & -0.10 & -0.30 & -0.15 & -0.02 \\ 0.03 & 1.49^* & -0.03 & 0.18 & -0.27 & 0.26 \end{bmatrix}$$

$$\text{SE}(\hat{R}_1)^b = \begin{bmatrix} 0.16 & 0.20 & 0.13 & 0.11 & 0.17 & 0.07 \\ 0.10 & 0.17 & 0.11 & 0.12 & 0.13 & 0.07 \\ 0.18 & 0.25 & 0.19 & 0.13 & 0.21 & 0.09 \\ 0.19 & 0.25 & 0.18 & 0.16 & 0.20 & 0.09 \\ 0.17 & 0.24 & 0.16 & 0.13 & 0.20 & 0.09 \\ 0.36 & 0.47 & 0.33 & 0.26 & 0.40 & 0.27 \end{bmatrix}$$

$\chi^2_6 = 24.5^*,\ 8.3$

[a] For notation, see table 2.3. The standard errors above and in table 2.9 are not based on the slightly incorrect formulae quoted in Hendry (1971) but on the correct variant thereof.
[b] Matrix of standard errors of the elements of $\hat{R}_1$.

dependence on consumer durable expenditure (similar to that reported by Evans, 1969, ch. 8) and a fall in inventories (*ceteris paribus*) in the quarter following a change in the vehicle registration letter.

The χ^2 test of parameter stability is significant in the first quarter but not in the second, and like the ALS evidence suggests that the autocorrelation may represent incorrect dynamic specification.

Such autocorrelation as is present in this model may not be completely accounted for by a first-order vector autoregressive process, and so a second-order scheme was estimated.[17] The final estimates are not presented here since the sample size is too small to accord these more than an illustrative status, but 12 $\hat{r}_{2ij}$ were greater than 0.4, $\hat{R}_1$ was unaltered apart from the first column which became almost zero, and the estimated structural coefficients were similar to those in table 2.8.

Finally, the results pertaining to (2.11) suggest estimating its vector equivalent $(u_t = R_4 u_{t-4} + \varepsilon_t)$, and there are a number of interesting aspects of these results, which are presented in table 2.9. First, 16 elements of $\hat{R}_4$ are greater than twice

Table 2.9 Autoregressive maximum likelihood $(m = 4)^a$

	ω^2	v^2	CORR
(i) $\hat{C}_d = 0.06Y_d + 33N + 0.64C_{d1} - 0.11C_{d2} + \hat{u}_{1t}$ 　　(0.03)　　(12)　　(0.11)　　　(0.10)	631	587	0.953
(ii) $\hat{C}_n = 0.14Y_d + 0.79C_{n1} + \hat{u}_{2t}$ 　　(0.06)　　(0.09)	562	515	0.997
(iii) $\hat{I} = -0.03\Delta Y + 0.10\Delta Y_1 + 0.70I_1 + 0.25I_2 + \hat{u}_{3t}$ 　　(0.08)　　(0.07)　　(0.12)　　(0.12)	815	907	0.989
(iv) $\hat{I}_v = 0.16\Delta Y + 0.35I_{v1} + 0.46I_{v2} + \hat{u}_{4t}$ 　　(0.08)　　(0.11)　　(0.13)	1299	1008	0.859
(v) $\hat{M} = 0.28I_v + 0.21Y_1 - 6.2P_m + \hat{u}_{5t}$ 　　(0.11)　　(0.02)　　(1.4)	959	617	0.979
(vi) $\hat{Y}_d = 0.14Y + 0.75Y_{d1} + \hat{u}_{6t}$ 　　(0.09)　　(0.10)	3441	3079	0.991

$$\hat{R}_4 = \begin{bmatrix} 0.38^* & -0.22 & -0.03 & -0.17 & -0.08 & -0.07 \\ -0.07 & 0.42^* & -0.08 & 0.10 & -0.17 & -0.03 \\ 0.82^* & -0.14 & -0.39^* & 0.33^* & -0.24 & 0.12 \\ 0.48^* & 0.82^* & -0.41^* & 0.07 & -0.76^* & 0.24^* \\ 0.92^* & 0.26 & -0.43^* & 0.17 & -0.37^* & 0.10 \\ 1.10^* & -1.34^* & 0.55 & 0.56 & -1.39^* & 0.20 \end{bmatrix}$$

$$\text{SE}(\hat{R}_4) = \begin{bmatrix} 0.18 & 0.19 & 0.14 & 0.12 & 0.20 & 0.06 \\ 0.16 & 0.16 & 0.13 & 0.10 & 0.16 & 0.07 \\ 0.22 & 0.22 & 0.17 & 0.15 & 0.21 & 0.08 \\ 0.23 & 0.24 & 0.20 & 0.18 & 0.24 & 0.09 \\ 0.20 & 0.20 & 0.15 & 0.14 & 0.18 & 0.07 \\ 0.43 & 0.41 & 0.33 & 0.29 & 0.40 & 0.15 \end{bmatrix}$$

$\chi_6^2 = 25.6^*, 23.9^*$

^{a}For notation, see table 2.3.

their standard error and, of the diagonal elements, only $\hat{r}_{224}$ is similar to its value in table 2.6. Thus, the earlier analysis invalidly assumed $\hat{R}_4$ to be diagonal, which may not vitiate its conclusions (this would depend on the results of applying equivalent specification tests to the system) but clearly indicates that the findings were not comprehensive. In view of the discussion in section 6, the result for Y_d is interesting and strongly confirms the mis-specification of this *ad hoc* equation. Despite the marked degree of autocorrelation, the structural coefficients are similar to the FIML estimates (unlike the results for $m = 1$), which perhaps reflects the smaller extent of bias arising from the dependence of y_{t-1} and y_{t-2} on u_{t-4} compared with u_{t-1}. However, the post-sample parameter stability test rejects the null hypothesis, leaving the researcher the task of respecifying the dynamics, testing the validity of the new over-identifying restrictions against the enlarged reduced form, and checking the autocorrelation structure of the re-estimated model.

9 Conclusion

The above results caution against the policy of simply estimating parameters and testing the (all too often uninteresting) null hypothesis of 'no relation'. Rather, it seems important to examine every aspect of a model as thoroughly as possible, since even if interminable revision is not practical, we should know what problems are untreated rather than just hope that they are absent. This applies to estimating autocorrelation schemes as much as structural parameters since invalid representation of mis-specified dynamics by an autoregressive process need not produce improved results.

On the positive side, the single-equation methods (ALS, AIV) at least highlighted the existence of mis-specification and provided clues to its solution even if they were inherently unable to reveal such problems as cross serial correlation. Since all the results for tables 2.1, 2.2, 2.4 and 2.6 required 20 s of CPU time, the 'single-equation' methods seem to provide value for money. This granted, the prevalence of autocorrelation when the observation period is a quarter or shorter and our reliance on data to determine lag relationships are strong arguments for automatically estimating them jointly rather than testing one conditional on dubious assumptions about the other. Certainly, there always exists a sufficiently stringent test that any model will fail; most of those considered above, however, are hardly in that category, and they seem to be a reasonable set of requirements that a structure should pass if it is proposed for policy analysis or control.

Appendix

C_{dt} Real consumption expenditure on durable goods, valued at market prices

C_{nt} Real consumption expenditure on all other goods and services, valued at market prices

I_t Real gross domestic fixed capital formation at market prices

I_{vt} Real value of the physical increase in stocks and work in progress at market prices

M_t Real value of imports of goods and services

G_t Real current government expenditure on goods and services at market prices

Y_{dt} Real total personal disposable income

Y_t Real gross domestic product at factor cost

P_{mt} Index of relative import prices

X_t Real value of exports of goods and services at market prices

T_t Real adjustment to factor cost (taxes on expenditure less subsidies)

N_t Dummy variable for the annual vehicle registration letter

All data except P_m and N are in 1958 prices, not seasonally adjusted and cover the period 1957(i)–1967(iv); they were taken from *Economic Trends*, October 1968, tables (A), (D) and (J). Two lags were created, and two observations were retained for the post-sample parameter stability test yielding a standard sample size of $40 - m$ for an mth-order autoregressive scheme.

P_m is a spliced index series of import unit values (compiled from various *Monthly Digests of Statistics*) divided by the implicit deflator of GDP. Real personal disposal income is derived from the series in current prices by dividing by the implicit deflator of aggregate consumption at market prices.

The identities in the system are

$$Y_t = C_{dt} + C_{nt} + I_t + I_{vt} + \mathrm{GXT}_t - M_t$$

where

$$\mathrm{GXT}_t = G_t + X_t - T_t \quad \text{and} \quad \Delta Y_t = Y_t - Y_{t-1}.$$

In tables 2.1–2.9, Z_j denotes Z_{t-j} as a shorthand.

Finally, the definition of N is as follows:

$N = -1$ for 1964(iv), 1965(iv), 1966(iv), 1967(ii)

$ = +1$ for 1965(i), 1966(i), 1967(i), 1967(iii)

$ = -\frac{1}{2}$ for 1962(iv), 1963(iv) $\Big\}$ to reflect a smaller impact when it was

$ = +\frac{1}{2}$ for 1963(i), 1964(i) $}$ initially introduced

$ = 0$ otherwise.

Notes

1   Relative to (say) data measurement errors, aggregation bias or omitted variable mis-specifications etc., these problems may not even be the most important.

2   Identities can be incorporated in (2.1) without undue difficulty.

3   The possible combination of autocorrelation and simultaneity without lagged endogenous regressors ($n = 0$) is not considered here, given the essentially dynamic nature of the model; for a discussion of techniques, see Amemiya (1966) and Wickens (1969).

4   A further possibility is to switch to estimation of the reduced form of (2.1) and (2.2) (see Hendry, 1971).

5   All the programs used in this study are described in Hendry (1970); note that when the underlying specification is valid, each of the above estimators either is, or is asymptotically equivalent to, a maximum likelihood estimator. For the iterative methods, the relevant likelihood function was first concentrated with respect to all unrestricted parameters (which includes the seasonal dummy variables in AML and FIML), and the resultant expression was maximized directly using a variant of Gauss–Seidel when $m = 1$ and a routine due to Powell (1965) when $m > 1$ for (iii) and (iv), and the routine developed by Powell (1964) in all other cases.

6   Since (2.2) can be reformulated as a set of 'final' form relationships in which each u_{jt} is a pth-order autoregression with a complex moving-average error which has both current and lagged covariances with equivalent errors on other equations, there is no necessary connection between the integer m in (2.2) and (2.10) unless all R_i are diagonal.

7   When $p = 1$, f_t can only be interpreted as a 'forecast error' if all the regressors are predetermined. This test deliberately ignores the asymptotically negligible sampling variances of the estimated parameters and hence should provide a stringent test in finite samples, as seems desirable when testing for possible previous type II errors.

8   This is certainly a crude approximation for what is a very large sector in most macro-models, but given a constraint on the size of the system feasible here, it seems preferable to the alternative mis-specification of treating Y_d as exogenous. Note that all the lag specifications could also arise from transformed rational approximations to distributed lag relationships as in Jorgenson (1965).

9   For example, the significant fourth-order autocorrelation found may indicate that the seasonal pattern is more complex than a time-invariant intercept shift between quarters (see Thomas and Wallis, 1971).

10 Because of AIV (see section 3 above) the set of instruments used for each equation also included all non-redundant regressors lagged one period.

11 $\chi^2_{(60)}$ depends on $\log(|\hat{\Omega}|/|\tilde{\Omega}|)$ where $\hat{\Omega} = T^{-1}\Sigma_{t=1}^{T}\hat{v}_t\hat{v}_t'$ and where $\hat{v}_t$ is the vector of reduced form residuals at time t; the circumflex and tilde denote unrestricted estimates and restricted estimates respectively. If, instead, one used

$$\frac{T}{T - h_1}\hat{\Omega} \text{ and } \frac{T}{T - h_2}\tilde{\Omega}$$

where the h_i are the average number of unconstrained parameters per equation in the unrestricted and restricted reduced forms (an approximate correction for degrees of freedom which might be considered), the resulting statistic unfortunately ceases to be valid, and converges to $\chi^2_{(n)} - n$.

12 Note how the negative autocorrelation implies positive values for the 'omitted' variables in (ii).

13 For C_d, although the overall likelihood ratio test (of (2.4) against (2.4) + (2.10)) does not allow rejection of the hypothesis that $\rho_i = 0$ ($i = 1, \ldots, 4$), two $\hat{\rho}_i$ are greater than twice their standard errors and $\hat{\rho}_4$ is close to this also.

14 This was suggested by one of the referees.

15 These are not corrected for degrees of freedom.

16 These are chosen for having the largest $\hat{r}_{ijl}$; standard errors of elements of $\hat{B}_j - \hat{R}_1\hat{B}_{j-1}$ are not available.

17 This helped to ascertain whether it was feasible to estimate a higher order scheme using the computational approach developed in Hendry (1971). In total, the problem involved maximizing a non-linear function of 114 parameters, transformed by concentrating the likelihood function to yield an expression which was more complex but depended

only on the 18 parameters in (i)–(vi). Although the computational cost was substantially greater than for $m = 1$ (to evaluate the likelihood function required about 1/6 s of CPU time on the London University CDC 6600), it proved possible to estimate such a process.

3

Testing Dynamic Specification in Small Simultaneous Systems: an Application to a Model of Building Society Behaviour in the United Kingdom

with Gordon J. Anderson

Preamble

The precedent of a five-year gap between initiation and completion of the previous chapter was slavishly followed for this one! The study was begun with Gordon Anderson in response to a challenge about the inability of econometrics to throw any light on the disequilibria induced by capital rationing. The challenge related to the difficulties believed to face small industrial firms in attracting outside capital financing, but as UK building societies were notorious for their mortgage rationing and were a well-defined sector with homogeneous and accurately measured data, an analysis of their behaviour seemed to offer excellent possibilities for success. Pride comes before a fall – it proved exceptionally difficult to establish unequivocal econometric evidence of rationing in a dynamic context, even though we knew it was present. Moreover, the model was too complicated to estimate with the existing computer technology.

Nevertheless, compared with chapter 2 a number of econometric methodology issues were significantly clearer to me by the time the paper was completed.

1   The order of testing must be general to simple, including commencing with the completely unrestricted reduced form (if that is estimable).

Reprinted from Intriligator, M.D. (ed.), *Frontiers of Quantitative Economics*, vol. IIIA, Amsterdam: North-Holland, 1977, ch. 8C. This is a totally revised version of Hendry (1975b), incorporating earlier work on capital rationing in building societies by D.F. Hendry and M.J. Webb and also drawing heavily on Anderson (1974). The research was supported by a grant from the Social Science Research Council to the Econometric Methodology project at the London School of Economics. The paper was completed while I was visiting at the Cowles Foundation, supported by grants from the National Science Foundation and the Ford Foundation at Yale University. We are indebted to John Spencer for providing the data from his study with C. St. J. O'Herlihy and to Frank Srba for invaluable help with the computer programming.

2   An acceptable model must be able to explain why other researchers found the results they reported, allowing both more powerful (predictive) tests of models, and going beyond data corroboration.

3   System autocorrelation could also be interpreted as a 'convenient simplification' when certain restrictions were satisfied, but not in general, although again this was solved only for the first-order case, and a system test for longer lags versus vector autoregression could be constructed.

The 'time-series versus econometrics' debate was at its misguided height, and so the other focus of the paper was an attempt to defuse this debate by integrating some of the good ideas from both approaches. On the one hand, the long-run equilibrium of the system was explicitly economic-theoretic and the short-run dynamics were guided by optimization theory albeit that only one lag was explicitly incorporated. This provided the skeletal framework for the model. On the other hand, the empirical equations were not to be restricted to the specific lag structure thus derived. Consequently, the resulting equations were explicitly formulated as growth rates related to levels to embed the time-series approach (which argued for analysing differenced data only, since levels were non-stationary) in an econometric system which nevertheless had a levels long-run solution to capture economic theory information.

At that stage, I was convinced that static-equilibrium economic theory was powerful enough to delineate how the non-stationary levels of economic variables would be related. To quote from the paper, 'there are ways to achieve stationarity other than blanket differencing . . . the theory input would appear to be "lost" unless levels variables are included'. The algebra naturally led to error correction mechanisms (ECMs) where levels disequilibria determined changes (including non-unit long-run responses). However, it was not until the struggle to resolve the problems of chapter 8 that I realized both that ECMs were a class of model with importantly different properties from most of the conventionally used classes (see chapter 4 for an analysis) and that Sargan (1964a) was again the key precursor. Equally, I was unaware of the important effects which the inherent non-stationarity in the original levels variables entailed for the distributions of many of the estimators and tests used, especially tests of the validity of the long-run theory. I merely asserted that (for example) ratios induced stationarity; it was much later that the formal idea of cointegration was introduced by Clive Granger (see chapter 19 for a brief discussion): this issue will recur in chapters 6 and 7.

Perhaps the most important aspect of the paper was its determined attempts at a constructivist methodology. It argued that the creation of theory models could be based on integrating long-run economic theory with control-theoretic dynamic adjustment, even for institutions without the conventional *raison d'être* of profit maximization. The initial evaluation of such theory models could occur without direct data implementation by checking whether they correctly predicted mis-specifications in existing empirical models and rejecting, extending or revising the theory accordingly. This was the precursor to the notion of encompassing extensively employed in chapter 8 and formalized in chapter 16 (also see Mizon (1984) and Mizon and Richard (1986) for test procedures and Hendry and Richard (1989) for a survey). Implementation of the empirical analogue of the theory was to be from the '*least* restricted hypothesis to the *most*' (italics in the original) analogous to that recommended by Ted Anderson (1971). That seemed to offer a feasible constructive data modelling strategy which avoided having dubiously to infer from test rejections how to generalize a manifestly incorrect model. The issue of where to commence a study in terms of the generality of the initial model was still assumed to be given by the theory. Moreover, although Grayham Mizon presented his paper on specification versus mis-specification testing at the same World Congress, we did not seriously investigate diagnostic testing of the initial system to ensure that later inferences would be based on a valid starting point.

The actual estimates of the model did not appear until much later (as Anderson and Hendry, 1984) since I was diverted into analysing many of the methodological issues highlighted by the following study, and testing their efficacy in other areas.

The key problem that remained (although I would not have verbalized it as such at the time) was how to discover useful empirical relationships if the economic theory was not essentially perfect. I had completely discarded the hope of omniscience and, because of the issues of identification and simultaneity and an increasing worry about the unrealism of autoregressive error representations, I returned to a detailed study of one equation from my chapter 2 model, namely the consumption function. This digression from analysing systems to focus on single equations was to last almost a decade, and all the empirical studies in part II are of individual equations. A clearer understanding of how to model systems, other than as groups of separately modelled single equations, only emerged (for me) in the late 1980s and is reported in Hendry et al. (1988) for stationary processes and in Hendry and Mizon (1991) for integrated data series. Nevertheless, the intent throughout was to develop better procedures for modelling systems, and the methods that have resulted are the product of intensive analysis of single-equation models and the consequent evolution of a general framework.

1   Introduction

The literature on estimating economic models from time-series data has revealed a considerable state of ferment in recent years. Conventional econometric approaches have been sharply questioned (see, for example, Granger and Newbold, 1974) and the forecasting ability of systems estimated by such methods has been criticized (see Cooper, 1972). Conversely, the main alternatives advocated, namely fitting autoregressive integrated moving average (ARIMA) equations (see Box and Jenkins, 1976) or the closely related 'control-theoretic' methods (see Astrom, 1970) are far from having unqualified support from practitioners (see Chatfield and Prothero, 1973; Wall and Westcott, 1974). As argued by the last authors and by Nerlove (1972), a crucial function is left to the 'mutually supportive roles of theory and measurement'.

The criteria which determine the selection of an ARIMA representation are roughly as follows: maximize the likelihood of the model transformed to be stationary and invertible, basing the initial specification on autocorrelation analysis of the data such that the chosen form is the most parsimonious without violating diagnostic checks on the residuals being 'white noise'. For a multiple input process, considerable judgement is required.

These criteria are basically sensible but minimal. Slight problems are that some economic variables are not well represented by ARIMA models (e.g. tax rates) and that there are ways to achieve stationarity other than blanket differencing. More importantly, emphasizing single-output models distracts attention from the joint dependence of economic variables and, by allowing almost no weight to theory or prior information accrued from other studies, including relevant variables, signs and magnitudes of parameters, orders of lags etc., exacerbates the difficulty of using short data series. Indeed, by placing all the initial emphasis on the (albeit important) dynamics–autocorrelation interaction it may underplay the multivariate aspect which remains of primary concern to the economist. On the other hand, initially examining only the multivariate relationship is equally unhelpful and it seems imperative to consider both *ab initio* (see chapter 2 and Zellner and Palm, 1974). Even then it is essential that the analysis be conducted in the context of an appropriate economic theory.

Unfortunately, although interdependence and dynamics have been accorded equal importance in general theoretical analysis (see, for example, Hicks, 1939), the latter has not been successfully developed for operational use. Economic theories remain for the most part of the long-run equilibrium–comparative statics variety and their practical value has been queried (see Nerlove, 1972). Also, since this is precisely the component which differencing (to achieve stationarity) will remove, the theory input would appear to be 'lost' unless levels variables are included.

Nevertheless, this paper is an attempt to integrate a 'long-run equilibrium' theory of the behaviour of building societies with a short-run control-theoretic model of their dynamic disequilibrium adjustment deliberately designed such that the equilibrium solution of the latter reproduces the former. The theory also suggests which data transformations may be useful (e.g. differencing, ratios etc.). While simple, it is based on established institutional evidence and Hendry (1975b) has shown that it includes three other extant models of building societies as special cases.

Finally, a sequential procedure for statistically testing the dynamics, autocorrelation and economic theory restrictions is developed, and we jointly apply these to the model of O'Herlihy and Spencer (1972) to investigate whether the economic theory predicts any mis-specifications of variables or dynamics, whether the statistical approach reveals any in practice (their system was estimated by two-stage least squares) and, if so, how closely these coincide with our anticipations from the theory.

2 Building Societies

These non-profit-making co-operative institutions (denoted BSs) dominate the UK mortgage market with their 70 per cent share, and they also hold 25 per cent of private financial assets. Most are members of the Building Societies Association, and they meet monthly to agree on mortgage and deposit interest rates, acting essentially as a cartel by quoting (for the most part) homogeneous figures. Mortgages have a standard life of 20–25 years, while deposits can be withdrawn on demand. Changes in either interest rate affect the *complete* stock immediately. Since the availability and price of mortgages have been important politically, BSs have been subjected to considerable indirect government pressure and/or help at various times. Revell (1973) provides an excellent discussion of their structure and functioning.

Clayton et al. (1974) investigated the objectives that BSs claim to set for themselves, Ghosh and Parkin (1972) and Ghosh (1974) considered their portfolio and debt behaviour, O'Herlihy and Spencer (1972) built a formal econometric model of their behaviour and estimated the existence and extent of credit rationing, the London Business School model of the UK economy contains a submodel of BS behaviour (see Renton, 1975, ch. 1) and Riley (1974) has developed a model for the Treasury based on time-series analysis methods (see Astrom, 1970). As discussed in Hendry (1975b), none of these studies is fully satisfactory, although all aid our understanding in different respects.

Since BSs constitute a homogeneous sector, problems of aggregation and measurement errors are likely to be of relatively less importance than usual. Conversely, the credit rationing for which these institutions are well known is a serious additional complication, as it seems to be chronic (rather than a transient 'switching of regimes' type) and endogenous to the system. Thus there may be no observations on the demand for mortgages schedule, which need not preclude estimating the effects of *changes* in demand but does rule out using the conventional market clearing equation to close the system for observability. Further, as BSs act as a group, the equally conventional 'Walrasian' equation of prices adjusting in response to excess demand is not valid either. Clearly 'chronic' rationing entails an ability to control both price and quantity (although 'transient' rationing could be a slowly evolving disequilibrium). As an operational criterion we use the following: if an increase in the mortgage interest rate induces a non-decrease in advances, *ceteris paribus*, then rationing was previously present.

The lack of identification of mortgage demand was solved by O'Herlihy and Spencer using 'prior' subjective information (primarily based on newspaper reports) formulated in dummy variables to proxy 'mild', $D(1)$, and 'strict', $D(2)$, rationing (see figure 3.1). Criticisms of this approach are its subjective nature, that it implies constant absolute magnitude effects of rationing, that the dummies are really endogenous and are not an 'explanation' of rationing, hence being difficult to use for forecasting, and that the method is highly specific to the BS sector. Our 'guideline' theory suggests that rationing is potentially present due to the inherent nature of how BSs make their decisions. Specifically, rationing seems to be generated by the efforts of BSs to reconcile conflicting objectives rather than to achieve a sole target such as profit maximization (compare Ghosh, 1974). To model this we adopt a 'managerial' type of theory based on the optimization of an objective function comprising several goals and subject to several (cost) constraints on the variability of the instruments to attain the targets. This is an explicitly dynamic 'control theory'

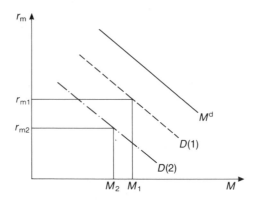

Figure 3.1   Mortgage interest rate r_m versus mortgage lending M: M^d, demand for mortgages perceived by building societies.

approach, but it only partly circumvents the awkward dilemma of postulating 'desired' variables separately determined outside of the optimization framework (see Theil, 1964).

We do not consider the overall portfolio allocation problem, however (see, for example, Ghosh and Parkin, 1972), but treat other assets as a single entity. A simple linear expository model of their long-run behaviour can be developed as follows.

2.1 Capital Account

$$A \equiv \text{LA} + \text{OA} + M \equiv D + R \equiv L \tag{3.1}$$

where the symbols denote respectively assets, liquid assets, other assets, mortgages, deposits, reserves and liabilities. We postulate that BSs plan to re-lend a constant proportion θ_1 of deposits as mortgages (this being their primary function as co-operative institutions):

$$M^s = \theta_1 D. \tag{3.2}$$

We also postulate that BSs hold a constant proportion θ_2 of their assets in liquid form,

$$\text{LA} = \theta_2 A, \tag{3.3}$$

accept all deposits offered,

$$D = D^s, \tag{3.4}$$

maintain a constant ratio θ_3 of reserves to assets,

$$R = \theta_3 A, \tag{3.5}$$

and, in equilibrium, they realize their plans. From equations (3.1)–(3.5) we have

$$\text{OA} = [1 - \theta_2 - \theta_1(1 - \theta_3)]A = \theta_4 A \tag{3.6}$$

and

$$D = (1 - \theta_3)A. \tag{3.7}$$

Finally, the private sector's equations for mortgage demand and deposit supply are

$$M^d = f(y, r_m, T, \text{PH}, M) \qquad \frac{\partial f}{\partial y} > 0 \qquad \frac{\partial f}{\partial r_m} < 0 \qquad \frac{\partial f}{\partial T} > 0 \qquad \frac{\partial f}{\partial M} < 0 \tag{3.8}$$

$$D^s = h(y, r_d, T, r_c, P)$$

$$\frac{\partial h}{\partial y} > 0 \qquad \frac{\partial h}{\partial r_d} > 0 \qquad \frac{\partial h}{\partial T} < 0 \qquad \frac{\partial h}{\partial r_c} < 0 \qquad \frac{\partial h}{\partial P} < 0 \tag{3.9}$$

where y is disposable income; r_m, r_d and r_c are pre-tax mortgage, deposit and competitive interest rates; PH and P are price indices for housing and all goods; and

T is the tax rate. BSs pay tax on interest earnings for depositors at a rate which differs slightly from the standard tax rate and they generally quote after-tax deposit interest rates: $r = r_d(1 - T)$.

2.2 Current Account

$$r_m M + r_c OA \equiv E + r_d D + S \tag{3.10}$$

where $E = \theta_5 A$ are management expenses (the inclusion of overheads does not materially affect the analysis) and S is the 'surplus' planned to equilibrate the reserve ratio. Dividing by A and rearranging:

$$r_d = \theta_5 \theta_6 + \theta_1 r_m - \theta_4 \theta_6 r_c + \theta_6 S/A \tag{3.11}$$

where $\theta_6 = 1/(\theta_3 - 1) < 0$. Let $K_t = (R/A)_t$. Then, if $A_t \approx (1 + g)A_{t-1}$ (say), $S/A = K_t - [1/(1 + g)]K_{t-1}$ (zero in stationary equilibrium), and if BSs do plan to have $K_t = \theta_3$ then, for given g, r_c, K_{t-1} and θ_i, equation (3.11) determines r_d as a function of r_m (the 'mark-up') or vice versa on renormalizing on r_m. Note that $\Delta(S/A)_t = - [1/(1 + g)]\Delta K_{t-1}$ if $K_t = \theta_3$.

This analysis leaves (for example) r_m to be determined, and, in the absence of a profit maximization motive, some other objective function must be postulated. The crucial point is that, if BSs do not equilibrate M^s and M^d, then, as a near monopoly which believes in keeping interest rates low (or is ordered to do so by the government), which does not seek to maximize S, *and* which plans to achieve its balance sheet goals, they will ration credit to control both price and quantity. Two extreme possibilities are (i) that the government dictates r_m on political grounds or (ii) that

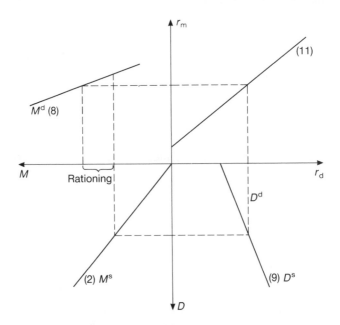

Figure 3.2   Behaviour of the theoretical model.

BSs do equilibrate M^s and M^d and so choose r_m as the implicit solution of

$$f(y, r_m, T, PH, M) = \theta_1 h(y, [\theta_5 \theta_6 + \theta_1 r_m - \theta_4 \theta_6 r_c + \theta_6 S/A], T, r_c, P). \quad (3.12)$$

Either way, given r_m, equation (3.11) determines r_d, equation (3.9) gives D, equation (3.2) gives M and so on. The system allows one to establish most of the anticipated comparative statics results for changes in y, r_c, T etc. when equation (3.12) operates. Figure 3.2 summarizes the behaviour of the model for an arbitrarily given low value r_m, and fixed y, r_c, PH, P, T. By abstracting from the dynamics we have implicitly taken

$$\Delta D = ND = 0 = NA = \Delta M \qquad (g = 0),$$

where ND and NA are net deposits and net advances respectively and

$$GD = WD \qquad GA = PR \qquad\qquad\qquad (3.13)$$

where the symbols denote respectively gross deposits, withdrawals, gross advances and principal repayments. Out of stationary equilibrium, to obtain

$$ND = GD - WD \quad \text{and} \quad NA = GA - PR \qquad\qquad (3.14)$$

the four components in equation (3.13) must be modelled. Note, however, that in equilibrium

$$PR = \frac{1}{n} M \qquad\qquad\qquad\qquad (3.15)$$

if the mortgage life is n years.

In disequilibrium, r_m and GA will not be constant and there will be premature terminations as well as routine repayments.

Given this 'long-run' framework we can formulate the objective function of BSs and introduce dynamics at the same time. As argued above, their prime objective is to achieve the long-run aim of re-lending a relatively constant fraction of their expected total deposits $\hat{D}_t$ as mortgages, but now $\hat{D}_t \neq D_t$ because of the stochastic nature of cash flows, unforeseen changes in y, r_c etc. At the same time they pay some attention to satisfying 'reasonable' mortgage applications and maintaining their long-run reserve ratio while attaching adjustment costs to changes in their instruments (if only to avoid 'bang-bang' control). Four other objectives or costs which do not affect the formal specification of the control rules but do alter the precise parameterization are as follows: maximizing the growth rate of assets, minimizing lending rates, adjusting faster the more they are out of equilibrium, and equilibrating interest rate differentials with the money market.

To facilitate comparison with existing models we take the objective function to be quadratic in the variables and to be one period only. This is because BSs do act as if they were myopic, but introducing a time horizon $t^* > 1$ in the objective function (equation (3.16) below) 'simply' creates leads in the analysis and first-period certainty equivalence applies (see Hay and Holt, 1975). However, the control is also equivalent to ignoring terminal conditions and the stability properties of this model are well known. The objective function of the model can be summarized as follows.

1 We measure the 'disutility' of 'disequilibrium' by $(M_t - \theta_1\hat{D}_t)^2$, even though such costs are probably asymmetric away from equilibrium.

2 Since $M_t - M_t^d = NA_t - NA_t^d$ and $NA_t = \min(NA_t^s, NA_t^d)$, we take the disutility of not supplying the required volume of housing finance to be $\alpha_1(NA_t - NA_t^d)^2$, thus assuming chronic rationing.

3 To achieve the desired reserve ratio requires the appropriate surplus, and, if θ_5 is constant, to model the BSs making marginal adjustments rather than re-evaluating the entire basis of the mark-up each period we include $\alpha_2[\Delta r_{mt} - (1/\theta_1)\Delta r_{dt} + \theta_4\theta_7\Delta r_{ct} - \theta_7\Delta(S/A)_t]^2$, on normalizing with respect to r_m in equation (3.11), with $\theta_7 = 1/\theta_1(1 - \theta_3)$. This term could also be interpreted as a cost of adjusting the differential.

4 Inertia to avoid high frequency oscillations in NA_t and r_{dt} seems desirable, but there are adjustment costs in any event arising from processing costs and destabilizing influences on the housing market for the former and administrative costs (perhaps less so with computers) and the creation of uncertainty for depositors concerning the latter. Thus we include $\lambda_1(\Delta NA_t)^2 + \lambda_2(\Delta r_{dt})^2$.

The objective function which results to determine BS behaviour is

$$c_t = \sum_{t=1}^{t^*} (1 + r_c)^{-t}\left[(M_t - \theta_1\hat{D}_t)^2 + \alpha_1(NA_t - NA_t^d)^2 + \lambda_1(\Delta NA_t)^2 \right.$$
$$\left. + \lambda_2(\Delta r_{dt})^2 + \alpha_2\left[\Delta r_{mt} - \frac{1}{\theta_1}\Delta r_{dt} + \theta_4\theta_7\Delta r_{ct} + \theta_8\Delta K_{t-1} \right]^2 \right] \qquad (3.16)$$

where $\theta_8 = \theta_7/(1 + g)$, and BSs seek to minimize this by choice of NA_t, r_{mt} and r_{dt}. Completely independent empirical support exists for formulating a myopic objective function (in which t^* denotes six months) with conflicting aims and emphasizing the goals of stable flows of funds; reserves in line with assets: re-lending the maximum, subject to achieving the desired liquidity ratio; attempting to satisfy the demand for housing finance; and *not* maximizing profits. This support is provided by Clayton et al. (1974), who conducted a questionnaire survey of how the Building Societies Association perceived the role of BSs in the housing market; they reached the conclusions noted in the previous sentence.

While c_t is not 'homogeneous' in its arguments and it would be preferable to deflate M, D and NA by A (say), we retain equation (3.16) for simplicity, with $t^* = 1$. Minimizing c_t with respect to NA_t, r_{mt} and r_{dt} yields the basic system equations (3.25), (3.27) and (3.28), closed by equations (3.23), (3.26) and (3.29)–(3.32), as follows.

$$\frac{1}{2}\frac{\partial c_t}{\partial NA_t} = \varepsilon_{1t} = (M_t - \theta_1\hat{D}_t) + \alpha_1(NA_t - NA_t^d) + \lambda_1\Delta NA_t \qquad (3.17)$$

$$\frac{1}{2}\frac{\partial c_t}{\partial r_{mt}} = \varepsilon_{2t} = -\alpha_1\left(\frac{\partial NA^d}{\partial r_m}\right)(NA_t - NA_t^d)$$

$$+ \alpha_2\left[\Delta r_{mt} - \frac{1}{\theta_1}\Delta r_{dt} + \theta_4\theta_7\Delta r_{ct} + \theta_8\Delta K_{t-1} \right] \qquad (3.18)$$

$$\frac{1}{2}\frac{\partial c_t}{\partial r_{dt}} = \varepsilon_{3t} = -\theta_1 \left(\frac{\partial \hat{D}}{\partial r_d}\right)(M_t - \theta_1 \hat{D}_t)$$

$$-\frac{\alpha_2}{\theta_1}\left[\Delta r_{mt} - \frac{1}{\theta_1}\Delta r_{dt} + \theta_4\theta_7\Delta r_{ct} + \theta_8\Delta K_{t-1}\right] + \lambda_2\Delta r_{dt} \qquad (3.19)$$

The ε_{it} represent optimization errors, but must also include any mis-specifications. Further

$$\Delta M_t = NA_t \qquad (3.20)$$

$$\Delta D_t = ND_t \qquad (3.21)$$

and

$$\hat{D}_t = D_{t-1} + \widehat{ND}_t \qquad (3.22)$$

where

$$\widehat{ND}_t = \beta_1 + \beta_2(B)ND_t + \beta_3\Delta r_{dt} + \beta_4\Delta r_{ct} + \beta_5\Delta y_t$$

$$(0 < \beta_2 \le 1, 0 < \beta_3, \beta_4 < 0, \beta_5 > 0) \qquad (3.23)$$

and $\beta_2(B)$ is a polynomial in the lag operator B. Note that equation (3.23) includes both 'rational' expectations and ARIMA models as special cases depending on what values the BSs use for the β_j. We obtain from these and equation (3.17)

$$NA_t = -\frac{1}{1+\lambda_1}(M_{t-1} - \theta_1 D_{t-1}) + \frac{\lambda_1}{1+\lambda_1}NA_{t-1} + \frac{\alpha_1}{1+\lambda_1}(NA_t^d - NA_t)$$

$$+ \frac{\theta_1}{1+\lambda_1}\widehat{ND}_t + \frac{\varepsilon_{1t}}{1+\lambda_1} \qquad (3.24)$$

or

$$NA_t = -\frac{1}{1+\lambda_1+\alpha_1}(M_{t-1} - \theta_1 D_{t-1}) + \frac{\lambda_1}{1+\lambda_1+\alpha_1}NA_{t-1}$$

$$+ \frac{\alpha_1}{1+\lambda_1+\alpha_1}NA_t^d + \frac{\theta_1}{1+\lambda_1+\alpha_1}\widehat{ND}_t + e_{1t}. \qquad (3.25)$$

As required, in equilibrium equation (3.25) reproduces equation (3.2). From equation (3.16) we have $0 < \lambda_1, \lambda_2, \alpha_1, \alpha_2 < 1$ if the first objective is the major one, and hence

$$0 < \frac{1}{1+\lambda_1+\alpha_1}, \frac{\lambda_1}{1+\lambda_1+\alpha_1}, \frac{\alpha_1}{1+\lambda_1+\alpha_1}, \frac{\theta_1}{1+\lambda_1+\alpha_1} < 1.$$

From equation (3.18), and assuming (possibly with additional lags) that equation (3.8) is approximated by

$$NA_t^d = \delta_1 y_t + \delta_2[r_{mt}(1 - T_t) - \dot{P}_t] + \delta_3 PH_t + \delta_4 M_{t-1} + v_{1t}$$

$$(0 < \delta_1, \delta_2 < 0, \delta_3?, -1 < \delta_4 < 0) \qquad (3.26)$$

where $\dot{P}_t$ denotes the rate of inflation, we obtain (neglecting variations in T_t)

$$\Delta r_{mt} = \frac{1}{\theta_1} \Delta r_{dt} - \theta_4 \theta_7 \Delta r_{ct} - \theta_8 \Delta K_{t-1} + \frac{\alpha_1 \delta_2}{\alpha_2} (NA_t - NA_t^d) + e_{2t}$$

$$\left(1 < \frac{1}{\theta_1}, \frac{\alpha_1 \delta_2}{\alpha_2} < 0, \theta_4 \theta_7 > 0, 0 < \theta_8 \right). \qquad (3.27)$$

Finally, from equations (3.19) and (3.23), and using equation (3.27) to eliminate Δr_{mt},

$$\Delta r_{dt} = \frac{\theta_1 \beta_3}{\lambda_2} (M_t - \theta_1 \hat{D}_t) + \frac{\alpha_1 \delta_2}{\lambda_2 \theta_1} (NA_t - NA_t^d) + e_{3t}$$

$$\left(0 < \frac{\theta_1 \beta_3}{\lambda_2}, \frac{\alpha_1 \delta_2}{\lambda_2 \theta_1} < 0 \right). \qquad (3.28)$$

Using equations (3.22) and (3.23) for $\hat{D}_t$, Δr_{dt} depends *positively* on Δr_{ct} and negatively on $M_{t-1} - \theta_1 D_{t-1}$. Note that all three control equations depend on the excess demand for mortgages. To close the system, an equation is required for D^s, which need not be equation (3.23) as the BSs could be using an incorrect model. To allow for different lag responses between deposits and withdrawals, we use

$$D_t^s = D_{t-1} + (GD_t^s - WD_t^s) + \text{interest credited } (I_t) \qquad (3.29)$$

with $GD_t = GD_t^s$ and $WD_t = WD_t^s$, so that $ND_t^s = I_t + GD_t^s - WD_t^s = ND_t$. Thus,

$$GD_t = \gamma_1(B) y_t + \gamma_2(B) r_{dt} + \gamma_3(B) r_{ct} + \gamma_4(B) \dot{P}_t + v_{2t}$$

$$(0 < \gamma_1 < 1, 0 < \gamma_2, \gamma_3 < 0, \gamma_4 < 0). \qquad (3.30)$$

A similar equation is postulated for WD_t, except that the signs of the coefficients will be reversed compared with equation (3.30), although the *net* effect (for ND_t) remains as for the γ_i. Finally, empirically

$$I_t \approx \mu \left(\frac{r_{dt} + r_{dt-1}}{2} \right) \left(\frac{D_t + D_{t-1}}{2} \right).$$

Equivalently we have

$$GA_t = NA_t + PR_t \qquad (3.31)$$

where PR_t is composed of routine repayments and premature terminations. If monthly payments are held constant an increase in r_{mt} will reduce PR_t, but for recently effected loans this effect will operate even if the length of life of the mortgage is held constant. Increased income and/or house prices will probably increase premature repayments. Thus, allowing for equation (3.15) and, with linearity, to explain changes in PR_t we propose (subject to additional lags)

$$\Delta PR_t = \phi_1 NA_{t-1} + \phi_2 \Delta y_t + \phi_3 \Delta r_{mt} + \phi_4 \Delta PH_t + \phi_5 \left(PR_{t-1} - \frac{1}{n} M_{t-1} \right) + v_{3t}$$

$$(0 < \phi_1 < 1, 0 < \phi_2, 0 > \phi_3, 0 < \phi_4, \phi_5 < 0). \qquad (3.32)$$

In equilibrium this reproduces equation (3.15). As argued in Hendry (1975b), dimensional analysis, homoscedasticity and stationarity all argue for logarithmic or ratio forms for all of these equations; we keep linearity, however, for comparison with O'Herlihy and Spencer.

Table 3.1 Single-equation estimates

(a) Original model, as reproduced[a] (see O'Herlihy and Spencer, 1972)

(1) $GD/P_t^* = 39r_t - 10r_{bt} + 44T_t + 0.06y/P_t + 0.62GD/P_{t-1} - 684$ $(s = 18.0)$
      (16)   (3)   (14)   (0.02)   (0.09)   (158)

(2) $WD/P_t^* = -23r_t + 9r_{bt} - 9T_t - 0.03y/P_t + 0.07D/P_{t-1} - 154$ $(s = 11.5)$
      (11)   (2)   (8)   (0.01)   (0.01)   (88)

(3) $GA/PH_t^* = 0.72GA/PH_{t-1} + 0.02y/P_t - 16D(1) - 29D(2) - 6$ $(s = 17.3)$
          (0.08)   (0.01)   (6)   (7)   (33)

(4) $PR_t^* = 0.20GA_t - 0.09GA_{t-1} + 0.72PR_{t-1} + 11$ $(s = 3.9)$
          (0.04)   (0.04)   (0.07)   (2)

(5) $r_{mt} = 0.96r_t + 0.35r_{mt-1} + 0.58$ $(s = 0.18)$
          (0.16)   (0.10)   (0.24)

(6) $r_t = -0.06K_t^0 - 0.16L_t^0 + 0.93r_{t-1} + 0.31$ $(s = 0.10)$
          (0.03)   (0.05)   (0.07)   (0.26)

(b) Reformulated model (see Anderson, 1974)

(1) $GD/P_t^* = -11(r_b - r)_t + 105r_t - 69r_{t-1} + 0.08y/P_t - 0.04y/P_{t-1}$ $(s = 18.2)$
          (5)   (60)   (54)   (0.09)   (0.03)

$+33T_t + 0.68GD/P_{t-1} - 554$
  (15)   (0.09)   (172)

(2) $WD/P_t^* = 8(r_b - r)_t - 0.03y/P_{t-1} - 9T + 0.07D/P_{t-1} + 112$ $(s = 9.6)$
          (2)   (0.01)   (6)   (0.01)   (65)

(4) $(PR_t - PR_{t-4}) = 0.17(GA_t - GA_{t-4}) - 0.06(GA_{t-1} - GA_{t-5})$ $(s = 3.9)$
                  (0.02)   (0.03)

$-3(r_{mt} - r_{mt-4}) + 0.57(PR_{t-1} - PR_{t-5}) + 3$
  (5)   (0.12)   (1)

(5) $r_{mt} = 0.66r_t - 0.55r_{mt-1} + 0.45$ $[\tilde{\rho}_1 = -0.34]$ $(s = 0.17)$
          (0.13)   (0.08)   (0.18)

(6) $(r_t - r_{t-1}) = -0.03K_t^0 - 0.18L_t^0 + 0.04(r_{bt-1} - r_{bt-2}) + 0.05$ $(s = 0.09)$
              (0.01)   (0.04)   (0.02)   (0.01)
                                              $[\tilde{\rho}_1 = -0.24]$
                                                  (0.11)

[a] Less four observations for forecasts. The sample size was 54 and s denotes the equation standard error. See table 3.3 for the complete set of definitions. An asterisk denotes that seasonal dummy variables were included but are not reported. Instrumental variables estimation was used where required. No respecification improving equation (3.3) was obtained, and ρ_1 denotes the first-order autoregressive error parameter.

Table 3.2 Forecast errors[a]

	GD/P			WD/P			GA/PH			PR			r_m			r		
	A	B	C	A	B	C	A	B	C	A	B	C	A	B	C	A	B	C
1969(ii)	20	−14	−19	19	12	14	16	16	17	16	11	13	−0.40	−0.25	−0.23	0.39	0.36	0.37
1969(iii)	−15	−20	−38	38	26	18	3	3	3	8	2	4	−0.31	−0.27	−0.30	−0.04	−0.03	0.03
1969(iv)	2	−6	−8	22	4	16	−17	−17	−15	7	0	1	−0.03	0.01	−0.02	−0.13	−0.18	−0.12
1970(i)	20	14	13	16	8	−5	1	1	4	1	7	5	−0.24	−0.18	−0.10	−0.04	−0.17	−0.01
A, χ_4^2	3.2			19.1*[b]			1.6			23.4*			9.4			18.6*		
B, χ_4^2	2.5			9.9			1.6			12.3*			5.7			20.4*		
C, χ_4^2	6.4			9.6			1.6			18.0*			4.8			16.8*		

[a] A, O'Herlihy and Spencer; B, Anderson (1974); C, O'Herlihy and Spencer re-estimated allowing for $u_t = \sum_{i=1}^{4} \rho_i u_{t-i} + \epsilon_t$.
[b] The asterisk denotes significance at the 0.05 level.

3 The Model of O'Herlihy and Spencer

The formulation of the model of O'Herlihy and Spencer is shown in table 3.1(a) (see table 3.2 for four one-period ahead forecasts). The gross deposits equation is similar to equation (3.9), as is that for withdrawals (compare equation (3.23)), and the principal repayments equation is (very roughly) $\Delta PR_t = \phi_1 \Delta GA_t$. Given

Table 3.3 Definitions[a]

Variable	Definition	Source
GD_t	Gross increase in shares and deposits outstanding, net of interest credited to accounts during period t	*Financial Statistics*
WD_t	Withdrawals of shares during period t	*Financial Statistics*
PR_t	Repayments of mortgage principal during period t	*Financial Statistics*
NA_t	Net advances of principal during period t	*Financial Statistics*
r_{mt}	Average rate of interest charged on new mortgages during period t	*Financial Statistics*
r_t	Average rate of interest offered, post tax, on deposits during period t $(= r_{dt}(1 - T_t))$	*Financial Statistics*
ND_t	GD_t + interest credited to accounts $-$ WD_t	*Financial Statistics*
LQ_t	Liquidity ratio $\times$ 100 where the liquidity ratio is cash and 'non-mortgage' investments as a fraction of total assets at the end of period t	*Financial Statistics*
r_{bt}	Average rate of interest paid on bank deposits withdrawable at seven days' notice, during period t	*Financial Statistics*
r_{lt}	Average rate of interest paid by local authorities on short-term loans during period t	*Financial Statistics*
T_t	Standard rate of income tax expressed as a percentage payable during period t	Inland Revenue
y_t	Personal disposable income in current money terms	*Digest of Statistics*
P_t	General index of retail prices	*Digest of Statistics*
PH_t	Index of new house prices	*Digest of Statistics*
L_t^0, K_t^0	Liquidity and reserves constructions	O'Herlihy and Spencer
GA_t	$NA_t + PR_t$	O'Herlihy and Spencer
D_t	Deposit and shares total at end of period t	*Financial Statistics*
M_t	Mortgage total outstanding at the end of period t	*Financial Statistics*
Q_1, Q_2, Q_3	Seasonal dummy variables	Construction
$D(1), D(2)$	Mild and severe rationing dummy variables	O'Herlihy and Spencer

[a] The following is taken from *Financial Statistics*, notes, April 1972, with reference to building societies:

(1) Statistics are based on returns from a sample of about 85 societies with assets amounting to 90 per cent of total building society assets: all societies exceeding £50 million are included, two-fifths of societies with assets of £10 million to £50 million, and one-thirteenth of societies with assets of less than £10 million. Each year figures are reconciled with statutory returns made to the Registrar of Friendly Societies by all building societies.

(2) Pre-1965 statistics are based on annual and quarterly samples smaller than the sample size now used (33 societies), together with annual statistics of the Registrar.

equations (3.31) and (3.15) we can expect very considerable simultaneity between these, and this expectation is supported by the extremely large coefficient on GA_t.

The gross advances equation can be interpreted as equation (3.24) with $GA_t - GA_t^d = \xi[D(1), D(2)]$ (see figure 3.1), $\widehat{ND}_t = a(y/P)_t$ and with $M_{t-1} - \theta_1 D_{t-1}$ omitted. Note that if this last term is reformulated in a stationary way as $(M/D)_{t-1} - \theta_1$ then this is approximately equal to $\{[1 - \theta_1(1 - \theta_3)] - LQ_{t-1}\}/(1 - \theta_3)$. Here $LQ = (A - M)/A$, which will be highly correlated with the form chosen by O'Herlihy and Spencer, namely

$$L_t^0 = \frac{\frac{1}{2}(LQ_{t-1} - 15.5)}{(19 - LQ_{t-1})(LQ_{t-1} - 12)} \tag{3.33}$$

as the denominator is always positive. Both the mortgage and deposit interest rate equations are formulated in levels: the former is made a geometric distributed lag of r and so equation (3.27) predicts a number of omitted variables while the latter depends negatively on L_t^0 (see the previous sentence) and on K_t^0 (a transform of K_t similar to L^0) such that the dependent variable could easily be made Δr_t (compare equation (3.28)). Given these theoretical predictions of mis-specification, we next develop a statistical theory for testing the formulation of the system.

4 Statistical Testing of Dynamic Specification in Small Simultaneous Systems

The determination of an appropriate lag structure in dynamic models is still primarily treated as an empirical matter, generally resolved by experimenting with a set of lagged regressors using a relevant estimator (e.g. ordinary or two-stage least squares). This can yield very misleading results in view of the well-known lagged dependent variable–autocorrelated error bias, especially in simultaneous equations systems (see Hendry, 1975a). However, an econometric approach which explicitly recognizes the interaction between the equation dynamics and the stochastic specification was developed by Sargan (1964a) and can be generalized as follows.

Consider a model given by (for $l \geqslant 1$ chosen *a priori*: e.g. $l = 1$ or $l = 4$)

$$By_t + Cz_t + Dy_{t-1} = u_t \tag{3.34}$$

where $u_t = Fu_{t-l} + \varepsilon_t$, $\varepsilon_t \sim NI(0, \Sigma)$, with *restricted* reduced form

$$y_t = \Pi_1 z_t + \Pi_2 y_{t-1} + v_t \tag{3.35}$$

where $v_t = \Phi v_{t-l} + \omega_t$, $\Pi_1 = -B^{-1}C$ and $\Pi_2 = -B^{-1}D$, $\Phi = B^{-1}FB$. The transformed reduced form (eliminating the autocorrelation) is

$$y_t = \Pi_1 z_t + \Pi_2 y_{t-1} + \Phi y_{t-l} - \Phi \Pi_1 z_{t-l} - \Phi \Pi_2 y_{t-l-1} + \omega_t. \tag{3.36}$$

Equivalently, we have an *unrestricted* version of equation (3.35):

$$y_t = P_1 z_t + P_2 y_{t-1} + \xi_t \tag{3.37}$$

where $\xi_t = G\xi_{t-l} + w_t$, and its transformation

$$y_t = P_1 z_t + P_2 y_{t-1} + G y_{t-l} - G P_1 z_{t-l} - G P_2 y_{t-l-1} + w_t. \tag{3.38}$$

Finally, we could ignore the autoregressive restriction in equation (3.38):

$$y_t = Q_1 z_t + Q_2 y_{t-1} + Q_3 z_{t-l}^0 + Q_4 y_{t-l-1} + Q_5 y_{t-l} + e_t \tag{3.39}$$

where z_{t-l}^0 are all the non-redundant regressors in z_{t-l}. Comparing equation (3.37) with equation (3.39) indicates that the variables omitted from the former ($Q_3 z_{t-l}^0 + Q_4 y_{t-l-1} + Q_5 y_{t-l}$) are being approximated by a first-order vector autoregressive process of lag l in ξ_t. This approximation will, of course, be valid if equation (3.37) *is* the true model, in which case estimating equation (3.39) will be inefficient. The converse does not hold, and there are many situations in which mis-specified dynamics cannot be well approximated by error autocorrelation, hence producing inconsistent estimates in equation (3.37). However, in the first situation, the likelihood values of equations (3.37) and (3.39) should be similar, whereas in the second, that for equation (3.39) should be 'considerably' larger than the likelihood for equation (3.37). Obviously, if $l = 1$, $Q_5 \equiv 0$.

This observation leads to a sequential testing procedure for the various restrictions (see, for example, Anderson, 1971, ch. 6.4). The symbol L_η denotes the log-likelihood value when the error on the equation is η. The chosen order of testing is such that each hypothesis is investigated without conditioning on untested assumptions about a further hypothesis to be investigated, i.e. from the *least* restricted hypothesis to the *most*. Despite this apparently very natural approach, most empirical work appears to proceed in the opposite direction and, indeed, investigators generally conduct tests *only* within equation (3.34) and for $l = 1$ and F either zero or diagonal (the latter being required for autoregressive instrumental variables (AIV) to be valid). Appropriate technology does exist, however, for conducting the required tests (see Hendry, 1971), and it is not too expensive (see Hendry and Tremayne, 1976). Our sequence is as follows.

H_a: the autoregressive restriction on equation (3.38) is valid. If this is true then

$$2(L_e - L_w) \underset{A}{\sim} \chi^2_{m^* n} \tag{3.40}$$

for m regressors in z_{t-l}^0, where $m^* = m$ if $l = 1$, and $m^* = m + n$ if $l > 1$.
If H_a is rejected then the system requires dynamic respecification (go to H_d).
If H_a is not rejected proceed to test H_b.

H_b: $G = 0$ in equation (3.38). If this is true then

$$2(L_w - L_\xi) \underset{A}{\sim} \chi^2_{n^2} \tag{3.41}$$

for n equations. If H_b is rejected use 'autoregressive' estimators; otherwise use 'white noise' estimators. Next we have

H_c: $\Pi_i = P_i$ (i.e. $P_1 = -B^{-1}C, P_2 = -B^{-1}D$). If this is true then either

$$2(L_w - L_\omega) \underset{A}{\sim} \chi^2_N \tag{3.42}$$

if H_b was rejected or

$$2(L_\xi - L_\nu) \underset{\textstyle\sim}{_A} \chi^2_N \tag{3.43}$$

if H_b was not rejected, for N over-identifying restrictions. (Before proceeding from H_b to H_c one could also test whether G was diagonal: H_a and H_b assumed it unrestricted. If the diagonality refers to F, it could be tested after H_c.) If H_c is rejected then the over-identifying restrictions are invalid and the exclusion restrictions in equation (3.34) require modification (or the underlying theory is false). Finally, if H_a is rejected one could attempt to respecify the dynamics by testing

$$H_d : Q_{3i} = Q_{4i} = Q_{5i} = 0.$$

This last test is intended to denote testing rows and/or columns of the Q_3, Q_4, Q_5 matrices for significance, and it could be based on appropriate modifications of the methods proposed in multivariate analysis (see, for example, Anderson, 1958, ch. 8). For the usual sample sizes and numbers of reduced form regressors in econometrics, some 'degrees of freedom' adjustments seem appropriate and those used below are of the form

$$(T - K_3)^{-1}\hat{W}'\hat{W} \quad \text{for} \quad \hat{\Omega}_w \tag{3.44}$$

where $W' = (w_1, \ldots, w_T)$ and (for example)

$$2(1 - h/T)(L_e - L_\xi) \underset{\textstyle\sim}{_A} \chi^2_{n^2 + nm}. \tag{3.45}$$

for $h = K_1 + \frac{1}{2}(n + K_2 + 1)$ with $K = K_1 + K_2$ regressors in equation (3.39), $K_1 = n + k, K_2 = n + m^*$ and k exogenous variables, so that $K_3 = 2n + k$.

Generalizing the analysis for longer lags in y_t in the initial formulation is straightforward; doing so for higher orders of autocorrelation is not, however, as it raises potential non-nesting problems. However, even if $l = 1$ and n is small (3–6 say) the ARIMA representations derived from equation (3.39) will have very high order lags (in the empirical analysis we chose $l = 1$ since initially guessing lags which are slightly too short seems a reasonably likely mistake).

Conversely, specializing the analysis to individual equations using the autoregressive error generalization of limited information maximum likelihood, or its asymptotic equivalent of AIV, yields the approach developed by Sargan (1964a). Since this special case has already proved useful in revealing dynamic mis-specifications in empirical research (see, for example, chapter 2) and is not expensive computationally, we first re-estimated the O'Herlihy and Spencer model by AIV to test (for each equation separately) the validity of the autoregressive restriction (H_a for a *structural* equation), the significance of the autoregressive parameter (H_b for $n = 1$) and also the implicit hypothesis of zero residual autocorrelation of higher order (see Pierce, 1971). Taking account of this information we produced a revised system with no residual autocorrelations other than, where required, a valid first-order autoregressive error. The results for this revised system are reported in table 3.1(b). The respecification brings the system closer to our theoretical form and improves its forecasting performance (other than r), but the forecast tests indicate that significant mis-specifications remain (see table 3.2). However, just re-estimating the original equations by AIV with a fourth-order autoregressive error (compare Wallis, 1972a) produced an equivalent improvement in the forecast accuracy as shown in table 3.2. We conclude that while there is some benefit in using AIV and its related tests, relative to two-stage least squares, to yield consistent estimates, all these individual equation estimators rely on the validity of the untested hypotheses that F is diagonal and that both H_a and H_c are valid. The importance of this is that we cannot really *a priori* expect these hypotheses to hold and hence we are making the 'maintained' hypothesis have less prior plausibility than many of the 'null' hypotheses that we are seeking to test – anticipating rejection.

Even when all these implicit hypotheses are valid, AIV remains inefficient asymptotically compared with full information estimation (note the results in Rothenberg, 1973, ch. 5). Both arguments emphasize the potential advantages of estimating and testing the system as a whole, and, although 54 observations is hardly a large sample for a six-equation model, it seems worth examining the practical value of the various tests applied to the original O'Herlihy and Spencer specification.

The non-linearity relating GA and GA/PH precludes a direct application of our analysis to their model, but if we revise it slightly (and quite reasonably) to use PR/PH instead of PR, so that all values are in real terms, then the model does become linear. The results for the various test statistics are shown in table 3.4. (Equation (3.42) is adjusted using $K_1 = 4 + 6 + [22/6]$, $K_2 = K - K_1 = 9$.) Two points of note are that the small sample size means that the degrees of freedom (df) adjustment has a major impact on equation (3.45) and that the validity of the over-identifying restrictions is clearly rejected (H_c), even if the results for H_a and H_b are equivocal.

Apart from the equation for PR, the restricted reduced form of the original model can be obtained by solution, while the unrestricted reduced form can be estimated directly. We have also done this subject to a different (but similar) approximation from that used for table 3.4, namely, making PR depend on $(GA/PH)_{t-1}$ instead of on GA_{t-1} in the reduced form. These unrestricted and solved reduced form estimates (ignoring PR_t in the latter and GA_{t-1} in both) are presented in table 3.5, and there are a number of major differences between them. Most importantly, in the unrestricted form the rationing dummies are *not* significant in GA/PH, but they *are* in GD/P, while L_t^0 is significant in GA/PH. Thus the dummies appear to represent unexpected downward shifts in the supply of deposits, and if the supply of advances is not formulated as a 'processing' equation the dummies naturally proxy a fall in advances. This result conforms closely with the theory in section 2. It should be noted (when interpreting the remaining coefficients) that r_{mt-1} and r_{t-1} are very

Table 3.4 Asymptotic χ^2 statistic values

Equation	Unadjusted	Adjusted	df
3.40	76		48
3.41	75		36
3.42	204	122	56
3.45	151	41	84

Table 3.5 Unrestricted reduced form estimates[a]

	D(1)	D(2)	T_t	r_{bt}	$(y/P)_t$	$(D/P)_{t-1}$	L_t^0	K_t^0	$(GD/P)_{t-1}$	$(GA/PH)_{t-1}$	PR_{t-1}	r_{mt-1}	r_{t-1}
(GD/P)*	−19.0 (2.4)*[b]	−26.0 (2.6)*	45.0 (3.7)*	−16.0 (4.0)*	0.06 (4.0)*	0.08 (3.9)*	−21.0 (1.5)	−30.0 (3.5)*	0.29 (2.2)*	−0.26 (1.6)	−0.71 (1.3)	−15.0 (1.5)	−35.0 (1.5)
(WD/P)*	2.0 (0.4)	1.0 (0.2)	−15.0 (1.9)	8.0 (3.5)*	−0.05 (5.5)*	0.07 (5.3)*	2.5 (0.3)	18.0 (3.3)*	0.06 (0.8)	−0.13 (1.4)	0.59 (1.8)	−7.0 (1.1)	8.0 (0.5)
(GA/PH)*	7.0 (1.2)	−3.0 (0.5)	−5.0 (0.6)	−2.0 (0.5)	0.02 (1.4)	−0.01 (0.4)	45.0 (4.3)*	7.6 (1.1)	0.42 (4.2)*	0.39 (3.2)*	−0.18 (0.4)	−0.7 (0.1)	−16.0 (0.9)
PR*	3.0 (1.3)	1.0 (0.4)	−9.0 (2.5)*	−0.8 (0.7)	−0.002 (0.4)	0.01 (1.0)	−3.8 (0.9)	1.4 (0.6)	0.18 (4.6)*	0.08 (1.8)	0.29 (1.9)*	2.1 (0.7)	2.6 (0.4)
100r_m^*	−14.0 (1.6)	−12.0 (1.0)	4.0 (0.3)	2.4 (0.6)	0.04 (2.4)*	0.04 (1.5)	−17.0 (1.1)	−15.0 (1.6)	−0.2 (1.6)	0.04 (0.2)	−1.2 (2.0)*	30.0 (2.5)*	64.0 (2.6)*
100r^*	−6.0 (1.1)	8.0 (1.1)	0.2 (0.3)	2.8 (1.2)	−0.003 (0.3)	0.04 (3.2)*	−16.0 (1.7)	−5.0 (1.0)	−0.04 (0.4)	−0.13 (1.3)	−0.55 (1.6)	9.4 (1.5)	40.0 (2.8)*

[a] The s values (adjusted for degrees of freedom) are 15.3, 9.4, 11.9, 4.5, 0.16, 0.09 (t values in parentheses).
[b] The asterisk on the t value denotes significance at the 0.05 level.

Table 3.6 Solved reduced form estimates[a]

	D(1)	D(2)	T_t	r_{bt}	$(y/P)_t$	$(D/P)_{t-1}$	L_t^0	K_t^0	$(GD/P)_{t-1}$	$(GA/PH)_{t-1}$	PR_{t-1}	r_{mt-1}	r_{t-1}
(GD/P)*			44	−10	0.06		−6.0	−2.0	0.62				35
(WD/P)*			−9	9	−0.05	0.07	4.0	1.0					−21
(GA/PH)*	−16	−29			0.02					0.72			
100r_m							−16	−6				35	92
100r							−16	−6					93

collinear, but many of the other coefficients in common between the two reduced forms have markedly similar values.

5 Conclusion

The statistical tests of the various implicit hypotheses (and such hypotheses are often made in time-series studies) revealed a number of mis-specifications in the BS model we have examined. The new estimates suggest appropriate ways of revising the formulation of the model and, despite the 'pre-test' problems in doing this (see, for example, Bock et al., 1973), we believe its justification is considerably enhanced by the existence of independent predictions from a theoretical analysis that such mis-specifications would indeed occur.

Further, corroborating the predictions endows the theory with some credibility. However, to estimate our own model efficiently requires a relatively complicated computer program generalizing the method in Hendry (1971) to systems with non-linear cross-equation restrictions on the parameters. This program has now been developed, and we intend to report our results from it at a later date.

4

Dynamic Specification

with Adrian R. Pagan and
J. Denis Sargan

Preamble

Despite the anachronism, the book seemed to need a forward look based on hindsight. This chapter written jointly with Adrian Pagan and Denis Sargan for *The Handbook of Econometrics* serves that purpose. It is the fruit of several SSRC-financed research programmes at the LSE, developments at CORE and related research at the Australian National University. It offers a route map in terms of an exposition of dynamic specification, a typology of simple dynamic models, an introduction to many of the concepts analysed below and a brief overview of the methodological framework. Chapters 16 and 17 offer more formal analyses of the concepts and framework respectively but require a great deal more knowledge of econometric theory and the background ideas. As noted above, chapter 18 also tries to exposit the ideas from a different angle, namely in terms of an applied example, and chapter 19 reviews the approach.

This chapter evolved out of a number of diverse yet related strands. Denis Sargan had completed the formalization of his COMFAC procedure for single equations and its generalization to systems. Grayham Mizon and I had completed two studies of COMFAC and its relation to dynamic specification and error correction (chapters 6 and 7). Adrian Pagan and I had written a survey of the distributed lag literature during his visit to CORE. The typology of models had evolved as a convenient teaching tool for my econometrics lectures at LSE. Jean-François Richard had formulated the concept of weak exogeneity and together with Rob Engle we were seeking to explore its implications (chapter 15). Jean-François and I had also made considerable progress in clarifying the conceptual basis of the methodology (chapters 16 and 17), originally written as chapters for a monograph on *Dynamic Econometrics* (which is still in progress!). And I had carried out numerous empirical studies (chapters 6–11), which firmly demolished most of my previously held views on how to do empirical research.

Reprinted from Griliches, Z. and Intriligator, M.D. (eds), *Handbook of Econometrics*, vol. II, Amsterdam: Elsevier, 1984, ch. 18. We are grateful to Jean-François Richard for his helpful advice, and to James Davidson, Rob Engle, Clive Granger, Andrew Harvey, Svend Hylleberg and Timo Teräsvirta for comments on an earlier draft. Financial support from the Social Science Research Council to the Programme in Methodology, Inference and Modelling at the London School of Economics and from the Centre for Operations Research and Econometrics at the Catholic University of Louvain-la-Neuve is gratefully acknowledged.

The attempt to write this chapter forced us to try and integrate the disparate strands into a coherent whole.

I cannot tell what my co-authors learned from or thought about the attempt, nor is it possible in retrospect to decide which papers prompted the most important reappraisal of my views. Nevertheless, from the group of papers in which I was involved (being written between 1978 and 1982) I realized at last what the essential difficulty was with my earlier empirical studies: the equation or model to be estimated was obtained from a theoretical derivation and was made stochastic by adding on an appropriately behaved 'error term'. The distributions of the dependent variables were then derived from those of the error terms and that generated the likelihood function for estimation, inference etc. It all seemed coherent. Implicitly, however, it still assumed omniscience. In a theory framework, the model obtained is a function of the assumptions made and as such is freely created by its proprietor. In an empirical framework, the *data* are given, and so the distributions of the dependent variables are already fixed by what the data generation process created them to be – I knew that from Monte Carlo. But I kept missing the obvious point until Jean-François drove it home during my CORE visit: the consequence of given data and a given theory model is that *the error is the derived component*, and one cannot make 'separate' assumptions about its properties. My model derivations were in essence back to front, and I had to reverse the process and obtain the error's distribution from that of the data distributions in empirical modelling (for a detailed exposition, see Hendry, 1987).

The present chapter is a half-way house down that road. Some sections embody the data → error route and others the error → data route. The former induces notions of model design, reparameterizations etc., and the latter induces notions of mis-specification, model revision and so on. Thus, as a route map it is more analogous to a sixteenth-century map of the New World than a twentieth-century map of the Americas. Nevertheless, it is intended to be a guide to what at the time were new explorations, and so I hope it helps to that end.

Now a brief guide to the chapter and its relation to later chapters.

Section 1 is closely related to (and based on) the more extensive discussion in chapter 8 as to why dynamic specification poses such awkward issues when the 'correct' model is not known *a priori*.

Section 2.1 then explains the analysis of exogeneity, developed more fully in chapter 15, and the overall model reduction framework, described in detail in chapter 17. Next, section 2.2 summarizes chapter 13, part I. Sections 2.3–2.5 are not covered elsewhere in this volume and offer a general discussion of the problems involved in dynamic specification. They include consideration of the economic theoretic basis for alternative models, and the interpretability of dynamic equations. The typology of single-equation dynamic models in section 2.6 builds on a preliminary idea initially advanced in chapter 8, and first published in chapter 17 (but omitted from that chapter in this reprint in view of its inclusion here). The typology seeks to clarify the properties of the many different model types which occur in the later chapters and in empirical work generally. It reveals that the results obtained on fitting a given model type are highly dependent on the type selected. Only by estimating unrestricted dynamic models can one ascertain the extent to which results are an artefact of the type used. This reinforces the arguments in Sims (1972a, 1974a). In particular, the discussions about model types (b), (c) and (g) are useful for chapters 6 and 7, and those about (f) and (h) for chapters 8–11. Chapter 19 updates the typology.

Section 4 provides a more extensive discussion of error correction models, which arose in chapter 3 (without being so named therein) and will play a major part in the later empirical studies. Finally, section 5 develops the generalization of the approach to systems of equations. For reasons of space, most of section 3 and all of section 5 of the original have been omitted here; they respectively analysed finite distributed lags and the dynamic–stochastic specification interaction based on the type (g) model. The interested reader is referred to the original for further details, noting that *The Handbook of Econometrics* is certainly not the least accessible publication form I have used!

1 Introduction

Dynamic specification denotes the problem of appropriately matching the lag reactions of a postulated theoretical model to the autocorrelation structure of the associated observed time-series data. As such, the issue is inseparable from that of stochastic specification if the finally chosen model is to have a purely random error process as its basic 'innovation', and throughout this chapter dynamic and stochastic specification will be treated together. In many empirical studies, most other econometric 'difficulties' are present jointly with those of dynamic specification but to make progress they will be assumed absent for much of the discussion.

A number of surveys of dynamic models and distributed lags already exist (see, *inter alia*, Griliches, 1967; Wallis, 1969; Nerlove, 1972; Sims, 1974a; Maddala, 1977; Thomas, 1977; Zellner, 1979a), while Dhrymes (1971) treats the probability theory underlying many of the proposed estimators. Nevertheless, the subject matter has advanced rapidly and offers an opportunity for critically examining the main themes and integrating previously disparate developments. However, we do not consider in detail: (a) Bayesian methods (see Drèze and Richard (1984) for background and Guthrie (1976), Mouchart and Orsi (1976) and Richard (1977) for recent studies); (b) frequency domain approaches (see, in particular, Sims, 1974a; Engle, 1976; Espasa, 1977; Granger and Watson, 1984); nor (c) theoretical work on adjustment costs as discussed, for example, by Nerlove (1972). Although theories of intertemporal optimizing behaviour by economic agents are continuing to develop, this aspect of the specification problem is not stressed below since, following several of the earlier surveys, we consider that as yet economic theory provides relatively little prior information about lag structures. As a slight caricature, economic-theory based models require strong *ceteris paribus* assumptions (which need not be applicable to the relevant data generation process) and take the form of inclusion information such as $y = f(z)$ where z is a vector on which y is claimed to depend. While knowledge that z may be relevant is obviously valuable, it is usually unclear whether z may in practice be treated as 'exogenous' and whether other variables are irrelevant or are simply assumed constant for analytical convenience (yet these distinctions are important for empirical modelling).

By way of contrast, statistical-theory based models begin by considering the joint density of the observables and seek to characterize the processes whereby the data were generated. Thus, the focus is on means of simplifying the analysis to allow valid inference from submodels. Throughout the chapter we shall maintain this distinction between the (unknown) data generation process and the econometric model postulated to characterize it, viewing 'modelling' as an attempt to match the two. Consequently, both aspects of economic and statistical theory require simultaneous development. All possible observables cannot be considered from the outset, so that economic theory restrictions on the analysis are essential; and while the data are the result of economic behaviour, the actual statistical properties of the observables corresponding to y and z are also obviously relevant to correctly analysing their empirical relationship. In a nutshell, measurement without theory is as valueless as the converse is non-operational.[1] Given the paucity of dynamic theory and the small sample sizes at present available for most time series of interest, as against the manifest complexity of the data processes, all sources of information have to be utilized.

Any attempt to resolve the issue of dynamic specification first involves developing the relevant concepts, models and methods, i.e. the deductive aspect of statistical analysis, prior to formulating inference techniques. In an effort to reduce confusion we have deliberately restricted the analysis to a particular class of stationary models, considered only likelihood-based statistical methods and developed a typology for interpreting and interrelating dynamic equations. Many of our assumptions undoubtedly could be greatly weakened without altering, for example, asymptotic distributions, but the resulting generality does not seem worth the cost in complexity for present purposes. In a number of cases, however, we comment parenthetically on the problems arising when a subset of parameters changes. Nevertheless, it is difficult to offer a framework which is at once simple and unambiguous and encompasses a comprehensive range of phenomena yet allows 'economic theory' to play a substantive role without begging questions as to the validity of that 'theory', the very testing of which may be a primary objective of the analysis.

Prior to the formal analysis it seems useful to illustrate by means of a relatively simple example why dynamic specification raises such difficult practical problems. Consider a consumption–income (C-Y) relationship for quarterly data given by

$$\Delta_4 \ln C_t = \delta_0 + \delta_1 \Delta_4 \ln Y_t^n + \delta_2 \Delta_4 \ln C_{t-1} + \delta_3 \ln (C/Y^n)_{t-4} + \varepsilon_t \tag{4.1}$$

where $\Delta_4 x_t = x_t - x_{t-4}$, ln is logarithm to the base e, ε_t is *assumed* to be white noise and Y_t^n is 'normal' income such that

$$\ln Y_t^n = 0.1 \sum_{i=0}^{3} (4 - i) \ln Y_{t-i}. \tag{4.2}$$

The unrestricted distributed lag relationship between $\ln C_t$ and $\ln Y_t$ has the form

$$\ln C_t = \delta_0 + \sum_{i=0}^{m} (\alpha_i \ln C_{t-i-1} + \beta_i \ln Y_{t-i}) + \varepsilon_t. \tag{4.3}$$

When $\delta' = (0, 0.5, 0.25, -0.2)$ (but this is unknown) (4.3) has coefficients

j	0	1	2	3	4	5	6	7	
$\ln C_{t-j}$	-1	0.25	0	0	0.80	-0.25	0	0	(4.4)
$\ln Y_{t-j}$	0.2	0.15	0.10	0.05	-0.12	-0.09	-0.06	-0.03	

Under appropriate conditions on Y_t, estimation of the unknown value of δ (or of δ_0, α, β) is straightforward, and so this aspect will not be emphasized below. However, the formulation in (4.1)–(4.4) hides many difficulties experienced in practice and the various sections of this chapter tackle these as follows.

Firstly, (4.1) is a single relationship between two series (C_t, Y_t) and, at best, is only a part of the data generation process (denoted DGP). Furthermore, the validity of the representation depends on the properties of Y_t. Thus, section 2.1 investigates conditional submodels, their derivation from the DGP, the formulation of the DGP itself, and the resulting behaviour of $\{\varepsilon_t\}$ (whose properties cannot be arbitrarily chosen at convenience since, by construction, ε_t contains everything not otherwise explicitly in the equation). To establish notation and approach, estimation, inference and diagnostic testing are briefly discussed in section 2.2, and are followed in section 2.3 by a more detailed analysis of the interpretation of equations like (4.1). However, dynamic models have many representations which are equivalent when no tight specification of the properties of $\{\varepsilon_t\}$ is available (section 2.4) and this compounds the difficulty of selecting equations from data when important features (such as m in (4.3), say) are not known *a priori*. Nevertheless, the class of models needing consideration sometimes can be delimited on the basis of theoretical arguments and section 2.5 discusses this aspect. For example, (4.1) describes a relatively simple situation in which agents make annual decisions, marginally adjusting expenditure as a short distributed lag of changes in 'normal' income and a 'disequilibrium' feedback to ensure a constant static equilibrium ratio of C to Y (or Y^n). This model constrains the values in (4.3) to satisfy $1 - \Sigma\alpha_i = \Sigma\beta_i$ *(inter alia)* although appropriate converse reformulations of (4.3) as in (4.1) are rarely provided by economic theory alone.

Since (4.3) has a complicated pattern of lagged responses (with 11 non-zero coefficients in (4.4)) unrestricted estimation is inefficient and may yield very imprecise estimates of the underlying coefficients (especially if m is also estimated from the data). Consequently, the properties of restricted dynamic models representing economic data series are important in guiding parsimonious yet useful characterizations of the DGP and section 2.6 offers a typology of many commonly used choices. For example, (4.1) is an 'error correction' model (see also section 4.2) and, as shown in (4.4), negative effects of lagged Y on C may be correctly signed if interpreted as arising from 'differences' in (4.1). Note, also, that long lags in (4.3) (e.g. $m = 7$) need not entail slow reactions in (4.1) (e.g. from (4.4) the median lag of Y^n on C_t is one quarter). The typology attempts to bring coherence to a disparate and voluminous literature.

This is also used as a framework for structuring the more detailed analyses of finite distributed lag models in section 3 (not included here) and other dynamic formulations in section 4 (which include partial adjustment models, rational distributed lags and error correction mechanisms). Moreover, the typology encompasses an important class of error autocorrelation processes (due to common factors in the lag polynomials), clarifying the dynamic–stochastic link and leading naturally to an investigation of stochastic specification in the original section 5 (not included here).

While the bulk of the chapter relates to one-equation submodels to clarify the issues involved, the results are viewed in the context of the general DGP and so form an integral component of system dynamic specification. However, multidimensionality also introduces new issues and these are considered in section 5 of this chapter (originally section 6) together with the generalized concepts and models pertinent to systems or submodels thereof.

Since the chapter is already long, we do not focus explicitly on the role of expectations in determining dynamic reactions. Thus, on one interpretation, our analysis applies to derived equations which, if expectations are important, confound the various sources of lags (see Sargent, 1981). An alternative interpretation is that by emphasizing the econometric aspects of time-series modelling, the analysis applies howsoever the model is obtained and seeks to be relatively neutral as to the economic theory content (see, for example, chapter 16).

2 Data Generation Processes

2.1 Conditional Models

Let x_t denote a vector of n observable random variables, X_0 the matrix of initial conditions, where $X_t^1 = (x_1 \ldots x_t)'$ and $X_t = (X_0' X_t^{1'})'$. For a sample of size T, let $D(X_T^1 | X_0, \theta)$ be the joint data density function where $\theta \in \Theta$ is an identifiable vector of unknown parameters in the interior of a finite-dimensional parameter space Θ. Throughout, the analysis is conducted conditionally on θ and X_0, and the likelihood function is denoted by $\mathcal{L}(\theta; X_T^1)$. The joint data density is sequentially factorized into

$$D(X_T^1 | X_0, \theta) = \prod_{t=1}^{T} D(x_t | X_{t-1}, \theta). \tag{4.5}$$

It is assumed that the conditional density functions in (4.5) have the common functional form

$$x_t | X_{t-1} \sim N(\mu_t, \Omega) \qquad \text{with } \mu_t = \mathcal{L}(x_t | X_{t-1}, \theta) \tag{4.6}$$

where $x_t - \mu_t = v_t$ is an 'innovation' and, by construction,

$$\mathcal{E}(v_t x_{t-j}') = 0 \qquad \forall j \geqslant 1$$

so that

$$\mathcal{E}(v_t v_{t-j}') = 0 \qquad \forall j \geqslant 1.$$

Implicitly, we are ignoring important issues of aggregation (over agents, space, time, goods etc.) and marginalization (with respect to all other variables than those in x_t) by assuming that (4.5) is an adequate statistical representation for a DGP. Hopefully, this conflation of the concepts of DGP and model, due to deliberate exclusion of other difficulties, will not prove confusing. Concerning the economic behaviour determining x_t, we suppose economic agents to form *contingent plans* based on limited information (see Bentzel and Hansen, 1955; Richard, 1980). Such plans define *behavioural relationships* which could correspond to optimizing behaviour given expectations about likely future events, allow for adaptive responses and/or include mechanisms for correcting previous mistakes. To express these in terms of x_t will require marginalizing with respect to all unobservables. Thus, assuming linearity (after suitable data transformations) and a fixed finite lag length (m) yields the model

$$\mu_t = \sum_{i=1}^{m} \pi_i x_{t-i}. \tag{4.7}$$

In (4.7) the value of m is usually unknown but in practice must be small relative to T. The corresponding 'structural' representation is given by

$$Bx_t + \sum_{i=1}^{m} C_i x_{t-i} = \varepsilon_t, \tag{4.8}$$

with $\varepsilon_t = Bv_t$ and $B\pi_i + C_i = 0$, where B and $\{C_i\}$ are well-defined functions of θ and B is of rank n $\forall \theta \in \Theta$ (strictly, the model need not be complete in that (4.6) need only comprise $g \leqslant n$ equations to be well defined: see Richard, 1979).

From (4.5)–(4.8), $\varepsilon_t \sim IN(0, \Sigma)$ where $\Sigma = B\Omega B'$ but, as will be seen below, this class of processes does not thereby exclude autocorrelated error representations. Also, while not considered below, the model could be generalized to include, for example, autoregressive conditional heteroscedasticity (Engle, 1982a).

Direct estimation of $\{\pi_i\}$ is generally infeasible (see, however, section 5.3 and Sargent and Sims, 1977) and in any case still involves important assumptions concerning parameter constancy, the choices of n and m and the constituent components of x_t. Generally, econometricians have been more interested in conditional submodels suggested by economic theory and hence we partition x_t' into $(y_t' z_t')$ and factorize the data densities $D(x_t | X_{t-1}, \theta)$ and likelihood function correspondingly as

$$D(x_t | X_{t-1}, \theta) = D_1(y_t | z_t, X_{t-1}, \phi_1) D_2(z_t | X_{t-1}, \phi_2),$$

where (ϕ_1, ϕ_2) is an appropriate reparameterization of θ, and

$$\mathcal{L}(\theta; X_T^1 | X_0) = \prod_{t=1}^{T} \mathcal{L}_1(\phi_1; y_t | z_t, X_{t-1}) \prod_{t=1}^{T} \mathcal{L}_2(\phi_2; z_t | X_{t-1}). \tag{4.9}$$

Certain parameters, denoted ψ, will be of interest in any given application because of either their 'invariance' to particular interventions or their relevance to policy or to testing hypotheses suggested by the associated theory etc. If ψ is a function of ϕ_1 alone, and ϕ_1 and ϕ_2 are variation free, then z_t is *weakly exogenous* for ψ and fully efficient inference is possible from the partial likelihood $\mathcal{L}_1(\cdot)$ (see Koopmans, 1950a; Florens and Mouchart, 1980a; Richard, 1980; Geweke, 1984; and chapter 15). Thus, the model for z_t does not have to be specified, making the analysis more robust, more comprehensible and less costly, and hence facilitating model selection when the precise specification of (4.8) is not given *a priori*. Indeed, the practice whereby $\mathcal{L}_1(\cdot)$ is specified in most econometric analyses generally involves many implicit weak exogeneity assertions and often proceeds by specifying the conditional model alone, leaving $\mathcal{L}_2(\cdot)$ to be whatever is required to 'complete' $\mathcal{L}(\cdot)$ in (4.9). That ψ can be estimated efficiently from analysing only the conditional submodel does *not* entail that z_t is predetermined in

$$B_{11}y_t + B_{12}z_t + \Sigma C_{1i}x_{t-i} = \varepsilon_{1t} \tag{4.10}$$

(using an obvious notation for the partition of B and $\{C_i\}$), but merely that the model for z_t does not require joint estimation with (4.10).

If, in addition to being weakly exogenous for ψ, the following holds for z_t,

$$D_2(z_t \mid X_{t-1}, \phi_2) \equiv D_2(z_t \mid Z_{t-1}, Y_0, \phi_2) \qquad (t = 1, \ldots, T), \qquad (4.11)$$

so that lagged ys are uninformative about z_t given Z_{t-1}, and hence y does not Granger-cause z (see Granger, 1969; Sims, 1977a; Geweke, 1984), then z_t is said to be *strongly exogenous* for ψ. Note that the initial choice of x_t in effect required an assertion of strong exogeneity of x_t for the parameters of other potentially relevant (economic) variables. Also, as shown in section 2.6, case (g), if (4.11) does not hold, so that y does Granger-cause z, then care is required in analysing model formulations which have autocorrelated errors since z will also Granger-cause such errors.

The remainder of this chapter focuses on dynamic specification in models like (4.10) since these encompass many of the equation forms and systems (with a 'linearity in variables' caveat) occurring in empirical research. For example, the system

$$B^* x_t + \sum_{i=1}^{m^{\bullet}} C_i^* x_{t-i} = u_t \qquad (4.8^*)$$

where

$$u_t = \sum_{i=1}^{r^{\bullet}} R_i^* u_{t-i} + \varepsilon_t,$$

with $m^* + r^* = m$, can be re-expressed as (4.8) with non-linear relationships between the parameters. However, unique factorization of the $\{\pi_i\}$ into $(B^*, \{C_i^*\} \{R_i^*\})$ requires further restrictions on $\{R_i^*\}$ such as block diagonality and/or *strong* exogeneity information (see Sargan, 1961; and section 5.1).

2.2 Estimation, Inference and Diagnostic Testing

Since specific techniques of estimation, inference and diagnostic testing will not be emphasized below (for a discussion of many estimation methods, see Dhrymes, 1971; Zellner, 1979a; and chapter 17) a brief overview seems useful. At a slight risk of confusion with the lag operator notation introduced below, we denote $\log_e$ of the relevant partial likelihood from (4.9) by[2]

$$L(\psi) = \sum_{t=1}^{T} L(\psi; y_t \mid z_t, X_{t-1}). \qquad (4.12)$$

In (4.12), ψ is considered as an argument of $L(\cdot)$, when z_t is weakly exogenous and (4.8) is the DGP. Let

$$q(\psi) = \frac{\partial L(\cdot)}{\partial \psi} \quad \text{and} \quad Q(\psi) = \frac{\partial q(\cdot)}{\partial \psi'}. \qquad (4.13)$$

The general high dimensionality of ψ forces summarization in terms of maximum likelihood estimators (denoted MLEs), or appropriate approximations thereto, and under suitable regularity conditions (most of which are satisfied here granted

(4.6)) – see, for example, Crowder (1976) – MLEs will be 'well behaved'. In particular if the roots of

$$\left| I - \sum_{i=1}^{m} \pi_i g^i \right| = 0 \tag{4.14}$$

(a polynomial in g of order no greater than nm) are all outside the unit circle, then when $\hat{\psi}$ is the MLE of ψ

$$T^{1/2}(\hat{\psi} - \psi) \underset{a}{\sim} N(0, V_\psi), \tag{4.15}$$

where $V_\psi = -\text{plim } TQ(\hat{\psi})^{-1}$, and is positive definite. Note that $\hat{\psi}$ is given by $q(\hat{\psi}) = 0$ (with $Q(\hat{\psi})$ negative definite) and numerical techniques for computing $\hat{\psi}$ are discussed in Dent (1980) and in Quandt (1984). Phillips (1980) reviews much of the literature on exact and approximate finite sample distributions of relevant estimators. If (4.8) is not the DGP, a more complicated expression for V_ψ is required although asymptotic normality still generally results (see, for example, Domowitz and White, 1982).

Note that $q(\psi) = 0$ can be used as an estimator generating equation for most of the models in the class defined by (4.10) when not all elements of ψ are of equal interest (see Hausman, 1975; and chapter 13).

To test hypotheses of the general form H_0: $F(\psi) = 0$, where $F(\cdot)$ has continuous first derivatives at ψ and imposes r restrictions on $\psi = (\psi_1 \ldots \psi_k)'$, three principles can be used (see Engle, 1984), namely: (a) a Wald test, denoted W (see Wald, 1943); (b) the maximized likelihood ratio, LR (see, for example, Cox and Hinkley, 1974, ch. 9); and (c) the Lagrange multiplier, LM (see Aitchison and Silvey, 1960; Breusch and Pagan, 1980; Engle, 1982b). Since (a) and (c) are computable under respectively the maintained and the null hypotheses alone, they are relatively more useful as their associated parameter sets are more easily estimated. Also, whereas (b) requires estimation of both restricted and unrestricted models, this is anyway often necessary given the outcome of either the W or LM tests. Because of their relationship to the unrestricted and restricted versions of a model, W and LM tests frequently relate respectively to tests of specification and mis-specification (see Mizon, 1977b), i.e. within and outside initial working hypotheses. Thus (see Sargan, 1980a) W forms apply to common factor tests, whereas LM forms are useful as diagnostic checks for residual autocorrelation. Nevertheless, *both* require specification of the 'maintained' model.

Formally, when (4.8) is the DGP, $\mathscr{E}q(\psi) = 0$ and $\mathscr{E}Q(\psi) = -\mathscr{I}(\psi)$, with $T^{-1/2}q(\psi) \underset{a}{\sim} N[0, \bar{\mathscr{I}}(\psi)]$, where $\bar{\mathscr{I}}(\cdot) = \text{plim } T^{-1}\mathscr{I}(\cdot) = V_\psi^{-1}$. Then we have the following.

1   From (4.15), on H_0: $F(\psi) = 0$

$$T^{1/2}F(\hat{\psi}) \underset{a}{\sim} N(0, J'V_\psi J) = N(0, V_F), \tag{4.16}$$

where $J = \partial F(\cdot)/\partial \psi$. Let $\hat{J}$ and $\hat{V}_F$ denote evaluation at $\hat{\psi}$; then on H_0

$$W_F = TF(\hat{\psi})'\hat{V}_F^{-1}F(\hat{\psi}) \underset{a}{\sim} \chi_r^2 \qquad (\hat{V}_F = \hat{J}'\bar{\mathscr{I}}(\hat{\psi})^{-1}\hat{J}). \tag{4.17}$$

Furthermore if W_a and W_b are two such Wald criteria based upon two sets of constraints such that those for W_a are obtained by adding constraints to those characterizing W_b, then

$$(W_a - W_b) \underset{\text{a}}{\sim} \chi^2_{r_a - r_b} \quad \text{independently of } W_b \underset{\text{a}}{\sim} \chi^2_{r_b}. \tag{4.18}$$

Such an approach adapts well to commencing from a fairly unconstrained model and testing a sequence of nested restrictions of the form $F_i(\psi) = 0, i = 1, 2, \ldots$, where $r_i > r_{i-1}$ and rejecting $F_j(\cdot)$ entails rejecting $F_l(\cdot)$, $l > j$. This occurs, for example, in a 'contracting search' (see Leamer, 1984), and hence W is useful in testing dynamic specification (see Anderson, 1971, p. 42; Mizon, 1977a; Sargan, 1980a).

2 Let $\tilde{\psi}$ denote the MLE of ψ subject to $F(\psi) = 0$; then

$$\text{LR}_F = 2[L(\hat{\psi}) - L(\tilde{\psi})] \underset{\text{a}}{\sim} \chi^2_r, \quad \text{if } H_0 \text{ is true.} \tag{4.19}$$

3 Since $\tilde{\psi}$ is obtained from the Lagrangian expression

$$L(\psi) + \lambda' F(\psi), \quad \text{using } q(\psi) + J\lambda = 0, \tag{4.20}$$

then, when H_0 is true,

$$\text{LM}_F = Tq(\tilde{\psi})' \bar{\mathscr{I}}(\tilde{\psi})^{-1} q(\tilde{\psi}) = T\tilde{\lambda}' \tilde{J}' \bar{\mathscr{I}}(\tilde{\psi})^{-1} \tilde{J}\tilde{\lambda} \underset{\text{a}}{\sim} \chi^2_r, \tag{4.21}$$

and hence the test is also known as the 'efficient score' test (see Rao, 1973).

Note that $q(\hat{\psi}) \equiv 0$, whereas $F(\tilde{\psi}) \equiv 0$, the converses not holding. Also (4.17), (4.19) and (4.21) show the three tests to be asymptotically equivalent both under H_0 and under the sequence of local alternatives $H_T: F(\psi) = T^{-1/2}\delta$ (for constant δ). All three tests are non-central χ^2_r with non-centrality parameter $\delta' V_F^{-1}\delta$ and are therefore consistent against any *fixed* alternative (i.e. $T^{-1/2}\delta$ constant).[3] As yet, little is known about their various finite sample properties (but see Berndt and Savin, 1977; Evans and Savin, 1982; and chapter 7).

It must be stressed that rejecting H_0 by any of the tests provides evidence only against the validity of the restrictions and does not necessarily 'support' the alternative against which the test might originally have been derived. Also, careful consideration of significance levels is required when sequences of tests are used. Finally, generalizations of some of the test forms are feasible to allow for (4.8) not being the DGP (see Domowitz and White, 1982).

2.3 Interpreting Conditional Models

For simplicity of exposition and to highlight some well-known but important issues we consider a single-equation variant of (4.10) with only one lag, namely

$$y_t = \beta_1 z_t + \beta_2' x_{t-1} + e_t. \tag{4.22}$$

There are (at least) four distinct interpretations of (4.22) as follows (see, for example, Wold, 1959; Richard, 1980).

1 Equation (4.22) is a *regression equation* with parameters *defined by*

$$\mathscr{E}(y_t \mid z_t, x_{t-1}) = \beta_1 z_t + \beta_2' x_{t-1}, \tag{4.23}$$

where $e_t = y_t - \mathscr{E}(y_t | \cdot)$ so that $\mathscr{E}(z_t e_t) = 0$ and $\mathscr{E}(x_{t-1} e_t) = 0$. When (4.23) holds, $\beta = (\beta_1 \beta_2')'$ minimizes the variance of e.

Whether β is or is not of interest depends on its relationship to ψ and the properties of z_t (e.g. β is clearly of interest if ψ is a function of β and z_t is weakly exogenous for β).

2   Equation (4.22) is a *linear least-squares approximation* to some dynamic relationship linking y and z, chosen on the *criterion* that e_t is purely random and uncorrelated with (z_t, x_{t-1}). The usefulness of such approximations depends partly on the objectives of the study (e.g. short-term forecasting) and partly on the properties of the actual DGP (e.g. the degree of non-linearity in $y = f(z)$, and the extent of joint dependence of y_t and z_t): see White (1980a).

3   Equation (4.22) is a *structural relationship* (see, for example, Marschak, 1953) in that β is a constant with respect to changes in the data process of z_t (at least for the relevant sample period) and the equation is *basic* in the sense of Bentzel and Hansen (1955). Then (4.22) directly characterizes how agents form plans in terms of observables and consequently β is of interest. In economics such equations would be conceived as deriving from *autonomous* behavioural relations with structurally invariant parameters (see Frisch, 1938; Haavelmo, 1944; Hurwicz, 1962; Sims, 1977a). The last interpretation is the following.

4   Equation (4.22) is derived from the *behavioural relationship*

$$\mathscr{E}(y_t | X_{t-1}) = \gamma_1 \mathscr{E}(z_t | X_{t-1}) + \gamma_2' x_{t-1}. \tag{4.24}$$

If

$$\varepsilon_{2t} = z_t - \mathscr{E}(z_t | X_{t-1}), \tag{4.25}$$

then e_t is the composite: $e_t = \varepsilon_{1t} - \gamma_1 \varepsilon_{2t}$ so that $\mathscr{E}(e_t \varepsilon_{2t}) \neq 0$ in general and depends on γ_1.

More generally, if $\mathscr{E}(z_t | X_{t-1})$ is a non-constant function of X_{t-1}, β need not be structurally invariant, and if incorrect weak exogeneity assumptions are made about z_t, then *estimates* of γ need not be constant when the data process of z_t alters.

That the four 'interpretations' are distinct is easily seen by considering a data density with a non-linear regression function $((1) \neq (2))$ which does not coincide with a non-linear behavioural plan $((1) \neq (4), (2) \neq (4))$ in which the presence of $\mathscr{E}(z_t | X_{t-1})$ inextricably combines ϕ_1 and ϕ_2, thereby losing structurality for all changes in ϕ_2 (i.e. (3) does not occur). Nevertheless, in stationary linear models with normally distributed errors, the four cases 'look alike'.

Of course, structural invariance is only interesting in a non-constant world and entails that, in practice, the four cases will behave differently if ϕ_2 changes. Moreover, even if there exists some structural relationship linking y and z, failing to specify the model thereof in such a way that its coefficients and ϕ_2 are variation free can induce a loss of structurality in the estimated equation to interventions affecting ϕ_2. This point is important in dynamic specification as demonstrated in the following section.

2.4 The Status of an Equation

Any given dynamic model can be written in a large number of equivalent forms when no tight specification is provided for the error term. The following example illustrates the issues involved.

Suppose there existed a well-articulated, dynamic but non-stochastic economic theory (of a supply–demand form) embodied in the model

$$Q_t = \alpha_1 Q_{t-1} + \alpha_2 I_t + \alpha_3 P_t + v_{1t}, \tag{4.26}$$

$$P_t = \alpha_4 P_{t-1} + \alpha_5 C_t + \alpha_6 Q_{t-1} + v_{2t}, \tag{4.27}$$

where Q_t, P_t, I_t and C_t are quantity, price, income and cost, respectively, but the properties of v_{it} are not easily pre-specified given the lack of a method for relating *decision* time periods to observation intervals (see Bergstrom (1984) for a discussion of continuous-time estimation and discrete approximations). It is assumed below that (C_t, I_t) is weakly, but not strongly, exogenous for $\{\alpha_i\}$, and that (4.26) and (4.27) do in fact correspond 'reasonably' to basic structural behavioural relationships, in the sense just discussed.

First, consider (4.26); eliminating lagged Qs yields an alternative dynamic relation linking Q to I and P in a distributed lag:

$$Q_t = \sum_{i=0}^{\infty} (a_{2i} I_{t-i} + a_{3i} P_{t-i}) + u_{1t}, \tag{4.28}$$

where $a_{ji} = \alpha_1^i \alpha_j \, (j = 2, 3)$. Alternatively, eliminating P_t from (4.26) using (4.27) yields the reduced form

$$Q_t = \pi_1 Q_{t-1} + \pi_2 I_t + \pi_3 C_t + \pi_4 P_{t-1} + e_{1t}, \tag{4.29}$$

which in turn has a distributed lag representation like (4.28) but including $\{C_{t-j} | j \geq 0\}$ and excluding P_t. Further, (4.27) can be used to eliminate all values of P_{t-j} from equations determining Q_t to yield

$$Q_t = \beta_1 Q_{t-1} + \beta_2 Q_{t-2} + \beta_3 I_t + \beta_4 I_{t-1} + \beta_5 C_t + w_{1t}, \tag{4.30}$$

transformable to the distributed lag

$$Q_t = \sum_{i=0}^{\infty} (b_{3i} I_{t-i} + b_{4i} C_{t-i}) + \eta_{1t} \tag{4.31}$$

(where the expressions for b_{ji} as functions of α_k are complicated), which is similar to (4.28) but with $\{C_{t-i}\}$ in place of $\{P_{t-i}\}$.

Manifestly, the error processes of the various transformations usually will have quite different autocorrelation properties and we have

$$u_{1t} = \alpha_1 u_{1t-1} + v_{1t},$$

$$e_{1t} = v_{1t} + \alpha_3 v_{2t},$$

$$w_{1t} = e_{1t} - \alpha_4 v_{1t-1},$$

$$\eta_{1t} = \beta_1 \eta_{1t-1} + \beta_2 \eta_{1t-2} + w_{1t}.$$

Almost all of these errors are likely to be autocorrelated, with correlograms that may not be easy to characterize simply and adequately, emphasizing the link of dynamic to stochastic specification.

In the illustration, all the 'distributed lag' representations are *solved* versions of (4.26) + (4.27) and if estimated unrestrictedly (but after truncating the lag length!) would produce very inefficient estimates (and hence inefficient forecasts etc.). Consequently, before estimating any postulated formulation, it seems important to have some cogent justifications for it, albeit informal ones in the present state of the art: simply asserting a given equation and 'treating symptoms of residual auto-correlation' need not produce a useful model.

Indeed, the situation in practice is far worse than that sketched above because of two additional factors: mis-specification and approximation. By the former is meant the possibility (certainty?) that important influences on y_t have been excluded in defining the model and that such variables are not independent of the included variables. By the latter is meant the converse of the analysis from (4.26) + (4.27) to (4.31), namely that *theory* postulates a general lag relationship between Q_t and its determinants I_t, C_t as in (4.31) (say), and to reduce the number of parameters in b_{3i} and b_{4i} various restrictions are imposed. Of course, a similar analysis applies to all forms derived from (4.27) with P_t as the regressand. Moreover, 'combinations' of any of the derived equations might be postulated by an investigator. For an early discussion, see Haavelmo (1944).

For example, consider the case where C_t is omitted from the analysis of (4.26) + (4.27) when a 'good' time-series *description* of C_t is given by

$$d_1(L)C_t = d_2(L)Q_t + d_3(L)I_t + d_4(L)P_t + \zeta_t, \qquad (4.32)$$

where $d_i(L)$ are polynomials in the lag operator L, $L^k x_t = x_{t-k}$ and ζ_t is 'white noise', independent of Q, P and I. Eliminating C_t from the analysis now generates a different succession of lag relationships corresponding to (4.28)–(4.31). In turn, each of these can be 'adequately' approximated by other lag models, especially if full allowance is made for residual autocorrelation. Nevertheless, should the stochastic properties of the DGP of any 'exogenous' variable change (such as C_t in (4.32)), equations based on eliminating that variable will manifest a 'structural change' even if the initial structural model (4.26) + (4.27) is unaltered. For this reason, the issue of the validity of alternative approximations to lag forms assumes a central role in modelling dynamic processes. A variety of possible approximations are discussed in section 3 of the original paper and, in an attempt to provide a framework, section 2.6 outlines a typology of single-equation dynamic models. First, we note a few quasi-theoretical interpretations for distributed lag models.

2.5 Quasi-theoretical Bases for Dynamic Models

First, equations with lagged dependent variables arise naturally in situations where there are types of adjustment costs like transactions costs, search costs, optimization costs etc. and/or where agents react only slowly to changes in their environment owing to habit, inertia or lags in perceiving changes and so on. Thus economic agents may attach monetary or utility costs to instantaneous alteration of instruments to achieve plans fully. Even when there are no adjustment costs, slow reactions are likely because of the uncertainty engendered by the future and the lack of perfect capital and futures markets. Although formal modelling of such costs is still badly developed – Nerlove (1972) and Sims (1974a) provide references and discussion – it appears that what optimal rules there are prove to be extraordinarily complex and, given the fact that only aggregates are observed, such theory would seem to be only a weak source of prior information. In fact it is not impossible that distributed lags between aggregate variables reflect the distribution of agents through the population. For example, if agents react with fixed time delays but the distribution of the length of time delays across agents is geometric, the aggregate lag distribution observed will be of the Koyck form. In the same way that Houthakker (1956) derived an aggregate Cobb–Douglas production function from individual units with fixed capital–labour ratios, some insight might be obtained for the format of aggregate distributed lags from similar exercises (see, for example, Trivedi, 1982).

However, it seems likely that many agents use simple adaptive decision rules rather than optimal ones although, as Day (1967) and Ginsburgh and Waelbroeck (1976) have shown, these have the capability of solving quite complex optimization problems. A further example of the potential role of these adaptive 'rules of thumb' arises from the monetarists' contention that disequilibria in money balances provide *signals* to agents that their expenditure plans are out of equilibrium (e.g. Jonson, 1976) and that simple rules based on these signals may be adopted as the costs are low and information value high. Stock–flow links also tend to generate models with lagged dependent variables.

In any case, state-variable feedback solutions of optimization problems often have alternative representations in terms of servomechanisms of a form familiar to control engineers, and it has been argued that simple control rules of the type discussed by Phillips (1954, 1957) may be more robust to mis-specification of the objective function and/or the underlying economic process (see Salmon and Young, 1978; Salmon, 1979a). For quadratic cost functions, linear decision rules result and can be expressed in terms of proportional, derivative and integral control mechanisms. This approach can be used for deriving dynamic econometric equations (see, for example, chapter 3), an issue discussed more extensively below. Since such adaptive rules seem likely solutions of many decision problems (see, for example, Marschak, 1953) lagged dependent variables will commonly occur in economic relationships. Thus, one should not automatically interpret (say) 'rational lag' models such as (4.26) as approximations to 'distributed lag' models like (4.28); often the latter will be the solved form, and it makes a great deal of difference to the structurality of the relationship and the properties of the error term whether an equation is a solved variant or a direct representation.

Next, finite distributed lags also arise naturally in some situations such as order–delivery relationships, or from aggregation over agents etc. and often some knowledge is available about properties of the lag coefficients (such as their sum being unity or about the 'smoothness' of the distribution graph). An important distinction in this context is between imposing restrictions on the *model*, such that (say) only steady-state behaviour is constrained, and imposing restrictions on the *data* (i.e. constraints binding at *all* points in time). This issue is discussed at greater length in chapter 8 and noted again in section 2.6, case (h).

Thirdly, unobservable expectations about future outcomes are frequently modelled as depending on past information about variables included in the model, whose current values influence y_t. Eliminating such expectations also generates more or less complicated distributed lags which can be approximated in various ways although, as noted in section 2.3, case (4), changes in the processes generating the expectations can involve a loss of structurality (see, for example, Lucas, 1976). Indeed, this problem occurs on omitting observables also, and although the conventional interpretation is that estimates suffer from 'omitted variables bias' we prefer to consider omissions in terms of eliminating (the orthogonalized component of) the corresponding variable with associated transformations induced on the original parameters. If all the data processes are stationary, elimination would seem to be of little consequence other than necessitating a reinterpretation of coefficients, but this does not apply if the processes are subject to intervention.

Finally, observed variables often are treated as being composed of 'systematic' and 'error' components in which case a lag polynomial of the form $d(L) = \Sigma_{i=0}^m d_i L^i$ can be interpreted as a 'filter' such that $d(L)z_t = z_t^*$ represents a systematic component of z_t and $z_t - z_t^* = w_t$ is the error component. If y_t responds to z_t^* according to some theory, but the $\{d_i\}$ are unknown, then a finite distributed lag would be a natural formulation to estimate (see, for example, Godley and Nordhaus (1972) and Sargan (1980b) for an application to models of full-cost pricing). Conversely, other models assert that y_t only respond to w_t (see, for example, Barro, 1978) and hence restrict the coefficients of z_t and z_t^* to be of equal magnitude, opposite sign.

As should be clear from the earlier discussion but merits emphasis, any decomposition of an observable into (say) 'systematic' and 'white noise' components depends on the choice of information set: white noise on one information set can be predictable using another. For example

$$V_{1t} = \sum_{j=0}^m \gamma_j \nu_{jt-j} \tag{4.33}$$

is white noise if each of the independent ν_{jt-j} is, but is predictable apart from $\gamma_0 \nu_{0t}$ using linear combinations of lagged variables corresponding to the $\{\nu_{jt-j}\}$. Thus, there is an inherent lack of uniqueness in using white noise residuals as a criterion for data coherency, although non-random residuals do indicate data 'incoherency' (see Granger (1983) and chapter 10 for a more extensive discussion). In practice, it is possible to estimate all the relationships derivable from the postulated DGP and check for mutual consistency through mis-specification analyses of parameter values, residual autocorrelation, error variances and parameter constancy (see chapter 8). This notion is similar in principle to that underlying 'non-nested' tests (see Pesaran and Deaton, 1978) whereby a correct model should be capable of predicting the residual variance of an incorrect model and any failure to do this demonstrates that the first model is not the DGP (see, for example, Bean, 1981). Thus, ability to account for previous empirical findings is a more demanding criterion of model selection than simply having 'data coherency': i.e. greater power is achieved by adopting a more general information set than simply lagged values of variables already in the equation (for a more extensive discussion, see chapter 16).

Moreover, as has been well known for many years,[4] testing for predictive failure when data correlations alter is a strong test of a model since in modern terminology (excluding chance offsetting biases) it indirectly but jointly tests structurality, weak exogeneity and appropriate marginalization (which includes thereby both dynamic and stochastic aspects of specification). A well-tested model with white noise residuals and constant parameters (over various subsamples), which encompasses previous empirical results and is consonant with a pre-specified economic theory seems to offer a useful approximation to the DGP.

2.6 A Typology of Single Dynamic Equations

In single-equation form, models like (4.22) from the class defined in (4.6) and (4.7) are called autoregressive distributed lag (AD) equations and have the general expression

$$d_0(L)y_t = \sum_{j=1}^{k} d_j(L)z_{jt} + \varepsilon_{1t}, \tag{4.34}$$

where $d_i(L)$ is a polynomial in L of degree m_i. Thus, (4.34) can be denoted $AD(m_0, m_1, \ldots, m_k)$ although information on zero coefficients in the $d_i(L)$ is lost thereby. The class has $\{\varepsilon_{1t}\}$ white noise *by definition* and so not all possible data processes can be described parsimoniously by a member of the $AD(\cdot)$ class; for example, moving-average errors (which lead to a 'more general' class called ARMAX – see section 4) are formally excluded but, as discussed below, this raises no real issues of principle. In particular, AD(1, 1) is given by

$$y_t = \beta_1 z_t + \beta_2 z_{t-1} + \beta_3 y_{t-1} + \varepsilon_{1t}, \tag{4.35}$$

which for present purposes is assumed to be a structural behavioural relationship wherein z_t is weakly exogenous for the parameter of interest $\beta' = (\beta_1\beta_2\beta_3)$, with the error $\varepsilon_{1t} \sim IN(0, \sigma_{11})$. Since all models have an error variance, (4.35) is referred to for convenience as a three-parameter model. Although it is a very restrictive equation, rather surprisingly AD(1, 1) actually encompasses schematic representatives of nine distinct types of dynamic model as further special cases. This provides a convenient pedagogical framework for analysing the properties of most of the important dynamic equations used in empirical research, highlighting their respective strengths and weaknesses, and thereby, we hope, bringing some coherence to a diverse and voluminous literature.

Table 4.1 summarizes the various kinds of model subsumed by AD(1, 1). Each model is only briefly discussed; cases (a)–(d) are accorded more space in this section since cases (f), (h) and (i) are considered in greater detail in section 4 (cases (e) and (g) are considered in sections 3 and 5 respectively of the original paper).

The nine models describe very different lag shapes and long-run responses of y to x, have different advantages and drawbacks as descriptions of economic time series, are differentially affected by various mis-specifications and prompt generalizations which induce different research avenues and strategies. Clearly (a)–(d) are

Table 4.1 Model typology

Type of model	Equation	Restrictions on (4.35)	Generalization $\left(\sum_0^n\right)$
(a) Static regression	(4.36) $y_t = \beta_1 z_t + e_t$	$\beta_2 = \beta_3 = 0$	$y_t = \sum \beta_{1j} z_{j,t} + e_t$
(b) Univariate time series	(4.37) $y_t = \beta_3 y_{t-1} + e_t$	$\beta_1 = \beta_2 = 0$	$y_t = \sum \beta_{3j} y_{t-j-1} + e_t$
(c) Differenced data/ growth rate	(4.38) $\Delta y_t = \beta_1 \Delta z_t + e_t$	$\beta_3 = 1,\ \beta_2 = -\beta_1$	$\Delta y_t = \sum \beta_{1j} \Delta z_{j,t} + \sum \beta_{3j} \Delta y_{t-j-1} + e_t$
(d) Leading indicator	(4.39) $y_t = \beta_2 z_{t-1} + e_t$	$\beta_1 = \beta_3 = 0$	$y_t = \sum\sum \beta_{2jk} z_{j,t-k-1} + e_t$
(e) Distributed lag	(4.40) $y_t = \beta_1 z_t + \beta_2 z_{t-1} + e_t$	$\beta_3 = 0$	$y_t = \sum\sum \beta_{1jk} z_{j,t-k} + e_t$
(f) Partial adjustment	(4.41) $y_t = \beta_1 z_t + \beta_3 y_{t-1} + e_t$	$\beta_2 = 0$	$y_t = \sum \beta_{1j} z_{j,t} + \sum \beta_{3j} y_{t-j-1} + e_t$
(g) Common factor (autoregressive error)	(4.42) $\begin{cases} y_t = \beta_1 z_t + u_t \\ u_t = \beta_3 u_{t-1} + e_t \end{cases}$	$\beta_2 = -\beta_1\beta_3$	$\left.\begin{array}{l} y_t = \sum\sum \beta_{1jk} z_{j,t-k} + \sum \beta_{3j} y_{t-j-1} + u_t \\ u_t = \sum \rho_l u_{t-l-1} + e_t \end{array}\right\}$
(h) Error correction	(4.43) $\Delta y_t = \beta_1 \Delta z_t + (1 - \beta_3)(z - y)_{t-1} + e_t$	$\sum \beta_i = 1$	$\Delta y_t = \left\{ \begin{array}{l} \sum\sum \beta_{1jk} \Delta z_{j,t-k} + \sum \gamma_{lj} \Delta y_{t-j-1} \\ \qquad + \phi\left[\sum \lambda_l z_l - y \right]_{t-1} + e_t \end{array}\right.$
(i) Reduced form/ dead start	(4.44) $y_t = \beta_2 z_{t-1} + \beta_3 y_{t-1} + e_t$	$\beta_1 = 0$	$y_t = \sum\sum \beta_{2jk} z_{j,t-k-1} + \sum \beta_{3j} y_{t-j-1} + e_t$

one-parameter models whereas (e)–(i) are two-parameter models and, on the assumptions stated above, all but (g) are estimable by ordinary least squares (OLS) (whereas (g) involves iterative least squares). Each case can be interpreted as a model 'in its own right' or as derived from (or an approximation to) (4.35) and these approaches will be developed in the discussion.

The generalizations of each 'type' in terms of increased numbers of lags and/or distinct regressor variables naturally resemble each other more than do the special cases chosen to highlight their specific properties, although major differences from (4.34) persist in most cases. The exclusion restrictions necessary to obtain various specializations from (4.34) (in particular, (4.36)–(4.40) and (4.44)) seem difficult to justify in general. Although there may sometimes exist relevant theoretical arguments supporting a specific form, it is almost always worth testing whatever model is selected against the general unrestricted equation to help gain protection from major mis-specifications.

(a) *Static regression* models of the general form

$$y_t = \sum_j \beta_j z_{jt} + e_t \qquad (4.45)$$

rarely provide useful approximations to time-series data processes (but see Hansen, 1982). This occurs both because of the 'spurious regressions' problem induced by the observations being highly serially correlated (see Yule, 1926; Granger and Newbold, 1974), with associated problems of residual autocorrelation and uninterpretable values of R^2, and because the assertion that (4.45) is structural with z_t weakly exogenous for β has not proved viable in practice. While equilibrium economic theories correctly focus on interdependence and often entail equations such as $y = f(z)$ where linearity seems reasonable, imposing (4.45) on *data* restricts short-run and long-run responses of y to z to be identical and instantaneous. It seems preferable simply to require that the dynamic model *reproduces* $y = f(z)$ under equilibrium assumptions; this restricts the class of model but not the range of dynamic responses (see (h)). Finally, for forecasting y_{t+j}, (4.45) requires a prior forecast of z_{t+j} and so lagged information is needed at some stage and seems an unwarranted exclusion from behavioural equations.

(b) In contrast, *univariate time-series* models focus only on dynamics but often serve as useful data-descriptive tools, especially if selected on the criterion of white noise residuals (see Box and Jenkins, 1976). A general stationary form is the autoregressive moving-average (ARMA) process

$$\gamma(L)y_t = \delta(L)e_t, \qquad (4.46)$$

where $\gamma(L)$ and $\delta(L)$ are polynomials of order m_0, m_1 (with no redundant factors), and (4.46) is denoted ARMA(m_0, m_1) with (4.37) being ARMA(1, 0). Equations like (4.37) can be suggested by economic theory and, for example, efficient markets and rational expectations models often have $\beta_3 = 1$ (see, for example, Hall, 1978; Frenkel, 1981), but for the most part ARMA models tend to be derived rather than autonomous. Indeed, every variable in (4.8) has an ARMA representation[5] (see, for example, Zellner and Palm, 1974; Wallis, 1977) but such reformulations need not be structural and must have larger variances. Thus, econometric models which do not fit better than univariate time-series processes have at least mis-specified dynamics, and if they do not forecast 'better'[6] must be highly suspect for policy analysis (see, *inter alia*, Prothero and Wallis, 1976).

In principle, all members of our typology have generalizations with moving-average errors, which anyway are likely to arise in practice from marginalizing with respect to autoregressive or Granger-causal variables, or from measurement errors, continuous time approximations etc. However, detailed consideration of the enormous literature on models with moving-average errors is precluded by space limitations (see section 4.1 for relevant references). In many cases moving-average errors can be quite well approximated by autoregressive processes (see, for example, Sims, 1977a, p. 194), which are considered under (g) below, and it seems difficult to discriminate in practice between autoregressive and moving-average approximations to autocorrelated residuals (see, for example, Hendry and Trivedi, 1972).

(c) *Differenced data* models resemble (a) but after transformation of the observations y_t and z_t to $y_t - y_{t-1} = \Delta y_t$ and Δz_t. The filter $\Delta = 1 - L$ is commonly applied on the grounds of 'achieving stationarity', to circumvent awkward inference problems in ARMA models (see Box and Jenkins, 1976; Fuller, 1976; Phillips, 1977; Evans and Savin, 1981; Harvey, 1981a) or to avoid 'spurious regressions' criticisms. Although the equilibrium equation that $y = \beta_1 z$ implies $\Delta y = \beta_1 \Delta z$, differencing fundamentally alters the properties of the error process. Thus, even if y is proportional to z in equilibrium, the solution of (4.38) is indeterminate and the estimated magnitude of β_1 from (4.38) is restricted by the relative variances of Δy_t to Δz_t. A well-known example is the problem of reconciling a low marginal with a high and constant average propensity to consume (see chapter 8, and compare Wall et al., 1975, and Pierce, 1977). In any case, there are other means of inducing stationarity, such as using ratios, which may be more consonant with the economic formulation of the problem.

(d) *Leading indicator* equations like (4.39) attempt to exploit directly differing latencies of response (usually relative to business cycles) wherein, for example, variables like employment in capital goods industries may 'reliably lead' GNP. However, unless such equations have some 'causal' or behavioural basis, β_2 need not be constant and unreliable forecasts will result; thus econometric models which indirectly incorporate such effects have tended to supersede leading indicator modelling (see, *inter alia*, Koopmans, 1947; Kendall, 1973).

(e) As discussed in section 2.4, *distributed lags* can arise either from structural–behavioural models or as implications of other dynamic relationships. Empirically, equations of the form

$$y_t = \alpha(L)z_t + e_t, \tag{4.47}$$

where $\alpha(L)$ is a polynomial of order m_1, frequently manifest substantial residual autocorrelation (see, *inter alia*, many of the $AD(0, m_1, \ldots, m_k)$ equations in Hickman (1972) or, for example, new housing 'starts–completions' relationships in Waelbroeck (1976)). Thus, whether or not z_t is *strongly* exogenous becomes important for the detection and estimation of the residual autocorrelation. 'Eliminating' autocorrelation by fitting autoregressive errors imposes 'common factor restrictions' whose validity is often dubious and merits testing (see (g) and Sargan, 1980a), and even after removing a first-order autoregressive error the equation may yet remain prey to the 'spurious regressions' problem (see Granger and Newbold, 1977a). Moreover, collinearity between successive lagged zs has generated a large literature attempting to resolve the profligate parameterizations of unrestricted estimation (and the associated large standard errors) by subjecting the $\{\alpha_j\}$ to various 'a priori constraints'. Since relatively short 'distributed lags' also occur regularly in other $AD(\cdot)$ models, and there have been important recent technical developments, the finite distributed lag literature is briefly noted in section 3.

(f) *Partial adjustment* models are one of the most common empirical species and have their basis in optimization of quadratic cost functions where there are adjustment costs (see Eisner and Strotz, 1963; Holt et al., 1960). Invalid exclusion of z_{t-1} can have important repercussions since the shape of the distributed lag relationship derived from (4.41) is highly skewed with a large mean lag when β_3 is large even though that derived from (4.35) need not be for the same numerical value of β_3: this may be part of the explanation for apparent 'slow speeds of adjustment' in estimated versions of (4.41) or generalizations thereof (see, especially, studies of aggregate consumers' expenditure and the demand for money in the United Kingdom). Moreover, many derivations of 'partial adjustment' equations like (4.41) entail that e_t is autocorrelated (see, for example, Maddala, 1977, ch. 9; Kennan, 1979; Muellbauer, 1979) so that OLS estimates are inconsistent for the β_i (see Malinvaud, 1966) and have inconsistently estimated standard errors, and residual autocorrelation tests like the Durbin–Watson statistic are invalid (see Griliches, 1961; Durbin, 1970). However, appropriate LM tests can be constructed (see Godfrey, 1978; Breusch and Pagan, 1980). Finally, generalized members of this class such as

$$\gamma(L)y_t = \sum_{i=1}^{K} \delta_i z_{it} + e_t \tag{4.48}$$

have unfortunate parameterizations since 'levels' variables in economics tend to be highly intercorrelated.

(g) *Common factor* representations correspond one-to-one to autoregressive error models and most clearly demonstrate the dynamic–stochastic specification link in terms of 'equation dynamics' versus 'error dynamics' (see Sargan, 1964a, 1980a; and chapters 6 and 7). To illustrate the principles involved, reconsider (4.35) written in lag operator notation (with $\beta_1 \neq 0$):

$$(1 - \beta_3 L)y_t = \beta_1 \left[1 + \frac{\beta_2}{\beta_1} L \right] z_t + e_t, \tag{4.35*}$$

where both lag polynomials have been normalized. Under the condition

$$-\beta_3 = \beta_2/\beta_1 \quad \text{or} \quad \beta_1\beta_3 + \beta_2 = 0, \tag{4.49}$$

the lag polynomials coincide and constitute a *common factor* of $1 - \beta_3 L$. Dividing both sides of (4.35*) by $1 - \beta_3 L$ yields

$$y_t = \beta_1 \left[\frac{1 + (\beta_2/\beta_1)L}{1 - \beta_3 L} \right] z_t + \frac{e_t}{1 - \beta_3 L} = \beta_1 z_t + u_t, \tag{4.50}$$

where

$$u_t = \beta_3 u_{t-1} + e_t. \tag{4.51}$$

Consequently, the equations

$$y_t = \beta_1 z_t + u_t \qquad (\mathrm{AD}(0,0)) \tag{4.52}$$

$$u_t = \beta_3 u_{t-1} + e_t \qquad (\mathrm{AD}(1))$$

uniquely imply and are uniquely implied by

$$y_t = \beta_1 z_t + \beta_3 y_{t-1} - \beta_1 \beta_3 z_{t-1} + e_t \qquad (\mathrm{AD}(1,1)). \tag{4.53}$$

Usually, $|\beta_3| < 1$ is required; note that (4.52) can also be written as

$$y_t^+ = \beta_1 z_t^+ + e_t, \tag{4.54}$$

where $z_t^+ = z_t - \beta_3 z_{t-1}$ is a 'quasi-difference' and the operator $1 - \beta_3 L$ 'eliminates' the error autocorrelation.

This example highlights two important features of the AD($\cdot$) class. First, despite formulating the class as one with a white noise error, it does *not* exclude autoregressive error processes. Second, such errors produce a *restricted* case of the class and hence the assumption of an autoregressive error *form* is testable against a less restricted member of the AD($\cdot$) class. More general cases and the implementation of appropriate tests of common factor restrictions are discussed in section 5 of the original paper.

The equivalence of autoregressive *errors* and common factor dynamics has on occasion been misinterpreted to mean that autocorrelated *residuals* imply common factor dynamics. There are many reasons for the existence of autocorrelated residuals including omitted variables, incorrect choice of functional form, measurement errors in lagged variables and moving-average error processes as well as autoregressive errors. Consequently, for example, a low value of a Durbin–Watson statistic does *not* uniquely imply that the errors are a first-order autoregression and automatically 'eliminating' residual autocorrelation by assuming an AD(1) process for the error can yield very misleading results.

Indeed, the order of testing is incorrect in any procedure which tests for autoregressive errors by assuming the existence of a common factor representation of the model: the validity of (4.49) should be tested before assuming (4.52) and attempting to test therein H_b: $\beta_3 = 0$. In terms of commencing from (4.35), if and only if H_a: $\beta_2 + \beta_1 \beta_3 = 0$ is true will the equation have a representation like (4.52) and so only if H_a is *not* rejected can one proceed to test H_b: $\beta_3 = 0$. If H_b is tested alone, conditional on the belief that (4.49) holds, then failure to reject $\beta_3 = 0$ does not imply that $y_t = \beta_1 z_t + e_t$ (a common mistake in applied work) nor does rejection of H_b imply that the equations in (4.52) are valid. It is sensible to test H_a first since only if a common factor exists is it meaningful to test the hypothesis that its root is zero. While (4.52) is easily interpreted as an approximation to some more complicated model with the error autocorrelation simply acting as a 'catch all' for omitted variables, unobservables etc. a full behavioural interpretation is more difficult. Formally, on the one hand, $\mathscr{E}(y_t|X_{t-1}) = \beta_1 z_t + \beta_3 u_{t-1}$ and hence agents adjust to this shifting 'optimum' with a purely random error. However, if the $\{u_t\}$ process is viewed as being autonomous then the first equation of (4.52) entails an immediate and complete adjustment of y to changes in z, but if agents are perturbed above (below) this 'equilibrium' they will stay above (below) for some time and do not adjust to remove the discrepancy. Thus, (4.52) also characterizes a 'good/bad fortune' model with persistence of the chanced-upon state in an equilibrium world. While these paradigms have some applications, they seem likely to be rarer than the present frequency of use of common factor models would suggest, supporting the need to test autoregressive error restrictions before imposition. The final interpretation of (4.53) noted in section 5 of the original paper serves to reinforce this statement.

Despite these possible interpretations, unless y does *not* Granger-cause z, then z Granger-causes u. If so, then regressing y_t on z_t when $\{u_t\}$ is autocorrelated will yield an inconsistent estimate of β_1, and the residual autocorrelation coefficient will be inconsistent for β_3. Any 'two-step' estimator of (β_1, β_3) commencing from these initial values will be inconsistent, even though (a) there are no explicit lagged variables in (4.52) and (b) fully iterated maximum likelihood estimators are consistent and fully efficient when z_t is weakly exogenous for β (see chapter 13 for a survey of estimators in common factor equations). Finally, it is worth emphasizing that, under the additional constraint that $\beta_3 = 1$, model (c) is a common factor formulation.

(h) *Error correction models* such as (4.43) are a natural reparameterization of AD($\cdot$) equations when

$$\left(\sum \beta_i - 1\right) = \delta = 0. \tag{4.55}$$

If $\beta_3 \neq 1$, the steady-state solution of (4.43) for $\Delta z = g = \Delta y$ is

$$y = \frac{(1 - \beta_1)g}{1 - \beta_3} + z = k(g) + z, \tag{4.56}$$

and hence $y = z$ in static equilibrium, or $Y = K(g)Z$ (more generally) when y and z are ln Y and ln Z, respectively (see Sargan, 1964a; and chapter 11). Thus, (4.55) implements long-run proportionality or homogeneity and ensures that the dynamic equation reproduces in an equilibrium context the associated equilibrium theory. Moreover, $H_0: \delta = 0$ is easily tested, since (4.35) can be rewritten as

$$\Delta y_t = \beta_1 \Delta z_t + (1 - \beta_3)(z - y)_{t-1} + \delta z_{t-1} + e_t, \tag{4.57}$$

which anyway offers the convenient interpretation that agents marginally adjust y_t from y_{t-1} in response to *changes* in z_t (β_1 being the short-run effect), the previous *disequilibrium* $(z - y)_{t-1}$ ($(1 - \beta_3)$ being the 'feedback' coefficient) and the

Table 4.2   Parameter values for other models when (4.57) is homogeneous

(a) $\beta_1 = 1 - \beta_3 = 1$	(b) $\beta_1 = 1 - \beta_3 = 0$	(c) $1 - \beta_3 = 0$
(d) $\beta_1 = \beta_3 = 0$	(e) $\beta_3 = 0$	(f) $\beta_1 = 1 - \beta_3$
(g) $\beta_1 = 1$	(i) $\beta_1 = 0$	

previous *level* z_{t-1} (which is irrelevant under proportionality). Since many economic theories have proportional forms in static equilibrium, error correction models might be expected to occur frequently. Indeed, an important property of (4.43) is that, when $\delta = 0$, (4.57) coincides with (4.43) and all of the other models in this typology become special cases of (4.43). Thus, given $\delta = 0$ a modelling exercise which commenced from (4.43) even when one of the *other* types represented the actual DGP would involve no mis-specification and which other special case was correct would be readily detectable from the values of the parameters in (4.43) given in table 4.2. The converse does *not* hold: fitting any of (a)–(g) when (h) is true but table 4.2 restrictions are invalid induces mis-specifications, the precise form of which could be deduced by an investigator who used (h). Thus, when $\delta = 0$, error correction is essentially a necessary and sufficient model form and it is this property which explains the considerable practical success of error correction formulations in encompassing and reconciling diverse empirical estimates in many subject areas (see, *inter alia*, Henry et al., 1976; Bean, 1977; Cuthbertson, 1980; Davis, 1982; and chapters 3, 8 and 11). In an interesting way, therefore, (4.43) nests 'levels' and 'differences' formulations and, for example, offers one account of why a small value of β_1 in (c) is compatible with proportionality in the long run, illustrating the interpretation difficulties deriving from imposing 'differencing filters'.

(i) Equation (4.44) could constitute either the *reduced form* of (4.35) on eliminating z_t (assuming its process to be AD(1, 1) also, or a special case thereof) or a 'deadstart' model in its own right. For example, if $z_t = \lambda z_{t-1} + \varepsilon_{2t}$ and (4.35) is the behavioural equation, (4.44) is also 'valid' with parameters

$$y_t = (\beta_2 + \beta_1 \lambda) z_{t-1} + \beta_3 y_{t-1} + e_t, \qquad e_t \sim \text{IN}(0, \sigma_{11} + \beta_1^2 \sigma_{22}) \qquad (4.58)$$

but is no longer structural for changes in λ, and λ is required for estimating β. Indeed if $\delta = 0$ in (4.55), (4.58) will not exhibit proportionality unless $\beta_1(1 - \lambda) = 0$. Also, $\beta_2 + \beta_1 \lambda < 0$ does not exclude $y = z$ in equilibrium, although this interpretation will only be noticed if (y_t, z_t) are *jointly* modelled.

Conversely, if (4.44) is structural because of an inherent lag before z affects y, then it is a *partial adjustment type* of model, and other types have deadstart variants in this sense.

Distributed lags often have autocorrelated errors and other dynamic models usually embody short distributed lags. Since generalizations can blur important distinctions, the preceding typology is offered as a clarifying framework.

3 Finite Distributed Lags

3.1 A Statement of the Problem

A finite distributed-lag relationship has the form

$$y_t = \sum_{i=1}^{n} W_i(L)z_{it} + u_t, \tag{4.59}$$

where

$$W_i(L) = \sum_{j=m_i^0}^{m_i} w_{ij} L^j, \tag{4.60}$$

and is a member of the AD$(0, m_1, \ldots, m_n)$ class. For ease of exposition and notation, attention is centred on a bivariate case, namely AD$(0, m)$ denoted by

$$y_t = \sum_{j=m^0}^{m} w_j z_{t-j} + u_t = W(L)z_t + u_t, \tag{4.61}$$

where $\{z_t\}$ is to be treated as 'given' for estimating $w = (w_{m^0}, \ldots, w_m)'$, and u_t is a 'disturbance term'. It is assumed that sufficient conditions are placed upon $\{u_t\}$ and $\{z_t\}$ so that OLS estimators of w are consistent and asymptotically normal (e.g. that (4.8) is the DGP and is a stable dynamic system with w defined by $\mathcal{E}(y_t | Z_{t-m^0})$).

Several important and interdependent difficulties hamper progress. First, there is the issue of the status of (4.61), namely whether it is basic or derived and whether or not it is structural, behavioural etc. or just an assumed approximation to some more complicated lag relationship between y and z (see sections 2.3 and 2.4). Unless explicitly stated otherwise, the following discussion assumes that (4.61) is structural, that $u_t \sim \text{IN}(0, \sigma_u^2)$ and that z_t is weakly exogenous for w. These assumptions are only justifiable on a pedagogic basis and are unrealistic for many economics data series; however, most of the technical results discussed below would apply to short distributed lags in a more general dynamic equation. Second, $W(L)$ is a polynomial of the same degree as the lag length and, for highly intercorrelated $\{z_{t-j}\}$, unrestricted estimates of w generally will not be well determined. Conversely, it might be anticipated that a lower order polynomial, of degree $k < m$ say, over the same lag length might suffice, and hence one might seek to estimate the $\{w_j\}$ subject to such restrictions. [Section 3.2 (not included here) considered some possible sets of restrictions whereas section 3.4 discussed methods for 'weakening' lag weight restrictions. 'Variable lag weights' wherein the $\{w_j\}$ are dependent on economic variables which change over time were considered in section 3.6.

However, n, m^0 and m are usually unknown and have to be chosen jointly, and this issue was investigated in section 3.3 together with an evaluation of some of the consequences of incorrect specifications. Further, given that formulations like (4.61) are the correct specification, many alternative estimators of the parameters have been proposed and the properties of certain of these were discussed in section 3.5 and related to sections 3.2 and 3.4.

Frequently, equations like (4.61) are observed to manifest serious residual auto-correlation and section 3.6 briefly considered this issue as well as some alternative specifications which might facilitate model selection.]

4 Infinite Distributed Lags

4.1 Rational Distributed Lags

Almost all individual estimated equations in macroeconometric systems have been members of the general class of autoregressive moving-average models with 'explanatory' variables, denoted by ARMAX($\cdot$) and written as

$$\alpha_0(L)y_t = \sum_{j=1}^{n} \alpha_j(L)z_{jt} + \alpha_{n+1}(L)e_t \qquad e_t \sim \text{IN}(0, \sigma_e^2) \tag{4.62}$$

where

$$\alpha_i(L) = \sum_{j=0}^{m_i} \alpha_{ij} L^j \qquad \alpha_{0,0} \equiv \alpha_{n+1,0} \equiv 1, \tag{4.63}$$

and there are *no* polynomial factors common to *all* the $\alpha_j(L)$. Then (4.62) is said to be ARMAX($m_0, m_1, \ldots, m_n, m_{n+1}$) (generalizing the AD($\cdot$) notation with the last argument showing the order of the moving-average error process). The $\{z_{jt}\}$ in (4.62) are not restricted to be 'exogenous' in the sense defined in section 2, and could be endogenous, weakly or strongly exogenous or lagged values of variables endo-genous elsewhere in the systems, and might be linear or non-linear transformations of the original (raw) data series. However, it is assumed that the parameters of (4.62) are identifiable and constant over any relevant time period.

The formulation in (4.62) can be expressed equivalently as

$$y_t = \sum_{i=1}^{n} \frac{\gamma_i(L)}{\delta_i(L)} z_{it} + \frac{\phi(L)}{\rho(L)} e_t, \tag{4.64}$$

where all common factors have been cancelled in the ratios of polynomials. An important special case of (4.64) is where $\phi(L) = \rho(L)$ (i.e. $\alpha_0(L) = \alpha_{n+1}(L)$ in (4.62)) which we call the rational distributed lag (RDL),

$$y_t = \sum_{i=1}^{n} \frac{\gamma_i(L)}{\delta_i(L)} z_{it} + e_t = \sum_{i=1}^{n} w_i(L)z_{it} + e_t, \tag{4.65}$$

and like the AD($\cdot$) class, RDL is defined here to have white noise disturbances relative to its information set. Equation (4.65) generalizes (4.59) to infinite lag responses. Thus, ARMAX($\cdot$) is RDL with ARMA($\cdot$) errors or AD($\cdot$) with MA($\cdot$) errors, and if any denominator polynomial is of non-zero order some of the derived lag distributions are infinite. Relative to the class defined by (4.62) the parameter spaces of AD($\cdot$) and RDL($\cdot$) models constitute a set of measure zero in the general parameter space. In practical terms, however, all the models in this chapter constitute more or less crude first approximations to complicated underlying economic pro-cesses and, for high-order lag polynomials, provide rather similar data descriptions.

Indeed, if all the roots of the $\delta_i(L)$ $(i = 1, \ldots, n)$, $\rho(L)$ and $\phi(L)$ polynomials in (4.64) lie outside the unit circle, by expanding the inverses of these polynomials as power series, a wide range of alternative approximations can be generated (extending the analysis in section 2.3 above). But selecting equations purely on the basis of 'goodness of approximation' is of little comfort if the resulting model does not correspond to either a behavioural or a structural relationship, and as stressed below derived parameters (such as mean lags, long-run outcomes etc.) can differ greatly between 'similar' approximations.

Consequently, the choice of model *class* relevant to empirical research does not seem to us to be an issue of principle but a matter of whether (a) the formulation is coherent with available theory and/or prior information concerning structural/behavioural relationships, (b) the parameterization is parsimonious with easily understood properties and (c) the equation is easily manipulated, estimated (when its form is known) and selected (when the exact orders of all the lag polynomials, relevant regressors etc. are not known *a priori*). These criteria may conflict since simple easily estimated equations may not provide the most parsimonious representations or may be non-structural etc. Moreover, if the unknown DGP takes one form (e.g. an error correction AD(1, 1)) but an encompassing model is investigated (say, ARMAX(1, 1, 1)), then parsimony cannot be claimed even if a 'minimal representation' of the dynamics is selected. For example, (4.43) becomes

$$y_t = \frac{\beta_1 + (1 - \beta_3 - \beta_1)L}{1 - \beta_3 L} z_t + \frac{e_t}{1 - \beta_3 L} = \frac{\gamma_{10} + \gamma_{11}L}{1 - \delta_{11}L} z_t + \frac{e_t}{1 - \rho_1 L}, \quad (4.66)$$

which necessitates four rather than two parameters in the absence of knowledge that $\delta_{11} = \rho_1$ and $\gamma_{10} + \gamma_{11} = 1 - \delta_{11}$, the imposition of which restrictions depends on the relevant behavioural theory. Conversely, an inadequate dynamic–stochastic representation entails inconsistency of parameter estimates and a loss of structural invariance, so both data coherency and theory validity are necessary, and such considerations must take precedence over arguments concerning approximation accuracy, generality of class etc.

An important consequence for econometric analysis (as against data description) is that closely similar dynamic model specifications can entail rather different behavioural implications. To isolate some of the differences, consider the three simplest cases of partial adjustment (PA), error correction (ECM) and RDL, with one strongly exogenous variable $\{z_t\}$, each model defined to have white noise disturbances relative to its information set:

$$\Delta y_t = \gamma(\beta z_t - y_{t-1}) + u_t \qquad \text{(PA)} \qquad (4.67)$$

$$\Delta y_t = \alpha \Delta z_t + \gamma(\beta z_{t-1} - y_{t-1}) + v_t \qquad \text{(ECM)} \qquad (4.68)$$

$$y_t = [1 - (1 - \gamma)L]^{-1} \gamma \beta z_t + e_t \qquad \text{(RDL).} \qquad (4.69)$$

The three models have the same non-stochastic static equilibrium solution, namely

$$y = \beta z = y^e \quad \text{(say),} \qquad (4.70)$$

and so could be interpreted as alternative implementations of a common theory. Expressed in ECM form, however, (4.67) and (4.69) are

$$\Delta y_t = \gamma \Delta y_t^e + \gamma (y_{t-1}^e - y_{t-1}) + u_t \qquad \text{(PA)} \qquad (4.71)$$

$$\Delta y_t^* = \gamma \Delta y_t^e + \gamma (y_{t-1}^e - y_{t-1}^*) \qquad \text{(RDL)} \qquad (4.72)$$

where $y_t = y_t^* + e_t$. Thus, both (4.67) and (4.69) constrain the response to changes in y^e and to past disequilibria to be the same, a strong specification which may well be at variance with observed behaviour (compare the arguments for the 'optimal partial adjustment' model in Friedman, 1976). Also, the disequilibria in the PA and ECM models are measured differently from those of the RDL in that the latter are relative to y_{t-1}^* rather than y_{t-1}. Accordingly, an RDL formulation is appropriate to behaviour wherein agents ignore the impact of past disturbances on the measured data, concentrating instead upon the 'permanent' component y_{t-1}^* so that disturbances in any period are *not* transmitted into future behaviour unlike in PA and ECM models.

Which formulation of the impact on plans of past disturbances is most appropriate to any particular situation must be an empirical matter, although in general the truth probably lies at neither extreme since adjustments to pure shocks are likely to differ from responses to past plans; and equation disturbances are anyway composites of measurement errors and *all* mis-specifications as well as shocks. Since the RDL form in (4.69) generalizes easily to

$$y_t = [1 - (1 - \gamma)L]^{-1}(\alpha \Delta z_t + \beta \gamma z_{t-1}) + e_t, \qquad (4.73)$$

which still has (4.70) as its static solution but corresponds to

$$\Delta y_t^* = \alpha \Delta z_t + \gamma (\beta z_{t-1} - y_{t-1}^*) \qquad \text{(with } \alpha \text{ unrestricted)}, \qquad (4.74)$$

the real distinction between $AD(\cdot)$ and RDL lies in their respective stochastic specifications. Yet investigators alter error assumptions for convenience without always acknowledging the consequential changes entailed in *behavioural* assumptions.

With the conventional practice of 'allowing for autocorrelated residuals', distinctions between model types become hopelessly blurred since disturbances in ARMAX($\cdot$) models are transmitted k periods into the future if $\phi(L)/\rho(L)$ is of degree k in L (and hence k is infinite if $\rho(L)$ is not of degree zero).

The literature on ARMAX models and all their special cases is vast and it is quite beyond the scope of this chapter to even reference the main relevant papers, let alone adequately survey the results (see, among many others, Aigner, 1971; Nicholls et al., 1975; Osborn, 1976; Wallis, 1977; Harvey and Phillips, 1979; Zellner, 1979a; Anderson, 1980; Palm and Zellner, 1980; Davidson, 1981; Harvey, 1981a, section 7.3; and the references therein). When all z_{it} are strongly exogenous in (4.64) separate estimation of $\gamma_i(\cdot)/\delta_i(\cdot)$ and $\phi(\cdot)/\rho(\cdot)$ is possible (see Pesaran (1981), who also derives several LM-based residual diagnostic tests). However, this last result is not valid if any of the z_i are Granger-caused by y in the model information set, nor will conventionally estimated standard errors provide a useful basis for model selection until the residuals are white noise. [The general issue of stochastic specification was considered in section 5, not included here.]

4.2 General Error Correction Mechanisms

There is a close relationship between error correction formulations and 'servo-mechanism' control rules (see Phillips, 1954, 1957). In chapter 9, α and γ in (4.68) are interpreted as parameters of 'derivative' and 'proportional' feedback controls, introducing the additional interpretation of stock variables in flow equations as 'integral controls'. Also, Nickell (1985) derives the ECM as the optimal decision rule for an infinite horizon quadratic optimization problem when the 'exogenous' variables are neither static nor random walk processes and Salmon (1979a) demonstrates that state-variable feedback rules can be reparameterized in servomechanism (and hence, if appropriate, in ECM) form. Thus, the ECM specification is compatible with 'forward-looking' as well as 'servomechanistic' behaviour, and since many static-equilibrium economic theories yield proportionality or homogeneity results (or are transformable thereto), this model form has a potentially large range of applications.

Suppose that a given static theory entails (in logarithms) that

$$y = \lambda_0 + \lambda_1 z_1 + (1 - \lambda_1)z_2 + \lambda_2 z_3 \tag{4.75}$$

and no theory-based dynamic specification is available. Then the following model at least ensures consistency with (4.75) in static equilibrium:

$$\Delta y_t = \beta_0 + \sum_{i=0}^{m_1} \beta_{1i}\Delta z_{1t-i} + \sum_{i=0}^{m_2} \beta_{2i}\Delta z_{2t-i} + \sum_{i=0}^{m_3} \beta_{3i}\Delta z_{3t-i}$$

$$+ \sum_{i=1}^{m_4} \beta_{4i}\Delta y_{t-i} + \gamma_1 (y - z_1)_{t-k_1} + \gamma_2 (z_1 - z_2)_{t-k_2} + \gamma_3 z_{3t-k_3} + e_t. \tag{4.76}$$

Such a formulation has a number of useful features. Firstly, the proportionality restriction is easily tested by adding y_{t-k_4} as a separate regressor, and non-rejection entails that (4.75) is the static solution of (4.76) for $\gamma_1 \neq 0$. Generally, low values of the m_i suffice to make e_t white noise and the resulting short distributed lags usually can be adequately represented by one or two Almon polynomial functions, so that the final parameterization is relatively parsimonious (see, for example, chapter 11). Also, the k_i are often unity (or four for quarterly – seasonally unadjusted – data); the parameterization is frequently fairly orthogonal (certainly more so than the levels of variables); and despite the 'common' lagged dependent variable coefficient (i.e. $1 + \gamma_1$) the formulation allows for very different lag distributions of y with respect to each z_i. Moreover, using Δy_t as the dependent variable helps circumvent the most basic 'spurious' regressions problem without losing long-run information from using differenced data only (compare, for example, Pierce, 1977). Also, using Δz_{jt-i} as regressors shows that 'level representations' (of y_t on z_{jt-i}) will have *negative* coefficients at some lag lengths but this does *not* preclude all the solved distributed lag weights from being positive. Furthermore, if (4.76) is a good data description when (4.75) is a useful equilibrium assertion, then omitting the feedback variables $(y - z_1)_{t-k_1}$, $(z_1 - z_2)_{t-k_2}$ and z_{3t-k_3} need not produce detectable residual autocorrelation, so that a model in differenced data alone might seem acceptable on a 'white-noise residual' criterion although it violates homogeneity (see, for example, chapter 8 and, as a possible example, Silver and Wallace, 1980). Finally, in practice, ECMs have successfully reconciled disparate empirical evidence in many areas, as discussed in section 2.6, case (h).

On a steady-state growth path, the solution of (4.76) entails that λ_0 in (4.75) depends on the growth rates of the z_i, a feature which has been criticized by Currie (1981). This issue is closely related to the existence of short-run (apparent) trade-offs (since sequences of above- or below-average values of Δz_is will lower or raise the ratios of y to the z_is in levels), and hence to the 'Lucas critique' of (1976) concerning the non-invariance of certain econometric equations to changes in policy rules. Also, Salmon and Wallis (1982) discuss the need for the input variables over the estimation period to 'stimulate' responses relevant to later behaviour if structurality is to be retained when policy alters the time profile of some z_{it}s as well as emphasizing the need to allocate dynamic responses correctly to expectation formation and behavioural responses. On both issues, again see Haavelmo (1944).

Constant-parameter linear models are only locally useful and adaptive processes in which the β_{ji} (say) depend on other functions (e.g. higher order differences) of the data merit consideration, so that 'trade-offs' in effect disappear if they entail exploiting information which actually ceases to be neglected when it becomes relevant. Sometimes, such models can be reparameterized as linear in parameters with non-linear variables acting as modifiers when they are non-constant. Also, note that the restriction of ECMs to cases in which y has a unit elasticity response to one variable (or a combination of variables) is not essential since 'logit' feedbacks with variable elasticities which eventually converge to unity are easily introduced (see, for example, chapter 17); other recent discussions are Salmon (1982), Kloek (1982) and Patterson and Ryding (1982).

We have not discussed partial adjustment models extensively since there are already excellent textbook treatments, but it is interesting that ECM is equivalent to partial adjustment of $y - z$ to Δz in (4.68) (not of y to z unless $\alpha = \gamma\beta$). Thus, on the one hand, care is required in formulating to which variable the PA principle is applied, and, on the other hand, the equivalence reveals that the ECM in (4.68) is most heavily dampening of discrepancies from equilibrium due to once-for-all impulses in z_t (so Δz_t goes $\ldots, 0, \delta, -\delta, 0, \ldots$) than of permanent changes in the level of z_t, and least for changes in the growth rate of z_t (although integral corrections and higher order derivative responses help mitigate the last two). In the case $\beta = 1, \alpha \neq \gamma$ in (4.68), if the DGP is an ECM but this is approximated by a PA model, the impact effect of z on y is generally underestimated although the derived mean lag need not be overestimated since the coefficient of y_{t-1} can be downward biased. Specifically, rewriting (4.68) (for $\beta = 1$) as

$$y_t = \gamma z_t + (\alpha - \gamma)\Delta z_t + (1 - \gamma)y_{t-1} + v_t \tag{4.77}$$

when z_t is highly autoregressive, the impact effect will be estimated for PA at around γ (rather than α) and the feedback coefficient at around $1 - \gamma$, whereas if Δz_t is sufficiently negatively correlated with y_{t-1} the mean lag will be underestimated. This issue coveniently leads to the general topic of derived statistics in AD($\cdot$) models.

4.3 Derived Statistics

Given the general equation (4.62), there are many derived statistics of interest including long-run responses, roots of the lag polynomials, summary statistics for the solved lag distributions etc., and approximate or asymptotic standard errors of these can be calculated in many cases (subject to various regularity conditions). The general problem is: given $\hat{\theta} \underset{\text{app}}{\sim} N(\theta, V)$ for a sufficiently large sample size T, to compute $f(\hat{\theta}) \underset{\text{app}}{\sim} N[f(\theta), \Omega]$ where, to first order, $\Omega = JVJ'$ and $J = \partial f(\cdot)/\partial\theta'$ (which, if necessary, can be computed numerically as in Sargan, 1980a). Of course, normality could be a poor approximation when $f(\theta)$ corresponds to (say) a latent root or the mean lag (see, for example, Griliches (1967) who discusses asymmetrical confidence intervals), but in the absence of better approximations it seems more useful to quote the relevant values of $f(\hat{\theta})$ and $\hat{\Omega}$ than provide no summaries at all. However, the mean lag can be a misleading statistic for lag distributions that are highly asymmetrical and is meaningless if the derived lag weights are not all of the same sign. For many distributions, it could be more useful to quote some of the fractiles rather than the first two moments (e.g. the median lag and the time taken for nine-tenths of the response to be completed): as an illustration, when $\beta = 1$ in (4.68), $\alpha = 0.5$ and $\gamma = 0.05$ yields a mean lag of ten periods yet has a median lag of one period and 70 per cent of the adjustment has taken place by the mean lag (but 90 per cent adjustment takes 31 periods!). Changing γ to 0.1 halves the mean lag but does not alter the median lag or the percentage response at the mean lag, while reducing the number of periods at which 90 per cent response is reached to 15. For skew distributions there seems little substitute to presenting several fractiles (or some measure of the skewness).

At first sight it may seem surprising that derived estimates of long-run responses might have large standard errors given that the typical spectral shape of economic variables has much of the power near the origin (i.e. in low frequency components) – see Granger (1966). There is no paradox here, however, since highly auto-regressive series also have primarily low frequency components yet may provide little long-run information about relations between variables. Alternatively expressed, the long run of (4.62) for $n = 1$ is $y = [\alpha_1(1)/\alpha_0(1)]z = Hz$, and if $\alpha_0(L)$ has a root close to unity, estimates of H can fluctuate wildly for seemingly small changes in $\{\hat{\alpha}_{0j}\}$. Thus, valid theoretical information about H can be of immense value in empirical analysis and, for example, if $H = 1$, switching from unrestricted estimation of (4.65) to (4.68) can substantially reduce parameter standard errors (and hence forecast error variances). Conversely, for highly autoregressive series much of the sample variability may be due to the dynamics and until this is partialled-out a misleading picture of the economic interrelationships may emerge (not just from 'spurious' regressions, but also the converse of attenuating important dependences). For econometric research, there seems little alternative to careful specification of the dynamics – and hence of the 'error term' (as discussed in section 5 of the original paper). Note that reparameterizations of the original formulation (4.62) can allow direct estimation of the long-run response and/or mean lag etc. as in Bewley (1979).

5 Dynamic Specification in Multi-equation Models

5.1 Identification with Autoregressive Errors

The problems that arise in multi-equation models are very similar to those discussed in earlier sections: to introduce suitable lag structures which represent correctly our *a priori* economic intuitions about the behaviour of the variables in the long and the short period, but which are not limited by an over-simplistic specification of the lags in the system nor made over-complex by the confusion of the basic dynamics of the economy with the stochastic processes generating the errors in the system.

Consider the latter problem first. Suppose that in lag operator notation we write the structural equations in the form

$$A(L)x_t = B(L)y_t + C(L)z_t = u_t, \qquad t = 1, \ldots, T, \tag{4.78}$$

where $A(L) = (B(L), C(L))$ is a matrix of polynomials in the lag operator L, with specified maximum lags on each variable, x_t is a vector of observed variables, made up of n endogenous variables y_t and m strongly exogenous variables z_t, and u_t is the vector of errors on the structural equations, all in period t. $B(L)$ is a square matrix such that B_0 (the zero-lag coefficient matrix) is non-singular. Suppose now that the u_t are generated by an ARMA process of the form

$$R(L)u_t = S(L)e_t, \tag{4.79}$$

where $R(L)$ and $S(L)$ are square matrix lag polynomials of degree r and s respectively, and $R_0 = S_0 = I_n$. Our general econometric methodology first requires us to discuss identification for such models. We can find sufficient conditions for identification by formulating the problem as follows. Eliminating u_t between equations (4.78) and (4.79) we obtain

$$R(L)A(L)x_t = S(L)e_t. \tag{4.80}$$

Writing this in the form

$$\mathbf{\Psi}(L)x_t = S(L)e_t, \tag{4.81}$$

where

$$\mathbf{\Psi}(L) = R(L)A(L), \tag{4.82}$$

consider conditions which ensure that the factorization is unique for a given $\mathbf{\Psi}(L)$ with a given maximum lag on each variable. Clearly, if $A(L)$ and $R(L)$ satisfy (4.82), then $HA(L)$ and $HR(L)H^{-1}$ satisfy

$$H\mathbf{\Psi}(L) = (HR(L)H^{-1})(HA(L)),$$

and if there are no prior restrictions on the covariance matrix of e_t, then if we write $A^*(L) = HA(L), R^*(L) = HR(L)H^{-1}, S^*(L) = HS(L)H^{-1}$ and $e^* = He_t$, the model consisting of equations (4.78) and (4.79) with stars on the lag matrices is observationally equivalent to (4.80). Conditions similar to those discussed by Hsiao (1984) are necessary for identification. Sufficient conditions for identification are as follows:

1   equation (4.81) is identified when $\boldsymbol{\Psi}_0$ is of the form $\boldsymbol{\Psi}_0 = (\boldsymbol{I}: \boldsymbol{\Psi}_{02})$, and the only constraints specify the minimum lag on each variable (sufficient conditions for this are those given by Hannan (1970) and discussed by Kohn (1979) and Hsiao (1984));

2   conditions which ensure that there is a unique factorization for (4.82) subject to the same maximal lag conditions, and $\boldsymbol{B}_0 = \boldsymbol{I}$;

3   standard conditions for identification, which ensure that linear or non-linear constraints on the coefficients of $A(L)$ are only satisfied if $H = I$, discussed by Hsiao.

However, Hsiao does not deal with conditions of type (2), and these will be discussed briefly here. Necessary and sufficient conditions for identification are given by Sargan (1983) when only the maximum lags on the variables are specified. The conditions depend on the presence or absence of latent roots of the $A(L)$ polynomial. $A(L)$ has a latent root λ if, for some non-zero vector h,

$$h'[A(\lambda)] = 0'. \tag{4.83}$$

A necessary condition for there to be more than one solution is that (4.83) is satisfied for some λ and h. (The paper referred to above gives a slightly different formulation which makes it easier to discuss cases where $A(z)$ has an infinite latent root.) This condition is also sufficient, provided that a factorization condition is satisfied which can be taken to have a prior probability of unity.

A necessary condition that the model is not locally identified is that $A(z)$ and $R(z)$ have a latent root λ in common, in the sense that for some non-zero vector h (4.83) is satisfied and for some non-zero vector k

$$R(\lambda)k = 0.$$

This is a sufficient condition that the Jacobian (first-order derivative) conditions for identification are not satisfied. But even if the Jacobian is not full rank, it does not follow that the model is not locally identified. This is discussed in the above paper.

The estimation of the model has two stages. The first is to decide on the various lags on the different variables, and on the autoregressive and moving-average processes. Suitable test procedures are required for this and they will be discussed in section 5.2.

Given the specification of these maximum lags then parameter estimation can proceed using maximum likelihood procedures, or procedures asymptotically equivalent to these. For a complete model, if a numerical optimization program which does not require analytical derivatives of the likelihood function, such as a conjugate gradient procedure or one using numerical differentiation, is used to optimize the likelihood function, it is no more difficult to fit a model of the form (4.80) than a less restricted model of form (4.81), since all that is required as an addition to a program for producing maximum likelihood estimates of (4.81) is a subroutine for computing the coefficients of $\boldsymbol{\Psi}(L)$ as functions of the unconstrained elements of $A(L)$ and $R(L)$.

It can be argued that since, in using ARMA models for the generation of the errors in econometric models, we are merely making use of convenient approximations, there might be considerable advantages (at least in the stage of making preliminary estimates of the model to settle its economic specification provisionally) in using a model with a fairly high order autoregressive specification and a zero-order moving-average specification. In practice the time to compute moving-average specifications can be large when the latent roots of the moving-average matrix polynomials tend to move towards the unit circle, and the convergence properties of autoregressive specifications may be much better. Chapter 13 contains a discussion of estimators for $S(L) = 0$ which are asymptotically equivalent to maximum likelihood estimators for models of this type but which may be lower in computing requirements.

For 'incomplete' models it may be necessary to modify the model before it is feasible to estimate it. The simplest way of defining the modified model is to retain both equations (4.78) and (4.79) but now to allow $B(L)$ to be a rectangular matrix. Thus, it is assumed that the errors on the incomplete model are generated by an ARMA model, which involves only the errors on the set of equations to be estimated. Note that starting from a complete set of equations whose errors are generated by an ARMA model, by eliminating the errors of the equations whose coefficients are not to be estimated, it is possible to obtain a higher order ARMA process generating the errors on the equations to be estimated. Thus the current formulation is of some generality. One method of estimating the incomplete system is to use a set of instrumental variables. These can be chosen rather arbitrarily initially, but as the specification is refined a set can be chosen which is efficient if the model is linear in the variables. Generalizing to the case where the $A(L)$ coefficients depend in a general non-linear way on a set of p parameters forming a vector Θ, the estimators can be regarded as minimizing a criterion function of the form

$$\det[\hat{\Omega}^{-1}(E'Z^+)(Z^{+\prime}Z^+)^{-1}(Z^{+\prime}E)], \tag{4.84}$$

where E is the matrix of white noise errors or 'innovations' in the ARMA process and $\hat{\Omega}$ is some preliminary consistent estimate of the variance matrix of e_t. Z^+ is the matrix of instrumental variables, which may include lagged values of the predetermined variables. If the $A(L)$ coefficients considered as functions of Θ have continuous first-order derivatives in some neighbourhood of the true value $\bar{\Theta}$ the instrumental variables estimates will be as efficient as the corresponding limited information maximum likelihood estimates if it is possible to express the expectations of $[\partial A(L)/\partial\Theta_i]x_t$, conditional on all lagged values of y_t, as linear functions of the z_{jt}^+ for all j, and for all i. This result follows from the discussion of Hausman (1975), and in the case of a purely autoregressive specification is most easily satisfied by using as instrumental variables the current values of z_t and the lagged values of x_t up to and including the rth-order lag. When the ARMA model contains a moving-average process, it is difficult to produce estimates of the conditional expectations from an incomplete model, but if the latent roots of the moving-average process are not too close to the unit circle there may be a comparatively small loss of efficiency in using x_{t-s} up to some maximum s^*, which is such that the total number of instrumental variables is not more than a fixed proportion (say 40 per cent) of the sample size. With such a set of instrumental variables an iterative minimization of (4.84) is possible, by computing $u_t = A(L)x_t$ and

$$e_t = S(L)^{-1}R(L)u_t \tag{4.85}$$

recursively for given values of the parameters, starting from the values $e_0 = e_{-1} = e_{-2} = e_{-3} = \ldots = e_{-(s-1)} = \mathbf{0}$. This procedure may not be optimal in a model with no exogenous variables, where end corrections corresponding to u_t being a stationary time series might give better results, but in a model with an autoregressive side there seems to be no simple alternative to the crude assumptions for e_t listed above. The recursive generation of e_t, $t \geqslant 1$, uses the equation (4.85) in the form

$$e_t = [I - S(L)]e_t + R(L)u_t, \qquad t = 1, \ldots, T,$$

noting that $I - S(L)$ has a zero-order coefficient matrix equal to zero. Recent discussions of estimators for models with vector moving-average error processes include Osborn (1977), Reinsel (1979), Anderson (1980) and Palm and Zellner (1980).

5.2 Reduced Form, Final Form and Dynamic Multipliers

From (4.78) it is of some interest to discuss the behaviour of y_t in response to changes in the z_t, particularly when some of the z_t may be regarded as government-controlled variables which can be changed independently so as to affect the level of the y_t variables. The standard reduced form of the model can be written

$$y_t = -B_0^{-1}B^*(L)Ly_t - B_0^{-1}C(L)z_t + B_0^{-1}u_t,$$

where

$$B(L) = B_0 + LB^*(L)$$

and $B^*(L)$ has a degree one less than that of $B(L)$. This equation is useful for directly simulating the impact of a change in z_t. Two types of dynamic multiplier can be distinguished: (i) the impact multiplier; (ii) the cumulative multiplier. The first considers the impact of a unit change in an element of z_t in time period t on all subsequent values of y_t; the second considers the change in y_s, $s \geqslant t$, if an element of z_τ is changed by one unit for all $\tau \geqslant t$. Since the second multiplier is obtained from the impact multiplier by summation for all $\tau \leqslant s$, only the impact multiplier will be considered here. Suppose that we wish to consider the impact multipliers for some subset of elements of z_t, which we form into a vector z_t^*, and denote the corresponding rows of $C(L)$ by $C^*(L)$. Then clearly, if we denote the change in z_t^* by Dz_t^*, the corresponding endogenous-variable changes $Dy_\tau, \tau \geqslant t$, will be obtained by solving the equation

$$B(L)Dy_\tau = -C^*(L)Dz_\tau^*, \qquad \tau = t, t + 1, \ldots,$$

where $Dz_\tau^* = 0$ if $\tau \neq t$. If we write for the solution

$$Dy_\tau = \Pi(L)Dz_\tau^*,$$

then the coefficients Π_s give the impact multipliers, in period $\tau = t + s$, of the change in z_t^* in period t.

Formally, we may write

$$\Pi(L) = -[B(L)]^{-1}C^*(L),$$

but a more practical computing procedure is to solve sequentially the equations

$$B(L)\Pi(L) = -C^*(L) \tag{4.86}$$

for $\Pi_s, s = 0, 1, \ldots$. In fact it is better to use the reduced form, and if we write

$$P_1(L) = B_0^{-1}B(L) = \sum_{i=0}^{k_1} P_{1i}L^i,$$

$$P_2(L) = B_0^{-1}C^*(L) = \sum_{i=0}^{k_2} P_{2i}L^i,$$

then the equations (4.86) are equivalent to

$$\sum_{i=1}^{j} P_{1(j-i)}\Pi_i = P_{2j}, \qquad j = 0, \ldots, \infty, \tag{4.87}$$

where

$$P_{ji} = 0 \text{ if } i > k_j \qquad (j = 1, 2).$$

These can be solved for Π_j sequentially noting that in the jth equation the matrix coefficient of Π_j is $P_{10} = I$. Asymptotic standard errors for the Π_j can be computed in the usual way, expressing them as functions of the $B(L)$ and $C(L)$, and using implicit differentiation to obtain the first derivatives from (4.86) (see, for example, Goldberger et al., 1961; Theil and Boot, 1962; Brissimis and Gill, 1978).

The final equations of Tinbergen (see Goldberger, 1959) are obtained by multiplying equation (4.78) by adj $B(L)$ where this is the adjoint matrix of $B(L)$ considered as a matrix polynomial. Since

$$\text{adj } B(L) \cdot B(L) = \det B(L) \cdot I,$$

we can then write

$$[\det B(L)]y_t = -\text{adj } B(L) \cdot C(L)z_t + \text{adj } B(L)u_t. \tag{4.88}$$

A possible method of testing models which is particularly appropriate for comparison with ARIMA statistical time-series models (used, for example, by Zellner and Palm, 1974; Wallis, 1977) is to estimate a model of the form (4.88) first, neglecting the constraints that every endogenous variable has the same scalar lag polynomial on the left-hand side of (4.88). Thus, unconstrained ARMA explanations of each y_{it} in terms of lagged z_t are estimated by single-equation ARMA maximum likelihood estimation. Then tests are made to check that the coefficients of the lag polynomials applied to the $y_{it}, i = 1, \ldots, n$, are all the same. There are severe difficulties in doing this successfully. First, if there are more than two endogenous variables, and more than one lag on each endogenous variable in (4.78), then det $B(L)$ and adj $B(L) \cdot C(L)$ are both of at least the fifth degree in L, and in models which are at all realistically treated as complete econometric models the degree must be much larger than this. This of course requires a large sample before asymptotic theory can be a good approximation, since each equation to be estimated will contain a large number of variables of various lags. If the total number of lags on the variables in the final equation form (4.88) is determined by significance tests then there is an obvious probability that the subsequent tests will reject the constraints that all the y_{it} are subject to the same lag operator. Indeed, there is no reason why the unconstrained estimates of the longer lagged coefficients should be significantly different from zero. The true values of these coefficients can be expected to be small if the model is stable since the higher order coefficients contain the products of many latent roots all less than one in modulus. Thus, it would be better to allow the maximum lag to be determined by feasibility. Even then, the size of model may have to be small to estimate unconstrainedly the set of equations of the final form. Finally, there are many implicit restrictions on the coefficients of adj $B(\cdot)$ which it is difficult to put in explicit form. Since, unless the right-hand-side polynomials satisfy these implicit constraints, the constraint that all the left-hand-side polynomials are the same is of little interest, it appears that starting from the unconstrained final equation is not really an adequate way of testing the specification of realistic econometric models. Moreover, parameter constancy in derived equations like (4.88) relies on all the equations in (4.78) being structurally invariant.

If the z_t are regarded as generated by ARMA processes, so that

$$D(L)z_t = F(L)\varepsilon_t, \tag{4.89}$$

where ε_t is a white noise series, then we can eliminate z_t from (4.88) using (4.89) to give

$$B(L)y_t = -C(L)D(L)^{-1}F(L)\varepsilon_t + u_t$$

or

$$[\det D(L)]B(L)y_t = -C(L)[\text{adj } D(L)]F(L)\varepsilon_t + [\det D(L)]u_t. \tag{4.90}$$

The error term on (4.90) contains a complicated moving average of the ε_t, and if u_t itself is generated by a general ARMA stochastic model then the stochastic specification is even more complicated. Assuming for simplicity that $u_t = S(L)e_t$, where e_t is white noise, there is a corresponding final form:

$$[\det D(L)][\det B(L)]y_t = -[\text{adj } B(L)]C(L)[\text{adj } D(L)]F(L)\varepsilon_t$$

$$+ [\text{adj } B(L)][\det D(L)]S(L)e_t. \tag{4.91}$$

Equation (4.91) gives separate ARMA-type representations for each element of y_t. Note that the autoregressive polynomial $[\det D(L)][\det B(L)]$ will generally be the same for each y_{it} (the exception occurs if a recursive structure can be set up by partitioning y_t into subsections). For a given y_{it}, the right-hand side of (4.91) also can be represented as a single moving-average process, the maximum lag of which is the same as the maximum lag in the terms of the right-hand side of (4.91). Note, however, that this new representation neglects the detailed correlation structure of the different components of the right-hand side of (4.91) and so loses a great deal of information which is contained in the specification (4.91). Thus, using the individual ARMA equations to forecast y_{it} would give less accurate forecasts than using the detailed model (4.91), and the use of original model (4.78) to forecast should also give more accurate forecasts than (4.91). With a correctly specified system, this should be true for an estimated model. And in estimating the model it will be found that greater efficiency in the estimation of the coefficients of (4.91) is obtained by first estimating (4.80) and (4.89) taking account of any appropriate constraints and then substituting the resulting estimates of $A(L)$, $S(L)$, $D(L)$ and $F(L)$ into equation (4.91) to give ARMA equations for the individual y_{it}. For an example of some relevant applied work see Prothero and Wallis (1976), and for a different emphasis, Zellner (1979a). Also, Trivedi (1975) compares ARMA with econometric models for inventories.

The suggested alternative for testing the specification is that the original model or its reduced form is estimated using the maximal feasible lags. Then constraints reducing the order of the lags in each reduced form equation are tested using asymptotic t or F ratio tests (Wald test) or by using likelihood ratio tests (see Sargan (1978) and, for an example, chapter 3).

5.3 Unconstrained Autoregressive Modelling

Alternatively, one may consider, following Sargent and Sims (1977), the possibility of an autoregressive representation for the economy in which the distinction between endogenous and exogenous variables is ignored. In an effort to estimate the dynamics of the system with no *a priori* constraints, the equations are written in the form

$$y_t = P(L)y_{t-1} + e_t,$$ (4.92)

where $P(L)$ is an unconstrained matrix lag polynomial of maximum lag q and e_t is a white noise vector. This can be regarded as a linear approximation to an autoregressive representation of the stochastic model generating y_t if the y_t are stationary time series (see Hannan, 1970) with the e_t being approximations to the innovations in the y_t. If the y_t are non-stationary but Δy_t are stationary, then a set of equations of the form (4.92) may still be a good approximation but unit latent roots should occur in the latent roots equation for the system. However, there may be problems if we consider (4.92) as an approximation to an ARMA system of the form

$$S(L)^{-1}B(L)y_t = e_t,$$ (4.93)

if $S(L)$ has roots close to the unit circle. In particular, if the true system is of ARMA form in a set of endogenous variables y_t^*, and the equations are mis-specified by taking a subset of variables y_t which includes the first differences of the corresponding variables y_t^*, then corresponding differences of white noise will occur in the errors of the ARMA model for the y_t. Thus, over-differencing the variables will invalidate the Wold autoregressive representation and the corresponding finite autoregressive representation will not hold; Sims has tended to work with levels variables in consequence. With the length of sample available for estimating the equations by multiple regression, it is necessary to work with a relatively small model and to restrict q rather drastically. Sargent and Sims (1977) also considered models which contain index variables, which in effect introduce non-linear restrictions in the coefficients $P(L)$ by requiring each y_{it} to depend upon past values of k index variables, $k < n$, where n is the number of variables y_t. It is to be expected that when the number of regression equations is allowed to increase to be of the same order as T, the estimated coefficients become sensitive to changes in the variables. Sims interprets his results by considering the effect of an innovation in a particular variable on later values of the other variables, but the interpretation is complicated by the correlation between the contemporaneous innovations on the different variables (see, for example, Sims, 1980). Additionally, marginalizing with respect to elements of y_t^* other than those retained in y_t will produce an ARMA form as in (4.93) unless none of the excluded variates Granger-causes the y_t, and as in all derived representations, strong assumptions are necessary to ensure parameter constancy.

5.4 Alternative Forms of Disequilibrium Model

The simplest model of disequilibrium is that of Samuelson–Tobin in which the tendency of economic variables to their equilibrium values is modelled by introducing an equilibrium static equation for each endogenous variable:

$$y_t^* = y_e(z_t),$$

where this is a vector of equilibrium values of n endogenous variables expressed as functions of a set of m exogenous variables. Writing $\Delta y_t = y_t - y_{t-1}$ the Samuelson–Tobin model is (see, for example, Samuelson, 1947)

$$\Delta y_t = D(y_t^* - y_{t-1}) + u_t, \tag{4.94}$$

where D is an arbitrary square matrix. The simplest special case is where D is a positive diagonal matrix, with every diagonal element satisfying

$$0 < d_{ii} < 1.$$

This type of model can be regarded as derived from an optimal control problem where the function whose expected values is to be minimized is

$$\sum_{t=1}^{S} [(\Delta y_t')W\Delta y_t + (y_t^* - y_t)'M(y_t^* - y_t)]. \tag{4.95}$$

As $S \to \infty$, the optimal control solution when $\mathscr{E}(y_{t+s}^* | Y_t^*) = y_t^*$ is

$$\Delta y_t = D(y_t^* - y_{t-1})$$

where, if $K = I - D$, then

$$K + K^{-1} = 2I + W^{-1}M,$$

or, if we write

$$K^* = W^{1/2}KW^{-1/2},$$

$$K^* + K^{*-1} = 2I + W^{-1/2}MW^{-1/2}.$$

Now if W and M are both positive definite the matrix on the right-hand side is positive definite such that every latent root is real and greater than 2. K^* can then clearly be chosen to be symmetric, so that every root is real, and if λ_k is a root of K^* and λ_m a corresponding root of $W^{-1/2}MW^{-1/2}$, then

$$\lambda_k + \lambda_k^{-1} = 2 + \lambda_m.$$

We can pick K^* such that λ_k satisfies

$$0 < \lambda_k < 1,$$

provided that M is non-singular, and $K = W^{-1/2}K^*W^{1/2}$ and has the same set of latent roots.

This choice of K is appropriate, since unstable solutions cannot be optimal. Then for $D = I - K$ we have that $\lambda_d = 1 - \lambda_k$, and so

$$0 < \lambda_d < 1. \tag{4.96}$$

Note that if W is a diagonal matrix then D is symmetric. Of course without prior knowledge of W and M it is difficult to specify D, and even the constraints that D has real latent roots satisfying (4.96) are difficult to enforce.

The generalization of the model (4.94) to more complicated time lags is obvious, but perhaps rather arbitrary. Using the lag operator notation a general formulation would be

$$C(L)\Delta y_t = D(L)(y_t^* - y_{t-1}) + u_t, \tag{4.97}$$

where $C(L)$ and $D(L)$ are matrix polynomials of any order. However, if y_t^* is being written as an arbitrary linear function of current and lagged values of a set of exogenous variables, then (4.97) may contain some redundancy and in any case a useful simplification may be obtained by considering either of the following special cases:

$$\Delta y_t = D(L)(y_t^* - y_{t-1}) + u_t \tag{4.98}$$

or

$$C(L)\Delta y_t = D(y_t^* - y_{t-1}) + u_t. \tag{4.99}$$

If no attempt is made to put constraints on the $C(L)$ and D matrices in (4.99), a further transformation can be considered by using this form with the restriction that D is diagonal and C_0 (the zero-order coefficient matrix in $C(L)$) has its diagonal elements equal to one, or perhaps better that $D = I$ and C_0 is unrestricted. In specifying $y_t^* = y_e(z_t)$ when there are linear restrictions on these equilibrium functions each of which affects only one element of $y_e(z_t)$ such forms (rather than the more usual assumption that $C_0 = I$) have the advantage that the corresponding restriction affects only one equation of (4.99).

If there are restrictions on $C(L)$ and D, then an equivalent model with an arbitrary lag on $y_t^* - y_{t-1}$ may make a better formulation if the rather *ad hoc* economic considerations to be considered below are applied. It is less easy to formulate an optimal control approach which will give significant restrictions on $C(L)$ and D. Thus, for example, if we write

$$\tilde{y}_t = \begin{pmatrix} y_t \\ y_{t-1} \\ \cdot \\ \cdot \\ \cdot \\ y_{t-f} \end{pmatrix} \qquad y_t^+ = \begin{pmatrix} y_t - y_t^* \\ y_{t-1} - y_{t-1}^* \\ \cdot \\ \cdot \\ \cdot \\ y_{t-f} - y_{t-f}^* \end{pmatrix},$$

then a loss function of the form

$$\sum_{t=1}^{S} (y_t^{+\prime} M^+ y_t^+) + \sum_{t=1}^{S} (\Delta \tilde{y}_t)' W^+ (\Delta \tilde{y}_t)$$

leads to optimal control equations of the form (4.97) (with the property that if y_t^* is held constant the adjustment equations are stable) but further restrictions, along the lines that the latent roots are all real, are not appropriate, since the results for the first-order case are dependent on the special separability assumption for the loss function used in the first-order case. (For a discussion of optimal control closed loop paths see Chow (1975).)

A possibility of some importance, which prevents the normalization $D = I$, is that D is in fact singular. This arises particularly where there are identities corresponding to exact equations satisfied by the whole set of endogenous variables, or where some variables react so quickly during the unit time period that the general equation of type (4.99) becomes inappropriate. If the partial equilibrium for this variable is stable, and is attained within the unit time period, then a static equation, or a dynamic equation obtained by differencing the static equation, is introduced into the model.

This possibility can be found in applied studies from various fields, for example in models of wage–price inflation (as in Sargan (1980a) or Laidler and Cross (1976)), models of entrepreneurial behaviour (as in Brechling (1973) or Nadiri and Rosen (1969)), models of consumer behaviour (as in Phlips (1978) or Deaton (1972a)), or models of portfolio choice (as in Tobin (1969)).

Somewhat similar specializations in the form of the general adjustment equations occur where there are buffer variables, such as cash in portfolio choice models, or inventories in some models of firm behaviour, or hours worked in models of labour demand. Buffer variables in the short period are regarded as absorbing the consequences of disequilibrium. Here if a sufficiently short time period is employed it may be appropriate to assume that the change in the buffer variable is determined by an appropriate overall identity.

If it is known how agents formulate $\mathscr{E}(y_{t+s}^* | Y_t^*)$, and a loss function of the form (4.95) is appropriate, then a useful theory-based dynamic specification can be derived. For example, if y_t^* is generated by $\Delta y_t^* = A \Delta y_{t-1}^* + V_t$, then the solution linear decision rule is

$$\Delta y_t = D_1 \Delta y_t^* + D_2 (y_t^* - y_{t-1}) + u_t, \tag{4.100}$$

which is a system error-correction form (see section 2.6; chapter 3; and Nickell, 1985). In (4.100), D_1 and D_2 depend on A, W and M such that $D_1 = 0$ and $D_2 = D$

in (4.94) if $A = 0$, and an intercept in the y_t^* equation would produce an intercept in (4.100) (so that the decision rules would depend on the growth rate of y_t^* in a log-linear model). Similarly, a rational expectations assumption in models with strongly exogenous variables provides parameter restrictions (see Wallis (1980), noting that the vector of first derivatives of the likelihood function provides an estimator generating equation for the model class, in the sense of section 2.2, suggesting fully efficient computationally cheap estimators and highlighting the drawbacks of 'fixed point' methods). Nevertheless, stringent diagnostic testing of models must remain an essential component of any empirical approach to dynamic specification (see chapter 2 and Sargan, 1980a).

Finally, where the economic model is set up in a form which makes it depend on a discrete decision period, and the unit time period is inappropriate, the use of continuous-time-period models, and the discrete-time-period approximations to them discussed by Bergstrom (1984), may considerably improve the dynamic specifications of the model whenever there are valid *a priori* restrictions on the continuous-time model.

Notes

1 This is a very old point, but bears repetition: 'all induction is blind, so long as the deduction of causal connections is left out of account; and all deduction is barren so long as it does not start from observation' (taken from J.N. Keynes, 1890, p. 164). Also, it has long been seen as essential to treat economic theory as a 'working "first approximation to reality" in statistical investigations' – see Persons (1925).

2 Strictly, (4.12) relates to ϕ_1 but ψ is used for notational simplicity; $L(\cdot)$ can be considered as the reparameterized concentrated likelihood if desired.

3 For boundary points of θ, the situation is more complicated and seems to favour the use of the LM principle – see Engle (1984). Godfrey and Wickens (1982) discuss locally equivalent models.

4 See, for example, Marget's (1929) review of Morgenstern's book on the methodology of economic forecasting.

5 Implicitly, therefore, our formulation excludes deterministic factors, such as seasonal dummies, but could be generalized to incorporate these without undue difficulty.

6 It is difficult to define 'better' here since sample data may yield a large variance for an effect which is believed important for policy but produces inefficient forecasts. A minimal criterion is that the econometric model should not experience predictive failure when the ARMA model does not.

Part II
The Development of Empirical Modelling Strategies

Chapters 2 and 3 chart the state of play up to about 1975, highlighting the problems I saw confronting empirical research, and some of the developments seeking to resolve those problems. In fact, five branches of my research were growing more or less contemporaneously: (1) Monte Carlo; (2) computer implementation; (3) empirical applications; (4) econometric technology; and (5) methodology.

1 The ostensible role of Monte Carlo had been to study by simulation the finite sample behaviour of econometric estimators and tests in situations which were too complicated to analyse. However, I had become interested in the methodology of Monte Carlo, and sought to tackle its two main problems of specificity (results may depend in unknown ways on the points chosen for study from the parameter space) and imprecision (a different set of replications would generate a different outcome for a given point in the parameter space). Techniques for resolving both were used in my first study (with Pravin Trivedi in 1972), where we estimated regressions linking (for example) biases to data generation process (DGP) parameter values in order to increase generality (a form of response surface) and used antithetic variates to reduce imprecision. My (1973) asymptotic theory analysis of the Monte Carlo results obtained by Steve Goldfeld and Richard Quandt (1972) suggested reformulating the response surface approach by using asymptotic outcomes as regressors. In effect, this led me to explain the deviation of the finite sample outcome from its asymptote, rather than from zero.

Denis Sargan showed me how to relate this idea to the variance reduction technique known as control variables, essentially using the Monte Carlo estimate of the asymptotic behaviour as a within-experiment control for the simulated finite sample behaviour. This led to a series of papers (Hendry and Harrison, 1974; Hendry and Srba, 1977; Hendry, 1979b) specifically on such techniques, the development being summarized in Hendry (1984a) and in the book about the Monte Carlo program called PC-NAIVE (see Hendry et al., 1991).

However, Monte Carlo methods also directly influenced my thinking about empirical methodology. As noted above, Monte Carlo helped clarify the distinction between the mechanism (or DGP) and the model (or econometric equation). Next, it helped me understand the notion that the 'errors' on an empirical model were a derived function of the properties of the DGP. Third, it highlighted the inadequacies of simple-to-general modelling strategies. Finally, it must have been an important background input to formulating the notion of encompassing which asks whether one empirical model can account for the results obtained by another: in a Monte Carlo context, where the numerical values of the DGP parameters are known, it is possible to numerically calculate what results any model fitted to data from that DGP should produce in a sufficiently large sample. Thus, one could always account for the results of estimated models when the DGP was known; the next step was to ask if one could do so using an estimated model *as if it* were the DGP (see chapter 8).

Several Monte Carlo studies are reported in part II, although of these only the study of COMFAC with Grayham Mizon in 1980 is substantive (chapter 7).

2 Partly from writing Monte Carlo programs and partly because of extending the econometric software of AUTOREG (reviewed in chapter 14), much of my time was spent programming computers; and debugging the code! I was ably assisted by Robin Harrison, Andy Tremayne and Frank Srba at the LSE; and Neil Ericsson, Yock Chong, Adrian Neale and Jurgen Doornik at Oxford, but the task was endless (and still continues with PC-GIVE, PC-FIML and PC-NAIVE to this day). Program development is rather like solving detective mysteries: incorrect results appear under some circumstances and the bug (or bugs) have to be detected from the evidence in the output, apprehended and corrected – without creating further errors. I find programming a very challenging activity and have always felt that the intellectual effort involved is seriously underestimated by those who have never tried to write computer code exceeding a hundred lines. PC-GIVE now comprises over 65,000 lines of code, and I regard it as one of my major contributions to empirical econometrics. As noted in the Introduction, it explicitly embodies the methodology, the evolution of which is the subject of this book.

There has always been a constant interaction between computer implementation and econometric theory and methodology in my research. Chapters 13 and 14 exemplify the impact on econometric theory, but I cannot now articulate specific instances where the feedback from programming onto methodology was fundamental until I tried to develop PC-FIML in 1984–6. There, my thinking about system modelling was radically changed by the exigencies of writing coherent software (see Hendry et al., 1988).

3 In 1972, house prices in London virtually doubled in about three months and I became intensely interested in analysing that phenomenon. The ensuing research endogenized house prices in the building society model of chapter 3, and in turn led to studies of new construction and new house prices with Neil Ericsson (see Ericsson and Hendry, 1985; Hendry, 1986a). The house price equation itself was not published until 1984 (referenced as Hendry (1984b) from Hendry and Wallis (1984)) but even by 1976–7, I was using my model successfully to predict the next housing boom and to test out my ideas about data analysis in a situation of considerable personal relevance.

My other main area of empirical application between 1974 and 1978 was consumers' expenditure, and that topic is amply covered below, as is money demand which became the focus of my interest around 1977. Since most of part II is about the interaction between empirical studies and the evolution of the methodology, I will not comment further on that aspect here.

4 Empirical research and programming both require disproportionately large time inputs relative to their professional evaluation, have very long gestation lags (as the reader must have noted by now) and are difficult to publish. Thus, they cannot be recommended as ways to establish or develop a career, and especially cannot be recommended as methods of fulfilling publication commitments for grant-awarding bodies. Developing new technology (estimators, tests, distributions etc.), however, is relatively straightforward, fairly rapid for the most part and easy to publish when the result is 'new' and 'correct'. Moreover, 'sophisticated tools' or 'new frills on established tools' seem to carry excess glamour and can be recommended as an excellent career route. This may partly reflect the risk aversion of editors (empirical results are often controversial, whereas no-one attacks 'correct theory' however dull and otiose it may be) but is also a product of professional refereeing practices (empirical work is usually reviewed by a subject area specialist and a specialist econometrician, one of whom is almost bound to find a 'mistake' or regard the results as obvious). Of course, it is also the product of the manifest methodological fact that destruction is valid and all too easy for empirical models of complicated data processes, whereas construction is invalid in general and extremely hard in practice. A resolution of this prevalent problem is offered by the methodology which evolves in this book, namely to treat all empirical research findings as part of a progressive research process, not as final answers. Thus, the correct criteria are whether a study improves over previous knowledge in the relevant area, and not whether the result is a new law which can be carved in stone (for a similar view, see Pagan, 1987).

The last claim was not the view of economics editors in the 1970s, and probably is not their view even now, so how did I survive? The obvious answer is correct – I published theory papers intermittently. The main ones, other than on Monte Carlo, were (1971), (1975a) and (1976a), as well as Hendry and Tremayne (1976), although only the (1976a) piece is reprinted here (as chapter 13), partly as it was easily the most important of these contributions and partly because it had an important, if indirect, impact on the communication of the methodology as follows.

A substantial fraction of the space in many econometrics textbooks is devoted to linear simultaneous equations estimators, of which there are dozens. Deriving these, their limiting distributions and their asymptotic equivalences consumed a considerable proportion of the time when teaching econometrics courses, with the opportunity cost that far less time could be devoted to the intrinsically more difficult problems of econometric modelling. By discovering a single simple formula from which all known (and many other) estimators could be derived, and their asymptotic relationships seen at once, a massive amount of time and intellectual energy were freed for other topics. The formula (which I called an estimator generating equation) was based on earlier work of Jim Durbin (1963) which has only recently appeared in print (Durbin, 1988). Jerry Hausman independently evolved a closely related approach in his 1975 paper.

5 By 1975, econometric methodology had become a theme in its own right, and Aris Spanos kept directing me towards related ideas in other subjects, especially the philosophy of science literature. I am embarrassed to admit that I had virtually no professional contact with my colleagues in that discipline while at LSE, although I knew several of them socially. In retrospect, I probably saw myself as trying to solve specific empirical puzzles and modelling problems rather than attacking method-ological issues (with a capital M). In any case, economist friends often joked that those who could not do anything else did methodology, and I was not yet ready to contemplate the ultimate decline that I did methodology! Fortunately, Aris per-suaded me to read several of Karl Popper's books (1961, 1963, 1968) as well as those by Thomas Kuhn (1970) and Imre Lakatos (1974), which fostered my interest in scientific methodology (as chapter 1 will have confirmed). I learned a great deal about invalid practices, became convinced of the essential role of progressive research strategies and gradually realized that no valid constructive methodology could be promulgated. Nevertheless, to use an analogy suggested by Gene Savin, while random searching for gold might strike a vast hoard, and sound geological study could lead to a failed search, most investors would back a company using the latter over the former.

Despite completing several time-consuming empirical studies, it was clear that I did not know how to do empirical research, nor could I teach students how to do it in anything like a structured way. The role of destructive testing was reasonably clear but no constructive approaches seemed justifiable.

Three events helped clarify the way ahead, although their outcomes are reported in exactly the reverse order in chapters 5, 6 and 8. First, I was working with James Davidson on modelling aggregate consumers' expenditure and the impact of measurement errors on parameter estimates, where we had a number of puzzling results. I still remember the afternoon in the LSE Economics Research Centre when we suddenly realized that the type of model in chapter 3 characterized a *class* which had the generic property of reconciling long-run equilibria with dynamic trajectories. It did not take long to show that it was the same type of model as in Sargan (1964a) and, most importantly for our pressing needs, it accounted for most of the mass of seemingly conflicting evidence we had accumulated about consumers' expenditure in the United Kingdom. The model class in question is that of error correction mechanisms (ECMs), which are exposited in chapter 4 above and are investigated and applied in chapter 8 below. The later discovery of the important role played by inflation (following Deaton, 1977) then resolved the remaining anomalies (or so we thought).

Second, I had tried unsuccessfully in mid-1975 to generalize to higher order error processes Denis Sargan's (1964a) test (see chapter 4, section 2.6, case (g)) for the validity of a first-order autoregressive error against the alternative of one-period-longer lags. In retrospect, the basic problem with my attempt was that the hypotheses were unordered, and sometimes non-nested, which was in turn a result of viewing the problem as simple to general. In a remarkably quick response, Denis formulated the general concept of common factors in dynamic equations, extending his earlier results to sequences of Wald tests and implementing the new method in a computer algorithm (called COMFAC) which inherently had to operate from the general to the simple. These results were eventually published as Sargan (1980a), and they led Grayham Mizon to write his (1977a) paper on the selection of dynamic models, which also exploited a general-to-specific framework to develop naturally ordered sequences of hypotheses, an approach he had advocated and applied to functional forms in Mizon (1977b) (written several years earlier).

COMFAC yielded a nearly complete understanding of autoregressive errors in dynamic equations and confirmed the inappropriateness of the conventional approach to mopping-up residual autocorrelation. While both of these notions (error correction and COMFAC) are technical developments, they had important methodological implications. Consequently, Grayham Mizon and I felt that an exposition was needed, leading to chapter 6, which was written after chapter 8 was completed, even though it appeared in print earlier. I have also put the other paper on COMFAC with Grayham as chapter 7, although it was completed much later (1980). Grayham had been working in 1975 at Statistics Canada on the demand for durable goods and saw that study as a convenient vehicle for trying out COMFAC procedures. Following chapter 8 and our 1978 paper, we became involved in investigating the behaviour of other model types (note the dismal performance of the ECM we tried) and in studying the finite sample properties of COMFAC, which accounts for the delay. The interaction between Monte Carlo evidence and empirical research was close in the overall LSE approach and yet is not well represented in this volume, so that chapter 7 usefully emphasizes that interplay as well as illustrating several aspects of both Monte Carlo and data analysis.

Third, despite having completed chapter 3 by mid-1975, I became inadvertently embroiled in the 'time series versus econometrics' debate, and responded in chapter 5. Although it was published first, chapter 5 was written after the first draft of chapter 8; however, it also fed back to influence how we completed the DHSY study (as it has since been referenced; usually pronounced 'daisy'). Had the order of the research been the same as that of the publications, some of the mistakes in chapter 8 might have been avoided, as we shall see below.

The remaining chapters of part II arose as consequences of each other and reactions to chapters 5–8, and illustrate the progressive research strategy in operation. Thomas von Ungern-Sternberg (then at LSE) proposed a number of potential improvements to DHSY, and chapter 9 reveals that he was correct. The role of inflation could be interpreted primarily as proxying income mis-measurement; an integral correction mechanism was needed in addition to the ECM, and, by *not* going from the general to the simple at every stage, several of the inferences in DHSY on the roles of seasonality and liquid assets were awry.

Chapter 10 was necessary to test DHSY against the model type proposed by Hall (1978) and was a step in the formalization of encompassing as an independent construct in model evaluation.

Chapter 11 sought to extend the methodology to account for apparent predictive failure and was explicitly general to simple. It was the empirical stimulus to the formalization recorded in part III since many of the concepts were imprecise at the time the chapter was written, but it helped popularize ECMs. Chapter 11, part (ii), is a later evaluation, which also benefited from a progressive step reported in Trundle

(1982). Finally, chapter 12 is a review of much of my work on money demand; it is rather polemical, but at the time I was experiencing great difficulty in publishing empirical studies in the journals whose readership I arrogantly thought needed to know about these developments.

5

On the Time-Series Approach to Econometric Model Building

Preamble

On this occasion, the first chapter of a new part does need a brief preamble of its own.[1]

Chapter 5 is a critique of a critique presented at a conference at the Federal Reserve Bank of Minneapolis in 1975; Christopher Sims (1977a) (who edited the conference volume in which it appeared) called my piece 'somewhat ascerbic'. The 1973 oil crisis had proved to be a large shock to OECD economies, and an even larger one to their macroeconometric models. Many of these systems mis-predicted badly and their credibility fell sharply within the profession. Views differed widely as to why such predictive failure occurred and ranged from taking the outcome as corroboration of pre-held beliefs that such models were nearly useless, through regarding it as evidence of their incorrect (Keynesian) economic theory basis, or seeing the problem as a reflection of inappropriate methodology, to extending the systems to incorporate oil sectors and significant influences from oil prices, thereby attributing the problem to a mis-specification which by implication was now corrected. Criticisms abounded, as did proposals for solutions. My own view was that the concept of macroeconometric systems based on stochastic–dynamic equations which did not assume that all markets cleared and all agents correctly foresaw the future remained a sensible basis for a research programme. The flaws with their present incarnation lay in inappropriate research tactics, particularly due to using excessively restrictive equation specifications where many of the constraints were imposed without testing.

In effect, I concurred with many of the criticisms extant in the literature, but dissented from most of the proposed solutions, as these seemed equally open to criticism in turn. The alternatives I suggested undoubtedly also had drawbacks, but the idea that all research – whether theoretical, methodological or empirical – should form part of a steady progression had already begun to seem the central concept (see the penultimate paragraph of the chapter).

Many of the points in chapter 5 had occurred in my earlier work and I was certainly not the first to enunciate them anyway. However, those made explicitly concern

Reprinted from Sims, C.A. (ed.), *New Methods in Business Cycle Research*, Minneapolis, MN: Federal Reserve Bank of Minneapolis, 1977, pp. 183–202. This research was undertaken in part while the author was visiting at the Cowles Foundation, Yale University, supported by grants from the National Science and Ford Foundations. He is grateful to Kenneth F. Wallis for valuable comments on an earlier draft of the paper and to Stephen M. Goldfeld, Cheng Hsiao, Charles F. Manski and Thomas J. Rothenberg for helpful discussions about the material herein.

1   the relationships between non-stationarity, differencing and error correction models,
2   the inappropriate assumption that residual autocorrelation corresponded to autoregressive errors (i.e. that common factors were present without conducting COMFAC tests),
3   the proliferation of competing models, and how to reduce their number, and
4   the fact that the quality of empirical research could be improved at low cost.

Clearly, (1) relates closely to the views in chapter 3, and had already been advocated as a resolution of the debate between time-series analysts and quantitative economists. However, I still assumed that long-run economic theory information could be implemented to produce stationary variables and blithely ignored any need to review the underlying distributional theory when the raw data were non-stationary. These lacunae helped to prompt the counter-critique in Granger (1981b) which led on to the theory of cointegration he enunciated in Granger and Weiss (1983), Granger (1986) and Engle and Granger (1987) (see chapter 19).

Equally, (2) is a brief exposition of Sargan (1964a) with the benefit of drafts of Sargan (1980a). Chapters 6 and 7 focus on this issue and the intimately related one of general-to-simple modelling. I remain convinced that COMFAC is a crucial modelling concept as it reveals that autoregressive errors are a special case of dynamic models and hence are a restriction of a model, and not a generalization as presented in most textbooks. A widespread understanding of that point (and a corresponding revision of the textbooks!) would probably yield the largest single improvement in the quality of time-series econometrics.

Point (3) is a pre-statement of the notions embodied in chapter 8, which derived from chapter 3's attempt at 'theory encompassing'. The analysis is tentative and vague, although the principle is clearly stated.

Finally (4) reflects upon the issue of 'quality control' through rigorous testing in empirical econometrics, based on the belief that, properly used, econometrics in the sense of the 'mutual penetration of quantitative economic theory and statistical observation' (Frisch, 1933) could deliver useful empirical relationships, for testing economic theory, predicting and policy making.

On the positive side, this chapter was a precursor to the power function response surfaces in chapter 7 and in later papers such as my 1984 Monte Carlo survey and Chong and Hendry (1986). At the conference, and during the year I spent in the USA between 1975 and 1976, kindly hosted by Yale University and then the University of California at Berkeley, I also learned that my approach was not generally regarded as being a development of 'traditional' econometrics but was viewed as 'atheoretical'. At the time – having only just completed chapter 3 – I found this reaction very odd, but in retrospect I can see that two facets of my approach probably induced it. First, my modelling methods were becoming increasingly data based since my worst mistakes in earlier studies had derived from not carefully analysing the data prior to modelling it. Second, the economic theory models I found most useful either were of long-run equilibria or, if dynamic, were feedback mechanisms rather than expectations equations. Intertemporal optimization theories were becoming the basis for a substantial fraction of applied econometrics in North America, and the resulting models inherently involved expectations, usually assumed to be rational in the sense of Muth (1961). Thus, the epithet 'atheoretical' probably connoted 'not intertemporal optimization' rather than the view espoused by Thomas Sargent and Christopher Sims in the second paper on which chapter 5 comments (see, for example, Gilbert, 1986).

Note

1   The original title was 'Comments on Granger–Newbold's "Time-series approach to econometric model building" and Sargan–Sims' "Business cycle modeling without pretending to have too much *a priori* economic theory"'. It has been abbreviated as above for convenience.

1 Introduction

It is certainly impossible to disagree with Granger and Newbold (1977a) on the desirability of incorporating the best features of time-series analysis into econometric practice. Moreover, many of Granger and Newbold's criticisms of econometric modelling are obviously valid and should be implemented as rapidly as possible in the conduct of empirical research. Indeed, econometricians have voiced similar criticisms of current methodology, and the additional support of Granger–Newbold will hopefully increase the probability of changing the state of the art in an appropriate direction.

Nevertheless, one must not misconstrue the *solution* to such criticisms since it would be equally unproductive to adopt *only* a time-series approach which neglected econometric methods. Also, since econometrics has derived benefit from a time-series-based critique, it would seem useful to undertake the converse in the hope of facilitating further interaction. Thus, I shall first consider whether more appropriate econometric methodology than ordinary least squares (OLS) with only Durbin–Watson statistic diagnostic testing can help resolve the 'nonsense regressions' problem and then discuss certain difficulties which can arise in selecting appropriate univariate autoregressive moving-average (ARMA) models for stationary data series. Next, the role of differencing will be examined, and finally the systems case will be briefly considered.

At the outset, however, Granger and Newbold are incorrect in suggesting that econometrics has not been much concerned with lag structures and/or with attempting to overcome *ad hockery* in theories which incorporate lags (see, among others Koyck, 1954; Nerlove, 1958; Fisher, 1962; Jorgenson, 1966; Dhyrmes, 1971). Further, contrary to an impression also supported by Naylor et al. (1972), econometric estimation is not and never has been synonymous with *simultaneous* equations estimation. Considerable attention has been devoted to estimating models with autocorrelated residuals, including both autoregressive schemes (see Cochrane and Orcutt, 1949; Sargan, 1959; Fisk, 1967) and moving-average representations (see Klein, 1958; Phillips, 1966; Trivedi, 1970). I certainly agree that all too often autocorrelation has been treated as a 'nuisance' and that usually only low-order processes have been examined, but this is not universal.[1] These comments are not intended as an apologia; rather they are an attempt to stress that the 'two philosophies' are not as distinct as Granger and Newbold initially suggest.

2 Autocorrelation Transforms Applied to Non-stationary Data Series

The results in tables I and II of Granger and Newbold (1977a) provide two salutary warnings:

1   do not misinterpret the 'significance' of regression coefficients based on highly autoregressive data when equations have high R^2 but low Durbin–Watson statistic values;

2 mechanical use of the Cochrane–Orcutt transformation to 'correct' autocorrelation will not solve the problem of spurious significance when residual autocorrelation actually represents mis-specified dynamics (compare Prais, 1975).

These criticisms are certainly valid, but may be labelled as applying to 'poor average' practice. Thus, a more appropriate procedure would include the test for the validity of the autoregressive transform proposed by Sargan (1964a) and described again below. Further, this test provides a constructive diagnostic statistic for one important aspect of dynamic specification (see chapter 2). Indeed, such a procedure has interesting implications when applied to the 'spurious regressions' problem discussed by Granger and Newbold.

Consider their equation

$$Y_t = \beta_1 + \beta_2 X_t + e_t \tag{5.1}$$

where Y_t and X_t are independent IMA(1,1) processes. Direct OLS estimation of (5.1) produces the results Granger and Newbold show in their table I. If the (false) assumption is made that the low Durbin–Watson values arise from the process

$$e_t = \rho e_{t-1} + v_t \qquad |\rho| < 1 \tag{5.2}$$

then applying the Cochrane–Orcutt procedure generates the outcomes in their table II. The autocorrelation transform reduces but does not completely remove the spurious significance problem.

However (5.1) and (5.2) are equivalent to

$$Y_t = \beta_1(1 - \rho) + \beta_2 X_t - \rho\beta_2 X_{t-1} + \rho Y_{t-1} + v_t \tag{5.3}$$

which is a restricted version of

$$Y_t = \gamma_1 + \gamma_2 X_t + \gamma_3 X_{t-1} + \gamma_4 Y_{t-1} + w_t. \tag{5.4}$$

Sargan (1964a) proposed testing the validity of the autoregressive restriction in (5.3) using the result that, if k valid restrictions are imposed, then twice the natural logarithm of the likelihood ratio is asymptotically distributed as χ_k^2. If v_t in (5.3) is normally distributed (as it is in Granger and Newbold's study) then

$$z_1 = T \ln\left(\sum \hat{v}_t^2 \Big/ \sum \hat{w}_t^2\right) \underset{A}{\sim} \chi_k^2 \tag{5.5}$$

when (5.4) *is* the unrestricted version of (5.3). On the other hand, if the apparent autocorrelation in (5.1) arises because it is a mis-specified approximation to (5.4), the latter will produce a better fit than (5.3) and hence too large a value for z_1. It would be interesting to know how often (5.5) led to the rejection of (5.3) against (5.4) at a conventional significance level for χ_1^2 in Granger and Newbold's autoregressive integrated moving-average (ARIMA) model. I hazard the guesses that z_1 would reject (5.3) reasonably frequently relative to the number of cases of spurious significance in table II and also that, in (5.4), X_t and X_{t-1} would now rarely have a significant effect – certainly their individual coefficients could not generally be significant because of collinearity and this finding should prompt a further revision of the dynamic specification.

Precisely how one proceeds at this stage will depend on the status of the theory relating Y_t to X_t. If the study is simply an exploratory empirical modelling of the data set, then it would seem reasonable to repeat the analysis described above with (5.4) constituting the new baseline; alternatively, one could recommence the exercise using a specialization of (5.4) obtained by deleting regressors with t values smaller in absolute value than some positive number c (e.g. c might be unity). Either way, provided that the refitting is conducted allowing for w_t to be autocorrelated (compare chapter 2), then it is hard to see why an approximately correct model could not be detected even for the paradigm used by Granger and Newbold. Clearly, these suggestions could be checked in a simulation study similar to that reported by Granger and Newbold.

As with any iterative model revision approach (including Box–Jenkins methods), preliminary test biases may be a serious problem.[2] Thus, Peck (1975) provides simulation evidence that (on a median absolute error criterion) for almost all values of the autoregressive error parameter ρ in (5.2) the maximum likelihood estimator allowing for autocorrelation like (5.2) is superior to most other estimators based on preliminary tests of the significance of ρ for most significance levels (except, of course, automatic rejection of $H_0 : \rho = 0$). On the other hand, this supports the principle (suggested above) that refitting should always allow for potential auto-correlation and that (5.2) is a simple and inexpensive process to estimate using modern computing equipment.[3]

Nevertheless, (5.4) is still an incorrect approximation to the ARIMA process

$$Y_t = Y_{t-1} + \eta_t + b^* \eta_{t-1} \tag{5.6}$$

which actually generated the data, and even if the X_t regressors were deleted (5.4) would continue to remain inappropriate if the autocorrelation in w_t was assumed to be autoregressive. [This remark raises the issue of the consequences of using incorrect approximations to ARMA or ARIMA processes, and since Granger and Newbold have described allowance for autoregressive errors like (5.2) as 'naive', section 3 of the original paper considered such incorrect approximations in some detail for simple ARMA models.]

3 Differencing Economic Time Series

Granger and Newbold recommend the use of first differences to achieve (more) stationary series and so avoid the problems discussed by Granger and Newbold (1974). There certainly do exist cases where differencing can be helpful, but it is not a universal panacea (no mechanical procedure ever is in econometrics). This occurs because there are two distinct interpretations of a difference transformation *to an equation*.

Operator Form

In this mode, $\Delta = 1 - B$ (where B is the lag operator) is considered to operate on an equation (taking (5.4) as an example), transforming

$$Y_t = \gamma_1 + \gamma_2 X_t + \gamma_3 X_{t-1} + \gamma_4 Y_{t-1} + w_t \qquad (5.7)$$

to

$$\Delta Y_t = \gamma_2 \Delta X_t + \gamma_3 \Delta X_{t-1} + \gamma_4 \Delta Y_{t-1} + \Delta w_t. \qquad (5.8)$$

An intercept in (5.8) would correspond to a trend term in (5.7), and the auto-correlation properties of the error term are completely altered since Δw_t is white noise if (and only if) w_t is a random walk.

Restriction Form

An equation in first differences can also be obtained from (5.7) by imposing the parameter restrictions that $\gamma_2 = -\gamma_3$ and $\gamma_4 = 1$ which yields

$$\Delta Y_t = \gamma_1 + \gamma_2 \Delta X_t + w_t. \qquad (5.9)$$

In this case, if the restrictions are valid, the interpretation of both the intercept and the error term are *unaltered* and (5.9) implies the exclusion of ΔX_{t-1} and ΔY_{t-1} compared with (5.8). Equally important is that if (5.9) *is* the true data generation process for some series Y_t, X_t such that ΔY_t, ΔX_t and w_t are stationary and w_t is white noise, then so must be the error w_t on the equation (5.7) in levels (see Granger and Newbold, 1974). Further, the validity of the difference restriction seems to be testable since, on the null hypothesis, w_t is stationary and the variables X_{t-1} and Y_{t-1} added to (5.9) should have zero coefficients; indeed the test is just one of their joint significance when included in (5.9). In this context (5.8) becomes an incorrect specification (falsely including ΔX_{t-1} and ΔY_{t-1} and excluding the intercept) and has a moving-average error with a coefficient of -1. However, new problems of 'spurious significance' should not afflict Granger and Newbold's procedures unless these are carelessly applied, since always proceeding from the most parsimonious case should ensure detection of (5.9) before (5.8) is reached. It is also worth repeating that the original problem (of obtaining 'nonsense' results if $\gamma_2 = 0$ but Y_t is regressed on X_t without including Y_{t-1}) still lurks in the background.

Nevertheless, in econometric terms the problem with differencing is not over, since both (5.8) and (5.9) have unacceptable features as *universally valid* types of formulation for economic systems. Let $y_t = \ln Y_t$ and $x_t = \ln X_t$ when Y and X are, say, consumption and income. Then (5.9) has *no* equilibrium solution (or is zero if $\gamma_1 = 0$), and the time paths that y_t can describe are independent of the states of disequilibrium existing in the period prior to observation. Since there are more ways of obtaining stationarity than differencing, the choice of which transformation to adopt should be based on economic theory considerations. Marginal adjustments do suggest differencing, and Fisher (1962) has argued in favour of difference formulations for short-run analysis because they avoid the need to specify the long-run behaviour of the process under study (compare chapter 3). On the other hand, long-run unit elasticities suggest the use of ratios. Reconsider (5.7) written as

$$\Delta y_t = \gamma_1 + \gamma_2 \Delta x_t + \gamma_5 (y_{t-1} - x_{t-1}) + w_t \qquad (5.10)$$

$(y_{t-1} - x_{t-1} = \ln(Y_{t-1}/X_{t-1}))$. This imposes the weaker (but still testable) restriction that $1 - \gamma_4 = \gamma_2 + \gamma_3 = -\gamma_5 > 0$ and produces an equation such that

1 the mean lag in levels is long but finite, and most of the adjustment occurs in the first period;
2 the long-run elasticity of Y with respect to X is unity, but the propensity varies with the growth rate of X;
3 the time path of y_t is dependent on previous disequilibrium states;
4 the equation has sensible steady-state and equilibrium properties.

Such a formulation is excluded if *only* differenced variables are considered. A model of the form (5.10) helps explain the very low long-run consumption–income elasticities reported by Wall et al. (1975) who estimate equations like (5.9) (excluding all levels variables) using bivariate modelling techniques based on a Box–Jenkins transfer function approach. Moreover, the Q statistic failed to indicate the existence of this mis-specification.[4]

4 Simultaneous Equations Systems

The above analysis has deliberately ignored the problem of contemporaneous feedbacks affecting the relationship under study in order to isolate some specific difficulties which I felt merited attention. Simultaneity is well known to introduce a host of additional problems including non-unique identification of structural relations (in the econometricians' sense), bias and inconsistency in structural parameters estimated by least squares procedures (which can create spuriously significant relationships as well as camouflaging the very existence of the inconsistencies), bias in residual autocorrelations towards white noise and so on (see, for example, Hendry, 1975a). Thus, Teräsvirta (1976) has demonstrated that the relevant variant of the Q statistic does not have a χ^2 distribution in systems with feedback. It seems as difficult to justify the use of Box–Jenkins transfer functions for *structural* estimation (compare Wall et al., 1975) as it is to justify two-stage least squares estimation of dynamic models with autocorrelated errors (see Hendry and Harrison, 1974); both inappropriate applications are likely to yield seriously biased estimates.

The eight-step method proposed by Granger and Newbold is, of course, designed to avoid the immediately preceding objections (also compare Wall and Westcott, 1974). On the one hand, the discussion in previous sections suggests that there are problems involved in correctly identifying appropriate univariate ARMA processes, that diagnostic tests may lack power to detect certain inadequacies and that differencing is not fully valid in an interesting class of dynamic models. The impact of such difficulties for bivariate modelling exercises seems to deserve investigation. However, if the results are only intended for forecasting purposes, these problems in no way proscribe the use of Granger and Newbold's approach as a *supplement* to other methods (although its labour intensity might!). Specifically, such forecasts could provide a formidable opponent for econometric systems to try and out-perform, and the pooling of forecasts from these rather different sources seems to merit greater empirical application (see, for example, Nelson, 1972).

5 Conclusion on Granger and Newbold

A thorough understanding of time-series analysis is an essential component of the intellectual tool-kit of econometricians studying time-series data – but it remains only one of many ingredients. Granger and Newbold have helpfully pointed out problems of potential relevance to that non-negligible proportion of applied work which neglects time-series considerations. One symptom of that neglect may be the less than totally impressive forecasting record of macroeconometric systems (see Naylor et al., 1972).

My major doubts concern how to remedy such a situation. This paper has investigated the possibility that time-series methods may be plagued by difficulties similar to those which trouble econometric model builders, although the consequences of mis-specifying ARIMA models are obviously rather different from the consequences of mis-specifying econometric systems. Some practical evidence has accumulated, however, since there have been several recent empirical studies comparing time-series models with econometric equivalents (see *inter alia* Zellner and Palm, 1974; Trivedi, 1975; Prothero and Wallis, 1976). Such studies also serve to highlight how similar the 'two philosophies' are by interpreting ARIMA processes as representing the (unrestricted) final forms of the same systems for which the econometrician seeks estimates of the structural equations. For short data series, valid structural information from economic theory must be of considerable importance for estimation efficiency and both Trivedi (1975) and Prothero and Wallis (1976) find that the econometric model fits rather better over the sample period. Unfortunately, such evidence is not incompatible with the econometric system also forecasting less well.

Nevertheless, I suspect that generalizations of econometric techniques specifically designed for multivariate times series will prove more useful in the medium term than any purely data-based approach. Such developments are feasible and are applicable to simultaneous equations systems of more than two variables (see chapter 3). Moreover, the modelling can be closely linked to (and test) the relevant economic theory, hopefully producing the joint outputs of understanding and reasonable forecasts.

6 On Business Cycle Modelling without Pretending to Have Too Much *a priori* Economic Theory

The Sargent and Sims (1977) generalization of factor analysis to the frequency domain is a most useful addition to the range of techniques currently available for investigating time-series data. Existing time domain methods comprise a variety of specializations of vector ARMA representations and of econometric systems, with occasional use (in economics) of factor analysis. In the frequency domain there are spectral analysis, spectral estimation of econometric models and now the Sargent–Sims 'specfac' analysis.

All these methods can be conveniently interpreted as seeking to provide parsimonious (but different) parameterizations of the matrix of cross-spectra of the endogenous variables (denoted by $Sy(\omega)$ for $\omega \in (0,\pi)$). Thus, a (vector) ARMA process assumes that $Sy(\omega)$ can be closely approximated by a (matrix) rational function; spectral analysis assumes constancy of the spectrum within certain neighbouring frequency band groups and variation between groups (i.e. a step-function form); and an econometric model assumes some specialization of an ARMA process for the error (often a constant over all frequency bands) and parameterizes $Sy(\omega)$ from this and the observed spectral matrix of the 'exogenous' variables. In their unobservable k-index model, Sargent and Sims postulate that $2\pi Sy(\omega) = H_1(\omega) + H_2(\omega)$ where $H_1(\omega)$ is symmetric positive semi-definite of rank k, and $H_2(\omega)$ is diagonal. Assuming that y is normally distributed, maximum likelihood estimates of H_1 and H_2 can be obtained together with information about the relative likelihoods of various values of k.

In practice, each data series is first separately pre-whitened by fitting a fifth-order autoregressive process with constant and trend, and r frequency bands are used so that when a value of $k > 1$ is chosen it is not obvious how parsimonious the resulting description is. Nevertheless, it is clear that new insights into the coherence structure of a data set can be achieved by using 'specfac', and the development of an operational algorithm must be warmly welcomed.

However, I must question the *motivation* underlying the Sargent–Sims approach. Certainly, 'important statistical regularities are missed by large scale models'. But this does not imply that one must seek substitutes for conventional econometric methods, as opposed to producing complements (which is how I prefer to interpret the role of the papers presented by Granger and Newbold and Sargent and Sims), together with some (perhaps substantial) revision and re-emphasis within econometrics.

On the one hand, the claimed proliferation of non-nested theories suggests that researchers are not building successively on previous results by rejecting these in the course of establishing more general models (which yet remain as parsimonious as the data will tolerate). This demands a more rigorous application of methodology, not its abandonment. Too often 'parsimony' in an econometric model relates to unwarranted and unnecessary assumptions about properties of the error process. When little is known concerning an *auxiliary* hypothesis, every effort should be made to avoid assumptions whose failure will produce serious inconsistencies. Conversely, one can often fruitfully exploit assumptions whose invalidity only produces inefficiency, unless this means a very large increase in variance. For example, when estimating the structural form of a simultaneous system one can *arbitrarily* restrict the error covariance matrix and/or the reduced form parameters without affecting consistency.[5] Considerable simulation evidence comparing 'full' and 'limited' information estimators suggests that even the efficiency loss of doing this is small. Compare such a situation with that of estimating a dynamic equation with an *ignored* autocorrelated error; doing so can produce large inconsistencies as well as serious inefficiencies in estimation and forecasting. A further example is that an omitted first-order autoregressive error can be approximated by including one lag longer in every variable in the equation with consistent but inefficient results, whereas the converse is not true, in general.

A closely related point is that the particular parameterization adopted for a behavioural relationship should often be selected on the criterion of generating near orthogonal regressors to reflect agents' use of independent sources of information relevant to their decisions (see chapter 8). This has the added advantages of circumventing collinearity problems and of minimizing any potential biases arising from (unsuspected) omitted variables. There remain many other constructive ways of directly improving econometric practice. Thus, it does not seem useful to concentrate on obtaining possibly spurious 'improved estimation efficiency' by using, say, instrumental variables based on solved reduced forms if the cost is neglecting autocorrelation and dynamic specification problems.

These comments assume that econometrics should strive to remain quantitative economics and not become just statistical modelling. The latter certainly provides an alternative answer to the proliferation of economic theories – by eschewing them totally. But this has the consequence that there is no paradigm to guide new research or integrate and summarize achieved findings, and hence little progress results. Sargent and Sims note that the possible conclusions from 'specfac' need not corroborate all conceivable economic theories; however, the deliberate avoidance of much *a priori* input also means that it is unlikely to lead to the exclusion of many theories either.

Overall, I agree with the thrust of the criticisms which both Granger and Newbold and Sargent and Sims make of existing methods. Nevertheless, I am not persuaded that *new* methods of business cycle research are the optimal response for correcting inadequacies in econometric systems as against a (major?) redirection of attention towards solving problems the existence and seriousness of which are well known. [The appendix on power functions is omitted to avoid overlap with chapter 7.]

Notes

1 For counter-examples to each of these statements, see Sargan (1964a) and Wallis (1972a) – note that the former also provides the test statistic for second-order autocorrelated residuals which Granger–Newbold request, but see Durbin (1970) for a slight correction.

2 See, for example, Bock et al. (1973) and for a discussion of sequential testing procedures for autocorrelation see Mizon (1977a).

3 Higher order autoregressive schemes are also relatively easy to estimate.

4 For a more detailed discussion and an application to the consumption–income relationship, see chapter 8.

5 See the 'estimator generating formula' in chapter 13.

6

Serial Correlation as a Convenient Simplification, not a Nuisance: a Comment on a Study of the Demand for Money by the Bank of England

with Grayham E. Mizon

Preamble

Because of their intimate links and common emphases, the two papers on COMFAC with Grayham Mizon come in sequence. Although their publication was separated by two years, there was considerable overlap in the periods during which the research was undertaken. As noted earlier, the development of COMFAC started at LSE in 1975, but the analysis of its implications, its finite sample statistical properties and its empirical performance continued into 1979, by which time Grayham had left LSE for Southampton University. The immediate stimulus to this chapter was a paper by Graham Hacche (then at the Bank of England) on modelling broad money demand. I was editing econometrics papers for the *Economic Journal*, and when Tony Courakis submitted a comment on Hacche's paper, Grayham Mizon and I decided to comment as well since we were unhappy about the use of differenced data in econometric modelling.

Thus, chapter 6 was written as an exposition of COMFAC, and reiterates the analysis of the first-order autoregressive error case described in chapter 2 but with an entirely different emphasis. Now we focus on the conceptual aspects, with the unrestricted dynamic model having primacy and autocorrelated errors being a potential way of reducing the parameterization. In earlier work, because of the implicit simple-to-general approach, the same statistic was treated as merely another check on the initial autoregressive error model against a less restricted, but perhaps uninteresting, alternative. The approach is forcefully general to simple in a sequential simplification strategy, although the application is actually to equation

Reprinted from *Economic Journal*, 88 (September 1978) 549–63. This research was financed in part by a grant from the Social Science Research Council to the Programme in Quantitative Economics at LSE. The idea of writing this paper arose during the refereeing process of Tony Courakis's note, and we are grateful to him for supplying his data. We are also indebted to Denis Sargan for permission to quote extensively from his two unpublished papers on COMFAC, to Stephen Yeo for his comments on a previous draft and to Frank Srba for undertaking all the calculations described below.

evaluation, not to model construction. A clear distinction is drawn between residual autocorrelation and error autoregression: the former could be due to many possible causes and hence did not entail the latter. Conversely, assuming an autoregressive error representation was identical to assuming a set of common factors in the dynamic model and hence was a restriction of that model and not a generalization as I had viewed the matter in chapter 2, and as many textbooks still do.

Non-stationarity and differencing again arise as major issues of contention. We interpreted differencing as imposing a common factor and setting its value at unity, so that it became a testable restriction on a dynamic model. Many of our arguments happen to remain correct, but we took no account of the different distributional properties of the tests when unit roots existed in the individual data series. Wayne Fuller (1976) had considered that case, and David Dickey and he developed those procedures in their 1979 and 1981 papers. In discussion, Gene Savin (then at Cambridge University) questioned our assumption that t statistics remained valid when there were unit roots in the time series. Naturally, Monte Carlo seemed the obvious way to investigate such an issue and so we simulated a two-equation process with one unit root equation and one equation with an error correction mechanism (ECM). At conventional critical values, the t test on the latter's coefficient rejected about 5 per cent of the time under the null when there was no ECM feedback, and more often under the alternative, which we now call cointegration, and so we concluded that we were not far wrong! As Aneuryn Evans and Gene Savin (1981) later discovered, we were just lucky.[1] The distribution is skewed under the null, but in the cases we had simulated, the 5 per cent critical value of $|t|$ did occur in the neighbourhood of 2 (see Dolado et al. (1990) for a review).

That simple Monte Carlo took several days to create, run and analyse in 1977–8 using NAIVE on a mainframe computer. To gauge possible gains in productivity since then and to cross-check our earlier findings, I re-ran the experiments in 1989 using PC-NAIVE (see Hendry et al., 1991). It took less than five minutes to recreate the data generation process and model, just over an hour to calculate 10,000 replications on an 80386 computer, and about ten minutes to analyse the results including the graphs reproduced below. The data generation process was

$$\Delta y_t = 0.5\Delta x_t + 0.0(y - x)_{t-1} + \varepsilon_{1t} \qquad \varepsilon_t \sim IN\left[\begin{pmatrix} 0 \\ 0 \end{pmatrix}, \begin{pmatrix} 1 & 0 \\ 0 & 3 \end{pmatrix}\right]$$

$$\Delta x_t = \qquad\qquad\qquad \varepsilon_{2t} \qquad t = 1, \ldots, 100,$$

where the first equation is estimated by least squares. The rejection frequency for the t test that the ECM coefficient was zero yielded $P(|t| \geq 2) = 0.052\,(\pm 0.004)$. The empirical density function of t from the experiment is shown in figure 6.1, standardized to have a zero mean and unit variance, and reveals a nearly normal distribution. Our earlier Monte Carlo had indeed yielded the 'correct' result. However, $\hat{P}(t \leq -2) = 0.040$ and $\hat{P}(t \geq 2) = 0.012$ and so most of the 5 per cent rejection frequency is in the lower tail as predicted.

In fact, the hour it took the computer to calculate the simulations included doing the experiment recursively at every sample size from $T = 10$ to $T = 100$. Figure 6.2 records the frequency with which $|t| \geq 2$ occurred at each T, so that the outcomes are shown for 90 experiments in all. The test rejection frequency is sample-size dependent but remains in the interval (0.045, 0.058) near to, but overestimating, the nominals per cent level. Kremers et al. (1992) provide a theoretical explanation for this result in terms of the signal-to-noise ratio, so such an outcome seems related to the finding in Hylleberg and Mizon (1989). Note that the overall research productivity gain during the decade needs to be measured in terms of several orders of magnitude!

When writing chapter 6, we worried about prior seasonal adjustment of the data. Ken Wallis's 1974 paper had revealed that dynamic specification could be distorted by pre-filtering

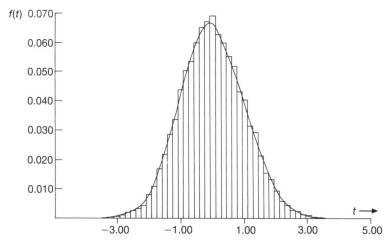

Figure 6.1 Frequency distribution of the t test on an ECM under H_0 when $T = 100$.

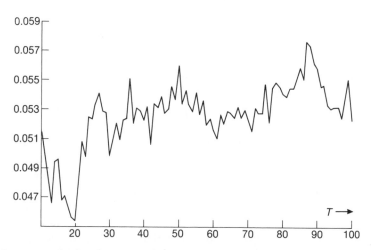

Figure 6.2 t test rejection frequency for an ECM under H_0.

data, when different filters were applied to each of the variables entering a relationship. We also knew from DHSY the extent to which results changed from adjusted to unadjusted data, but for comparability we accepted Graham Hacche's data exactly as he had analysed them.

Finally, we were concerned that econometrics was drifting away from integrating economic analysis with statistical theory and towards time-series modelling, so we sought to relate the conventional long-run money demand theory to our empirical estimates in a similar way to that used in chapter 3. Since chapter 8 (DHSY) was essentially completed, ECMs were separately delineated and their properties seemed promising – perhaps more so in the event than our fondest hopes, given later research on cointegration.

Notes

1 Or unlucky perhaps, since otherwise we might have stumbled over cointegration notions before Clive Granger formulated this idea.

1 Introduction

Tests of serial correlation in residuals have been used to check model adequacy for many years and the d statistic of Durbin and Watson (1950) and the h statistic of Durbin (1970) have become important tools in the model building kit of social scientists in general, as well as of economists. Similarly, the increased availability of computing facilities has made possible the estimation of most forms of model (whether single equations or simultaneous systems) with serially correlated error processes, parameterized as autoregressions and/or moving averages, or even not parameterized using spectral methods (see, *inter alia*, Osborn, 1976; Espasa, 1977; and chapter 13). The ability to 'allow for' serial correlation without great difficulty is well reflected in the applied economics/econometrics literature (see, for example, Pindyck and Rubinfeld, 1976). However, is serial correlation correctly viewed as a nuisance for which 'allowance' is required or does such a view of serial correlation represent a misunderstanding of its nature? The purpose of this note is to suggest that serial correlation can be interpreted as a convenient way of representing dynamic relationships, following the 'common factor' analysis of autoregressive error processes proposed by Sargan (1980a) (also see Mizon, 1977a).[1] We hope that our exposition may encourage a reappraisal by empirical researchers of serial correlation in residuals, clarify its relationship to dynamic specification and yield insight into some problems of applying 'black-box' time-series methods to economics data. The analysis leads to using sequential statistical procedures to test a number of important hypotheses which are all too often arbitrarily assumed to be valid. Evidence acquired from the tests can be incorporated in a model based on general economic considerations to produce an adequate approximation to the process generating the data. *If* the model chosen at the termination of the selection process has an autoregressive error, then it will be seen that this *is* a convenient simplification and *not* a nuisance, since it allows a reduction in the number of parameters required to specify the data generation process. As a consequence, there is a gain in estimation efficiency without loss of consistency.

The next section presents the *conceptual* aspects of the common factor approach to investigating dynamic equations, while the third section applies the technique to one of the demand for money equations obtained by Hacche (1974) to illustrate the *practical* value of the method. However, we believe that several aspects of the methodology so well exposited by Hacche are not generally valid in economics and if widely adopted could misdirect empirical econometric research using time-series data. Thus, we offer a critique of certain other features of Hacche's methodology, these being in any case intimately connected with the problems of dynamic specification and serial correlation. To avoid any possible confusion over similarity of name with the completely different technique of 'factor analysis' (see Anderson,

1958), in what follows we have chosen to refer to Sargan's common factor method as COMFAC, which is the name of the relevant computer program developed by Sargan and Sylwestrowicz (1976a).

2 COMFAC Analysis

Consider a stable linear regression equation relating a variable y_t to its own lagged value and to the current and lagged values of a regressor variable x_t:

$$y_t = \beta_1 y_{t-1} + \gamma_0 x_t + \gamma_1 x_{t-1} + v_t, \tag{6.1}$$

where $|\beta_1| < 1$ and v_t has a zero mean, a constant variance σ^2 and is serially independent. Models similar to (6.1) occur frequently in empirical econometrics (see many of the equations comprising the macroeconomic systems described in Renton, 1975). Define the lag operator L such that $L^n y_t = y_{t-n}$ and rewrite (6.1) as

$$y_t = \beta_1 L y_t + \gamma_0 x_t + \gamma_1 L x_t + v_t$$

or

$$(1 - \beta_1 L) y_t = (\gamma_0 + \gamma_1 L) x_t + v_t. \tag{6.2}$$

In this alternative (but equivalent) notation, equation (6.1) is seen to result from multiplying the dependent variable y_t by a first-order polynomial in the lag operator L and multiplying the regressor variable x_t by another first-order polynomial in L.

If the parameter γ_1 is equal to $-\beta_1 \gamma_0$, then equation (6.2) becomes

$$(1 - \beta_1 L) y_t = \gamma_0 (1 - \beta_1 L) x_t + v_t \tag{6.3}$$

so that the terms involving y_t and x_t have a common factor of $1 - \beta_1 L$ and hence the polynomials in L multiplying y_t and x_t have a common root[2] of β_1. Dividing both sides of equation (6.3) by the common factor yields

$$y_t = \gamma_0 x_t + \frac{v_t}{1 - \beta_1 L} = \gamma_0 x_t + u_t, \tag{6.4}$$

where

$$u_t = \frac{v_t}{1 - \beta_1 L}$$

or

$$u_t = \beta_1 u_{t-1} + v_t,$$

from which it is seen that u_t is generated by a first-order autoregressive process. Consequently, if the model (6.1) with one-period-lagged variables satisfies the restriction $\gamma_1 = -\beta_1 \gamma_0$, then the polynomials in the lag operator have a common root and (in our terminology) this root is the serial correlation coefficient of a first-order autoregressive error process when (6.1) is written as a static model with the error term u_t. Thus, the fact that u_t is generated by a first-order autoregression is actually a convenience (and not a nuisance to be eliminated) in that model (6.4) only requires the three parameters β_1, γ_0 and σ^2 to be estimated rather than the four parameters β_1, γ_0, γ_1 and σ^2 of model (6.1). It is true that while ordinary least squares can be used to estimate (6.1), the estimation of (6.4) involves more 'complicated' techniques, but this is not a serious problem given the wide availability of computationally efficient (and very fast) programs implementing the Cochrane–Orcutt technique (for a survey, see chapter 13). The benefit from estimating (6.4) rather than (6.1) when the common root restriction $\gamma_1 = -\beta_1\gamma_0$ is valid is the improved statistical efficiency of the parameter estimates.

Whether or not such a common root restriction *is* valid could be tested as in Sargan (1964a) by comparing the goodness of fit of model (6.1) with that of model (6.4).[3] Nevertheless, it must be emphasized that estimating the 'static model'

$$y_t = \gamma_0 x_t + u_t \tag{6.5}$$

and using the Durbin–Watson d statistic calculated from the residuals $\hat{u}_t$ to test whether u_t is serially independent (against the alternative of a first-order autoregression) is *not* a test of the common root restriction. In fact, it can be seen from the derivation of (6.4) that the d statistic tests whether the common root β_1 is zero conditional on the (arbitrary and untested) assumption that a common root formulation is valid. Of course, *if* (6.4) constituted the true model then the common root restriction would be valid and the d test would provide a valid check for autocorrelation. Conversely, when (6.1) has a common factor, it can be simplified to a static model with an autoregressive error. Thus, there is a one-to-one correspondence between common factor dynamics and autoregressive errors. This statement does *not* entail that *residual* autocorrelation (revealed by a significant d statistic for example) derives from such a source.

Equation (6.1) is obviously more general than equation (6.3) and hence there exists an infinity of situations in which the dynamic behaviour cannot be summarized accurately by an autoregressive error; that is, a common factor cannot necessarily be found. Expressed somewhat differently, comparison of (6.1) with (6.4) shows that the variables $\beta_1 y_{t-1} + \gamma_1 x_{t-1}$ in (6.1) are omitted from (6.4) and are being approximated by the error autoregression $\beta_1 u_{t-1}$. Consider the case when $\gamma_1 \neq -\beta_1\gamma_0$. An investigator who commenced from (6.5) (without an estimated autoregressive error) would usually observe a significant value of d calculated from the residuals $\hat{u}_t$. This reflects the fact that (6.4), with a non-zero common root, will usually provide a better approximation to (6.1) (especially in terms of goodness of fit) than will (6.5) where the root is further restricted to be zero (see Hendry, 1975a). Frequently, a significant d will lead to an attempt to allow for the observed autocorrelation, which entails estimating (6.4). However, the approximation of (6.1) by (6.4) could still be very poor and a conventional mis-specification analysis indicates that substantial coefficient biases will usually occur, yielding misleading values for impact and long-run multipliers, mean lags etc. In other words, residual autocorrelation may reflect little more than dynamic mis-specification, which is a well-known but frequently ignored result. The appropriate strategy is to commence from the general model and investigate how far it can be simplified legitimately. Such an approach will be consistent whichever of the contending equations, (6.1), (6.4) or (6.5), constitutes the true model.

Before developing the generalization of the above analysis, we turn to a special case of the model with one-period lags and a common root which has assumed undue importance in empirical work. This is equation (6.3) with $\beta_1 = 1$, which produces a simple regression model in the first differences (rather than the levels) of the variables:

$$\Delta y_t = \gamma_0 \Delta x_t + v_t, \tag{6.6}$$

when $\Delta = 1 - L$. The use of differences to transform trending series to approximate stationarity has been advocated by Box and Jenkins (1976) and their model building strategy appears to be gaining in popularity in economics (see Naylor et al., 1972). Granger and Newbold (1974; 1977b, ch. 4) have forcefully described the pitfalls awaiting economists who use regressions based on the levels of trending variables and have emphasized the long famous 'spurious' (or nonsense) regressions problem (see Yule, 1926). Nevertheless, instances of nonsense equations are not unknown in applied economics.[4] Granger and Newbold suggest that the danger is especially large when the warning of a significant d statistic has been ignored[5] and, to circumvent this problem, also propose the use of differenced variables. However, while we accept that there are situations in which differencing is fully appropriate (namely, when there is a common root of unity), there are also situations in which it can cause problems as serious as those it aims to solve (see chapter 5). For example, if the true model is

$$y_t = \gamma_0 x_t + \varepsilon_t \tag{6.7}$$

where ε_t is a white noise error, but because y_t and x_t have trends a model in differences is used,

$$\Delta y_t = \gamma_0 \Delta x_t + \omega_t,$$

then the error $\omega_t = \Delta \varepsilon_t$ is a moving average with a coefficient of -1, swapping one awkward problem (potentially spurious fits) for another (an error process with a root of minus unity). It is interesting to note that such 'over-differencing' of the variables in a linear regression will result in the first-order serial correlation coefficient of the errors being close to -0.5, a phenomenon often found in studies using differences (e.g. Hacche, 1974). Prothero and Wallis (1976) note that a similar difficulty can occur also with 'seasonal differences' (i.e. using $1 - L^4$ on quarterly seasonally unadjusted data in an attempt to remove seasonal factors). However, if the true model is equation (6.7) and the tentative working hypothesis is equation (6.1), then there is a common root but its value is *zero* and the COMFAC approach should detect this and allow the redundant dynamics or autocorrelation to be eliminated.

It might be objected that one cannot know *a priori* that (6.7) is the true model, and since economic time series often have strong trends, any model formulated in levels is a potential candidate for the spurious regressions phenomenon. A careful distinction is essential at this stage since we agree with the statement in the previous sentence, but do *not* agree that analysing only differenced variables will necessarily provide a good solution to the problem. Rather, it seems desirable to be able to *test* the hypothesis that the appropriate model should be formulated in differences by testing the hypothesis of a unit common root against the alternative of a model which contains one more lagged value of both y_t and x_t with unrestricted coefficients. A test of this last hypothesis can be effected by first testing whether there *is* a common root in the alternative model, and if this hypothesis is not rejected, then testing whether that root is unity. Such a procedure takes advantage of the fact that the hypothesis of a common root of unity is a composite hypothesis, and that the constituent hypotheses ((i) there is a common root and (ii) that root is unity) form a uniquely ordered nest – see Mizon (1977a). For example, when the appropriate model is a static equation with autocorrelation like (6.4) (in the levels of y_t and x_t with $|\beta_1| < 1$), then such a two-step procedure (in reasonable sample sizes) with a high probability should *not reject* the common root hypothesis (i) (there being a common root of β_1 in the equation $y_t = \gamma_0 x_t + \beta_1 y_{t-1} - \beta_1 \gamma_0 x_{t-1} + \varepsilon_t$), but then hypothesis (ii) that the root is unity should be rejected (unless β_1 is close to unity). If the appropriate model is (6.1) with $\gamma_1 \neq -\beta_1 \gamma_0$, then (i) itself should be rejected.

A crucial point about such an approach is that it will be valid even if the underlying variables are 'spuriously' related in levels but unrelated in differences. This can be seen as follows. Reformulate the maintained hypothesis (6.1) as

$$\Delta y_t = \gamma_0 \Delta x_t + (\beta_1 - 1) y_{t-1} + (\gamma_0 + \gamma_1) x_{t-1} + v_t. \tag{6.8}$$

If equation (6.6) is valid (for any value of γ_0), then the coefficients of y_{t-1} and x_{t-1} must both be zero in (6.8).[6] A common root entails $\gamma_1 = -\beta_1 \gamma_0$ and that root is unity if also $\beta_1 = 1$ in which case (6.8) does specialize to (6.6). Hence the composite hypothesis of a unit root can be tested by testing the joint significance from zero of the coefficients of y_{t-1} and x_{t-1} in (6.8). Moreover, if v_t in equation (6.6) is a white noise (or stationary) error, then v_t in (6.8) must be also and hence so must v_t in (6.1). Indeed equations (6.1) and (6.8) are really identical, and the parameters of either can be derived uniquely from the parameters of the other. Of course, the same is true of estimates of the parameters: $\hat{\gamma}_0$, $\hat{\gamma}_1$ and $\hat{\beta}_1$ derived from (6.8) must be identical to the values obtained by direct estimation of (6.1) and the validity of such estimates cannot be affected by whether the transformation to the differenced form (6.8) is made before or after estimation. Moreover, a model in differences like (6.6) can always be rewritten as a model in levels like (6.1) (with parametric restrictions of the form $\beta_1 = 1$ and $\gamma_0 = -\gamma_1$) and the error process will be unaffected by such a reformulation. Thus, if differencing is a valid solution to the spurious regression problem, then so must be the inclusion of lagged values of *all* the variables. However, we have demonstrated above that it is not always valid to take the converse path of reducing a general dynamic relationship in levels to a simpler equation in differences only, since there may not be any common factors.

Although the preceding analysis has been restricted to the case of a one-period lag and one regressor only, the main points apply in general for higher order lags and more than one regressor. Thus consider the equation

$$\beta(L)y_t = \gamma(L)x_t + \delta(L)z_t + v_t, \tag{6.9}$$

where $\beta(L)$, $\gamma(L)$ and $\delta(L)$ are scalar polynomials in L of orders p, q and r respectively. It is possible for $\beta(L)$, $\gamma(L)$ and $\delta(L)$ to have at most l common roots (where $l = \min(p, q, r)$) and if in fact there are $n \leqslant l$ common roots, then there exists a polynomial $\rho(L)$ of order n common to $\beta(L)$, $\gamma(L)$ and $\delta(L)$. Therefore

$$\beta(L) = \rho(L)\beta^*(L) \qquad \gamma(L) = \rho(L)\gamma^*(L) \qquad \delta(L) = \rho(L)\delta^*(L)$$

or

$$[\beta(L):\gamma(L):\delta(L)] = \rho(L)[\beta^*(L):\gamma^*(L):\delta^*(L)], \tag{6.10}$$

where $\beta^*(L)$, $\gamma^*(L)$ and $\delta^*(L)$ are polynomials of order $p - n$, $q - n$ and $r - n$ respectively. Consequently, using (6.10), (6.9) can be rewritten as

$$\rho(L)\beta^*(L)y_t = \rho(L)\gamma^*(L)x_t + \rho(L)\delta^*(L)z_t + v_t \tag{6.11}$$

so that

$$\beta^*(L)y_t = \gamma^*(L)x_t + \delta^*(L)z_t + u_t, \tag{6.12}$$

where

$$\rho(L)u_t = v_t \tag{6.12a}$$

which means that the error term u_t in (6.12) is generated by an autoregressive process of order n. The reduction in the number of parameters from the general model (6.9) is $2n$ (or kn for k different regressors) which can greatly enhance estimation efficiency. Also, the computational cost of estimating the parameters of (6.12) + (6.12a) by non-linear optimization need be incurred only when the COMFAC algorithm indicates that such a model is a reasonable description of the data process. As earlier, if $\rho(L)$ has a factor $\Delta = 1 - L$ such that $\rho(L) = (1 - L)\rho^*(L)$, then (6.12) can be modified to

$$\beta^*(L)\Delta y_t = \gamma^*(L)\Delta x_t + \delta^*(L)\Delta z_t + u_t \tag{6.13}$$

with

$$\rho^*(L)u_t = v_t.$$

The above analysis assumes that the orders of the lag polynomials are known and in practice this will not be the case. Two approaches could be adopted to solve this, both being two-stage decision procedures which commence from the most general (unrestricted) model which it seems reasonable to consider but sequentially simplify it in different ways. Either way, the lengths of the longest lags must be specified *a priori* (p, q, r in (6.9) for example). In the first method, sequential tests for reducing the order of the dynamics are conducted as in Anderson (1971, ch. 3.2) until a test value exceeding the chosen critical limit is obtained. Then the COMFAC algorithm is applied to the equation so selected, maintaining the overall lag length at the value found during the first stage (see Sargan, 1980a). Alternatively, the common factor technique could be applied directly to the model as specified *a priori* and then the equation could be simplified later by testing for zero roots from the set of n common roots extracted.[7] Since we wish to test a sequence of (implicit) common root hypotheses about an existing model, we have adopted the second approach in the next section.

A formal discussion of the computer algorithm COMFAC for implementing the common root tests is provided in Sargan (1980a), with an extension in Sargan and Mehta (1983). We have used the Wald test form described in the former paper since the controlled simulation study in chapter 7 suggests that this test has reasonable power properties in finite samples for models like (6.1) when the common factor restriction is invalid. Briefly, the approach works as follows. First, the coefficients and their variance matrix in the general unrestricted equation (equation (6.9)) are estimated by the desired method (say, ordinary least squares): denote these results by $\hat{b}$ and $\hat{V}$. The restrictions in (6.10) are equivalent to requiring a (vector) non-linear function of b, denoted $f(b)$, to be zero: for example, in equation (6.1) the restriction takes the form that $\gamma_1 + \beta_1 \gamma_0 = 0$. The (asymptotic) variance matrix of $f(\hat{b})$ is given by $S = J'VJ$ when $J = \partial f/\partial b'$ and hence $f(\hat{b})'\hat{S}^{-1}f(\hat{b})$ will be distributed as a central χ^2 variate in large samples when the restrictions $f(b) = 0$ are valid. The degrees of freedom of the χ^2 will be equal to the number of restrictions being tested. The appropriate numerical algorithms in COMFAC have been implemented by Sargan and Sylwestrowicz (1976a) for use with the program GIVE.

3 Demand for Money Study of Hacche (1974)

There are five very closely related issues which concern us about the approach in Hacche (1974), namely: stationarity and differencing; dynamic specification; serial correlation; seasonal adjustment (denoted SA below) of the data and the formulation of the regression model. The first three of these issues have been the subject of the previous section but to clarify our approach we must record some important points relating to SA of data and equation formulation.

Lag polynomials like $\beta(L)$ and $\gamma(L)$ can also be interpreted as linear *filters* since an 'adjusted' series such as $y_t^* = \beta(L)y_t$ (say) will have certain frequencies attenuated or enhanced relative to the original series y_t, depending on the values of the parameters in $\beta(L)$ (e.g. the difference filter $\Delta = 1 - L$ heavily attenuates low frequency (trend) components of y_t). Wallis (1974) demonstrates that the widely used US Bureau of the Census method II, variant X-11, procedure can be adequately characterized as a two-sided lag polynomial of the form

$$\lambda(L) = \sum_{j=-m}^{m} \lambda_j L^j \qquad (\lambda_j = \lambda_{-j})$$

and hence 'seasonally adjusted' data take the form $y_t^a = \lambda(L)y_t$. If two series y_t and x_t are related by the equation

$$\beta(L)y_t = \gamma(L)x_t + v_t \tag{6.14}$$

and are subject to separate SA procedures using filters $\lambda(L)$ and $\mu(L)$ such that $y_t^a = \lambda(L)y_t$ and $x_t^a = \mu(L)x_t$, then the relationship between the adjusted series must be of the form

$$\beta(L)y_t^a = \gamma(L)x_t^a + w_t, \tag{6.15}$$

where

$$w_t = \lambda(L)v_t + \gamma(L)[\lambda(L) - \mu(L)]x_t. \tag{6.16}$$

When a relationship between series is involved, the error term will contain the 'omitted variables' $\gamma(L)[\lambda(L) - \mu(L)]x_t$ unless the same SA filter is used for both series, and the transformed error $\lambda(L)v_t$ will not be white noise unless the filter used for y_t eliminates the original 'seasonal noise' in v_t. Otherwise, as Wallis shows, inappropriately applied SA procedures can create serial correlation and dynamic specification problems which lead to inconsistent and inefficient estimates. The data series used by Hacche appear to have been separately adjusted and, in particular, interest rates were not adjusted using the same filter as for the money stock, which could cause seasonal bias problems (see experiment B in Wallis, 1974). We must emphasize that it only seems silly to subject a non-seasonal variable like interest rates to an SA filter because a concept appropriate to adjusting a series is being incorrectly applied in the context of filtering a relationship (a related comment applies to differencing a relationship in order to remove trends from variables). Note, also, that if any filter which reduced v_t to white noise in (6.16) was one-sided then from (6.14)

$$\lambda(L)\beta(L)y_t = \lambda(L)\gamma(L)x_t + w_t, \tag{6.17}$$

where $w_t = \lambda(L)v_t$ is white noise by hypothesis and hence $\lambda(L)$ corresponds to a non-redundant common factor in the unrestricted dynamic equation relating the unadjusted levels of the variables (if v_t in (6.14) is white noise, then the common factor in (6.17) is redundant). We conclude that SA of the variables in a relationship is appropriate when it is designed to remove noise at seasonal frequencies, in which case it is also usually necessary (see Sims, 1974b). Nevertheless, as comparison of (6.14) and (6.15) highlights, correct SA should not alter the lag structure. If one anticipated long lags (e.g. four periods) prior to SA, then these should still occur after SA. Thus, use of SA data does *not* justify confining tests of dynamic specification to one or two lags only (see chapter 8). Further, if $\lambda(L) \neq \mu(L)$ then SA will alter the lag structure and little can be deduced validly about the underlying dynamic reactions from the estimated lag coefficients.

The equation specifications adopted by Hacche take the general form (see Hacche, 1974, p. 258)[8]

$$\Delta \ln\left(\frac{M}{P}\right)_t = b_0 + b_1 \Delta \ln Y_t + b_2 \Delta \ln(1 + r_t) + b_3 \Delta \ln\left(\frac{M_{t-1}}{P_t}\right) + v_t, \tag{6.18}$$

where $v_t = \rho v_{t-1} + \varepsilon_t$ with ε_t assumed to be white noise. In equation (6.18), ln denotes $\log_e$ and M, P, Y and r are as defined in Hacche (1974) and Courakis (1978) with M being (nominal) M3 holdings of the personal sector, Y personal disposable income at 1970 prices, P the implicit deflator of Y and r the yield on consols; M, Y and P are seasonally adjusted. The value of ρ was chosen by Hacche using a rough grid search over $-1 < \rho < 1$ by steps of 0.2, selecting $\hat{\rho}$ to minimize $\Sigma \varepsilon_t^2$ (Hacche does not state if the quoted standard errors were conditional on the estimated value of ρ).

Consider a general unrestricted log-linear model relating M to Y, P and r:

$$\ln M_t = c_0 + \sum_{j=0}^{J} [\alpha_j \ln Y_{t-j} + \gamma_j \ln P_{t-j} + \delta_j \ln(1 + r_{t-j}) + \beta_j \ln M_{t-1-j}] + e_t.$$

$$(6.19)$$

We chose a maximum lag of four periods ($J = 4$) for the regressors in (6.19) partly because the data were quarterly and partly because the sample size of 51 observations did not merit trying for more than 22 coefficients.[9] Compared with equation (6.18), the restrictions imposed by Hacche on (6.19) to obtain (6.18) with six coefficients are as follows: (i) a common root of unity (corresponding to Δ); (ii) a common root of ρ; (iii) two common roots of zero (corresponding to the maximum lag lengths in (6.18), transformed to remove the autoregressive error, of one period for P_t, two periods for Y_t and r_t and three periods for M_t); (iv) a unit elasticity of M with respect to P.

The four common factors provide 12 restrictions, with the three fixed values of the roots and the unit elasticity providing the remaining four restrictions on (6.19) to yield (6.18). Consequently, the extraction of four common factors from (6.19), corresponding to roots of $(1, \rho, 0, 0)$ will reproduce the dynamic specification in (6.18). We note from tables A and B in Hacche (1974) that all the estimates of ρ are either -0.6 or -0.4 and that no other useful diagnostic information is provided about residual autocorrelation. Moreover, although we have used least squares for comparability with Hacche's results, we doubt the validity of treating Y_t, P_t and r_t as exogenous.[10] Also, we stress that the dynamic specification of (6.18) must be rejected against (6.19) either if four common factors can be rejected in (6.19) or even should four common factors be found, if the corresponding roots differ significantly from $(1, \rho, 0, 0)$.

Space precludes our discussing the issue of 'multicollinearity' in a time-series context but we note that, although few of the coefficients in the unrestricted estimation of (6.19) are 'individually significant' (see table 6.1), whatever 'collinearity' may be present need not prevent the rejection of the hypothesis of four common roots (see below). By comparison with (6.19), estimation of (6.18) (by method 5.1 in chapter 13) for the whole sample period yields[11]

$$\Delta \ln\left(\frac{M}{P}\right)_t = 0.002 + 0.13 \Delta \ln Y_t + 0.89 \Delta \ln(1 + r_t) + 0.33 \Delta \ln\left(\frac{M_{t-1}}{P_t}\right)$$
$$(0.003) \quad (0.10) \qquad\qquad (0.37) \qquad\qquad\qquad (0.17)$$

$$+ 0.20 v_{t-1}$$
$$(0.18)$$

$$\hat{\sigma} = 0.0119 \qquad \chi_{12}^2 = 6.7.$$

$$(6.20)$$

The R^2 for the equation without the autoregressive error is 0.42 ($\hat{\sigma} = 0.0118$). $\hat{\sigma}$ is the equation standard error adjusted for degrees of freedom and coefficient standard errors are shown in parentheses. χ_{12}^2 is the Box–Pierce random residual correlogram test: see Pierce (1971).

Note that this equation 'passes' the conventional time-series diagnostic test. The solved coefficients from (6.20) for the levels of the variables are shown in table 6.2.

Table 6.1 Equation (6.19) with $J = 4$

Variable	$j = 0$	$j = 1$	$j = 2$	$j = 3$	$j = 4$
$\ln M_{t-1-j}$	0.92 (0.22)	−0.05 (0.28)	−0.17 (0.28)	−0.22 (0.29)	0.30 (0.23)
$\ln(1 + r_{t-j})$	0.90 (0.39)	−0.82 (0.66)	−0.99 (0.76)	1.28 (0.81)	−0.63 (0.68)
$\ln Y_{t-j}$	0.22 (0.13)	0.05 (0.15)	0.14 (0.15)	0.01 (0.15)	0.20 (0.13)
$\ln P_{t-j}$	0.59 (0.25)	−0.71 (0.42)	0.94 (0.59)	−0.99 (0.60)	0.24 (0.39)

$c_0 = -2.40$ (3.63); $R^2 = 0.9995$; $\hat{\sigma} = 0.0096$.

Table 6.2 Solved coefficients from equation (6.20)

Variable	$j = 0$	$j = 1$	$j = 2$
$\ln M_{t-1-j}$	1.53	−0.46	−0.07
$\ln(1 + r_{t-j})$	0.89	−1.07	0.18
$\ln Y_{t-j}$	0.13	−0.16	0.03
$\ln P_{t-j}$	0.67	−0.80	0.13

The use of $\Delta \ln(M_{t-1}/P_t)$ would entail a coefficient of -0.33 on $\Delta^2 \ln P_t$ if the model was reformulated using $\ln(M/P)_{t-1}$ (see Goldfeld (1973) and compare (6.21) below). These numbers differ considerably from the results in table 6.1.

First, sequentially testing for the existence of one, two, three or four common factors in (6.19) yields the results shown in table 6.3. Three common factors can be extracted without 'loss of fit' but the fourth produces a large value for the test statistic, supporting the hypothesis that invalid restrictions are being imposed.[12] To check that this outcome did not arise purely from the choice of $J = 4$ in (6.19), we

Table 6.3 Common factor tests of equation (6.19)

Common factor	Value of statistic	Degrees of freedom
First	0.20	3
Second	0.54	3
Third	2.57	3
Fourth	9.71	3

Table 6.4 Equation (6.19) with $J = 2$

Variable	$j = 0$	$j = 1$	$j = 2$
$\ln M_{t-1-j}$	0.92 (0.19)	0.03 (0.26)	−0.10 (0.18)
$\ln(1 + r_{t-j})$	0.88 (0.38)	−0.77 (0.58)	−0.50 (0.55)
$\ln Y_{t-j}$	0.24 (0.12)	−0.03 (0.13)	0.09 (0.12)
$\ln P_{t-j}$	0.69 (0.21)	−0.81 (0.35)	0.26 (0.34)

$c_0 = 0.53$ (2.18); $R^2 = 0.9993$; $\hat{\sigma} = 0.0099$.

Table 6.5 Roots of the lag polynomials in (6.19)

$J = 4$			
ln M	0.61 ± 0.56i	0.84	−0.51 ± 0.55i
ln$(1 + r)$	0.51 ± 0.54i	1.28	−1.31
ln Y	0.54 ± 0.77i		−0.86 ± 0.97i
ln P	0.30 ± 0.57i	1.11	−0.59
$J = 2$			
ln M	0.74	−0.25	0.48
ln$(1 + r)$	1.24	−0.55	
ln Y	0.02 + 0.61i	0.02−0.61i	
ln P	1.10	−0.14	

also applied the test to the unrestricted estimates of (6.19) with $J = 2$ (i.e. this tests (i) and (ii) conditional on (iii)). The coefficient estimates are reported in table 6.4 and the χ_3^2 test statistic values for the two separate common factors are 1.63 and 9.03 respectively, and so again there is evidence against Hacche's formulation. The roots of the polynomials in (6.19) for $J = 4$ and $J = 2$ are reported in table 6.5.

For theoretical reasons discussed in chapter 8 we would find it surprising if unit root restrictions were appropriate for economic time series. Equations formulated like (6.18) provide no mechanism for disequilibria between the *levels* of the variables (M, P, Y, r) to influence the time path of M. Moreover, all long-run information in the data is lost by choosing the filter $1 - L$. To illustrate a form of model which is not rejected against (6.19), which avoids all of the theoretical objections to (6.18) and which has interesting short-run dynamic behaviour with reasonable long-run properties, we estimated an analogue of the model used in chapter 8. This also demonstrates with great clarity precisely why the common factor hypotheses implicit in Hacche's model are invalid. Specifically, we obtained

$$\Delta \ln \left(\frac{M}{P}\right)_t = 1.61 + 0.21 \, \Delta \ln Y_t + 0.81 \, \Delta \ln (1 + r_t) + 0.26 \, \Delta \ln \left(\frac{M}{P}\right)_{t-1}$$
$$\quad (0.65) \ (0.09) \qquad\quad (0.31) \qquad\qquad\quad (0.12)$$

$$\quad - 0.40 \, \Delta \ln P_t - 0.23 \ln \left(\frac{M}{PY}\right)_{t-1} - 0.61 \ln (1 + r_{t-4})$$
$$\quad\quad (0.15) \qquad\quad (0.05) \qquad\qquad (0.21)$$

$$\quad + 0.14 \ln Y_{t-4}, \qquad\qquad\qquad\qquad\qquad\qquad (6.21)$$
$$\quad\quad (0.04)$$

$$\hat{\sigma} = 0.0091 \qquad R^2 = 0.69 \qquad \chi_{12}^2 = 6.4 \qquad \chi_5^2 = 1.02 \qquad \chi_1^2 = 0.7.$$

χ_5^2 tests for extracting one common factor from the generalization of (6.21) in which every variable also occurs with one further lag and χ_1^2 tests whether the corresponding root is zero: these two statistics show no indication of dynamic mis-specification or serial correlation in the residuals from (6.21) of one lag longer. It is possible that higher order lags may be significant and, although economic theory suggests that this is unlikely, such a possibility highlights the importance of the choice of the maintained hypothesis.

Table 6.6 Solved coefficients from equation (6.21)

Variable	$j = 0$	$j = 1$	$j = 2$	$j = 3$	$j = 4$
$\ln M_{t-1-j}$	1.03	-0.26	0.00	0.00	0.00
$\ln(1 + r_{t-j})$	0.81	-0.81	0.00	0.00	-0.61
$\ln Y_{t-j}$	0.21	0.02	0.00	0.00	0.14
$\ln P_{t-j}$	0.60	-0.63	0.26	0.00	0.00

The solved coefficients from (6.21) are recorded in table 6.6.[13]

The most obvious point about (6.21) is that it has four variables (with individually significant coefficients) which were omitted from (6.20). Moreover, the last three variables are *level* effects and strongly reject the hypothesis that there is a common root of unity (see equation (6.8) above). A major point about (6.21) is that it is simply a reformulated (though restricted) *levels* equation and the close match between the coefficients in tables 6.1 and 6.6 shows the advantages of such a formulation. The specific choice of parameters in (6.21) was not made to highlight this aspect, although we would stress that any investigator committed to analysing only data in differenced form – for whatever philosophical reasons – could never detect such a relationship. Rather, the form of (6.21) was based on the desire to enter separate decision variables with sensible economic interpretations for both long-run and short-run influences on the demand for money. Thus the coefficient of $\Delta \ln P_t$ shows a negative influence due to the rate of inflation, although, in equilibrium, the long-run elasticity of M with respect to P in (6.21) is unity. Next, previous disequilibria in the relationship between the levels of 'real' money and 'real' income affect current demand through the (inverse) 'velocity' measure $\ln(M/PY)_{t-1}$. Moreover, as shown below, this same variable allows one to derive a sensible long-run steady-state money demand function. The interest rate and income effects at four-period lags may be due in part to the inappropriate use of separate SA filters for the various data series, but long-run considerations suggest including some level measure of interest rates; the significant income coefficient immediately rejects the hypothesis of a long-run unit income elasticity.

Consider a steady-state growth path along which

$$\Delta \ln Y_t = \pi_1 \qquad \Delta \ln P_t = \pi_2 \qquad \Delta \ln(1 + r_t) = \pi_3 \qquad \Delta \ln M_t = \pi_4,$$

all of these growth rates being constants (which could be zero). Since (6.21) describes a stable difference equation with roots of 0.59 and 0.45, the time paths of the variables will converge to (taking $\pi_3 = 0$)

$$\pi_4 - \pi_2 = 1.61 + 0.21\pi_1 + 0.26(\pi_4 - \pi_2) - 0.40\pi_2 - 0.23 \ln(M/PY)$$
$$-0.61 \ln(1 + r) + 0.14 \ln Y \tag{6.22}$$

and hence

$$M/PY = K(1 + r)^{-2.6} Y^{0.6} (1 + \dot{p})^{-1.7},$$

where

$$K \approx \exp[7 + \pi_1 + 3.2(\pi_2 - \pi_4)] \tag{6.23}$$

using $\Delta \ln P = \ln(1 + \dot{p})$ (although our choice of formulation in (6.23) is obviously not unique). The long-run interest elasticity of M with respect to r evaluated at the mean of r yields -0.2 and the absolute value of this elasticity increases as r increases. However, the impact elasticity is positive in (6.21) and, if r_t increased steadily, the income velocity of M_t would appear to decrease and only later increase if plotted against r_t (see chart B in Hacche). Similar comments apply to the effects of $\dot{p}$.

The large income elasticity may reflect the considerable upsurge in M following the introduction of competition and credit control policies in 1971. Indeed, since we concur with the arguments presented by Hacche (1974) and Goodhart (1978) that aggregate relationships for M3 like any of those presented above are not appropriate for the post-1971 period as important variables are omitted, we have not attempted further economic modelling of the M/PY relationship (although we would expect equations of the form of (6.21) to provide a better basis for future research than equations like (6.18)). Nevertheless, it is worth stressing that the dynamic model (6.21) seems consonant with the time-series properties of the data and yields a long-run solution which appears to be fully consistent with standard economic theory statements of the demand for money function (see, *inter alia*, Artis and Lewis, 1976; Friedman, 1956, ch. 1; Johnson, 1971, ch. 13).

4 Conclusion and Summary

This paper has attempted to clarify the nature of serial correlation and its relationships with dynamic specification, differencing and seasonal adjustment using the common factor interpretation proposed by Sargan (1980a). The problems inherent in imposing arbitrary restrictions were stressed and compared with the alternative of commencing from a general dynamic relationship and sequentially simplifying it according to the information in the data. The COMFAC algorithm was applied to the demand for money function of Hacche (1974) and provided evidence against his dynamic specification in the differences of the variables. An alternative model in levels, which nevertheless avoided any 'spurious' regressions problems, was estimated and tested. The derived long-run properties of the levels model seemed sensible and its coefficients were close to those of the general dynamic relationship. We conclude that it is perfectly feasible to test differencing and serial correlation restrictions in practice, and that 'econometric' models appropriately formulated can prove superior to 'time-series' descriptions which explicitly ignore long-run information in the data.

Notes

1 Although we do not explicitly consider situations in which serial correlation derives from incorrect functional form, much of the analysis would apply to attempts to represent such autocorrelation by an autoregressive scheme.

2   The root of the polynomial $1 - \beta_1 L = 0$ is $1/\beta_1$ and for single equations this is the usual terminology (see Granger and Newbold, 1977b). However, economics is a multivariate subject and on a matrix interpretation β_1 corresponds to a latent root of the equation $|\lambda I - \beta_1| = 0$. For this reason we refer to β_1 as the (latent) root and for stability and stationarity our terminology requires that roots lie inside the unit circle. The idea of common roots also occurs in the literature on autoregressive moving-average models (see Box and Jenkins, 1976) where the roots are common to all the variables *and the error term*. Thus, the occurrence of such roots poses identification problems, and we shall refer to this situation as one having *redundant* roots.

3   This is actually a likelihood ratio test which differs from the sequence of Wald tests proposed by Sargan (1980a) and used in the approach described below.

4   See, for example, the Letters to the Editor of *The Times*, April 1977.

5   One does not have to be a time-series analyst to doubt the credibility of equations in which $R^2 > d$, yet economists regularly publish such results (see, for example, Mizon (1974) and the models in Waelbroeck (1976)).

6   A further interesting transformation of (6.8) is

$$\Delta y_t = \gamma_0 \Delta x_t + (\beta_1 - 1)(y_{t-1} - x_{t-1}) + (\gamma_0 + \gamma_1 + \beta_1 - 1)x_{t-1} + v_t.$$

This emphasizes that the *change* in y_t depends on the *change* in x_t, the 'disequilibrium' between the *levels* of y_t and x_t in the previous period, and the level of x_{t-1} (which measures any departure from a long-run unit elasticity if y_t and x_t are in logarithms): see equation (6.21) below.

7   A common root of zero entails the factor $1 - 0L$ and imposing the zero for any root which is negligible shortens the lag length by one for every variable; this could reflect initial over-inclusion of lagged variables.

8   Hacche's model, its justification and the assumptions whose validity is in question are set out clearly in Courakis (1978, pp. 539–42).

9   As the exercise was illustrative and the sample of 35 observations from 1963(i) to 1971 (iii) proved too small for sensible estimates of (6.19) when $J = 4$, most of our estimates are based on fitting equations to the entire sample period provided by Courakis (1963(i)–1975(iii)). We have used r_t unlagged rather than lagged one quarter as in Hacche, and the variable $1 + r_t$ denotes $100 + R_t$ where R_t is measured in percentages.

10   The parameter values input to the COMFAC algorithm can be estimated in any desired way, and hence using instrumental variables or maximum likelihood estimates creates no additional complications.

11   These and the ensuing results should be contrasted with those in Courakis (1978) to obtain a full picture, especially regarding the elasticity estimates shown in Courakis's table 4, p. 546.

12   Strictly, since we are choosing the largest of four test statistics, we need to set the type I error of each test at about 0.01 to have an overall 5 per cent size and hence we cannot reject the unrestricted four-roots hypothesis with 95 per cent confidence. However, the largest χ_3^2 is significant at the 0.025 level, providing 90 per cent confidence in the overall test outcome.

13   If both $\Delta \ln(1 + r_{t-2})$ and $\Delta \ln P_{t-2}$ are added to (6.21), they have coefficients of -0.79 (0.48) and 0.26 (0.27) respectively and raise R^2 to 0.71.

7

An Empirical Application and Monte Carlo Analysis of Tests of Dynamic Specification

with Grayham E. Mizon

Preamble

This 1980 follow-up to chapter 6 resulted from trying to use COMFAC as a sequential simpli-fication device in empirical analysis, and not being very successful. Such an outcome might have been due to the poor power properties of the procedure, and the Monte Carlo sections address that issue. Alternatively, unsuccessful outcomes could arise from COMFAC being a poor representation of economic agents' behaviour. At the time, we inclined to the latter view and so tried various other model reduction devices, retaining COMFAC as a destructive testing device for invalid 'autocorrelation corrections'. Also note the strong caveat about arbitrarily imposing error correction representations without testing their data coherency; and the discussion of diagnostic testing of the initial model.

By the time chapter 7 appeared, the closely related work at CORE on model reduction had begun to provide a theoretical rationale for general-to-simple, leading directly to the formaliza-tion of part III. Using the terminology in Spanos (1986), the evolving framework distinguished between the statistical model used to characterize the data (i.e. the initial general specification) and the econometric model, which must be interpretable in terms of the underlying economic theory and be a valid simplification of the statistical model. Thus, unless COMFAC restrictions had an economic theoretical basis (which chapter 4 suggested was limited) there seemed little reason to seek such a simplification. Nevertheless, simplification procedures in general became central to the approach.

The empirical section of this chapter involves many of the same difficulties as we confronted for UK money demand, including seasonality (especially of farmers' incomes), lag length

Reprinted from *Review of Economic Studies*, 47 (1980) 21–45. An earlier version of this paper, based on work done while Mizon was visiting the Current Economic Analysis Division of Statistics Canada during August and September 1975, was presented at the European Meeting of the Econometric Society, Helsinki, in August 1976. The financial and research assistance provided by Statistics Canada, and the valuable computational assistance provided by Frank Srba and Tony Chan at LSE, and Peter Smith at Southampton, are gratefully acknowledged. The authors also wish to thank Denis Sargan for his advice and for the use of his COMFAC program to calculate the Wald criteria, and are indebted to Stephen Yeo for his comments and help in interpreting the Canadian data.

This research was supported in part by a grant from the Social Science Research Council to the Quan-titative Economics Programme at LSE.

selection, the choice of simplification and the constancy of the chosen specification. While the focus is on dynamic specification, the treatment is much more like succeeding than preceding studies. Thus, like chapters 1 and 4, chapter 7 is one of the main bridges between my pre- and post-1980 views in this volume, noting that the first and seventh chapters appeared in 1980, whereas chapter 4 was partly written during a six-month visit to CORE in 1980 and more clearly reveals the influence of Jean-François Richard's thinking on mine.

1 Introduction

The shortage of detailed information from economic theory to determine the dynamic structure of economic relationships has long been recognized (e.g. Nerlove, 1972), and has caused some researchers recently to rely almost exclusively on the methods of time-series analysis for model building with economic time-series data. Furthermore, a number of studies of the forecasting performance of econometric models *vis à vis* that of time-series models (e.g. Naylor et al., 1972; and further references in Prothero and Wallis, 1976) have been interpreted as demonstrating the superiority of time-series model building methodology over that of econometrics. To the extent the econometric models have been based on static economic theory, with dynamics possibly introduced via serially correlated error processes, or have been in the mould of simple models involving first-order dynamics such as the partial adjustment and adaptive expectations models, the implied criticism of econometric modelling is probably valid. However, econometricians need not restrict the range of models and techniques in this way, for they are fortunate in being able to combine structural information from economic theory (especially for long-run equilibrium or steady-state behaviour) with the techniques of time-series analysis *and* those of econometrics. We believe that the econometrician's search for an acceptable representation of the process generating the data being analysed is made easier by the use of both economic theory and the methods of time-series analysis, and that the latter are complementary to econometric methods rather than substitutes for them. Rather than abandoning an econometric approach to modelling altogether and using 'black-box' time-series methods, we favour an approach which uses reasonable statistical procedures to test various hypotheses (which are too often arbitrarily selected and *assumed* to be valid), contained within a general unrestricted model, and then incorporates this evidence in a model whose structure is suggested by general economic considerations, to obtain an adequate approximation to the data generation process.

Our aim in this paper is to employ some of the statistical procedures for determining dynamic specification, first proposed in Sargan (1964a) and extended by Sargan (1980a) (see also Mizon, 1977a; and Sargan and Mehta, 1983), to illustrate how their use, together with the guidelines provided by the economic theory of the demand for durable goods, can lead to the selection of a useful model of Canadian expenditure on consumer durables. Since the tests of dynamic specification used do not have high power against *all* alternative hypotheses, and only their asymptotic properties have been analysed, we also perform a controlled simulation study of the small sample size and power characteristics of the Wald and likelihood ratio tests of common factor restrictions, and the Lagrange multiplier (proposed by Godfrey, 1978; Breusch and Pagan, 1980), Wald and likelihood ratio tests for residual autocorrelation.

Another important purpose of this simulation study is to illustrate the value of a computationally inexpensive Monte Carlo analysis of problems not yet having analytical solutions. In doing this we emphasize the importance of using analytical information (especially from asymptotic theory) to control the simulation, the value of a carefully chosen experimental design, and the use of response surfaces as convenient summaries which help reduce the specificity of Monte Carlo results.

Procedures for determining dynamic specification in econometric equations are briefly discussed in the next section. This is followed by an analysis of the demand for consumer durables (excluding automobiles) equation from a quarterly econometric model of Statistics Canada. The Monte Carlo methods to be used for analysing the finite sample properties of test statistics whose asymptotic distribution is known are described in section 4 and then applied in section 5 to investigate two of the specification tests used in the empirical study. The final section provides a brief summary and the conclusion.

2 Testing Procedures

Perhaps the most common analysis of dynamic specification undertaken by econometricians has been distributed lag analysis, in which a major concern has been to achieve acceptable finite parameterizations of possibly infinite distributed lags, with a primary aim of making parameter estimation feasible and simple. Though the distributed lag literature contains much analysis of the problem of choosing the shape of lag distributions, little attention has been paid to determining empirically the value of the maximum lag in such relationships (or in the case of rational distributed lags to determining the polynomial orders); for example, Dhrymes (1971) in a whole book on distributed lags devotes four pages to the determination of their order. However, for Almon distributed lags Godfrey and Poskitt (1975) have considered the problem of determining the optimal order of an approximating polynomial given the order of the distributed lag, Trivedi and Pagan (1979) present an extended analysis of this problem, and Sargan (1980b) suggests tests of hypotheses about the maximum lag. Additionally, it is very common to find empirical economic studies which use time-series data but fit equations based on static models (e.g. the estimation of Cobb–Douglas or constant elasticity of substitution production functions and the estimation of demand equation systems), and only when significant serial correlation in the residuals is observed are dynamic formulations adopted. However, since the Durbin–Watson and Durbin h statistics (see Durbin, 1970) are the most common tests of mis-specification used in this context, the prevalent dynamic formulations are ones with first-order (or occasionally simple fourth-order for quarterly data) autoregressive errors, and so *untested* common factor restrictions are imposed which can lead to the acceptance of models with mis-specified dynamic structure and hence result in incorrect inferences about mean lags and long-run elasticities and propensities – see chapter 6. The following analysis provides a framework within which these problems can be tackled, by having a general unrestricted dynamic model as the maintained hypothesis and systematically simplifying in the light of the sample evidence. This can be done in many ways since there is no unique ordering of the hypotheses under consideration and below we examine testing for the presence of common factors and the order of dynamics. Indeed one of the essential features of the procedure for determining dynamic specification outlined in Sargan (1980a) (and denoted COMFAC below) is that it starts from the most general model to be considered (i.e. including the maximum number of lags) and tests sequentially whether restricted versions of it are consistent with the data. This is in marked contrast with the common practice of starting with the simplest (i.e. most restricted) model and attempting to determine whether it is necessary to consider a more general one. The contrast between the tests of specification of the former approach (which systematically tests restricted models within a general maintained hypothesis) and the tests of mis-specification of the latter approach (which tests the need to consider more general models usually without a specified maintained hypothesis) is emphasized and discussed in Mizon (1977b).

The class of models considered has the form

$$\theta(L)'x_t = w_t \tag{7.1}$$

where $\theta(L)$ is a vector of $k+1$ polynomials in the lag operator L of orders m_0, $m_1, m_2, \ldots, m_k$ respectively, with $\theta_0(L)$ operating on the normalized or dependent variable y_t, and $\theta_j(L)$ operating on the regressor variable z_{jt}, $j = 1, 2, \ldots, k$. The values of m_j, $j = 0, 1, 2, \ldots, k$ which denote the largest lag for each variable are taken to be sufficiently large that the error w_t may be treated as serially independent with zero mean and constant variance σ_w^2. This class of model is denoted $AD(m_0, m_1, \ldots, m_k)$ for autoregressive–distributed lag with the relevant orders shown in parenthesis and the number of different regressor variables equal to k. The model (7.1) for the maximum polynomial orders $\bar{m}_0, \bar{m}_1, \bar{m}_2, \ldots, \bar{m}_k$, which must be specified *a priori*, forms the maintained hypothesis. Two specializations are considered having the forms

$$\rho(L)\alpha(L)'x_t = \varepsilon_t \tag{7.2a}$$

when $\rho(L)$ is a scalar polynomial in L of order r, $\alpha(L)$ is a vector of $k+1$ polynomials in L of orders $l_0, l_1, \ldots, l_k$, and the error ε_t is white noise, and

$$\theta^*(L)'x_t = v_t \tag{7.2b}$$

where the restrictions on $\theta(L)$ to define $\theta^*(L)$ are chosen on the basis of economic theory considerations relating to the likely decision variables of agents, a point amplified below.

Concentrating on (7.2a) first, comparison of (7.1) and (7.2a) shows that (7.2a) will be valid if $\theta(L)$ in (7.1) satisfies

$$\rho(L)\alpha(L) = \theta(L) \tag{7.3}$$

which implies that the polynomials in $\theta(L)$ have a *common factor* of $\rho(L)$. However, (7.2a) can be written alternatively, but equivalently, as

$$\alpha(L)'x_t = u_t$$
$$\rho(L)u_t = \varepsilon_t \tag{7.4}$$

which is a dynamic linear model with errors generated by an autoregression of order r so that $\alpha(L)$ represents systematic dynamics and $\rho(L)$ error dynamics as in Mizon (1977a). Of course, it is possible that serially correlated errors arise because of an underlying moving average, or combined autoregressive moving-average process rather than an autoregressive process, but because moving-average error processes pose identification, estimation and testing problems we consider autoregressive error processes only. However, the correlogram for a moving-average process can be reasonably approximated by an autoregressive process (see chapter 5), and indeed the Lagrange multiplier test for residual serial correlation does not depend on whether the underlying process is moving average or autoregressive (see Godfrey, 1978).

Empirically to determine the dynamic specification of the model (7.1) as a specialization of the type (7.2a) it is necessary to determine the order of dynamics (i.e. the length of lag for each variable $\hat{m}_j \leqslant \bar{m}_j$, $j = 0, 1, \ldots, k$) and to test whether the factorization (7.3) of $\theta(L)$ is consistent with the data for some value of r, $\hat{r} \leqslant \min(\hat{m}_j)$. This is formally equivalent to determining the orders of systematic dynamics $l_0, l_1, \ldots, l_k$ and the order of error dynamics r, and this equivalence suggests the following procedures. It is noted though that the empirical implementation of these two approaches, despite their formal equivalence, might lead to different model choices.

One procedure first determines how many common factors are consistent with the data at the chosen significance level, within the maintained hypothesis, and secondly tests for zero roots among the set of $\hat{r}$ common roots extracted. The first stage of this procedure can use the COMFAC algorithm with unrestricted parameter estimates for the maintained hypothesis obtained by any desired estimation methods such as ordinary least squares (OLS) or instrumental variables (IV).

The second stage requires parameter estimates for the model $\rho_{\hat{r}}(L)\alpha_{m-\hat{r}}(L)'x_t = \varepsilon_t$ and these can be obtained by method 5.1 in chapter 13. A property of this procedure is that the lag lengths can only differ across variables to the extent that the *a priori* specified values of maximum lag, $\bar{m}_j$ ($j = 0, 1, \ldots, k$) differ. This procedure is illustrated in the next section as it can be a useful approach when it is desired to test a set of common factor restrictions.

An alternative procedure first conducts sequential tests for reducing the order of dynamics until a test statistic exceeds the chosen critical value, and secondly uses the COMFAC algorithm to test how many common factors there are in the model of type (7.1) (but with lag lengths fixed at the values determined in the first stage). The determination of the order of dynamics in the first stage can be done for all $k + 1$ variables simultaneously, or for each variable separately, but in either case the test statistics can be compared with critical values from the central χ^2 distribution asymptotically, though with small sample corrections and degrees of freedom adjustments they can be compared with the critical values of the F distribution. If all the regressors are predetermined, the first stage only requires the unrestricted estimation of the parameters of the maintained hypothesis which can be done by OLS, and OLS parameter estimates will also be appropriate for COMFAC in stage two for the model of form (7.1) with the orders of dynamics determined by the first stage. It is only when the order of common factors has been determined that the 'more complicated' estimation methods are needed.

The details of these and other procedures are discussed in Mizon (1977a), but it is relevant to emphasize that for each of the two stages within each procedure the hypotheses to be tested form a uniquely ordered sequence, and that provided the testing is carried out as indicated in Anderson (1971, ch. 3.2) (i.e. beginning with the most general model and sequentially testing more restricted models), the tests induced in each stage will have high power asymptotically. It should be noted, though, that the hypotheses in each of the two stages are uniquely ordered because they are concerned solely with the order of dynamics (maximum lags) and the number of common factors. We are in practice, of course, interested in additional hypotheses, and this makes it more difficult to make statements about statistical power. Similarly, since the stages of the two-stage procedures are not independent it is not easy to determine the power of the procedures as a whole, though all the tests involved will reject any fixed invalid hypothesis with probability unity as the sample size tends to infinity, and section 5 contains simulation evidence on their small sample behaviour.

The determination of the number of common factors that can be extracted from models of the form (7.1) without significant loss of fit is an important part of the procedures described above. In fact, this problem consists of testing the sequence of hypotheses

$$\rho_r(L)\alpha_{m-r}(L) = \theta_m(L) \tag{7.5}$$

for $r = 0, 1, 2, \ldots, \underline{m}$ when $\underline{m} = \min(\bar{m}_i)$ and $\theta_m(L)$ is the vector of $k+1$ polynomials in L for the maintained hypothesis. The common factor restrictions implicit in (7.5) can be written generally as $f(\theta) = 0$, so that given unrestricted parameter estimates $\hat{\theta}$ such that

$$T^{1/2}(\hat{\theta} - \theta) \underset{a}{\sim} N(0, \sigma_w^2 V)$$

(which implies that

$$T^{1/2}[f(\hat{\theta}) - f(\theta)] \underset{a}{\sim} N(0, \Omega)$$

where $\Omega = \sigma_w^2(JVJ')$ with $J = \text{plim}(\partial f/\partial \theta'))$, the Wald testing principle can be used to yield the test statistic $\eta_3 = Tf(\hat{\theta})'\hat{\Omega}^{-1}f(\hat{\theta})$. When $H_0: f(\theta) = 0$ is true, η_3 is asymptotically distributed as a central χ^2 variate with R (usually $R = rk$ when there are r common factors as in (7.5)) degrees of freedom. Although the estimates of θ are easily obtained, the restrictions $f(\theta) = 0$ and their derivatives can be complicated to compute, as the following examples illustrate. First, consider the linear regression model $y_t = \gamma z_t + u_t$ when $u_t = \rho u_{t-1} + \varepsilon_t$, $|\rho| < 1$, so that the common factor restricted transformed structure is $y_t = \rho y_{t-1} + \gamma z_t - \rho\gamma z_{t-1} + \varepsilon_t$, which is to be compared with the unrestricted model $y_t = \theta_0 y_{t-1} + \theta_1 z_t + \theta_2 z_{t-1} + w_t$. The constraint implicit in moving from the unrestricted model to the restricted transformed structure is $f(\theta) = \theta_2 + \theta_0\theta_1 = 0$. This is discussed by Sargan (1964a), and is seen to be easily parameterized and tested. Second, consider the slightly more general model (which is more likely to be encountered in practice): $y_t = \beta y_{t-1} + \gamma_0 z_t + \gamma_1 z_{t-1} + u_t$ with $u_t = \rho u_{t-1} + \varepsilon_t$, $|\rho| < 1$. The restricted transformed structure here is $y_t = (\rho + \beta)y_{t-1} - \rho\beta y_{t-2} + \gamma_0 z_t + (\gamma_1 - \rho\gamma_0)z_{t-1} - \rho\gamma_1 z_{t-2} + \varepsilon_t$ which has four parameters to be estimated compared with the unrestricted model $y_t = \theta_0 y_{t-1} + \theta_1 y_{t-2} + \theta_2 z_t + \theta_3 z_{t-1} + \theta_4 z_{t-2} + w_t$ which has five. Hence there is one restriction implicit in the restricted model, but it is more difficult to parameterize, for the mapping between the restricted and unrestricted parameters

$$\theta_0 = \rho + \beta \qquad \theta_2 = \gamma_0 \qquad \theta_4 = -\rho\gamma_1$$

$$\theta_1 = -\rho\beta \qquad \theta_3 = \gamma_1 - \rho\gamma_0$$

implies the restriction

$$\theta_4 + \hat{\rho}\theta_3 + \hat{\rho}^2\theta_2 = 0 \quad \text{when} \quad \hat{\rho} = -(\theta_4 + \theta_1\theta_2)/(\theta_3 + \theta_0\theta_2).$$

Therefore even for this *second*-order dynamics example the calculation of the Wald test statistic is complicated, and the degree of complexity increases with the order of dynamics and the number of common factors being tested. These considerations led Sargan (1980a) to note that the constraints $f(\theta) = 0$ can be expressed in the form that a certain matrix, whose elements consist of the θ coefficients and zeros, should have a given rank, which can in turn be translated into equivalent determinantal conditions. We have adopted Sargan's approach in this study and used the numerical algorithms, called COMFAC, developed by Sargan and Sylwestrowicz (1976a) for use with the program GIVE. It should be noted that the use of the Wald testing principle means that the computational expense of estimating the parameters corresponding to *all* hypotheses, which is required for likelihood ratio tests, is avoided. This is especially important when methods more complicated than OLS have to be used, and problems associated with multiple optima can be expected – see Sargan and Mehta (1983). Statistically the two principles lead to asymptotically equivalent tests, and since the COMFAC algorithm is computationally inexpensive and easy to use, the Wald test seems preferable to the likelihood ratio test, unless it has poorer finite sample properties. Since the simulation study of the finite sample behaviour of both tests in section 5 below does not provide any clear grounds for preferring either test, the computational advantage of the Wald test led us to use that form.

An important choice in using any of the sequential testing procedures outlined above is that of significance levels. Clearly, in order to control the probability of type I error for a procedure as a whole it is necessary to choose the significance levels for each test in the sequence of tests carefully. For example, the second procedure mentioned above has a significance level of $\delta_a = 1 - [1 - \varepsilon(a)]^n$ for the sequence of tests for reducing the order of dynamics – stage (a) – when n is the maximum number of tests possible in the sequence and $\varepsilon(a)$ is the significance level common to all tests in this sequence. The value of n will be determined by the maintained maximum order of dynamics and any *a priori* specified minimum order of dynamics for stage (a); it should be noted that it is not necessary to use the same significance level for all tests in the sequence; in fact $\delta_a = 1 - \Pi_{i=1}^n [1 - \varepsilon_i(a)]$ if the $\varepsilon_i(a)$ differ for all tests. Stage (b) tests for the number of common factors and the significance level for this sequence of tests is $\delta_b = 1 - \Pi_{i=1}^{\hat{m}} [1 - \varepsilon_i(b)]$, or $1 - [1 - \varepsilon(b)]^{\hat{m}}$ if a common $\varepsilon(b)$ is used for all tests when $\hat{m}$ is the order of dynamics determined in stage (a). The significance level for the procedure as a whole is more difficult to derive because stages (a) and (b) are not statistically independent.

However, it is possible to use the Bonferroni inequality to provide a lower bound $\bar{p}$ on the probability of *not* making a type I error. If δ is the overall significance level then $1 - \delta \geqslant \bar{p} = 1 - \delta_a - \delta_b$ when δ_a and δ_b are as defined above. As an example, consider a case when $\bar{p}$ is chosen as 0.9 (i.e. the overall significance level will be at most 10 per cent) and δ_a and δ_b are both 0.05; then if $n = 4$, $\varepsilon(a)$ will have to be 0.0128 with critical values corresponding to a probability of 0.0064 for two-sided alternatives. The value of $\varepsilon(b)$ would be similarly determined depending on the value of $\hat{m}$. Hence for this example the significance levels used for the individual tests in the sequences of stages (a) and (b) would have to be approximately 1 per cent in order to ensure that the procedure's significance level is no more than 10 per cent. This point is often ignored in applied studies, in which typically a series of tests is performed using conventional significance levels for each test, so that the overall significance level can be very large. However, to the extent that the consequences of inconsistency are believed to be more serious than those of inefficiency in estimation, the implicit choice of large significance levels might be reasonable. Such judgements, and decisions in practice, though, are not independent of the degree of generality of the chosen maintained hypothesis.

The above discussion has concentrated on particular procedures for determining dynamic specification, but these are only a part of a specification search. The problem of model choice or specification search can be profitably thought of and approached as a decision problem. The decision criterion might be a measure of forecasting accuracy and/or the desire to gain detailed structural information about the process generating the data relevant to the problem. The actions then consist of the choice of functional form, of the set of variables (including the length of lag on variables as well as selection from a set of different variables), of the error structure and of the data set. There will usually be many alternatives for each category of action mentioned above, and relative to the most general models to be considered most of these alternatives can be generated by sets of restrictions, so that there will be a collection of hypotheses from which an acceptable subset has to be chosen. Searches relative to a specified set of models have been categorized into specification and mis-specification searches by Mizon (1977b). Specification searches start with an *a priori* maintained hypothesis H_m, and then systematically search for a subset (which might consist of one model) of acceptable models within H_m. The hypotheses considered in such local searches usually form a composite hypothesis, so that the problems caused by lack of structure or unique ordering amongst them arise, but these problems can be reduced by exploiting the structure or ordering that does exist, and by imposing some structure on the remaining hypotheses. In fact, this is precisely what is done in the discussion above of testing for common factors and lag lengths. The economic theory considerations which lead to (7.2b) as a restricted version of (7.1) provide another form of specification search. Since these specification searches are attempting to find an acceptable simplification of H_m they have been called simplification searches by Leamer (1978).

An obvious difficulty with any specification search procedure is the choice of H_m, and even if the specification searches are done efficiently they may result in a poor choice of model if H_m was chosen badly. In order to guard against this possibility tests of mis-specification can be conducted which will check the adequacy of the chosen H_m. The Durbin–Watson and the diagnostic test statistics of time-series analysis are usually employed in exactly this way. Many of these mis-specification searches use Lagrange multiplier (LM) test statistics, as opposed to the Wald (W) or likelihood ratio (LR) test statistics which are usually associated with specification searches. Although the three test statistics (W, LR and LM) for a particular null hypothesis against a given alternative have the same asymptotic distribution, and the differences in their computational costs are known for particular examples, little is known about their small sample behaviour. In section 5 therefore we conduct a Monte Carlo analysis of the three test statistics for a widely used test of mis-specification, that for first-order autocorrelation in dynamic models.

In the next section we illustrate the use of specification and mis-specification searches in a model of consumers' expenditure on non-automobile durable goods in Canada. COMFAC is used as a sequential simplification procedure within a general maintained hypothesis. The results indicate that it is rarely possible to reject an autoregressive error specification, but the simulation findings in section 5 encourage us to emphasize that failure to reject a hypothesis does not necessarily imply its acceptance, and so we look for alternative simplifications using economic theory considerations.

3 Empirical Application

As an illustration of the practical use and empirical performance of these procedures for determining dynamic specification we now analyse a model of Canadian expenditure on consumer durables (excluding automobiles, expenditure on which is markedly affected by the Auto Pact with the USA), which is one of the equations from Statistics Canada's quarterly econometric model. The set of explanatory variables consists of those that either appeared in the 1975 version of the quarterly model or were considered for inclusion in it. The data are for the aggregate Canadian economy, quarterly and seasonally unadjusted for the period 1960(i)–1976(ii), giving a total of 66 observations, the last six of which are used for parameter constancy tests. As the number of lagged variables created was varied, the exact sample size used for estimation is recorded in each instance below. The dependent variable C is the per capita constant dollar expenditure on consumer durables excluding automobiles in 1971 prices. The current dollar expenditure figures divided by this series provide the implicit deflator for non-automobile consumer durable expenditure P_D. The income series used, Y, is per capita current dollar personal disposable income deflated by the implicit deflator P_T for total consumer expenditure on durables and non-durables in 1971 prices. This income series includes net income received by farm operators from farming operations which is highly seasonal, being negative for all but the third quarter of many years. It seems unreasonable to believe that the economic agents receiving this income base their durable expenditure decisions quarter by quarter on such a variable, and this is precisely the type of situation in which 'permanent income' concepts seem most relevant. To focus attention on other issues, however, the analysis was conducted without disaggregating income, but since the model chosen had a seasonally varying average propensity to spend (equivalent to a simple form of seasonal adjustment), this pre-simplification is unlikely to have seriously distorted the results. In any case, very similar results were obtained using a 'smoothed' series for farm income (of a quarter of annual income). The relative price variable PR was calculated as P_D/P_T and further details concerning all these series can be obtained from the Statistics Canada publication *National Income and Expenditure Accounts*, volume 3, September 1975.

The general form of model considered below was $AD(m_0, m_1, m_2)$ as in equation (7.1) with $k = 2$, the dependent variable being $c = \log C$ (lower case letters denote the natural logarithm of upper case variables) with $y = \log Y$ and $p = \log PR$ as regressor variables and the intercept varying seasonally.[1] The model form assumed for a steady-state growth path of all the variables was

$$C/Y = K_i Y^{\lambda_1} PR^{\lambda_2}$$

where K_i varies seasonally and depends (potentially) on the growth rates of Y and/or PR. Out of steady state, the precise lag structure cannot be specified *a priori* and since the quarterly data series provided a sample of 66 observations a relatively general maintained hypothesis for the orders of the dynamic reactions was selected, with maximum lags $\bar{m}_j$ set at 8 for all j. This formulation allowed a great deal of flexibility in the determination of the dynamic structure, particularly for the implied shape and length of the distributed lag relationship between c and the regressors p and y. OLS estimation was used throughout as any contemporaneous feedback from c to y seemed unlikely to be important. Also, for models with $\hat{m} = 4$, the likelihood ratio criterion proposed in Sargan (1964a) suggested that models in the logarithms of the variables were preferable to models in levels.

The correlograms of the series c_t, y_t and p_t are shown in table 7.1, and as with many economic time series, the correlograms are slow to die out. Also, there is marked seasonality in the c_t and y_t series, although not in phase.

Given the seasonal pattern it is not obvious how to determine the model specification; in particular it is possible that most non-zero coefficients occur at seasonal lags, so that testing for successively shorter lags than the pre-specified maximum lags need not be optimal. Similarly the seasonal behaviour in c might be represented well by the seasonality in y and p, with or without seasonal dummy variables. The hypotheses corresponding to these alternatives provide an example of a set of hypotheses which are not ordered, so that alternative testing procedures can yield different results. Nevertheless, some simplification seemed desirable and so we chose to test for successively shorter lags, anticipating $m = 4$ as a relatively parsimonious compromise. Although the results we report include seasonal dummy variables we also investigated models without them, but simplification and data-instigated searches

Table 7.1   Correlograms for c, y, p over eight periods

Variable	$j = 1$	$j = 2$	$j = 3$	$j = 4$	$j = 5$	$j = 6$	$j = 7$	$j = 8$
c_{t-j}	0.82	0.89	0.81	0.98	0.79	0.86	0.77	0.96
y_{t-j}	0.88	0.84	0.88	0.99	0.87	0.81	0.86	0.98
p_{t-j}	0.96	0.93	0.92	0.92	0.86	0.80	0.78	0.77

always led us to models which included them. The sequence of tests to determine the order of lag length resulted in $\hat{m} \leq 4$, the value of the test for H_0: $m = 4$ against H_1: $m = 5$ being 1.27, consonant with a variate approximately distributed as $F(4, 27)$ on H_0. Table 7.2 records the estimates for $\hat{m} = 4$.

In table 7.2, coefficient standard errors are shown in parentheses, $\hat{k}_0$ is the intercept, $\hat{k}_j$ ($j = 1, 2, 3$) are the coefficients of the seasonal dummies, T denotes the sample size, s is the standard deviation of the residuals and Σ denotes the sum of the lag coefficients. The four test statistics $\eta_7(T_2)$, $\eta_6(T_2, T - \kappa)$, $\eta_5(n - 4)$ and $\eta_M(n/2)$ are respectively asymptotically distributed as $\chi^2_{T_2}$, $F(T_2, T - \kappa)$, χ^2_{n-4} and $\chi^2_{n/2}$ on their nulls and in pairs test parameter constancy (see chapter 11 and Chow, 1960) and residual autocorrelation (see Pierce, 1971; Godfrey, 1978; also section 5 below), with T_2 post-sample observations, κ parameters in the estimation equation and n residual autocorrelations. The lag polynomial in c_t has two pairs of complex roots ($0.40 \pm 0.22i$ and $-0.26 \pm 0.43i$) and apart from a number of redundant parameters and some ill-determined individual coefficient estimates, the equation seems to be an adequate description of the data on c_t.

In steady-state growth with $\Delta_1 c = g_1$, $\Delta_1 y = g_2$, $\Delta_1 p = g_3$, the long-run solution for the model in table 7.2 is

$$C = K_i Y^{1.3} PR^{-0.55} \tag{7.6}$$

where $K_i = \exp(-2.52 + 0.35Q_1 + 0.25Q_2 + 0.54Q_3 - 2.21g_2 - 1.55g_3)$ and Q_i denotes the ith seasonal, noting that $g_1 = 1.3g_2 - 0.55g_3$ from equation (7.6). Thus, K_i falls as either g_2 or g_3 increases, and (for $g_2 = 0.006, g_3 = 0.012$) varies from a high of 0.13 for the fourth quarter to a low of 0.08 for the first quarter so that C/Y behaves seasonally both directly through K_i and indirectly through any seasonality in Y and PR. Finally, C is income elastic but price inelastic.

Several simplifications of the model with $\hat{m} = 4$ seemed worth investigating. First, we tested the hypothesis that the dynamic structure could be represented by an error autoregression and applied the COMFAC procedure to the estimates in table 7.2, obtaining the results shown in table 7.3. Setting the overall test size at 10 per cent, the hypothesis of three (of fewer) common factors cannot be rejected whereas four common factors can be. Nevertheless, the estimates in table 7.2 are not very consonant with the hypothesis of an AD(1, 1, 1) model with third-order autoregressive errors since (for example) the coefficients of y_{t-2} and p_{t-2} are far larger than the corresponding coefficients at $t - 1$. Indeed, estimation of such a model (from AD(1, 1, 1) and $\eta_M(3)$ initial values) yielded the marked increase in s to 0.025

Table 7.2 Estimates for AD(4, 4, 4) with constant and three seasonal dummy variables

Variable	$j = 0$	$j = 1$	$j = 2$	$j = 3$	$j = 4$	Σ
c_{t-j}	-1	0.30 (0.16)	-0.05 (0.16)	0.09 (0.17)	-0.05 (0.16)	-0.71
y_{t-j}	0.42 (0.21)	-0.05 (0.22)	0.39 (0.21)	0.21 (0.18)	-0.04 (0.18)	0.93
p_{t-j}	-0.62 (0.31)	-0.69 (0.53)	1.24 (0.55)	-0.75 (0.57)	0.43 (0.43)	-0.39
k_j	-1.79 (0.57)	0.25 (0.08)	0.18 (0.08)	0.38 (0.09)	–	

$T = 55$ $R^2 = 0.9948$ $s = 0.0227$ $\eta_7(6) = 12.7$ $\eta_6(6, 37) = 0.93$

$\eta_5(8) = 15.1$ $\eta_M(6) = 3.5$

Table 7.3   Tests of COMFAC restrictions

No. of common factors	Direct tests		Incremental tests	
	Degrees of freedom	Value of test statistic	Degrees of freedom	Value of test statistic
1	2	0.47	2	0.47
2	4	1.24	2	0.77
3	6	6.09	2	4.85
4	8	32.01	2	25.92

shown in equation (7.7) (possibly because of multiple optima problems – see Sargan and Mehta, 1983):

$$\hat{c}_t = \underset{(0.33)}{-0.98} + \underset{(0.04)}{0.32Q_{1t}} + \underset{(0.04)}{0.12Q_{2t}} + \underset{(0.05)}{0.38Q_{3t}} + \underset{(0.16)}{0.66c_{t-1}} + \underset{(0.15)}{0.69y_t} - \underset{(0.22)}{0.25y_{t-1}}$$

$$\underset{(0.22)}{-1.03p_t} + \underset{(0.28)}{0.80p_{t-1}} + \hat{u}_t \tag{7.7}$$

$$\hat{u}_t = \underset{(0.21)}{-0.54\hat{u}_{t-1}} - \underset{(0.20)}{0.58\hat{u}_{t-2}} - \underset{(0.19)}{0.19\hat{u}_{t-3}}$$

$$T = 52 \qquad s = 0.0250 \qquad \eta_7\,(6) = 19.8 \qquad \eta_5(8) = 10.5$$
$$\eta_3^*\,(6) = 18.6$$

where $\eta_3^*(6)$ denotes the likelihood ratio test of three common factor restrictions based on the values of the restricted and unrestricted versions of the AD(4, 4, 4) model. Hence the likelihood ratio test indicates the rejection of the common factor restrictions which the COMFAC analysis had suggested were data admissible, providing an empirical illustration of the simulation findings in section 5. It is interesting to record that when estimating the AD(1, 1, 1) model (without auto-regressive errors) $\eta_5\,(11) = 14.2$ whereas $\eta_M\,(6) = 17.0$, indicating that the latter is a more useful diagnostic statistic.

Failure to reject a hypothesis does not entail that it must be accepted, and as COMFAC may be rejecting invalid common factor restrictions too infrequently (see section 5) we decided to investigate alternative ways of reducing the dimensionality of the parameter space.

Note that the 'error correction' model proposed in chapter 8 has a specification which makes invalid common factor restrictions in a general dynamic model difficult to reject, and yet, if these are accepted, biased parameter estimates, and derived moments of the lag distributions, result. In fact, the 'annual decision taking' formulation excluding seasonal dummies is easily rejected, the estimates being

$$\widehat{\Delta_4 c_t} = \underset{(0.09)}{-0.29} + \underset{(0.19)}{0.98\Delta_4 y_t} - \underset{(0.18)}{0.40\Delta_1\Delta_4 y_t} - \underset{(0.04)}{0.12\,(c_{t-4} - y_{t-4})} - \underset{(0.30)}{1.39\Delta_1 p_{t-1}}$$

$$\underset{(0.30)}{-1.64\Delta_1 p_{t-3}} \tag{7.8}$$

$$T = 54 \qquad R^2 = 0.6492 \qquad s = 0.0316 \qquad \begin{array}{l} \eta_7(6) = 5.1 \qquad \eta_6(6, 48) = 0.81 \\ \eta_5(8) = 12.0 \qquad \eta_M(6) = 4.2 \end{array}$$

Although this is not a nested special case of table 7.2 (because of the presence of y_{t-5}), s has increased by almost 40 per cent, partly through excluding the seasonal dummies and partly because a unit income elasticity has been imposed. However, we believe that these estimates are worth recording as a caution against imposing an *untested* model on data since on conventional criteria (parameter 'significance', signs and magnitudes, forecast accuracy, and random residual correlogram) such a fitted model would often be judged 'acceptable'.

Inspection of the results in table 7.2 suggests another simplification in which $\hat{m}_0 = 1$, $\hat{m}_1 = 0$ and $\hat{m}_2 = 2$ (but with the price variables being $\Delta_1^2 p_t$ and $\Delta_1 p_t$) and searches in this direction found reasonable models. Similarly, specification searches using a 'smoothed' farm income series yielded models with variables which closely resembled an integral control mechanism (see Phillips, 1957), and these were reported in an earlier version of the paper. Hence our searches for a good approximation to the data generation process have illustrated the fact that there can be a set of models which are almost indistinguishable empirically but have different interpretations.

The data-instigated simplification we finally chose was $\hat{m}_0 = 1$, $\hat{m}_1 = 3$ and $\hat{m}_2 = 4$ but with the sum of the price coefficients restricted to be zero (equivalent to using $\dot{p}$ in place of p), and estimation yielded

$$\begin{aligned} (\widehat{c - y})_t = {} & -1.46 + 0.29Q_{1t} + 0.25Q_{2t} + 0.39Q_{3t} + 0.44c_{t-1} - 0.84\Delta_1^2 y_t \\ & (0.22) \ \ (0.05) \qquad (0.04) \qquad (0.04) \qquad (0.11) \qquad (0.15) \\[4pt] & + 0.45\Delta_1^2 y_{t-1} - 2.22\Delta_1 y_{t-1} - 0.20y_{t-3} - 0.63\Delta_1^2 p_t - 1.82\Delta_1 p_{t-1} \\ & \ \ (0.18) \qquad\quad (0.42) \qquad\quad (0.16) \qquad (0.29) \qquad (0.33) \\[4pt] & - 0.83\Delta_1 p_{t-3} \\ & \ \ (0.30) \end{aligned} \qquad (7.9)$$

$$T = 54 \qquad R^2 = 0.977 \qquad s = 0.0227 \qquad \begin{array}{l} \eta_7(6) = 6.5 \qquad \eta_6(6, 42) = 0.68 \\ \eta_5(11) = 14.9 \qquad \eta_M(6) = 5.9 \end{array}$$

The reformulation of both regressors and regressand was selected to achieve 'sensible' decision variables which would be relatively orthogonal, and the substantial reduction in the estimated standard errors of the seasonals reflects the 'success' of the choice (subject to some discounting for having several tries!). The smaller values of η_6 and η_7, however, are encouraging and support the use of the restrictions (which are obviously not data rejectable). The derived parameter estimates are recorded in table 7.4 and equation (7.10) reports the steady-state solution. Thus

$$C = K_i^* Y^{1.43} (1 + \dot{p})^{-1.18} \qquad (7.10)$$

where

$$K_i^* = \exp(-2.61 + 0.52Q_1 + 0.45Q_2 + 0.70Q_3 - 2.25g_2),$$

and $\dot{p}$ denotes the *annual* rate of inflation in PR ($\dot{p} = 4g_3$); with $g_2 = 0.006$, K_i^* ranges from 0.07 to 0.15. Since $\eta_6 < 1$, the value of s will be somewhat smaller

Table 7.4   Solved coefficients from equation (7.9)

Variable	$j = 0$	$j = 1$	$j = 2$	$j = 3$	$j = 4$	Σ
c_{t-j}	-1	0.44	0	0	0	-0.56
y_{t-j}	0.16	-0.09	0.48	0.25	0	0.80
p_{t-j}	-0.63	-0.56	1.19	-0.83	0.83	0
k_j	-1.46	0.29	0.25	0.39	–	

Table 7.5   AD(4, 4, 4) over the entire sample

Variable	$j = 0$	$j = 1$	$j = 2$	$j = 3$	$j = 4$	Σ
c_{t-j}	-1	0.37 (0.14)	-0.05 (0.15)	0.09 (0.16)	0.03 (0.14)	-0.56
y_{t-j}	0.41 (0.18)	-0.11 (0.21)	0.34 (0.19)	0.20 (0.18)	-0.09 (0.17)	0.75
p_{t-j}	-0.69 (0.27)	-0.40 (0.47)	1.16 (0.49)	-1.09 (0.53)	0.84 (0.37)	-0.18
k_j	-1.47 (0.43)	0.26 (0.08)	0.19 (0.07)	0.37 (0.09)	–	

$T = 61$ $R^2 = 0.9956$ $s = 0.0226$ $\eta_5(8) = 9.2$ $\eta_M(6) = 3.2$

when (7.9) is estimated from the entire sample, and as a final comparison the unrestricted AD(4, 4, 4) model was re-estimated including the six forecast observations, with the results shown in table 7.5.

In many respects, the main advantage of a simplification search is well illustrated by these estimates since the *restricted* solved coefficients for $T = 54$ are closer to the unrestricted estimates which are based on the longer sample, a result consistent with equation (7.9) being an accurate approximation to the underlying data generation process.

4 Monte Carlo Methods

Most studies of properties of econometric tests in dynamic models have used either numerical integration or simulation methods to tabulate numerical values of 'sizes' and 'powers' (see, *inter alia*, Maddala and Rao, 1973; Guilkey, 1974; Kenkel, 1974; L'Esperance and Taylor, 1975; Peck, 1975; Tillman, 1975). Investigators have generally conceded that the main drawbacks of their approaches comprise the following:

1   the results obtained are specific to the parameter values considered;
2   simulation estimates are imprecise even when based on a large number of replications;
3   tabulation strains the memory without producing much insight.

The objectives of this section are to develop some *simple* methods which attempt to avoid the objections in (1)–(3) and to apply such methods to investigate the behaviour in finite samples of several of the tests of dynamic specification used above, including likelihood ratio and Wald tests for common factors and Lagrange multiplier tests for residual autocorrelation.

To achieve these aims, we consider large sample approximations to the power functions of the tests at any chosen nominal significance level, and then 'calibrate' the approximations for finite samples using response surfaces which relate simulation estimates to the asymptotic formulae. The analytical results highlight the factors determining power at any nominal significance level, and the response surfaces reveal the asymptotic approximations to be quite useful for the classes of model which we have investigated (more accurate approximations could be obtained by retaining higher order terms in T^{-M} with $M > 1$ (see Lee, 1971) using, for example, Edgeworth expansions (see Davis, 1971; Sargan, 1976)).

The principles underlying our approach are relatively standard but for expository purposes are developed for a very simple situation which can be generalized to the multivariate case. Thus we consider testing the hypothesis $H_0: \alpha = \alpha_0$ using a Wald test (see Wald, 1943; Aitchison, 1962) for the model

$$y_t = \alpha y_{t-1} + \varepsilon_t \quad \text{where} \, |\alpha| < 1, t = 1, \ldots, T, \tag{7.11}$$

and

$$\varepsilon_t \sim \text{NI}(0, \sigma_\varepsilon^2). \tag{7.12}$$

In large samples, the least squares (which is equivalent to the maximum likelihood) estimator $\hat{\alpha}$ of α has the distribution

$$\frac{T^{1/2}(\hat{\alpha} - \alpha)}{(1 - \hat{\alpha}^2)^{1/2}} \underset{a}{\approx} \text{N}(0, 1), \tag{7.13}$$

and hence

$$\frac{T(\hat{\alpha} - \alpha)^2}{1 - \hat{\alpha}^2} \underset{a}{\approx} \chi^2(1, 0) \tag{7.14}$$

where $\chi^2(n, \mu^2)$ denotes a non-central χ^2 variate with n degrees of freedom and non-centrality parameter μ^2 (central if $\mu = 0$). To test H_0 against $H_1: \alpha \neq \alpha_0$ at nominal (and large sample) significance level δ, one computes

$$\eta_1 = \frac{T(\hat{\alpha} - \alpha_0)^2}{1 - \hat{\alpha}^2} \tag{7.15}$$

and rejects H_0 if $\eta_1 \geq d_1$ where $\text{prob}[\chi^2(1, 0) \geq d_1] = \delta$.

When H_0 is false, the large sample power of η_1 can be evaluated against a sequence of alternative hypotheses given by

$$\alpha = \alpha_0 \pm \gamma/T^{1/2} \quad \text{for fixed } \gamma > 0 \tag{7.16}$$

(see, for example, Kendall and Stuart, 1961, ch. 25; Durbin, 1970). From (7.13), when (7.16) holds,

$$\frac{T^{1/2}(\hat{\alpha} - \alpha_0)}{(1 - \hat{\alpha}^2)^{1/2}} \underset{a}{\approx} \text{N}(\mu, 1) \tag{7.17}$$

where

$$\mu = \gamma/(1 - \alpha^2)^{1/2}$$

and hence

$$\eta_1 \underset{\text{a}}{\sim} \chi^2(1, \mu^2)$$

noting that

$$\mu^2 = \frac{\gamma^2}{1 - \alpha^2} = \frac{T(\alpha - \alpha_0)^2}{1 - \alpha^2}. \tag{7.18}$$

The large sample power of η_1 to reject H_0 against H_1 for any chosen values of $(\alpha, \delta, \gamma, T) = \psi$ is given by $\text{prob}[\chi^2(1, \mu^2) \geq d_1]$ and this can be calculated from the area of the relevant non-central χ^2 distribution lying in the interval $[d_1, \infty]$. However, some insight into the properties of the test can be obtained by using the well-known approximation to the non-central χ^2 of a proportion of the familiar central χ^2 adjusted to have the same first two moments (but different degrees of freedom). Thus (see Kendall and Stuart, 1961, ch. 24),

$$\chi^2(n, \mu^2) \approx h\chi^2(m, 0) \tag{7.19}$$

where

$$h = \frac{n + 2\mu^2}{n + \mu^2} \qquad m = \frac{n + \mu^2}{h}. \tag{7.20}$$

These values of h, m ensure that the two χ^2s in (7.19) have the same first two moments, namely:

$$\mathscr{E}[h\chi^2(m, 0)] = hm = n + \mu^2 \tag{7.21}$$

and

$$\mathscr{E}[h\chi^2(m, 0) - hm]^2 = 2h^2m = 2(n + 2\mu^2).$$

Consequently, the approximate and large sample power P^* of η_1 given ψ is (using (7.19) and (7.20))

$$P^*(\eta_1 | \psi) = \int_{h^*}^{\infty} \mathrm{d}\chi^2(m, 0) \tag{7.22}$$

where $h^* = d_1/h$, $h = (1 + 2\mu^2)/(1 + \mu^2)$ and $m = (1 + \mu^2)^2/(1 + 2\mu^2)$. The following interesting properties of η_1 are revealed by (7.22).

1 If H_0 is true, $\mu = 0$ so that $h = 1 = m$ and hence

$$P^*[\eta_1 | (\alpha_0, \delta, 0, T)] = \int_{d_1}^{\infty} \mathrm{d}\chi^2(1, 0) = \delta \tag{7.23}$$

confirming the appropriate nominal and large sample size of the test.

2 If $\alpha \neq \alpha_0$, $\mu^2 \to \infty$ with T, so that $h \to 2$ and $m \to \infty$. Therefore, $P^* \to \int_{0.5d_1}^{\infty} \mathrm{d}\chi^2(\infty, 0) = 1$ so that the test is consistent and rejects H_0 against any *fixed* alternative with probability unity for sufficiently large T (this determined the choice of alternative in (7.16)).

3 As γ increases for fixed T, μ^2 and m increase monotonically and so the power also increases towards unity; conversely, the probability of type II error increases

as δ falls and hence d_1 increases. Heuristically, the power of η_1 given ψ arises from the fact that its *actual* distribution depends on a χ^2 with m degrees of freedom centred on hm, whereas it is being compared with a critical value d_1 based on a central χ^2 with one degree of freedom; as m increases, the probability of η_1 exceeding d_1 tends to unity.

4   The large sample power P^* of η_1 is easily and cheaply calculated from (7.22) for any choice of ψ (although m need not be integer, (7.22) can be computed for the nearest integers on both sides of m and an approximate value calculated by linear interpolation). Alternatively, P^* could be computed directly from $\text{prob}[\chi^2(1, \mu^2) \geqslant d_1]$.

To summarize, equation (7.22) highlights in a simple analytical formula the way in which the factors α, δ, γ, T determine the large sample power of η_1 to reject H_0 against the sequence (7.16). As such, the approach seems to provide a reasonable compromise between a highly labour-intensive analysis (such as Phillips, 1977) and a computer-intensive simulation (like Orcutt and Winokur, 1969). Moreover, P^* can be used as a statistical control for between-experiment variation in simulation estimates of $P = \text{prob}(\eta_1 \geqslant d_1 | \psi)$, to improve the accuracy with which power functions are determined when T is finite (compare the equivalent for moments of estimators in Hendry and Srba, 1977). The actual power[2] $P(\psi)$ is, of course, unknown and the naive Monte Carlo estimate $\hat{P}$ is the proportion of times that $\eta_1 \geqslant d_1$ in N random replications. Since

$$\text{var}(\hat{P}) = P(1 - P)/N \tag{7.24}$$

to produce a 95 per cent confidence interval of ± 0.01 requires $N = 40,000(1 - P)P$ (e.g. $N = 3600$ for $P = 0.1$ or 0.9; $N = 10,000$ for $P = 0.5$; and $N = 1900$ for $P = 0.05$ or 0.95) (see Sargan, 1976). Thus, for a reasonable number of values of $\psi \in \Psi$ (the parameter space under consideration), an inordinately expensive experiment would be required to achieve accurate and general results.

The main interest in a test's properties would seem to be accurate estimation (or evaluation) of P as a function of ψ: $P = \phi(\psi)$ (say), rather than just P at a few isolated points in Ψ. The simulation equivalent is a *response surface* relating $\hat{P}$ to the design variables through an appropriate choice of $\phi(\cdot)$: $\hat{P} = \phi^*(\psi) + \varepsilon$ where ε is a composite of the error in approximating $\phi(\cdot)$ by $\phi^*(\cdot)$ and the error in estimating P by $\hat{P}$. The form of $\phi^*(\cdot)$ *should* ensure that all power estimates and predictions lie in the interval $[0, 1]$ and that identical results occur from studying type II errors rather than powers. Moreover, it seems efficient to include P^* as one of the determinants of $\hat{P}$ to evaluate the accuracy of the asymptotic approximations discussed above.

These considerations rule out a large number of potential candidates for $\phi^*(\cdot)$ (including, for example, the linear approximations tried in an earlier version of this paper, which additionally suffer from a 'spurious regressions' problem since $\hat{P} \approx P^*$ at very low and very high powers, ensuring a high R^2 independently of the quality of the fit over most of the region of interest, revealed by a low Durbin–Watson statistic when the data from the experiments were ordered according to the value of the non-centrality parameter!).

We chose the function

$$\frac{P}{1-P} = \left(\frac{P^*}{1-P^*}\right)^{\beta_1} \exp[g(\psi)] \tag{7.25}$$

implemented in the form (see Cox, 1970, ch. 6)

$$H^{1/2} \ln\left(\frac{\hat{P} - k_N}{1 - \hat{P} - k_N}\right) = \beta_1 H^{1/2} \ln\left(\frac{P^*}{1-P^*}\right) + H^{1/2} g(\psi) + \nu \tag{7.26}$$

denoted by

$$L^*(\hat{P}) = \beta_1 L(P^*) + g^*(\psi) + \nu,$$

where

$$H = F(N - F)/(N - 1) \quad \text{and} \quad k_N = (2N)^{-1} \quad \text{for} \quad N\hat{P} = F \text{ rejections.}$$

In (7.26), the dependent variable should have roughly a unit variance around $[NP(1 - P)]^{1/2} \ln[P/(1 - P)]$ and consequently the adequacy of the approach can be evaluated by (a) $\beta_1 = 1$, (b) $\sigma_\nu = 1$, (c) $g(\cdot) = 0$, as well as by the R^2 from

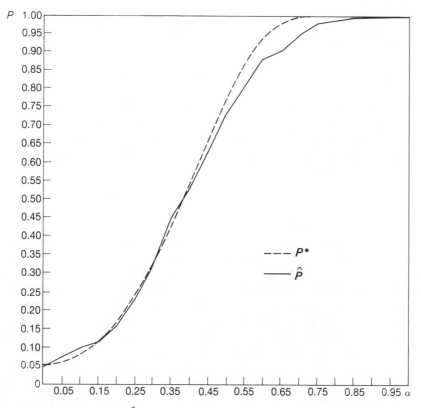

Figure 7.1 Plots of P^* and $\hat{P}$ for $T = 25$.

estimating (7.26) (compare the 'Stein–James smoothing' proposed by Effron and Morris, 1975).

Note that $H = 0$ if $F = 0$ or N and observations for which this occurred, or where $P^* \geqslant 0.9999$, were deleted from the regression. Thus, unlike other experiments, 'extreme' points provide no information if the experimental evidence is summarized via $\hat{P}$ and, for example, (7.26).[3]

To illustrate the above analysis, 20 experiments were conducted from $\alpha = 0$ (0.05) 0.95 with $\alpha_0 = 0$, $\delta = 0.05$, $T = 25$, $\sigma_\varepsilon^2 = 1$ (without loss of generality) using $N = 800$, re-using identical random numbers *between* experiments. Although only $\alpha > 0$ was considered, the two-sided test η_1 was used with $d_1 = 3.84$. Figure 7.1 shows plots of P^* and $\hat{P}$ and it is clear that P^* increasingly overestimates $\hat{P}$ as α increases from 0.5 until $P^* \approx 1$. This finding suggests trying $g(\psi) = \beta_2 \alpha^2 / (1 - \alpha^2) = \beta_2 \mu^2 / T$ as an additional regressor with P^* (δ and T being omitted since they were not varied) and estimation yielded

$$\widehat{L^*(\hat{P})} = 0.908 L(P^*) - 1.05 H^{1/2}(\mu^2/T) \qquad (7.27)$$
$$\phantom{\widehat{L^*(\hat{P})} = } (0.053) \qquad\quad (0.29)$$

$$R^2 = 0.97 \qquad d = 0.95 \qquad s = 2.44 \qquad \eta_6(4, 14) = 0.25$$

(with $\hat{P}$ ordered as in figure 7.1), where $\eta_6(T_2, T_1 - \kappa)$ is the Chow test described in section 2 for $T_2 = 4$ (randomly chosen) experiments retained for prediction, from a model with κ regressors estimated from T_1 observations.

A similar outcome resulted for $T = 50$ (see figure 7.2), with a much steeper power function ($\hat{P} \approx 1$ for $\alpha \geqslant 0.65$), slight underestimation of P^* at low powers and larger underestimation for $0.75 \leqslant P^* \leqslant 0.95$. Such results are approximately what would be anticipated in view of the Edgeworth expansion for the t ratio (7.13) provided by Phillips (1977), and starkly reveal the defects of a simulation study relative to an analytical derivation. The term in μ^2/T is reminiscent of the form of inconsistency response surface found by Hendry and Srba (1977) and hence it was decided to modify equation (7.25) to allow $\beta_1 = \beta_1^* + \beta_2^*/T$ which yields a class of response surfaces given by

$$L^*(\hat{P}) = \beta_1^* L(P^*) + \beta_2^* L(P^*)/T + g^*(\psi) + \nu \qquad (7.26^*)$$

and this is the formulation used in section 5 below.

As a basis for studying much more complicated situations, given the number of approximations involved (the assumption that η_1 has a χ^2 distribution, the approximation to the non-central χ^2 in (7.19), the use of asymptotically valid values of P^* and relatively inaccurate estimates of P) the results are rather encouraging. Indeed, R^2 is close to unity, the regression accurately predicts the four randomly chosen values of α, and $\tilde{\beta}_1$ is not 'significantly' less than unity. However, $\tilde{\beta}_2$ is 'significantly' different from zero, the fitted regression exhibits significant residual autocorrelation because P^* overestimates the simulation-based power values at high power[4] and s is much in excess of unity. These disadvantages are offset by the erratic behaviour of $\hat{P}$ despite $N = 800$ (note that P^* is a zero variance asymptotically unbiased, though biased, estimator of P), and in fact the 95 per cent confidence intervals for P at 0.05 (or 0.95) and 0.5 are ± 0.016 and ± 0.036. When the experiments were

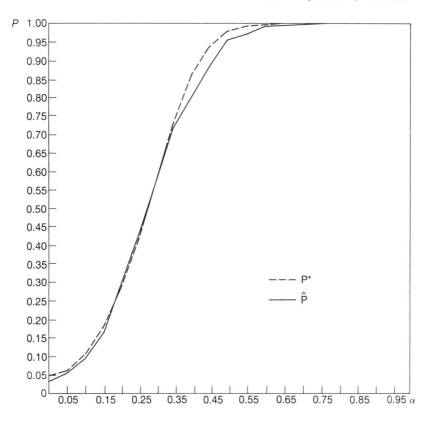

Figure 7.2   Plots of P^* and $\hat{P}$ for $T = 50$.

re-run using $N = 400$, $\hat{P}$ sometimes decreased as α increased, demonstrating the unreliability of crude simulation. In contrast, P^* provides an analytical result which is inexpensive to compute and yields insight into the behaviour of the test. Overall, the mixed $\hat{P}$, P^* calibration approach seems sufficiently worthwhile to use for investigating other tests of dynamic specification.

5 The Finite Sample Properties of the Tests

The class of relationship under study is $AD(m_0, m_1)$:

$$\theta_0(L)y_t = \theta_1(L)z_t + w_t \quad \text{where } w_t \sim NI(0, \sigma_w^2), \tag{7.28}$$

and z_t is generated by

$$z_t = \lambda z_{t-1} + v_t \quad \text{with } v_t \sim NI(0, \sigma_v^2) \quad \text{and} \quad E(v_t w_s) = 0, \quad \forall t, s. \tag{7.29}$$

In fact, z_t is also stochastic in that it was generated separately for each replication rather than being held fixed in the N replications. The COMFAC algorithm developed by Sargan and Sylwestrowicz (1976a) can be used to form a sequence of

Wald tests for common factors in the lag polynomials of unrestricted dynamic equations like (7.28) using the test statistic

$$\eta_3 = Tf(\hat{\boldsymbol{\theta}})' \hat{\boldsymbol{\Omega}}^{-1} f(\hat{\boldsymbol{\theta}}) \tag{7.30}$$

which, as described in section 2, is asymptotically distributed as $\chi^2(r, 0)$ when H_0: $f(\boldsymbol{\theta}) = \boldsymbol{0}$ is true and imposes r restrictions. As with η_1, H_0 is rejected when $\eta_3 \geq d_r$ where $\text{prob}[\chi^2(r, 0) \geq d_r] = \delta$. The COMFAC algorithm for implementing η_3 was incorporated in NAIVE (see Hendry and Srba, 1977) for the simulation experiments.

When H_0 is false, the power of η_3 can be evaluated against the sequence of alternatives

$$f(\boldsymbol{\theta}) = T^{-1/2} \boldsymbol{\gamma} \quad \text{for fixed } \boldsymbol{\gamma} \tag{7.31}$$

such that

$$\eta_3 \underset{a}{\sim} \chi^2(r, \mu^2) \quad \text{with } \mu^2 = \boldsymbol{\gamma}' \boldsymbol{\Omega}^{-1} \boldsymbol{\gamma}. \tag{7.32}$$

Thus, to use the power approximation analysis described above requires calculation of

$$\mu^2 = Tf(\boldsymbol{\theta})' (\boldsymbol{JVJ}')^{-1} f(\boldsymbol{\theta}) / \sigma_w^2. \tag{7.33}$$

The population second moments of the data can be calculated from (7.28) and (7.29), thus determining V; and J, $f(\boldsymbol{\theta})$ and μ^2 are then evaluated for any given model. Note from (7.33) that the power of η_3 (at any chosen δ) depends on the sample size (T), the magnitude of the discrepancy from the common factor restrictions $(f(\boldsymbol{\theta}))$, the (asymptotic) variance of the unrestricted estimator of $\boldsymbol{\theta}$ $(\sigma_w^2 V)$ and the Jacobian from $\boldsymbol{\theta}$ to $f(\cdot)$. Having calculated μ^2, $P^*(\eta_3 | \boldsymbol{\psi})$ can be computed from the equivalent of (7.22).

The two special cases of (7.28) investigated were AD(1, 1) and AD(2, 1) respectively, testing for one common factor (i.e. $r = 1$) in both. In the first case

$$y_t = \theta_0 y_{t-1} + \theta_1 z_t + \theta_2 z_{t-1} + \theta_3 + w_t \tag{7.34}$$

so that $f(\boldsymbol{\theta}) = \theta_0 \theta_1 + \theta_2 = \gamma / T^{1/2}$ (obtained by setting $\theta_2 = \gamma / T^{1/2} - \theta_0 \theta_1$).[5] For each of the five values of $\gamma = 0 \ (0.5) \ 2$, nine independent experiments were

Table 7.6 Properties of COMFAC for AD(1, 1) when $\lambda = 0.9$

	T	θ_0	σ_w^2		0.0	0.5	1.0	1.5	2.0
							γ		
(i)	75	0	10	$\hat{P}$	0.03	0.03	0.04	0.05	0.06
				P^*	0.05	0.05	0.06	0.08	0.10
(ii)	25	0.8	1	$\hat{P}$	0.06	0.24	0.42	0.66	0.87
				P^*	0.05	0.17	0.43	0.71	0.91
(iii)	55	0.4	0.1	$\hat{P}$	0.04	0.50	0.99	1.0	1.0
				P^*	0.05	0.59	0.99	1.0	1.0

replicated with $\delta = 0.05$, $\theta_1 = \sigma_v^2 = 1$, $\theta_3 = 0$ (but estimated), using a Graeco–Latin 3×3 design generated from $T = (25, 55, 75)$, $\theta_0 = (0, 0.4, 0.8)$, $\lambda = (0.3, 0.6, 0.9)$ and $\sigma_w^2 = (0.1, 1.0, 10.0)$ (see Cochran and Cox, 1957, p. 146). The small value $N = 100$ was selected to see what levels of accuracy could be achieved at relatively low cost given the generality sought from 45 experiments. Note that $\hat{P}$ cannot be more accurate than two digits, and to illustrate typical results table 7.6 records the outcomes of $\hat{P}$ and P^* for the three sets of experiments with $\lambda = 0.9$.

The results for the 45 experiments were pooled to estimate the overall response surface between $\hat{P}$ and P^* with five randomly selected experiments retained for the prediction test:

$$L^*\widetilde{(\hat{P})} = 1.05L(P^*) + 0.37H^{1/2} \tag{7.35}$$
$$\quad\;\;(0.05) \qquad\quad (0.08)$$

$$R^2 = 0.92 \qquad s = 1.27 \qquad \eta_6(5, 38) = 0.68.$$

In this case, P^* provides a good approximation to the general behaviour of $\hat{P}$, noting that the standard errors of $\hat{P}$ at 0.05 and 0.5 are 0.022 and 0.050 respectively. The functional approximation is not rejected by the prediction test, the coefficient of P^* is not significantly different from unity, although the intercept is from zero, R^2 is high and s is quite close to unity. In fact, the central χ^2 approximation to η_3 also held well in terms of the first two moments as shown in equations (7.36) and (7.37), which record regressions of $\bar{\eta}_3$ on $\mathscr{E}[\chi^2(1, \mu^2)]$ and $\ln \mathrm{SD}(\eta_3)$ on $\ln \mathrm{SD}[\chi^2(1, \mu^2)]$ respectively:

$$\tilde{\bar{\eta}}_3 = 1.30\mathscr{E}(\cdot) - 40T^{-1} + 0.39 \tag{7.36}$$
$$\quad\;\;(0.04) \qquad (40) \qquad (1.1)$$

$$R^2 = 0.97 \qquad s = 2.9 \qquad \eta_7(5) = 10.3$$

$$\ln \widetilde{\mathrm{SD}(\eta_3)} = 1.06 \ln \mathrm{SD}(\cdot) + 2.7T^{-1} - 0.06 \tag{7.37}$$
$$\quad\;\;(0.03) \qquad\qquad (2.1) \qquad (0.07)$$

$$R^2 = 0.97 \qquad s = 0.15 \qquad \eta_7(5) = 4.7$$

where $\eta_7(T_2)$ is the χ^2 test of predictive accuracy for T_2 prediction observations first introduced in section 2.

For many practical purposes, P^* provides as adequate an approximation to the unknown P as does $\hat{P}$ for COMFAC applied to (7.34) but at a fraction of the cost.

To check our approach and obtain information on the comparative finite sample performances of two asymptotically equivalent tests, we also investigated the likelihood ratio (LR) test for a first-order common factor originally proposed by Sargan (1964a). For the same experiments (i.e. identical data) as the Wald test, the response surface corresponding to (7.35) was (using $\hat{P}_R$ to denote the simulation-estimated power of the LR test),

$$L^*\widetilde{(\hat{P}_R)} = 1.05L(P^*) + 0.48H^{1/2} \tag{7.38}$$
$$\quad\;\;(0.05) \qquad\quad (0.10)$$

$$R^2 = 0.91 \qquad s = 1.40 \qquad \eta_6(5, 38) = 0.67.$$

The performance of the two tests is clearly very similar in this simple case, and seems adequately described by the asymptotic approximation.

Turning next to the AD(2, 1) model, this was defined by

$$y_t = \theta_0 y_{t-1} + \theta_1 y_{t-2} + \theta_2 z_t + \theta_3 z_{t-1} + \theta_4 + w_t \tag{7.39}$$

with $w_t \sim NI(0, \sigma_w^2)$ and z_t generated by (7.29). $P^*(\eta_3 | \psi)$ was calculated as before using equations (7.31)–(7.33). To help comparability, a similar experimental design was selected, using the same values of γ, T, λ, σ_w^2 as earlier, with $\theta_2 = \sigma_v^2 = 1$, $\theta_4 = 0$ (but estimated), setting $\theta_0 = \xi + \rho$, $\theta_1 = -\xi\rho$ and $\theta_3 = -\rho + \gamma/T^{1/2}$ where $\rho = (0, 0.4, 0.8)$ and $\xi = (0, \pm 0.2, \pm 0.4, \pm 0.6, \pm 0.8)$. A 3×3 Graeco–Latin square was formed from the values of $(T, \lambda, \sigma_w^2, \rho)$ with a value of ξ being randomly assigned to each experiment, these sets of nine experiments then being conducted for each of the five values of γ, using $N = 200$ (again re-using the random numbers as γ varied). Both Wald and LR tests for common factors were conducted and table 7.7 records illustrative values of the tests' relative rejection frequencies in the experiments with $\lambda = 0.6$.

The estimated response functions were

$$\widetilde{L^*(\hat{P}_W)} = 0.76 L(P^*) + 1.7 H^{1/2} - 12(H/T)^{1/2} - 0.78 \sigma H^{1/2} \tag{7.40}$$
$$\quad\;\; (0.08) \qquad\quad (0.59) \qquad (3.6) \qquad\qquad (0.19)$$

$$R^2 = 0.81 \qquad s = 2.57 \qquad \eta_6(5, 36) = 0.3$$

and

$$\widetilde{L^*(\hat{P}_R)} = 0.95 L(P^*) - 13.4 L(P^*)/T - 24 H^{1/2}/T + 0.25 H^{1/2} \tag{7.41}$$
$$\quad\;\; (0.15) \qquad\qquad (5.6) \qquad\qquad\; (12) \qquad\quad (0.36)$$

$$R^2 = 0.75 \qquad s = 3.00 \qquad \eta_6(5, 38) = 0.3.$$

Both tests perform rather poorly in terms of the asymptotic approximation, although both (7.40) and (7.41) serve as reasonable descriptions of the experiments conducted, accurately predicting five randomly selected experimental outcomes.

The average sizes of the Wald and LR tests ($\gamma = 0$) were approximately 0.04 and

Table 7.7   Properties of COMFAC tests in AD(2, 1) when $\lambda = 0.6$

	T	ξ	ρ	σ_w^2		γ 0	0.5	1	1.5	2
(i)	55	0	0	1	P^*	0.050	0.051	0.053	0.062	0.081
					$\hat{P}_W$	0.035	0.025	0.040	0.045	0.075
					$\hat{P}_R$	0.060	0.080	0.090	0.115	0.145
(ii)	25	0.6	0.4	10	P^*	0.050	0.052	0.056	0.063	0.071
					$\hat{P}_W$	0.000	0.000	0.000	0.000	0.000
					$\hat{P}_R$	0.160	0.160	0.150	0.165	0.180
(iii)	75	-0.2	0.8	0.1	P^*	0.050	0.350	0.889	0.997	1.00
					$\hat{P}_W$	0.080	0.495	0.940	1.00	1.00
					$\hat{P}_R$	0.080	0.475	0.940	1.00	1.00

0.09 respectively, so that the latter deviates from its nominal significance level; however, the Wald test tended to reject infrequently at small sample sizes as table 7.7 illustrates.[6] Overall, even for AD(2, 1) models and $r = 1$, COMFAC had a fairly large type II error and we conjectured that this would worsen as the number of lags increased on the very limited comparison basis of the AD(1, 1) findings. The response surfaces for the first two moments of the tests suggest that on this criterion the Wald test is closer to the asymptotic approximation based on χ^2 than is the LR (see Sargan, 1980a) since

$$\tilde{\bar{\eta}}_{3W} = 0.94 \mathscr{S}(\cdot) - 73/T + 1.45 \tag{7.42}$$
$$\qquad (0.03) \qquad (20) \quad (0.58)$$

$$R^2 = 0.97 \qquad s = 1.49 \qquad \eta_7(5) = 0.7$$

$$\ln \widehat{\mathrm{SD}}(\eta_{3W}) = 1.12 \ln \mathrm{SD}(\cdot) - 25/T + 0.17 \tag{7.43}$$
$$\qquad\qquad (0.07) \qquad\qquad (4.4) \quad (0.13)$$

$$R^2 = 0.88 \qquad s = 0.32 \qquad \eta_7(5) = 5.0$$

$$\tilde{\bar{\eta}}_{3R} = 0.73 \mathscr{S}(\cdot) - 16/T + 1.12 \tag{7.44}$$
$$\qquad (0.04) \qquad (30) \quad (0.84)$$

$$R^2 = 0.90 \qquad s = 2.15 \qquad \eta_7(5) = 13.2$$

$$\ln \widehat{\mathrm{SD}}(\eta_{3R}) = 0.65 \ln \mathrm{SD}(\cdot) - 4.9/T + 0.48 \tag{7.45}$$
$$\qquad\qquad (0.05) \qquad\qquad (3.2) \quad (0.10)$$

$$R^2 = 0.81 \qquad s = 0.23 \qquad \eta_7(5) = 3.6.$$

Thus the first two moments of η_{3W} are close to those of the asymptotic approximation whereas substantial underestimation occurs for η_{3R}. These findings guided our use of the Wald test in the empirical section above, namely as an attempt to reject common factor representations without entailing selecting such a representation when it could not be rejected at conventional significance levels.

In the final set of experiments, we examined the performance of three asymptotically equivalent tests for first-order autocorrelation in dynamic models (conditional on knowing that a common factor representation existed), both to illustrate the approach for a well-studied problem and to compare the finite sample properties of the Lagrange multiplier (LM) based tests used in the empirical analysis above with those of Wald and LR form. In addition a 'portmanteau' LM test for fourth-order residual autocorrelation was investigated.

The data generation process was

$$y_t = \xi y_{t-1} + dz_{1t} + 0.5z_{2t} + u_t \qquad\qquad (t = 1, \ldots, T)$$

$$u_t = \rho u_{t-1} + \varepsilon_t \qquad\qquad\qquad \varepsilon_t \sim \mathrm{NI}(0, \sigma_\varepsilon^2)$$

$$\qquad\qquad\qquad\qquad\qquad\qquad\qquad\qquad\qquad\qquad \tag{7.46}$$

$$z_{1t} = 0.3z_{1t-1} + v_{1t} \qquad\qquad\qquad v_{1t} \sim \mathrm{NI}(0, 1)$$

$$z_{2t} = 0.87z_{2t-1} + v_{2t} - 0.15v_{2t-1} \qquad v_{2t} \sim \mathrm{NI}(0, 4)$$

with $\rho = (\pm 0.4, \pm 0.75)$, $d = (\pm 1, \pm 10)$, $\xi = (\pm 0.4, \pm 0.8)$, $T = (19, 39, 59, 76)$

and $\sigma_e^2 = 1$; ρ, d, c, T were used to generate a 4×4 Graeco–Latin square (set (i)) which was then replicated but with $\rho = 0$ (ii) and $\xi = 0$ (iii), to calibrate the significance level of the tests and check on any 'power loss' through incorrectly including the lagged dependent variable. Typical results (from the four experiments with $\rho = +0.4$) are shown in table 7.8, using the notation η^* for $\chi^2(1, \mu^2)$, η_W, η_R, η_M for the Wald, LR and LM tests of $H_0 : \rho = 0$, $\eta^*(4)$ for $\chi^2(4, \mu^2)$ and $\eta_M(4)$ for the LM test for fourth-order autocorrelation (note that $\eta_M(4) \approx \eta^*(4)$ with the same non-centrality parameter as η^* but different degrees of freedom). The power approximations described earlier were again used, and although μ^2 is a complicated function of the parameters of (7.46) it is easily computed using $\mu^2 = \ln(\sigma_{up}^2/\sigma_e^2)$ (where $\sigma_{up}^2 = \text{plim } T^{-1}\Sigma\tilde{u}_t^2$ and $\tilde{u}_t$ is the OLS residual) for the alternatives $\rho = \gamma/T^{1/2}$ with fixed γ. A nominal significance level of $\delta = 0.05$ (where $\text{prob}[\chi^2(n, 0) \geqslant d_n] = \delta$) was used for all the tests which were computed using $\eta_W = \hat{\rho}^2/\widehat{\text{var}(\rho)}$, $\eta_R = T \ln(\Sigma\tilde{u}_t^2/\Sigma\hat{e}_t^2)$ and $\eta_M = TR^2$, with R^2 calculated from the regression of $\tilde{u}_t$ on $(\tilde{u}_{t-1}, y_{t-1}, z_{1t}, z_{2t})$ (see Godfrey, 1978), where a circumflex denotes maximum likelihood estimator and $(1/T)\Sigma\hat{e}_t^2 = \hat{\sigma}_e^2$. $\eta_M(4)$ is TR^2 from regressing $\tilde{u}_t$ on $(\tilde{u}_{t-1}, \ldots, \tilde{u}_{t-4}, y_{t-1}, z_{1t}, z_{2t})$. Note that η_W and η_R are of the *form* of $TR^2/(1 - R^2)$ and $T \ln(1 - R^2)$ for suitably defined regressions (different from those of the LM test) and that $x \leqslant \ln(1 - x) \leqslant x/(1 - x)$ for $0 < x < 1$. Thus, although we have been unable to prove that $\eta_M \leqslant \eta_R \leqslant \eta_W$ for $H_0 : \rho = 0$ in model (7.46) (see Berndt and Savin, 1977) we conjecture that such a

Table 7.8 Autocorrelation test results

| | E_1 | | | E_2 | | | E_3 | | | E_4 | | |
	P	$\bar{\eta}$	SD	P	$\bar{\eta}$	SD	P	$\bar{\eta}$	SD	P	$\bar{\eta}$	SD
(i)												
η^*	0.37	3.8	3.6	0.75	7.8	5.4	0.91	11	6.5	0.97	14	7.4
η_W	0.37	4.8	6.9	0.66	7.7	6.3	0.80	9.3	6.4	0.88	14	9.3
η_R	0.30	3.5	4.1	0.66	6.8	5.1	0.80	8.7	5.6	0.90	13	7.6
η_M	0.27	2.4	2.6	0.57	5.5	4.0	0.78	7.4	4.7	0.88	11	6.1
$\eta^*(4)$	0.23	6.8	4.4	0.52	10.8	5.9	0.72	14	7.0	0.85	17	7.8
$\eta_M(4)$	0.10	5.2	2.9	0.32	8.2	4.2	0.46	10	5.0	0.76	14	6.1
(iii)												
η^*	0.37	3.8	3.6	0.74	7.8	5.4	0.85	9.7	6.1	0.97	14	7.4
η_W	0.33	4.5	6.9	0.64	7.4	6.2	0.79	8.7	7.1	0.93	15	9.4
η_R	0.30	3.3	4.0	0.63	6.6	5.1	0.80	8.2	6.1	0.93	13	7.6
η_M	0.26	2.4	2.6	0.57	5.3	4.0	0.73	6.6	4.0	0.91	12	6.1
$\eta^*(4)$	0.23	6.8	4.4	0.52	10.8	5.9	0.64	13	6.5	0.85	17	7.8
$\eta_M(4)$	0.08	5.2	2.8	0.34	8.1	4.3	0.43	9.5	4.3	0.76	14	6.1

Parameter values in (i)

	E_1	E_2	E_3	E_4
ξ	−0.4	−0.8	0.8	0.4
d	1	−10	−1	10
T	19	39	59	76

result holds for the mean values, a hypothesis supported by the finding that $\bar{\eta}_M \leqslant \bar{\eta}_R \leqslant \bar{\eta}_W$ in almost all the experiments we conducted (see, for example, table 7.8). A similar ordering was observed for the standard deviations of the tests so that no power or significance level implications follow from the inequality (although there was a tendency for $\hat{P}_M = \hat{P}(\eta_M) < \hat{P}(\eta_R) \approx \hat{P}(\eta_W))$.

The following response surfaces were obtained:

$$L^*(\widehat{\hat{P}_M}) = 1.06L(P^*) - 12.7L(P^*)/T - 9.1H^{1/2}/T - 0.20H^{1/2} \qquad (7.47)$$
$$\phantom{L^*(\widehat{\hat{P}_M}) =} (0.07) \qquad\quad (1.9) \qquad\quad (4.9) \qquad\quad (0.19)$$

$$R^2 = 0.90 \qquad s = 1.57 \qquad \eta_6(3, 41) = 1.5$$

$$L^*(\widehat{\hat{P}_W}) = 1.06L(P^*) - 10.8L(P^*)/T - 0.66H^{1/2}/T - 0.15H^{1/2} \qquad (7.48)$$
$$\phantom{L^*(\widehat{\hat{P}_W}) =} (0.07) \qquad\quad (1.7) \qquad\quad (4.2) \qquad\quad (0.16)$$

$$R^2 = 0.93 \qquad s = 1.38 \qquad \eta_6(3, 41) = 2.1$$

$$L^*(\widehat{\hat{P}_R}) = 1.08L(P^*) - 11.1L(P^*)/T - 2.9H^{1/2}/T - 0.10H^{1/2} \qquad (7.49)$$
$$\phantom{L^*(\widehat{\hat{P}_R}) =} (0.07) \qquad\quad (1.8) \qquad\quad (4.5) \qquad\quad (0.17)$$

$$R^2 = 0.92 \qquad s = 1.46 \qquad \eta_6(3, 41) = 1.6$$

$$L^*(\widehat{\hat{P}_{M4}}) = 0.90L(P_4^*) - 11.6L(P_4^*)/T - 24H^{1/2}/T - 0.06H^{1/2} \qquad (7.50)$$
$$\phantom{L^*(\widehat{\hat{P}_{M4}}) =} (0.10) \qquad\quad (3.1) \qquad\quad (5.6) \qquad\quad (0.19)$$

$$R^2 = 0.83 \qquad s = 1.93 \qquad \eta_6(3, 41) = 0.79$$

All three first-order autocorrelation tests deviate significantly from the asymptotic power function, with $\hat{P}_W$ having the smallest coefficient on $L(P^*)/T$ and $\hat{P}_M$ the largest as well as the largest on $1/T$, although the R^2 values are high and $\hat{\beta}_1^* \approx 1$. Moreover, $\eta_M(4)$ performed even worse than the three first-order autocorrelation tests with $P[\eta^*(4)]$ being much lower than $P(\eta^*)$ (as anticipated), and $P[\eta_M(4)]$ being much less than $P[\eta^*(4)]$, but it is hardly surprising that a 'portmanteau' test should have rather low power against specific alternatives, or that it is not close to its large sample distribution for $T \leqslant 60$. When $|\rho| = 0.75$, all the tests had near unit power for $T > 19$, and when $\rho = 0$, the average rejection frequencies of all the tests were around the nominal level of 0.05 (0.06, 0.065, 0.05 and 0.04 for η_W, η_R, η_M and $\eta_M(4)$ respectively). Since autocorrelation seems easy to detect when it is 'large' and is relatively unimportant when 'small' we conclude that the LM tests provide useful 'diagnostics' for modelling stationary dynamic processes.

Finally, to relate the asymptotic power function approach to the control variate (CV) methods used by Hendry and Srba (1977) in studying the distribution of $\hat{\rho}$ in

Table 7.9   Correlation of $\hat{\rho}$ and its control variate

	E_1	E_2	E_3	E_4
(i)	0.80	0.87	0.86	0.93
(ii)	0.78	0.90	0.92	0.95
(iii)	0.81	0.86	0.89	0.93

the present class of model, table 7.9 records the correlations of $\hat{\rho}$ with its CV for the four experiments reported in table 7.8. The correlations are all fairly high and increase rapidly with T, but for $T \neq 76$ the CV only accounts for about 80 per cent of the within-experiment variation in $\hat{\rho}$. Thus, both the CV and the response surface evidence suggest that the asymptotic approximations are useful but not fully adequate by themselves.

6 Summary and Conclusions

The paper describes some sequential simplification procedures for stationary, linear dynamic equations and applies these to model consumers' expenditure on non-automobile durable goods in Canada. Since only the asymptotic distributions of the various dynamic specification tests used (common factor and residual autocorrelation) are known, simple methods for studying their finite sample properties are developed, resulting in logistic response surfaces relating empirical rejection frequencies to asymptotic powers, where the latter are easily calculated numerically and the former are obtained by Monte Carlo simulation.

The simple log-linear model (7.9) proposed to explain expenditure on durables is judged to be consonant with the data, and does not suffer from predictive failure over the six quarters following the end of the estimation sample. However, several of the simplification procedures considered (e.g. COMFAC and the annual change model in chapter 8) did not prove useful, and since there are arguments favouring the use of relatively unrestricted models (see Leamer, 1978), (7.9) may not be the best choice of model. The choice of (7.9) does seem justified though, not least because it is easy to interpret and appears to have superior parameter constancy to other models that we considered. In advocating and employing specification searches which start from a general dynamic model and then systematically searching for reasonable simplifications that are data admissible, tests for common factors and residual autocorrelation are considered. These tests jointly form the basis of the procedures described in section 2 for determining dynamic specification. However, in the simulation study we analysed the small sample behaviour of these tests separately, leaving the analysis of their joint behaviour for future research.

Both the empirical and the simulation studies suggest that the common factor tests may have low power in rejecting invalid restrictions in even the simple models AD(1, 1) and AD(2, 1), and that the asymptotic distributions are rather crude, but nevertheless useful, approximations to the behaviour of the tests for sample sizes of less than 80 observations. In particular, for the AD(2, 1) model the Wald and LR common factor tests behave very differently from the asymptotic approximation, though the response surfaces do give an accurate description of the experiments conducted. Although the average size of the COMFAC test at 0.04 is less than that of the LR common factor test (0.09) and COMFAC does appear to have a large probability of type II error, which we conjecture would increase with the order of dynamics, the response surfaces for the first two moments of the test statistics' distributions suggest that the COMFAC distribution is closer to a χ^2 distribution than the distribution of the LR statistic is. We conclude, therefore, that in view of these simulation results and the fact that the Wald test is computationally easier to obtain than the LR common factor test (given the existence of the COMFAC algorithm), COMFAC can be usefully employed in attempts to reject common factor representations provided that the failure to reject at conventional significance levels does not entail selecting such a representation. This proviso is particularly important when COMFAC is being used as a part of a specification or simplification search, and less important when it is used as a diagnostic check. Hence COMFAC can be a useful tool in specification searching, but it must not be used uncritically.

The simulation evidence on the widely used diagnostic checks for residual autocorrelation is favourable, in that all three tests, Wald, LR and LM, easily detect autocorrelation when it is 'large', and when it is 'small' its detection is less important. Interestingly, the inequality $\eta_W \geqslant \eta_R \geqslant \eta_M$ appears to hold for the mean values of these residual autocorrelation tests, but even though the size of each of the tests is close to the nominal 5 per cent this has no power implications, since a similar inequality appears to hold between the standard deviations of the test statistics. It does mean, though, that the LM test will on average reject less frequently than the other two tests which is a reasonable feature for a test of mis-specification. Hence the evidence favours the use of the easily computed LM test for residual autocorrelation as a useful diagnostic for mis-specification, which has high power when common factor restrictions are valid and the error term manifests substantial first-order autocorrelation. Though clearly the portmanteau LM has low power against the specific alternative of first-order autocorrelation the simulation evidence does favour its use, and there is empirical evidence in section 3 that it is to be preferred to the conventional time-series portmanteau statistic of Pierce (1971).

Finally, we note that Monte Carlo simulation for problems not yet having analytical solutions, especially when the experimental design is carefully chosen and the results of asymptotic theory are used to calibrate the inter-experimental results via response surfaces, can be very useful without being computationally expensive.

Notes

1   Other potential regressors were considered in preliminary analysis, including r (the interest rate on three month Government of Canada treasury bills), $\Delta \ln P_T$ (the rate of inflation) and L (the sum of end of month currency in circulation plus demand deposits per capita). The first two were not retained as their total influence was empirically negligible in models with $\hat{m} = 4$, and the last was not used as it seemed an unhelpful variable, being a very poor proxy for either 'liquid assets' or an integral control mechanism.

2   Strictly, rejection frequency since the actual size may differ substantially from the nominal size δ.

3   James Davidson has suggested an alternative form of experimentation which deserves consideration, using a very large number of randomly generated values of ψ and analysing one replication per experiment.

4   This may be due in part to the smoothing caused by re-using the random numbers. Also note the very different sense in which we consider asymptotic approximations to be *useful* compared with (say) the tests on distribution functions used by Basmann et al. (1974) since

the t test of $\beta_2 = 0$ rejects the hypothesis that the $\hat{P}$ are observations from the P^* distribution at the 0.01 level.

5   Since V depends on θ_2, μ^2 is *not* invariant to sign changes in γ.

6   While re-using the random numbers as γ increases reduces the variability between such experiments, it has the undersirable effect of causing autocorrelation and hence (for example) the sequence of zero rejects for $\hat{P}_w$ in set (ii): on balance we would not adopt such a practice again.

8

Econometric Modelling of the Aggregate Time-Series Relationship between Consumers' Expenditure and Income in the United Kingdom

with J.E.H. Davidson, F. Srba and S. Yeo

Preamble

Since DHSY marked my real break from the conventional approach (described in the preamble to chapter 2), it may be helpful to sketch some of its antecedents. In the first half of the 1970s, consumption functions in the United Kingdom were not predicting well. I was still bruised from my encounter with trying to predict 1968 and failing miserably, and hence was puzzling over the causes of both massive and persistent mis-prediction. There were a number of papers by time-series protagonists claiming better prediction records than those of econometric systems (see, for example, Naylor et al., 1972; Cooper, 1972), and yet it was clear that their methods had to be special cases of econometrics techniques (see Zellner and Palm (1974) and Prothero and Wallis (1976) for formal analyses). The proliferation of incompatible consumption models was also worrying since at most one of them could be 'correct'. Why did our research methods not yield unique answers on common data sets?

During 1974–5, James Davidson and I had investigated quarterly versions of permanent income–life cycle models of the stereotypical kind found in macro systems, and confirmed that such equations were indeed dominated in terms of goodness of fit and predictive accuracy by simple time-series representations. The key issue was whether the underlying economic analysis was wrong or merely its implementation in an empirical model. My papers on mis-specification (1975a) and Monte Carlo (Hendry and Harrison, 1974) together with the general theoretical analysis of building society behaviour in chapter 3 had revealed (to me) how to

Reprinted from *Economic Journal*, 88 (December 1978) 661–92. This research was financed in part by a grant from the Social Science Research Council to the Econometric Methodology Project at the London School of Economics. Preparation of the initial draft of the paper was supported by grants from the National Science and Ford Foundations while Hendry visited at the Cowles Foundation, Yale University. Yeo gratefully acknowledges the financial assistance of a Canada Council Doctoral Fellowship. We are grateful to Gordon Anderson, Charles Bean, Jeremy Bray, Angus Deaton, John Flemming, Grayham Mizon and John Muellbauer for helpful comments on previous drafts.

reconcile conflicting evidence when the data generating process (DGP) was known or believed to be known, and so it seemed reasonable that an analogous notion could be used within a class of models even if the DGP was not known. Which class, if any, could possess such a property? I have no recollection of initially noticing any connections within this disparate set of problems, beyond the obvious point that knowledge of the 'correct' model would remove them all.

As noted earlier, the vital clue was provided by the concept of an error correction mechanism (ECM) (although ECMs have been used in chapters 5–7 above, DHSY was their source). The analogy to the mortgage–deposit ratio of chapter 3 was the consumption–income ratio and suddenly both the theories and the evidence seemed reconcilable. Yet again, Denis Sargan's (1964a) paper was the crucial precursor and must have been an important stimulus, although it was only after struggling with consumers' expenditure that I realized the general implications of his wage–price model. Moreover, despite having taught control theory and having been aware of Bill Phillips's papers on the uses of servomechanisms for economic policy (see Phillips, 1954; 1957), I did not immediately grasp the relationship between his notion of proportional feedback and ECMs as models for the behaviour of individual agents, although that gap was filled by 1977–8.

We next realized how to develop encompassing explanations which applied even when the DGP was unknown. If the ECM-based model was provisionally treated as the DGP, then we could understand the connection between the time-series equation and the permanent-income equation, using the ECM as an intermediary. In its simplest, form, the ECM was

$$\Delta c_t = \alpha + \beta \Delta y_t - \gamma(c - y)_{t-1} + \varepsilon_t \tag{1}$$

where $\varepsilon_t \sim \text{IN}(0, \sigma^2)$ and c, y denoted the logarithms of real consumers' expenditure C and real income Y respectively. The time-series model set γ to zero (i.e. excluded the ECM $\log(C/Y)_{t-1}$). Because growth rates Δy_t and disequilibria $(c - y)_{t-1}$ were little correlated, and the latter had a relatively small variance, the resulting equation had roughly the correct estimate of β and a residual standard error which was not greatly in excess of σ. By actually estimating β (i.e. the short-run coefficient) the time-series model would manifest a small income elasticity. But (1) could also be written as

$$c_t = \alpha + \beta y_t + (\gamma - \beta)y_{t-1} + (1 - \gamma)c_{t-1} + \varepsilon_t. \tag{2}$$

The permanent-income model which we considered set $\gamma - \beta$ to zero (i.e. excluded y_{t-1}). Since y_t and y_{t-1} were highly positively correlated, if $\gamma - \beta$ was negative then the estimate of β would be badly biased towards zero, and because $\{y_t\}$ had a large variance the fit would deteriorate considerably. Nevertheless, the sum of the coefficients of y_t and c_{t-1} would remain near unity (the value anticipated by many economic theories for the long-run income elasticity of consumption). Moreover, we had a new idea to explain the proliferation of incompatible empirical models: methodologies such as 'time-series' or 'theory calibration' acted like blinkers on a horse, namely to narrow vision, and the resulting estimates were perhaps more an artefact of the restrictions imposed by the methodology than a reflection of the properties of the data being analysed.

At that stage, we had discovered a general econometric model which was consistent with long-run economic theory and encompassed much of the empirical evidence, as well as making intuitive sense. Unfortunately, it predicted no better than existing equations! A further long lag ensued while we tried to ascertain what would explain the predictive failure (Frank Srba and Stephen Yeo were co-authors by then). This time, Angus Deaton's work came to the rescue (see Deaton, 1977) by suggesting an important role for (unanticipated) inflation in the consumption function. On the very first try with our ECM augmented by inflation (and its change) we struck gold: a well fitting and constant model which had no difficulty predicting the first half of the 1970s. Had Angus Deaton not proposed his 'unanticipated inflation' hypothesis, the DHSY model might have been stillborn, although as chapter 5 showed, many of the lessons learnt in its development were well taken prior to having obtained a complete explanation.

If it had not been totally obvious to me before, it was now manifest that methodology, however brilliantly conceived, was at best a *necessary* and not a sufficient ingredient for successful empirical research. Poor or restrictive methodology could preclude discovering useful models. To use a phrase due to John Herschel (1830), in 'the context of discovery' creative insights, serendipity and good luck were equally as essential as methodology, even though they were not yet susceptible to scientific analysis.

In writing chapters 3 and 8, the concept of a progressive research strategy had gradually evolved. The model of building society behaviour had first revealed that considerable improvements in understanding empirical phenomena could be achieved despite the model not being the 'final word' – indeed, Gordon Anderson and I felt we understood why most previous empirical models behaved as they did, even though our own had not yet been estimated. The ability of an ECM to account for the failure of other consumption function models despite being a manifestly false model (as it could not describe the 1970s prior to incorporating inflation effects) confirmed both the possibility and the value of viewing empirical modelling as part of a progressive sequence and not as a 'one-off' analysis forging economic laws. Aris Spanos had persisted in drawing my attention to the literature on the philosophy of science, especially Lakatos (1974), which helped clarify my thinking and provided an 'authority' to cite in support. These ideas play a major role in the rest of the story. In particular, we realized that most of the puzzles noted at the start of this preamble were interrelated and could be jointly reconciled.

A wide range of econometric issues is confronted in this chapter and an analysis is offered of each topic in isolation, and occasionally conjointly. To summarize the chapter the main issues were as follows.

1   We sought to account for the proliferation of rival models of consumers' expenditure, using a 'detective story' approach. The formal sequential simplification method still lay in the future despite chapter 3, but within the confines of our evolving methodology we developed 'locally general models' such as equation (8.20) below, which emphasized systematic dynamics relative to error dynamics (which imposed COMFAC restrictions). However, by not reverting to the general unrestricted specification when additional variables were tried, we made mistakes, especially about the importance of liquid assets, leading to chapter 9.

2   The ECM was formalized as a class of models, and was found to have good properties in a pilot Monte Carlo study. The role of error correction in encompassing was analysed along the lines of equations (1) and (2) above, and a preliminary typology of models was described (the precursor to chapter 4 above).

3   Parameter constancy and its obverse of predictive failure were major concerns, primarily because of the help the latter offered through its power to reject inadequate models.

4   Data graphs instantly revealed the flaws of the consumption equations reported in chapter 2! The data were highly seasonal (much more so for expenditure than income) and strongly trended, and the consumption–income ratio also trended (downwards).

5   The economic theory was used to structure the empirical analysis and delineate the class of theory-consistent models; within the class, the data determined the dynamics as well as the parameter estimates. Modelling was viewed as matching economic theory to data evidence.

6   Encompassing provided the guiding framework, based on a mixture of standardization

and embedding to create a common general model. We took this approach, rather than (say) non-nested tests, for three reasons. First, non-nested testing allowed the possibility that all the models might be rejected and hence did not fit comfortably with the notion of progressive research. Second, we wanted to account for the results obtained by previous researchers, not merely demonstrate that they were incorrect. Finally, we also wished to explain *why* the previous models had been selected, given that they were false as judged by the DHSY equation. This first attempt at 'selection encompassing' necessitated determining an equation which closely mimicked the DGP in those aspects relevant to consumers' expenditure and then analysing what the rival methodologies should have found when applied to such a DGP compared with what they did find. If the two matched, we could feel much more confident that the DHSY model really could account for all the available evidence.

7   We explicitly conditioned consumption on income despite the 'simultaneous equations problem'. I had undertaken a number of empirical, analytical and Monte Carlo studies of least squares and instrumental variables methods in simultaneous systems (see chapter 2; Hendry, 1973, 1975a, 1979b;[1] Hendry and Harrison, 1974). The overall findings suggested that dynamic mis-specification induced far larger biases than simultaneity, unless the latter corresponded to implicitly regressing a variable on itself when the true coefficient was zero (as in an identity $W \equiv X + Z$ where X is then regressed on W even though X does not actually depend on W). Although income could only be spent or saved, and hence appeared to have expenditure as a component, that was an *allocation* equation *given* income, not the equation *determining* income. Also, the anticipated coefficient of income in a consumption function was far from zero. The estimated income coefficients, which did not appear upward biased relative to their anticipated values, and the constancy of the final model suggested that the bias must be small, since any potential bias should change with changing data covariances. We reported instrumental variables estimates, which were also consistent with negligible biases, but these were conditional on a model specification selected by least squares. The concept of weak exogeneity, analysed in chapter 15, would have helped to sustain our analysis.

8   The differencing/unit roots issue is confronted and related to ECMs. It is amusing to recall my confidence that we had finally resolved that problem – immediately prior to the extensive later developments on cointegration (see chapter 19).

9   Multicollinearity was treated as an issue of 'choice of parameterization' rather than 'choice of regressors'. Orthogonalizing transformations were selected as corresponding to parameters of interest, and related to a simple theory-model of agent behaviour.

10   Seasonality and prior seasonal adjustment were discussed, with the preferred empirical solution being close to the recommended procedure of Box and Jenkins (1976) in that it involved four-period differences, but with a four-period lagged ECM as well. A crucial distinction was drawn between the effects of seasonal adjustment on procedures for estimating a known model and on procedures for selecting models. It could be very difficult to uncover the 'correct' equation from adjusted data.

11   Yet again, the time-series versus econometrics debate was noted. On this occasion, however, it was the predictive failure of the former, and not the latter, which provided decisive evidence favouring 'econometric' equations for forecasting.

12   Measurement error effects were studied since we had anticipated that these might be large, but yielded a blank.

13   A servomechanistic interpretation of behaviour was very much to the fore. This was only partly because the selected feedback model needed a rationalization. Since econometricians were also economic agents and yet had proved unable to predict future events at all satisfactorily despite detailed empirical studies, I did not believe that all other agents were somehow able to predict the future correctly. An important aspect of error correc-

tion is that it allows agents to make mistakes and yet maintain consistent long-run plans and so mimic the economists' view of rationality. That idea deserved exploration and DHSY offered a tentative formulation.

The next three chapters form a closely linked sequence in time, in ideas and in subject matter. They reflect an attempt to develop methodology through practical application and are both the precursors of and stimulants to much of the formal analysis in part III. They also illustrate a progressive sequence of empirical models, and demonstrate that econometric models can survive for sustained periods after their creation.

On the one hand, the substantive estimates in DHSY had an immediate practical impact in the United Kingdom. Many of the economy-wide econometric models tried a variant of it in their systems, and retained such an equation for the next six to eight years. However, some of the outcomes prompted considerable controversy. For example, embedding DHSY in the Treasury model led to a large number of sign changes on important multipliers: owing to the inflation effect, stimulating demand could have perverse effects if inflation rose more rapidly than real disposable income, inducing an offsetting fall in the consumption–income ratio. Bean (1977) provided a rigorous test of our findings which proved persuasive in the adoption of a similar formulation in the Treasury model. Thus, the DHSY equation was embodied in the main econometric model used for economic policy advice, yet for a prolonged period it did not suffer from the effects of the 'Lucas critique' (1976) despite the absence of explicit expectations formation.

On the other hand, the modelling strategy manifest in DHSY still seemed too much 'hit or miss'. Fortunately, it also presented many possible directions for improvement, and several of these are followed up below.

Note

1   First written in 1975.

1 Introduction

Although the relationship between consumers' expenditure and disposable income is one of the most thoroughly researched topics in quantitative economics, no consensus seems to have emerged in the United Kingdom about the short-run dynamic interactions between these two important variables. In support of this contention, we would cite the plethora of substantially different quarterly regression equations which have been reported by Byron (1970), Deaton (1972b, 1977), Ball et al. (1975), Bispham (1975), Shepherd et al. (1975), Wall et al. (1975), Townend (1976), Bean (1977) and chapter 2. Moreover, this list of studies is representative, rather than exhaustive.

The diversity of the published estimates is really surprising since most of the investigators seem to have based their regression equations on similar economic theories and seem to have used approximately the same data series. Specifically, therefore, we wish to explain why their results manifest quite dissimilar short-run multipliers, lag reactions and long-run responses. This requires examining the extent to which the estimates are mutually incompatible as well as their inconsistency with the empirical evidence. More generally, we hope to be able to specify which aspects of the methodology used were primarily responsible for creating the differences in the published results.

Close inspection of the above list of studies reveals that, despite their superficial similarities, they differ in many respects the importance of which is not obvious *a priori*. Initially, therefore, to highlight the issues involved we concentrated on three studies only (Hendry (chapter 2), Ball et al. (1975) and Wall et al. (1975), denoted H, B and W respectively). Rather than use the elegant but very technical theory recently developed for testing 'non-nested' models (see Pesaran and Deaton, 1978) we have chosen to 'standardize' those aspects of the three studies which do not seem crucial to explaining the original differences between the results. This allows analogues of the contending models to be embedded in a common framework within which nested tests are feasible. By stressing the implications for each model of the results obtained by others it will be seen below that our approach assigns a major role to mis-specification analysis (see Hendry (1979b) for a discussion of mis-specification theory in dynamic systems).

A proliferation of non-nested models is symptomatic of certain inappropriate aspects of present practice in econometrics. We would suggest that this problem can be mitigated to some extent by adopting the following principles. First, we consider it an essential (if minimal) requirement that any new model should be related to existing 'explanations' in a constructive research strategy such that previous models are only supplanted if new proposals account (so far as possible) for previously understood results, and also explain some new phenomena. Second, to avoid directionless 'research' and uninterpretable measurements, a theoretical framework is also essential. Unfortunately, much existing economic analysis relates to hypothetical constructs (for example, 'permanent income') and/or is based on unclearly specified but stringent *ceteris paribus* assumptions, and leaves many important decisions in formulating an operational model to *ad hoc* considerations (e.g. functional form, dynamic specification, error structure, treatment of seasonality etc.). Nevertheless, economic theory does furnish some helpful postulates about behaviour in steady-state environments and to guide an empirical analysis it seems sensible to incorporate such information as is available explicitly. Third, to be empirically acceptable, an econometric model obviously must account for the properties of the data (e.g. the autocorrelation function in a time-series study). It is not valid to 'accomplish' this aim simply by not looking for counter-evidence (e.g. by claiming the absence of autocorrelation in a dynamic equation on the basis of an insignificant value for a Durbin–Watson d statistic).

The combination of not encompassing previous findings, introducing *ad hoc* auxiliary assumptions and not rigorously testing data compatibility leaves plenty of room for a diversity of outcomes from model building even in a common theoretical framework with a common data set. Indeed, one could characterize 'econometric modelling' as an attempt to match the hypothetical data generation process postulated by economic theory with the main properties of the observed data. Any model which fails to account for the *gestalt* of results which are obtained from the data set cannot constitute the actual data generation process. Consequently, a further minimal requirement when modelling from a common data set is that the chosen model should explain both the *results* obtained by other researchers and *why* their research methods led to their published conclusions. The former usually can be achieved through the appropriate mis-specification analysis from a sufficiently general model which could be based on *a priori* theory (see, for example, chapter 3) or empirical considerations. Any theory gains some plausibility by an explanation of different empirical results, but a data-based construction always must be susceptible to a potential *post hoc ergo propter hoc* fallacy. However, given the research methods which any investigator claimed to use it is not trivial even from a data-based general model to explain why they reached certain conclusions. That the general model is not obtained by every investigator seems to depend on the operation of (self-imposed) constraints limiting the range of specifications, estimators, diagnostic tests etc. which are employed. Such arbitrary and unnecessary constraints can play a large role in determining the final equations selected and a further major objective of this chapter is to illustrate the advantages of using a wide range of different techniques (including both 'econometric' and 'time-series' methods) when analysing aggregate economic data.

We believe that considerable insight can be achieved by trying to explain the inter-relationships between the consumption function studies in chapter 2, Ball et al. (1975) and Wall et al. (1975). Our analysis proceeds by noting seven potential explanations for the main differences between these three studies, namely the choice of (i) data series, (ii) methods of seasonal adjustment, (iii) other data transformations, (iv) functional forms, (v) lag structures, (vi) diagnostic statistics and (vii) estimation methods. It proves possible to 'standardize' the models on a common basis for (i)–(iv) such that the major differences between the studies persist. This allows us to nest the standardized contending theories as special cases of a general hypothesis and test to see which (if any) are acceptable on statistical grounds. Such an approach leads to the selection on *statistical criteria* of the equation which we consider to be the least reasonable of the three on the basis of *economic theory* considerations. To account for this outcome we investigate the role of measurement errors in the data, but draw a blank. Next, we develop an econometric relationship (which was originally obtained as an empirical description of the data series) and show that it satisfies our desired theory criteria, fits as well as the previously best fitting equation and includes the rejected models as special cases. Moreover, this relationship is such that, if it were the true model, then it is reasonably easy to see in retrospect why the alternative research methods led to their various conclusions. Finally, we conduct a variety of tests on a modified version of our chosen model and show that it adequately accounts for the atypical consumption behaviour observed over the period 1971–5.

The data and the three econometric studies are described in sections 2 and 3 respectively. Sections 4 and 5 investigate the standardization aspects and multicollinearity respectively and in section 6 we consider the selection of the equation which performs 'best' on statistical criteria. Section 7 discusses the effects of certain of the data transformations on measurement errors. In section 8 we propose a possible explanation for all the previous results through a serious, but hard to detect, dynamic mis-specification, and conditional on this interpretation re-evaluate the role of (v)–(vii) above. Inflation effects are considered in section 9 and section 10 concludes the study.

It should be noted that throughout the chapter we are only concerned with expenditure excluding durables. Also, we must stress the most of the modelling described below was carried out during 1974–5 using data series in 1963 prices and estimating up to the end of 1970 only. Re-estimation using an extended data set in 1970 prices was undertaken in early 1977 without re-specifying any of the earlier equations and still terminating the estimation period in 1970. The data to the end of 1975 was used for testing and the additional equations based on Deaton (1977) were included at this stage.

2 The Data

Let Y_t denote personal disposable income, Cd_t consumers' expenditure on durable goods, S_t personal saving and C_t consumers' expenditure on all other goods and services, all variables being in constant prices. The main series used in this study are taken from *Economic Trends* (1976 Annual Supplement) and are quarterly, seasonally unadjusted in million pounds at 1970 prices. Although C_t and Cd_t are separately deflated, the series are such that $Y_t = C_t + Cd_t + S_t$. Figure 8.1 shows the time series of Y_t and C_t for the period 1958(i)–1976(ii) (the data for 1957 were used to create variables like $C_t - C_{t-4}$).

The salient features of the data are the strong trends in both C_t and Y_t, the magnitude and stability of the seasonal pattern in C_t compared with that of Y_t (although the seasonal shape has tended to become increasingly 'elongated' over time), the regularity of the 'output' series C_t compared with the 'input' series Y_t, and the marked change in the behaviour of the Y_t series after 1972. Detailed scrutiny reveals the presence of 'business cycles' which are more clearly seen in the transformed series $\Delta_4 Y_t = Y_t - Y_{t-4}$ and $\Delta_4 C_t$ graphed in figure 8.2 (Δ_4 is referred to below as the four-period or annual difference, as compared with the fourth dif-

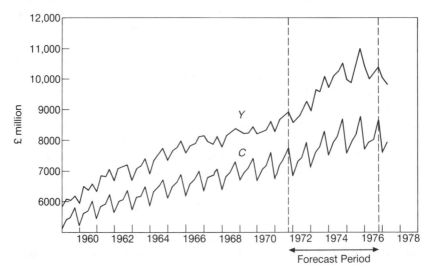

Figure 8.1 Time paths of personal disposable income Y and consumers' expenditure C.

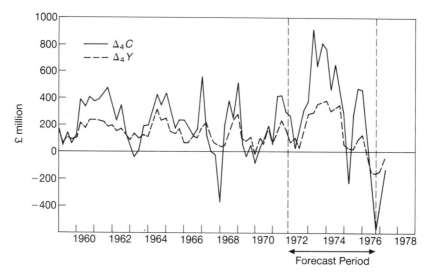

Figure 8.2   Four-period changes in data series.

ference Δ_1^4). Figure 8.2 also confirms the greater variance of the income series, and casual inspection suggests that using annual differences has removed most of the seasonality in both series. As shown in figure 8.3, the average propensity to consume (C_t/Y_t, denoted APC) has fallen steadily over the sample period from around 0.9 to under 0.8 although, as explained below, this evidence is still consonant with a long-run income elasticity of expenditure close to unity. If C_t is plotted against Y_t as in figure 8.4, marked differences in the average propensities to consume in the various

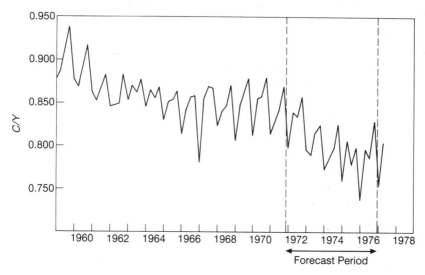

Figure 8.3   The average propensity to consume.

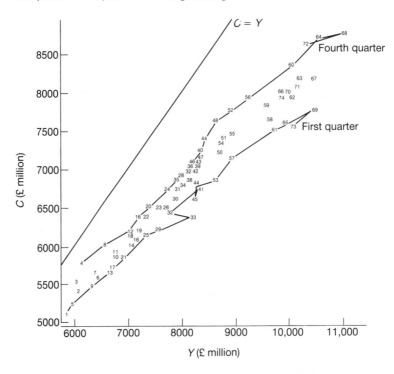

Figure 8.4   Scatter diagram of personal disposable income and consumers' expenditure.

quarters are clear. The upper and lower lines show the patterns of observations for the fourth and first quarters respectively. Finally, plotting $\Delta_4 C$ against $\Delta_4 Y$ yields a scatter diagram (see figure 8.5) in which the slope (marginal propensity to consume, MPC) of the 'short-run' consumption function is much smaller than that of the relationship portrayed in figure 8.4, and a wide range of values of $\Delta_4 C$ seems to be compatible with any given value for $\Delta_4 Y$. A closely similar picture emerges from the equivalent graphs of the logarithms of the data series, except that now the seasonal pattern for C_t does not appear to change over time (see figure 8.6). The

Table 8.1   Correlograms for C_t, Y_t, $\Delta_4 C_t$ and $\Delta_4 Y_t$

Lag	1	2	3	4	5	6	7	8
C	0.79	0.80	0.75	0.99	0.76	0.76	0.72	0.99
Y	0.95	0.95	0.93	0.97	0.93	0.93	0.91	0.96
$\Delta_4 C$	0.49	0.24	−0.02	−0.28	−0.23	−0.24	−0.02	−0.07
$\Delta_4 Y$	0.50	0.24	0.04	−0.33	−0.17	−0.16	−0.16	−0.02
Lag	9	10	11	12	13	14	15	16
C	0.72	0.73	0.67	0.99	0.68	0.68	0.60	0.98
Y	0.92	0.92	0.89	0.96	0.91	0.90	0.86	0.95
$\Delta_4 C$	−0.05	0.09	0.02	0.04	0.02	0.06	0.20	0.35
$\Delta_4 Y$	−0.03	0.01	−0.02	−0.03	−0.04	−0.08	0.04	0.18

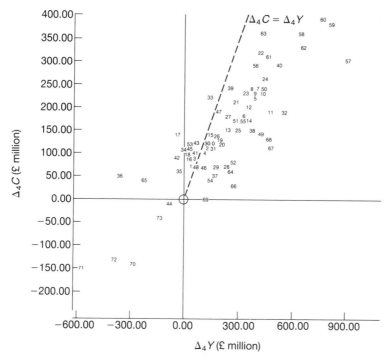

Figure 8.5   Scatter diagram of four-period changes.

correlograms for C_t, Y_t, $\Delta_4 C_t$ and $\Delta_4 Y_t$ over the period to 1970(iv) are shown in table 8.1.

From the slightly shorter data series 1957(i)–1967(iv) in 1958 prices, Prothero and Wallis (1976) obtained a number of univariate time-series models for C_t and Y_t, no

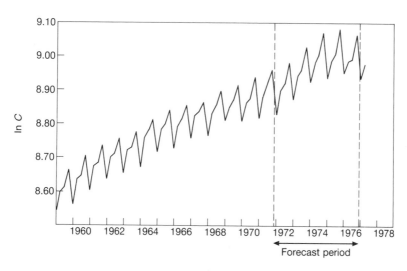

Figure 8.6   Logarithms of consumers' expenditure.

one of which was uniformly superior. Their most parsimonious descriptions were

$$\Delta_1 \Delta_4 C_t = (1 - 0.59L^4)\hat{\varepsilon}_t \qquad \hat{\sigma} = 32.0 \qquad \chi^2_{15} = 6.8 \tag{8.1}$$
$$(0.14)$$

$$\Delta_1 \Delta_4 Y_t = (1 - 0.58L^4)\hat{\varepsilon}_t \qquad \hat{\sigma} = 103.0 \qquad \chi^2_{15} = 9.6. \tag{8.2}$$
$$(0.18)$$

In (8.1) and (8.2), L denotes the lag operator such that $L^j C_t = C_{t-j}$, ε_t represents a white noise error process with estimated standard deviation $\hat{\sigma}$, and χ^2_{15} is the Box–Pierce (1970) test for a random residual correlogram. Such time-series descriptions show C_t and Y_t to obey similar equations but with the variance of the random component of Y_t nearly ten times as large as that of C_t.

3 Three Econometric Studies and their Research Methods

Since the main objective of this study is to explain why a large number of econometric descriptions of the data have been offered, there seems no need for a long section dealing with relevant economic theories. However, we do wish to stress that most theories of the consumption function were formulated to reconcile the low short-run MPC with the relative stability claimed for the APC over medium to long data periods (see *inter alia* Duesenberry, 1949; Brown, 1952; Friedman, 1957; Ando and Modigliani, 1963). Broadly speaking, all these theories postulate lag mechanisms which mediate the response of C_t to changes in Y_t (e.g. previous highest C_t, C_{t-1}, 'permanent income' and wealth respectively). Thus, the permanent income hypothesis (PIH) assumes that

$$C_t = \theta Y_{pt} + u_t, \tag{8.3}$$

where u_t is independent of Y_{pt} and has finite variance, and where Y_{pt} is 'permanent income'. Friedman (1957) approximated Y_{pt} using

$$(1 - \lambda L) Y_{pt} = (1 - \lambda) Y_t \tag{8.4}$$

to obtain

$$C_t = \theta(1 - \lambda) (1 - \lambda L)^{-1} Y_t + u_t, \tag{8.5}$$

while Sargent (1977) interprets this as a rational expectations formulation when Y_t is generated by

$$\Delta_1 Y_t = a + (1 - \lambda L)\varepsilon_t, \tag{8.6}$$

which would add an intercept to (8.5). Since Y_t is assumed exogenous, (8.3) and (8.6) ensure that C_t and Y_t will have similar time-series properties, and as Sargent (1977) shows

$$\Delta_1 C_t = \theta(1 - \lambda)\varepsilon_t + \theta a + u_t - u_{t-1}$$
$$= \theta a + (1 - \lambda^* L)\varepsilon^*_t, \tag{8.7}$$

where ε_t^* is white noise and λ^* depends on θ, λ, σ_u^2 and σ_ε^2. Since $\sigma_{\varepsilon^*}^2 > \sigma_u^2$, it is of course more efficient to analyse (8.5) than (8.7).

At the aggregate level, a steady-state form of the life cycle hypothesis (LCH) is exposited by Modigliani (1975) as

$$C_t = \alpha Y_t + (\delta - r)A_t, \tag{8.8}$$

where A_t is end period private wealth and r (the rate of return on assets), α and δ are constant. Out of steady state, α and δ (like θ in (8.3)) vary with a number of factors including the rate of interest and the expected growth of productivity. If capital gains and interest are included in income, then from (8.8) and the identity

$$A_t = A_{t-1} + Y_{t-1} - C_{t-1} \tag{8.9}$$

we can obtain

$$\Delta_1 C_t = \alpha \Delta_1 Y_t + (\delta - r)(Y_{t-1} - C_{t-1})$$

or

$$C_t = \alpha Y_t + (\delta - r - \alpha)Y_{t-1} + (1 - \delta + r)C_{t-1}, \tag{8.10}$$

which again produces a distributed lag model of C_t and Y_t.[1]

It is noticeable that neither the PIH nor the LCH is much concerned with seasonal patterns of expenditure and models based on such theories are often estimated from annual or from seasonally adjusted quarterly data series.

Against this background we can consider the three econometric studies.

(H) Hendry (chapter 2) estimated several equations of the form

$$C_t = a_0 + a_1 Y_t + a_2 C_{t-1} + \sum_{j=1}^{3} b_j Q_{jt} + \sum_{j=1}^{4} d_j Q_{jt} t + \varepsilon_t \qquad (t = 1, \ldots, T), \tag{8.11}$$

where Q_{jt} denotes a dummy variable for the jth quarter. He imposed various restrictions on the parameters, used a number of different estimators and considered various autocorrelation structures for ε_t. For example, assuming a constant seasonal pattern $(d_j = 0, j = 1, \ldots, 4)$, no autocorrelation and using raw data, 1957(i)–1967(iv) in 1958 prices, least squares estimation yielded (see H, table 2.1)

$$\hat{C}_t = 377 + 0.10 Y_t + 0.84 C_{t-1} + \hat{S}_t, \tag{8.12}$$
$$\quad\;\; (76)\;\; (0.06)\quad\; (0.09)$$

$$R^2 = 0.994 \qquad \hat{\sigma} = 30.4 \qquad DW = 2.6.$$

In (8.12) the numbers in parentheses are standard errors,

$$\hat{S}_t = \sum_{j=1}^{3} \hat{b}_j Q_{jt},$$

R^2 is the squared coefficient of multiple correlation, $\hat{\sigma}$ is the standard deviation of the residuals and DW is the Durbin–Watson statistic. Then testing (8.12) for (i) fourth-order autoregressive residuals, (ii) omitted four-period lagged values of

C_t, Y_t and C_{t-1} and (iii) an evolving seasonal pattern, H found that each of these three factors was present if allowed for *separately*. When included in combinations, however, they appeared to act as substitutes since only the last remained significant in the three sets of pairwise comparisons.

Consequently, H selected (8.11) (with ε_t assumed serially independent) as the best description of his data and obtained the following least squares estimates (instrumental variables estimates were similar):

$$\hat{C}_t = 1994 + 0.19Y_t + 0.22C_{t-1} + \hat{S}_t + \sum_{j=1}^{4} \hat{a}_j Q_{jt}t,$$

$$(369) \quad (0.04) \quad (0.14)$$

(8.13)

$$R^2 = 0.998 \qquad \hat{\sigma} = 17.6 \qquad DW = 2.2.$$

When selecting this outcome, all other potential mis-specifications were apparently deliberately ignored by H to highlight the problems of stochastic specification. Even granting this escape from sins of omission, there are several important drawbacks to econometric formulations like (8.11)–(8.13), and many of the following criticisms apply to other published regression equations. First, the assumed seasonal pattern is *ad hoc* and would yield meaningless results if extrapolated much beyond the sample period. Moreover, one of the more interesting aspects of the data (the regular seasonal pattern of C_t) is attributed to unexplained factors, where by contrast a model like

$$C_t = \sum_{i=1}^{4} \alpha_i Q_{it} Y_t$$

would at least correspond to the possible behavioural hypothesis of a different MPC in each quarter of the year. Second, since the derived mean lag and long-run (static equilibrium) MPC coefficients in (8.12) are given by $\hat{a}_2/(1 - \hat{a}_2)$ and $\hat{a}_1/(1 - \hat{a}_2)$ respectively, these can be altered considerably by minor changes in $\hat{a}_2$ when that coefficient is close to unity. In turn, $\hat{a}_2$ can vary markedly with different treatments of residual autocorrelation. Next, both the short-run and long-run MPCs are very small in (8.13) (yielding a long-run elasticity of about 0.2) and are radically different from the corresponding estimates in (8.12) although only the treatment of seasonality has changed. In part this is due to the inclusion of a trend in (8.13), but this is hardly an explanation and simply prompts the question as to why the trend is significant when one believes that the economic variables are actually determining the behaviour of C_t (most of the very close fit of (8.13) is due to the trend and seasonals). Finally, it is difficult to evaluate the plausibility of the results *as presented* in (8.12) and (8.13). For example, R^2 is unhelpful since the data are trending (see Granger and Newbold, 1974). Also, DW has both low power against high-order residual autocorrelation in static equations and an incorrect conventional significance level in dynamic equations[2] (see Durbin, 1970). No forecast or parameter stability tests are presented and the appropriateness of least squares is not obvious (although Hendry (chapter 2) did in fact publish forecast tests and other diagnostic checks and used less restrictive estimators).

Overall, with or without evolving seasonals, (8.11) does not seem to be a useful specification for studying consumption–income responses, however well it may happen to describe the data for a short time period.

(B) Ball et al. (1975) present an equation rather like (8.12) but based on seasonally adjusted data (abbreviated to SA below and denoted by a superscript a) for the period 1959(ii)–1970(iv), estimated by least squares:

$$(\widehat{C - G})_t^a = 185 + 0.23(Y - G)_t^a + 0.69(C - G)_{t-1}^a + (\hat{\phi}_1 D_t + \hat{\phi}_2 D_{t-1}),$$
$$\qquad\quad (65)\ (0.07) \qquad\qquad (0.09)$$

(8.14)

$$\bar{R}^2 = 0.99 \qquad \hat{\sigma} = 29.3 \qquad \text{DW} = 2.3.$$

D_t represents a dummy variable with zero values everywhere except for 1968(ii) when it is unity (1968(i) and (ii) are anomalous quarters owing to advance warning in the first quarter of 1968 of possible purchase tax increases in the second quarter; these duly materialized, and considerable switching of expenditure between these quarters resulted). G_t denotes direct transfer payments to individuals and, as specified in (8.14), G_t is immediately and completely spent. $\bar{R}^2$ is the adjusted value of R^2.

Many of the criticisms noted in H apply to (8.14) and, in addition, the use of SA data must be considered. Seasonal adjustment methods can be interpreted as filters applied to time series to remove frequency components at or near seasonal frequencies, such filters often being many-period weighted moving averages (e.g. 24 periods for quarterly data in the commonly used Bureau of Census Method II version X-11 program). In published statistics, single series tend to be separately adjusted. However, as documented by Wallis (1974), *separate* adjustment of series can distort the relationship between pairs of series and in particular can alter the underlying dynamic reactions. Thus, Wallis records a case of four-period lags being incorrectly identified as one period after SA and the possibility of such a dynamic misspecification applying to (8.14) merits investigation since earlier variants of (8.14) in the London Business School model based on unadjusted data used C_{t-4} as a regressor.

Note that the estimates in (8.14) again seem to imply a long-run (static equilibrium) elasticity of less than unity (MPC = 0.74, APC = 0.84) which is consistent with figure 8.3 and reasonably similar to (8.12) despite the very different treatment of seasonality.

(W) Wall et al. (1975) analyse total consumers' expenditure $C_t^* = Cd_t^a + C_t^a$ using SA data for 1955 (i)–1971 (iv) with estimation based on the transfer function methodology proposed by Box and Jenkins (1976). Their published model is

$$\dot{C}_t^* = 0.21 + 0.31\dot{Y}_t^a + 0.24\dot{Y}_{t-1}^a \quad \text{where} \quad \dot{x}_t = \frac{100(x_t - x_{t-1})}{x_{t-1}},$$
$$\qquad\quad (0.08)\quad\ (0.08)$$

(8.15)

$$R^2 = 0.56 \qquad \hat{\sigma} = 0.74.$$

The relative first-difference transformation was adopted to make the variables 'stationary'. Given their advocacy of Box–Jenkins methods, we assume that W estimated (8.15) with the residuals treated as 'white noise' because they had found no evidence of residual autocorrelation.

However, (8.15) has *no static equilibrium* solution and is only consistent with a steady-state growth rate of about 2 per cent per annum. Indeed, the *ad hoc* mean correction of 0.21 is 35 per cent of the mean of $\dot{C}^*$ and, as a consequence, the conventionally calculated long-run elasticity is 0.55. Moreover, (8.15) implies that any adjustment to income changes is completed within six months and is independent of any disequilibrium between the *levels* of C_t and Y_t. Also, the use of $C_t^* = C_t^a + Cd_t^a$ may entail some aggregation bias in view of the extra variables usually included in models of durables purchases (see, for example, Williams, 1972; Garganas, 1975). However, it is not surprising that (8.15) results from estimation based on data like that in figure 8.5.

4   A Standardized Framework

The studies listed as H, B and W above satisfy the requirement that approximately the same data set (C, Y) is involved in all three cases. Nevertheless, the results differ in many respects and are conditioned by very different auxiliary hypotheses. Indeed, the first problem is to find enough common elements to allow direct comparisons to be made! Our approach is to re-estimate close equivalents of (8.13)–(8.15) in a standard framework which tries to isolate which factors do, and which do not, induce differences in the results. We begin by examining the roles of the data period, seasonal adjustment procedures, data transformations and functional forms since it might be anticipated that small alterations to these should not greatly change the findings of any particular study.

We chose the data series graphed in figure 8.1, with the 20 observations for 1971(i)–1975(iv) being used purely for forecast tests.[3] The choice of data period did not seem to be too important, and we preferred raw to SA data for the reasons noted in the discussion of H and B, namely 'Wallis' effects' and our desire to 'model' the seasonal behaviour of C rather than filter it out. Sims (1974b) has pointed out that the use of raw data involves a potential risk of 'omitted seasonals' bias if there is also seasonal noise in the error on the equation of relevance; however, the estimates recorded below do not suggest the presence of such a problem.

A major assumption which we made in order to develop analogues of the various equations is that the closest equivalent of a transformation of the form $\Delta_1 Z_t^a = Z_t^a - Z_{t-1}^a$ (in SA data) is $\Delta_4 Z_t = Z_t - Z_{t-4}$ (in raw data), since both transformed variables represent changes net of seasonal factors (we have also estimated most of the analogue equations using SA data and report below on the negligible changes this induces). The *converse* equivalence is not valid, however, since dynamics should be unaltered when a linear filter is correctly applied to a relationship (see Wallis, 1974; and chapter 6). Also, we assumed that $\Delta_1 \ln x_t \approx \Delta_1 x_t / x_{t-1}$ (where ln denotes $\log_e$) and so could approximate W's variable $\dot{C}_t^*$ in SA data by $\Delta_4 \ln(C_t + Cd_t)$ in raw data.

Finally, models in differences can be related to those in levels by noting that there are two distinct interpretations of 'differencing', a point most easily demonstrated by the following relationship:[4]

$$x_t = \beta_1 w_t + \beta_2 w_{t-4} + \beta_3 x_{t-4} + \sum_{j=1}^{4} (\theta_j + \mu_j t) Q_{jt} + v_t, \tag{8.16}$$

where w_t is an exogenous regressor generated by a stationary stochastic process and v_t is a stationary error.

Differencing as a Filter or Operator

Applying the operation Δ_4 to equation (8.16) yields

$$\Delta_4 x_t = \beta_1 \Delta_4 w_t + \beta_2 \Delta_4 w_{t-4} + \beta_3 \Delta_4 x_{t-4} + \sum_{j=1}^{4} 4\mu_j Q_{jt} + \Delta_4 v_t \tag{8.17}$$

and hence the features which are altered comprise:

1 the elimination of trends and the re-interpretation of the constant seasonal pattern in (8.17) as corresponding with the evolving pattern in (8.16);
2 the autocorrelation properties of v_t (e.g. if $v_t = v_{t-4} + \nu_t$, where ν_t is white noise, then $\Delta_4 v_t$ is white noise, whereas if $v_t = \nu_t$, $\Delta_4 v_t$ is a four-period simple moving average with a coefficient of -1);
3 the form of all the non-dummy variables in (8.16) (which re-occur as annual differences in (8.17)).

Differencing as a Set of Coefficient Restrictions

Applying the restrictions $\beta_1 = -\beta_2$ and $\beta_3 = 1$ to (8.16) yields

$$\Delta_4 x_t = \beta_1 \Delta_4 w_t + \sum_{j=1}^{4} (\theta_j + \mu_j t) Q_{jt} + v_t. \tag{8.18}$$

Now, the changes from (8.16) are the elimination of w_{t-4} and x_{t-4} as independent regressors and the occurrence of the transformed variables $\Delta_4 x_t$ and $\Delta_4 w_t$. The interpretation of the constant and the seasonal pattern is unaltered and when the restrictions are valid the autocorrelation properties of v_t are unaffected – if v_t in (8.16) is white noise then so is v_t in (8.18) (contrast the arguments presented in Granger and Newbold, 1974). One immediate and obvious application of this interpretation is the converse step of deriving (8.16) from (8.18) which allows valid comparisons of models involving differenced variables with those using level variables.

Combining all the above approximations, we move from (8.15) via the equivalence of $\dot{C}_t^a$ with $\Delta_4 \ln C_t$ to

$$\Delta_4 \ln C_t = \delta_0 + \delta_1 \Delta_4 \ln Y_t + \delta_2 \Delta_4 \ln Y_{t-1} + e_t$$

$$= \delta_0 + (\delta_1 + \delta_2) \Delta_4 \ln Y_t - \delta_2 \Delta_1 \Delta_4 \ln Y_t + e_t, \tag{8.19}$$

which provides our version of (8.15). For comparison with equations in log-levels we use the unrestricted version of (8.19), namely

$$\ln C_t = \lambda_1 \ln Y_t + \lambda_2 \ln Y_{t-4} + \lambda_3 \ln Y_{t-1} + \lambda_4 \ln Y_{t-5} + \lambda_5 \ln C_{t-4} + \lambda_6 + e_t, \tag{8.20}$$

where (8.19) corresponds to imposing $\lambda_1 = -\lambda_2, \lambda_3 = -\lambda_4$ and $\lambda_5 = 1$ in (8.20). Since no seasonal dummy variables are introduced in (8.20) this procedure requires that Δ_4 in (8.19) removes any seasonal factors; some support for such a proposition is provided in figure 8.2 but this issue will be reconsidered below. We assumed that it was reasonable to use C_t in place of C_t^* in developing (8.19) for reasons presented above. Throughout, we have estimated most specifications in both linear and log-linear forms, comparing these where necessary using the likelihood criterion proposed by Sargan (1964a). Thus (8.19) can be compared through (8.20) and the linear-log mapping with whatever equivalents are chosen for (8.13) and (8.14) (we chose to use C_t rather than $C_t - G_t$ when approximating (8.14) to maintain closer comparison with both (8.15) and (8.11)).

The main justification for adopting the above approximations is simply that the important features of and differences between the results in (8.13)–(8.15) survive the standardization sequence. First, to illustrate the effects of changing the sample period to 1958(ii)–1970(iv) and using 1970 prices, re-estimation of (8.13) by least squares yields

$$\hat{C}_t = 2556 + 0.20Y_t + 0.35C_{t-1} + 83D_t^0 - 514Q_{1t} - 74Q_{2t}$$
$$\quad\;\; (537)\;\;(0.05)\quad(0.12)\qquad(33)\qquad(60)\qquad(57)$$

$$- 187Q_{3t} + 16.3t - 6.7Q_{1t}t - 2.2Q_{2t}t - 0.3Q_{3t}t, \qquad (8.21)$$
$$\quad (38)\qquad(3.7)\quad(1.3)\qquad(1.2)\qquad(1.2)$$

$$R^2 = 0.996 \qquad \hat{\sigma} = 39.4 \qquad \text{DW} = 2.2 \qquad z_1(20) = 130 \qquad z_2(15) = 25.$$

In (8.21), $D^0 = D_{t-1} - D_t$, which assumes that the 1968(i) announcement caused a switch in expenditure between quarters.[5] $z_1(k)$ is a test of parameter stability or one-period-ahead forecast accuracy using the actual future values of the regressors for the next k quarters. Letting f_t denote the forecast error, then

$$z_1(k) = \sum_{t=T+1}^{T+k} \left(\frac{f_t}{\hat{\sigma}}\right)^2,$$

which would be distributed as χ_k^2 in large samples if the parameters in (8.21) remained constant.[6] $z_2(l)$ is the Pierce (1971) residual correlogram statistic distributed as χ_l^2 in large samples when the residuals are serially independent.[7] The only noticeable differences between (8.13) and (8.21) are the change in $\hat{\sigma}$ due to the change in the base of the implicit deflator for C, and the increase in the coefficient of C_{t-1}. However, z_2 indicates the presence of significant autocorrelation (actually, of fourth order) and z_1 strongly rejects parameter stability (when comparing equations, it should be noted that z_1 is *not* a measure of *absolute* forecast accuracy).

Next, we estimated two analogues of (8.14) from the same sample, namely

$$\hat{C}_t = 509 + 0.18Y_t + 0.75C_{t-1} + 68D_t^0 - 812Q_{1t} + 32Q_{2t} - 169Q_{3t}, \qquad (8.22)$$
$$\quad (142)\;(0.08)\quad(0.11)\qquad(49)\qquad(63)\qquad(46)\qquad(26)$$

$$R^2 = 0.990 \qquad \hat{\sigma} = 62.0 \qquad \text{DW} = 2.1 \qquad z_1(20) = 190 \qquad z_2(15) = 86,$$

which, not surprisingly, is also similar to (8.12); and

$$\hat{C}_t = 734 + 0.28Y_t - 0.09\Delta_1 Y_t + 0.59C_{t-4} + 71D_t^0 - 251Q_{1t} - 92Q_{2t} - 81Q_{3t}$$
$$\quad (112) \; (0.06) \quad (0.06) \qquad (0.08) \qquad (44) \qquad (58) \quad (27) \quad (27)$$
$$(8.23)$$

$$R^2 = 0.993 \qquad \hat{\sigma} = 53.2 \qquad DW = 1.3 \qquad z_1(20) = 129 \qquad z_2(12) = 21,$$

which is reasonably similar to (8.14). ($\Delta_1 Y_t$ was included in (8.23) to allow for a one-lag income effect but DW still indicates considerable first-order residual autocorrelation.) Lastly, for (8.15)

$$\Delta_4 \hat{C}_t = 78.5 + 0.34\Delta_4 Y_t - 0.14\Delta_1\Delta_4 Y_t + 61\Delta_4 D_t^0, \tag{8.24}$$
$$\quad (10.1) \; (0.04) \qquad (0.04) \qquad (22)$$

$$R^2 = 0.70 \qquad \hat{\sigma} = 40.5 \qquad DW = 1.7 \qquad z_1(20) = 94.0 \qquad z_2(16) = 20.$$

We have quoted (8.24) in linear (rather than log) form for immediate comparison with (8.21)–(8.23) but, despite this change of functional form, (8.24) reproduces the main features of (8.15) (a long-run elasticity of about 0.5, a large and significant intercept and 'white noise' errors). All the re-estimated analogues are rejected by the forecast test, although this does not affect our ability to choose between them; an explanation for the overall poor forecasts is provided in section 9. Equation (8.22) also exhibits very marked four-period autocorrelation and re-estimation assuming an error of the form $u_t = \rho_4 u_{t-4} + \varepsilon_t$ yielded $\hat{\rho}_4 = 0.98$ (0.03), $z_2(12) = 22$ and $\hat{\sigma} = 42.9$. Consequently, all the models estimated from the raw data require some allowance for four-period effects.

A similar story emerges if SA data are used and seasonal dummies are omitted from all the models. Specifically for (8.22), (8.23) and (8.24) we obtained (for the rather different data period 1963(i)–1973(ii), forecasting 1973(iii)–1975(ii))

$$\hat{C}_t^a = 250 + 0.18Y_t^a + 0.75C_{t-1}^a + 101D_t^0, \tag{8.22a}$$
$$\quad (154) \; (0.04) \qquad (0.06) \qquad (29)$$

$$R^2 = 0.990 \qquad \hat{\sigma} = 39.3 \qquad DW = 2.5 \qquad z_1(8) = 35.5 \qquad z_2(9) = 8.4;$$

$$\hat{C}_t^a = 567 + 0.41Y_t^a - 0.20\Delta_1 Y_t^a + 0.44C_{t-4}^a + 81D_t^0, \tag{8.23a}$$
$$\quad (145) \; (0.03) \qquad (0.05) \qquad (0.05) \qquad (30)$$

$$R^2 = 0.990 \qquad \hat{\sigma} = 41.2 \qquad DW = 1.5 \qquad z_1(8) = 138 \qquad z_2(6) = 6.3;$$

$$\Delta_4 \hat{C}_t^a = 66 + 0.37\Delta_4 Y_t^a - 0.16\Delta_1\Delta_4 Y_t^a + 86\Delta_4 D_t^0, \tag{8.24a}$$
$$\quad (11) \; (0.03) \qquad (0.04) \qquad (23)$$

$$R^2 = 0.80 \qquad \hat{\sigma} = 43.9 \qquad DW = 1.8 \qquad z_1(8) = 26.2 \qquad z_2(10) = 20;$$

$$\Delta_1 \hat{C}_t^a = 21 + 0.31\Delta_1 Y_t^a - 0.11\Delta_1^2 Y_t^a + 69\Delta_1 D_t^0, \tag{8.15a}$$
$$\quad (8.6) \; (0.08) \qquad (0.05) \qquad (19)$$

$$R^2 = 0.52 \qquad \hat{\sigma} = 44.5 \qquad DW = 2.9 \qquad z_1(8) = 7.3 \qquad z_2(10) = 24.$$

These results support our contention that the choices of the exact data period and of the seasonal adjustment procedures do not markedly affect the *estimates* obtained, although it should be noted that the goodness of fit ranking of the models on SA data is the opposite of that prevailing with raw data. Only (8.24a) has an error variance close to its raw data counterpart, and hence the *selection* of equations is greatly altered by SA.

Thus (i)–(iv) can be eliminated as the main factors accounting for the differences in (8.13)–(8.15) and we can proceed to consider (v)–(vii) which represent more important differences in methodology. At this stage, our standardized analogues of (8.13)–(8.15) can be nested as special cases of the model

$$C_t = \xi_0 + \xi_1 Y_t + \xi_2 Y_{t-4} + \xi_3 \Delta_1 Y_t + \xi_4 \Delta_1 Y_{t-4} + \xi_5 C_{t-4} + \sum_{j=1}^{3} \xi_{5+j} Q_{jt}$$

$$+ \xi_9 D_t^0 + \xi_{10} D_{t-4}^0 + \xi_{11} C_{t-1} + \xi_{12} t + \sum_{j=1}^{3} \xi_{12+j} Q_{jt} t + \varepsilon_t, \tag{8.25}$$

and hence (8.21)–(8.24) can all be tested directly against the estimated version of (8.25).

5 On Multicollinearity

Can sensible estimates of (8.25) be obtained given the general misapprehension that 'severe collinearity problems are bound to be present'? To resolve this, consider the well-known formula (see, for example, Theil, 1971, p. 174)

$$\frac{\hat{\xi}_i^2}{\widehat{\text{var}}(\hat{\xi}_i)} = \frac{(T - m) r_i^2}{1 - r_i^2} \qquad (i = 1, \ldots, m), \tag{8.26}$$

where r_i is the partial correlation between the regressand and the ith regressor allowing for the influence of the other $m - 1$ regressors in the equation. The left-hand side of (8.26) is the square of the conventionally calculated t statistic to test $H_0: \xi_i = 0$.

A crucial point is that a partial correlation like r_i can *increase* as m increases to $m + n$ even if the n added variables are highly (but not perfectly) collinear *provided they are relevant to explaining the regressand*. Thus t values can increase even though the moment matrix requiring inversion in least squares becomes 'more singular' in the sense of having a smaller determinant or a smaller ratio of the least to the greatest eigenvalue (compare, for example, the analysis assuming that the true model is known in Johnston, 1972, ch. 5.7). In effect, the issue is that 'collinearity problems' are likely to occur in conjunction with omitted variables problems. If the n initially excluded regressors are important in determining the regressand, then adding them may well help resolve what appears to be a collinearity problem between the m originally included variables, since 'small' t values can arise from downward biases in $\hat{\xi}_i$ as well as from 'large' values of $\widehat{\text{var}}(\hat{\xi}_i)$. Consequently, it is not universally valid to assume that a group of badly determined estimates indicates the presence of collinearity (to be solved by reducing the dimensionality of the parameter space) rather than omitted variables bias (solved by increasing the dimensionality of the parameter space). To illustrate these points consider the following estimates of a special case of (8.25) (which incidentally immediately demonstrates some misspecification of (8.23)):

$$\hat{C}_t = 2516 + 0.24Y_t - 0.07\Delta_1 Y_t + 0.38C_{t-4} + 13t + 65D_t^0 + \hat{S}_t, \qquad (8.27)$$
$$(627)\ (0.06)\quad (0.06)\qquad (0.12)\qquad (4)\ (40)$$

$$R^2 = 0.994 \qquad \hat{\sigma} = 48.8 \qquad DW = 1.6 \qquad z_1(20) = 119 \qquad z_2(12) = 37.$$

Conventionally, $\Delta_1 Y_t$ is 'insignificant' (but see Bock et al. (1973) for an analysis of some of the consequences of using a 'preliminary test' estimator in which 'insignificant' regressors are excluded prior to re-estimation), and the trend coefficient is significant. Now compare (8.27) with the equation in which every regressor also re-occurs with a four-period lag:[8]

$$\hat{C}_t = 921 + 0.31Y_t - 0.09\Delta_1 Y_t + 0.65C_{t-4} + 4t - 0.25Y_{t-4}$$
$$(695)\ (0.05)\quad (0.05)\qquad (0.13)\qquad (5)\ (0.06)$$

$$+\ 0.16\Delta_1 Y_{t-4} + 0.16C_{t-8} + 67D_t^0 - 46D_{t-4}^0 + \hat{S}_t, \qquad (8.28)$$
$$(0.05)\qquad\quad (0.11)\qquad (33)\qquad (34)$$

$$R^2 = 0.997 \qquad \hat{\sigma} = 38.7 \qquad DW = 2.1 \qquad z_1(20) = 110 \qquad z_2(8) = 12.$$

Patently, despite including three more regressors, the t values for $Y_t, \Delta_1 Y_t$ and C_{t-4} are *all* considerably larger in (8.28) than in (8.27), whereas the trend coefficient has become negligible in (8.28) and reveals the possibility of explaining the behaviour of C_t by economic variables alone (the seasonal dummies are also insignificant in (8.28)).

6 Selection of the 'Best' Equation

We now return to choosing between the various equations on statistical criteria. Even before estimating (8.25) it can be seen that (8.28) encompasses (8.23) and allows immediate rejection of the latter. Moreover, adding C_{t-1} to (8.28) cannot worsen the goodness of fit and so (8.22) can be rejected also. Testing (8.21) proves more of a problem since in chapter 2, (8.21) was chosen in preference to an equation similar to (8.28) (but excluding $\Delta_1 Y_t, \Delta_1 Y_{t-4}$ and C_{t-8}) whereas for the present data (8.28) fits marginally better. Strictly, (8.28) is not nested within the (initially) general equation (8.25), although this is only because of the presence of the insignificant regressor C_{t-8} and so can be ignored. Direct estimation of (8.25) yields

$$\hat{C}_t = 1618 + 0.28Y_t + 0.14C_{t-1} + 0.40C_{t-4} - 0.15Y_{t-4} - 0.09\Delta_1 Y_t$$
$$(692)\ (0.06)\quad (0.15)\qquad (0.15)\qquad (0.06)\qquad (0.06)$$

$$+\ 0.11\Delta_1 Y_{t-4} + 91D_t^0 - 11D_{t-4}^0 + 7.6t + 212Q_{1t} + 180Q_{2t}$$
$$(0.06)\qquad\quad (34)\qquad (34)\qquad (4.4)\ (129)\qquad (77)$$

$$+\ 278Q_{3t} + 2.95Q_{1t}t + 3.88Q_{2t}t + 4.63Q_{3t}t, \qquad (8.29)$$
$$(104)\qquad (1.87)\qquad (1.60)\qquad (1.52)$$

$$R^2 = 0.997 \qquad \hat{\sigma} = 36.2 \qquad DW = 2.0 \qquad z_1(20) = 114.$$

The fit of (8.29) is little better than that of either (8.21) or (8.28) even though many of the four lagged variables and evolving seasonals appear to be significant on t tests.

Thus, given either set of variables, the additional explanatory power of the other set is small and so to a considerable extent we re-confirm their substitute roles. Relative to chapter 2, the four-period lags are more important in the larger sample.

The most interesting outcome is that (8.24) cannot be rejected against (8.29) by testing the joint significance of all the restrictions using an F test based on the residual sums of squares (F(12, 31) = 1.9). Thus at the chosen significance level (using, for example, the S method discussed by Savin, 1984) no other subset of the restrictions can be judged significant either; alternatively, individual t tests on restrictions would need to be significant at (at least) the 0.4 per cent level to preserve the overall size of the test at 5 per cent when considering 12 restrictions. On this basis, (8.24) seems to provide an adequate parsimonious description of the data (although other equations are also not significantly worse than (8.29) at the 5 per cent level), and it seems that the Δ_4 transform satisfactorily removes seasonality.

Moreover, if (8.24) were close to the correct data generation process then we would expect just the sort of result shown in (8.28) (the fits are similar, the lag polynomial in C_t has a root near unity, the seasonal dummies are insignificant and four-period lags of income variables have roughly equal magnitudes, opposite signs to current dated equivalents). Tentatively accepting such a hypothesis, (8.22) and (8.23) would constitute poor approximations to (8.24) and hence are easy to reject whereas (8.21) is a reasonable approximation and is not easily discarded (see figure 8.1 and 8.4). Also, the relationship between (8.24) and (8.28) corresponds closely with the interpretation of differences as arising from coefficient restrictions but does not cohere with the 'filtering' interpretation. The large change in the constant term is probably due to collinearity, since the exact unrestricted equivalent of (8.24) is

$$\hat{C}_t = 150 + 0.32Y_t - 0.33Y_{t-4} - 0.12\Delta_1 Y_t + 0.16\Delta_1 Y_{t-4}$$
$$\phantom{\hat{C}_t = } (76) \ (0.04) \quad (0.04) \quad\ \ (0.04) \qquad\ (0.04)$$

$$+ 0.995C_{t-4} + \hat{\phi}_1 D_t^0 + \hat{\phi}_2 D_{t-4}^0, \qquad\qquad (8.30)$$
$$ (0.04)$$

$$R^2 = 0.996 \qquad \hat{\sigma} = 40.7 \qquad DW = 1.8 \qquad z_1(20) = 82.9 \qquad z_2(12) = 19.$$

The coefficients of (8.30) correspond very closely with those of the unrestricted equation which would be anticipated if (8.24) validly described the expenditure relationship, although the large standard error of the intercept in (8.30) compared with (8.24) is a distinct anomaly requiring explanation in due course. In summary, the evidence points strongly to accepting (8.24) as the best simple description of the data despite the loss of long-run information and the theoretical drawbacks discussed in section 3.

7 Measurement Errors

Zellner and Palm (1974) note that difference transformations can substantially alter the ratio of the 'systematic' variance to the measurement error variance of time series. Since large measurement error variances in regressors can cause large downward biases in estimated coefficients (see, for example, Johnston, 1972, ch. 9.3) it is possible that the low-income elasticities in (8.24) could be caused by the effects of the Δ_4 transform enhancing relative measurement errors.

A formal mis-specification analysis of a simple model where observations are generated by a first-order autoregressive process with coefficient ψ_1 and first-order autoregressive measurement error with coefficient ψ_2 reveals that $\psi_1 > \psi_2$ is a necessary and sufficient condition for differencing to induce a relative increase in measurement error variance. The amount by which the measurement error bias in the coefficient of a differenced regression exceeds the corresponding bias in the regression in levels depends directly and proportionately on $\psi_1 - \psi_2$. Davidson (1975) found that data revisions were highly autoregressive, and although by itself this does not imply that the unknown errors also will be autoregressive, two other factors argue for the magnitude of $\psi_1 - \psi_2$ being small for Y_t. First, if there were large measurement errors in $\Delta_4 Y_t$ these would occur one period later in $\Delta_4 Y_{t-1}$ which would create a negative first-order moving-average error on (8.24) and we could find no evidence of this – nor did Wall et al. (1975) in their similar equation (8.15). Second, we re-estimated (8.24) by weighted least squares assuming a measurement error variance of 50 per cent of the variance of $\Delta_4 Y_t$ and yet there was no noticeable increase in the coefficients. All these points together, though individually rather weak, suggest that errors-in-variables biases do *not* explain the low long-run elasticities. Conversely, any simultaneity bias which might arise from least squares estimation would tend to cause upward biased coefficients and hence can be discarded as an explanation also. Thus we return to figure 8.2 and 8.5 which originally indicated the source of the problem: the variance of $\Delta_4 Y_t$ is much larger than that of $\Delta_4 C_t$ and so any model like (8.24) must end up having 'small' coefficients.

8 A Simple Dynamic Model

In one sense, the above results simply reproduce the familiar problem of reconciling short-run and long-run consumption behaviour. However, there is a more serious difficulty since the original set of models included several distributed lag variants of permanent income and/or life cycle theories (see section 3 above) and yet, in a direct comparison, the statistical evidence favoured the model which accounted for only short-run behaviour. Clearly, therefore, either some new implementation of the PIH or LCH is required or (assuming that we do not wish to canvass a new theory) an account must be provided of why the evidence takes the form which it does. Naturally, we prefer the latter course.

Fisher (1962) advocated using equations involving only differenced variables to facilitate the study of short-run behaviour without having to specify trend-dominated long-run components. The main defects in this strategy are that one loses almost all *a priori* information from economic theory (as most theories rely on steady-state arguments) and all long-run information in the data (yet Granger's 'typical spectral shape' suggests that economic data are highly informative about the long run: see Granger, 1966). Moreover, as noted when discussing (8.15), it seems inappropriate to assume that short-run behaviour is independent of disequilibria in the levels of the variables.

A simple modification of equations in differences can resolve these three problems. Consider a situation in which an investigator accepts a non-stochastic steady-state theory that $X_t = KW_t$, where K is constant on any given growth path but may vary with the growth rate. In logarithms, letting $x_t = \ln X_t$ etc., the theory becomes

$$x_t = k + w_t. \tag{8.31}$$

The differenced variable equivalent is

$$\Delta_1 x_t = \Delta_1 w_t. \tag{8.32}$$

However, to assume that (8.32) had a white noise error would deny the existence of any 'long-run' relationship like (8.31), and to assume that (8.31) had a stationary error process would cause a negatively autocorrelated error to occur on (8.32). Furthermore, the Δ_1 operator in (8.32) could just as validly have been Δ_4 – on all these points the theory is unspecific.

On the basis of (8.31), the investigator wishes to postulate a stochastic disequilibrium relationship between x_t and w_t, which will simplify to (8.31) in steady state. In the absence of a well-articulated theory of the dynamic adjustment of x_t to w_t, it seems reasonable to assume a general rational lag model of the form

$$\alpha(L)x_t = k^* + \beta(L)w_t + v_t, \tag{8.33}$$

where $\alpha(L)$ and $\beta(L)$ are polynomials in the lag operator L of high enough order that v_t is white noise. For simplicity of exposition we consider the situation where both polynomials are first order:

$$x_t = k^* + \beta_1 w_t + \beta_2 w_{t-1} + \alpha_1 x_{t-1} + v_t. \tag{8.34}$$

Clearly, (8.31) and (8.32) are the special cases of (8.34) when $\beta_2 = \alpha_1 = 0, \beta_1 = 1$, and $\beta_1 = -\beta_2 = 1, k^* = 0, \alpha_1 = 1$ respectively; these coefficient restrictions force behaviour to be in steady state at all points in time. However, to ensure that for *all* values of the estimated parameters, the steady-state solution of (8.34) reproduces (8.31) one need only impose the coefficient restriction $\beta_1 + \beta_2 + \alpha_1 = 1$ or

$$\beta_1 = -\beta_2 + \gamma \quad \text{and} \quad \alpha_1 = 1 - \gamma,$$

yielding the equation

$$\Delta_1 x_t = k^* + \beta_1 \Delta_1 w_t + \gamma(w_{t-1} - x_{t-1}) + v_t \tag{8.35}$$

(which is more general than (8.31) or (8.32) but less general than (8.34)). The specification of (8.35) is therefore guided by the long-run theory; there is no loss of long-run information in the data since (8.35) is a reformulated 'levels equation'; and compared with the 'short-run' model

$$\Delta_1 x_t = k^* + \beta_1 \Delta_1 w_t \tag{8.36}$$

the vital 'initial disequilibrium' effect is provided by $\gamma(w_{t-1} - x_{t-1})$. Consequently, (8.35) does indeed resolve the three problems noted above (it is straightforward to generalize the analysis to equations of the form of (8.33)). An important example of this class of model is the real-wage variable formulation used by Sargan (1964a).

In (8.35) consider any steady-state growth path along which

$$\Delta_1 \ln X_t = \Delta_1 x_t = g = \Delta_1 w_t.$$

Then the solution of (8.35) with $v_t = 0$ is

$$g = k^* + \beta_1 g + \gamma(w_{t-1} - x_{t-1}) \tag{8.37}$$

or, assuming $\gamma \neq 0$,

$$X_t = KW_t$$

where

$$K = \exp\left[\frac{k^* - g(1 - \beta_1)}{\gamma}\right] \tag{8.38}$$

(implicitly, in (8.31) $k = [k^* - g(1 - \beta_1)]/\gamma$). Thus for any constant growth rate, if $\gamma \neq 0$, (8.35) automatically generates a long-run elasticity of unity for all values of the parameters, whereas if $\gamma = 0$ the elasticity is β_1. Interpreting X_t as C_t and W_t as Y_t, then the derived APC ($=$ MPC in steady-state growth) is a decreasing function of the growth rate g, consonant with inter-country evidence (see Modigliani, 1975). Note that the above analysis remains valid even if $k^* = 0$ (in which case $K < 1$ for $\gamma, g > 0$ and $1 > \beta_1 > 0$), so that the theory entails no restrictions on the presence or absence of an intercept in (8.35).[9]

If, from the steady-state solution (8.38), the growth rate of W_t changes from g to g_1 the ratio of X to W will gradually change from K to

$$K_1 = \exp\left[\frac{k^* - g_1(1 - \beta_1)}{\gamma}\right]$$

and hence even prolonged movements in one direction of the observed X/W ratio do not rule out a long-run unit elasticity hypothesis for a *given* growth rate. If g is a variable, then $(X/W)_t$ will not be constant either, although the data will be consistent with a model like (8.35). The important implication of this is that a variable, or even trending, observed APC does not by itself refute a unit elasticity model (the unit elasticity restriction is easily tested in (8.35) by including w_{t-1} as a separate regressor and testing its coefficient for significance from zero). Estimation of (8.31) requires that the *data* satisfy a unit elasticity restriction (this will be false out of steady state) whereas estimation of (8.35) only requires that the *model* satisfy this restriction and that the data are consonant with the model.

The estimation of restricted dynamic models like (8.35) from finite samples does not seem to have been the subject of any investigations to date. Consequently, we undertook a pilot simulation study of least squares estimation of δ_1 and δ_2 in

$$\Delta_1 x_t = \delta_1 \Delta_1 w_t + \delta_2(w_{t-1} - x_{t-1}) + v_t \qquad (t = 1, \ldots, T) \tag{8.35*}$$

for

$$(\delta_1, \delta_2) = (0.5, 0.1), \quad v_t \sim \text{NI}(0, 1)$$

and

$$w_t = 0.8w_{t-1} + u_t$$

with $u_t \sim NI(0,9)$, independent of v_t. The results are shown in table 8.2 for 100 random replications. For $T \geqslant 34$, the biases are very small, SE provides an accurate estimate of SD and $H_0: \delta_i = 0$ is rejected with considerable frequency. This contrasts favourably both with the bias which would arise from estimating μ in a simple dynamic model of the form

$$x_t = \mu x_{t-1} + u_t$$

(where the bias is approximately equal to $-2\mu/T$ and so has the same sign but is about five times as large as the corresponding bias in $\hat{\delta}_2$ in table 8.2) as well as with the biases and the variances which would be obtained from unrestricted estimation of

$$x_t = \beta_1 w_t + \beta_2 w_{t-1} + \alpha_1 x_{t-1} + v_t. \tag{8.34}*$$

Thus there may be an 'estimation' advantage from formulating dynamic equations as in (8.35), although for small δ_2 it may not be easy to establish $\hat{\delta}_2$ as significant at the 0.05 level unless T is relatively large.

When the appropriate lag length in (8.35) is four periods, the resulting model can be written as

$$\left(\frac{X}{W}\right)_t = K^* \left(\frac{X}{W}\right)_{t-4}^{1-\gamma} \left(\frac{W_t}{W_{t-4}}\right)^{\beta_1 - 1}. \tag{8.39}$$

For small γ the historical seasonal pattern of the APC will persist with modifications from any 'seasonality' in $\Delta_4 \ln W_t$. Note that (8.35) and (8.39) are stable dynamic processes for $2 > \gamma > 0$, and that K is relatively robust to changes in the values of β_1 and $\gamma > 0$ (contrast the properties of the solved long-run MPC from (8.12)). However, K is not a continuous function of γ at $\gamma = 0$ (switching from zero to infinity) which reflects dynamic instability in (8.39) at $\gamma = 0$.

The solved distributed lag representation of (8.35) is

$$x_t = \frac{k^*}{\gamma} + \sum_{j=0}^{\infty} \mu_j w_{t-j} + u_t, \tag{8.40}$$

Table 8.2 Simulation findings for (8.35)*

T	$\hat{\delta}_1 - \delta_1$				$\hat{\delta}_2 - \delta_2$			
	14	34	54	74	14	34	54	74
Bias	0.010	−0.013	−0.003	0.003	−0.026	−0.009	−0.004	−0.007
SD	0.106	0.062	0.041	0.044	0.108	0.060	0.043	0.038
SE	0.090	0.058	0.044	0.038	0.105	0.060	0.045	0.039
H_0 rejected	99	100	100	100	15	41	60	82

SD, the sampling standard deviation; SE, the average estimated standard error; 'H_0 rejected', the frequency with which the null hypothesis $H_0: \delta_i = 0$ was rejected when the nominal test size was 0.05. The values for δ_1, δ_2 and σ_v^2/σ_u^2 were based on empirical estimates of analogous consumption functions.

where

$$u_t = (1 - \gamma)u_{t-1} + v_t$$

and

$$\mu_0 = \beta_1, \qquad \mu_j = (1 - \gamma)^{j-1}\gamma(1 - \beta_1) \qquad (j \geq 1).$$

The mean lag is $(1 - \beta_1)/\gamma$ which could be very large for γ close to zero, but, depending on the magnitude of β_1, much of the adjustment could occur instantaneously (for example, the median lag could be less than one period). If v_t is white noise, then (8.40) will manifest considerable autocorrelation for small γ, no matter how long a distributed lag is used for w_t.

The final feature of (8.35) is of crucial importance; *if* the growth rate g is relatively constant, then X_t will be approximately equal to KW_t and hence from (8.31) $x_{t-1} - w_{t-1} \approx k$. In such a state of the world, the intercept and $w_{t-1} - x_{t-1}$ would be almost perfectly collinear in (8.35). A similar collinearity also must affect any attempt to estimate (8.34) unrestrictedly. Although either regressor could be dropped without much loss to the goodness of fit, setting $k^* = 0$ does not affect the long-run behaviour (see (8.38) above) but setting $\gamma = 0$ does. This phenomenon at last provides a potential explanation both for the discrepant behaviour of the standard error of the intercept between (8.24) and (8.30) and for the low elasticity of the former equation, since the initial disequilibrium effect has been excluded from (8.24) but is still indirectly present in (8.30).

However, before considering empirical variants of (8.35) it seems worth commenting on the relationship between equations like (8.35) and the four main theories of consumers' behaviour discussed in section 3. First, it is clear that both (8.34) and (8.35) resemble Brown's (1952) model; also, the term $\gamma(w_{t-1} - x_{t-1})$ could be interpreted as a 'ratchet' to the 'short-run' relationship (8.36) (compare Duesenberry, 1949) although it is a 'ratchet' which operates in either direction for any sustained change in the growth rate of w_t. The distributed lag form (8.40) could be interpreted as an empirical approximation to 'permanent income' in a model which always satisfies a long-run steady-state unit elasticity postulate (see Friedman, 1957). Moreover, using $C_t = x_t$ and $Y_t = w_t$, (8.35) corresponds to a transformed 'life cycle' model. For example, the wealth model of Ball and Drake (1964) is the special case of (8.35) in which $\beta_1 = \gamma$ and Deaton (1972b) presents a modified life cycle model of the same form but with revaluations of wealth as an additional variable. More recently, Deaton (1977) presents a savings equation closely similar to (8.35) but with the rate of inflation as an additional regressor (this study is discussed in section 9 below). Similar reasoning applies to models using changes in liquid assets in consumption equations (see Townend, 1976).

Nevertheless, as stressed above, the transformations involved in deriving the PIH and LCH (or eliminating any stock variable) significantly affect the properties of the error process, and it is possible (at least in principle) to distinguish between the contending hypotheses on this basis, subject to requiring that the error on the 'true' model is white noise. Even so, it is exceedingly hard in practice to decide in a time-series context *alone* which relationships are 'autonomous' and which are merely 'good approximations'. In terms of modelling any relationship between C and Y, the only really definite conclusion is that it seems vital to include some factor to account for the effect represented by $w_{t-1} - x_{t-1}$.

Returning to the problem of reconciling the estimates in (8.24) and (8.30), consider the alternative restriction of dropping the intercept and retaining $C_{t-4} - Y_{t-4}$, which in log terms yields

$$\Delta_4 \widehat{\ln C_t} = 0.49\Delta_4 \ln Y_t - 0.17\Delta_1 \Delta_4 \ln Y_t - 0.06 \ln(C/Y)_{t-4} + 0.01\Delta_4 D_t^0, \quad (8.41)$$
$$\quad\quad\quad (0.04) \quad\quad\quad (0.05) \quad\quad\quad\quad (0.01) \quad\quad\quad\quad (0.004)$$

$$R^2 = 0.71 \quad\quad \hat{\sigma} = 0.0067 \quad\quad DW = 1.6 \quad\quad z_1(20) = 80.7 \quad\quad z_2(12) = 23.$$

A relationship like (8.41) can be derived from a simple 'feedback' theory in which consumers plan to spend in each quarter of a year the same as they spent in that quarter of the previous year ($\ln C_t = \ln C_{t-4}$) modified by a proportion of their annual change in income ($+ 0.49\Delta_4 \ln Y_t$), and by whether that change is itself increasing or decreasing ($-0.17\Delta_1 \Delta_4 Y_t$) (compare Houthakker and Taylor, 1970); these together determine a 'short-run' consumption decision which is altered by $-0.06 \ln(C_{t-4}/Y_{t-4})$, the feedback from the previous C/Y ratio ensuring coherence with the long-run 'target' outcome $C_t = KY_t$. The parameterization of (8.41) is determined by the choice of a set of plausible decision variables which incorporate relatively independent items of information, allowing agents to assess their reactions separately to changes in each variable. This seems a 'natural' parameterization to adopt and, as the small standard errors (8.41) show, the resulting parameters are precisely estimated. Moreover, if any omitted decision variables can be reformulated as orthogonal to the already included regressors, then the potentially serious problem of 'omitted variables bias' is transformed to a problem of estimation efficiency. In practical terms, previously estimated coefficients will not change radically as new explanatory variables are added (see equation (8.45) below). The use of transformed variables like $\Delta_4 \ln C_t$ etc. is *not* because we want to 'seasonally adjust' and/or achieve 'stationarity' (with the attendant loss of spectral power at low frequencies noted by Sims, 1974b) but because $\Delta_4 \ln C_t$ represents a sensible decision variable when different commodities are being purchased in different quarters of the year.

The significance value of z_1 in (8.41) reveals that other factors need to be included to provide a full account of the behaviour of C_t and this aspect is considered in section 9. Nevertheless, (8.41) seems consistent with the salient features of the data in figures 8.1–8.6 and straightforwardly explains the large difference between the short-run and long-run MPC. The impact elasticity is 0.32, rising to 0.49 after one quarter, the remaining 51 per cent of the adjustment taking a considerable time to occur, which matches the relatively small value of the variance of consumption relative to that of income noted earlier. With only three 'economic' variables, the model seems a reasonably parsimonious explanation of trend, cycle and seasonal components. Also it provides a suitable basis for discussing why the studies by H, B and W reached their published results.

First, a model like (8.41) could never be detected by any methodology in which the first step was to difference data and then only to investigate the properties of the differenced series (as Wall et al., 1975, do). Subject to that restriction, (8.24) (or its log equivalent) provides an excellent approximation in terms of goodness of fit despite its apparent lack of coherence with steady-state theory and long-run evidence.

Next, the lag structure of (8.41) could not be detected by researchers who only investigated lags of one or two periods and never used diagnostic tests for higher order residual autocorrelation (see Ball et al., 1975). The use of SA data does not justify neglecting higher-order lags. If a model like (8.39) constitutes the true data generation process then this should not be greatly altered by filtering out seasonal frequencies from the data. Indeed, re-estimating (8.41) on the SA data used earlier yields

$$\Delta_4 \widehat{\ln C_t^a} = 0.44 \Delta_4 \ln Y_t^a - 0.19 \Delta_1 \Delta_4 \ln Y_t^a - 0.06 \ln(C^a/Y^a)_{t-4} + 0.01 \Delta_4 D_t^0,$$
$$\quad (0.04) \qquad\qquad (0.05) \qquad\qquad (0.01) \qquad\qquad\quad (0.003)$$

$$(8.41a)$$

$$R^2 = 0.79 \qquad \hat{\sigma} = 0.0063 \qquad DW = 1.7 \qquad z_1(8) = 29.0 \qquad z_2(6) = 18.$$

The coefficients are very similar to those in (8.41), but the use of SA data has created considerable negative fourth-order residual autocorrelation (e.g. a coefficient at four lags of -0.7 in a tenth-order residual autoregression) which would induce any investigator who did not previously believe in a model like (8.41) to select an equation with considerably less emphasis on four-period effects.

Lastly, despite estimating equations with four-period lags similar to unrestricted variants of (8.41), Hendry (chapter 2) selected (8.11) as his preferred equation. The seasonal pattern for C_t seems to evolve whereas that for $\ln C_t$ does not (see figures 8.1 and 8.6 above) and hence the use of the untransformed data appears to have been one factor determining Hendry's choice. Further since C/Y was relatively constant over the period to 1967, the inclusion of an intercept in all the models considered by Hendry would greatly reduce the partial significance of four-period lagged variables. Both of these effects favour the incorrect selection of the evolving seasonals model as the best description of the data. Moreover, it is interesting that, if a model like (8.39) is assumed as a data generation process and w_t is highly correlated with w_{t-1}, then regressing x_t on w_t and x_{t-1} will yield estimates like those in (8.12) when the data are *not* prior seasonally adjusted, and the true partial coefficient of x_{t-1} is zero. In summary, therefore, (8.41) seems to have the requisite properties to explain why previous researchers' methodologies led to their published conclusions.

Finally, in terms of the levels of the variables, equation (8.39) becomes

$$x_t = k^* + \beta_1 w_t + (\gamma - \beta_1) w_{t-4} + (1 - \gamma) x_{t-4} + v_t. \tag{8.42}$$

Such an equation can be approximated closely by

$$x_t = k^{**} + \beta_1 w_t + u_t \quad \text{where} \quad u_t = (1 - \gamma) u_{t-4} + e_t. \tag{8.43}$$

The mis-specification of (8.42) as (8.43) entails restricting the coefficient of w_{t-4} to be $\gamma \beta_1 - \beta_1$ instead of $\gamma - \beta_1$. This mis-specification will be negligible for small γ and $\beta_1 > 0$. Consequently, it is easy to approximate incorrectly the four-period dynamics by fourth-order autocorrelation. Since γ is small, imposing the further restriction that the autocorrelation coefficient is unity will not noticeably worsen the fit and provides an alternative sequence whereby an incorrect differenced model might be selected (for a more general discussion of this last issue see chapter 6).

9 Inflation Effects

Deaton (1977) has presented evidence for a disequilibrium effect of inflation on consumers' expenditure, which he interprets as consumers mistaking unanticipated changes in inflation for relative price changes when sequentially purchasing commodities. Since the forecast period contains inflation rates which are considerably greater than any observed during the sample used for estimation (the graph of $\Delta_4 \ln P_t$, where P_t is the implicit deflator of C_t, is shown in figure 8.7), Deaton's analysis offers a potential explanation for the poor forecast performance of all the estimated models.

In view of the functional form of the models (8.24) and (8.41), the regressors $\Delta_4 \ln P_t$ and $\Delta_1 \Delta_4 \ln P_t$ were included to represent the level and rate of change of inflation. Retaining the same sample and forecast periods yielded the results shown in equations (8.44) and (8.45) respectively (for comparability, we have chosen the log equivalent of (8.24)):

$$\Delta_4 \widehat{\ln C_t} = \underset{(0.04)}{0.022} + \underset{(0.05)}{0.34 \Delta_4 \ln Y_t} - \underset{(0.05)}{0.16 \Delta_1 \Delta_4 \ln Y_t} + \underset{(0.003)}{0.01 \Delta_4 D_t^0}$$

$$\underset{(0.07)}{-0.21 \Delta_4 \ln P_t} - \underset{(0.14)}{0.15 \Delta_1 \Delta_4 \ln P_t}, \tag{8.44}$$

$$R^2 = 0.81 \qquad \hat{\sigma} = 0.0055 \qquad DW = 1.8 \qquad z_1(20) = 146 \qquad z_2(16) = 15;$$

$$\Delta_4 \widehat{\ln C_t} = \underset{(0.04)}{0.47 \Delta_4 \ln Y_t} - \underset{(0.05)}{0.21 \Delta_1 \Delta_4 \ln Y_t} - \underset{(0.02)}{0.10 \ln (C/Y)_{t-4}}$$

$$+ \underset{(0.003)}{0.01 \Delta_4 D_t^0} - \underset{(0.07)}{0.13 \Delta_4 \ln P_t} - \underset{(0.15)}{0.28 \Delta_1 \Delta_4 \ln P_t}, \tag{8.45}$$

$$R^2 = 0.77 \qquad \hat{\sigma} = 0.0061 \qquad DW = 1.8 \qquad z_1(20) = 21.8 \qquad z_2(12) = 19.$$

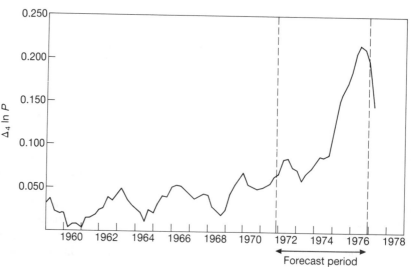

Figure 8.7 Annual rate of change of prices.

Both equations confirm Deaton's result that inflation was significantly reducing consumers' expenditure prior to 1971. Also, the inclusion of inflation effects in (8.45) has resolved the forecast problem: the considerable fall in the APC after 1971 (see figure 8.3) can be explained by the sharp increase in inflation and the five-year-ahead *ex post* predictions from (8.45) satisfy the parameter stability test (figure 8.8 shows the plots of $\Delta_4 \ln C_t$ and $\Delta_4 \widehat{\ln C_t}$ over the period to 1975(iv)). Nevertheless, simply including the two additional regressors does not of itself guarantee an improved forecasting performance as z_1 in (8.44) shows. This outcome is easy to understand on the hypothesis that (8.45) constitutes the 'true' model, since the behaviour of C/Y is negatively influenced by changes in P_t and so the approximation of C/Y by a constant is very poor over the forecast period. Consonant with this argument, and illustrating the robustness of the parameter choice in (8.41), the only parameter estimate to be substantially altered by the inclusion of $\Delta_4 \ln P_t$ and $\Delta_1 \Delta_4 \ln P_t$ is the coefficient of $\ln(C/Y)_{t-4}$. The fact that (8.44) has a lower value of $\hat{\sigma}$ than (8.45) is evidence against suppressing the intercept, and indeed an intercept is significant if added to (8.45). However, $\ln(C/Y)_{t-4}$ loses significance if this is done and $z_1(20) = 137$. Thus, (8.44) and (8.45) exhibit an interesting conflict between goodness of fit and parameter stability as criteria for model selection. Bearing in mind that the forecast period is very different in several respects from the estimation period, the predictive accuracy of (8.45) is rather striking. Adding this to the earlier theoretical arguments, we have no hesitation in dropping the constant term instead of $\ln(C/Y)_{t-4}$.

On a steady-state growth path with constant annual real income growth rate g and inflation rate μ, (8.45) yields the solution

$$C = KY \quad \text{where} \quad K = \exp(-5.3g - 1.3\mu). \tag{8.46}$$

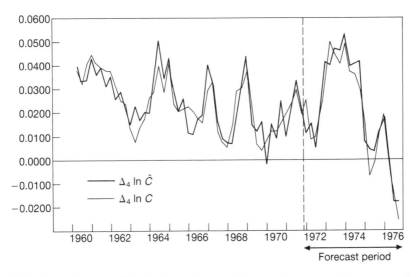

Figure 8.8 Actual and predicted values of annual change in consumption.

When $g = 0.02$ and $\mu = 0.05$ (as roughly characterized the 1960s) $K = 0.84$, whereas if μ increases to 0.15, K falls to 0.74 (which is similar to the 1970s). Variations in the rate of inflation induce substantial changes in the ratio of C to Y.

There are a number of theories in addition to Deaton's which would lead one to anticipate significant inflation effects in (8.45). For example, during periods of rapid inflation, the conventional measure of Y_t ceases to provide a good proxy for 'real income' (note that equation (8.9) above holds when capital gains and losses are accounted for in Y_t) and $\Delta_4 \ln P_t$ etc. 'pick up' this effect. Models like (8.10) based on the LCH but transformed to eliminate wealth should manifest negative inflation effects of the form $\Delta_4 \ln P_t$ through the erosion of the real value of the liquid assets component of A_t. Although one might expect agents to alter the composition of their wealth portfolio by shifting into real assets such as housing when inflation is rapid, it is not clear how this would affect expenditure decisions. In terms of empirical evidence, Townend (1976) found a real net liquid assets variable N to be significant in his specification of the consumption function together with negative inflation effects (based on Almon lags). Using Townend's data for N_t (1963(iii)–1975(i), retaining the last two years' data for a forecast test) the only form which yielded significant results when added to (8.45) was $\Delta_1 \ln N_t$ (which could be due in considerable measure to the joint endogeneity of C_t and N_t):

$$\Delta_4 \widehat{\ln C_t} = 0.47\Delta_4 \ln Y_t - 0.28\Delta_1 \Delta_4 \ln Y_t - 0.05 \ln(C/Y)_{t-4}$$
$$\quad\ \ (0.04) \qquad\quad (0.05) \qquad\qquad (0.02)$$

$$-0.27\Delta_1 \Delta_4 \ln P_t + 0.008\Delta_1 D_t^0 + 0.11\Delta_1 \ln N_t + 0.01\Delta_4 \ln P_t, \quad (8.47)$$
$$\ (0.17) \qquad\qquad (0.003) \qquad\ (0.05) \qquad\qquad (0.06)$$

$$R^2 = 0.86 \qquad \hat{\sigma} = 0.0059 \qquad DW = 1.8 \qquad z_1(8) = 41 \qquad z_2(12) = 26.$$

The main impacts of adding $\Delta_1 \ln N_t$ to (8.45) are the halved coefficient of $\ln(C/Y)_{t-4}$ (in an LCH framework, these are proxies) and the dramatic change to almost zero in the coefficient of $\Delta_4 \ln P_t$, consistent with the hypothesis that $\Delta_4 \ln P_t$ is a proxy for the erosion of the value of liquid assets from inflation. Nevertheless, the effect of accelerating inflation retains a large negative coefficient. The marked deterioration in the forecast performance of (8.47) suggests an incorrect specification and hence we decided to omit N_t from further consideration, attributing its significance in (8.47) to simultaneity.[10]

To test the validity of the various restrictions imposed on (8.45) (price level homogeneity, exclusion restrictions and the unit income elasticity) we estimated the general unrestricted model

$$\ln C_t = \sum_{j=0}^{5} (\alpha_j \ln Y_{t-j} + \beta_j \ln P_{t-j}) + \sum_{j=1}^{5} \lambda_j \ln C_{t-j} + \varepsilon_t. \tag{8.48}$$

The results are shown in table 8.3, and table 8.4 records the equivalent values derived from the restricted model (8.45) (it seemed spurious to include five lagged values of D_t^0 in (8.48), although doing so does not greatly alter the results, $\hat{\sigma}$ falling to 0.0059). The restrictions are not rejected on a likelihood ratio test, and indeed the two sets of estimates are rather similar. Moreover, to two decimal digits, $\Sigma\hat{\beta}_j = 0$

Table 8.3 Unrestricted estimates of (8.47)

j	0	1	2	3	4	5
$\ln C_{t-j}$	–	0.12 (0.17)	0.02 (0.04)	–0.06 (0.04)	0.98 (0.05)	–0.11 (0.17)
$\ln Y_{t-j}$	0.25 (0.06)	0.10 (0.08)	–0.06 (0.07)	0.11 (0.07)	–0.18 (0.07)	–0.16 (0.08)
$\ln P_{t-j}$	–0.59 (0.21)	0.50 (0.29)	–0.23 (0.24)	0.12 (0.24)	0.44 (0.28)	–0.24 (0.21)

$R^2 = 0.997$; $\hat{\sigma} = 0.0062$; DW $= 2.2$.

Table 8.4 Solved estimates from (8.45)

j	0	1	2	3	4	5
$\ln C_{t-j}$	–	0	0	0	0.90	0
$\ln Y_{t-j}$	0.26	0.21	0	0	–0.16	–0.21
$\ln P_{t-j}$	–0.41	0.28	0	0	0.41	–0.28

and $\Sigma\hat{\alpha}_j \approx 1 - \Sigma\hat{\lambda}_j$, favouring the hypotheses of price homogeneity and a unit elasticity for income.

Finally, re-estimation of (8.45) assuming $\Delta_4\ln Y_t$, $\Delta_1\Delta_4\ln Y_t$, $\Delta_4\ln P_t$ and $\Delta_1\Delta_4\ln P_t$ to be endogenous and using instrumental variables[11] yielded the outcome

$$\Delta_4\widehat{\ln C_t} = 0.48\Delta_4\ln Y_t - 0.20\Delta_1\Delta_4\ln Y_t - 0.12\Delta_4\ln P_t - 0.28\Delta_1\Delta_4\ln P_t$$
$$\quad (0.04) \qquad\quad (0.06) \qquad\qquad (0.07) \qquad\qquad (0.18)$$

$$\qquad\quad - 0.09\ln(C/Y)_{t-4} + 0.007\Delta_4 D_t^0, \qquad\qquad (8.45)^*$$
$$\qquad\quad (0.02) \qquad\qquad (0.004)$$

$$\hat{\sigma} = 0.0061 \qquad \text{DW} = 1.7 \qquad z_1(20) = 22 \qquad z_2(12) = 19 \qquad z_3(10) = 16,$$

where $z_3(l)$ is the test for validity of the choice of instrumental variables discussed by Sargan (1964a) and is distributed as χ_l^2 in large samples when the instruments are independent of the equation error. It is clear that the coefficient estimates and the goodness of fit are hardly altered, providing no evidence of simultaneity biases.

An interesting result emerges from estimating (8.45) over the entire sample period (to 1975(iv)):

$$\Delta_4\widehat{\ln C_t} = 0.48\Delta_4\ln Y_t - 0.23\Delta_1\Delta_4\ln Y_t - 0.09\ln(C/Y)_{t-4} + 0.006\Delta_4 D_t^*$$
$$\quad (0.03) \qquad\quad (0.04) \qquad\qquad (0.01) \qquad\qquad (0.002)$$

$$\qquad\quad - 0.12\Delta_4\ln P_t - 0.31\Delta_1\Delta_4\ln P_t, \qquad\qquad (8.45)^{**}$$
$$\qquad\quad (0.02) \qquad\quad (0.10)$$

$$R^2 = 0.85 \qquad \hat{\sigma} = 0.0062 \qquad \text{DW} = 2.0 \qquad z_2(12) = 23.$$

D_t^* is D_t^0 extended to allow for the introduction of VAT (see note 5). Manifestly, the coefficient estimates and $\hat{\sigma}$ are hardly changed from (8.45), as would be expected given the value for $z_1(20)$ on equation (8.45). R^2 has therefore increased, and the coefficient standard errors are smaller, especially for $\Delta_4\ln P_t$. However, the equivalent long-period estimates of (8.44) alter considerably, with $\hat{\sigma}$ increasing to 0.0063 and $z_2(16)$ to 28. Thus, the overall data set does not offer much evidence against deleting the intercept, and strongly favours retaining $\ln(C/Y)_{t-4}$. From the longer sample period, a significant coefficient for $\Delta_4 \ln Y_{t-2}$ also can be established, creating a 'smoother' distributed lag of C_t on Y_t.

10 Summary and Conclusions

A simple dynamic model which conforms with a range of theoretical requirements and matches all the salient features of the data was used to explain various recently published relationships between consumers' expenditure on non-durables and disposable income. Extended to allow for the effects of inflation noted by Deaton (1977), the model produces an acceptable set of post-sample predictions over 20 quarters using the actual data for incomes and prices. While noting the implications of the analyses of Leamer (1974, 1975) for an exercise like that described above, we feel that our 'prejudiced search for an acceptable model' has not been fruitless. We conclude that it is worthwhile trying to explain the *complete* set of existing findings; that restrictions derived from economic theories can be valuable in econometric modelling if correctly implemented to restrict the *model* but not the *data*; the seasonal adjustment of data can confuse the *selection* of an appropriate dynamic specification; that 'multicollinearity' is not necessarily resolved by restricting the parameter space rather than by enlarging it; and that econometric relationships can predict accurately over periods in which the behaviour of the regressors is sufficiently different that mechanistic time-series methods will fail. However, we do not conclude that our model represents the 'true' structural relationship since there are several important issues which have not been considered (including changes in income distribution and direct wealth effects). Hopefully, our methods, models and results will facilitate future work on these problems.

Notes

1   The derivation of (8.10) is less convincing if a white noise error is included in (8.8), since the error on (8.10) would be a first-order moving average with a root of minus unity, reflecting the inappropriateness of differencing (8.8).

2   DW is quoted below as a conventional statistic (from which, for example, Durbin's h test could be calculated if desired).

3   We ignored the two observations for 1976 as being liable to considerably larger revisions than the earlier data.

4   Equations involving variables denoted by x_t and w_t are used to illustrate simplified versions of principles which can be generalized validly to the relationship between C and Y.

5   The introduction of VAT in 1973 was treated as being similar to the 1968(i)–(ii) budget effect and hence we projected D_t^0 as $+1$, -1 in 1973(i)–(ii). This improved the forecast accuracy in these quarters and demonstrated the value of investigating 'special effects'.

6   A significant value for z_1 indicates *both* an incorrect model *and* a change in the stochastic properties of the variables in the 'true' data generation process of C_t, whereas an insignificant value for z_1 only shows that the latter has not occurred and is fully con-

sistent with an incorrect model for C_t (see Hendry, 1979b). Note that a large value of z_1 occurs when the variance of the forecast errors is large relative to the variance of the sample residuals.

7   The results of Hendry (chapter 5) and Davis et al. (1977) suggest that 'small' values of z_2 should be treated with caution and do not necessarily indicate the absence of residual autocorrelation.

8   Equation (8.28) can be derived from (8.27) by assuming that the residuals in (8.27) follow a simple fourth-order autoregressive process, and then carrying out the usual 'Cochrane–Orcutt' transformation, but ignoring the parameter restrictions implied by the autoregressive transform.

9   If $k^* = 0$, then $K = 1$ when $g = 0$. Consequently, care must be exercised when simulating to *equilibrium* a model containing equations of the form of (8.35) for a subcategory of expenditure.

10 Other regressors which were added to (8.47) without yielding significant results were unemployment, the relative price of durables to non-durables and short-term interest rates. The largest t value was for $\Delta_1 \Delta_4 \ln(\text{unemployment})$ and Bean (1977) reports a significant value for this variable in a variant of (8.45). Note that, if the significance of $\Delta_1 \ln N_t$ is due to simultaneity, then the vanishing of the *direct* effect of $\Delta_4 \ln P_t$ on $\Delta_4 \ln C_t$ provides no evidence on the 'erosion of the value of real liquid assets' hypothesis.

11 The instruments used were $\ln Y_{t-j} (j = 1, \ldots, 5)$, $\ln P_{t-j} (j = 1, 4, 5)$, $\ln F_{t-j}$, $\ln E_{t-j}$, $\ln I_{t-j} (j = 0, \ldots, 4)$ (where F_t, E_t, I_t respectively denote the real value of current government expenditure, exports and gross domestic fixed capital formation) and the predetermined variables in the regression.

9

Liquidity and Inflation Effects on Consumers' Expenditure

with Thomas von Ungern-Sternberg

Preamble

The printer's ink was scarcely dry when Thomas von Ungern-Sternberg noted three important problems with the DHSY specification.

1   If consumption did not equal income, an asset stock must be altering: why was there no feedback onto expenditure behaviour of changes in that asset? Integral correction mechanisms offered a potential solution, and a tighter link to control theory of the form in Phillips (1954, 1957). In turn, this clarified error correction mechanisms generally, and allowed an encompassing explanation for the evidence on liquid assets in DHSY.
2   Could we discriminate between the many possible explanations for the role of inflation? Was it unanticipated effects as in Deaton (1977), money illusion or mis-measurement of real income due to ignoring the impact of inflation on the values of nominal assets and nominal interest rates? The last of these seemed the most fruitful.
3   Deleting the seasonal dummies in DHSY seemed a mistake in retrospect: the seasonality would gradually die out in the form DHSY selected. Reintroducing seasonals resolved one of DHSY's 'paradoxes', namely why the goodness of fit with the intercept exceeded that with the error correction mechanism term, although the resulting model (with an intercept) predicted badly.

We immediately began to investigate these ideas.

By this stage, the notion of a progressive research strategy for empirical modelling was explicit, sustained by encompassing. I still viewed encompassing as applied mis-specification analysis since specific test procedures were still several years away from development (see Mizon (1984), Mizon and Richard (1986) and the survey in Hendry and Richard (1989)), as was the formalization of the concept of encompassing (chapter 16). The empirical analysis

Reprinted from Deaton, A.S. (ed.), *Essays in the Theory and Measurement of Consumers' Expenditure*, Cambridge: Cambridge University Press, 1981, ch. 9. This research was financed in part by a grant from the Social Science Research Council to the Quantitative Economics Programme at the London School of Economics. Valuable assistance from Frank Srba is gratefully acknowledged. We are indebted to Charles Bean, Angus Deaton. Robert Engle, George Hadjimatheou, Jean-François Richard, Tom Rothenberg, Mark Salmon and Pravin Trivedi for helpful comments on an earlier version of the paper, although we do not hold them responsible for the residual errors.

certainly included the least restricted hypothesis, but again only as a test baseline, not as part of a reduction sequence. However, the implicit inconsistency between analysis proceeding from general-to-simple within a study, but being simple-to-general across studies (an issue initially raised by Bob Marshall) was not even noticed. This lacuna is probably due to my then prevailing belief that non-nested testing was different in kind from nested testing. Given two non-nested models, no unique route existed for nesting them, and so any particular choice always seemed arbitrary. One of the useful insights from the theory of reduction is that the wrong question is being posed: at an earlier stage in the reduction process, the two models were nested and hence remain comparable despite their apparent non-nesting. As Mizon and Richard (1986) show, encompassing can resolve the problem and, in doing so, reveals that a nesting model is implicitly present in non-nested tests, since tests against that nesting model are equivalent to tests between the competing models. Thus, the nesting model is instrumental. Moreover, in a progression between studies, to avoid inconsistencies it is imperative to retain the complete sequence of variables used previously, i.e. each new study should re-commence from the entailed general model embedding all the earlier studies (see Ericsson and Hendry, 1989).

That last point resolved the conundrum as to why DHSY find that liquid assets are irrelevant, and yet they transpire to be crucial in this chapter. In DHSY, the test of the importance of liquid assets is conditional on maintaining a unit elasticity of expenditure with respect to income, which in turn is tested when liquid assets are excluded; however, the general model requires letting income enter unrestrictedly and, on doing so, liquid assets are found to be significant.

The related issue is the status of the variables in a stock–flow model. The economic analysis assumes that the flow of consumption relative to that of income depends on the (log of the) ratio of the asset stock to the flow of income, where the nominal stock is the cumulation of all past values of nominal income less nominal consumption (i.e. cumulated nominal saving). Inflation erodes the nominal stock and interest receipts augment it. In a stationary world, there is no difficulty in maintaining such a formulation. However, if the income process is non-stationary, due to an evolving component (integrated of order one, denoted I(1) in the terminology introduced by Granger (1981b), entailing the need to difference once to eliminate the evolving component), then so is consumption and hence, in general, so is saving. Thus, the stock will generally be I(2) and considerable care is needed to ensure that the econometric equation is balanced in that all of its variables can be written as I(0). The research agenda implicit in that difficulty, namely how to ascertain the degree of integration of time series and their transformations and how to check that models can be written in terms of I(0) variables etc., has been the focus of a vast amount of subsequent research (see *inter alia* Engle and Granger, 1987; *Oxford Bulletin*, 1986; Banerjee et al., 1992). As ever in applied research, all these insights lay in the future and could not be drawn upon at the time.

Follow-ups evaluating the later success of the HUS model (as it inevitably became known) are provided in chapter 18, Hendry et al. (1990b) and Carruth and Henley (1990).

1 Introduction

In a recent study of the time-series behaviour of consumers' expenditure in the United Kingdom, Davidson et al. (1978) (denoted DHSY below: see chapter 8 in this volume) presented results for an equation in constant (1970) prices relating consumers' expenditure on non-durables and services (C) to personal disposable income Y and the rate of change of prices P:

$$\Delta_4 c_t = \alpha_1 \Delta_4 y_t + \alpha_2 \Delta_1 \Delta_4 y_t + \alpha_3 \Delta_4 p_t + \alpha_4 \Delta_1 \Delta_4 p_t + \alpha_5 (c_{t-4} - y_{t-4}) + \alpha_6 \Delta_4 D_t + \varepsilon_t$$
$$(9.1)$$

In (9.1), lower case letters denote $\log_e$ of corresponding capital letters, P_t is the implicit deflator of C_t, $\Delta_j = (1 - L^j)$ where $L^k x_t = x_{t-k}$ and ε_t is assumed to be a white noise error process. D_t is a dummy variable for 1968(i) and (ii) and for the introduction of VAT.

DHSY selected equation (9.1) using the criteria that it

1 encompassed as special cases most previous empirical models relating C_t to Y_t,
2 was consonant with many steady-state economic theories of non-durable consumption,
3 explained the salient features of the available data,
4 provided a simple dynamic model in terms of plausible decision variables of economic agents,
5 helped explain why previous intestigators had selected their (presumed incorrect) models and
6 exhibited an impressive degree of parameter constancy over 20 quarters after the end of the estimation sample (through a period of rapid change in P and C/Y).

Nevertheless, DHSY did *not* conclude that (9.1) represented a 'true' structural relationship and three issues merited immediate re-examination, namely liquidity effects, the role of inflation and the treatment of seasonality.

Although DHSY obtained negative results when investigating liquid asset effects in (9.1), Professor Sir Richard Stone established a significant influence for cumulated savings on consumers' expenditure using annual data (see, for example, Stone, 1966; 1973). Moreover, the dynamic specification of (9.1) is logically incomplete as some latent asset stock must be altering when total expenditure is unequal to income. Alternatively expressed, in the terminology of Phillips (1954) and (1957), the formulation in (9.1) includes derivative and proportional control mechanisms but omits *integral* control, and the influence of liquid assets is considered below as an observable proxy for such an integral control. This interpretation is close to the spirit of Professor Stone's approach. Integral correction mechanisms are analysed in section 2, together with a pilot Monte Carlo study of the finite sample properties of least squares estimators in such models.

Several theories have been offered to account for the direct influence of inflation on savings (see, for example, Deaton, 1977; Bean, 1978; and the references cited therein) and in section 3 we consider the model developed in Ungern-Sternberg (1978) based on the mis-measurement of real income in inflationary conditions. The resulting equation avoids the problem in (9.1) that, as inflation increases, C/Y falls without a positive lower bound.

The empirical evidence for the United Kingdom is re-examined in section 4 using an extension of (9.1) which allows for a seasonally varying average propensity to consume and thereby explains one of the 'paradoxes' noted by DHSY. Section 5 concludes and summarizes the study.

Since (9.1) accounts for much previous empirical research relating C to Y in the United Kingdom, we commence from DHSY's model and supplant it by an equation which still satisfies the six criteria noted above. Although the resulting model remains parsimonious, is data coherent and exhibits a fair degree of parameter constancy, it is undoubtedly far from being the final resolution of this complex subject. It is offered as a further step in that scientific progression which has been a hallmark of Professor Stone's research.

2 Integral Correction Mechanisms

Simple dynamic models based on 'error correction' feedbacks as in (9.1) are important in linking equations formulated in *levels* with those formulated in *differences* of the original variables. Further, an error correction mechanism (denoted ECM) has many interesting dynamic and econometric properties (see, for example, Sargan, 1964a, DHSY; and chapter 11) and, appropriately specified, can ensure that an estimated equation reproduces as its steady-state solution the economic theory from which it was derived, thus facilitating rigorous testing of theories. Consequently, (9.1) provides an example of a useful class of dynamic equations.

Nevertheless, (9.1) has a major flaw as a complete account of the dynamic behaviour of flow variables. Consider the simplest example of an ECM relating two variables denoted by w_t and x_t:

$$\Delta_1 w_t = \gamma_1 \Delta_1 x_t + \gamma_2 (x_{t-1} - w_{t-1}) + v_t \tag{9.2}$$

where $v_t \sim \text{NI}(0, \sigma_v^2)$ and $\mathscr{E}(x_t v_s) = 0 \, \forall t, s$, with $1 > \gamma_1$, $\gamma_2 > 0$. The non-stochastic steady-state solution of (9.2) when $\Delta_1 x_t = g$ must have $\Delta_1 w_t = g$ and hence

$$W = KX \quad \text{where} \quad K = \exp\left[(\gamma_1 - 1)g/\gamma_2 \right] \tag{9.3}$$

and (9.2) is stable provided that $2 > \gamma_2 > 0$. However, the convergence of W_t to its steady-state growth path following any disturbance is monotonic and if $\gamma_1 < 1$ then w_t converges to $x_t + k$ from below (above) when x_t increases (decreases) (note that, in terms of stabilizing W/X, $\Delta_1 x_t$ has the appropriate negative coefficient). Consequently, even when $K = 1$ ($k = 0$) there is a cumulative under-adjustment if x_t is steadily increasing or decreasing. If w_t is an expenditure and x_t an accrual then some stock of assets is implicitly altering and for decreases in x_t, the asset stock is essential to finance the 'over-spending'.

In the terminology of Phillips (1954, 1957), (9.2) incorporates derivative ($\Delta_1 x_t$) and proportional ($x_{t-1} - w_{t-1}$) control mechanisms, but *no* integral control ($\Sigma_{j<t}(x_j - w_j)$). Such an integral can be interpreted most easily by introducing a state variable A_t (which may or may not be observable) defined by (using end-of-period definitions)

$$A_t \equiv A_{t-1} + X_t - W_t \tag{9.4}$$

In terms of the original variables, A_t is the integral of past discrepancies between X and W. Whether or not integral control mechanisms (denoted ICMs) influence behaviour is, from this viewpoint, simply a matter of dynamic specification. Nevertheless, economic theory is far from being devoid of alternative interpretations (for example, Pissarides (1978) presents a theoretical analysis of the role of liquid assets in consumption which yields conclusions similar to those obtained below) and we record with interest that Phillips (1954, p. 310) considered the 'Pigou effect' to be an integral regulating mechanism inherent in the economy.

Indeed, many previous researchers have incorporated integral variables in expenditure equations, including the explicit use of cumulated savings by Stone (1966, 1973), liquid assets (see, *inter alia*, Zellner et al., 1965; Townend, 1976) and wealth (see Ball and Drake, 1964; Deaton, 1972b, 1976; and Modigliani, 1975). However, since there are many econometric relationships in which integral effects are potentially relevant but do not appear to have been used previously (such as wage-price equations) we develop the simplest form of model which extends (9.2) to allow for an ICM, following an approach similar to that of Deaton (1972b) and chapter 3.

To focus attention on the dynamic specification, we assume that a prior steady-state utility maximization exercise leads agents to seek to maintain constant ratios both between W and X as in (9.2) and between A and X (*ceteris paribus*), namely: $W^e = K^* X$ and $A^e = B^* X$ where ^{e} denotes 'dynamic equilibrium'. For consistency with (9.4) in steady state, $K^* = 1 - [g/(1 + g)]B^*$. Either linear or log-linear decision rules could be formulated, but since we want the latter in order to generalize (9.2) (noting also that both DHSY and Salmon (1979b) found that Sargan's (1964a) likelihood criterion favoured log-linear models for C_t), (9.4) has to be replaced by its steady-state approximation:

$$\Delta_1 a_t^e = H^* (x_t - w_t^e) \tag{9.5}$$

where $H^* = (1 + g)/B^*$. The long-run targets can be written in logarithms as

$$w_t^e = k^* + x_t, \qquad a_t^e = b^* + x_t \tag{9.6}$$

Since the actual outcomes are stochastic, and (9.4) rather than (9.5) holds for the observed data, disequilibria can occur. To model agents assigning priorities to removing these, a quadratic loss function is postulated where the first two terms are the relative costs attached to discrepancies occurring between planned values (w_t^p and a_t^p) and their respective steady-state outcomes. Further, to stabilize behaviour when the environment remains constant (i.e. to avoid 'bang-bang' control in response to random fluctuations), agents attach costs to changing w_t^p from w_{t-1}. However, when the primary objectives are to attain (9.6), it does not seem sensible to quadratically penalize changes in w_t^p when it is known that w_t^e has changed. Thus there is an offset term to allow more adjustment at a given cost when w_t^e has changed than when it is constant. By comparison, partial adjustment models enforce quadratic adjustment costs irrespective of how much the target is known to have changed.

Collecting together these four terms in a one-period loss function yields

$$q_t = \lambda_1 (a_t^p - x_t - b^*)^2 + \lambda_2 (w_t^p - x_t - k^*)^2$$
$$+ \lambda_3 (w_t^p - w_{t-1})^2 - 2\lambda_4 (w_t^p - w_{t-1}) (x_t - x_{t-1}) \tag{9.7}$$

where $\lambda_i \geqslant 0$ ($i = 1, \ldots, 4$). Allowing for the possibility that the current value of x_t might be uncertain, $\mathscr{E}(q_t)$ has to be minimized with respect to w_t^p (or a_t^p), taking into account that (9.5) holds for planned quantities. The deliberately myopic formulation in (9.7) naturally leads to a 'servomechanism' solution when x_t is known, or more generally on setting $\partial \mathcal{L}(q_t)/\partial w_t^p$ to zero:

$$\Delta_1 w_t = \theta_0 + \theta_1 \Delta_1 \tilde{x}_t + \theta_2 (x_{t-1} - w_{t-1}) + \theta_3 (a_{t-1} - x_{t-1}) + u_t \tag{9.8}$$

where $\Delta_1 \tilde{x}_t = \mathcal{L}(x_t) - x_{t-1}$, $w_t - w_t^p = u_t \sim \text{NI}(0, \sigma_u^2)$ independently of w_t^p and the $\theta_i \in (0, 1)$ are given by

$$\theta_0 = \frac{\lambda_2 k^* - \lambda_1 H^* b^*}{\psi} \qquad \theta_1 = \frac{H^* \lambda_1 (H^* - 1) + \lambda_2 + \lambda_4}{\psi}$$

$$\theta_2 = \frac{H^{*2} \lambda_1 + \lambda_2}{\psi} \qquad \theta_3 = \frac{H^* \lambda_1}{\psi} \qquad \psi = H^{*2} \lambda_1 + \lambda_2 + \lambda_3$$

The three variables in (9.8) correspond respectively to derivative, proportional and integral control mechanisms as required; the equivalent partial adjustment cost function would constrain $\theta_1 + \theta_3$ to equal θ_2 (which, in the absence of an ICM, entails having prior information that $\theta_1 = \theta_2$, i.e. that x_{t-1} does not occur in the equation).

The planning rule for w_t given by the above approach is of the form advocated by Richard (1980), where agents' behaviour is described by conditional expectations functions, but agents have no control over the variability around the function. Indeed, the uncertain and highly variable nature of real income makes a feedback control model like (9.8) an attractive behavioural possibility for expenditure. Also, the inclusion of specific mechanisms for correcting past mistakes makes the white noise assumption for u_t more tenable.

Let $x_t - \tilde{x}_t = \varepsilon_t \sim \text{NI}(0, \sigma_\varepsilon^2)$; then (9.8) holds with $\Delta_1 \tilde{x}_t$ replaced by $\Delta_1 x_t$ and u_t by $v_t = u_t - \theta_1 \varepsilon_t$ where $\mathcal{L}(x_t v_t) = -\theta_1 \sigma_\varepsilon^2$. Conversely, time aggregation could introduce simultaneity between x and the equation error for the observation period even if x_t is weakly exogenous in the decision time period (see Richard, 1980); these two effects will be offsetting and are in principle testable, but, for the remainder of this paper, both are assumed to be absent.

Equation (9.8) seems to be the simplest generalization of (9.2) which incorporates an integral control and it yields a non-stochastic steady-state solution when $\Delta_1 x_t = g = \Delta_1 w_t = \Delta_1 a_t$ given by

$$\frac{W}{X} = D \left(\frac{A}{X} \right)^\phi \tag{9.9}$$

where $\phi = \theta_3/\theta_2 > 0$ and $D = \exp\{ [\theta_0 - (1 - \theta_1)g]/\theta_2 \}$. Moreover, (9.5) (for planned magnitudes) and (9.8) imply that

$$\Delta_1 a_t = H^* [\theta_3 (x_{t-1} - a_{t-1}) - \theta_0 + (1 - \theta_2) (x_{t-1} - w_{t-1})$$

$$+ (1 - \theta_1) \Delta_1 x_t - u_t^0] \tag{9.10}$$

(where u_t^0 deviates from u_t by a term involving the product of the disequilibria in the two endogenous variables). Consequently, in non-stochastic steady state

$$A = BX \quad \text{or} \quad a = b + x \tag{9.11}$$

and hence

$$W = KX \quad \text{or} \quad w = k + x \tag{9.12}$$

where $k = -gB/(1 + g)$ (i.e. $K = 1 - gB/(1 + g)$), and

$$b + MB = (b^* + MB^*) + (\lambda_4 - \lambda_3)k^*/\lambda_1 \tag{9.13}$$

when $M = \lambda_3 k^*/\lambda_1 (1 + g)$. Expanding $b + MB$ in a first-order Taylor series around b^* yields $b = b^* + (\lambda_4 - \lambda_3)gk^*/(g\lambda_1 - \lambda_3 k^{*2}) = b^* + O[g/(1 + g)]$.

Equations (9.11) and (9.12) reproduce the forms of the 'desired' relationships in (9.6), and show that the long-run ratios depend on the agents' aims and on the losses attached to the various terms in the objective function (9.7). Since only two alternatives are allowed (e.g. spending W_t or saving $\Delta_1 A_t$), $W = X$ when $g = 0$, but in practice this restriction need not hold for a subcategory of expenditure.

The dynamic reaction of w_t to exogenous changes in x_t can be expressed in the form

$$\Psi(L)w_t = \Phi(L)x_t \tag{9.14}$$

and $\Psi(\cdot)$ is the same for the autoregressive–distributed lag representation of a_t (using (9.5) and (9.10)), where

$$\Psi(L) = \{1 - [1 + (1 - \theta_2) - \theta_3 H^*]L + (1 - \theta_2)L^2\}$$

$$= \sum_{i=0}^{2} \psi_i L^i \tag{9.15}$$

Equation (9.15) is identical to the lag polynomial of the simple multiplier–accelerator model and has stable roots since $0 < \theta_2$, $\theta_3 H^* < 1$, the roots being a complex conjugate pair if $(\theta_3 H^*)^{1/2} > \frac{1}{2}(\theta_2 + \theta_3 H^*)$, in which case the adjustment path is oscillatory with period of oscillation given by $2\pi/\delta$ where $\cos \delta = -\psi_1/2\psi_2^{1/2}$ (for an exposition see Allen, 1963, ch. 7).

Changes in x_t have an impact elasticity of $\theta_1 (1 - \theta_1)$ on w_t (a_t), and for $\theta_1 \neq 1$, discrepancies are created between the actual values of A_t and W_t and their 'equilibrium' levels BX and KX respectively, *both* of which are partly corrected in the next period. In fact, even if $\theta_1 = 1$, the ECMs are still required to correct for stochastic variation (i.e. unless $u_t = 0 \; \forall t$) or for 'unanticipated' changes in x_t, when that variable is not known for certain until the end of the period.

Rather little is known about the finite sample properties of least squares estimators of the θ_i in (9.8), both when the equation is correctly specified and when the lag structure has been wrongly formulated. The case $\theta_3 = 0$ was investigated by DHSY and here we consider the one set of parameter values $(\theta_0, \theta_1, \theta_2, \theta_3) = (-0.1, 0.5, 0.3, 0.1)$ at sample sizes $T = (20, 40, 60, 80)$ when (i) the model is correctly formulated, (ii) the ICM is omitted and (iii) both the ICM and the proportional ECM are omitted. $\sigma_u^2 = 1$, $\sigma_e^2 = 0$ and x_t was generated by

$$x_t = 0.8x_{t-1} + e_t$$

with $e_t \sim \text{NI}(0, 9)$. The first 50 values of each data series were discarded in every replication, and each experiment was replicated 400 times, identical random numbers being used across the three sets of experiments. Normalizing on $\lambda_1 = 1$, the underlying parameter values are $(\gamma_2, \gamma_3, \gamma_4) = (0.97, 2.58, 1.10)$ with $g = 0$ and $h^* = -1$. These parameter values were selected to mimic the empirical results reported below; the chosen model has a static equilibrium solution given by

$$w = x \qquad a = 1 + x$$

with the roots of the $\Psi(L)$ polynomial being $0.8 \pm 0.245i$. To investigate the usefulness of autocorrelation diagnostic tests as indicators of the dynamic mis-specifications, rejection frequencies for Lagrange multiplier (LM) based tests of first- and (general) fourth-order residual autocorrelation were computed (see Godfrey, 1978; Breusch and Pagan, 1980). The results for $T = 80$ are recorded in table 9.1 (similar outcomes were obtained at the other sample sizes), and several features merit note.

First, the simulation findings reveal no new problems for estimating correctly specified single equations involving integral control variables since, although a_t is generated by a cumulative process as in (9.4), $a_t - x_t$ is stationary as shown in equation (9.10). In case (i), the coefficient biases are small and SD $\approx$ SE with the residual autocorrelation tests having approximately the right empirical significance levels as found more generally in chapter 7. Dropping the ICM does *not* cause very large biases in $\hat{\theta}_1$ and $\hat{\theta}_2$ but does bias the intercept to zero; s^2 is biased upwards by almost 30 per cent and the LM tests detect significant autocorrelation in the residuals only 11 per cent of the time. Further, the equilibrium solution remains $w = x$ so that this mis-specification would seem to be very difficult to detect. Consequently, these findings are consistent with 'true' models like (9.8), generating data which are apparently well explained by equations like (9.2) (as reported by DHSY, for example). Except for a further large increase in s^2, the outcome is not much changed by also dropping the proportional ECM (note the results obtained by Wall et al, 1975).

Thus, although $a_t - x_t$ is highly autoregressive, dropping $a_{t-1} - x_{t-1}$ does not

Table 9.1   Simulation findings for (9.8) at $T = 80$

		θ_1	θ_2	θ_3	θ_0	s^2	$z_4(1)$	$z_4(4)$
(i)	Bias[a]	0.00	0.01	0.01	−0.01	0.00	0.06	0.04
	SD	0.04	0.05	0.02	0.13			
	SE	0.04	0.05	0.02	0.12			
(ii)	Bias	−0.01	−0.03	–	0.10	0.29	0.11	0.11
	SD	0.04	0.04	–	0.04			
	SE	0.04	0.05	–	0.13			
(iii)	Bias	−0.04	–	–	0.10	0.76	0.16	0.06
	SD	0.05	–	–	0.05			
	SE	0.05	–	–	0.15			

[a] For coefficient estimates, bias denotes the simulation estimate of $\mathscr{E}(\hat{\theta}_i - \theta_i)$, and for $z_4(i)$ (the LM test for ith order residual autocorrelation) shows the per cent rejection frequency of the null of no autocorrelation.
SD, the sampling standard deviation; SE, the average estimated coefficient standard error; –, the parameter in question was not estimated (and hence has a bias of $-\theta_j$). The sampling standard error of the estimated bias is SD/20.

cause detectable autocorrelation in the residuals. This is important given that the derivation of equations like (9.12) is often ostensibly by differencing a stock–flow relationship (see, for example, ch. 8, p. 187); such interpretations are not unique because of the two formulations of 'differencing' noted by DHSY (p. 191), and (9.2) can be obtained from a linear equation relating w_t to x_t and a_t either by filtering or by imposing invalid coefficient restrictions on the integral control, with very different implications for the error process. It should be noted that Mizon and Hendry (chapter 7) found the LM autocorrelation tests to have reasonable rejection frequencies when the error was generated as an autoregressive scheme.

There are obviously a large number of steps from obtaining simple error correction models like (9.8) to empirical implementation, of which aggregation over agents and time, and the choice of a proxy for A_t, are perhaps the most important in the present context. A proper treatment of aggregation is beyond the scope of this chapter, but (9.8) still provides a useful guide to equation formulation in terms of interpretable and relatively orthogonal variables.

For C_t, the stock of real net liquid assets of the personal sector (denoted by LA_t) seems to play a role analogous to that of A_t (complicated by portfolio adjustments in response to changes in rates of return on other assets and durable expenditure, jointly denoted by N_t):[1]

$$\mathrm{LA}_t = (1 - \Delta_1 p_t)\mathrm{LA}_{t-1} + Y_t - C_t - N_t$$

Thus, in logarithms,

$$\Delta_1 \mathrm{la}_t = -\Delta_1 p_t + H(y_t - c_t) - \eta_t \tag{9.16}$$

where $H = Y/\mathrm{LA}$, η_t depends on N_t (and changes in H) and the variability of η_t is assumed to be small relative to that of $\Delta_1 p_t$ and $y_t - c_t$. The data for $P_t\mathrm{LA}_t$ are taken from the various issues of *Financial Statistics* (see, for example, table 10.3 in the June 1979 issue where $P_t\mathrm{LA}_t$ is the total identified less bank advances). In fact, the form of equation (9.16) points directly to the issue examined in the next section.

3 Real Income and Inflation

The measure of personal disposable income used by DHSY is the 'conventional' series reported in *Economic Trends* and comprises wages, salaries, earnings of the self-employed, rents, net interest receipts, dividends and transfer payments less direct taxes, all revalued using the implicit deflator for total consumers' expenditure. Since the personal sector is a substantial net creditor (see *Economic Trends*, 1978, p. 291), interest receipts are a non-negligible fraction of Y; moreover, as inflation increases, nominal interest rates tend to rise, thereby increasing the interest component of Y. It seems inappropriate to measure 'real income' as increasing in such a situation, since the large nominal interest receipts are offset by capital losses on all monetary assets, which are *not* being deducted from the income variable used (Townend (1976) makes a related point, but does not estimate such an effect). It is easy to understand why the national income accounts should wish to calculate income as the sum of readily observable components, avoiding hard to measure and rather volatile changes in the real values of a spectrum of assets. However, if Y^*, the real income *perceived* by consumers, differs from Y, then consumption functions based on Y will manifest predictive failure when the correlation between Y and Y^* alters.

Hicks (1939, ch. 14) discusses the many difficulties involved in defining and measuring real income when interest rates and prices (and expectations about these) are changing. One improvement over Y might be 'that accrual which would leave real wealth intact', but despite recent improvements in the available statistical evidence we doubt our ability to construct such a quarterly time series relevant to consumers' expenditure. Indeed, to the extent that Y^* differs from Y, it must do so by some easily observable magnitude.

Since most households are aware of their liquid asset position and since the personal sector's losses on liquid assets are a major component of its overall financial loss during inflationary periods, $\dot{p}$LA (where $\dot{p}$ denotes the rate of inflation) seems a prime candidate for relating perceived to measured income. Moreover, aggregate data on net liquid assets (which comprise, very roughly, 20 per cent of wealth and 40 per cent of financial assets) seem reasonably accurate and will occur in our models as the basis of the ICM in any case. Thus the simplest initial hypothesis is that $Y^* = Y - \beta\dot{p}$LA where β has been introduced to account for any scale effects due to wrongly choosing measures for $\dot{p}$ or LA; note that if $\beta = 1$ (i.e. if the loss on our measure of net liquid assets is the variable which consumers perceive as negative income), then (9.16) could be rewritten as $\Delta_1 la_t = H^0(y_t^* - c_t) - \eta_t$ where $H^0 = Y^*/$LA.

More or less inclusive measures proxying A_t could be chosen, and the validity of these is open to test on the data. For example, the choice of LA entails that agents react asymmetrically to erosion of their deposits in building societies as against their mortgages from the same institutions, but, to the extent that such variables behave similarly, the scaling will be corrected by β (for example, building society mortgages are about 40 per cent of LA and are very highly correlated with LA). A two-year moving average of the quarterly inflation rate of the retail price index R was selected for $\dot{p}$ (i.e. $\dot{p} = \Delta_8 \log_e R_t/8$).

To give some idea of the magnitude of the correction to real income involved in Y^*, if $\beta = 1$ and $\dot{p} = 0.05$ (per quarter) then, using LA/$Y = 3$, $Y^* = Y[1 - \dot{p}(\text{LA}/Y)] = 0.85Y$, inducing a dramatic reduction in the income measure. As $\dot{p}$ increases, LA falls, so that $\dot{p}$LA/Y does not increase without bound, unlike the linear term in $\Delta_4 \ln P_t$ in (9.1). Further, when $\dot{p}$ is small, Y^* and Y are very highly correlated and this breaks down only when inflation increases substantially; consequently, if $C = f(Y^*)$ but models attempted to explain C by Y, then such equations would fail only when $\dot{p}$ altered rapidly. Moreover, the increase in $\dot{p}$ in the 1970s in the United Kingdom is closely correlated with the fall in LA/Y (see figures 9.1 and 9.2) and hence including $\dot{p}$ alone as a linear regressor (as DHSY do, for example) would provide an excellent proxy for $\dot{p}$LA/Y: i.e.

$$\log_e\left[Y\left(1 - \beta\dot{p}\frac{\text{LA}}{Y}\right)\right] \approx y - \left(\beta\frac{\text{LA}}{Y}\right)\dot{p}. \tag{9.17}$$

The converse also holds, of course, but our hypothesis seems potentially able to account for the existing evidence.

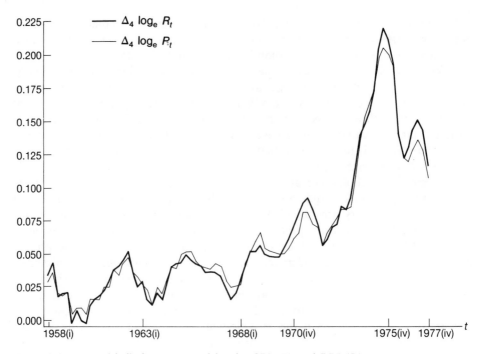

Figure 9.1 Annual inflation measured by the CPI (P) and RPI (R).

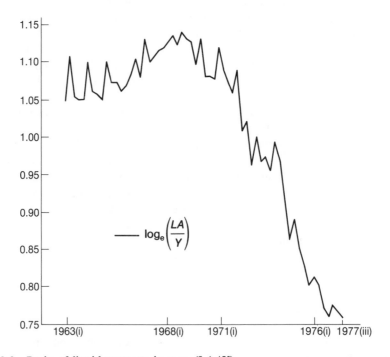

Figure 9.2 Ratio of liquid assets to income (LA/Y).

Alternatively expressed, assuming that the long-run income elasticity of consumption is unity, the apparent fall in C/Y during the 1970s must be due in large part to mis-measurement of the denominator; one simple check on the credibility of this hypothesis is the behaviour of C/Y^* (which should be more nearly constant than C/Y). Figure 9.3 shows the time series of $c_t - y_t$ and $c_t - y_t^*$ (for $\beta = 0.5$) and confirms that the use of Y_t^* has greatly stabilized the consumption–income ratio. The main test of the hypothesis is, of course, whether the resulting model performs as well as (9.1) on the six criteria of section 1, which includes satisfying all the diagnostic tests in section 4 below.

It should be stressed that the use of Y^* is in principle complementary to the theory in Deaton (1977), although in practice the explanations are likely to be more nearly substitutes. Our model is also distinct from the hypothesis that the fall in C/Y is due solely to consumers rebuilding their real liquid assets; certainly an ICM (like a real balance effect) implies that C/Y will fall when LA/Y has fallen, but this is a joint determinant together with the increase in $\dot{p}$. Since our model uses LA/Y^* as the ICM (which also falls less than LA/Y) and since DHSY accounted fully for the fall in C/Y using $\dot{p}$, the correction to Y constitutes a major part of the explanation for the rise in the observed savings ratio. We note that the London Business School (1980) model also requires both inflation and integral effects, although their specification is rather different from equation (9.27) below.

4 Empirical Evidence for the United Kingdom

For ease of comparability, we retained DHSY's data definitions and, so far as possible, their actual data series, extending the sample to 1977(iv) (no further data being

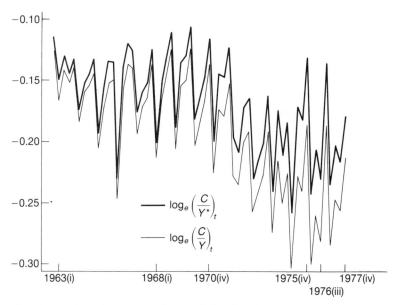

Figure 9.3   Time series of $c_t - y_t$ and $c_t - y_t^*$ for $\beta = 0.5$.

available in 1970 prices) but curtailing the early period to 1962(iv) owing to the lack of observations on liquid assets prior to this date. Also, the implicit deflator of $C(P)$ was replaced by R (the two data series are very highly correlated as shown in figure 9.1). Re-estimating equation (9.1) from 1963(i) and testing its predictions for 1973(i)–1977(iv) yields

$$\widehat{\Delta_4 c_t} = 0.50\Delta_4 y_t - 0.26\Delta_1\Delta_4 y_t - 0.076(c_{t-4} - y_{t-4}) + 0.01\Delta_4 D_t - 0.089\dot{p}_t$$
$$\quad\ (0.04)\qquad (0.05)\qquad\quad (0.017)\qquad\qquad\qquad (0.004)\qquad (0.051)$$

$$\qquad\quad - 0.253\Delta_1\dot{p}_t \qquad\qquad\qquad\qquad\qquad\qquad\qquad\qquad\qquad (9.18)$$
$$\qquad\quad (0.151)$$

$$T = 40 \qquad R^2 = 0.785 \qquad s = 0.0066 \qquad d = 2.1 \qquad z_1(20) = 49.8$$
$$z_3(20, 34) = 1.3 \qquad z_2(8) = 11 \qquad z_4(6) = 3.1.$$

In (9.18), $\dot{p}_t = \Delta_4 \log_e R_t$, T denotes the estimation sample size, s is the standard deviation of the residuals, $z_1(20)$ and $z_2(8)$ are the χ^2 predictive test and the Box–Pierce statistic as reported by DHSY, and $z_3(20, 34)$ and $z_4(6)$ are the Chow test of parameter constancy and the Lagrange multiplier test for residual autocorrelation respectively. Note that if $z_1(n) > n$ then the numerical values of parameter estimates provide inaccurate predictions, but z_3 could still be less than unity so that, with the best re-estimated parameter values, s will not increase.

While the greatly changed behaviour of $\dot{p}_t$ means that the last 20 observations on c_t are far from easy to predict, the predictive performance of (9.18) is distinctly less impressive than that over the DHSY forecast period of 20 quarters (which included the first 12 observations of the present forecast set). Re-estimation over the entire sample yields

$$\widehat{\Delta_4 c_t} = 0.51\Delta_4 y_t - 0.25\Delta_1\Delta_4 y_t - 0.082(c_{t-4} - y_{t-4}) + 0.01\Delta_4 D_t - 0.132\dot{p}_t$$
$$\quad\ (0.03)\qquad (0.05)\qquad\quad (0.013)\qquad\qquad\qquad (0.003)\qquad (0.022)$$

$$\qquad\quad - 0.036\Delta_1\dot{p}_t \qquad\qquad\qquad\qquad\qquad\qquad\qquad\qquad\qquad (9.19)$$
$$\qquad\quad (0.151)$$

$$T = 60 \qquad R^2 = 0.866 \qquad s = 0.0070 \qquad d = 1.9 \qquad z_2(8) = 11$$
$$z_4(6) = 1.8$$

confirming the change in parameter values (especially for $\Delta_1\dot{p}_t$) and the increase in s. Although the values of z_2, z_3 and z_4 in (9.18) are not significant, the evidence in (9.19) suggests that it may be possible to improve on the DHSY specification using the ideas developed in sections 2 and 3.

One direct check (which could have been undertaken before proceeding but in fact was computed later) is to test the null hypothesis that $\beta = 0$ by applying to (9.19) the LM test proposed in Engle (1982b). Engle's statistic (based on (9.17)) rejects the null at the 5 per cent significance level, and while rejection cannot be taken as corroborating any given alternative hypothesis, it does confirm the potential for improvement and is consistent with the argument in section 3.

First, DHSY's steady-state assumption that $C = KY$ seems questionable in view of the strong and persistent seasonal behaviour of C/Y (see figure 9.3). A steady-state solution of the form $C = K_i Y$ (where K_i varies seasonally) is more plausible

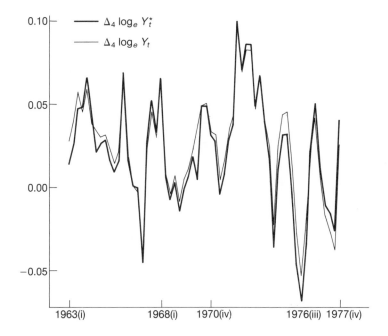

Figure 9.4   Time-series plots of $\Delta_4 y_t$ and $\Delta_4 \hat{y}_t^*$.

on the basis of their own analysis and suggests an error correction mechanism of the form $\log_e (C/K_i Y)_{t-4}$ which could be implemented by either geometrically 'seasonally adjusting' Y or adding seasonal dummies. Indeed, seasonal dummy variables are significant if added to (9.1) which thereby fits better than equation (8.44) of DHSY, resolving their conflict (p. 205) between goodness of fit and parameter constancy. In most results reported below, the K_i were estimated unrestrictedly as coefficients of seasonal dummies, although very similar results were obtained when C/Y was corrected using the quarterly sample means.

Second, DHSY's test for the significance of liquid assets by adding LA to (9.1) is inappropriate as it forces the steady-state solution to be $C/Y = Kf(\text{LA})$ which is dimensionally incorrect (scale changes in LA alter C/Y); it seems more reasonable to anticipate that $C/Y = Kf(\text{LA}/Y)$. Such a mistake would have been avoided had the authors estimated the least restricted model in their class (see table 9.2 below), but omitting the ICM did *not* induce autocorrelated residuals.

Third, the analysis in section 3 requires recomputing real income using $Y_t^* = Y_t - \beta \dot{p} \text{LA}_{t-1}$ (with $\dot{p} = \frac{1}{8}(\dot{p}_t + \dot{p}_{t-4})$, henceforth denoted by $\bar{p}_t$). Since β enters non-linearly in y^*, initial estimates were obtained using a grid search over $0 \leqslant \beta \leqslant 1$ by steps of 0.1 for a specification similar to (9.18) but excluding $\dot{p}_t$ and $\Delta_1 \dot{p}_t$ and including $(\overline{\text{la}} - \bar{y}^*)_{t-1} = \log_e (\Sigma_{i=1}^4 \text{LA}_{t-i} / \Sigma_{i=1}^4 Y_{t-i}^*)$. The minimum residual sum of squares for various sample periods lay in the interval [0.4, 0.6] and $\hat{\beta} = 0.5$ was selected for most of the subsequent regression analysis (see figure 9.4 for the time-series plots of $\Delta_4 y_t$ and $\Delta_4 y_t^*$).

Conditional on $\hat{\beta} = 0.5$, $(\dot{p}_t, \ldots, \dot{p}_{t-4})$ were insignificant ($F_{25}^5 = 1.8$) if added to the otherwise unrestricted log-linear equation

Table 9.2 Unrestricted estimates of (9.20) with $\beta = 0.5$

j	0	1	2	3	4	5	6
c_{t-j}	-1.0	-0.04 (0.12)	-0.05 (0.09)	0.29 (0.11)	0.61 (0.13)	–	–
y^*_{t-j}	0.26 (0.04)	0.19 (0.06)	0.06 (0.06)	-0.10 (0.07)	-0.10 (0.06)	-0.17 (0.05)	-0.04 (0.04)
la_{t-j}	–	0.29 (0.10)	-0.39 (0.17)	0.10 (0.17)	0.07 (0.11)	–	–
Q_{jt}	0.03 (0.20)	-0.05 (0.02)	-0.03 (0.01)	-0.04 (0.01)	–	–	–
D_{t-j}	0.01 (0.004)	–	–	–	-0.01 (0.003)	–	–
$T = 51$	$R^2 = 0.9978$	$s = 0.0053$	$z_1(6) = 33.5$	$z_2(8) = 14.0$	$z_3(6, 30) = 1.7$		

The roots of $\alpha(L) = 0$ are 0.95, -0.78, -0.10, $\pm 0.90i$.

$$c_t = \sum_{i=0}^{n} [\alpha_i c_{t-i-1} + \gamma_i y^*_{t-i} + \delta_i la_{t-i-1} + \xi_i Q_{it}] + \mu_1 D_t + \mu_2 D_{t-4} + \varepsilon_t \qquad (9.20)$$

(where $n = 3$ for c, la and Q and 6 for y^*) and table 9.2 reports the estimates obtained for (9.20). The s value is substantially smaller than DHSY report for their unrestricted model, $\hat{\delta}_i$ and $\hat{\xi}_i$ being individually significantly different from zero at the 0.05 level. Because of the shorter sample period, only six observations have been retained for parameter constancy tests and, while both z_1 and z_3 are unimpressive, the parameterization is profligate (the equivalent z_3 value using Y in place of Y^* is 2.13).

The long-run solution of (9.20) derived from table 9.2 is

$$c = k_i - 8.3g + 0.57y^* + 0.38 \text{ la}$$
$$\quad (7.8) \quad (0.14) \quad (0.20)$$

where k_i varies seasonally, g is the quarterly growth rate of y^* and la, and numerically computed asymptotic standard errors of the derived parameters are shown in parentheses. The sum of the coefficients of y^* and la is not significantly different from unity (0.95 (0.10)) but, as discussed by Currie (1981), the coefficient of g is badly determined and is not significantly different from zero.

Such results are consistent with the theory developed in section 2, but a more parsimonious restricted specification facilitates interpretion of the data. First, for the derivative term, the results in DHSY and Bean (1978) suggest using a distributed lag in $\Delta_4 y^*_t$ and the simple Almon polynomial (see Sargan, 1980b) $Ay^*_t = \Sigma_{i=0}^2 (3 - i) \Delta_4 y^*_{t-i}$ adequately captures this. Note that Ay^*_t is, in effect, 'self-seasonally adjusted', and continuing this idea for the ICM suggests using $(\overline{la} - \bar{y}^*)_{t-1}$ as defined above; likewise, the proportional ECM takes the form $(c - k_i - y^*)_{t-4}$ discussed earlier. Finally, to strengthen derivative control and dampen any potential oscillatory behaviour generated by the ICM, $\Delta_1 la_{t-1}$ was also included as a regressor (see table 9.2). Thus, the restricted dynamic model to be estimated is of the general form

$$\Delta_4 c_t = \alpha_1 Ay^*_t + \alpha_2 (c - y^*)_{t-4} + \alpha_3 (\overline{la} - \bar{y}^*)_{t-1} + \alpha_4 \Delta_1 la_{t-1} + \alpha_5 \Delta_4 D_t$$

$$+ \sum_{j=0}^{3} \alpha_{j+6} Q_{jt} + u_t \qquad (9.21)$$

Estimation of this specification yielded

$$\widehat{\Delta_4 c_t} = 0.082 Ay^*_t - 0.20(c - y^*)_{t-4} + 0.074(\overline{la} - \bar{y}^*)_{t-1} + 0.24\Delta_1 la_{t-1}$$
$$\quad (0.005) \qquad (0.05) \qquad\qquad (0.018) \qquad\qquad (0.07)$$

$$+ 0.009\Delta_4 D_t - 0.098 - 0.017 Q_{1t} - 0.007 Q_{2t} - 0.003 Q_{3t} \qquad (9.22)$$
$$\quad (0.002) \qquad (0.025) \quad (0.004) \qquad (0.003) \qquad (0.003)$$

$T = 47 \qquad R^2 = 0.928 \qquad s = 0.0052 \qquad z_1(6) = 4.9 \qquad z_3(6, 38) = 0.6$
$z_2(8) = 19.5 \qquad z_4(6) = 11.2.$

Since the $z_4(6)$ value indicated significant fourth-order residual autocorrelation, the simple autoregressive form $u_t = \rho_4 u_{t-4} + \varepsilon_t$ was assumed and re-estimation provided the equation.

$$\widehat{\Delta_4 c_t} = 0.083Ay_t^* - 0.18(c - y^*)_{t-4} + 0.072(\overline{la} - \overline{y}^*)_{t-1} + 0.22\Delta_1 la_{t-1}$$
$$\quad\;\; (0.004) \qquad (0.05) \qquad\qquad (0.015) \qquad\qquad\quad (0.06)$$

$$+ 0.010\Delta_4 D_t - 0.094 - 0.016Q_{1t} - 0.007Q_{2t} - 0.003Q_{3t} \qquad\qquad (9.23)$$
$$(0.002) \qquad (0.021) \;\; (0.004) \qquad (0.002) \qquad (0.002)$$

$$\hat{\rho}_4 = -0.33$$
$$\quad\; (0.15)$$

$$T = 47 \qquad s = 0.0050 \qquad z_1(6) = 5.7 \qquad z_5(5) = 4.0 \qquad z_6(6,38) = 0.7$$

where z_6 is an approximate F test of parameter constancy based on the change in s^2 when the sample size is increased. Figure 9.5 shows the plot of the actual data and the fit of (9.23), including the six 'prediction' observations. Since $z_1(6) \approx 6$ and $z_6 < 1$, parameter constancy is ensured when the sample is extended to include the last six observations and (in contrast to (9.18)) s will fall; re-estimation yielded

$$\widehat{\Delta_4 c_t} = 0.083Ay_t^* - 0.16(c - y^*)_{t-4} + 0.072(\overline{la} - \overline{y}^*)_{t-1} + 0.19\Delta_1 la_{t-1}$$
$$\quad\;\; (0.004) \qquad (0.04) \qquad\qquad (0.009) \qquad\qquad\quad (0.06)$$

$$+ 0.009\Delta_4 D_t - 0.091 - 0.015Q_{1t} - 0.007Q_{2t} - 0.004Q_{3t} \qquad\qquad (9.24)$$
$$(0.002) \qquad (0.013) \;\; (0.003) \qquad (0.002) \qquad (0.002)$$

$$\hat{\rho} = -0.30$$
$$\quad\; (0.14)$$

$$T = 53 \qquad s = 0.0049 \qquad z_5(5) = 5.2.$$

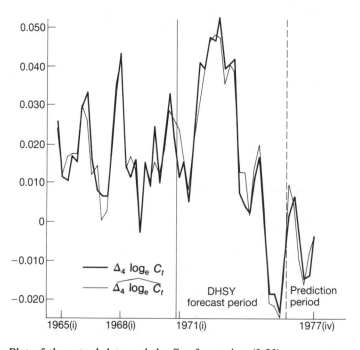

Figure 9.5   Plot of the actual data and the fit of equation (9.23).

In both (9.23) and (9.24), $z_5(5)$ denotes the likelihood-ratio-based χ^2 test of the autoregressive error 'common factor' restrictions (see Sargan, 1964a; and chapter 7).

There are many interesting features of these results which deserve comment. First, s is less than 0.5 per cent of C and, even in terms of tracking the quarterly movements in the annual growth rate, the equation fits extremely well. Compared with (9.19) (the most comparable sample period), the s value is over 30 per cent smaller. Further, the proportional ECM coefficient is nearly twice as large as in (9.19), reflecting the omitted seasonals bias of the latter, although the sum of the income change coefficients is almost identical. All the individual coefficients are well determined and the diagnostic statistics (including the parameter constancy tests) are insignificant, and yet the last six observations seem to 'break' a collinearity between $(\overline{la} - \bar{y}^*)_{t-1}$ and the intercept, judging by the fall in their standard errors (this could be due to the marked upturn in LA_t which occurred during 1977).

Finally, given that the integral control is close to the cumulated real savings measure used in Stone (1973) and Deaton (1976) it is interesting that the R^2 of (9.24) (without the fourth-order autoregressive error) is 0.934, similar to values previously obtained using *annual data* for changes in C_t.

Despite the many steps and approximations from the simple theory of section 2 to equations like (9.21), the results are readily interpretable in terms of the parameters of (9.5)–(9.7) above. The static solution of (9.24) (i.e. when $g = 0$) is

$$c - y^* = -0.55 + 0.44(la - y^*) - 0.088Q_1 - 0.041Q_2 - 0.026Q_3 \qquad (9.25)$$
$$(0.07) \ (0.08) \qquad\qquad (0.009) \quad (0.011) \quad (0.012)$$

Taking $b^* = 1.1$ (the mean of $\overline{la} - \bar{y}^*$ prior to 1970) and normalizing $\lambda_1 = 1$ yields $\lambda_2 = 0.65$ (from ϕ), $\lambda_3 = 3.9$ (from θ_3) and $\lambda_4 = 1.9$ (from θ_1); the over-identifying restrictions can be used as a consistency check and the λ_i and b^* imply $\theta_0/\theta_2 = -0.48$ as against -0.55 in (9.25). Note the efficiency gain in estimating ϕ relative to the solution from (9.20).

If the *annual* growth rate of Y is $g > 0$, the two values of θ_0/θ_2 match more closely and the term $2.7g$ must be subtracted from (9.25). The λ_i are hardly altered for $g = 0.025$ (the sample average was 0.022) and b^* differs from b by about 0.02 per cent. Eliminating $la - y^*$ from (9.25) using $b^* = 1.1$ and $g = 0.025$ yields

$$c - y^* = -0.22Q_1 - 0.17Q_2 - 0.16Q_3 - 0.13Q_4 \qquad (9.26)$$

which compares closely with the time series shown in figure 9.3. If LA/Y^* depended on any outside variables (such as interest rates) then these would enter (9.26) as a 'reduced form' effect.

The full long-run impact of $\dot{p}$ in (9.25) is hard to obtain, but neglecting any behavioural dependence of LA/Y^* on $\dot{p}$, using $e^{b^*} = B^* = 3$ yields $c = y - 0.38\mu - \Sigma_1^4 k_i Q_i$, where μ is the *annual* rate of inflation. This is a much smaller inflation effect than that obtained by DHSY, primarily because of the downward bias in their coefficient of $(c - y)_{t-4}$ and their omission of an ICM.

As a check on the choice of $\hat{\beta} = 0.5$, equation (9.24) was re-estimated using non-linear least squares to compute the optimal value of β, in an equation which set $\hat{\rho}_4$ to zero and used the quarterly sample means to compute $C_t/K_i Y_t^*$ (denoted by $(c^a - y^{*a})_t$ below) to economize on parameters:

$$\widehat{\Delta_4 c_t} = 0.082 A y_t^* - 0.21 (c^a - y^{*a})_{t-4} + 0.089 (\overline{la} - \bar{y}^*)_{t-1} + 0.15 \Delta_1 la_{t-1}$$
$$\quad (0.004) \qquad (0.04) \qquad\qquad\qquad (0.011) \qquad\qquad\qquad (0.05)$$

$$+ 0.010 \Delta_4 D_t - 0.123 \qquad\qquad\qquad\qquad\qquad\qquad (9.27)$$
$$\quad (0.003) \qquad (0.018)$$

$$\hat{\beta} = 0.44$$
$$\quad (0.12)$$

$$T = 52 \qquad R^2 = 0.936 \qquad s = 0.0049 \qquad d = 2.04$$

(d is the Durbin–Watson statistic value). The results in (9.27) are consistent with the initial choice of $\hat{\beta}$ as 0.5 and suggest little bias in the quoted standard errors from conditioning on $\hat{\beta}$. Similar results were obtained when estimating equations like (9.27) over different sample periods (see Ungern-Sternberg, 1978) although point estimates of β were not well determined in smaller sample sizes.

Lastly, as a weak test of parameter constancy, equation (9.21) with $\hat{\beta} = 0.5$ was used to predict the 20 quarters on which (9.18) was tested:

$$\widehat{\Delta_4 c_t} = 0.085 A y_t^* - 0.27 (c - y^*)_{t-4} + 0.099 (\overline{la} - \bar{y}^*)_{t-1} + 0.36 \Delta_1 la_{t-1}$$
$$\quad (0.009) \qquad (0.10) \qquad\qquad\qquad (0.043) \qquad\qquad\qquad (0.16)$$

$$+ 0.010 \Delta_4 D_t - 0.137 - 0.022 Q_{1t} - 0.006 Q_{2t} - 0.003 Q_{3t}$$
$$\quad (0.003) \qquad (0.058) \quad (0.008) \qquad (0.003) \qquad (0.003)$$
$$\qquad\qquad\qquad\qquad\qquad\qquad\qquad\qquad\qquad\qquad (9.28)$$

$$\hat{\rho}_4 = -0.36$$
$$\quad (0.22)$$

$$T = 33 \qquad s = 0.0052 \qquad z_1(20) = 44.4 \qquad z_6(20, 23) = 0.75 \qquad z_5(5) = 2.1$$

In contrast to (9.19), there is no evidence of significant parameter changes although, as shown in table 9.3, the correlation structure of the main regressors altered radically between the estimation and prediction periods. Indeed, fitting (9.21) to *only* the last 20 observations provides the estimates (setting ρ_4 to zero given the sample size)

$$\Delta_4 c_t = 0.086 A y_t^* - 0.17 (c - y^*)_{t-4} + 0.067 (\overline{la} - \bar{y}^*)_{t-1} + 0.12 \Delta_1 la_{t-1}$$
$$\quad (0.009) \qquad (0.07) \qquad\qquad\qquad (0.018) \qquad\qquad\qquad (0.07)$$

Table 9.3   Data correlations

1964(iv)–1972(iv)	$\Delta_4 c_t$	Δy_t^*	$(c - y^*)_{t-4}$	$(\overline{la} - \bar{y}^*)_{t-1}$	$\Delta_1 la_{t-1}$
			1973(i)–1977(iv)		
$\Delta_4 c_t$		0.94	0.22	0.71	0.46
$A y_t^*$	0.85		0.25	0.56	0.41
$(c - y^*)_{t-4}$	0.18	0.22		-0.09	0.34
$(\overline{la} - \bar{y}^*)_{t-1}$	-0.25	-0.38	0.04		0.12
$\Delta_1 la_{t-1}$	0.19	0.07	-0.17	-0.15	

$$+ 0.007\Delta_4 D_t - 0.085 - 0.017 Q_{1t} - 0.010 Q_{2t} - 0.009 Q_{3t} \qquad (9.29)$$
$$(0.002) \qquad (0.016) \quad (0.007) \qquad (0.004) \qquad (0.005)$$

$T = 20 \qquad s = 0.0047 \qquad R^2 = 0.97 \qquad d = 1.74 \qquad z_7(9, 35) = 0.74$
$\hat{\phi} = 0.39 \ (0.23)$

(where $z_7(9, 35)$ is the covariance F test between $T = 53$ and the two subsamples, all with $\rho_4 = 0$). The estimates in (9.28) and (9.29) are remarkably similar to those given in table 9.3 and strongly suggest that the relationship under study is not simply a conditional regression equation (see Richard, 1980). Supporting this contention, re-estimation of (9.23) using t, c_{t-1} and the lagged regressors as instrumental variables for Ay_t^* yielded almost identical results with $s = 0.0050$, $z_8(6) = 4.3$ (an asymptotically valid χ_6^2 test of the independence of the instruments and the error), $\hat{\phi} = 0.40 \ (0.07)$ and $z_1(6) = 5.8$.

5 Summary and Conclusions

Three extensions of the model presented in chapter 8 are considered, namely integral correction mechanisms, a re-interpretation of the role of their inflation variable and a re-specification of the seasonal behaviour of consumers' expenditure on non-durables and services (C) in the United Kingdom. For the first of these, we adopt an approach similar to that of Stone (1966, 1973) (who used cumulated real savings in an annual model) which leads to the use of the ratio of liquid assets to income (LA/Y) in the empirical equation as a proxy for integral control. The second extension involves the recalculation of real income by subtracting a proportion of the losses on real liquid assets due to inflation $(\dot{p})$ and yields a ratio of consumption to perceived income (Y^*) which is substantially more stable than the ratio of the original series. Allowing for a seasonally varying average propensity to consume (K_i) produces a model with a steady-state solution given by

$$\frac{C}{Y^*} = K_i \left(\frac{LA}{Y^*}\right)^{0.44} \qquad (9.30)$$

where $Y^* = Y - \frac{1}{2}\dot{p}LA$ and where K_i also depends on the growth rate of real income. The dynamic formulation of (9.30) satisfies the equation selection criteria proposed by DHSY and both simulation evidence and analysis are used to explain how they managed to choose an incorrect model (with mis-specifications not detectable by their diagnostic statistics) which nevertheless provided a reasonable approximation to (9.28) above over their sample period.

The results are consistent with Stone's findings and, like Deaton (1976) and Townend (1976), we confirm the importance of some cumulative measure in explaining C in the United Kingdom. In addition, the hypothesis that real income is seriously mis-measured in times of inflation is supported by the data and plays a major role in accounting for the sharp fall in C/Y during the 1970s (compare Siegel, 1979).

Strikingly similar results have also been obtained for equivalent equations using West German semi-annual data (see von Ungern-Sternberg, 1978), providing strong additional support for our hypothesis concerning the negative income effects of inflation on consumers' expenditure.

Note

1   Strictly, the first term should be $(1 + \Delta_1 p_t)^{-1}$, the result quoted being accurate only for small values of $\Delta_1 p_t$.

10

Interpreting Econometric Evidence: The Behaviour of Consumers' Expenditure in the United Kingdom

with James E.H. Davidson

Preamble

Consumption function studies were almost becoming a treadmill! Partly to update and test the DHSY and HUS specifications, and partly to check whether they encompassed Robert Hall's (1978) formulation, James Davidson and I returned to the topic in early 1980. We sought to evaluate Hall's model on UK data both by direct testing and by encompassing it via eliminating the contemporaneous income term from DHSY. The former could only reject the Hall model whereas the latter could reject either model or even both. In addition, we tried to tackle the 'feedback versus feedforward' debate then becoming prominent in the wake of Robert Lucas (1976) paper.

The way I had used economic theory in previous empirical studies was becoming critically questioned at seminar presentations, so despite the major role which I thought theory formulations had played in chapters 3 and 6–9, a latent criticism of 'measurement without theory' lurked in the background. As noted in chapter 5 above, the issue is probably more one of the interpretation of the implications of economic analysis rather than its presence or absence, especially concerning intertemporal optimization by economic agents. Chapter 17 considers some of the associated issues and the papers by Salmon (1982), Nickell (1985) and Pagan (1985) all offer insights into the close links between feedback and feedforward representations of economic behaviour. Certainly, the styles of this chapter and of the paper it was criticizing (i.e. Hall, 1978) are very different, but I think the objectives of using theory-based empirical models to understand data phenomena and improve theory are the same for both.

The concept of weak exogeneity was in the process of formalization (see Richard, 1980; and chapter 15), as were the basic concepts discussed in chapter 16, and some of these ideas appear in the analysis, including innovations and encompassing. At the time, we did not perceive the powerful encompassing implications which changing marginal processes

Reprinted from *European Economic Review*, 16 (1981) 177-92. Paper presented at the International Seminar in Macroeconomics, Oxford, June 23-24, 1980. We are indebted to Frank Srba for valuable assistance and to John Muellbauer and participants at the conference for helpful comments. This research was financed in part by the International Centre for Economics and Related Disciplines and the Social Science Research Council.

(here, income, liquid assets and inflation) entailed for conditional models (such as consumption functions). These implications would have clarified the Lucas critique and provided a more general test of expectations–based models. The merging of the notions of encompassing and predictive failure depended on the prior development of super exogeneity (see chapter 15 and Engle and Hendry, 1989) and the formalization of encompassing (see chapter 16), and first appears in Hendry (1988b) and Favero and Hendry (1989).

Concerning the substantive findings, the empirical results favoured the error correction mechanism over the model proposed by Hall both on criteria of direct testing and encompassing. Nevertheless, even the 'best' *ex ante* predictor of the change in aggregate consumers' expenditure had surprisingly little explanatory power. The final follow-up study of consumers' expenditure is left until chapter 18 since its objective was more to exposit the evolving methodology in the context of consumers' expenditure, as a familiar illustration, rather than to offer new substantive evidence *per se* (see Hendry et al. (1990b) for an update on DHSY).

1 Introduction

In two chapters in this volume (chapter 8, denoted DHSY, and chapter 9, denoted HUS), an attempt was made to account for the empirical findings of most published 'aggregate consumption function' studies based on UK quarterly time-series data. Their approach involved specifying a number of criteria which any chosen empirical model should satisfy and they sought to select a simple equation which was not only data coherent and consistent in broad outline with the main theories of consumers' expenditure but also explained why previous studies obtained the results they reported and had not selected the 'best' equation. In both DHSY and HUS, the *Gestalt* of data evidence strongly favoured error correction formulations for the dynamic response of real consumers' expenditure on non-durables (C) to real personal disposable income (Y) – the latter chapter also included real personal sector liquid assets (LA) as an 'integral' correction. Moreover, although both papers were primarily concerned with methodological issues, their finally chosen equations seem to have continued to track the data with the anticipated accuracy despite further changes in both the expenditure–income ratio and the data intercorrelations (see, for example, Davies, 1979).

One important approach was not investigated in either study, namely the model based on a permanent income/life cycle theory of consumers' expenditure where agents hold rational expectations about future real income accruals. As an implication of that approach, Hall (1978) deduced that C_t should follow a 'random walk', i.e.

$$C_t = \alpha_0 + \alpha_1 C_{t-1} + v_t, \tag{10.1}$$

where $\alpha_1 > 1$ allows for a trend, and v_t is 'white noise' independent of past values of income. Fitting such an equation to quarterly (seasonally adjusted) data for the United States, Hall found that (10.1) provided an adequate description of the data in that such an equation seemed to have random residuals, and lagged income did not appear significantly if added. These findings were interpreted as supporting the postulated theory. Since the results in DHSY and HUS encompassed an equation like (10.1) as a special case and were not necessarily incompatible with such a data process it seemed worth investigating the validity of (10.1) for UK data.

The following framework is proposed for interpreting the econometric evidence, given that the forms of equation in DHSY and HUS survived a range of tests and encompassed most empirical models other than (10.1). If C_t were a random walk with a completely autonomous error process (so (10.1) defines the true model) then it is inconceivable that any of the other estimated equations could have survived predictive failure tests. Consequently, we follow Hall in interpreting (10.1) as an implication of the data generation process, but consider the situation in which a log-linear error correction mechanism (ECM) defines the true model and income is strongly exogenous. For clarity, different symbols are used, bearing the interpretation that (X, Q) are (C, Y) respectively.

$$\Delta_1 x_t = \gamma_1 \Delta_1 q_t + \gamma_2 (q - x)_{t-1} + v_t, \tag{10.2}$$

$$q_t = \lambda q_{t-1} + u_t, \tag{10.3}$$

where lower-case letters denote logarithms of corresponding capitals, $\Delta_j x_t = (x_t - x_{t-j})$, and $0 < \gamma_1, \gamma_2 < 1$, with

$$\begin{bmatrix} u_t \\ v_t \end{bmatrix} \sim \text{IN} \left(\begin{bmatrix} 0 \\ 0 \end{bmatrix}, \begin{bmatrix} \sigma_u^2 & 0 \\ 0 & \sigma_v^2 \end{bmatrix} \right). \tag{10.4}$$

Regarded as a servomechanism, (10.2) enables agents to maintain $X = KQ$ (where $K = \exp[(\gamma_1 - 1)g/\gamma_2]$ in a world of stochastic variation around any steady-state growth path with constant growth rate $\Delta_1 q = g$. Thus (10.2) is consistent with the proportionality aspect of the permanent income hypothesis, but otherwise is based on 'feedback' rather than 'anticipation' assumptions. Equation (10.3) is interpreted purely as a data description (see table 10.4(c) below) and issues of log versus linear, the endogeneity or 'exogeneity' of q etc. are discussed later. For the moment, it suffices to note that (10.2) is estimable by least squares under the assumptions stated and has an error variance of σ_v^2.

However, if an investigator only considered lagged regressors, then since (10.2) can be re-expressed as

$$x_t = \beta_1 q_t + \beta_2 q_{t-1} + \beta_3 x_{t-1} + v_t, \tag{10.5}$$

where $\beta_1 = \gamma_1$, $\beta_2 = \gamma_2 - \gamma_1$ and $\beta_3 = 1 - \gamma_2$, eliminating q_t using (10.3) yields

$$x_t = \pi_1 q_{t-1} + \pi_2 x_{t-1} + w_t, \tag{10.6}$$

where $\pi_1 = \beta_2 + \beta_1 \lambda$, $\pi_2 = \beta_3$ and $w_t = v_t + \gamma_1 u_t$. The apparent equilibrium solution of (10.6) no longer yields proportionality between X and Q (unless $\lambda = 1$); also, π_1 typically will be small as β_1 and β_2 usually have opposite signs (with $\pi_1 < 0$ possible); next, (β_1, β_2) can be recovered *only* by jointly modelling the x and q processes so that q_{t-1} is not weakly exogenous for the β_i in (10.6) and finally, even when (10.2) is structural, (10.6) is *not* for interventions which affect the data generation process of q_t (see chapter 15). Consequently, direct estimation of the parameters of (10.6) is inefficient and could induce an incorrect decision to delete the 'insignificant' regressor q_{t-1}, leading to the selection of an equation like (10.1),

$$x_t = \theta x_{t-1} + \varepsilon_t, \tag{10.1'}$$

as the 'appropriate' model. Moreover, the deletion of q_{t-1} need not cause notice-able *residual* autocorrelation in (10.1').

This analysis is most easily understood by simulating the three models ((10.2), (10.6) and (10.1')) when (10.2)–(10.4) defines the data generation process (analogous results obtain allowing for x to Granger-cause q, but add little additional insight and so are not reported below). The data generation process in the Monte Carlo analysis used 'typical' values for the parameters based on DHSY, namely $(\beta_1, \beta_2, \beta_3) = (0.5, -0.4, 0.9)$, $\lambda = 0.95$, $\sigma_v^2 = 1$, $\sigma_u^2 = 10$ and $T = 74$, and repli-cated (10.2)–(10.4) 200 times, using NAIVE (see chapter 14). The intercept was esti-mated for every model, $\{q_t\}$ was generated independently in each replication, and the first 20 initial data values were discarded.[1] A circumflex denotes the 'econo-metric' estimate and an overbar denotes the mean simulation outcome. The following simulation statistics are reported:

$\bar{\delta}$	mean value of the coefficient $\hat{\delta}$ of the relevant regressor
SD	sampling standard deviation of $\hat{\delta}$
SE	mean estimated standard error of $\hat{\delta}$
F	proportional rejection frequency of the null H_0: $\delta = 0$
$\bar{\sigma}^2$	mean residual variance
η_k	proportional rejection frequency of the Lagrange multiplier test for general kth-order residual autocorrelation

In the tables, figures in parentheses denote standard errors; all tests are at 5 per cent nominal significance levels.

First, the results for equation (10.2) are as might be anticipated (see table 10.1). Not surprisingly, the ECM adequately characterizes the data and closely reproduces the population parameters; the two autocorrelation tests reject slightly less often than their nominal levels (but within two standard errors). Solving for $(\hat{\pi}_1, \hat{\pi}_2)$ from estimates of (10.2) + (10.3) should yield standard errors of around (0.04, 0.04)

Table 10.1 Simulation results for equation (10.2)

Regressor	δ	$\bar{\delta}$	SD	SE	F	η_1	η_4	$\bar{\sigma}^2$
Δq_t	0.50	0.50 (0.003)	0.04	0.04	1.00	0.04 (0.01)	0.03 (0.01)	1.00
$(q - x)_{t-1}$	0.10	0.12 (0.003)	0.04	0.04	0.92			

Table 10.2 Simulation results for equation (10.6)

Regressor	δ	$\bar{\delta}$	SD	SE	F	η_1	η_4	$\bar{\sigma}^2$
q_{t-1}	0.075	0.090 (0.006)	0.08	0.07	0.32	0.06 (0.01)	0.03 (0.01)	3.5
x_{t-1}	0.90	0.83 (0.007)	0.10	0.09	1.00			

Table 10.3   Simulation results for equation (10.1′)

Regressor	δ	$\bar{\delta}$	SD	SE	F	η_1	η_4	$\bar{\sigma}^2$
x_{t-1}	0.98	0.93	0.05	0.04	1.00	0.10	0.09	3.6
		(0.004)				(0.02)	(0.02)	

(these figures are based on using $\text{var}(\hat{\lambda}) = (1 - \lambda^2)/T$ and the asymptotic covariance matrix of $\hat{\delta}$ and obtaining $\text{var}(\hat{\pi}_i)$ from the formula in Goldberger et al. (1961)).

Next, the simulation estimates of equation (10.6) are presented in table 10.2. Both standard errors are almost twice as large as in table 10.1 and $H_0: \pi_1 = 0$ is rejected only a third of the time, so the loss of efficiency is important. $\bar{\sigma}^2$ correctly estimates $\sigma_v^2 + \gamma_1^2 \sigma_u^2$ and, as earlier, η_1, η_4 reject at about the 5 per cent level.

Finally, if the investigator deleted q_{t-1} so that equation (10.1′) was estimated, we have table 10.3, where $\delta = \theta$ is *defined* by $\text{plim}_{T \to \infty} (\Sigma x_t x_{t-1}/\Sigma x_{t-1}^2)$; interestingly, $\bar{\delta} - \delta \approx -(1 + 3\delta)/T$, the usual formula for the bias to $O(T^{-1})$.

Although q is highly autoregressive, and both q_t, q_{t-1} are excluded, neither η_1 nor η_4 detect residual autocorrelation more than a small percentage of the time, and 'invalid' tests (such as Durbin–Watson) should perform even worse. Given that $\bar{\sigma}^2$ is close to that obtained for equation (10.6), it is easy to see how (10.1′) might be selected when (10.2) is the true model and q is exogenous, but (for whatever reason) only lagged regressors were considered.

The models used by DHSY and HUS are certainly more complicated than (10.2) and the framework is not intended to imply that the equivalent of $\hat{\pi}_1$ must be insignificant for UK data (in fact, y_{t-1} enters significantly below). The analysis does show, however, that the same model (here (10.1)) can be implied by 'contradictory' theories and hence, while observing an 'implication' of a theory provides a check on its data consistency, it does not really offer 'support'.

Before testing (10.1), it is clearly essential to re-establish the validity of the empirical equivalents of the analogue models, and in the interval since DHSY and HUS selected their equations, new data (on a new, 1975, price index basis) have accrued which allow a powerful independent test of their formulations (see section 2). Following this, the implications for the Hall model are derived from HUS using the empirical equivalent of (10.3) and, against this, (10.1) is tested. The evidence leads to rejection of (10.1) but seems consistent with HUS and so section 4 briefly examines the issues of simultaneity and data coherency. Finally, the interpretation of equations in terms of 'forward'- versus 'backward'-looking behaviour is reconsidered and suggests that there is less incompatibility between the various approaches than might appear at first sight.

2 A Reappraisal of DHSY and HUS

Equations (10.7) and (10.8) respectively report least squares re-estimates of these two models based on the 1975 price index data;[2] all series are quarterly, seasonally *un*adjusted and in constant prices over the period 1964(i) ($T = 1$) to 1979(iv) ($T = 64$) with C, Y, LA as defined above and P and D denoting the retail price index and the dummy variable (for 1968(i)–(ii) and the introduction of value added tax) used by HUS. As earlier, lower-case letters denote $\log_e$ of corresponding capitals and Δ_j denotes a *j*-period difference. Thus, the DHSY model yields

$$\widehat{\Delta_4 c_t} = 0.48\Delta_4 y_t - 0.27\Delta_1\Delta_4 y_t - 0.11(c - y)_{t-4} - 0.14\Delta_4 p_t - 0.34\Delta_1\Delta_4 p_t$$
$$\qquad (0.05) \qquad (0.07) \qquad\quad (0.02) \qquad\qquad (0.05) \qquad (0.20)$$

$$+ 0.01\Delta_4 D_t,$$
$$\quad (0.003)$$

(10.7)

$T = 6, 44 + 20f \qquad R^2 = 0.73 \qquad \hat\sigma = 0.0088$

$z_1(20, 33) = 0.6 \qquad z_2(20) = 25 \qquad z_3(8) = 9.3 \qquad z_4(6) = 5.7,$

where

$T = a, b + nf$	denotes estimation from (a, b) and prediction over the next n observations
$\hat\sigma$	residual standard deviation
$z_1(n, T - K)$	F test of parameter constancy due to Chow (1960) for n post-sample observations and K regressors
$z_2(n)$	asymptotically equivalent χ^2 test (see chapter 11)
$z_3(l)$	Box–Pierce autocorrelation statistic based on the residual correlogram
$z_4(l)$	Lagrange multiplier test for *l*th-order error autocorrelation (i.e. η_l above)

Figure 10.1 shows the graph of $\Delta_4 c_t$ and the fit/predictions from (10.7) (note that 'prediction' means using known values for the regressors, with parameter estimates held fixed). The estimates in (10.7) are closely similar to those reported in DHSY, parameter constancy is maintained over the prediction period and no evidence is present of residual serial correlation. Also, extending the estimation sample to $T = 6$, $56 + 8f$ (so that only completely new observations are retained for the predictive failure tests) yields $\hat\sigma = 0.0083$, $z_1(8, 45) = 0.8$, $z_2(8) = 8$, $z_4(6) = 5.7$. These empirical results corroborate those reported independently by Bean (1977) and Davies (1979) and provide further empirical support for the theoretical arguments developed in Deaton (1980).

Next,

$$\widehat{\Delta_4 c_t} = 0.084\sum_0^2 (3 - i)\Delta_4 y_{t-i}^a - 0.15(c - y^a)_{t-4} + 0.068(la - y^a)_{t-4}$$
$$\qquad (0.007) \qquad\qquad\qquad\qquad (0.06) \qquad\qquad\quad (0.018)$$

$$+ 0.01\Delta_4 D_t - 0.15\Delta_1 R_{t-3}^* - 0.079 - 0.013Q_{1t} - 0.009Q_{2t} - 0.007Q_{3t},$$
$$\quad (0.002) \qquad (0.09) \qquad\quad (0.023) \quad (0.005) \qquad (0.004) \qquad (0.003)$$

(10.8)

$T = 7, 60 + 4f \qquad \hat\sigma = 0.0078 \qquad \hat\rho_1 = 0.31\ (0.16)$

$z_1(4, 43) = 0.3 \qquad z_2(4) = 2 \qquad z_5(5) = 7.1 \qquad z_3(7) = 8.9,$

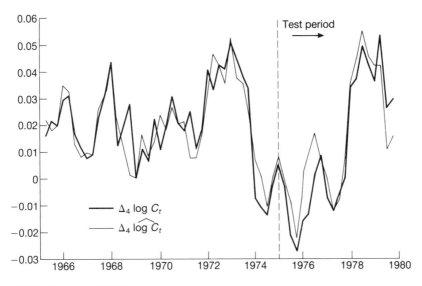

Figure 10.1 Equation (10.7).

where $y^a = \log_e (Y - \dot{p}\text{LA})$ and $\dot{p}$ is an eight-quarter moving average of the rate of change of the retail price index, $R^* = R(1 - T_y) - \Delta_4 p$, where R is the local authority three-month interest rate and T_y is the standard marginal rate of income tax, Q_{it} are seasonal dummy variables, $\hat{\rho}_1$ is the estimated first-order autoregressive error coefficient and $z_5(k)$ is the likelihood ratio test of the common factor restriction (see Sargan, 1964a, 1980a).

The specification in (10.8) differs slightly from HUS, but $\Delta_1 R_{t-3}^*$ is not significant[3] (and has a t value of about 0.6 if $\Delta_1 \text{la}_{t-1}$ is added, which in turn has a t of 1.7 and reduces $\hat{\rho}_1$, supporting the HUS formulation) and the use of the single-period value of $\text{la} - y^a$ (rather than a four-period moving average) improves both the fit and the predictions and removes the four-period autocorrelation found by HUS. Figure 10.2 shows the graph of (10.8) and figure 10.3 provides the time series of $c - y$ and $c - y^a$ to demonstrate the effects of adjusting the income series for inflation-induced losses on liquid asset holdings. As with (10.7), the estimates are similar to those reported earlier (and seem robust to the noted changes in specification), and exhibit parameter constancy despite the dramatic changes which occurred in $c - y^a$ after 1976 (note that the adjusted expenditure–income ratio reaches a peak in 1976 prior to falling sharply). Since $z_1(\cdot)$ and $z_2(\cdot)$ are Lagrange multiplier-based tests, it is legitimate under the null to test other periods for parameter constancy after model fitting, and doing so for $10f$ (using $\Delta_1 \text{la}_{t-1}$ as a regressor) yields $z_1(10, 37) = 1.1$, $z_2(10) = 31$, $\hat{\sigma} = 0.0073$. While parameter constancy is not rejected, z_2 indicates that the estimates are not well determined over the shorter estimation period.

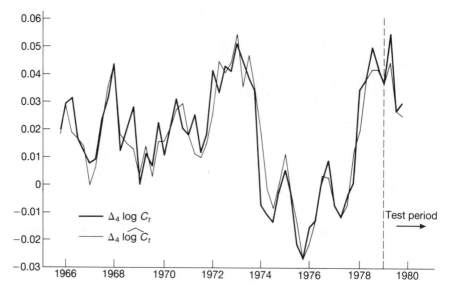

Figure 10.2 Equation (10.8).

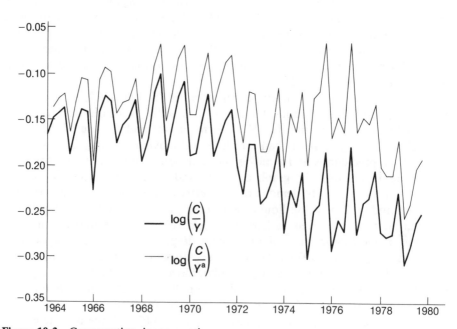

Figure 10.3 Consumption–income ratios.

The long-run steady-state constant growth 'equilibrium' solutions from (10.7) and (10.8) have the form

$$\frac{C}{Y} = B(g, \dot{p}) \left(\frac{LA}{Y}\right)^{\phi},$$
(10.9)

where $\phi = 0, 0.45$ in (10.7) and (10.8) respectively and $B(\cdot)$ depends negatively on the growth rate of Y (g) and inflation ($\dot{p}$). Long-run proportionality as in (10.9) is a well-known attribute of both permanent income and life cycle theories, as is a negative dependence on g. The presence of LA/Y can be rationalized in several ways when capital market imperfections and uncertainty prevail (see, for example, Flemming, 1973; Pissarides, 1978). Note that although the solution (10.9) takes the same form for (10.7) and (10.8) under the static equilibrium condition that LA/Y is constant, marginalizing with respect to all current and lagged values of LA is an unnecessary restriction on the information set which would be counterproductive if the partial correlations between included and excluded variables altered.

The empirical equivalent of (10.3) is reported in table 10.4(c) below, and using this to eliminate current y_t from (10.8) yields[4]

$$c_t \approx 0.31 y_{t-1} + 0.17 y_{t-2} - 0.17 y_{t-4} - 0.14 y_{t-5} - 0.08 y_{t-6} + 0.85 c_{t-4}$$

$$+ 0.2 la_{t-1} - 0.2 la_{t-2} + 0.07 la_{t-4}$$
(10.10)

Thus, on the hypothesis that (10.8) describes the data generation process, the data evidence suggests that lagged y and lagged la should influence c_t given lagged cs.

3 The Hall Model

If C_t is determined by permanent income (Y_t^p) and the latter is the discounted rational expectation of future income accruals, since innovations to the information set are white noise, Hall (1978) deduced that C_t would follow a random walk[5] with drift or trend as in (10.1). As noted above, the empirical evidence for the United States quoted by Hall is consistent with such a hypothesis.

Below, log-linear rather than linear models are used, but this change seems inconsequential, and UK evidence favours the former. However, Hall's data seem to have been seasonally adjusted and, depending on the filter used for the different series, the results could be distorted thereby (see Wallis, 1974; and DHSY). Although it is unlikely that the substance of the arguments would be changed radically by the use of adjusted versus raw series, the fit of (10.1) requires re-interpretation in terms of filtered data, and application to unadjusted data (as herein) involves substantially different lag lengths.

The unrestricted fifth-order autoregression for c_t suggested the following analogue of (10.1) (see Prothero and Wallis, 1976):

$$\widehat{\Delta_4 c_t} = 0.72 \Delta_4 c_{t-1} + 0.01 \Delta_4 D_t + 0.006$$
(10.11)
$$\phantom{\widehat{\Delta_4 c_t} = } (0.25) \phantom{\Delta_4 c_{t-1} + } (0.004) (0.006)$$

$T = 8, 44 + 20f \qquad \hat{\sigma} = 0.0110 \qquad \hat{\rho}_1 = 0.19\ (0.32)$

$z_1\ (20, 33) = 1.3 \qquad z_2\ (20) = 26 \qquad z_5\ (1) = 0.5 \qquad z_3\ (7) = 7.0.$

Figure 10.4 provides the time-series graph, and at first sight the tracking performance appears satisfactory. However, the standard deviation of $\Delta_4 c_t$ is only 0.0195 and the $\pm 2\hat{\sigma}$ interval from (10.11) is ± 0.0220; specifically, on the six occasions when $\Delta_4 c_t$ changed by more than ± 0.022, the model's prediction error/residual fell outside the $\pm 2\hat{\sigma}$ interval four times, and of 29 sign changes in $\Delta_1 \Delta_4 c_t$ (i.e. when $\Delta_4 c_t$ changed direction) (10.11) had the opposite sign (for $\Delta_1 \Delta_4 \hat{c}_t$) on 21 occasions! Nevertheless, the residuals from (10.11) are not detectably autocorrelated, which entails that all other lagged values of c_t are potentially legitimate instrumental variables.

It should be clear that neither (10.1) nor (10.11) is claimed to be the data generation process; both are *derived* models and there are many objections to arguing that the *true* consumption equation is a random walk with an autonomous error process generated independently of Y, LA etc., not least the fact that random walks can drift anywhere and so produce C much in excess of Y. Rather, the stochastic implications obtained by Hall can be expressed succinctly as: no other potential lagged variables Granger-cause the residuals in (10.1) (see Granger, 1969; and chapter 15).

On methodological grounds, to test (10.1) (or, here, (10.11)) adequately against other models, all the additional variables should be included at the outset. First testing c_t on y_{t-j} $(j \geq 1)$ alone, then on la_{t-j} $(j \geq 1)$ alone etc. can seriously bias the outcome. Thus, table 10.4(a) reports the estimates for a model of the form

$$c_t = \sum_{j=0}^{n} \left(\alpha_j c_{t-j-1} + \beta_j y^a_{t-j-1} + \gamma_j la_{t-j-1} + \delta_j R^*_{t-j-1} + \lambda_j Q_{jt} \right)$$

$$+ \theta_0 D_t + \theta_1 D_{t-4} + u_t, \tag{10.12}$$

where n is 5 for y^a, 4 for c and 3 for Q, la and R^* (in table 10.4(b), δ_j is set to zero for all j).

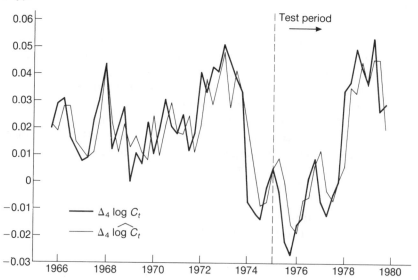

Figure 10.4   Equation (10.11).

Table 10.4 Least squares estimates of the unrestricted consumption equation

j	0	1	2	3	4	5	6
(a)							
c_{t-j}	-1	0.59 (0.22)	-0.09 (0.17)	0.42 (0.16)	0.71 (0.17)	-0.17 (0.24)	–
y^a_{t-j}	–	0.20 (0.09)	0.03 (0.10)	-0.19 (0.10)	-0.13 (0.11)	-0.25 (0.11)	0.01 (0.10)
la_{t-j}	–	0.21 (0.19)	-0.50 (0.22)	0.10 (0.23)	0.07 (0.14)	–	–
R^*_{t-j}	–	0.05 (0.19)	0.11 (0.24)	-0.28 (0.27)	0.21 (0.19)	–	–
Q_{jt}	0.10 (0.35)	-0.06 (0.02)	-0.01 (0.02)	-0.04 (0.02)	–	–	–
D_{jt}	0.02 (0.01)	–	–	–	-0.01 (0.01)	–	–

$T = 7$, $58 + 6f$ $\quad R^2 = 0.994 \quad \hat\sigma = 0.0083$
$z_1(6, 27) = 1.0 \quad z_2(6) = 12 \quad z_3(7) = 14.6 \quad z_4(6) = 8$

j	0	1	2	3	4	5	6
(b) Least squares estimates excluding the real interest rate							
c_{t-j}	-1	0.52 (0.20)	-0.07 (0.16)	0.40 (0.15)	0.71 (0.16)	-0.13 (0.23)	–
y^a_{t-j}	–	0.21 (0.08)	0.03 (0.09)	-0.19 (0.09)	-0.14 (0.10)	-0.22 (0.10)	-0.02 (0.09)
la_{t-j}	–	0.32 (0.12)	-0.51 (0.19)	-0.00 (0.20)	0.10 (0.12)	–	–
Q_{jt}	0.03 (0.32)	-0.06 (0.02)	-0.01 (0.02)	-0.04 (0.02)	–	–	–
D_{jt}	0.02 (0.01)	–	–	–	-0.01 (0.01)	–	–

$T = 7$, $58 + 6f$ $\quad R^2 = 0.993 \quad \hat\sigma = 0.0079$
$z_1(6, 31) = 1.9 \quad z_2(6) = 19 \quad z_3(7) = 9.7 \quad z_4(6) = 5$

j	0	1	2	3	4	5	6
(c) Autoregressive model for adjusted real income							
y^a_{t-j}	-1	0.58 (0.18)	0.34 (0.22)	-0.12 (0.24)	-0.07 (0.24)	0.12 (0.20)	–
Q_{jt}, t	1.4 (1.3)	-0.05 (0.02)	-0.01 (0.01)	-0.01 (0.02)	-0.001 (0.001)	–	

$T = 6$, $44 + 20f$ $\quad R^2 = 0.97 \quad \hat\sigma = 0.020$
$z_1(20, 29) = 1.0 \quad z_2(20) = 40 \quad z_3(7) = 5.0 \quad z_4(6) = 6$

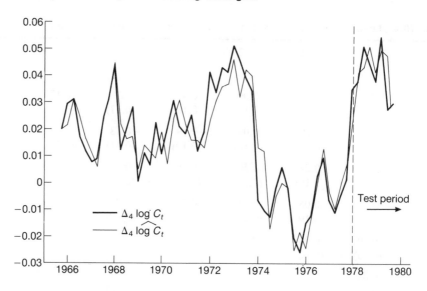

Figure 10.5   Equation (10.13).

Although such over-parameterized regressions must be treated with care, several lagged variables are individually significant rejecting the strong implications underlying (10.1). Indeed, the estimates in table 10.4(b) correspond reasonably to the solved 'reduced form' (10.10) which obtains on marginalizing (10.8) with respect to current y, using the empirical data process reported in table 10.4(c). Further, directly reparameterizing table 10.4(b) yields

$$\widehat{\Delta_4 c_t} = 0.12\,\Delta_4 y^a_{t-1} + 0.54\,\Delta_4 c_{t-1} + 0.40\,\Delta_1\,\mathrm{la}_{t-1} + 0.01\,\Delta_4 D_t + 0.003$$
$$\phantom{\widehat{\Delta_4 c_t} = }(0.06)\qquad\quad (0.12)\qquad\quad (0.09)\qquad\quad (0.003)\qquad (0.003)$$

$$- 0.001\,Q_{1t} + 0.002\,Q_{2t} + 0.007\,Q_{3t},\qquad\qquad (10.13)$$
$$(0.004)\qquad (0.004)\qquad (0.004)$$

$T = 8,56 + 8f \qquad R^2 = 0.82 \qquad \hat{\sigma} = 0.0089$

$z_1(8,41) = 1.7 \qquad z_2(8) = 16 \qquad z_3(8) = 9.4 \qquad z_4(8) = 3.0.$

This fits and predicts only slightly worse than (10.7) (DHSY) and, noting that the predictions are still *ex ante*, is a substantial improvement over (10.11). Figure 10.5 shows the time-series track of (10.13). Clearly, while the residuals from (10.11) may be white noise, components thereof are functions of lagged observables and hence are Granger-caused by both y and la.

4 Analysis of Results

4.1 Endogeneity of Y_t

One reason why investigators are sometimes reluctant to include Y_t in consumption functions is that Y_t and C_t are believed to be simultaneously determined and hence an (upward) biased coefficient will result from regression estimates. This is testable by using as instruments an appropriate set of lagged variables which might help agents to predict Y_t at time $t - 1$, and on both HUS and Hall's arguments, all other lagged variables are appropriate; in particular lagged Cs are valid. However, measurement errors in Y induce biases in the opposite direction and DHSY and HUS both note that instrumental variable estimates of (10.7) and (10.8) are almost identical to those quoted above.

There is clearly a time aggregation problem in using an observation period of a quarter when agents may be revising decisions monthly or even weekly, and shorter observation period data would provide a more powerful test of the alternative models, but it is hard to establish evidence of sufficiently strong within-quarter feedbacks from C_t to Y_t to yield serious biases in the parameters of interest. It must be stressed that the fact that C_t and Y_t are linked by identities is irrelevant to the status of Y_t as 'endogenous' or 'predetermined': to argue otherwise is to confuse the properties of the *measurement* system with those of the data generation processes which *determine* outcomes: an identity is simply a constraint and *per se* cannot determine anything (see, *inter alia*, Buiter, 1980; Spanos and Taylor, 1984; and compare Sargent, 1978). In any case, hazarding to predictive failure when data correlations change jointly tests putative structurality, and weak exogeneity (see chapter 15). Consequently, if some structural consumption function existed, but (10.7) or (10.8) did not reasonably approximate this or Y_t was not weakly exogenous for its parameters (e.g. because of simultaneity) then regression estimates should manifest predictive failure (especially for (10.7) which was initially selected from pre-1971 data). Since such has not occurred, the evidence does not support an assertion that including Y_t induces substantial simultaneity bias in models of C_t. The coherence of (10.10) with the estimates in table 10.4(b) further supports such an interpretation.

4.2 Data Coherency

Much empirical research treats a model as being data coherent if its fit deviates only randomly from the observations. The converse, namely that non-random residuals imply data incoherency, is certainly true; but although there are many necessary conditions for model adequacy, there do not appear to be any sufficient conditions in a scientific discipline. The terms 'random errors' and 'white noise' are often used loosely to refer to serially uncorrelated time series, but strictly white noise disturbances should be defined as innovations which are unpredictable relative to a given information set (see Granger, 1983). Typically, diagnostic tests for randomness in residuals are simply tests for autocorrelation. However, in checking for data coherency it is clear that a somewhat more general information set than the past history of the series itself is appropriate. Serially uncorrelated series may be largely predictable from other lagged information; for example,

$$w_t = \sum_{j=0}^{\infty} \gamma_j v_{j,t-j} \tag{10.14}$$

is serially independent when all the $v_{j,t-j}$ are, and yet all but $\gamma_0 v_{0t}$ is predictable in principle from lagged data. Moreover, processes with a strong intertemporal component may still be serially uncorrelated, as for example

$$u_t = \sum_{i=0}^{\infty} \rho^i \varepsilon_{1t-i} + \varepsilon_{2t} \tag{10.15}$$

which contains an infinite moving average but is 'white noise' if $\mathscr{E}(\varepsilon_{1t}\varepsilon_{2t-1}) = -\rho\mathscr{E}(\varepsilon_{1t}^2)/(1 - \rho^2)$.

Hence, the criterion of uncorrelated residuals is a very weak test of model adequacy – indefinite numbers of models which are 'data coherent' on this criteria will exist. It is found for example (see HUS) that deleting $(q - x)_{t-1}$ from (10.2) does not create detectable autocorrelation. We reiterate the stress which DHSY placed on the need to account for all other relevant empirical findings before according plausibility to an estimated model.

5 'Forward-looking' versus 'Backward-looking' Behaviour

The original derivations of (10.7) and (10.8) placed stress on their servomechanism interpretations since minimal assumptions about the 'rationality' and/or 'intelligence' of agents were required: (10.7) and/or (10.8) mimic 'rational' behaviour seeking to achieve a target like (10.9) in a steady-state world, without needing any 'expectational' hypotheses. Nevertheless, feedback control rules frequently correspond to reformulations of state-variable feedback solutions of forward-looking optimal control problems (see, for example, Salmon and Young, 1978; Salmon, 1979a); indeed, the basic form of ECM first obtained by one of the authors arose naturally in an optimal control context (see chapter 3). Moreover, Nickell (1985) has derived a range of circumstances in which ECMs are the *optimal* responses of agents in a dynamic environment using optimal predictors of regressor variables. These arguments re-emphasize the non-uniqueness of interpretations of empirical findings as 'support' for postulated theories in non-experimental disciplines: feedback and forward-looking behaviour can 'look alike' in many states of nature if deliberately designed experimental perturbations of expectations are excluded. In fact, D_t is a dummy precisely for such 'experiments' (albeit, inadvertently conducted) and demonstrates that agents are fully capable of anticipatory behaviour – yet to date, we seem to lack general ways of modelling such events. Overall, the problem is not one of reconciling error correction or expectational interpretations, but of distinguishing their separate influences.

Notes

1 Technically, there are difficult inference problems for processes like (10.1) when α_1 is 'near' the unit circle (see Phillips, 1977; Evans and Savin, 1981) and hence the analogue Monte Carlo considers only stationary processes; but pilot experiments suggested that similar results obtained for $\lambda = 1.02$.

2 *See Economic Trends*, Annual Supplement of January 1980 and the issue of May 1980.

3   R^* was tried as a 'control' to partial out any changes in real interest rates. In fact, $\Delta_1 la_{t-1}$ retains a similar coefficient to that reported by HUS if $\Delta_1 R_{t-3}$ is excluded (namely 0.2), and this is used below in deriving equation (10.10).

4   In fact, c_{t-1} 'Granger-causes' y_t if added to table 10.4(c) (see Granger, 1969) and incorporating this feature would further improve the 'match' with later results.

5   John Muellbauer pointed out to us that an error on the relationship linking C_t to Y_t^p would produce a negative moving-average error on (10.1) (and hence bias the least squares estimates of α_1) which need not be detectable by, for example, a Durbin–Watson test; see Muellbauer and Winter (1980) for a related discussion.

11

Predictive Failure and Econometric Modelling in Macroeconomics: the Transactions Demand for Money

Preamble

A natural question to ask of the approach adopted by DHSY was 'will it work in other subject matter areas?' The opportunity to test an answer was presented immediately after DHSY was published when another demand for money study was reported by the Bank of England which included models in levels only and in differences only. If encompassing worked, it should be possible to develop a unique model; and given the role error correction had played in both chapter 6 and DHSY to reconcile long-run and short-run models, a similar approach looked very promising for the transactions demand for money.

A major change in the emphasis of the methodology had taken place between 1976 and 1978, following Jean-François Richard's realization of the important parallels with the approach at CORE. Many of the concepts in DHSY dovetailed with the CORE ideas, and conversely many of their ideas both clarified and extended the DHSY approach. In particular, the concept of models being reductions of the underlying data generation process (DGP), due to eliminating some variables and conditioning on others, neatly formalized both that aspect of DHSY and my related contemporaneous Monte Carlo research. Moreover, the reduction approach explained the sense in which error processes were *derived* rather than *autonomous* and hence why models could be designed to satisfy pre-selected criteria (such as Durbin–Watson statistic values of 2). But if errors and hence models could be designed, what 'design' criteria should be adopted? Attempting to resolve that issue leads directly to chapter 16.

A useful side effect of the DHSY–CORE merger was to relate the methodology much more closely to the extant statistical literature, where concepts of reduction to sufficient statistics,

Reprinted from Ormerod, P. (ed.), *Economic Modelling*, London: Heinemann, 1979, ch. 9. The research was supported in part by a grant from the Social Science Research Council to the Quantitative Economics Programme at the London School of Economics. I am grateful to Richard Coghlan for supplying his data, and to Jeremy Bray, Richard Coghlan, Charles Goodhart, Lawrence Klein, Grayham Mizon, Adrian Pagan, Morris Perlman and Deane Terrell for helpful comments on earlier versions of the paper. All of the results reported below are based on the author's AUTOREG Computer Programme Library and I am greatly indebted to Frank Srba for his invaluable assistance in undertaking and evaluating the calculations.

conditioning on ancillary statistics, marginalizing etc. were standard (see, for example, Barndorff-Nielsen, 1978).

The methodological point of importance arising from the research reported in the present chapter is the re-emphasis on commencing from general models and sequentially reducing these to parsimonious data representations as in chapters 3 and 6. Since empirical models were reductions of the DGP by marginalizing and conditioning, to apply that idea explicitly in data analysis required that one should begin from the most unrestricted yet feasible mimic of the DGP and reduce it to a model (maquette?) thereof. Consequently, a simple-to-general approach is compared directly with a general-to-simple approach in a practical context, much to the benefit of the latter.

I continued to regard the 'time-series versus econometrics' debate to be misplaced. As chapter 3 argued, the autoregressive integrated moving-average (ARIMA) model form used by time-series advocates could be viewed as a special case of an econometric model form in which the information from related variables was ignored. Logically, therefore, ARIMA models should never outperform econometric models on economics data, and their doing so in any instance must be due to the latter mis-specifying the dynamics. Consequently, any successes of ARIMA models simply reveal the importance of dynamics in econometrics, and a major theme of chapter 11 is to analyse the implications of that finding. However, what I did *not* realize at the time is that the issue of model forms (on which others also had focused) must be a red herring. With hindsight, the obvious question is why econometric equations did not *in practice* embed the ARIMA reductions as special cases, and that is an issue of *modelling methods*. Box and Jenkins (1976) had laid out systematic procedures for discovering useful data representations in a restricted model class (for univariate processes) when the researcher did not know how the data were generated. Econometric models needed the same type of methodology: since the DGP was unknown, the data had to be systematically analysed to develop a useful statistical summary, which was the objective of the general-to-simple strategy. However, the general model, which constituted the initial point of the data analysis, depended on both economic analysis (the 'cognitive' stimulus to including potential determinants) and previous empirical evidence (the 'physical' stimulus). If applied studies are to be validly encompassed later, they have to be included unrestrictedly from the outset. Once an acceptable or *congruent* statistical model is developed, it has to be interpretable either through existing theory or by forging new theoretical analyses. Conjectures can be tested against the statistical baseline to see if they lie in the space of acceptable models, and the finally chosen econometric model must be a parsimonious representation of the well-established statistical model (i.e. one of the acceptable conjectures). This approach evolves in chapter 16 and is emphasized in Spanos (1986).

Thus, the section on the flaws of simple-to-general methods, which includes as a special case merely imposing a prior theory onto data, is really the key to why econometric model forms were not functioning well in practice. The chapter only relates it in a negative way to the time-series debate, however, by showing that both a structural break in a marginal process and model mis-specification are necessary for predictive failure and the latter is indicated if time-series representations of the variable of interest do not also manifest structural breaks.

The other crucial idea deriving from Jean-François Richard's work was that of weak exogeneity (see Richard, 1980) with its emphasis on efficient conditional inference about parameters of interest. The first aspect led to a reconsideration of conditioning on contemporaneous variables and the construct of weak exogeneity (see chapter 15) and the second, through a concern with constant parameters, led to super exogeneity. The present chapter stresses the issue of constancy versus non-constancy, its interpretation and its role in model selection. More recently, the development of good graphical facilities on personal computers has allowed a focus on recursive procedures for more intensively investigating parameter constancy and evaluating invariance (see Hendry and Neale, 1987; Hendry, 1988b; Engle and Hendry, 1989).

The applications of error correction mechanisms (ECMs) to both data modelling and encompassing are also discussed in the context of processes experiencing regime shifts and, again, ECMs are able to account for the available evidence. However, since different econometric specifications have different susceptibilities to changes elsewhere in the economy, it is important to evaluate a range of models when testing the adequacy of any particular claim.

The chapter includes a re-evaluation of a variant of my model using new data, taken from section 7 of chapter 17 (published four years afterwards). As with later tests of the constancy of DHSY, the evidence reveals that the out-of-sample performance is comparable with in-sample fit, even though the models were explicitly data based. While such an outcome could have been due to good luck, it was at least consistent with the view that data-basing improved rather than hindered forecasting performance. By chapter 18, I had realized that an important distinction helped clarify why such an outcome was possible, namely the distinction between the intrinsic validity of a model (a property of the model, independently of how it was discovered) and the initial credibility of the selected model (which might depend on the discovery route): see Johnston (1984, ch. 12) for a similar analysis. And as chapter 18 records, I also realized that this dichotomy was a special case of Karl Popper's (1969) distinction between conjectures and refutations.

More recent updates of the same model are provided by Hendry and Mizon (1991b), who test the weak exogeneity of the conditioning variables for the parameters of interest in a system of I(1) variables, and Hendry and Ericsson (1991b), who extend the sample to 1989, demonstrate constancy of the same equation with a modification of the measure of opportunity cost to reflect financial innovation, and test super exogeneity and invariance.

1 Introduction

It is widely recognized that instability in an estimated econometric equation provides little evidence about the stability or otherwise of the sought-after economic relationship. This is especially true of research into demand for money functions where it has proved far from easy to establish stable empirical relationships for the United Kingdom (see, for example, Hacche, 1974; Artis and Lewis, 1976; Hamburger, 1977). Attempts to account for observed instability have included the possibility of mis-specification (excluded variables and incorrect exogeneity assumptions), and the coincidence of a major policy change (competition and credit control in 1971) with the commencement of apparent parameter change. However, for the transactions demand equation, mis-specified exogeneity and policy change explanations are not very convincing and recently Coghlan (1978) presented evidence for relatively stable M1 relationships common to both the 1960s and 1970s.

The term 'stability' in the preceding paragraph related to the constancy over time of the estimated parameters in an equation and not to the latent roots of the dynamics of a model being such as to yield convergence to equilibrium or steady state. As the latter usage is well established, the former will be called 'predictive accuracy' since econometric formulations which are constant over time will provide 'accurate' predictions of a regressand given the correct values of the regressors where 'accurate' denotes 'within the anticipated forecast confidence region'. (The chapter is not concerned either with *ex ante* forecasts – where these depend on any judgemental factors such as intercept adjustments, *ad hoc* parameter modifications, exogenous variables projections etc. – or with 'absolute' forecast accuracy measures.) Conversely, 'predictive failure' indicates that the model formulation can be rejected against an unspecified alternative using post-estimation sample data.

The linkages of structural breaks and mis-specifications to predictive failures are discussed in section 2 together with some alternative forecast test procedures. The role of 'simple-to-general' modelling methods as a potential factor leading to mis-specification is considered in section 3 using transactions demand models for illustration. The converse strategy of 'general to simple' is briefly reviewed in section 4, followed in section 5 by an analysis of 'error correction' feedback mechanisms in dynamic equations, and their effect on predictive accuracy for M1. Section 6 concludes the study.

The chapters by Davidson et al. (chapter 8) on modelling consumers' expenditure and Hendry and Mizon (chapter 6) on testing the specification of M3 equations are sufficiently closely related in framework to obviate reconsidering many of the econometric issues raised therein. In particular, the problems of seasonal adjustment of data and multi-collinearity, the importance of explaining the *Gestalt* of previous findings and the sequential testing of common factors for autocorrelation will *not* be discussed below in order to highlight the additional material and keep the paper to a sensible length (see Coghlan (1978) for an evaluation of a number of previously reported M1 equations). In his interesting and thorough study of money demand in the United States, Goldfeld (1973) also considered a wide range of specification issues, although these differ somewhat from the problems emphasized below. Pagan (1977) adopted a similar approach to testing implicit econometric assumptions in a study of M1 demand in Australia and concluded that inappropriate research techniques leading to mis-specification could adequately account for the observed apparent instability. And general model selection procedures for dynamic equations were discussed by Mizon (1977a).

2 Predictive Failure and Model Mis-specification

Over the last few years, researchers monitoring macroeconomic relationships appear to have needed to revise their models frequently to counteract what are loosely classified as 'structural breaks'. Certainly, many important changes have occurred recently, including the oil crisis, the move from (adjustable) fixed to (controlled) floating exchange rates, the introduction of the competition and credit control regulations, trade liberalization following the United Kingdom's entry into the EEC etc., all of which probably altered certain economic relationships. Moreover, theoretical arguments have been adduced that 'structural equations' may not be constant, rapidly adjusting to incorporate changes in policy rules and depending on 'rational expectations' about future events (see, for example, Sims, 1980). Consequently, it is easy to rationalize the predictive failure of an econometric system on the grounds that some 'structural break' occurred, although this is both vacuous unless the precise structural break factors are themselves specified and very unconvincing if extrapolative models continue to forecast with reasonable accuracy!

Further, while a *genuine* structural break in a relationship may be sufficient to induce predictive failure in that equation, it is not necessary in the following sense: if all the true structural equations in a system remained unaltered but the behaviour of some exogenous variables changed, then all mis-specified econometric approximations to the equations of that system could manifest 'shifts' (i.e. *apparent* structural breaks).[1] To account for the phenomenon of predictive failure, the hypothesis of mis-specified econometric relationships interacting with the changed behaviour of a small number of variables (arising from the major breaks noted above) is undoubtedly not novel. However, it is sufficiently constructive and parsimonious relative to postulating shifts in a wide range of underlying economic relationships to merit careful consideration. Also it has some prior plausibility since few researchers would maintain that previous model specifications were correct, and there are some empirical findings which seem to provide illustrations of such interactions.

First, concerning the issue of correct model specification, all situations in which a 'naive' time-series model (see Box and Jenkins, 1976; Granger and Newbold, 1977b) outperforms the corresponding 'econometric' system constitute *prima facie* evidence that the latter suffers from mis-specification (*at a minimum*, dynamic and/or stochastic). Even a relatively rudimentary handling of system dynamics and autocorrelation seems to produce models which are superior to univariate autoregressive integrated moving-average (ARIMA) descriptions (see Prothero and Wallis, 1976) and although this is obviously a weak criterion, more detailed analysis can yield improvements over 'transfer function' models (see chapter 8). Conversely, inadequate treatment of the dynamic–stochastic specification leaves open the possibility that mechanical predictors which correctly model the main dynamics of the data generation process may be more accurate than resource intensive systems which are coherent in terms of economic theory but econometrically mis-specified (see, for example, Cooper, 1972).

Second, while *residual* autocorrelation can arise from error autocorrelation, it is at least as likely to derive from the many forms of potential mis-specification which afflict time-series modelling, including ignored simultaneity, omitted variables, measurement errors and incorrect functional form as well as dynamic–stochastic specification mistakes. However, since residual autocorrelation refers to something that is *not* included in a model, then *whatever its source* it again indicates mis-specification. The problems involved in 'removing' such autocorrelation by simply assuming some error process and incorporating it in the model are discussed in chapter 6. Noting that most of the models reported in Hickman (1972) manifested substantial residual autocorrelation, no surprise should have been expressed at Cooper's findings. In order to highlight the issues just discussed, section 3 examines in some detail the effects of inappropriately modelling a 'sensible' economic relationship.

Turning to examples of mis-specification interacting with the changed behaviour of a variable, the greatly increased rate of inflation ($\dot{p}$) in the United Kingdom in the mid-1970s would have induced shifts in all *estimated* equations which excluded $\dot{p}$ if the *true* structural relationships depended on $\dot{p}$ or any variable highly dependent on $\dot{p}$. Moreover, earlier variations in $\dot{p}$ need not have been so large or so persistent in one direction as to induce predictive failure, yet at the same time could have been adequate for estimating the correct specification *had it been proposed*. In particular, Deaton (1977) demonstrates the effect of $\dot{p}$ on savings behaviour prior to 1970 and Davidson et al. (chapter 8) confirm the equivalent effect on consumers' expenditure and highlight the large shifts which occurred later in the 1970s in consumption equations excluding $\dot{p}$. Further, it must be stressed that the excluded variables need not be previously *unthought of* effects but could be functions of variables which were already included in *some* (but incorrect) *form* – witness the predictive failure of the Wall et al. (1975) equation extended to include $\dot{p}$ but having the dynamic specification mistake reported in chapter 8. A similar outcome is recorded below in section 5 for some transactions demand for money functions.

Of course, mis-specification *per se* is not sufficient for predictive failure since, under unchanged structure in stationary stochastic systems completely incorrect equations will continue to forecast within the accuracy limits anticipated from their error variances (see, for example, Hendry, 1979b). For example, univariate ARIMA models constitute approximations to the final form equations of econometric systems (see Zellner and Palm, 1974; Prothero and Wallis, 1976), and hence should forecast reasonably so long as the underlying structure does not alter. A similar result holds for other derivable relationships, whether or not these have white noise errors. Conversely, an ARIMA model ceasing to predict within the anticipated confidence interval for any variable is evidence of a change in the behaviour of that variable either directly or through a change in its final form determination. Morever, the latter is liable to affect several equations and hence it may be possible to detect which variables(s) have changed. Consequently, by examining the concomitant behaviour of the predictions from 'econometric relationships', 'time-series models' etc., constructive revision strategies are possible which could facilitate rapid model improvement during periods of change.

When model specification is incorrect in unknown ways, there is no single 'best' modelling method, and the idea in the previous paragraph tries to exploit the information provided by different equation formulations having different susceptibilities to mis-specification. In such a context, 'time-series' models can be a valuable adjunct to econometric systems, although they are certainly not an adequate substitute. Whatever model is conjectured as a tentative working hypothesis, reasonable effort should be devoted to testing it, learning its weak points and discovering which aspects of the data generation process are not yet explained, and comparison with ARIMA descriptions is a useful part of this activity. (For an excellent and much more detailed discussion of the issues in 'specification searches' see Leamer (1978).)

To summarize: rejecting an equation on a test of forecast accuracy implies either that it has experienced a real structural break or that it is mis-specified and the behaviour of a relevant variable has changed, whereas not rejecting is compatible with considerable mis-specification. This provides the framework for interpreting the prediction findings reported in the following sections.

A small technical issue concerns the choice of forecast test since different tests have power against different alternatives and often make different auxiliary assumptions about (for example) the constancy of error variances, whether regressors are fixed or stochastic and whether the equation is correctly specified (for an exposition of a number of tests see Fisher, 1970).

Let $y_1 = X_1\beta_1 + u_1$ and $y_2 = X_2\beta_2 + u_2$ be models for estimation and prediction periods of length T_1 and T_2 respectively with $u_i \sim N(0, \sigma_i^2 I)$, the former sample providing estimates b_1 and s_1^2 for β_1 ($\kappa \times 1$) and σ_1^2. Let $f_2 = y_2 - X_2 b_1$ be the post-estimation-sample residuals, and assume that $\text{var}(b_1) = \sigma_1^2 (X_1'X_1)^{-1}$ (which entails assuming a correctly specified model for the estimation period); then Chow (1960) showed that

$$z_5 (T_2, T_1 - \kappa) = f_2'V^{-1}f_2/T_2 s_1^2 \sim F(T_2, T_1 - \kappa)$$

on $H_0 : \beta_1 = \beta_2, \sigma_1^2 = \sigma_2^2$

where $V = I + X_2 (X_1'X_1)^{-1} X_2'$. Note that if s^2 is based on the entire sample of $T = T_1 + T_2$ observations, and $h = (T - \kappa)/(T_1 - \kappa)$, then $z_5 = (hs^2 - s_1^2)/(h - 1)s_1^2$ and hence $z_5 \gtrless 1$ as $s^2 \gtrless s_1^2$. Consequently, z_5 will assume large values if either $\beta_1 \neq \beta_2$ or $\sigma_1^2 \neq \sigma_2^2$ as seems appropriate when testing for predictive failure (for example, $\beta_1 = \beta_2$ with $\sigma_1^2 \neq \sigma_2^2$ could occur if a new set of variables orthogonal to X started to influence y during the prediction period).

For stochastic regressors, z_5 is only approximately distributed as F and so an asymptotically equivalent test which neglects the variation due to estimating β_1 is also reported, namely $z_4(T_2) = f_2'f_2/s_1^2 \sim \chi_{T_2}^2$ in large samples when H_0 is true. Thus z_4 simply compares within- and post-sample residual variances (neither test measures 'absolute' forecast accuracy).

More detailed study of parameter constancy could be undertaken using, for example, n-step-ahead simulations and/or recursive residuals (see Brown et al., 1975) but z_4 and z_5 will suffice for the purposes of this study.

3 'Simple-to-general' Modelling Methods

A non-negligible fraction of empirical econometrics can be characterised as *excessive presimplification with inadequate diagnostic testing* (see Leamer, 1974). By this is meant that investigators:

1 commence from theories which are drastic abstractions of reality (usually of a long-run steady-state world subject to stringent *ceteris paribus* assumptions concerning all but a very small number of variables);
2 formulate highly parsimonious relationships to represent their theories (see many of the equations reported in Hickman, 1972; Renton, 1975; Waelbroeck, 1976);
3 estimate their equations from the available data using techniques which are 'optimal' only on the assumption that the highly restricted model is correctly specified;
4 test a few of the assumptions explicitly or implicitly underlying the exercise (such as the conventional investigation of residual autocorrelation);
5 revise the specification in the light of the evidence acquired; and
6 re-estimate accordingly.

While it is not impossible to end with a sensible model from a very restrictive start using 'iterative model building' methods, success manifestly depends on the thoroughness with which diagnostic testing is pursued: commencing from a simple model and not rigorously testing it is a reasonably certain path to concluding with a mis-specified relationship.

An example which provides somewhat of a caricature of the above process without invidiously criticizing any specific study is as follows. Let M, P, X, r denote the nominal money stock, price level, real income and nominal interest rate respectively, and assume that a consensus theoretical specification of the transactions demand for money function is given by

$$\frac{M}{P} = f(X^e, r^e, \dot{p}^e) \tag{11.1}$$

where X^e denotes 'expected' or 'permanent' income etc as appropriate (see, *inter alia*, Friedman, 1956, ch. 1; Johnson, 1971, ch. 13; Goldfeld, 1973; Hacche, 1974; Artis and Lewis, 1976; Hamburger, 1977; Coghlan, 1978). Adding the auxiliary assumptions that f defines a multiplicative function, that expectations are static and that there is a long-run unit elasticity of M/P with respect to X yields the 'inverse-velocity' equation

$$\frac{M}{PX} = Kr^\alpha (1 + \dot{p})^\beta \tag{11.2}$$

with α, $\beta < 0$, and K assumed constant. With the further assumptions that (11.2) does not hold exactly but has a multiplicative error $\exp(\varepsilon_t)$ at time t where $\varepsilon_t \sim \mathrm{NI}(0, \sigma^2)$, that the relevant data for M, P, X, r are nominal M1, the implicit deflator of X, constant (1970) price total final expenditure (all quarterly, seasonally adjusted) and local authority three-month interest rates respectively, and that r_t and $\dot{p}_t$ are independent of ε_t, then maximum likelihood estimation of (11.2) (i.e. ordinary least squares after taking logarithms to base e, denoted ln) for the period 1963(i)–72(i) yields

$$\ln\left(\widehat{\frac{M}{PX}}\right)_t = \underset{(0.12)}{-0.09} - \underset{(0.06)}{0.14 \ln r_t} - \underset{(2.2)}{6.7 \Delta \ln P_t} \tag{11.3}$$

$$R^2 = 0.37 \qquad s = 0.067 \qquad T = 32$$

where T denotes the number of observations in the estimation sample (five lags were created). The estimates of α and β have the 'right signs', 'sensible orders of magnitude' and seem to be 'significantly different from zero at the 5 per cent level', although the goodness of fit is not spectacular.

Since (11.3) 'corroborates' the *a priori* theory, some investigators might stop at this stage. Others might proceed to test diagnostically various of the (arbitrary) pre-simplifying assumptions noted earlier, and as the data are time series the assumed absence of serial correlation is an obvious candidate. Indeed the Durbin–Watson statistic (DW) has the value 0.45 indicating significant residual autocorrelation in (11.3). *If* this derived from a first-order autoregressive error and *if* all the other assumptions made above were correct, then the quoted estimates of α, β would be unbiased but inefficient and their standard errors would be downward biased. Consequently $\hat{\alpha}$ and $\hat{\beta}$ may not in fact be 'significantly different from zero at the 5 per cent level' as claimed above. However, it is easy to 'allow for' such an error process and (iterative) Cochrane–Orcutt yields (method 5.1 in chapter 13)

$$\ln\left(\widehat{\frac{M}{PX}}\right)_t = -0.49 - 0.02 \ln r_t - 0.54 \, \Delta \ln P_t \tag{11.4}$$
$$\quad\quad\quad (0.11) \ (0.03) \quad\quad (0.55)$$

$$\hat\rho = 0.94$$
$$\quad (0.04)$$

$$s = 0.019 \quad\quad T = 32$$

where $\hat\rho$ denotes the estimated first-order autoregressive error coefficient.

The estimates in (11.4) are not very consonant with the interpretation offered in the previous paragraph since the parameter estimates have changed drastically and neither economic variable retains a significant coefficient; such a finding is more reminiscent of an omitted variable effect where the lagged error has approximated the (unknown) missing regressor. Moreover, as $\hat\rho$ is very close to unity and has reduced s by a factor of over 3, the results in (11.3) and (11.4) imply that just regressing $\ln(M/PX)_t$ on its own lagged value would yield an R^2 of about 0.95 which suggests a potential candidate for the omitted regressor. Thus, the interpretation of the *residual* autocorrelation as *error* autocorrelation is suspect.

Possible paths from (11.4) begin to multiply rapidly, but two obvious routes for some would be (i) to impose $\hat\rho = 1$ and re-estimate (11.4) in first differences (see the discussion in chapter 6 of the model estimated by Hacche (1974) and the analysis in section 5 below), or (ii) to check whether the residual autocorrelation derived from invalidly restricting the model through price homogeneity and the unit income elasticity, which yields

$$\widehat{\ln M_t} = 7.6 + 0.18 \ln X_t + 0.84 \ln P_t - 0.12 \ln r_t + 0.17 \, \Delta \ln P_t \tag{11.5}$$
$$\quad\quad (2.9) \ (0.30) \quad\quad (0.17) \quad\quad (0.02) \quad\quad (0.76)$$

$$T = 32 \quad\quad R^2 = 0.75 \quad\quad s = 0.019 \quad\quad DW = 0.93.$$

At first sight, the unit income elasticity restriction appears to be rejected in (11.5) (indeed $\ln X_t$ has an 'insignificant' coefficient), whereas price homogeneity does not, but while DW is considerably larger than in (11.3) it still indicates significant residual autocorrelation which invalidates the t tests just quoted! Again, 'allowing for' autocorrelation yields

$$\widehat{\ln M_t} = 8.9 + 0.04 \ln X_t + 1.00 \ln P_t - 0.06 \ln r_t - 0.53 \, \Delta \ln P_t \tag{11.6}$$
$$\quad\quad (2.4) \ (0.25) \quad\quad (0.17) \quad\quad (0.03) \quad\quad (0.51)$$

$$\hat\rho = 0.79$$
$$\quad (0.25)$$

$$T = 32 \quad\quad s = 0.016$$

Now the evidence favours price homogeneity but a near zero income effect – and that in a 'transactions' demand for money equation! Imposing a unit income elasticity restriction as in (11.3) may produce a more 'sensible' equation and could even improve the forecast performance if it happened to be closer to reality than a zero effect, but it will hardly increase understanding of the data and leaves unexplained the puzzle of why a non-unit coefficient was obtained in the first place.

Since much applied work is a 'prejudiced search for an acceptable model' (see Leamer, 1975), anyone who considered the evidence in (11.6) to be unacceptable would presumably re-specify the equation and/or seek a further test for constructive revision. One possible diagnostic is to test the common factor restriction imposed by assuming an autoregressive error in (11.4) and (11.6) (see Sargan, 1964a; also chapter 6 for an exposition). Doing so using a likelihood ratio test yields $z_1(2) = 7.6$ for (11.4) and $z_1(3) = 17.2$ for (11.6), where on the hypothesis of a valid autoregressive error representation $z_1(k)$ is distributed as χ_k^2 in large samples. Thus, in both cases the common factor hypothesis is rejected at the 5 per cent level, revealing that the residual autocorrelation does not derive from a first-order autoregressive error.

Such an outcome highlights a major problem with the 'specific-to-general' approach, namely that every test is conditional on arbitrary assumptions which are to be tested *later*, and if these are rejected all earlier inferences are invalidated, whether 'reject' or 'not reject' decisions. Until the model adequately characterizes the data generation process, it seems rather pointless trying to test hypotheses of interest in economic theory. A further drawback is that the significance level of the unstructured sequence of tests actually being conducted is unknown.

Nevertheless, continuing as earlier to expand the model on the basis of every negative outcome, the relevant generalization of (11.4) given $z_1(2)$ is

$$\ln\widehat{\left(\frac{M}{PX}\right)}_t = \underset{(0.03)}{0.05} - \underset{(0.03)}{0.02}\ln r_t - \underset{(0.65)}{0.70}\,\Delta\ln P_t + \underset{(0.06)}{0.88}\ln\left(\frac{M}{PX}\right)_{t-1}$$

$$\underset{(0.03)}{-0.03}\ln r_{t-1} + \underset{(0.64)}{0.46}\,\Delta\ln P_{t-1} \tag{11.7}$$

$T = 32 \qquad R^2 = 0.96 \qquad s = 0.017 \qquad DW = 2.4 \qquad z_2(11) = 14$
$z_3(6) = 4.7$.

In (11.7), $z_2(k)$ denotes the Pierce (1971) residual correlogram test, and $z_3(l)$ is the Lagrange multiplier test for lth-order residual autocorrelation, distributed as χ_l^2 in large samples when the errors are white noise (see Godfrey, 1978; Breusch and Pagan, 1980). Again, the fit has improved and now there is no strong evidence of residual autocorrelation. Moreover, in steady-state growth, (11.7) yields

$$\frac{M}{PX} \approx K^* r^{-0.4}(1 + \dot{p})^{-2.0} \tag{11.8}$$

where $K^* \approx \exp[0.4 + 8(g_3 + g_2 - g_1)]$ and $g_1, g_2 = 1 + \dot{p}$ and g_3 are the steady-state growth rates of M, P and X respectively. In turn, (11.8) implies that $g_1 = g_2 + g_3$ and hence K^* is simply $\exp(0.4)$ in such a state of the world. It must be stressed that the assumptions on which (11.8) is based (specifically, an accommodating money supply to meet whatever demand requires) preclude 'inverting' the equation to 'explain', for example, P or $\dot{p}$; g_1 is the *result* of $g_2 + g_3$ because of the *assumed* behaviour of agents in demanding money *given* $\dot{p}$, X and r. Note that the apparently 'insignificant' coefficients of r and $\dot{p}$ actually imply large long-run effects and that the mean lags of $\ln M$ with respect to $\ln X$ and $\ln r$ are zero and almost two years respectively. Overall, (11.7) is consonant with the original theory (11.2), 'passes' the diagnostic tests presented and accounts for 96 per cent of the sample variance of velocity.

A similar analysis could be applied to (11.6) but we have followed the story far enough, and will mimic the random stopping point aspect associated with this approach. The final diagnostic is simply to check the parameter constancy of all the equations quoted above for the period following the introduction of competition and credit control (namely the 20 quarters 1972(ii)–77(i)); the outcomes for z_4 are

Equation	(11.3)	(11.4)	(11.5)	(11.6)	(11.7)
$z_4(20)$	42	73	399	72	59 .

Since z_4 measures forecast accuracy relative to s, equation (11.7) performs best by a wide margin, although all five equations are rejected.[2] This outcome is a good illustration of a predictive failure which might be attributed to a 'structural break' following competition and credit control. Nevertheless, on the evidence presented below, it is probably due to dynamic mis-specification combined with the changed time-series properties of X, P, r since a generalization of (11.7) satisfies the z_4 test over the same forecast period (see section 5).

The objective of this section has been to stress some of the difficulties inherent in the specific-to-general econometric modelling approach using a relatively simple specification as a baseline, and it is irrelevant that in practice investigators might commence from models with slightly longer lag structures if these still do not represent the general maintained hypothesis. It is important to distinguish this approach from one in which the general model really is defined at the start of the analysis but all specializations thereof are estimated to check their mutual consistency. An analogy would be in testing for nth-order autocorrelation; for computational reasons the models are estimated from simple to general but the sequence of *tests* is conducted from highest order to lowest order (see Anderson, 1971). While not entirely in this second category, the 'detective' approach of reconciling all the evidence adopted in chapter 8 attempts to conduct its analysis within a reasonably well-defined framework, although in fact the initial general working hypothesis is later found to be false.

4 From the General to the Specific

In an attempt to avoid the difficulties just discussed, it seems natural to consider the converse method: intended overparameterization with data-based simplification. Commencing from the most general model which it seems reasonable (or possible) to maintain, sequential testing procedures are used to select a data coherent specialization. This re-emphasizes the distinction Mizon (1977b) draws between tests of specification (within a maintained hypothesis, and often based on Wald's test procedure (1943) such as the common factor sequence of tests in Sargan (1980a)) and tests of mis-specification (diagnostic tests for greater generality than initially assumed and often based on the Lagrange multiplier or efficient score procedure as used above for autocorrelation (see Aitchison and Silvey, 1960; Rao, 1973; and, for recent developments, Godfrey, 1978; Breusch and Pagan, 1980; Engle, 1982b).

The main problems in the general-to-specific methodology are (i) that the intention may not be realized – the chosen (ostensibly general) model could actually comprise a very special case of the data generation process, so that diagnostic testing remains important; (ii) data limitations – sample size or the information content of the data may be inadequate; (iii) there is no uniquely 'best' sequence for simplifying the model – different approximations which have similar sample likelihoods may forecast very differently; and (iv) the individual tests will often have large type II error probabilities if the overall sequence is not to have a high type I error.

Nevertheless, so little hard evidence exists about lag responses that it can be worth estimating the unrestricted 'rational lag' equation as a baseline, choosing a maximal lag length according to any available evidence (e.g. as 4 or 5 for quarterly data series because of seasonal dynamics). Such an approach has in fact yielded reasonable results for testing a money demand function proposed by Hacche (1974) (see chapter 6) and for investigating transactions demand equations in the interesting study undertaken by Coghlan (1978). Commencing from unrestricted distributed lag representations of (11.2) having the general form

$$\ln M_t = C + \sum_{j=0}^{J} (\alpha_j \ln X_{t-j} + \beta_j \ln P_{t-j} + \gamma_j \ln r_{t-j} + \delta_j \ln M_{t-j-1}) + u_t \quad (11.9)$$

Coghlan concluded that satisfactory parsimonious representations of the data generation process (on the basis of goodness of fit, the *Gestalt* of the sample evidence, similarity to (11.9) and short-run post-sample parameter constancy) were given by (for 1964(i)–71(iv), *t* ratios in parentheses; from Coghlan (1978), table B)

$$\widehat{\ln M_t} = 0.41 \ln X_t - 0.11 \ln X_{t-3} + 0.92 \ln P_{t-1} - 1.20 \ln P_{t-2}$$
$$\quad (1.9) \qquad\quad (0.5) \qquad\qquad (1.9) \qquad\qquad (1.7)$$

$$+ 0.71 \ln M_{t-1} + 0.74 \ln P_{t-3} - 0.31 \ln P_{t-4} - 0.06 \ln r_t \qquad (11.10a)$$
$$\quad (5.7) \qquad\qquad (1.0) \qquad\qquad (0.6) \qquad\qquad (2.7)$$

$$\bar{R}^2 = 0.99 \qquad s = 0.013 \qquad DW = 1.9$$

$$\Delta \widehat{\ln M_t} = 0.44 \, \Delta \ln X_t + 0.46 \, \Delta \ln X_{t-1} + 0.20 \, \Delta \ln X_{t-2} + 0.89 \, \Delta \ln P_{t-1}$$
$$\quad\quad (1.8) \qquad\qquad (2.0) \qquad\qquad (1.1) \qquad\qquad (1.9)$$

$$- 0.69 \, \Delta \ln P_{t-2} + 0.25 \, \Delta \ln P_{t-3} - 0.05 \, \Delta \ln r_t - 0.02 \, \Delta \ln r_{t-1}$$
$$\quad (1.3) \qquad\qquad (0.5) \qquad\qquad (1.9) \qquad\qquad (0.8)$$

$$- 0.04 \, \Delta \ln r_{t-2} \qquad (11.10b)$$
$$\quad (1.4)$$

$$\bar{R}^2 = 0.29 \qquad s = 0.014 \qquad DW = 2.0.$$

Specifically, for the same sample period as for (11.3) to (11.7) estimation of (11.10b) yields

$$\Delta \widehat{\ln M_t} = 0.51 \, \Delta \ln X_t + 0.51 \, \Delta \ln X_{t-1} + 0.24 \, \Delta \ln X_{t-2} + 0.92 \, \Delta \ln P_{t-1}$$
$$\quad\quad (0.27) \qquad\qquad (0.27) \qquad\qquad (0.22) \qquad\qquad (0.50)$$

$$-0.74 \, \Delta \ln P_{t-2} + 0.26 \, \Delta \ln P_{t-3} - 0.04 \, \Delta \ln r_t - 0.03 \, \Delta \ln r_{t-1}$$
$$\quad (0.56) \qquad\qquad (0.56) \qquad\quad (0.03) \qquad\quad (0.03)$$

$$-0.03 \, \Delta \ln r_{t-2} \qquad\qquad\qquad\qquad\qquad\qquad\qquad (11.11)$$
$$\quad (0.03)$$

$T = 32 \qquad R^2 = 0.49 \qquad s = 0.014 \qquad \mathrm{DW} = 2.0 \qquad z_4(20) = 37.5$
$z_2(12) = 12 \qquad z_5(20, 23) = 0.85.$

This equation both fits better than (11.7) and has distinctly better parameter constancy properties: neither z_4 nor z_5 rejects the hypothesis of predictive accuracy at the 1 per cent level (the graphs of the actual and predicted values from (11.11) are shown in figure 11.1). The relative parameter stability can be seen by estimating (11.11) from the sample 1963(i)–76(iii) (retaining the last two data points for the z_4 test):

$$\Delta \widehat{\ln M_t} = 0.33 \, \Delta \ln X_t + 0.42 \, \Delta \ln X_{t-1} + 0.25 \, \Delta \ln X_{t-2} + 1.15 \, \Delta \ln P_{t-1}$$
$$\qquad\quad (0.13) \qquad\quad (0.13) \qquad\qquad (0.12) \qquad\qquad (0.24)$$

$$-0.91 \, \Delta \ln P_{t-2} + 0.50 \, \Delta \ln P_{t-3} - 0.04 \, \Delta \ln r_t - 0.01 \, \Delta \ln r_{t-1}$$
$$\quad (0.28) \qquad\qquad (0.28) \qquad\quad (0.02) \qquad\quad (0.02)$$

$$-0.07 \, \Delta \ln r_{t-2} \qquad\qquad\qquad\qquad\qquad\qquad\qquad (11.12)$$
$$\quad (0.02)$$

$T = 48 \qquad R^2 = 0.71 \qquad s = 0.014 \qquad \mathrm{DW} = 1.9 \qquad z_4(2) = 3.8$
$z_2(12) = 14.$

The value of R^2 has increased but, as anticipated from z_5, s has not and so there is minimal evidence of predictive failure despite the fact that the sample correlations of the variables indicate a marked change in behaviour pre- and post-1971 (table 11.1 reports the correlation matrices for the variables in the closely related specification to (11.12) discussed below). Clearly, *if* (11.12) did constitute the correct structural equation, rejection of the constancy of the econometric equations (11.3)–(11.7) is unsurprising and provides no evidence about the existence of *some* stable transactions demand relationship. Since only the dynamic specification has changed this appears to be an excellent example of the hypothesis of section 2. Coghlan (1978) reports similar constancy properties for (11.10a) (see his chart A).

The formulation of models like (11.11) and (11.12) in terms of differenced variables only has been criticized on a number of grounds in chapter 8 and chapter 6. Moreover, it seems essential to consider some modified specification in the *levels* of the variables which encompasses *both* (11.10a) and (11.10b) in order to account for their manifest similarity and constancy despite (apparently) very different long-run properties. Further, there is room for improvement in forecast accuracy, since the z_4 test would reject (11.11) at the 5 per cent level. 'Error correction' mechanisms provide a convenient way of achieving all these aims; hence we now consider the role of feedbacks in dynamic models and investigate their contribution to explaining predictive failure in transactions demand functions.

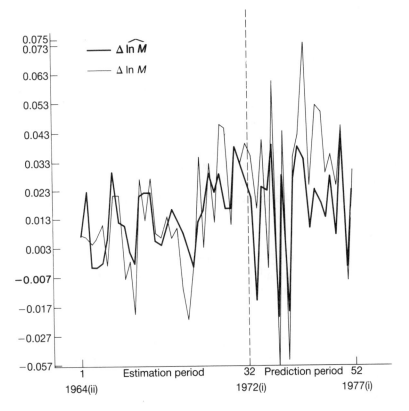

Figure 11.1 Equation (11.11).

Table 11.1 Data correlation matrices

Subperiod	Whole period	1	2	3	4	5	6	7	8
1 $\Delta \ln \left(\dfrac{M}{P} \right)_t$			0.30	−0.46	−0.61	−0.19	0.07	0.01	−0.25
2 $\displaystyle\sum_{i=0}^{2} \Delta \ln X_{t-i}$	0.31			0.18	−0.01	−0.39	−0.43	0.36	−0.42
3 $\displaystyle\sum_{i=0}^{2} \Delta \ln r_{t-i}$	−0.52	−0.24			0.24	−0.21	−0.33	0.26	−0.24
4 $\Delta^2 \ln P_t$	−0.24	0.30	0.00			−0.15	−0.24	0.17	−0.04
5 $\Delta \ln P_{t-2}$	0.08	0.12	−0.34	−0.01			0.84	−0.82	0.73
6 $\Delta \ln P_{t-3}$	0.30	−0.13	−0.47	−0.11	0.39			−0.83	0.66
7 $\ln \left(\dfrac{M}{PX} \right)_{t-1}$	−0.31	0.06	0.49	0.09	−0.52	−0.58			−0.82
8 $\ln r_{t-2}$	0.09	−0.24	−0.36	−0.17	0.34	0.33	−0.73		

5 Feedback Mechanisms in Differenced Models

Consider the following simple dynamic model[3] relating a variable denoted by y_t to a single regressor denoted by x_t:

$$\Delta \ln y_t = \theta_0 + \theta_1 \Delta \ln x_t + \theta_2 \ln(x_{t-1}/y_{t-1}) + \varepsilon_t \tag{11.13}$$

where $0 \leqslant \theta_2 < 1$ and $\varepsilon_t \sim \text{NI}(0, \sigma_\varepsilon^2)$. Provided that $\theta_2 \neq 0$, (11.13) defines a stable dynamic equation in the levels of y_t and x_t with a mean lag given by $\mu = (1 - \theta_1)/\theta_2$ and a median lag of (approximately) $\psi = [0.7 + \ln(1 - \theta_1)]/\theta_2$ (for $\theta_1 \leqslant 0.5$). In non-stochastic steady-state growth with $\Delta \ln x_t = g = \Delta \ln y_t$, the solution to (11.13) yields

$$y_t = Kx_t \tag{11.14}$$

where $K = \exp\{-[(1 - \theta_1)g - \theta_0]/\theta_2\}$ so that (11.13) characterizes a process with long-run unit elasticity, for all values of θ_0, θ_1 and $\theta_2 \neq 0$. When g is constant, $\ln(y_{t-1}/x_{t-1}) \approx \ln K = k$, and in such a state of the world

$$\Delta \ln y_t = \theta_0^* + \theta_1 \Delta \ln x_t + \varepsilon_t^* \tag{11.15}$$

where $\theta_0^* = \theta_0 - \theta_2 k$ and ε_t^* is approximately white noise, and hence a simple differenced data model will adequately describe the data. In terms of the levels of the variables, an equation of the form

$$\ln y_t = \phi_0 + \phi_1 \ln x_t + v_t \tag{11.16}$$

will generally exhibit substantial autocorrelation,[4] well approximated by $v_t = (1 - \theta_2)v_{t-1} + \varepsilon_t$ which, for small θ_2, will be close to unity, supporting the choice of (11.15). Alternatively, adding the lagged dependent variable to (11.16) will produce a partial adjustment model with little obvious residual autocorrelation, but usually having estimates of θ_1 and $1 - \theta_2$ which are biased towards zero, so that μ and ψ are respectively underestimated and overestimated.

In all of these mis-specified models, a *change* in the growth rate of x_t will induce an apparent 'structural break' due entirely to the incorrect dynamic formulation, yet (11.13) will continue to track the data with an error variance of σ_ε^2. To be appropriate for all possible time paths of x_t, a model like (11.13) which incorporates an 'error correction' mechanism seems essential: by way of contrast, (11.15) entails that economic agents ignore disequilibria between the levels of y_t and x_t. It seems more reasonable to assume that long-run relationships are followed because of the disequilibrium effect $\theta_2 \ln(x_{t-1}/y_{t-1})$ rather than because agents never make mistakes.

Two objections which have been made to formulations like (11.13) are that

1 the 'long-run' outcome (11.14) is surely irrelevant in practice and hence there is no real presumption favouring 'levels' over 'differences' formulations and
2 the mean lag of models with small values of θ_2 may entail implausibly slow adjustment whereas (11.15) demonstrates very rapid adjustment.

These objections indicate misunderstandings concerning the roles of equilibrium and adjustment in econometrics. First, the 'long run' given by (11.14) does not relate solely to what will occur in future as $t \to \infty$; instead, unless the growth rate of x_t has been constantly changing, then *currently* observed data generated by (11.13) will reflect a relatively constant ratio of y_t to x_t. Second, while (11.15) manifests rapid adjustment in terms of changes, it also shows *infinitely slow* adjustment to any levels relationship; conversely (depending on the parameter values), most of the adjustment in (11.13) can occur instantaneously (i.e. $\psi < 1$). The longer *mean* lag reflects the use by agents of the 'low-frequency filter' (y_{t-1}/x_{t-1}) such that their current behaviour is modified by the 'long-run' information in (11.14) embodied in the lagged ratio. Thus, care is required in interpreting a long mean lag derived from a distributed lag model estimated in levels, since such an outcome is not incompatible with rapid adjustment (in the median lag sense) combined with a slower equilibrating error correction mechanism; for example, $(\theta_1, \theta_2) = (0.5, 0.1)$ implies $\mu = 5$ but $\psi = 0$.

This analysis indicates that a model like (11.15) with white noise errors could, for certain time-paths, provide a reasonable approximation to (11.13) without contradicting the existence of a 'long-run' relationship between the levels of the variables such as (11.2). Moreover, this is one way in which the mutual stability of (11.10a) and (11.10b) could be reconciled since the former can be rewritten as

$$\Delta \widehat{\ln M_t} = 0.41 \, \Delta \ln X_t + 0.12 \, \Delta \ln X_{t-1} + 0.12 \, \Delta \ln X_{t-2} + 0.63 \, \Delta \ln P_{t-1}$$

$$- 0.57 \Delta \ln P_{t-2} + 0.17 \Delta \ln P_{t-3} - 0.06 \, \Delta \ln r_t - 0.06 \, \Delta \ln r_{t-1}$$

$$- 0.29 \ln \left(\frac{M}{PX} \right)_{t-1} - 0.06 \ln r_{t-2} - 0.14 \ln P_{t-4} + 0.01 \ln X_{t-3}.$$

$$(11.10c)$$

Consequently, both (11.10a) and (11.10b) are special cases of an unrestricted equation of the form of (11.10c) which generalizes (11.13), obtained by imposing different parameter restrictions,[5] and the very success of both (11.10a) and (11.10b) in describing the one data series points strongly towards requiring an error correction model to account for all the observed characteristics of previously estimated models as analysed above.

To investigate the possibility of feedback mechanisms for M1 models, consider adding the following regressors to equation (11.12):

$\ln (M/PX)_{t-1}$ corresponding to $\ln (y_{t-1}/x_{t-1})$ in (11.13)

$\ln r_{t-2}$ which allows interest rates to influence the long-run ratio of M to PX

a constant   to 'pick up' scale effects.

Including $\ln (M/PX)_{t-1}$ as a regressor in (11.12) imposes both price homogeneity and a unit elasticity of M with respect to X in steady state, although these two hypotheses are easily tested by including $\ln P_{t-1}$ and $\ln X_{t-1}$ as separate regressors. Further modifications of (11.12) incorporated in (11.17) are the choice of $\Delta \ln(M/P)_t$ as the regressand and the inclusion of $\Delta^2 \ln P_t$ as a regressor (restricting $\Delta \ln P_{t-1}$ to entering through that variable).

Since Coghlan's analysis used most of the sample data, the modified regression was first estimated for the same period as (11.12) and tested over the four observations 1976(ii)–77(i) which yielded

$$
\widehat{\Delta \ln\left(\frac{M}{P}\right)_t} = \underset{(0.15)}{0.28} \Delta \ln X_t + \underset{(0.15)}{0.34} \Delta \ln X_{t-1} + \underset{(0.14)}{0.24} \Delta \ln X_{t-2} - \underset{(0.23)}{1.1} \Delta^2 \ln P_t
$$

$$
- \underset{(0.26)}{0.81} \Delta \ln P_{t-2} + \underset{(0.29)}{0.44} \Delta \ln P_{t-3} - \underset{(0.02)}{0.05} \Delta \ln r_t - \underset{(0.02)}{0.03} \Delta \ln r_{t-1}
$$

$$
- \underset{(0.02)}{0.05} \Delta \ln r_{t-2} - \underset{(0.04)}{0.09} \ln\left(\frac{M}{PX}\right)_{t-1} - \underset{(0.016)}{0.033} \ln r_{t-2} + \underset{(0.022)}{0.026}
$$

(11.17)

$T = 48$ $R^2 = 0.78$ $s = 0.013$ $DW = 2.0$ $z_4(4) = 5.9$
$z_2(11) = 18$ $z_3(6) = 8.4$.

The actual t values for the last two coefficients are 2.04 and 2.10 respectively, and the new variables have the anticipated signs and sensible magnitudes. Indeed (11.17) is close to what might have been expected given the results in (11.10a) and (11.10b) by, in effect, encompassing the two non-nested models.

The similarity of the sets of coefficients on the short distributed lags of $\Delta \ln X_t$ and of $\Delta \ln r_t$ suggests reformulating (11.17) by imposing identical coefficients to economize on parameters (i.e. zero-order Almon polynomials); this yields

$$
\widehat{\Delta \ln\left(\frac{M}{P}\right)_t} = \underset{(0.09)}{0.28} \left(\sum_{i=0}^{2} \Delta \ln X_{t-i}\right) - \underset{(0.01)}{0.04} \left(\sum_{i=0}^{2} \Delta \ln r_{t-i}\right) - \underset{(0.21)}{1.2} \Delta^2 \ln P_t
$$

$$
- \underset{(0.24)}{0.88} \Delta \ln P_{t-2} + \underset{(0.27)}{0.50} \Delta \ln P_{t-3} - \underset{(0.04)}{0.09} \ln\left(\frac{M}{PX}\right)_{t-1}
$$

$$
- \underset{(0.012)}{0.034} \ln r_{t-2} + \underset{(0.018)}{0.027}
$$

(11.18)

$T = 48$ $R^2 = 0.77$ $s = 0.013$ $DW = 2.0$ $z_4(4) = 6.1$
$z_5(4, 40) = 1.01$ $z_2(11) = 15$ $z_3(6) = 7.2$.

The restrictions have lowered the coefficient standard errors without noticeably lowering R^2 and hence are not data rejected. Note that

$$
\sum_{i=0}^{2} \Delta \ln z_{t-i} \equiv (1 - L^3) \ln z_t,
$$

where L is the lag operator.

In steady state, the solution to (11.18) can again be written as in (11.2) with $K = \exp(0.3 - 1.8g_3)$, $\alpha = -0.38$ and $\beta = -4.4$ (using $g_3 = g_1 - g_2$). This indicates 'long-run' elasticities of M with respect to r and $\ln(1 + \dot{p})$ of -0.38 and $-4.4 \ln(1 + \dot{p})$ (compare Cagan (1956) and note that β in (11.2) has units of 'quarters').

The solved coefficients from (11.12) and (11.18) in terms of the levels of the variables are shown in table 11.2 together with the direct estimates of the general

Table 11.2 Estimated and derived coefficients for equation (11.9) for the complete sample

i	0	1	2	3	4
(a) Equation (11.9)					
$\ln M_{t-i-1}$	0.72(0.19)	0.07(0.22)	−0.22(0.20)	0.08(0.17)	0.12(0.15)
$\ln X_{t-1}$	0.20(0.19)	0.24(0.20)	−0.07(0.19)	−0.28(0.21)	0.13(0.20)
$\ln r_{t-i}$	−0.04(0.02)	−0.01(0.03)	−0.04(0.03)	0.03(0.03)	−0.03(0.03)
$\ln P_{t-i}$	0.18(0.30)	1.08(0.48)	−1.52(0.58)	0.97(0.72)	−0.52(0.43)
	$\hat{C} = 0.30(0.78)$	$R^2 = 0.999$	$s = 0.014$	DW = 2.1	
(b) Equation (11.12)					
$\ln M_{t-i-1}$	1.0	–	–	–	–
$\ln X_{t-i}$	0.33	0.09	−0.17	−0.25	–
$\ln r_{t-i}$	−0.04	0.03	−0.06	0.07	–
$\ln P_{t-i}$	–	1.2	−2.1	1.4	−0.50
(c) Equation (11.18)					
$\ln M_{t-i-1}$	0.91	–	–	–	–
$\ln X_{t-i}$	0.28	0.09	0	−0.28	–
$\ln r_{t-i}$	−0.04	0	−0.03	0.04	–
$\ln P_{t-i}$	−0.20	1.5	−2.1	1.4	−0.50

unrestricted equation (11.9). The fits of (11.12) and (11.18) are not significantly different from the fit of (11.9), and the coefficient estimates are all reasonably similar. Also, note that the lagged dependent variable coefficient is closer to unity in (11.18) than in, for example, (11.10a) as anticipated from the simulation findings in chapter 8.

It remains to investigate how the re-specification of the dynamics has affected the constancy of the relationship, remembering that since many of the models were originally established from considering the complete sample period, their fitting with similar coefficients to subperiods is less impressive than say the predictive test on new raw data used in (11.11). Nevertheless, since there is some chance of a negative outcome because of predictive failure, it may be possible to refute the hypothesis that the revised equation adequately characterizes the data for the subsample:

$$\Delta \ln \widehat{\left(\frac{M}{P}\right)}_t = \underset{(0.23)}{0.42} \left(\sum_{i=0}^{2} \Delta \ln X_{t-i}\right) - \underset{(0.01)}{0.03} \left(\sum_{i=0}^{2} \Delta \ln r_{t-i}\right) - \underset{(0.41)}{0.89} \Delta^2 \ln P_t$$

$$- \underset{(0.49)}{0.62} \Delta \ln P_{t-2} + \underset{(0.55)}{0.23} \Delta \ln P_{t-3} - \underset{(0.05)}{0.07} \ln \left(\frac{M}{PX}\right)_{t-1}$$

$$- \underset{(0.020)}{0.019} \ln r_{t-2} + \underset{(0.032)}{0.006} \tag{11.19}$$

$T = 32 \qquad R^2 = 0.48 \qquad s = 0.014 \qquad$ DW $= 2.1 \qquad z_4(20) = 27.6$
$z_5(20, 24) = 0.77 \qquad z_2(11) = 12 \qquad z_3(6) = 3.0.$

The model shows a fair degree of parameter constancy, having smaller 'forecast' errors than (11.11) for 15 of the 20 observations (see figure 11.2) reflected in the

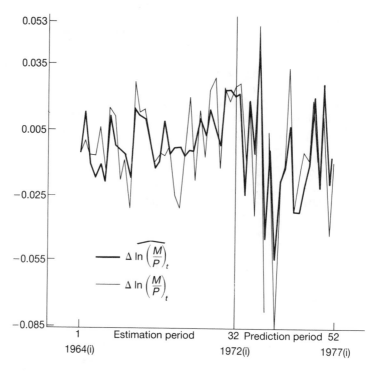

Figure 11.2   Equation (11.19).

substantially smaller and insignificant value of $z_4(20)$. Thus the error correction feedback does seem to play a useful role when 'tracking' data over a reasonably long period. Given the large change in the correlation structure of the data shown in table 11.1,[6] the existence of constant parameters in (11.19) seems to provide a powerful argument for considering it to be a good approximation to a 'structural relationship', and a further improvement over (11.11).

As a postscript, it may be noted that $\Delta \ln P_t$ effectively cancels from all the equations (11.17)–(11.19) and hence a more parsimonious specification can be obtained by using $\Delta \ln(M_t/P_{t-1})$ as the regressand. Since three new observations appeared during work on this chapter, it seemed of interest to fit this last model to the longest estimation sample used above and predict the seven observations 1976(ii)–77(iv) which yielded

$$\Delta \ln \widehat{\left(\frac{M_t}{P_{t-1}}\right)} = \underset{(0.28)}{0.86}\,\Delta \ln X_t^* - \underset{(0.023)}{0.119}\,\Delta \ln r_t^* - \underset{(0.23)}{0.90}\,\Delta \ln P_{t-2} + \underset{(0.26)}{0.54}\,\Delta \ln P_{t-3}$$

$$- \underset{(0.036)}{0.096}\ln\left(\frac{M}{PX}\right)_{t-1} - \underset{(0.011)}{0.035}\ln r_{t-2} + \underset{(0.017)}{0.026} \qquad (11.20)$$

$$T = 49 \qquad R^2 = 0.65 \qquad s = 0.013 \qquad z_1(5) = 4.5 \qquad z_2(11) = 15$$
$$z_3(6) = 6.5 \qquad z_4(7) = 8.1 \qquad z_5(7, 42) = 0.75 \qquad F(14, 27) = 0.56.$$

In (11.20), $\Delta \ln y_t^* = \frac{1}{3} \Sigma_{i=0}^2 \Delta \ln y_{t-i}$ (the average growth rate) and $F(14, 27)$ denotes the F test against the fit of (11.9), which reveals no evidence of invalid restrictions (as might be expected given the data-based selection of (11.20)). Such an equation has only one more parameter than (11.7), yet describes far richer dynamic reactions embodied in relatively sensible functions of the data. Moreover, the formulation allows very different lag patterns for each of X, r, P (despite having a 'common' exponential tail due to the lagged dependent variable coefficient of 0.904); indeed these may be found surprising since, for X_t, μ and ψ are only 1.4 and 0.6 *quarters* (with 96 per cent of the adjustment to income changes occurring within nine months), while for r_t the corresponding figures are 7.9 and 4 quarters (with 40 per cent of adjustment occurring within nine months).

6 Summary and Conclusions

Following a discussion of predictive failure, attention is focused on the possibility that it derives from mis-specification interacting with the changed behaviour of a few variables; a precedent is inflation effects on the consumption function as in chapter 8. A potential explanation for mis-specification in terms of inappropriate modelling procedures is examined in section 3, and the alternative approach of sequentially simplifying a general relationship is briefly discussed in section 4. The demand for the narrow money stock is used as an illustration in both sections and in section 5, where slight modifications of the demand for M1 equations proposed by Coghlan (1978) demonstrate the importance of a disequilibrium component which incorporates an error correction feedback mechanism. The resulting model yields a sensible long-run equation relating velocity to interest rates and inflation and predicts up to 20 quarters ahead with reasonable accuracy. If a relationship in the *levels* of the variables does exist, then any 'differenced' equation could only be valid close to a steady-state time path, and hence, although perhaps adequate for short-run forecasting, would provide another instance conforming with 'Goodhart's law' if used as a basis for policy changes (see Goodhart, 1978). Equation (11.20) may well suffer the same fate (e.g. if important variables are omitted), but the specification does at least seem to have theoretical plausibility and fairly constant parameters despite a substantial change in the behaviour of the rate of inflation, real income and interest rates. Moreover, it highlights how apparent 'structural breaks' in simpler equations (like (11.3)–(11.7)) need reflect no more than dynamic mis-specification. Finally, the analysis emphasizes the potential advantages when the dynamics are uncertain of considering the most general (theory-based) maintained hypothesis at the start of the analysis, and sequentially simplifying it in a data-coherent way.

Perhaps the most serious criticism of the section 4 approach is the possibility that the data provide inadequate information to enable the 'correct' model to be selected. Indeed, few investigators would have retained the results in (11.9) or (11.11) had such relationships even been fitted prior to 1971. Since it is infeasible to estimate (11.19) from 32 observations only, the proposed approach could not have been implemented at the time. Nevertheless, the outcome seems much more satisfactory than that which concluded section 3 and strongly suggests that estimating rather general dynamic representations of the economic theory should be part of any time-series modelling exercise.

7 An Empirical Illustration*

with Jean-François Richard

To evaluate the finally chosen model (11.20), we now test it against data which have become available only since that study was completed. To simplify notation, lower-case letters denote the logarithms of the corresponding capitals, except for r_t, and Δ_j denotes a j-period difference. The earlier model was proposed on the basis that, for the existing data, it satisfied all of the test statistics reported, which entails empirically satisfying the relevant model design criteria discussed in chapter 17. This included accounting for most previous findings of M1 equations in the United Kingdom. For the overall sample 1963(i)–1980(ii) (less four lags), ordinary least squares re-estimation yields

$$\Delta_1(m_t - p_{t-1}) = 0.73\left(\tfrac{1}{3}\Delta_3 x_t\right) - 0.12\left(\tfrac{1}{3}\Delta_3 r_t\right) - 0.57\Delta_1^2 p_{t-2} - 0.26\Delta_1 p_{t-3}$$
$$-0.074(m - p - x)_{t-1} - 0.038r_{t-2} + 0.041 + \hat{e}_t, \qquad (11.21)$$

$$T = 66 \qquad R^2 = 0.64 \qquad \hat{\sigma} = 0.013 \qquad z_5(20, 38) = 1.2 \qquad z_5(7, 52) = 1.6$$
$$z_3(6, 52) = 1.2 \qquad z_1(5) = 9.3 \qquad \eta_4(1) = 0.1 \qquad \eta_5(20, 38) = 0.8,$$

where the coefficients on the right-hand side of (11.21) have standard errors 0.27, 0.02, 0.19, 0.20, 0.020, 0.009 and 0.015 respectively. Note that in (11.21) we are using a Lagrange multiplier interpretation of the Chow tests for 1978(iv)–1980(ii) and for 1975(iii)–1980(ii). In addition, $\eta_4(1)$ is the Lagrange multiplier test for first-order autoregressive conditional heteroscedasticity, i.e.

$$\mathscr{E}(e_t^2|e_{t-1}) = \phi_0 + \phi_1 e_{t-1}^2 \qquad (0 \leqslant \phi_1 < 1)$$

(Engle, 1982a), distributed as $\chi^2(1)$ asymptotically under the null that $\phi_1 = 0$; $z_1(5)$ is the maximized likelihood ratio test for a common factor in the first-order autoregressive generalization of (11.21) asymptotically distributed as $\chi^2(5)$ under the null; and $\eta_5(j, T - k - j)$ is the general functional-form–heteroscedasticity test from White (1980b), distributed in large samples as $F(j, T - k - j)$ on the null of homoscedasticity.

Further descriptive statistics are provided by figure 11.3 which shows the time-series graph of $\Delta_1(m_t - p_{t-1})$ and the fit of (11.21); and the following features of the standardized residuals $\{\hat{e}_t/\hat{\sigma}\}$ from (11.21): maximum, 2.2; minimum, −2.0; skewness, 0.03; excess kurtosis, −0.4. There is no evidence of any problems of 'outliers' and the first four moments are not unlike those of a normal distribution.

Even though the final seven observations could not have been used in selecting the specification, the model 'survives' all the tests including that of parameter

---

*Reprinted from *International Statistical Review*, 51 (1983) 141–3.

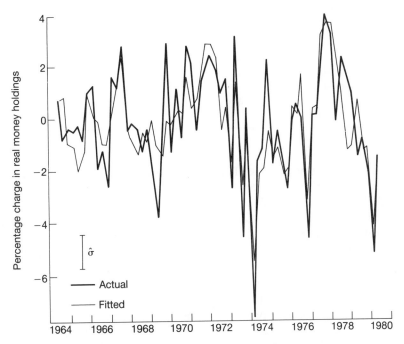

Figure 11.3   Time series of changes in demand for money and fit of (11.21) $(\Delta_1(m_t - p_{t-1}))$.

constancy when (11.4) fails. Indeed, the estimated error variance of (11.21) is about 2 per cent (!) of that of (11.4), and even in terms of residual standard deviations the best of the earlier equations has a value more than double that of $\hat{\sigma}$ in (11.21). Consequently, it seems worth commenting on the interpretation of this model.

First, the specification is an error correction form which reproduces (11.2) in static equilibrium. More generally, consider a steady-state growth path along which r, $\Delta_1 x = g$ and $\Delta_1 p = \dot{p}$ are constant, and if we note that $\Delta_1 m = g + \dot{p}$ from (11.22), the dynamic equilibrium equation derived from (11.21) is

$$\frac{M}{PX} = \exp(0.55 - 3.7g)r^{-0.51}(1 + \dot{p})^{-3.6} \qquad \eta_6(4) = 643.0 \qquad (11.22)$$

where the coefficients on the right-hand side have standard errors of 0.23, 5.0, 0.13 and 2.4 respectively. Although the derived coefficients in (11.22) have relatively large standard errors, the $\eta_6(\cdot)$. Wald statistic value strongly rejects the null of no association and the solved model is in accord with the initial theory in (11.2). Nevertheless, the underlying unrestricted levels equation corresponding to (11.21) has complicated dynamics, as shown in table 11.3, but is summarized using seven estimated parameters for lag *functions* selected as being data coherent and non-collinear decision variables, e.g. $\frac{1}{3}\Delta_3 x_t$ is the average growth rate of real income over the previous three quarters. Since the residual standard error of the general model estimated unrestrictedly is 1.3 per cent of M, the simplification from potentially 20

Table 11.3 Derived lag coefficients from (11.21)

	$j = 0$	$j = 1$	$j = 2$	$j = 3$	$j = 4$
m_{t-j}	–	0.926	–	–	–
x_{t-j}	0.24	0.074	–	−0.24	–
r_{t-j}	−0.04	–	−0.038	0.04	–
p_{t-j}	–	1.074	−1.57	0.88	−0.31
1	0.041	–	–	–	–

parameters to seven is acceptable. The lag reactions of M to changes in X, r, P are all very different: that for X is very fast (as seems sensible for transactions demand), whereas that for $\Delta_1 p$ is very slow.

It is clear from figure 11.3 that (following a policy change) the data variance increased substantially after 1971. Even so, (11.21) is not rejected by parameter constancy tests. This supports both the weak exogeneity assumptions about x_t and r_t, and the structural invariance of the model, especially since the policy authorities sought to control either interest rates or money supply differentially over most of the sample period. Also, since (11.21) has residuals which are not detectably different from white noise against an information set including up to seven lags of m, it should not prove easy to develop univariate time-series models which 'outperform' it in terms of goodness of fit or parameter constancy. While the overall forecasting performance of M from a submodel for all the variables obviously cannot be decided on the basis of (11.21) alone, parameter constancy in (11.21) seems a necessary condition for such an exercise to be useful; note that the largest quarter to quarter change in $\Delta_1(m_t - p_{t-1})$ is over $6\hat{\sigma}$.

In any case, structural modelling is undertaken for other purposes than simply forecasting, e.g. policy analysis, testing of theories, and it is noteworthy that (11.21) explains why the error on (11.4) was not white noise and encompasses that earlier model. The predictive failure of (11.4) can be explained in terms of changes in the correlations of its regressors with those in (11.21) between sample and forecast periods, with the derived parameters of (11.4) not being invariants for such changes. For a recent evaluation of models like (11.21), see Trundle (1982).

We conclude on an interpretative note. How demand for M1 responds to changes in interest rates which in turn lower both real incomes and inflation (as in recent UK monetary policy) depends on the 'true' numerical magnitudes of all the responses. The evidence in (11.21) reveals that M1 could increase or decrease as r rises and, say, $\Delta_1 p$ falls, depending on the sizes of their changes. Thus, to understand why M1 might rise as r rises (but, for example, $\Delta_1 p$ is falling) or fall as r falls (but, for example, X is falling) even though a negative relation is anticipated, a structural invariant multivariate model of agents' behaviour seems essential; and useful characterizations seem feasible.

Notes

1   Richard (1980) has recently described how such a situation can be confused with a 'switch of regimes'.

2   The 5 per cent level for χ^2_{20} is 31.4; the 1 per cent level is 37.6.

3   The arguments presented below are additional to those discussed in chapter 8 and chapter 6 and reference should be made to those chapters for a more complete analysis of the properties of the dynamic model (11.3), and the problems of differencing.

4   As indeed will any distributed lag representation.

5   Equation (11.7) can also be expressed as a special case of (11.10c) with both short- and long-run unit income elasticities and a mean lag of zero.

6   Note that the correlations in the upper triangle of table 11.1 are for the whole period of 52 observations and so include the 32 data points used to compute the correlations in the lower triangle.

12

Monetary Economic Myth and Econometric Reality

Preamble

The concluding chapter of this Part is a polemical follow-up to chapter 11. It attempts to exposit the important concepts from chapters 5–11 in the context of empirical modelling of money demand. It also critically comments on the range of debates then raging about econometric methodology. In fact, Hendry and Mizon (1990), which is a direct response to Ed Leamer's (1983) challenge to 'take the con out of econometrics', was being written at the same time and, like chapter 12, had the analyses of chapters 15–17 as a basis.

Part of the explanation for the polemical nature of the chapter was my frustration with economic policy in the United Kingdom. I had acted as a special adviser to the Treasury and Civil Service Select Committee of the House of Commons on Monetary Policy (see Hendry, 1981) and endorsed the Committee's report which highlighted the complete lack of empirical evidence for many of the assertions on which the government of Margaret Thatcher based its economic policy. The Committee's advice was ignored at the time, although by the second half of the 1980s monetary policy more closely resembled what they suggested. Because the chapter was written for a new journal specifically concerned with policy issues, and since econometric evidence was increasingly cited in policy debates, it provided a suitable vehicle for criticizing other methodologies and other evidential claims.

In the chapter it is argued that empirical econometric equations do not just chance to 'break down' out of sample, having been constant within sample: rather, many models have already 'broken down' on the available data before being published, but their proprietors are unaware of this because they have not rigorously tested for constancy. New observations merely highlight the pre-existing failure. Thus, regime changes play a vital role in helping to eliminate poor specifications, and hence are a help and not just a problem.

A distinction is explicitly drawn between the constructive and destructive modes of econometric research. In the former (Herschel's (1830) 'context of discovery') non-econometric influences such as luck, brilliance, serendipity and creativity are crucial if new congruent models are to be developed: there do not seem to be any sufficient conditions for how to

Reprinted from *Oxford Review of Economic Policy*, (1985) 72–84. I am greatly indebted to Chris Allsopp for considerable help and encouragement in preparing this paper and to John Muellbauer for valuable comments. The research was supported in part by grant B00220012 from the Economic and Social Research Council.

discover valid empirical models. For example, one could in principle dream the answer without recourse to data or stumble over the same answer after analysing hundreds of regressions. Nevertheless, different methods of model construction can and do differ radically in their research efficiency, and general-to-simple offers the best prospect from that viewpoint.

Conversely, in the latter, or destructive, mode (Herschel's 'context of evaluation') econometric testing is generally applicable since tests can be obtained with known behaviour under the null that the model to be tested is valid (analytically in large samples or by simulation for a customized problem). Consequently, conditional on believing their own model, the proprietors of that model should agree to the legitimacy of the relevant test, and hence be persuaded by its outcome.

Two issues arise: (1) how to define the null of model validity; and (2) what tests to select.

1   Since models restrict data in many ways, a taxonomy of information is needed to delineate what aspects of model validity are testable. Such a taxonomy in fact follows directly from the theory of reduction given the sequence of steps needed to derive any model from the data generation process. A null hypothesis corresponds to each element of the taxonomy and rejecting that null reveals model invalidity (subject to resolving (2), of course). The concept of *congruency*, which summarizes satisfying all the ingredients in the taxonomy, then characterizes a valid model (see chapters 16 and 17 for the formal analysis). It was while editing this paper that Christopher Allsopp suggested the use of the word 'congruent' to describe the match in all salient respects between a model and the data, to replace the acronym 'TADC' of chapter 16. Teun Kloek has suggested that this choice is not entirely felicitous since the mathematics usage (e.g. congruent triangles or matrices) interrelates two objects of the same kind whereas the present sense appears to relate different objects. A partial resolution of this linguistic difficulty is to note that a triangle can also be congruent with the top of a (sliced off) triangular pyramid, where different objects are compared. Alternatively, once the data are fully characterized by the Haavelmo distribution (the joint density of all the observables: see, for example, Spanos, 1986; Hendry et al., 1989) congruency is a relation between the model and the Haavelmo distribution, so that similar entities are being compared.

2   A different set of considerations (drawing on both economics and statistics) is needed to delineate the alternatives against which testing is worthwhile. The power functions of many econometric tests depend only on the distance, and not the direction, of any departure from the null, and for alternatives close to the null, many different departures turn out to be locally equivalent (see, for example, Godfrey and Wickens, 1982). However, different statistics for testing a given null may have very different powers to reject that null when it is false, depending on the properties of the data generation process. Thus, no test need dominate all others across different states of nature. Despite the importance of such issues, they are too technical to analyse in a volume such as this. The interested reader is referred to Cox and Hinkley (1974), Lehmann (1959) and White (1990).

The structure of destructive testing also reveals that there can be no *sufficient* conditions for model validity in an empirical social science. An innovation relative to one information set may prove explicable on another; human behaviour may alter, and so future parameters may differ from present ones; and so on. However, a stringent list of *necessary* conditions exists and places tight requirements on a model even to be deemed well designed or congruent with all the available evidence.

A background development during the period 1978–82 was the introduction of microcomputers, heralding the personal computer (PC) revolution. Prior to 1980, empirical work was conducted with cumbersome and unfriendly batch programs tailored to specific mainframe computers: most of these machines existed in small numbers and they usually differed dramatically from other computers in how they operated, thus creating no incentives to develop powerful, friendly or transportable software. PCs, however, were produced by the million and were largely standardized (though compatibility has steadily waned as the diversity of PC manufacturers has increased), and so huge incentives were created for software development – and as we all know, the market responded. Econometrics was no exception despite the relatively small size of the discipline. Much of my leisure time since 1982 has been spent rewriting AUTOREG (see chapter 14) for PCs to meet the much higher standards of power, presentation and ease of use expected by PC users. Chapter 12 was my first substantive field trial of the PC-GIVE module and, like the Monte Carlo example noted above, revealed a gigantic leap in productivity: from once being an arduous six-month task, model evaluation could be undertaken at home in one evening! Moreover, it was both much more fun (aided by colour graphics and a reliable and flexible program specifically designed in the light of all the work reported in this book) and yielded a higher quality product, as judged against the criteria underlying congruency. Further developments to PC-GIVE since 1984 have again increased both the productivity of empirical researchers and the quality of the resulting models relative to those prevalent in the 1970s (see chapter 19, and Hendry, 1989).

The substantive results in section 6 below indicated that the M1 demand equation (modified to a simpler specification following work by John Trundle (1982) at the Bank of England) remained on course and did not exhibit predictive failure on a further extension of the data, which included the 1979 policy change to emphasizing monetary control. This finding in turn yielded a clue to a deeper evaluation of super exogeneity and hence to tests which potentially could confirm or refute the Lucas (1976) critique (see Hendry, 1988b; Engle and Hendry, 1989). The section re-analysing Friedman and Schwartz (1982) briefly describes the results by Hendry and Ericsson in 1983, which eventually appeared in print during 1991 (Hendry and Ericsson, 1991a), and section 7 notes Baba et al. (1992).

Finally, section 6 has a prediction about the response of the UK clearing banks to interest being taxed at source. I note that interest-bearing chequing accounts have since proliferated, and deposit account interest rates match those on offer from building societies. Hendry and Ericsson (1991b) present a model of M1 which incorporates this innovation.

1 Present Controversy: a Funeral Pyre or the White Heat of Technical Advance?

Few of the main macroeconomic forecasting systems can produce sensible forecasts without the tender loving care of their proprietors. Many econometric equations in common use show significant deterioration in the accuracy with which they characterize data as time passes. And many economists are sceptical about empirical evidence, feeling it lacks 'credibility'. Monetary relationships have the dubious distinction of being among the leaders in this field, as witnessed by the very large mispredictions of M1 models in the United States over what is now known as the 'missing money' period (1973–6) as well as during the recent 'great velocity decline' (1979–82). In the United Kingdom, models of M1 and M3 demand experienced large 'structural breaks' following the competition and credit control regulation changes and the move to floating exchange rates. Perhaps it is no suprise that 'Goodhart's law' should have been formulated with respect to money demand equations.

These factors are closely interrelated and in part represent different facets of the same underlying problem – a problem of methodology. Somewhat as a caricature, the conventional approach in empirical economics is as follows: (i) postulate an arbitrary theory (arbitrary in the literal sense of being at the free choice of the investigator); (ii) find a set of data with the same names as the theory variables (such as 'money', 'incomes', 'interest rates', 'inflation' etc.); (iii) make a range of auxiliary simplifying assumptions (e.g. choosing a linear model, assuming away measurement errors); (iv) fit the theory-model to the data to see the degree of match. Corroboration is sought, and accepted, with minimal testing to check whether rejection is possible against interesting alternative hypotheses (such as non-random errors, and changing parameters). Consequently, very few models are rejected and a plethora of disparate empirical results coexists (even when mutually contradictory in terms of claimed *empirical* findings!). For general surveys of monetary econometric equations, see Desai (1981b) and Laidler (1985).

An objective observer should indeed be sceptical: the approach just sketched is inherently non-scientific and it would be surprising if it threw light on anything more than the investigators' personal prejudices. Nevertheless, this is not a necessary state of affairs: had many of the models just caricatured been tested on *pre-existing* data, they would have been found to have broken down already – all that later data did was to highlight the various hidden defects. Models which are in fact not constant within sample are an unreliable basis for post-sample forecasting, let alone policy.

Poor methodology and poor models alone, however, are not sufficient to explain model failure for the following reason. If the world were constant (in that economic data were generated by an unchanging mechanism), so would be econometric representations of it, *however badly specified and/or untested*. If the world did not change, the falsity or invalidity of models could not be revealed. Thus, changes in the properties of economics data are necessary to account for the observed phenomenon of predictive failure and model breakdown. Of course, the last decade of turbulence has been amply adequate to that task. Unfortunately once it is granted that changes do occur in the data generation process, that alone is potentially a sufficient explanation for model failure. How then is one to distinguish between legitimate appeals to a 'regime shift' (such as oil shocks or floating exchange rates) upsetting an otherwise 'good' model, and the same claim being an excuse for the deserved failure of a poor model?

There are two factors which can help to discriminate:

1 Can specific events be appealed to as likely potential causes of the claimed shift (e.g. the switch from fixed to floating exchange rates, or the formation of OPEC)?
2 What has happened over the same historical period to purely extrapolative forecasting devices (such as the well-known Box–Jenkins methods)?

If extrapolative methods have not failed, and no obvious external source of regime change is specified. . . . The point hardly needs elaboration, especially as a third check has already been alluded to, namely the extent to which the claimed relationships have survived rigorous within-sample testing.

Several authors have recently added to the chorus of complaints about the validity/credibility of econometric evidence. Lucas (1976) argued that model failures were often due to ignoring the crucial role of expectations in economic behaviour and deduced his notorious 'policy critique' from this assertion. Yet *documented* empirical instances where this critique has been shown to be the main (let alone the sole) explanation for an equation's breakdown are exceedingly rare. Sims (1980) argued that macroeconomics provided no useful theory information for guiding econometric research, characterizing existing approaches as 'incredible'. His proposed solution of allowing the data to play a direct and much larger role in empirical analysis than it does in the straitjacket of the 'conventional' approach has much merit, but in my view swings too far. In particular, his unrestricted equations inextricably mix features which are relatively variable with those which are potentially more constant, rendering the whole non-constant. The perceptive reader will note the contradiction between the Lucas and Sims critiques since the former appears to be arguing for more reliance on theory, and Sims for less.

More fuel has been added to the pyre of econometrics by Leamer (1983) in a piece entitled 'Let's take the con out of econometrics'. He argues that models are fragile and whimsical, meaning that claimed empirical results (like 'interest rates negatively affect money demand') are easily 'reversed' by relatively minor changes in model specification and that many econometric results reflect the whims and prejudices of investigators as much as the information content of the data. He proposes one technique called 'extreme bounds analysis' which generates the complete range of coefficient estimates which investigators with widely different beliefs could produce from a given set of data. However, Leamer has been taken to task by McAleer et al. (1985) who argue that his proposed approach is unreliable because it eschews rigorous testing of models against data evidence. The present writer shares their views in large part (having argued in chapter 1 that the three golden rules of econometrics are test, test and test).

What is the justification for my standpoint, and does it throw light both on the existing controversies and on appraising claimed empirical evidence? The next section seeks to answer these questions. Then in section 3 we consider a simplified framework for model evaluation, based on a crucial departure from a conventional analysis, namely that the world is always evolving and in a state of flux and hence econometric methods must be tailored to cope with this inherent difficulty. The primary objectives then become isolating and calibrating the constancies of the existing social framework; not eternal constants, since there are no permanent inviolable laws in a social science, but current behavioural rules that evolve slowly relative to the changes in the observed data. Finally, sections 4–7 will illustrate this expository analysis with empirical evidence from studies of the demand for money.

2 Construction and Destruction: Pious Hope versus Hard Reality

For most of my professional life, I have been writing articles critical of econometric practice (what not to do and why you should not do it), while developing computer software to implement a rather different approach. The basis of my viewpoint is that all *constructive* suggestions are invalid in that the correct way to learn about the world depends on how it is constructed – which is not known until after the learning has occurred. Thus, any methodological prescription must be open to counter-examples: the 'truth' could be discovered by 'wrong' methods (cf. Kepler's attempts to fit the regular solids into his planetary orbits) or by chance (Eureka!) and not by painstaking scientific endeavour (which happened, say, to lack a crucial insight into a problem). Nevertheless, the possibility that drunken prospectors might find gold by falling down and sticking their pick in does not mean that geological science is irrelevant to gold mining. Thus, I advocate an approach which combines construc-tionist aspects in a basically destructive methodology: crudely put, by eliminating the worst models, we are left with the less bad ones. Moreover, an essential prere-quisite for tentatively accepting a model is that it can explain previous findings, including why such models broke down when they did. This we have called an encom-passing strategy (cf. chapter 8 and Mizon, 1984). A new model supplants existing models only if it accounts for the phenomena they can explain and some additional features (especially any previous anomalies). Application of this principle yields a progressive sequence of models, which at the worst are summaries of previous research and at best (subject to all the criteria to be noted shortly) may usefully characterize certain features of the economy.

Various search strategies are open to modellers trying to develop adequate if simplified characterizations of economic behaviour, and, in turn, any formal strategies can be subjected to prior statistical analysis to examine their likely proper-ties (e.g. the frequency with which they select the correct model, or a close approx-imation to it, in a situation where we generate artificial data from known structures). Most formal strategies are woefully poor. For example, fitting models without first looking at the data is wonderful if your model chances to coincide with reality, and rather unhelpful otherwise. Revising it in the light of later evidence to elimi-nate the worst misfits ensures that it matches where it touches – but otherwise leads to invalid inference. The explanation for this last assertion is simple in a complex world: if many factors determine an outcome and only one or a few are allowed for, their estimated effects are contaminated by the effects of the excluded factors (unless they chance to be all mutually uncorrelated). Moreover, a revision process of gradually expanding a model and stopping at the first insignificant improvement maximizes the initial contamination and hence maximizes the likelihood of false inferences.

The converse of starting with as unrestricted or general a model as the data will sustain minimizes the contamination effects but spreads the explanation so thinly that it can be difficult to recognize what are the main determinants. Thus, a simplification search is needed which may differ between investigators, data sets and choices of elimination rules. While open to reasonable objections, nevertheless this approach does seem in practice to produce more robust and interesting models than other routes I have tried. And since all constructive routes are invalid, the only objec-tive at the present stage is to eliminate models that are really poor representations of the data.

The valid aspect of econometrics is its destructive role. It does not make one many friends, but it does help to take the con out of *economics*. Once a model has been developed (by any method whatsoever) its construction excludes many features of the world. For example, if a model is claimed to have random errors, or constant parameters and so on, such claims are testable conditional on temporarily accepting the model as a valid description of the data. A test (or set of tests) can be derived which the builder of the model is bound to accept as valid given his model, and a reject outcome is as close to a conclusive result as a social science can ever come. New data, new tests and new rival models also provide unprejudiced evidence against which to evaluate any existing model, but frequently the investigator's own data set is more than adequate to refute the claimed results.

To recap, no method of constructing a model is necessarily bad or good, but some methods seem in practice to deliver more robust findings. Specifically, general models properly simplified have been of some value in generating useful approximations to economic behaviour. One reason for this is that rejection on a range of tests within sample is ruled out by the design and construction of such models. Thus, as claimed, the worst contenders have been eliminated so that 'better' ones remain. These can then be tested as new evidence accrues, but in any case must encompass previous findings and hence summarize existing knowledge in a progressive research sequence. Rigorous testing of models against data and against each other is a crucial aspect of this approach (with appropriate care in allowing for the number of tests conducted when appraising the overall findings), and it applies to Lucasian, Simsian and Leamerian modelling strategies alike. By requiring encompassing of previous models, one requires encompassing of their failures as well as of their successes and that is the aspect which tends to throw most light on the appraisal of claimed empirical findings. Obviously, mutually contradictory results could not coexist in this methodology. However, alternative hypotheses could, although few areas of economics suffer from a plethora of competing models which fully account for all the empirical evidence.

The natural question to arise is: what tests should be conducted? Presumably, an infinite number of potential tests exists (most still undreamt of by economists) but only a small select number could be applied to any data set. Thus, the next section addresses the issue of what types of information are relevant and a minimal set of associated tests which might be used. It must be stressed that such tests are of *necessary* conditions for models not to be invalid. No sufficient conditions for validating models can exist in an empirical science; and failure to reject one of the necessary conditions does not establish that the model is valid, but only that it is not demonstrably invalid. Finally, corroboration of theoretical claims is an extremely weak form of 'favourable' evidence since not only can false premises entail correct conclusions, but it can happen that each of several items of evidence apparently 'confirming' a theory when taken together refute that theory (cf. the earlier discussion on contamination from excluded influences).

3 Evaluation Criteria: or More Than You Ever Wanted to Know about Testing Models

The complete set of information available to an investigator comprises (i) the data deemed relevant, (ii) existing subject-matter theory (iii) the structure of the measurement system and (iv) the data that other investigators have used (non-overlapping with (i)). Each of (i) and (iv) can be divided with respect to any particular data point into (a) previous data, (b) current data and (c) future data. Thus, we have an eightfold partition of all the information. Model evaluation consists of testing models against each of these subsets.

For example, the claim that a model adequately characterizes the available data history (i) (a) translates into the proposition (usually called the null hypothesis) that deviations of the model's fit from the actual outcome are relatively 'small' and non-systematic. This null can be tested against several interesting alternatives corresponding to different forms of systematic lack of fit (e.g. the errors or model residuals are correlated over time, or have a variance which changes over time). Similarly, any claim to characterize (i)(c) corresponds to an assertion of parameter constancy over time, which is directly testable. Without wishing to conduct an extensive enumeration of all the possible claims and tests, note that (iv)(a) concerns tests for historical encompassing of rival models (which must include previous models) and (iv)(c) concerns forecast encompassing (can the model explain the forecasting performance of rival models?). The large technical literature deriving tests and examining their properties for samples which realistically reflect the characteristics of economic data need not concern us. The important point is that usable tests do exist, are available (many of the tests are embodied in the better econometric software packages including, for example, the AUTOREG library) and have clear implications for testing others' models.

In fact, we have scaled a sufficient height to obtain an overview of the fires burning below. Conventional modelling assumes that the model and data process coincide at the outset; i.e. that the data were actually generated by the factors in the model plus a random innovation impinging from nature. As such, *any* misfit should lead to rejection of the model. Instead, to rescue their pet hypotheses, investigators may run literally 'hundreds of regressions' (cf. Friedman and Schwartz, 1982, p. 266), hoping that one of these will 'corroborate' their ideas. Thus, difficulties are camouflaged or papered over, not revealed; the resulting models are not robust and it is little wonder they break down when confronted with new data and/or new economic policies. As asserted earlier, they do not even adequately characterize existing data.

The alternative is to view modelling in a more engineering spirit – that is, as a matter of designing models to achieve certain (albeit limited) objectives. Thus, the model is viewed as an inherently simplified mimic of behaviour, not a facsimile of the data process, and its unexplained component (residual) is *derived* as 'everything not elsewhere specified'. Then, one designs the model such that (i)(a) the residual is unsystematic (i.e. is an innovation or 'news' relative to the available data) and has a relatively constant variance; (i)(b) the variables treated as given are ones which economic agents could act contingently upon; (i)(c) the parameters are as constant as possible on subsets of the existing data; (ii) it is consistent with theory; (iii) it is admissible given the properties of the measurement system (e.g. predictions of prices are positive, or of unemployment are less than 100 per cent etc.); and (iv) it encompasses previous models (either historically or that and their forecasts). An important ingredient of this design process is to structure the model so that its explanatory factors are as little intercorrelated as feasible while corresponding to the sort of decision variables economic agents might actually use (e.g. rates of growth, interest differentials etc.).

Models designed in such a way seem to describe the data relatively robustly. In each case, the model is not justified by how it was constructed, but by how it performs against new evidence. A year's embargo on publishing empirical claims after submission to a journal to allow new data to accrue for a 'post-script' set of tests would be a useful check on the validity of claims. The charge that 'data-mining' occurs is germane only to the extent that by ignoring the implications of using a data-based modelling strategy one is (mis)led to select weak models. It is not a justifiable complaint in general since the converse of building models without knowing what features of the data even need explanation seems like a reversion to the worst practices of scholasticism. Further, by adopting the modelling strategy proposed above, one should *never* need to run hundreds of regressions.

On the one hand, seen as a sharp critical razor, econometrics is far from being in a mess; its major problem is that the speed of generation of garbage has usually exceeded that of its incineration by professionals – leaving nature to do the job instead. However, the availability of standardized microcomputers and the consequential international compatibility of data and software should soon allow rapid testing and replication exercises, leading to the demolition of many of the at present conflicting assertions. On the other hand, if a model based on sensible theory and designed on pre-1978 data continues to perform as anticipated for the following 20–30 quarters, then the theory-based critical assertions of Lucas and Sims or the statistical objections of Leamer seem irrelevant: it behoves them to explain why such an event occurred given that other models do not have good track records over a similar period. This is especially true in the United Kingdom since the Thatcher experiment seems to have perturbed the economy more than any other domestic regime has succeeded in doing since 1921. Of course, even well-designed models remain *models*: they are not 'truth' in any definable sense, merely having residuals which have not yet been explained. The progressiveness of the strategy is reflected in an improving sequence of interrelated, successively encompassing models, and in the class of economic and statistical theory issues these raise. For one example, still not completed by any means, but helping to resolve an important ingredient of all macroeconomic systems – the consumption function – see chapters 8, 9, 10 and 18; Davis (1982), Harnett (1984), Pesaran and Evans (1984) and Bollerslev and Hylleberg (1985).

4 Empirical Illustration A: or Assertion versus Empirical Evidence

A supposed cornerstone of the monetarist viewpoint is the recent book by Friedman and Schwartz (1982). It received generally favourable reviews as a work of scholarship (cf. Laidler, 1982; Goodhart, 1982; Mayer, 1982; although see Congdon, 1983; Moore, 1983; *per contra*). A wide range of claims concerning the behaviour of monetary economies was made by Friedman and Schwartz and they asserted that these claims were consistent with the long-run historical evidence. A remarkable feature of their book is that none of the claims was actually subjected to *test* (cf.

Hendry and Ericsson, 1991a). Rather, equations were reported which did not manifestly contradict their theories and this non-contradiction was taken for 'corroboration'. On close examination, quite a number of their claims were not econometrically testable, but the 'stability of the demand for money as a function of a small number of arguments' could be tested. The most obvious test was a split-sample one (fitting their model separately to each half of the data period) and this rejected parameter constancy. In addition, the basic claim of 'price homogeneity' (that nominal money is proportional to the price level *ceteris paribus*) also could be rejected as could the specification of the equation (e.g. a trend was significant if added). And this was despite their having a poorly fitting money demand model with a standard error of around 5 per cent of the money stock (when residuals are large, tests which seek to discriminate between hypotheses have low power to do so). Testing may be destructive, but since Friedman and Schwartz immediately drew major policy implications from their study, it may prove less destructive of economic well-being to highlight unsubstantiated claims and poor models prior to their policy implementation.

5 Regime Shifts: or Why Econometrics Textbooks Need to be Rewritten

The vast bulk of the theory of econometrics is predicated on a 'constant world' assumption. The methods of Sims explicitly require stationarity, and most of the classical econometrics problems (identification, estimation etc.) implicitly assume unchanging parameters in the processes which generate the data. As a simplifying assumption to allow the subject to develop, one cannot but admire what has been achieved. As a description of reality, it is wildly off target, for one of the most pervasive problems in econometrics is model breakdown, bringing us full circle to the starting point of this essay. Hopefully, the explanation is now clearer. All models are crude simplifications, but many are hopelessly crude because of the methods used in their formulation, which camouflaged their inherent flaws: i.e. they were very badly designed. The first hot blast of post-sample reality ensured the conflagration of these straw-houses. In chapter 11 I discuss the extent to which model failure can be traced to mis-specification in a world of change which does not rule out the possibility of establishing relatively constant relationships for the same dependent variables over the same historical epochs. And, following the encompassing strategy, the model I present reveals why earlier ones failed.

Therefore, if all but good models manifest parameter non-constancy, then identifying/selecting/isolating the constant relationships becomes a major objective of econometrics. In that case, many of the earlier 'problems' of econometric theory disappear. For example, how to tell whether a fitted equation is a supply or a demand curve or a mixture is not a serious issue if only one of the two schedules is constant: find the constant one. This in fact re-emphasizes the main point behind the early analyses of 'identification' (summarized by Working, 1927). Likewise, the high intercorrelations of economic time series seemed to jeopardize our ability to select the relevant explanatory factors: however, if the correlations are not constant and one seeks a constant relationship, then discrimination becomes far easier (include the 'wrong' variables and the equation fails when the correlations alter). With turbulence, data become informative between rival claims and few models survive – a far cry from the present proliferation of contending 'explanations'.

6 Empirical Illustration B: UK Money Demand Re-revisited

In a series of studies commencing in 1978, the demand for narrow money in the UK (M1 measure) was modelled using the approach described above (cf. chapters 11 and 17 and Trundle, 1982). The follow-up analyses have suggested that the originally selected model has remained remarkably constant over the period since 1977 (the end of the then available data set) even though substantial changes have occurred in the authorities' policy objectives and control rules. As part of a parallel investigation of the demand for M1 in the United States (Baba et al., 1992), we returned to test the recent performance of my earlier model for the United Kingdom. One change adopted to match the US data was to use gross national product GNP as the measure of income in place of the earlier Total Final Expenditure series (TFE); the other data series were the same (including being quarterly seasonally adjusted, unfortunately). The model assumes that in a static equilibrium state, agents wish to hold money M in proportion to their nominal income PI (where I is real income) but hold less as inflation $\dot{p}$ and/or interest rates R rise:

$$M = KPI(1 + R)^{\alpha}(1 + \dot{p})^{\beta} \tag{12.1}$$

with $\alpha, \beta < 0$. The graph of M/PI is shown in figure 12.1 and well represents a 'flight from money'. It is readily verified empirically that the precise choice of income

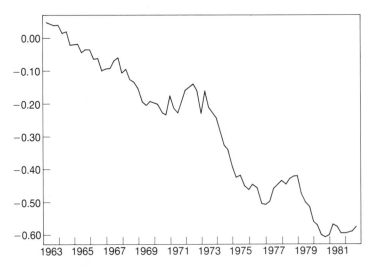

Figure 12.1   Log(M/PI).

measure does not alter the findings already reported. For example in chapter 11 a caricature model was estimated – intended to show the results of applying the conventional methodology. If this model is refitted to the period 1963(i)–1972(ii) using GNP data we obtain

$$\widehat{(m - p - i)}_t = 0.33 - 0.19r_t - 5.4\,\Delta_1 p_t \tag{12.2}$$
$$(0.12)\ (0.06)\quad (1.7)$$

$$T = 32 \qquad R^2 = 0.42 \qquad s = 6.2\% \qquad \text{DW} = 0.7$$

where T is the sample size, M is M1, I is constant price GNP, P is the GNP price deflator, R is the local authority three-month interest rate, at annual rates, lower-case letters denote logarithms of corresponding capitals and $\Delta_1 x_t = x_t - x_{t-1}$. Also s is the standard deviation of the residuals and conventional standard errors are shown in parentheses.

By the usual criteria of corroboration this model does not look too bad – and could possibly be accepted, or even applied in a policy context. However, if the sample is extended to 1977(i) ($T = 52$) the standard deviation rises to 8.7 per cent, and for the period up to 1982(iv) to 12.7 per cent. Thus the 'badness of fit' doubles, and the coefficients change by around 100–200 per cent, although they do retain 'the right signs'. Thus, forecasts from an equation such as (12.2) would have been very poor: it is a badly designed model.

To mimic the earlier study and to illustrate the methods outlined above, a general dynamic equation relating m to p, i and R with up to four lags in every variable was fitted for the period 1961(i)–1977(i) and then simplified to yield an interpretable, parsimonious model. (The choice of R, rather than log R follows from Trundle, 1982.) The selected equation, which fits dramatically better than the 'caricature', is

$$\Delta_1 \widehat{(m - p)}_t = 0.40\,\Delta_1 i_{t-1} - 0.52R_t - 0.86\,\Delta_1 p_t - 0.11\,(m - p - i)_{t-2}$$
$$(0.16) \qquad\quad (0.11) \quad\ (0.17) \qquad\ (0.02)$$

$$- 0.26\,\Delta_1(m - p)_{t-1} + 0.040 \tag{12.3}$$
$$(0.09) \qquad\qquad\qquad (0.006)$$

$$T = 52 \qquad R^2 = 0.62 \qquad s = 1.5\% \qquad z(3) = 0.4.$$

Here, $z(\cdot)$ is an appropriate test for residual autocorrelation of up to and including third order (distributed as F(3, 43) if the residuals are not autocorrelated). Although the lag structure is somewhat different from the model reported in the earlier studies, this is due to using the level rather than the logarithm of interest rates and to the use of GNP. However, the main features of the earlier study are reproduced including large negative interest rate and inflation elasticities, a feedback of 10 per cent from previous 'disequilibria' between money and income (measured by $m - p - i$) and a residual standard deviation of 1.5 per cent (against 1.3 per cent for TFE over the same period, suggesting that it may be a slightly better measure of 'transactions' for M1).

Now, testing the above restricted model on the period up to 1982(iv) yields

$$\Delta_1 \widehat{(m - p)}_t = 0.37\,\Delta_1 i_{t-i} - 0.58R_t - 0.80\,\Delta_1 p_t - 0.10\,(m - p - i)_{t-2}$$
$$(0.13) \qquad\quad (0.07) \quad\ (0.12) \qquad\ (0.01)$$

$$- 0.28\,\Delta_1(m - p)_{t-1} + 0.041 \tag{12.4}$$
$$(0.07) \qquad\qquad (0.005)$$

$$T = 75 \qquad R^2 = 0.71 \qquad s = 1.3\% \qquad z(4) = 0.3.$$

The coefficients are hardly altered and the model actually fits quite a bit better notwithstanding the Lucas/Sims/Leamer critiques and the Thatcher experiment! The residuals have a variance of 1 per cent of that of the caricature model. Incidentally, these results were obtained in one evening on a personal computer using the author's interactive programme PC-GIVE and did not require any 'trials' not reported (the simplification sequence took four steps following the more detailed structuring proposed in Hendry, 1986a). The choice of variables produces very low intercorrelations, the largest being -0.68 between R_t and $(m - p - i)_{t-2}$ with all but two being under $\frac{1}{2}$. Figure 12.2 shows the one-step-ahead fit of the model against the actual data, based on the whole sample.

In a hypothetical 'static state' when all change has ceased (except inflation at a constant rate), our equation suggests that

$$M = 1.5PI(1 + R)^{-5.6}(1 + \dot{p}_a)^{-1.9} \tag{12.5}$$

where $\dot{p}_a$ is annual inflation and, like R, is (for example) 0.05 for 5 per cent. Thus the elasticity of M with respect to R is about -0.56 at $R = 10$ per cent; and a rise in inflation from say 5 per cent to 10 per cent lowers M/PI by about 9 per cent. These estimates are similar to the magnitudes we found in the United States although other substitution, innovation and volatility effects were included in the latter study (and the residual standard deviation was under 0.4 per cent).

Since 1982, the annual rate of inflation has fallen considerably (although UK interest rates have not) and hence a rising ratio of M/PI would correspond to agents' desires to hold idle money balances. Taking $\dot{p}_a$ as dropping from 12 per cent to 4 per cent, with R constant, a 'neutral' policy should envisage M/PI rising by around

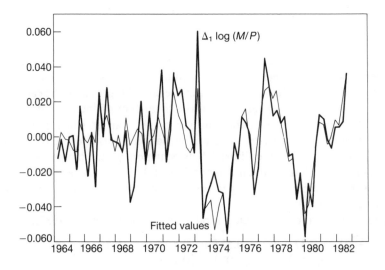

Figure 12.2 Fitted and actual values of $\Delta_1 \log(M/P)$.

12 per cent (more if R also fell). Notice that, despite being well above the going inflation rate, such a rise would *not* be inflationary: rather it would reflect the reduced costs of holding idle money, and hence the increased desire for 'liquidity'. There are clear implications for the 'stringency' of any set of monetary targets.

A standard blunder with equations of the form estimated above is to 'invert' them to 'determine' the price level or nominal income or interest rates etc. This is an invalid and indeed rather meaningless step warned against in chapter 11. The equation is predicated on the assumption that agents could obtain the M1 balances they desired and is a contingent behavioural rule given interest rates, inflation and incomes. Then agents choose to hold on average the amounts of M1 predicted by the equation. This conditional model is constant across changes which destroy other models (the caricature *inter alia*) and the technical term for its parameters is that they are super exogenous to the historical interventions of the authorities. Such equations cannot be inverted and still remain constant. That is, attempting to explain $\dot{p}$ by the obverse of our model should produce predictive failure. That is a testable proposition.

Indeed we have the following contrast between (a) for 1963(i)–1972(iv)

$$\widehat{\Delta_1 p_t} = -0.03\,\Delta_1 m_t - 0.040 R_t + 0.17\,\Delta_1 i_{t-1} + 0.04\,\Delta_1 (m-p)_{t-1}$$
$$\quad\;\; (0.07) \qquad (0.11) \qquad (0.06) \qquad\;\; (0.08)$$

$$-0.042\,(m-p-i)_{t-2} + 0.12 \tag{12.6}$$
$$\;\;(0.016) \qquad\qquad\quad (0.008)$$

$$T = 32 \qquad R^2 = 0.36 \qquad s = 0.6\% \qquad DW = 1.3 \qquad z(2) = 1.9$$

and (b) for 1963(i)–1977(iv)

$$\widehat{\Delta_1 p_t} = 0.09\,\Delta_1 m_t + 0.17 R_t - 0.14\,\Delta_1 i_{t-1} - 0.14\,\Delta_1 (m-p)_{t-1}$$
$$\quad\;\; (0.11) \qquad (0.14) \quad (0.13) \qquad\;\; (0.11)$$

$$-0.045\,(m-p-i)_{t-2} - 0.002 \tag{12.7}$$
$$\;\;(0.023) \qquad\qquad\quad (0.009)$$

$$T = 52 \qquad R^2 = 0.53 \qquad s = 1.2\% \qquad DW = 1.3 \qquad z_3(3) = 4.1.$$

Thus the residual standard error has *doubled* although that for our money demand equation was unchanged at 1.4 per cent over these two periods. Although (12.6) and (12.7) describing $\Delta_1 p_t$ have smaller percentage standard errors than the corresponding models for $\Delta_1 (m-p)_t$, this does not mean they are 'better' models. The standard deviations of inflation and real money are 1.6 per cent and 2.4 per cent respectively for 1963(i)–1977(iv), and even a simple second-order autoregression for $\Delta_1 p_t$ has a residual standard error of only 1.0 per cent. Whatever was 'causing inflation' during the mid-1970s, it was not a constant relationship based on the inverse of the demand for M1 equation. In fact, while the specification of equation (12.4) corresponds to received wisdom in terms of formulating M1 demand as a demand for *real* money, the empirical evidence here and in the United States points directly to agents planning in *nominal* terms in the short run. First, note that $\Delta_1 (m-p)_t \equiv \Delta_1 m_t - \Delta_1 p_t$. If the $\Delta_1 p_t$ component of the dependent variable is taken to the right-hand side (the model is linear in such variables and is *invariant* under linear transformations of its variables) the coefficient of inflation becomes $+0.20\,\Delta_1 p_t$ (0.12)

and hence is statistically insignificant. In effect $\Delta_1 p_t$ vanishes so that one could not logically invert the model to explain inflation. Of course, in the 'long run', agents adjust their nominal money holdings in line with nominal income and hence eventually demand real money in relation to real income. But that is consequential on prices changing, not directly causative of their doing so. In technical terms, it is invalid to switch the endogenous–exogenous status of the variables while preserving the same parameters. The one constancy between (12.6) and (12.7) is the *negative* coefficient of $(m - p - i)_{t-2}$!

Does this mean that 'money did not cause inflation'? First, we must confront the 'helicopter problem' – surely prices would rise if pound notes were scattered in large volumes from the air (or by post as Alfred Marshall discussed in his evidence to the Committee on Bimetallism almost a century ago (see Marshall, 1926))? Indeed, but in such an experiment I believe equations like those promulgated above would 'break down' dramatically. Panic could well ensue with a complete collapse of faith in currency (so it is back to cigarettes – or cowrie shells?). War might erupt, who knows? Certainly not the economist nor the econometrician. In periods of catastrophic change, human behaviour patterns are not constrained to reproduce previously manifested historical forms: we are nothing if not creatures of innovation. Perhaps the one useful moral of this train of argument is – don't try the experiment.

This view might be seen as an extreme Lucasian one, but it is not. For a wide range of interventions (e.g. tax changes, rules on deduction of tax at source of income, financial innovation, and possibly even hyper-inflation), the model presented above has some chance of characterizing the outcome as long as the contingent structure is retained. Only the violation of the latter is *prima facie* disastrous for the reasons just discussed.

Our analysis suggests one possible way of accounting for the failure of 'monetarist' predictions to explain macroeconomic outcomes under the so-called Thatcher experiment. The stereotypical 'Friedmanite' model of a stable demand for money confronting an 'exogenously' controlled supply with equilibrium achieved by adjustments in the price level requires money demand equations with nominal money being exogenous. But the models above are of *endogenous* nominal money. And if the authorities' control rules have altered, then by being a constant relationship our equation is neither a supply function nor confounded therewith. Consequently, the evidence is wholly counter to that stereotypical view, and conclusions based on that view are unlikely to describe reality.

An amusing prediction is possible from our work concerning the impact of the recent decision to deduct tax on interest at source from the clearing banks. R_t above is *not* tax adjusted (quite unlike our US models where tax is an important determinant of M1 demand).[1] Indeed, using $R(1 - T)$ where T is the standard rate of tax actually worsens the goodness of fit of the overall model, albeit slightly. Since R_t is supposed to measure the opportunity cost of holding money, one is led to the view that tax on interest earnings is not being fully paid. If so, clearing banks could either experience an out-flow of funds once tax becomes inevitable, or be forced to increase their interest rates to offset such a tendency (or money holders are simply irrational). To model this effect within the present equation would probably involve a switch to defining interest rates as $R(1 - T)$ once deductibility is enforced.

7 Empirical Illustration C: US Money Demand Explained

As noted above, in joint work with Baba and Starr, we have been modelling M1 demand in the United States. As in the United Kingdom the ratio of M1 to nominal GNP has fallen substantially during the last 20 years. Our study proposes ways of accounting for this through financial innovation and the volatility of long-term interest rates, and allows for taxes, inflation, substitution between competing assets, and dynamic adjustment. We are able to establish a relatively constant equation which also accounts for the failures of previous models during the 'missing money' episode and following the new operating procedures of the Federal Reserve Bank in 1979(iv) (for previous surveys, see Judd and Scadding, 1982; Laidler, 1985). The value of s varies over the range 0.36–0.39 per cent for a variety of subsamples of the data and all the 'new' items incorporated in our approach seem necessary to explain the observed behaviour of M1. The modelling is as for the United Kingdom, the model is similar to a generalization of (12.4), and the results are numerically remarkably close for the common parameters (the α and β analogues are -4.8 and -1.6 respectively although the US income elasticity is 0.5). Thus, nominal M1 money seems endogenously determined by the private sector's demands to hold it, and the 'inversion' to determine prices or inflation fails as badly as it did on the UK data.

Overall, the model fits about as well as most of the best previous representations (and its residual variance is about one-fiftieth of that of the equation reported in Cooley and Le Roy (1981) who dispute the uniqueness of the sign on the interest rate coefficient).

8 Conclusion

Economic analysis is an essential tool for understanding how monetary economies function. Its use, however, is severely curtailed and often counter productive unless it is firmly based on empirical evidence. That evidence is frequently econometric in nature but, unfortunately, much of the existing empirical work is not credible and has not produced constant relationships. Thus a further precondition to understanding is the rigorous econometric testing of empirical assertions.

The logic of that view was presented above. It may seem that this casts econometrics in a destructive role and that few empirical claims would stand up to rigorous testing. If this is the case then well and good: it is far better that uncertainties and ignorance should be recognized than that invalid models should be used as a basis for policy. Since the proof of these puddings is in their eating, some dumplings were sampled. Testing was revealed as a powerful device for highlighting invalid assertions, despite the latter being apparently 'corroborated' by empirical evidence.

But the need for rigorous testing can also be seen in a more constructive light: to eliminate bad models and point the way to better. A strategy was outlined involving the simplification of general dynamic equations to parsimonious characterizations of the data which are then susceptible to reasonably powerful within-sample tests. Though such a procedure is open to legitimate objections as a means of constructing models, so too, in principle, are all other 'constructive' methodologies. The one valid rule – think of the truth at the start – is not a little unhelpful. Precisely how best to find 'good' empirical models is mainly a matter of research efficiency, productivity and 'flair'. The *validity* of the entailed claims is established on post-sample evidence, no matter how the model was developed.

The suggested modelling strategy yielded constant characterizations of the holdings of M1 in the United Kingdom and United States, which are interpretable as demand functions. The resulting models were predicated on the endogeneity of M1 – despite 'targeting' or attempted control by the monetary authorities. Hence they do *not* sustain the common procedure of inverting the relationship whereby the price level is derived as an equilibrium or market clearing outcome given the money supply. Moreover, such equations are not likely to be invariant to switches in the exogeneity of M1, given their contingent nature.

To establish any point to a policy of controlling M1, a different paradigm is required, in which the mechanism by which money influences prices is articulated and tested. Since the demand for M1 changes greatly as inflation, real incomes, disequilibria etc. alter, there is nothing in the analysis that precludes M1 from having an important macroeconomic role when economic agents are perturbed from their 'equilibrium' demands. Only the claim that prices can be determined by inverting the M1 demand equation is discredited given the empirical constancy of the conditional model, despite changes in the data properties.

Finally, the constancy of the estimated equations may still not be an adequate basis for policy (though of course they are more useful than equations which have broken down). They are conditional on a given state of financial institutions and technology, and as new assets are 'invented' or develop in response to changing circumstances, their yields will influence the demand for money. (Witness money market mutual funds and 'supernow' accounts in the United States; perhaps interest-bearing building society cheque accounts will greatly influence even the conservative British in due course.) Econometrically, this can be allowed for once the relevant agents' reactions are measurable to recover the behavioural constancies; for policy, however, the equation appears to shift.

Monetary relationships are among the most susceptible to these effects (cf. Goodhart, 1978), making some past policy recommendations look less appetizing in retrospect than the prospects claimed at the time. Thus while rigorous econometric testing can dispose of some monetary myths, and can offer constant characterizations of the data which are historically useful, their relevance to policy needs to be carefully assessed. Money demand models remain useful when either it is known that financial innovations will not occur or, if they will occur, their quantitative effects can be anticipated. A necessary, though insufficient, basis is careful empirical modelling of the past.

Notes

1 This phenomenon vanished on the revised data set reported in Baba et al. (1992), bringing the results slightly closer to those found for the United Kingdom.

Part III
Formalization

Many facets interact to determine the ultimate success or failure of an empirical study. Luck may save poor methodology; or bad econometrics may wreck a creative theory; clever thinking or valuable insights can point up the crucial ingredients or reformulations needed for a useful model to emerge from an inadequate starting point; or, despite the best available methodology, technology and intellect, the problem under study may have no solution. Since we are empirically investigating social behaviour it is unimaginable that *sufficient conditions* can be stated which will *guarantee* the success of any given study: succinctly, methodology alone is inadequate.

However, the preceding argument does not entail that methodology is worthless. That there is no 'best' way does not imply that all ways are equally good. Despite its inadequacy, an important role remains for methodology, and consequently for concepts and strategies which sustain modelling. Since good ideas can be lost by poor implementation, including inappropriate estimation, there are many necessary conditions for the empirical success of a model. In this third part of the book, such conditions are formulated as requirements for models to be congruent data representations, and most of the following papers are concerned with analysing the attributes of congruency.

The five chapters in this part are respectively concerned with estimation, computation, conditioning, model concepts and an overall framework for analysing economic time series. Chapter 13 develops the notion of an estimator generating equation (EGE) for linear simultaneous systems estimators (briefly discussed in chapter 4). The EGE is a simple formula based on the first derivatives of the likelihood function, from which almost all estimation methods for a given model class can be derived. By summarizing the topic of linear systems estimation, which often comprised a substantial part of textbook treatments, attention can be refocused on other problems – and economists should be the last scientists to ignore the implications of opportunity cost! The EGE idea can also be applied to models with errors in variables (see Hendry, 1976b) and a further follow-up to 'incomplete systems' is described in chapter 17.

The EGE idea helped my research in an indirect, but important, way. The paper helped establish my reputation as an econometric theorist in terms of conventional professional criteria, making it easier for me to explore unconventional ideas, and yet hope to publish them. The status quo in any scientific endeavour represents the cumulation of the ideas, methods and concepts deemed successful over its history, and this rightly imparts a conservative bias against new ideas or approaches. In addition, the existing participants have invested heavily in their present intellectual capital, and new developments, especially new routes, are initially resisted since they threaten the value of that capital. However, recent entrants stand to gain most by adopting the latest ideas because this strategy both takes them fastest to the research frontier and circumvents the need to become masters of the knowledge so painfully acquired by earlier entrants. Consequently, over time new ideas percolate through a profession despite initial resistance.

Unfortunately, new entrants with genuinely new ideas often find these extremely difficult to publish because of the conservative bias and because it can be hard to explain a new idea in terms of existing concepts. If the innovative new entrants do not have excellent pedagogical skills, their ideas may languish. However, a previously established reputation facilitates publication and so allows the ideas a fighting chance: at the margin, it helps to be respected by the editor of a journal even if that respect is for rather different contributions. Of equal importance is that one's ego is far less dented by a one-line referee's report which characterizes a hard-won new idea as 'rubbish, which the author has said three times before': an established figure has some grounds for his or her cognitive rationalization that the referee is an idiot, whereas for a new entrant the third or fourth devastating denunciation can induce total despair and abandonment of the idea, or the profession.

In my own microcosmic case, I (and my co-authors!) certainly received some damning reports, but I also received constructive and encouraging ones. Papers rejected outright by some journal often were invited by another; and despite some adverse reactions to various aspects of the developing methodology, yet other journals commissioned specially written papers to exposit or clarify the approach that was evolving. Nevertheless, the certainty of employment in my post at the London School of Economics, and the fact that I became quite widely known after this chapter was published, were at least facilitating factors. If I wished to dissent from prevailing views and approaches then I could do so securely, irrespective of whether or not that dissent would lead to a fruitful outcome.

To return to the overview of this part, chapter 14 is only the tip of the iceberg of programming but it serves both as an overall exposition of the methodological framework pre-1980 and as a description of the mutual interdependence between computational considerations based on numerical analyses and on statistical analyses. Then chapter 15 is devoted to an analysis of exogeneity which is a key concept for both conditional single-equation models (as used throughout part II) and open simultaneous systems. Moreover, the process of precisely formalizing one modelling concept both highlighted the need to formalize others and suggested a framework for doing so, namely the theory of reduction. Chapter 16 resulted as a first attempt at formalization, and chapter 17 followed as an overview of the whole approach, which also reconsiders many of the themes developed in earlier chapters.

The main drawback to segmenting the book between empirical applications and formalizations of the concepts and strategies is the false impression it may create that the two evolved separately. Each aspect interacted closely with the others: empirical puzzles stimulated conceptual and methodological developments, which had to be programmed for future applied research, often requiring a Monte Carlo study of small-sample performance. The resulting framework clarified some earlier difficulties but revealed others as well as highlighting previously unnoticed phenomena, thereby inducing a continuing cycle.

One may legitimately ask of a methodology which espouses an empirically progressive research strategy whether it itself is progressive. This question has two aspects: (i) is there excess content to the methodology, namely does it clarify problems beyond those which the methodology was created to explain?; and (b) is any of that excess content corroborated and found to improve empirical research? Part IV offers a brief evaluation. First, we must formalize the methodology, and part III is the attempt.

13

The Structure of Simultaneous Equations Estimators

Preamble

Chapter 13 needs a separate preamble. Its primary aim at the time of writing was to downplay the prominence of optimal estimation methods in econometrics textbooks and thereby allow more attention to be devoted to other aspects of modelling. Building on the papers by James Durbin (written in 1963) and Denis Sargan (1958) (and, of course, Koopmans, 1950b), the score equations determining the full information maximum likelihood (FIML) estimator in a complete linear simultaneous system are reinterpreted as an estimator generating equation (EGE) for all systems and single-equation estimators.[1] Thus, dozens of extant estimators are encapsulated in a simple expression, which also reveals how to generate new estimators as desired. Moreover, whether any given estimator is consistent and efficient can be ascertained directly from its method of generation using the EGE. While the chapter is relatively long, that is only because it actually demonstrates how to obtain most existing estimators from the EGE. Once the theorem is proved, however, only the EGE and a few salient special cases need to be taught.

The EGE idea actually occurred to me in the middle of a lecture on FIML when I was deriving equation (13.13) below based on Durbin's unpublished (1963) paper (Durbin, 1988). At that point, it needed only a minor change to the software code of FIML to produce any other estimator. In its personal computer reincarnation, PCFIML has over 12,000 lines of code; of that, the total for the EGE is under 40 lines (or about 200 if one includes the code for obtaining all the possible reduced form matrices). Estimation of a given model is the minor part of the program that a minor, albeit essential, tool in modelling deserves. From my perspective, the EGE achieved its immediate objective in so far as I ceased to research into econometric estimation techniques and was able to concentrate my attention on empirical analyses and modelling tools and methods, both in teaching and research. This was an essential step for me in consolidating all the methods on which I had previously worked as well as greatly simplifying the underlying computer programs.

Over the years, a number of readers have enquired about the notation of chapter 13,

Reprinted from *Journal of Econometrics*, 4 (1976) 51–88. Revised version of a paper presented to the 1974 Econometric Conference at Grenoble. I am grateful to Grayham Mizon, Jean-François Richard, Denis Sargan and Kenneth Wallis for helpful discussions about the material herein. This research was supported by a grant from the Social Science Research Council.

specifically the use of implicit selection and vectorizing operators together with the matrix form of the econometric model, rather than (say) the more conventional explicit selection matrix and the vec($\cdot$) operator with a vector model as is usual for ordinary least squares or three-stage least squares. The answer is that writing the program FIML described in chapter 14 helped to define the EGE formalization! In computer code, it is natural to write the score in the compact form of equation (13.8) below, for any size of system with any linear mapping from the coefficient matrix (denoted A) to the parameter vector (θ). Models are then defined by specifying which elements of A correspond to θs, and that mapping can be written as a vector of integers (e.g. θ_1 comes in position $(1, 4) = 4$ of A, θ_2 in position $(2, 3) = n + 3$ of A if A is $k \times n$ and so on). The vector of integers is the only selection operator needed by the program and, in addition, it allows easy and accurate model specification or respecification on the computer.

The other aspect stressed in the present chapter is the close link between optimal estimation and numerical optimization. First, estimators are viewed as numerical rules or algorithms for approximating the solution of the score, and are classified by their choice of initial values, number of iterations and approximation to the Hessian of FIML. This class of different statistical approximations must be distinguished from the class of alternative numerical optimization methods which implement FIML in different ways (e.g. Newton–Raphson or conjugate directions etc.) but are all equal on convergence. Second, in COMFAC problems, many ostensibly different estimators transpire to be just different optimization algorithms (see section 5 below). Interestingly, numerical efficiency and statistical efficiency are also closely linked: one step of a numerically efficient (second-order convergent) method from consistent initial values is statistically (asymptotically) efficient; and not iterating a numerically inefficient algorithm can lead to a statistically inefficient estimator. This idea was later applied to Monte Carlo in Hendry and Srba (1977) and to recursive updating in Neale (1988). A brief overview of the links between optimization and estimation is also offered in chapter 14.

The EGE idea was extended to models with errors in variables in my comment on a paper by Ted Anderson (1976). The main point of that comment was that instrumental variables and weighted regression methods were just different solutions of the same basic expression, with the surprise that the former were far more robust to mis-specification of the error covariance matrix. The original EGE is also extended to so-called 'incomplete' systems in chapter 17. Potentially, the EGE notion applies much more widely and in joint research with Ken Wallis we have derived an EGE for the class of rational expectations models discussed in Wallis (1980) which both reveals the existence of some non-iterative yet fully (asymptotically) efficient estimators and shows why fixed-point methods usually do not work (analogous to case 5.4 below). Generalized method of moments (GMM) estimators are based on a similar principle to the EGE (see, for example, Hansen, 1982) and both approaches exploit the claimed orthogonality between a set of instrumental variables and an unobservable error term, weighted by the appropriate covariance matrix. Jerry Hausman (1975) uses this basic property of instrumental variables to derive FIML as an instrumental variables estimator. The construct of an EGE is also closely related to the notion of an efficient estimating equation analysed by Godambe (1976) and Godambe and Thomson (1974), although I was unaware of that literature at the time.

The issue of modelling a simultaneous system is not discussed in this chapter; an early approach was noted in chapter 3 with its follow-up in Anderson and Hendry (1984), and my most recent ideas are described in Hendry et al. (1988) in the context of PCFIML and in Hendry and Mizon (1991) for cointegrated processes. Most of the empirical studies in part II are single-equation analyses, in part because it was unclear (to me) until recently how to model systems *ab initio* (especially so until it became clear how to model the special case of a single-equation system) and in part because the concepts are usually easier to explain in simple cases. Chapter 19 briefly comments on system modelling issues.

Note

1   Durbin's paper appeared in *Econometric Theory*, 1988.

1 Introduction

In the three decades since Haavelmo's (1943) analysis of the consequences of failing to treat the joint endogeneity of economic variables appropriately, there has developed a vast literature proposing estimators and deriving their asymptotic sampling distributions, interrelationships and comparative advantages etc. It is demonstrated in this chapter that almost all simultaneous equations estimators can be interpreted as numerical approximations to the full information maximum likelihood (FIML) estimator, and hence one simple formula can be obtained which encompasses all of them and highlights their close basic similarities despite the present apparent diversity. This clarifies the situation concerning asymptotic equivalences, while allowing the numerical variants to induce very different finite sample properties.

   A similar approach was adopted in the original paper to the large class of estimators designed for equations with autoregressive error processes, but is not reproduced here.

   It should be noted that as our primary purpose is an exposition of the interrelationships between a vast array of methods, rigour is sacrificed (if necessary) where this enhances clarity.

2 Simultaneous Equations Estimators

As a basic statistical framework, we shall use the following set of assumptions, which could be generalized in many ways with little additional complexity.[1] The true structural model is known to have the specification

$$AX' = BY' + CZ' = E',\tag{13.1}$$

where

$$A = (B:C) \qquad X' = (x_1 \ldots x_T) \qquad x_t' = (y_t':z_t'),$$

so that

$$X = (Y:Z) \text{ and } E' = (\varepsilon_1 \ldots \varepsilon_T).$$

B is an $n \times n$ non-singular matrix of (unknown) fixed parameters of the endogenous variables y_t and C is an $n \times k$ matrix of (unknown) fixed parameters of the strictly exogenous variables z_t. There are adequate, exact, valid, prior zero restrictions on B and C such that every required parameter is identifiable given a suitable normalization rule, usually $b_{ii} = -1$ $(i = 1, \ldots, n)$. The z_t are measured without error and have a distribution function which is independent of the parameters of (13.1) and ε_t, and $T^{-1}Z'Z$ is positive definite with a finite probability limit H. The additive error ε_t is distributed as $NI(0, \Sigma)$, where Σ is unrestricted *a priori* apart from being positive definite and finite. We shall usually also assume $T > n + k$. The circumflex, tilde and overbar will respectively denote maximum likelihood, instrumental variables (IV) and least squares estimators.

As is well known (see Koopmans and Hood, 1953) the log likelihood function L is given by

$$T^{-1}L(B, C, \Sigma|X) = K_0 + \log\|B\| - \tfrac{1}{2}\log|\Sigma| - \tfrac{1}{2}\text{tr}\,[\Sigma^{-1}A\,(X'X/T)A\,'\,],\,(13.2)$$

where A and Σ are now considered as arguments of L, and not as the true parameters (to simplify notation). Clearly the FIML parameter estimates are those which maximize L subject to the *a priori* restrictions on A.

For any matrix $D = (d_1 \ldots d_m)$, let $D^{v\prime} = (d_1' \ldots d_m')$ and let superscript u denote a selection operator to choose only unrestricted elements of a matrix. Thus $\delta = A^v$ includes all the elements of A, whereas $\phi = \delta^u = A^{vu} \equiv A^r$ ($\nu_u \equiv r$ denoting *retained* elements being the combined operator) yields the vector of *a priori* unrestricted structural parameters.

Using the invariance property of maximum likelihood, maximize (13.2) with respect to Σ^{-1} by solving $\partial L/\partial \Sigma^{-1} = 0$, which yields

$$\Sigma = A(X'X/T)A', \tag{13.3}$$

and then solve $\partial L/\partial \phi = 0$, which implies

$$[(B'^{-1}:0) - \Sigma^{-1}A(X'X/T)]^r = 0, \tag{13.4}$$

so that (13.3) + (13.4) is the set of (non-linear) equations to be solved for the FIML estimator of A. However, the approach of Durbin (1988) yields a more convenient expression. From (13.3),

$$B'^{-1} = \Sigma^{-1}A(X'X/T)A'B'^{-1} = T^{-1}\Sigma^{-1}AX'(Y - Z\Pi'), \tag{13.5}$$

where the reduced form of (13.1) is

$$Y = Z\Pi' + W, \tag{13.6}$$

with $W' = B^{-1}E'$, and

$$\Pi = -B^{-1}C, \tag{13.7}$$

so that we also have $X = (Y:Z) = ZQ' + (W:0)$ where $Q' = (\Pi':I)$.

Substituting (13.5) in (13.4) therefore yields

$$q = [\Sigma^{-1}A(X'Z/T)Q']^r = 0. \tag{13.8}$$

Maximum likelihood estimators of A and Σ must satisfy (13.3), (13.7) and (13.8) (to be mutually reconciled) as these are necessary conditions for maximizing L; a check that a global maximum has been achieved can be conducted using (13.2) as a criterion function. However, given any data matrix X and a model specification, this is purely a numerical problem, although one which involves solving a set of non-linear equations. Expressed in general terms, we seek $\max_\theta L(\theta)$ where θ is the vector of all the parameters in L (i.e $(A:\Sigma)$) and to achieve this we could adopt an iterative rule of the form

$$\theta_{j+1} = \theta_j + \lambda_j G_j g_j \qquad j = 1, \ldots, J, \tag{13.9}$$

where θ_1 is the vector of initial values, J is the number of iterations (which could be determined arbitrarily or be a variable dependent on some convergence criterion), g_j is a vector of search directions, G_j is a modifying matrix to define the metric for the problem (both g_j and G_j being functions of θ_j) and λ_j is a scalar to determine the step length to maximize $L(\theta_{j+1})$. We shall consider different algorithms to be induced by varying the formulae determining any of $(\theta_1, \lambda, G, g, J)$. Two closely related classes must now be clearly distinguished:

1   choices which just induce different algorithms for *implementing* FIML;
2   choices which (either deliberately or inadvertently) produce algorithms *approximating* FIML.

Choices within class (1) imply that $L(\theta)$ is used as a criterion function to monitor the progress of the iteration so that, assuming no multiple optima difficulties and a suitably stringent test for convergence, iteration is carried out to convergence and (to the limits of numerical accuracy) we obtain $\hat{\theta}$ and $L(\hat{\theta})$. Variation within (1) therefore relates to *computational efficiency* and, while this is of considerable importance, we postpone a detailed discussion until section 5 to concentrate on class (2).

When (13.8) is evaluated at (13.3) and (13.7), it is dependent only on ϕ and a formulation equivalent to (13.9) is to seek solutions to $q(\phi) = 0$. However, we could also derive *approximate* solutions in this way, and this in fact transpires to be a dramatically convenient approach to characterizing (2) which unifies all existing simultaneous equations estimation theory since, if the algorithms approximating FIML are well defined, they constitute estimation rules. Thus, consider the possible class of estimators approximating (13.8), (13.3) and (13.7)

(i) $[\Sigma_2^{-1} A_3 (X'Z/T) Q_1']^r = 0,$

where

(ii) $\Sigma_2 = A_2 (X'X/T) A_2'$

and

(iii) $Q_1' = (\Pi_1' : I),$

with

(iv) $\Pi_1 = -B_1^{-1} C_1.$ \hfill (13.10)

In (13.10) the subscripts denote that *different* estimators could be used in each expression, the numbers showing the order in which the estimators are often obtained, with the possibility that (for example) Π_1 depends on the same estimator of A as Σ_2 etc. Every member of this class is a numerical approximation to the maximum likelihood solution commencing from different initial values and/or iterating a different number of times (including not iterating). Since (iii) and (iv) are definitions and (ii) is the 'obvious' estimator of Σ (as $AX' = E'$), the formula essentially centres on (i), which is a relatively simple expression. But, conditional on any given values for Q_1 and Σ_2, (i) is *linear* in A, and so constitutes a *generating equation* for econometric estimators in that variations in the choice of Q_1 and Σ_2 generate almost all known estimators for A. Thus, the formulae for almost all econometric estimators for linear simultaneous equations are just specializations of (13.10). This not only achieves a major economy of teaching and memory, but clarifies the structure of large groups of estimators and their asymptotic equivalences and consolidates the current proliferation of methods.[2] In the next two sections, we apply this theorem to systems (structural and reduced forms) and individual equation estimators respectively.

3 Systems Methods

3.1 Full Information Maximum Likelihood

We use the notation that a circumflex denotes a maximum likelihood estimator (see Koopmans, 1950b, ch. 2; Hood and Koopmans, 1953, ch. 6); then the FIML estimator solves (13.10) for $\hat{\phi}$ such that the *same* $A_j = \hat{A}$ occurs in all four terms from which both $\hat{\Sigma}$ and $\hat{Q}$ are derived. Granted the usual regularity conditions for maximum likelihood estimation (see Kendall and Stuart, 1961, ch. 18), we then have (throughout, $\sim$ denotes 'asympotically distributed as')

$$T^{1/2}(\hat{\phi} - \phi) \sim N(0, G^{-1}),$$

where

$$G = \text{plim}\,(\partial q/\partial \phi')|_{\phi=\hat{\phi}} \tag{13.11}$$

(a possible choice for G_j in (13.9)) and

$$q = \left\{ \left[A \left(\frac{X'X}{T} \right) A' \right]^{-1} A \left(\frac{X'Z}{T} \right) (-C'B'^{-1} : I) \right\}^r, \tag{13.12}$$

and so q is (13.8) evaluated at (13.3) and (13.7) and is the expression for $-\partial L_0/\partial \phi$ where L_0 is the *concentrated* likelihood function. However,

$$\text{plim} \left(\frac{\partial q}{\partial \phi'} \right) = \text{plim}\, \frac{\partial}{\partial \phi'} \left[\Sigma^{-1} A \left(\frac{X'Z}{T} \right) Q' \right]^r$$

$$= \text{plim}\, \frac{\partial}{\partial \phi'} \left[\Sigma^{-1} \left(\frac{E'Z}{T} \right) Q' \right]^r, \tag{13.13}$$

and hence, although Σ^{-1} and Q' depend on ϕ through (13.3) and (13.7) respectively, since $\text{plim}\,(E'Z/T) = 0$, terms involving their derivatives with respect to ϕ in (13.13) are asymptotically negligible for *any* consistent estimator of A. Conversely, variations in estimating Σ and Q will not affect the asymptotic distribution of $\hat{A}$ subject to the minimal condition that the estimators of Σ and Q are consistent. Let

$$(D \otimes F) = (f_{ij}D),$$

so that

$$(DRF)^v = (D \otimes F')R^v. \tag{13.14}$$

Then from (13.13), dropping the asymptotically negligible terms,

$$G = (\Sigma^{-1} \otimes QHQ')^u, \tag{13.15}$$

where superscript u denotes selecting rows and columns corresponding to unrestricted a_{ij} prior to inversion.

The reason that FIML requires iterative solution is that, to maximize the likelihood, it must reconcile all the relationships between the data and the parameters such that the latter are *mutually* consistent at all sample sizes. Nevertheless, (13.13) shows that, provided they are consistent, sampling variability in the estimators of Q and Σ does *not* affect the asymptotic distribution of $\hat{\phi}$. Re-expressed in numerical terms, *iterating* with respect to consistent estimators of Q and Σ leaves the asymptotic distribution of $\hat{\phi}$ unaffected. Thus, there is an infinitely large class of asymptotically efficient estimators derivable by solving (13.10)(i) conditional on consistent estimators of Q and Σ and this in fact includes *all* methods known at present. Further, even if Q_1 and Σ_2 are *not* consistent for Q and Σ, providing plim $T^{-1}Z'E = 0$, every solution of (13.10)(i) yields a consistent estimator for A (see section 5 for numerical optimization methods).

3.2 Three-stage Least Squares

This method was proposed by Zellner and Theil (1962). In (13.10), evaluate Σ_2 using (consistent) two-stage least squares (2SLS) or IV estimates for A_2 (denoted $\tilde{\Sigma}_2$) and replace Q_1' by $\bar{Q}' = (\bar{\Pi}' : I)$ (an overbar denotes least squares), where[3]

$$\bar{\Pi} = Y'Z(Z'Z)^{-1} \tag{13.16}$$

is the *unrestricted* reduced form estimator of Π so that (iv) is ignored. Since $\bar{Q}Z'X = X'Z(Z'Z)^{-1}Z'X = X'MX$, for $M = Z(Z'Z)^{-1}Z'$, normalizing the diagonal of B and vectoring (13.10)(i) yields (on cancelling T^{-1} and using $y = (Y')^v$)

$$(\tilde{\Sigma}_2^{-1} \otimes X'MX)^u \phi_3 = (\tilde{\Sigma}_2^{-1} \otimes X'M)^u y, \tag{13.17}$$

which is readily verified to be three-stage least squares (3SLS) (compare Madansky, 1964; Sargan, 1964b).

3.3 Iterated Three-stage Least Squares

If (13.17) is iterated numerically revising only Σ_2 from (13.10)(ii) the convergence point will in general differ (numerically) from FIML for all finite T, leaving the asymptotic distribution unaffected (see Dhrymes, 1973). However, (13.17) could equally be written as

$$(\tilde{\Sigma}_2^{-1} \otimes \bar{Q}Z'X)^u \phi^* = (\tilde{\Sigma}_2^{-1} \otimes \bar{Q}Z')^u y, \tag{13.18}$$

and iterating this with respect to both Σ and Q using (ii) and (iv) will yield FIML on convergence (revising Q as well would add negligibly to the computational cost).

Indeed, it corresponds to a 'block' Gauss–Seidel solution of (13.10), successively linearizing it in the form (13.18). Writing $\tilde{X} = Z\bar{Q}'$ provides an IV interpretation (see Hausman, 1975). Alternatively, since $X = ZQ' + (W:0)$ and plim $T^{-1}Z'W = 0$, replacing the remaining X in (13.18) by $Z\bar{Q}'$ provides a 'two-stage' interpretation (i.e. replacing the regressors by their 'systematic' components):

$$(\tilde{\Sigma}_2^{-1} \otimes \bar{Q}Z'Z\bar{Q}')^u \phi^* = (\tilde{\Sigma}_2^{-1} \otimes \bar{Q}Z')^u y. \tag{13.19}$$

This is obviously the same as (13.17) but could be expressed more generally as

(i) $\quad (\Sigma_2^{-1} \otimes Q_1Z'ZQ_1')^u \phi_3 = (\Sigma_2^{-1} \otimes Q_1Z')^u y$

or as

(ii) $\quad (\Sigma_2^{-1} \otimes \tilde{X}'\tilde{X})^u \phi_3 = (\Sigma_2^{-1} \otimes \tilde{X}')^u y \tag{13.20}$

for $\tilde{X} = ZQ_1'$.

Further, these are all obvious special cases of (13.19). However, for $Q_1 \neq \bar{Q}$, (13.20) cannot be written explicitly as (13.10), and hence (13.13) cannot be used as the criterion for deciding on asymptotic efficiency. Indeed, the efficiency of ϕ_3 *does* now depend on that of Q_1 and will be asymptotically efficient if and only if Q_1 is at least as efficient as $\bar{Q}$. Thus, for example, 2SLS values of Q_1 will *not* suffice in (13.20) even though they would in (13.18). Further, the consistency of ϕ_3 depends on the consistency of Q_1.

Another alternative would be to replace X in (13.10)(i) by its 'systematic' component ZQ_1', but now if Q_1 satisfies the *a priori* restrictions on A, namely $AQ = 0$, the next iteration simply reproduces A_1.

3.4 Linearized Full Information Maximum Likelihood

Evaluate Σ_2 and Q_1 in (13.10) using the same consistent estimator $\tilde{A}$ of A, and solve for A_3. From section 3.1, this is equivalent to using the Newton–Raphson algorithm $(\tilde{\theta}, 1, G, q, 1)$ in (13.9). When $\tilde{A} - A$ is $O(1/T^{1/2})$, since Newton–Raphson is second order convergent, the one-step estimates solve (13.10)(i) to $O(1/T)$ (see Rothenberg and Leenders, 1964).

3.5 Iterated Instrumental Variables

Using any IV estimator of A, solve (13.10)(ii), (13.10)(iii) and (13.10)(iv) for $\tilde{\Sigma}$ and $\tilde{Q}$ and as before let $\tilde{X} = Z\tilde{Q}'$. Re-estimate A using (13.10)(i) written as

$$(\tilde{\Sigma}^{-1} \otimes \tilde{X}'X)^u \tilde{\phi} = (\tilde{\Sigma}^{-1} \otimes \tilde{X}')^u y. \tag{13.21}$$

Apart from the choice of initial values, this is identical to (13.18) and converges numerically to FIML if iterated using (13.10) (see Brundy and Jorgenson, 1971).

Generally, note that (13.10)(i) can be vectored as

$$(\Sigma_2^{-1} \otimes Q_1Z')^u (A_3X')^r = 0 \tag{13.22}$$

and that only the *consistency* of the parameters of the 'generalized instruments' affects the efficiency of A_3 (see equation (13.13) above). Heuristically, such instruments are 'optimal' as Σ^{-1} allows for the between-equation error correlations and heteroscedasticity while $\mathscr{E}(x_t | z_t) = Qz_t$. In dynamic models, 'simulation predictions' of x_t could be used instead of reduced form predictions, but this would not be fully efficient in correctly specified systems.

3.6 System κ-class

The system κ-class estimator considers $Q_1 Z$ as a 'unit' such that Q_1 cannot be *explicitly* written, using for some matrix κ^*

$$Q_1 Z' = \begin{bmatrix} (I - \kappa^*) Y' + \kappa^* \Pi_1 Z' \\ Z' \end{bmatrix} \tag{13.23}$$

(see Srivastava (1971) and Savin (1973), who considers $\kappa^* = \alpha I$ for scalar α). Now, however, irrespective of whether (13.23) is used in (13.20) or (13.22), the analysis in (13.13) cannot be applied and such estimators require separate proofs of their asymptotic efficiency. A point requiring care is that even if plim $\kappa^* = I$, so that (13.22) + (13.23) *satisfy* (13.10) *asymptotically*, and both $T^{-1} Q_1 Z' Z Q_1'$ and $T^{-1} Q_1 Z' X$ converge to QHQ', the resulting estimator will *not* be asymptotically efficient unless plim $T^{1/2} (\kappa^* - I) = 0$ (compare section 4.6 below).

All the above estimators therefore differ solely in the choice of initial values and iterative algorithm (where the latter subsumes the choice of number of iterations) for solving (13.10). Nevertheless, their finite sample behaviour can be radically different (as comparison of FIML and 3SLS dramatically illustrates), as can computational cost and the conditions necessary for the computability of the estimators. Manifestly, there remain infinitely many members of the class of asymptotically efficient estimators; some of these may well have better (finite) sampling properties than those already known, and/or cost less to calculate, but it seems a plausible conjecture that they are all specializations of (13.10), since it comprises the class of all approximations to FIML.

3.7 Reduced Form Estimation

If the complete system (13.1) is just identifiable,

$$AQ = B\Pi + C = 0 \tag{13.24}$$

has a unique solution for $(B: C)$ from any arbitrary Π. Π can therefore be estimated unrestrictedly and, if a maximum likelihood estimator is used, by invariance the values of $(B: C)$ from (13.24) will also be maximum likelihood. But (13.10)(i) can be rewritten as

$$[\Sigma_2^{-1} B_3 (I: -\Pi_3) X' Z Q_1']^r = [\Sigma_2^{-1} B_3 (Y'Z - \Pi_3 Z'Z) Q_1']^r = 0, \tag{13.25}$$

which has (13.16) as the solution noting that only the second 'block' corresponding to I in Q_1' is retained since there are no derivatives for coefficients of Y. If the system is in reduced form ($B = I$), but with exclusion restrictions, an immediate solution of (13.25) is

$$\Pi_3^r = [(\Sigma_2^{-1} \otimes Z'Z)^u]^{-1} (\Sigma_2^{-1} \otimes Z'Y)^r$$

(see Zellner, 1962), and plim $\Sigma_2 = \Sigma$ is sufficient for the efficiency of Π_3^r.

3.8 Minimum Distance Estimators

Expression (13.25) remains true if A is over-identified, although as this imposes restrictions on Π the efficient solution is no longer (13.16). Let $\Omega = B^{-1}\Sigma B'^{-1} = T^{-1}\mathscr{E}(W'W)$ be the reduced form error variance matrix (which is unrestricted if Σ is); then (13.25) becomes

$$[B_3'^{-1}(B_3'\Sigma_2^{-1}B_3)(Y' - \Pi_3 Z')ZQ_1']^r = [B_3'^{-1}\Omega_2^{-1}(Y'Z - \Pi_3 Z'Z)Q_1']^r$$

$$= 0. \tag{13.26}$$

As in (13.13), replacing Q_1 and Ω_2 by any consistent estimators will not affect the asymptotic distribution of Π_3, and one possible choice is $\bar{Q}$ and $\bar{\Omega} = T^{-1} \times Y'(I - M)Y$. Then (13.26) could be *iteratively* solved for B_3 and $\Pi_3 = -B_3^{-1}C_3$ as functions of ϕ. This is in fact the usual minimum distance estimator, alternatively derived from minimizing

$$\text{tr}[\bar{\Omega}^{-1}(\bar{\Pi} + B^{-1}C)Z'Z(\bar{\Pi} + B^{-1}C)']^u \tag{13.27}$$

as a function of ϕ, directly establishing its asymptotic equivalence to FIML (see Malinvaud, 1970, ch. 9; Rothenberg, 1973, ch. 4). If Q_1 and Ω_2 were also iteratively revised using (13.10), the convergence point in all sample sizes would provide FIML estimates of the restricted reduced form parameters (by invariance); this would add little to computational cost, while providing the value of the likelihood function at the optimum for inference.

Simultaneous least squares (see Brown, 1960; Dhrymes, 1972) is obtained by setting $\Omega_2 = I$ in (13.26) and hence cannot be asymptotically efficient in general.

3.9 Subsystem Estimation

A further variant is when good structural specifications are available for some equations while no reasonable theory exists concerning others or these equations are just identified. If the latter set are replaced by unrestricted reduced forms and the whole system is then estimated by FIML, a subsystem variant of limited information maximum likelihood is produced (see Hood and Koopmans, 1953, ch. 6). Also, Court (1973) has proposed a 3SLS equivalent (which will not improve the efficiency of estimation of the over-identified subset) from which more efficient reduced form estimates than (13.16) are obtained. This is (13.10)(i) written as

$$\left[\Sigma_2^{-1}\begin{pmatrix} B_d Y'Z + C_d Z'Z \\ Y_b'Z - \Pi_b Z'Z \end{pmatrix} Q_1'\right]^r = 0 \tag{13.28}$$

(where $B_d Y' + C_d Z' = E_d'$ is the well-specified subset (B_d being $n_1 \times n$, say) and $Y_b' - \Pi_b Z' = W_b'$ is the remainder) using $\tilde{\Sigma}_2$ for Σ_2 and $\bar{Q}$ for Q_1, and hence resulting in a variant of (13.17). Again, different consistent estimators of Σ and Q

could be adopted without affecting the asymptotic distribution.

Finally, note that (13.10) is *not* the correct expression for FIML when Σ is known to be diagonal, so that the various asymptotic equivalences cannot be claimed to hold, and in fact it is well known that FIML is more efficient asymptotically than 3SLS in that case.

4 Individual Equation Methods

Equation (13.10) also specializes to the class of estimators which recognizes the joint dependence of the regressors but neglects over-identifying information on all other equations. Since the consistency of Σ_2 for Σ is not necessary to ensure that A_3 is consistent for A, a *sufficient* condition for (13.10)(i) to hold is

$$(Q_1 Z' X a_{3i})^{\mathrm{u}} = 0 \qquad i = 1, \ldots, n. \tag{13.29}$$

This would be necessary if Σ was diagonal, but then (13.10) would not be the appropriate expression for FIML derivatives as just noted.

A more useful derivation is to consider (13.28) when $n_1 = 1$, with all equations except the ith exactly identified, the ith being the *first* row of A. Thus let $A' = (a_i : D')$, where $D = [\,(0 : I) : -\Pi_b\,]$, and let

$$\Sigma = \begin{pmatrix} h & \sigma' \\ \sigma & \Sigma^* \end{pmatrix} \quad \text{with} \quad \Sigma^{-1} = \begin{pmatrix} h^* & \omega' \\ \omega & \Phi \end{pmatrix}. \tag{13.30}$$

Then (13.28) becomes

$$\begin{pmatrix} h_2^* a_{3i}' X' Z Q_1' + \omega_2' D_4 X' Z Q_1' \\ \omega_2 a_{3i}' X' Z Q_1' + \Phi_2 D_4 X' Z Q_1' \end{pmatrix}^{\mathrm{r}} = 0. \tag{13.31}$$

Since $h\omega = -\Phi\sigma$, the second 'block' in (13.31) can be solved for Π_b in the form

$$\Pi_{4b} = \bar{\Pi}_b - \frac{\sigma_2}{h_2} (a_{3i}' \bar{Q})^{\mathrm{u}}, \tag{13.32}$$

and substituting this back into (13.31) yields (13.29) immediately.

As in (13.13), derivatives of Q_1 with respect to a_{3i} in (13.29) are asymptotically negligible (being multiplied by $T^{-1} Z' \varepsilon_i$) so that for any consistent estimator of Q all solutions of (13.29) yield asymptotically equivalent estimators of a_i with asymptotic variance matrix $\sigma_{ii} (QHQ')^{-1}$. Also, as before, variations in the choice of Q_1 generate all 'limited information' type estimators.

4.1 Limited Information Maximum Likelihood

Limited information maximum likelihood (LIML) solves (13.29) subject to (13.32) and (13.10)(ii), (13.10)(iii), (13.10)(iv), using the same estimator of a_i throughout (LIML and FIML coincide if all equations but the ith are just identified). Noting the equivalence between (13.30) and (13.3) so that

$$\Sigma = \frac{1}{T} \begin{pmatrix} a_i' X' X a_i & a_i' X' X D' \\ D X' X a_i & D X' X D' \end{pmatrix} = \begin{pmatrix} h & \sigma' \\ \sigma & \Sigma^* \end{pmatrix},$$
(13.33)

post-multiply (13.32) by $Z' X \hat{a}_i$ and substitute for σ and h from (13.33),

$$\hat{\Pi}_b Z' X \hat{a}_i = \bar{\Pi}_b Z' X \hat{a}_i - (\hat{D} X' X \hat{a}_i \hat{a}_i' \bar{Q} Z' X \hat{a}_i / \hat{a}_i' X' X \hat{a}_i)$$

$$= \bar{\Pi}_b Z' X \hat{a}_i - \hat{\lambda} \hat{D} X' X \hat{a}_i,$$

where

$$\hat{\lambda} = (\hat{a}_i' X' M X \hat{a}_i / \hat{a}_i' X' X \hat{a}_i),$$

and as $\hat{D} X' = Y_b' - \hat{\Pi}_b Z'$ we have

$$\hat{\Pi}_b Z' X \hat{a}_i = (1 - \hat{\lambda})^{-1} (\bar{\Pi}_b Z' X \hat{a}_i - \hat{\lambda} Y_b' X \hat{a}_i).$$
(13.34)

Thus $\hat{\lambda}$ is $O(1/T)$ and is the smallest latent root of $[(X' M X - \lambda X' X) a_i]^u = 0$ with $a_{i1} = -1$, and $\hat{a}_i$ is the corresponding latent vector. Finally, using (13.34) in (13.29) and deleting the first row (which provides the normalization) yields the more familiar expression for LIML (see Anderson and Rubin, 1949)

$$\left[\begin{pmatrix} Y_b' \\ Z' \end{pmatrix} (\hat{\lambda} I - M) X \hat{a}_i \right]^u = 0.$$
(13.35)

Alternatively, if the first row is retained, we have the expression

$$\left\{ \left[X' M X - \hat{\mu} \begin{pmatrix} \bar{\Omega} & 0 \\ 0 & 0 \end{pmatrix} \right] \hat{a}_i \right\}^u = 0,$$

where

$$\hat{\mu} = T \hat{\lambda} / (1 - \hat{\lambda}),$$
(13.36)

which generates the 'Ω class' of estimators recently proposed by Keller (1975), using other estimators of $\mu \Omega$ than $\hat{\mu} \bar{\Omega}$. Further, the preceding analysis immediately clarifies that the resulting estimator of a_i is consistent provided that the estimator of $\mu \Omega$ is $O(T^{1/2})$ (even if it is inconsistent) and efficient if it is $O(1)$ (or less). Because LIML enforces the estimates of Σ, D and Q all to be coherent with $\hat{a}_i$ using the maximum likelihood functional relationships, LIML is the hardest estimator to derive *explicitly* from (13.10); even so it is no more tedious than doing so via the concentrated likelihood function (see, for example, Klein, 1974).

4.2 Two-stage Least Squares

2SLS can be interpreted as either (13.29) using $\bar{Q}$ for Q_1 or (13.35) with $\hat{\lambda} = 0$ (note (13.34) if $\hat{\lambda} = 0$). Since $\bar{Q} = X' Z (Z' Z)^{-1}$, $\bar{X} = Z \bar{Q}' = M X$ and hence $X' \bar{X} = \bar{X}' \bar{X}$ (by the idempotency of M) so that a 'two-stage' formulation is valid (see Basmann, 1957; Theil, 1961; Theil also considers iterative 2SLS). Thus we have three forms for (13.29):

$$(\bar{Q} Z' X \tilde{a}_i)^u = (\bar{Q} Z' Z \bar{Q}' \tilde{a}_i)^u = (\bar{X}' \bar{X} \tilde{a}_i)^u = 0.$$
(13.37)

Nevertheless, this is only true because the resulting estimator remains a special case of (13.29).

4.3 Iterative Two-stage Least Squares

Since applying 2SLS to every equation is equivalent to using (13.20)(ii) with $\tilde{X}' = \bar{Q}Z'$ but $\Sigma_2 = I$, solving (13.37) even with *restricted* estimates of Q will not yield FIML efficient estimates of a_i. Further, if (subject to a normalization condition) the 'two-stage' formulation given by the middle expression in (13.37) is used but with the estimator of Q based on solved 2SLS estimates of A, as these cannot be ranked in asymptotic efficiency relative to $\bar{Q}$, the resulting estimator of a_i cannot be ranked relative to 2SLS (compare sections 3.3 and 4.7).

Also, the consistency of this estimator of a_i depends on Q_1 being consistent for Q. Finally, if the 'two-stage' form $(Q_1 Z' Z Q_1' a_{3i})^u$ is adopted for *all* the variables in X, from any values of Q_1 satisfying the *a priori* restrictions on A, $Q_1' a_{3i} = 0$ and the initial estimates are reproduced (see Basmann and Bakony, 1961).

4.4 Instrumental Variables

Equation (13.29) is an IV estimator using $\tilde{X}' = Q_1 Z'$ as the set of instruments, thus exploiting the independence of the exogenous variables and the errors (see Sargan, 1958). Further, as Q 'weights' the Zs in linear combinations for each Y_j according to how important a determiner of that Y_j the various Zs are in the reduced form this provides an 'optimal' set of instruments (compare McCarthy, 1972). Note that the IV estimator remains consistent even when plim $Q_1 \neq Q$, and that a vast range of choices for Q_1 exists. In particular we have $Q_1 = \bar{Q}$ (*2SLS*), $Q_1 = \hat{Q}$ (in (13.32)) (LIML) and also $Q_1 = \tilde{Q}$ which yields the iterated IV estimator.

4.5 Iterated Instrumental Variables

This iterated IV is the 'limited information' analogue of section 3.5 (see Brundy and Jorgenson, 1971). From any IV estimator $\tilde{A}$ of A, solve for $\tilde{Q}$ from (13.10)(iii) and (13.10)(iv) and compute

$$(\tilde{Q}Z' X a_i)^u = 0. \tag{13.38}$$

Further iteration will not affect the asymptotic distribution; note that IV and this estimator are computable for $k > T > m$ (m regressors) whereas 2SLS is not (see, however, Fisher and Wadycki, 1971).

4.6 κ-class

The κ-class uses (13.23) with $\kappa^* = \kappa I$ for $Q_1 Z'$ in (13.29) or can be obtained from $\kappa = 1/(1 + \lambda)$ for arbitrary λ in (13.35) and hence cannot be written explicitly as a product of Q and Z for $\kappa \neq 1$ or $1/(1 + \hat{\lambda})$ (see Theil, 1961). As noted above, a sufficient condition for consistency is plim $\kappa = 1$; but κ-class only have the same asymptotic distribution as LIML if plim $T^{1/2}(\kappa - 1) = 0$. Thus $\kappa = 1 \pm 1/T^{1/2}$ does *not* yield an LIML asymptotically efficient estimator, despite satisfying the estimator generating equation (13.29) asymptotically.

Eliminating the predetermined variables from (13.35), we can reformulate LIML (relating it to the least generalized residual variance principle) such that we require the smallest latent root of $|F_d - \lambda F_c| = 0$, where $F_d = Y_c' (I - M_c) Y_c$ and $F_c = Y_c' (I - M) Y_c$, Z_c and Y_c are all the included exogenous and endogenous regressors in the relevant equation, respectively, and $M_c = Z_c (Z_c' Z_c)^{-1} Z_c'$. Since κ-class comprises all values of κ, we have the well-known alternative interpretation that 2SLS is κ-class with $\kappa = 1$, and ordinary least squares (OLS) is κ-class with $\kappa = 0$ etc. (the choice of other appropriate values of κ has been considered by Nagar (1959) and Sawa (1973)).

A convenient summary of the effects of varying κ is provided by Farebrother (1974).

4.7 Fix Point

While fix point (FP) uses a reformulated interdependent (REID) system specification this does not preclude its derivation in the above framework (see Mosbaek and Wold, 1970; Maddala, 1971a; Lyttkens, 1973). Normalizing on the diagonal of B, in structural predictor form the REID specification has $B = (I - B^*)$ with B^* having zeros on its diagonal and postulates

$$Y' = B^* Y^{*\prime} - CZ' + W', \tag{13.39}$$

where $W' = (I - B^*)^{-1} E'$ as in (13.6),

$$Y^{*\prime} = \mathscr{E}(Y' | Y^{*\prime}, Z')$$

and hence

$$\mathscr{E}(Y^{*\prime} W) = \mathscr{E}(Z' W) = 0,$$

so that on taking expectations in (13.39)

$$Y^{*\prime} = B^* Y^{*\prime} - CZ' = -(I - B^*)^{-1} CZ' = \Pi Z'. \tag{13.40}$$

If Y^* was *known*, the coefficients in (13.39) could be estimated by OLS, but empirical implementation necessitates estimating Y^* which yields a non-linear problem in the parameters B^*, C, Y^*. One of the proposed algorithms (Mosbaek and Wold, 1970, p. 128) is as follows. Given any initial value Y_1 of Y^* (e.g. from $Y_1 = Z\Pi_1'$ with Π_1 based on 2SLS estimates of A) apply OLS to the empirical equivalent of (13.39). This involves regressing Y on Y_1 and Z to yield B_2^* and C_2 or, at the jth iteration,

$$Y' = B_j^* Y_{j-1}' - C_j Z' + W_j', \tag{13.41}$$

and one estimates B_j^* and C_j by OLS. From these generate Y_j using the empirical equivalent of (13.40) in *structural* form,

$$Y_j' = B_j^* Y_{j-1}' - C_j Z', \tag{13.42}$$

to update the iteration. The *fixed point* is defined by $B_j^* = B_{j-1}^*$, $C_j = C_{j-1}$, $Y_j = Y_{j-1}$ and hence if convergence occurs at the Jth iteration from (13.42) we have at $j = J$

$$Y_j' = -(I - B_j^*)^{-1} C_j Z' = \Pi_j Z', \tag{13.43}$$

as required from (13.40). The reduced form method of generating Y_j uses (13.43) for all values of j, although this might radically alter both the convergence properties and the values of B^*, C to which the iteration converges.

Despite the apparent gulf between this development and (13.10), FP is a straightforward special case of our generating formula using the modification to (13.20)(ii) with $ZQ_1' = \tilde{X} = (Y_j : Z)$ and $\Sigma_2 = I$, where Y_j is generated by either of the structural or reduced form methods. Thus FP is also an approximation to FIML, but by choosing (implicitly) $\Sigma_2 = I$ it is (under REID) inefficient relative to FIML. Further, by using a 'two-stage' reformulation (often called repeated least squares) the analysis in section 3.3 applies and the asymptotic distribution of the estimator of A depends on that of Q_1, such that if it converges it is asymptotically equivalent to iterative 2SLS. Thus, if (13.43) is used to generate Y_j (as in Edgerton, 1974), FP appears as an iterated 'two-stage' estimator, while an IV equivalent is provided in section 4.5. In comparing the various possibilities, Maddala (1971a) found that IV + (13.43) always converged (this is (13.38) applied to all equations and is LIML efficient), 'two-stage' + (13.42) was next best (this is FP), whereas the alternative pairings rarely converged. Since FP cannot be ranked in asymptotic efficiency compared with LIML, the 'two-stage' substitution has affected its statistical distribution while the generation of Y_j by (13.42) or (13.43) has equally clearly altered its numerical properties.

4.8 Single-equation Estimation

Trivially, if $n = 1$, (13.10) has OLS estimates as its solution.

Summarizing the development, the expression $(\Sigma^{-1} AX' ZQ')^r = 0$ defines the structure of simultaneous equations estimators and provides a simple means of creating new methods by using various estimators for Σ and Q, although this is an activity which by now must have a negligible marginal product.[4] All the available methods appear as numerical variants of (13.10), either of fixed s-steps (for small s) or iterative to convergence, using different initial values, treating ZQ_1' as two terms or as $\tilde{X}$, and solving the set of equations simultaneously or only partially. These variations can affect both the large- and the small-sample distribution properties, and (13.10) helps clarify these asymptotic equivalences as well as unifying the theory.

The former have been covered during the above discussion but space considerations prohibit surveying present research on the finite sample situation.

In closing this section, however, it seems worth pointing out that, to practitioners, the *true* structural specification of the system is rarely known and hence an equally valuable selection criterion between estimators is their robustness to misspecification. 'Two-stage' formulations (other than 2SLS) seem weaker here than IV estimates; equally, stochastic κ (LIML) also induces different susceptibility (see Fisher, 1966a). Greater information on this aspect seems desirable as it may be more important in guiding the choice of the estimator than formal small-sample properties assuming correct specification.

5 Single-equation Methods for Autoregressive Errors

The case $n = 1$ is denoted autoregressive least squares (ALS). While this is not a simultaneous equations problem any longer, similar principles apply and the interrelationships within this large subgroup can be substantially clarified by once more considering all the estimators as alternative numerical approximations to the maximum likelihood method. Further, this is a convenient problem for analysing case (1) in section 2, as it has all the essential non-linear complications while the two-parameter specialization (with one non-constant exogenous regressor) is a useful pedagogical device for graphical exposition of the various numerical optimization methods which have been proposed for implementing econometric estimators.

To simplify notation, write the equation of concern with unrestricted γ as

$$y = Z\gamma + w \qquad w = \rho w_l + e, \tag{13.44}$$

and let

$$Z^+ = Z - \rho Z_l, \tag{13.45}$$

so that

$$y^+ = Z^+\gamma + e.$$

Let $\theta = (\gamma, \rho)$, and note that the concentrated likelihood function (neglecting initial conditions), obtained by eliminating

$$\sigma^2 = T^{-1}e'e, \tag{13.46}$$

is

$$L(\theta) \propto -e'e = f(\theta).$$

Thus the estimator generating equation specializes to $(q = \partial f / \partial \theta)$

$$q(\theta) = \begin{bmatrix} Z^{+\prime}e \\ w_l'e \end{bmatrix} = 0. \tag{13.47}$$

Further, it is useful to record $-\partial q/\partial \theta$ (dropping asymptotically negligible terms):

$$\begin{bmatrix} Z^{+\prime}Z^+ & Z^{+\prime}w_l \\ w_l'Z^+ & w_l'w_l \end{bmatrix} = F(\theta). \tag{13.48}$$

5.1 Maximum Likelihood Estimation of (γ, ρ) (Autoregressive Least Squares)

The maximum likelihood estimator solves equation (13.47) for $\hat{\theta}$ which maximizes[5] $f(\theta)$, and since the equations are non-linear in γ and ρ some iterative algorithm must be adopted. The framework of section 2 is convenient, in particular equation (13.9),

$$\theta_{j+1} = \theta_j + \lambda_j G_j g_j \qquad j = 1, \ldots, J$$

and the set

$$(\theta_1, \lambda, G, g, J) = \Phi.$$

Stepwise Optimization

Choose $\Phi_a = (0, 1, (F^*)^{-1}, q, J)$ where F^* is F with $Z^{+\prime} w_l = 0$ which induces separate estimation of γ and ρ (see Cochrane and Orcutt, 1949). Since $q(\theta) = 0$ implies

$$\begin{pmatrix} Z^{+\prime} y^+ - Z^{+\prime} Z^+ \gamma \\ w_l' w - \rho w_l' w_l \end{pmatrix} = 0,$$

we have

(i)
$$\begin{pmatrix} \gamma \\ \rho \end{pmatrix} = \begin{pmatrix} (Z^{+\prime} Z^+)^{-1} Z^{+\prime} y^+ \\ (w_l' w_l)^{-1} w_l' w \end{pmatrix},$$
(ii)
$$\tag{13.49}$$

and hence the alternative stepwise interpretation which exploits the property that, given ρ, (13.49)(i) is linear in γ and, given γ, (13.49)(ii) is linear in ρ. These calculations are just successive OLS estimations and hence every step produces an increase in the likelihood and the procedure converges with probability unity (see Sargan, 1964a).

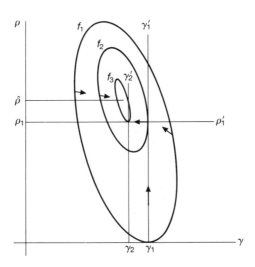

Figure 13.1 Iso-contours of the likelihood function: →, increasing values; subscripts, the number of the iteration.

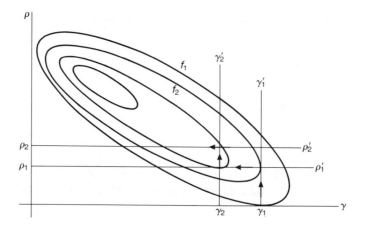

Figure 13.2 Iso-likelihood contours for correlated parameters.

For one regressor this is just 'axial search', a method which has received considerable criticism for its computational inefficiency (see Box et al., 1969; Dixon, 1972; Klein, 1974, p. 92). Figure 13.1 portrays the situation for exogenous Z. The plots show iso-contours of the likelihood function, with the arrow denoting increasing values and subscripts denoting the number of the iteration. Thus, γ_1 is the OLS estimate ignoring autocorrelation and ρ_1 is the estimate of ρ based on OLS residuals ($\approx \frac{1}{2}(2 - DW)$ where DW denotes the Durbin–Watson statistic.

From equation (13.48) using the same argument as in (13.13), if $y_1 \notin \{Z\}$ any consistent estimator of ρ will yield an asymptotically efficient estimator of γ and conversely (*hence* the diagnostic value of DW). But ρ_1 will be close to $\hat{\rho}$ only if the contours are approximately circular, or are 'vertical' ellipses. The rate of convergence (and the closeness to the optimum achieved by the first few steps) thus depends on the shape and slope of the contours and could be slow if these are elongated in a

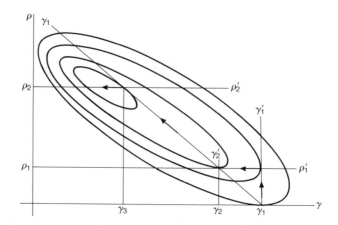

Figure 13.3 Direction of total progress after three axial searches.

direction which is parallel to neither axis. Such is likely to occur when the lagged dependent variable is a regressor, which illustrates why DW is then not a useful statistic (see figure 13.2). In effect, this is a criticism of the initial value $(0, 0)$ used to commence this algorithm, although in practice any pair $(\tilde{\gamma}, \tilde{\rho})$ could be used. Further, the choice of $\lambda_j = 1 \; \forall j$ is not optimal for dynamic equations and choosing λ_j to maximize $f[\theta_j + \lambda_j F^*(\theta_j)^{-1} q(\theta_j)]$ at every iteration (which is a scalar line search in the direction of total progress – see figure 13.3 and the section 'Conjugate Directions' below) considerably alleviates the slow convergence problem (especially if combined with sensible θ_1) while retaining the advantage of κ-dimensional conditional optimization without search.[6] Note that this section does *not* justify the use of *ad hoc* successive substitution methods, but merely the subset that corresponds to stepwise maximization of some criterion function (see section 5.4).

Grid Search

Since $-1 < \rho < 1$ for stationarity, the optimum can be located within ± 0.1 using a grid of steps of 0.1 (requiring the equivalent of 19 iterations of the above procedure). This corresponds to solving equation (13.49)(i) for successive least squares estimates of γ conditional on each value of $\rho \in \{-0.9, -0.8, \ldots, 0.9\}$, and choosing that $\tilde{\gamma}$ which yields the highest likelihood (see Hildreth and Lu, 1960). A 'finer' grid search by steps of 0.01 could then be undertaken for the interval of 0.2 which brackets $\tilde{\gamma}$. However, this would require a further 19 iterations to improve the precision to ± 0.01 and it seems definitely cheaper to switch to stepwise optimization at this point, as is often done (compare Klein, 1974, p. 92). A potential advantage of doing the first grid search is to reveal any multiple optima, provided that these are not sharp spikes. Graphically, of course, the grid is simply a series of 'line searches' (of the form $\rho_1 \rho_1'$ in figure 13.1) parallel to the γ axis by intervals of 0.1. Unlike stepwise optimization, it does not generalize usefully to other situations, including higher order autoregressive schemes. In terms of Φ, equation (13.9) is applied to stepwise optimization for $\theta = \gamma$ (i.e. ignoring equation (13.49)(ii)) with $J = 1$ but repeated for the grid over ρ using f purely as a criterion.

Newton–Raphson and Gauss–Newton

The Newton–Raphson and Gauss–Newton procedures use $\Phi_c = (\theta_1, 1, F^{-1}, q, J)$ (although λ_j chosen as suggested for stepwise optimization is not uncommon) (see Sargan, 1964a). If Z is strictly exogenous this will be slower than stepwise optimization as $Z^{+\prime} w_i = 0$ is approximately true. If $y_i \in \{Z\}$, $\theta_1 = 0$ is hopeless as then $F^{-1} q$ corresponds to regressing y on Z and y_i. If F in (13.48) is partition inverted, the first 'block' of $F^{-1} q$ is (for general θ_j)

$$\gamma_{j+1} = \gamma_j + (Z^{+\prime} M^* Z^+)^{-1} (Z^{+\prime} M^* e)|_{\theta = \theta_j}$$

$$= (Z^{+\prime} M^* Z^+)^{-1} (Z^{+\prime} M^* y^+)|_{\theta = \theta_j} \tag{13.50}$$

where $M^* = I - w_i (w_i' w_i)^{-1} w_i'$ so that $M^* Z^+$ are the residuals from regressing Z^+ on w_i. Thus Gauss–Newton is simply a stepwise method with the additional step of computing M^*Z^+ in place of Z^+ and so existing programs for stepwise optimization can be easily converted.[7] Combined with optimizing over λ_j and using consistent estimates $(\tilde{\gamma}, \tilde{\rho})$ for θ_1 this provides an inexpensive algorithm, which virtually always converges. Variants of Gauss–Newton (including those based on numerically evaluating first derivatives) have been extensively used for estimating moving-average error models (see *inter alia* Hendry and Trivedi, 1972; Williams, 1972; Marquardt, 1963; Box and Jenkins, 1976).

In graphical terms, q defines the gradient while $-F^{-1}$ is negative definite and defines the metric such that, for a quadratic, their product maps θ_1 into the maximum. Note that steepest descent is just $\Phi_s = (\theta_1, -1, I, q, J)$, but, if λ_j is optimized, this is the same as stepwise optimization for $k = 1$. Also quadratic hill climbing (see Goldfeld and Quandt, 1972) combines Φ_c and Φ_s in $\Phi_q = (\theta_1, 1, (F + \mu I)^{-1}, q, J)$, where μ is chosen to ensure that $(F + \mu I)$ is positive definite. This has been successfully used for autoregressive FIML, but for $n = 1$ is unlikely to surpass equation (13.50).

Variable Metric or Quasi-Newton

The variable metric or quasi-Newton estimator is $\Phi_d = (\theta_1, \lambda, G_j, q, J)$, where G_j evolves during the iteration by $G_{j+1} = G_j + D_j$ such that $G_1 = I$ and $G_J = F^{-1}$ (see Powell, 1972). Thus the Davidon–Fletcher–Powell (DFP) algorithm chooses

$$D_j = (\Delta\theta_j \Delta\theta_j' / \Delta\theta_j' \Delta g_j) - (G_j \Delta g_j \Delta g_j' G_j / \Delta g_j' G_j \Delta g_j), \tag{13.51}$$

where

$$\Delta\theta_j = \theta_{j+1} - \theta_j \quad \text{and} \quad \Delta g_j = q(\theta_{j+1}) - q(\theta_j),$$

whereas Broyden's rank-one algorithm uses ($J \geqslant k + 1$)

$$D_j = (\Delta\theta_j - G_j \Delta g_j)(\Delta\theta_j - G_j \Delta g_j)' / (\Delta\theta_j - G_j \Delta g_j)' \Delta g_j, \tag{13.52}$$

(see, for example, Dixon, 1972).

Applied to any non-linear maximum likelihood estimator (of which ALS is just an example) these make for reasonably fast algorithms which only require f and q to be programmed and hence are quite easy to implement if, for example, DFP is already 'packaged'.

Conjugate Directions

In fact, an important advantage of the conjugate directions approach is that it does not even require the first derivatives and operates from values of the likelihood function only (see Powell, 1964; Hendry, 1971). By appropriate use of the concentrated likelihood function to map the problem into the lowest possible dimensional space, it can provide a computationally efficient (and easily programmed) algorithm.

In two dimensions, the stepwise optimization approach was shown to be that of axial search. Now, after one search has been accomplished in each axis direction from $(\gamma_1, 0)$ to locate (γ_2, ρ_1), the direction of total progress is defined by the vector difference

$$\begin{pmatrix} \gamma_2 - \gamma_1 \\ \rho_1 \end{pmatrix}$$

and, since this shows the direction in which the parameter values are changing, it is a good direction to investigate, as is obvious from figure 13.3. The optimum in that direction can be located by any line search procedure (e.g. fitting a quadratic and choosing the optimum of the quadratic). Further, this defines a search direction which is not parallel to the original (perpendicular) axes but is closer to the elongation of the ellipses. In fact, since (γ_2, ρ_1) and $(\gamma_1, 0)$ are both maxima of the function in the direction of the γ axis (corresponding to different values of ρ), for a quadratic their difference is conjugate to that direction. Thus, a set of conjugate directions can be constructed by retaining all (non-collinear) directions of total progress. Further, given a set of conjugate directions, the maximum of a quadratic of k variables can be located by exactly one search in each direction. Thus, assuming that the likelihood function can be reasonably approximated by a quadratic in the neighbourhood of the optimum, Powell's algorithm will be quadratically convergent. In practice, however, for *this application*, because it does not exploit the bilinearity of the scalar autocorrelation case, it tends to be slower than stepwise optimization (for autoregressive FIML its performance is often impressive). Thus we have $\Phi_e = (\theta_1, \lambda, I, g, J)$ where g represents $k + 1$ search directions in each iteration for (γ, ρ) (updated as above) commencing from the co-ordinate axes.

Iterated to the same convergence accuracy these algorithms all define the *same* estimator (ALS), but we can also consider the class of approximations to (13.47). An additional notation is very convenient here, namely (noting that lagged values are always denoted by l) define

$$Z_1^+ = Z - \rho_1 Z_l,$$

$$e_2 = y_2^+ - Z_2^+ \gamma_2 \quad \text{etc.,} \tag{13.53}$$

so that we derive estimators by solving

$$\begin{array}{l} \text{(i)} \\ \text{(ii)} \end{array} \begin{bmatrix} Z_3^{+\prime} e_3 \\ (y_l - Z_l \gamma_2)^\prime e_2 \end{bmatrix} = 0. \tag{13.54}$$

If $y_l \in \{Z\}$ efficient estimation of $\gamma(\rho)$ is required for $\rho(\gamma)$.

5.2 Linearized Autoregressive Least Squares

Linearized ALS is in fact just one step of equation (13.50), i.e. $\Phi_2 = (\theta_1, 1, F_1^{-1}, q_1, 1)$, where $(\theta_1 - \hat{\theta}) = O(1/T^{1/2})$ (see Hatanaka, 1974). Hence from a first-order Taylor series expansion $(\theta_2 - \hat{\theta}) = O(1/T)$ and so one iteration produces an asymptotically efficient (if somewhat arbitrary) estimator. $\theta_1 = \tilde{\theta}$ based on purely exogenous regressors seems a reasonable choice. (Compare Sargan (1964a) and the following discussion.)

5.3 Two-step Estimation

Two-step estimation uses (13.54)(ii) to solve for ρ_2 from $\gamma_2 = \tilde{\gamma}$ (a consistent IV estimator) and then solves (13.54)(i) for γ_3 (actually the closely related Aitken expression is used: see Wallis, 1967). While not asymptotically efficient for dynamic equations (see Maddala, 1971b) the efficiency loss does not appear to be large (see Wallis, 1972b; Hatanaka, 1974). Thus $\Phi_2 = (0, 1, F^{*-1}(\theta_2), q(\theta_2), 1)$, where $\theta_2 = (\tilde{\gamma}, \rho_2)$.

Other variations are quite possible, but to repeat, if y_l is a regressor, non-iterative estimators other than those described in section 5.2 will not be fully efficient asymptotically.

5.4 Lagged Residual Methods

A rather different approach to 'treating' autocorrelation has been based on a modification of (13.44), namely (see Gupta, 1969; Feldstein, 1970)

$$y = Z\gamma + \rho w_l + e. \tag{13.55}$$

From any consistent estimator $\tilde{\gamma}$ of γ calculate $\tilde{w}$ from $(y - Z\tilde{\gamma})$, substitute this lagged for w_l in equation (13.55) and estimate γ and ρ by least squares. The method can be iterated, estimating at each step

$$y = Z\gamma_j + \rho_j(y_l - Z_l\gamma_{j-1}) + e_j, \tag{13.56}$$

until the fixed point $\gamma_j = \gamma_{j-1}$, $\rho_j = \rho_{j-1}$ is reached. Each stage of the iterate (except calculating $(y_l - Z_l\gamma_{j-1})$) requires the minimization of $e_j'e_j$ and at the optimum the estimates satisfy the non-linear restriction on the restricted transformed relationship of equation (13.45). But appearances can be deceptive for the formulation in terms of (13.56) stops this from being a fully efficient solution to (13.54). Heuristically, equation (13.54)(i) is obtained by allowing *both* γs in (13.56) to vary simultaneously whereas applying OLS to equation (13.56) holds the γ_{j-1} multiplying Z_l *fixed*. Indeed, the least squares equations for (13.55) are

$$\begin{pmatrix} Z' \\ w_l' \end{pmatrix} e = 0, \tag{13.57}$$

and hence for $\rho \neq 0$ these yield different results from equation (13.54). (I am grateful to Honor Stamler for this analysis.) In practice, recalculating w_l means that successive iterates of equation (13.56) can lead to increases in the residual sum of squares, and in addition are inefficient (compare section 4.7) and provide conditional standard errors (see Grether and Maddala, 1972).

6 Conclusion

Virtually every known (classical) econometric estimator for dynamic or static systems or single equations, with or without autoregressive errors, appears as a *numerical approximation* to the maximum likelihood (first derivative) equations. Further, this formulation clarifies for which 'nuisance' parameters efficient estimation is directly required and for which consistent estimation suffices (in not affecting the asymptotic distribution of the main parameters of interest). By appropriate choice of the numerical algorithm, asymptotically efficient estimators can be obtained in a few steps whereas the same number of steps using similar but less efficient algorithms yields statistically inefficient results. The forms of equations (13.10) and (13.47) generalize directly to higher order or vector autocorrelation, spectral estimation (see Espasa, 1977), non-linear parameters etc., and a similar approach could be adopted. Equally, the approach of section 5 can be applied to clarify alternative estimators for models with moving-average errors.

If criteria other than asymptotic efficiency and computational cost are used the choice of the approximation (if any) remains an open question. For example, problems of finite sample distribution (e.g. the existence of moments) or robustness may have to be judged against the powerful arguments in favour of using the likelihood for inference (see Edwards, 1972) and the objectivity of maximum likelihood estimators. Nevertheless, I hope that the present result helps elucidate the structure of simultaneous equations estimators so that such questions can be more easily tackled.

Notes

1 For example, by allowing for identities, lagged endogenous variables, non-normal errors etc., which do not affect the asymptotic results (see, for example, Mann and Wald, 1943).
2 Hausman (1975) has proposed an IV interpretation of FIML, providing an alternative grouping system. Also, compare Chow (1964) and Malinvaud (1970, ch. 19).
3 This can also be derived from (13.10); see equation (13.25).
4 For example, consider applying generalized least squares using a consistent estimator of Ω at each step estimating (13.41) in place of OLS; i.e. solve (13.20)(ii) with consistent Σ_2 etc.
5 Again ignoring initial conditions.
6 The standard errors of the estimated coefficients provided by these intermediate regressions are of course conditional standard errors which ignore the variability of the estimator of ρ; specializing (13.48) yields the correct result and this coincides with the conditional estimates only if $y_l \notin \{Z\}$.
7 Note that equation (13.50) is equivalent to regressing y^+ on Z^+ and w_l (compare Hatanaka, 1974).

14

AUTOREG: a Computer Program Library for Dynamic Econometric Models with Autoregressive Errors

with Frank Srba

Preamble

No matter how powerful and general econometric theory may become, it is only of operational value after it has been implemented in computer software. Like many other disciplines over the last quarter century, econometrics has been serviced by an ever increasing number of computer packages. Most econometric software has embodied an implicit methodology and modelling approach, but widely distributed programs have usually lagged some years behind the state-of-the-art technical econometric frontier. Consequently, a large share of my research time has always been devoted to programming in order to implement the various estimators, tests and modelling strategies discussed above, leading to the AUTOREG library described in the present chapter.

The evolution of AUTOREG mirrors the story of the methodological developments described in earlier chapters. Initially, the programs focused on 'optimal estimation' based on the implicit assumption that the dynamic models under study were more or less correctly specified. The tests offered were mainly tests of model specification, where the null was just a special case of an already estimated more general model. Then an increasing number of diagnostic tests was included for mis-specification (see, for example, Mizon, 1977a) gradually leading to the implementation of 'model building' procedures. In parallel, the Monte Carlo simulation programs evolved to allow the properties of the various new methods to be studied in finite samples, as well as to embody advances in Monte Carlo methods.

I have always found computer programming to be an intellectually challenging activity.

Reprinted from *Journal of Econometrics*, 12 (1980) 85–102. We are grateful to the Computer Unit at LSE for considerable help in preparing AUTOREG, to Ray Byron, Carol Hewlett, Grayham Mizon, Denis Sargan, Juri Sylwestrowicz, Pravin Trivedi and Ross Williams for invaluable advice at many stages during the last decade, to Robin Harrison and Andrew Tremayne for assistance in developing several of the programs and to Raija Thomson for organizing and typing much of the documentation for the library. Initial versions of most of the programs in AUTOREG were written by Hendry in partial fulfilment of the requirements for the PhD degree at London University. Developments to AUTOREG since July 1973 have been financed in part by a grant from the United Kingdom Social Science Research Council to the Econometrics Methodology and Quantitative Economics Projects at the London School of Economics.

It is extremely difficult to write software code that will function in the wide range of situations to which a user community will certainly subject it, often involving circumstances totally unanticipated by the programmer. Locating the source or sources of a given problem, and correcting it so that no further bugs are induced, involves similar considerations to empirical modelling: detective work, creative insights, discovery processes, luck and serendipity all play a role, combined with an understanding of the behaviour and complexities of simultaneous interdependences and dynamics. Moreover, the detection and elimination of a bug involves an uncertain time horizon and all too often represents the outcome of an apparently unconnected mistake whose consequences materialize only from an interaction with a rarely triggered state. The tactics of debugging are of course distinctly different from those of econometric modelling, since the code system does not itself adapt to changed inputs, allowing detailed 'experimentation' to determine the causes of errors. The strategy is nevertheless very similar – collect evidence, think hard, test conjectures and develop encompassing explanations for the phenomena observed during the experiments. Once you have successfully programmed an econometric technique, you really understand it. Thus, there is a useful direct symbiosis between the econometric technology and its implementation, as well as the indirect one of acquiring knowledge as to the practical performance of new proposals.

This chapter records the structure and state of AUTOREG in 1978–9 (in sections 5 and 6), and describes both its validation (section 7) and the relative costs of the different modules (section 8). In addition, it summarizes several of the theorems from chapter 13, to emphasize the distinctions between

1 the *discovery* problem of finding a suitable model specification (section 1),
2 the *estimation* problem of exactly or approximately solving the score equations via the estimator generating equation for a given model specification (section 2),
3 the *numerical* problem of maximizing any specific likelihood function $\mathscr{L}(\theta)$ (section 3), and
4 the *statistical* problem of formulating $\mathscr{L}(\theta)$ (section 1) and subsequently analysing the properties of estimators (section 4).

These four problems determined the structure of the software which thereby explicitly embodied the methodology of part II above. Thus, the numerical and statistical aspects were closely linked, the likelihood function was the core of every analysis and associated tests were based on the likelihood. Because statistical tests are relatively specific to the null and alternative envisaged and often raise no new issues of programming, the chapter under-represents their importance in the software library: as noted earlier, many users of AUTOREG regarded it as a tool kit for model destruction!

The developments envisaged in section 9 did in fact take place (see Chong and Hendry (1986, 1990) for the distributed array processor implementation, and Hendry (1986c, 1989) for descriptions of the data handling module), but these were not the major changes to come. Shortly after this chapter appeared, the microcomputer revolution brought forth inexpensive, yet powerful, standardized personal computers (PCs) with interactive graphics capabilities. High quality general software also rapidly appeared and stimulated concurrent advances in econometrics software. To exploit this technological advance and implement the continually evolving methodology, AUTOREG has been converted to a PC format in the form of the PC-GIVE and PC-NAIVE systems. As recorded in Hendry (1989), however, had I correctly appraised the effort that would be involved, I would not have started the conversion. First, the change from batch processing to menu-driven graphics-oriented interactive computing, with stringent checks to avoid 'crashing', increased the code size fivefold: I had guessed it would double. The resulting programs soon reached the upper bounds of PC capabilities. Second, PC users grew accustomed to excellent and powerful general packages for word processing, databases and spreadsheets, and demanded similar quality products in econometrics. A part-time programmer could not easily attain the required standards. Third, I had absorbed the implications of the approach described in chapters 15–17 and this necessitated a major restructuring of the econometrics routines (the 'hard software') as well as the surrounding code in which it was embodied ('soft software'). Fourth, new econometrics techniques and tests had appeared and the library needed to be extended to include them (especially recursive procedures). Finally, users demanded superior and detailed documentation, including explanations of the econometrics as well as the software.

The consequence was an almost total rewrite of the code which involved several thousand hours of evening and weekend input over six years and virtually overwhelmed me. Fortunately, compilers and linkers improved to cope with the increasing code size; and I benefited from Adrian Neale's skills and code in developing routines for PC-NAIVE (see Hendry and Neale, 1987). Despite the effort involved, I think the result is worthwhile. PC-GIVE offers an implementation of the methodology to anyone who wishes to adopt or try it; it has substantially improved my teaching with live classroom demonstrations; it sustains live presentations of empirical research to establish the credibility of econometric evidence; it has helped clarify system modelling (see Hendry et al., 1988); and it has dramatically reduced the time taken to complete empirical research. Indeed, chapter 12 already reflected the resulting leap in the productivity of empirical modelling relative to the mainframe batch processing underlying chapter 11. PC-NAIVE was released in March 1991, and it too is a boon to teaching through enabling the creation and revision of Monte Carlo experiments in about a minute and their execution by recursive simulation in a few minutes (see Hendry et al., 1991). Since the program is again menu driven, and almost uncrashable, it is easy to demonstrate the finite sample behaviour of econometric methods in the classroom. Thus, PC-AUTOREG has replaced the batch programs described in the following chapter but with a closely related interactive system (now into version 7: see Doornik and Hendry, 1992).

1 Econometric Background

The general model around which the AUTOREG Library is formulated comprises a linear dynamic simultaneous equations system with autoregressive errors of the form

$$\sum_{i=0}^{n} B(\theta)_i y_{t-i} + \sum_{i=0}^{l} C(\theta)_i z_{t-i} = u_t \qquad t = 1, \ldots, T, \tag{14.1}$$

where

$$\sum_{i=0}^{r} R_i u_{t-i} = e_t \qquad R_0 = I \tag{14.2}$$

and

$$\sum_{i=0}^{s} D_i z_{t-i} = v_t \qquad D_0 = I \tag{14.3}$$

with e_t and v_t being unobservable vectors of random variables which for analytical convenience are assumed to behave as

$$e_t \sim \text{NI}(0, \Omega) \qquad v_t \sim \text{NI}(0, \Phi) \qquad \mathcal{E}(e_t v_s') = 0 \qquad \forall t, s \tag{14.4}$$

where Ω and Φ are finite positive definite matrices.[1]

In (14.1), y_t and z_t are $p \times 1$ and $m \times 1$ vectors of observations on the jointly determined and 'exogenous' variables respectively. The κ non-zero non-normalized coefficents in the B_i and C_i matrices are functions of $k \leqslant \kappa$ unrestricted parameters θ, the appropriate restrictions being derived from whatever theory accounts for the determination of y_t. The system is assumed to be stationary and linear after suitable transformations of the discrete-time data series and hence all the roots of the polynominal matrices in h,

$$\sum_{i=0}^{n} B_i h^i \qquad \sum_{i=0}^{r} R_i h^i \qquad \sum_{i=0}^{s} D_i h^i,$$

must lie outside the unit circle.

Given (14.4), the log-likelihood function for (14.1) + (14.2) conditional on the zs and initial values of the ys is

$$L(\theta, R_1, \ldots, R_r, \Omega) = K_0 + T \ln \|B_0\| - \tfrac{1}{2} T \ln |\Omega| - \tfrac{1}{2} \mathrm{tr} \left(\Omega^{-1} \sum_{t=N}^{T} e_t e_t' \right), \quad (14.5)$$

where[2]

$$e_t = \sum_{i=0}^{r} R_i \left(\sum_{j=0}^{n} B(\theta)_j y_{t-j-i} + \sum_{j=0}^{l} C(\theta)_j z_{t-j-i} \right) \qquad (14.6)$$

and $N = \max(l + r + 1, n + r + 1)$. Clearly, $L(\cdot)$ is a very complicated function in a high dimensional space and hence considerable summarization is essential if any progress is to be made. This can be done in a number of stages.

First, $L(\cdot)$ itself may be summarized in terms of its first two derivatives (compare Edwards, 1972) leading to maximum likelihood estimation (MLE) (or quasi-MLE if e_t is not normally distributed). Let ψ denote the vector of unrestricted arguments of $L(\cdot)$ in (14.5) and let $L(\hat{\psi}) = \max_\psi L(\psi)$; then obtaining $\hat{\psi}$ given any data set is purely a numerical problem, albeit one requiring non-linear optimization methods and raising difficult issues of efficient computation and finding global rather than just local optima: optimization is considered in section 3 below.

Frequently, it is computationally efficient to locate $\hat{\psi}$ by solving $\partial L / \partial \psi = q(\psi)$ $= 0$ subject to $(\partial^2 L / \partial \psi \partial \psi')|_{\hat{\psi}} = Q(\hat{\psi})$ being negative definite and this suggests a further simplification through approximating the solution of $q(\psi) = 0$. Such an idea leads to the 'estimator generating equation' approach and is discussed in section 2.

Further valid summarization cannot be achieved in general simply by ignoring information (e.g. neglecting equations which are not of direct interest) since the joint occurrence of system autocorrelation and dynamics enforces system estimation techniques. However, special cases of (14.1) and (14.2) may occur either validly or as a result of the arbitrary imposition of restrictions. Such specializations are usually more tractable than the initial problem, and for computational efficiency require separate programs, as discussed in section 5.

All the preceding summaries of $L(\psi)$ can be classified as 'optimal estimation' in that, subject to some resource constraint, an investigator seeks the best estimates he can obtain for a pre-specified model. In practice, the correct specification of the model is unknown and so various estimators might be tried together with a range of tests of specification and mis-specification (see Mizon, 1977b) and AUTOREG is designed to aid such 'model building'. However, the same point leads to a distinction between the properties of the 'true' data generation process and those of the 'assumed' model and hence the need to study the behaviour of estimators and tests in both appropriate and inappropriate applications. In turn, numerical efficiency requires that, if this is to be done by stochastic simulation experiments, then an asymptotic analysis should be conducted at the same time. Consequently, numerical values of the data population second moments must be computed.

Consider the case $n = r = s = 1$ and $l = 0$ so that the transformed reduced form of (14.1) + (14.2) is given by

$$y_t = -B_0^{-1}[(B_1 - RB_0)y_{t-1} + (C_0D_1 - RC_0)z_{t-1} - RB_1y_{t-2} + (e_t + C_0v_t)]$$

$$= \pi_1 y_{t-1} + \pi_2 y_{t-2} + \pi_3 z_{t-1} + \omega_t, \tag{14.7}$$

and hence the system (14.1)–(14.3) can be represented in companion form as

$$\begin{pmatrix} y_t \\ y_{t-1} \\ z_t \end{pmatrix} = \begin{bmatrix} \pi_1 & \pi_2 & \pi_3 \\ I & 0 & 0 \\ 0 & 0 & D_1 \end{bmatrix} \begin{bmatrix} y_{t-1} \\ y_{t-2} \\ z_{t-1} \end{bmatrix} + \begin{bmatrix} \omega_t \\ 0 \\ v_t \end{bmatrix} \tag{14.8}$$

or, in an obvious notation,

$$f_t = \Delta f_{t-1} + \xi_t. \tag{14.9}$$

A similar procedure will yield the companion form of (14.1)–(14.3) for general values of n, r, s and l as a suitably stacked first-order vector autoregression as in (14.9) (a further reason for choosing the name AUTOREG for the library: note that stationarity requires all the eigenvalues of Δ to have modulus less than unity). By construction, $\mathscr{E}(\xi_t \xi_s') = 0$, $\forall t \neq s$, and letting $\mathscr{E}(\xi_t \xi_t') = \Gamma$ then

$$\mathscr{E}(f_t f_t') = M_0 = \Delta M_1' + \Gamma = \Delta M_0 \Delta' + \Gamma, \tag{14.10}$$

where

$$\mathscr{E}(f_t f_{t-1}') = M_1 = \Delta M_0 \tag{14.11}$$

and hence

$$M_0^v = (I - \Delta \otimes \Delta)^{-1} \Gamma^v, \tag{14.12}$$

where v denotes column vectoring and $\otimes$ the associated Kronecker product. Thus for given values of B_i, C_i, R_i, D_i, Ω and Φ, (Δ, Γ) can be formed and M_0, M_1 can be calculated from (14.11) and (14.12) (useful checks on the calculations are provided by common elements in M_0 and M_1). Finally, the appropriate terms from these population second moments can be used to calculate plims of estimators, asymptotic standard errors, control variables for Monte Carlo experiments and so on as described in more detail in section 4 (the actual Monte Carlo programs are described in section 6).

Several special features of the data generation process (14.9) were deliberately assumed above without comment to clarify the exposition, and are not an inherent limitation on the underlying econometric model. For example, measurement error problems can be tackled using certain of the instrumental variables estimators; variables which are redundant when lagged are usually automatically eliminated when testing dynamic specification and so on. More importantly, perhaps, the 'closure' assumption (14.3) is adopted purely for simplicity and it would not affect the basic analysis to allow lagged ys to influence z_t; in any case, such an assumption is testable should one wish to explain the behaviour of the z_t but it is assumed below that the likelihood function for z_t contains negligible information about θ (see Florens et al., 1976).

Further, the common factor restrictions embodied in (14.2) are also testable and provide additional evidence on the validity of the dynamic specification (see Sargan (1964a, 1980a) for the single-equation case and chapter 6 for an exposition and application; Sargan (1978) and Yeo (1978) discuss the vector case using Wald procedures, and Hendry and Tremayne (1976) provide a reduced form illustration based on the likelihood ratio principle).

The moving-average error case is not explicitly included in the library since many other investigators have developed algorithms (see, *inter alia*, Trivedi, 1970; Box and Jenkins, 1976; Osborn, 1976; Prothero and Wallis, 1976; Wall, 1976; Harvey and Phillips, 1979; with useful surveys provided by Aigner, 1971; Nicholls et al., 1975); also, to the orders of approximation involved in empirical research, autoregressive and moving-average errors seem reasonable proxies for each other (see Hendry and Trivedi, 1972; Godfrey, 1978). More general assumptions can be included without great difficulty: for example, using spectral methods (see Espasa and Sargan, 1977) leads to SPECFIML as implemented by Espasa (1977) using one of the AUTOREG programs as the basis.

Work on efficient treatment of missing data in dynamic systems (see Sargan and Drettakis, 1974) has also been implemented from the AUTOREG basis (see Drettakis, 1973).

If adequate data existed, direct estimation of the π_i in generalizations of (14.7) would be possible and would allow Wald tests of economic theory restrictions; generally, unfortunately, this is not possible, but interesting attempts at minimally constrained estimation are described in Sims (1977a, 1980). Finally, the existence of many different representations of the data (see, for example, Zellner and Palm, 1974; Prothero and Wallis, 1976; Hendry 1979b) poses very difficult problems for empirical research in the usual situation where the exact model specification is uncertain *a priori*; consequently, AUTOREG incorporates a large number of 'diagnostic tests' to aid 'model building' (see Leamer (1978) for an excellent discussion and critique of specification search procedures).

The inclusion of the likelihood term for initial conditions could significantly affect MLE final parameter values if any of the latent roots of the estimated dynamics were close to unity, since the asymptotic approximations involved cease to be accurate in such a situation. However, near non-stationarity may be better handled by reformulating the model than by arbitrarily imposing stationarity conditions and it is assumed that the former will be done so that (14.5) remains a good approximation to the complete log-likelihood function.

Aspects of program validation and development level are discussed in section 7 and approximate computing costs are noted in section 8. The concluding section describes some likely future developments.

2 Estimator Generation

Within the class of problems encompassed by (14.5) + (14.6), the present main constraint inhibiting frequency of use and/or the scale and complexity of problem which can be tackled is probably central processor unit (CPU) time. Since computational efficiency is of the essence, considerable effort has been (and is continuing to be) devoted to finding good procedures for the high-cost areas such as iterative optimization and stochastic simulation experiments. The theme of this and the next two sections is that these apparently dissimilar *numerical* areas are not only intimately interlinked but are also closely related to methods of *approximating* $q(\psi)$ which in turn may affect the *statistical* properties of the resulting procedure.

As noted above, once $L(\psi)$ is specified the statistical formulation is complete and locating the maximum of $L(\cdot)$ (either unrestrictedly or in any lower dimensional subspace) is a numerical problem. Any algorithm which is a well-defined rule mapping from a fixed data set to a unique[3] value of ψ denoted $\tilde{\psi}$ defines an estimator. All algorithms which attain $\hat{\psi}$ yield statistically equivalent results, but if an algorithm is selected which only ever calculates an *approximation* to $\max_\psi L(\psi)$ then this can affect the statistical properties of the estimator; i.e. depending on the algorithm, $\hat{\psi}$ and $\tilde{\psi}$ may or may not have equivalent statistical properties either in large or in finite samples. Conversely, different estimators can be interpreted as alternative numerical methods for approximating the optimum of $L(\cdot)$. As shown in chapter 13, this approach provides a convenient way of categorizing all extant econometric estimators through examining solutions of the equation $q(\psi) = 0$. To take a familiar example, where $r = 0$, let $A = (B_0 \ldots B_n C_0 \ldots C_l)$ and let $X = (x_1 \ldots x_T)'$, where $x_t' = (y_t' \ldots y_{t-n}'z_t' \ldots z_{t-l}') = (y_t' \; x_t^{*\prime})$ so that $Ax_t = e_t$ and $x_t = Hx_t^* + w_t$ with $\mathscr{E}(x_t^* w_t') = 0$; then $q(\theta)$ is given by

$$(\Omega^{-1}AX'X^*H')^\rho = 0. \tag{14.13}$$

where $(\;)^\rho$ denotes vectoring and retaining equations corresponding to unrestricted elements of A (i.e. $A^\rho = \theta$). Equation (14.13) defines the estimator generating equation (EGE) for the system $Ax_t = e_t \sim \mathrm{NI}(0, \Omega)$ and yields full information maximum likelihood (FIML), three-stage least squares (3SLS), limited information maximum likelihood (LIML), two-stage least squares (2SLS) etc. as solutions depending on the choices of estimators for the 'auxiliary' parameters Ω and H. Any consistent estimators for (Ω, H) will yield an estimator of A which is asymptotically equivalent to FIML whereas choosing the unit matrix for Ω and a consistent estimator for H yields the LIML-equivalent class and so on.

The important point about (14.13) is that, given any values for Ω^{-1} and H, the expression is linear in A and can be solved immediately. Thus a program written around (14.13) can produce a vast range of non-iterative estimators very flexibly and can use the output of (say) 3SLS to commence the optimization of $L(\cdot)$ for FIML. Of course, if one simply seeks *any* estimator which is asymptotically equivalent to FIML, then the program can be terminated after 3SLS or the full information instrumental variables estimator (FIVE) and in this sense the desired result has been achieved with considerable computational efficiency; although this may seem an unusual interpretation, obtaining non-iterative solutions and/or cheaply calculating good initial values are two important aspects of numerically efficient procedures.

3 Numerical Optimization

If FIML estimates are to be calculated, then Ω and H become functions of A, (14.13) becomes highly non-linear in θ and an iterative optimization method is required. Since the speeds of good and bad routines can differ by factors of many thousands, 'good' choices are of vital importance. Unfortunately the choice of a 'good' numerical optimization algorithm is not straightforward because no method is 'best' on all criteria (e.g. robustness, accuracy, flexibility, speed, scale independence and memory requirements) for all problems (e.g. varying numbers of parameters, forms of function etc.) in all circumstances (e.g. as machine structure and/or capital/labour costs vary). Nevertheless, reasonable choices are possible, although they tend to be problem and relative cost specific and primarily depend on the ease with which various analytical derivatives of $L(\cdot)$ can be calculated and programmed. Three situations of interest are when the following are available:

1 $L(\cdot)$ only;
2 $L(\cdot)$ and $q(\cdot)$ only;
3 $L(\cdot)$, $q(\cdot)$ and $Q(\cdot)$.

1   In the choice between conjugate directions such as the method of Powell (1964) and a variable metric method using finite differences such as Davidon–Fletcher–Powell (DFP, see, for example, Dixon, 1972) or Gill–Murray–Pitfield (1972) (GMP, see Wolfe, 1978) the latter seems generally much faster and (using the variant from the NAG library (1977)) rarely fails to converge. Note that having to program only $L(\cdot)$ trades considerable flexibility for altering programs against the costs of a (generally) slower algorithm.

2   When analytical first derivatives are also available, the corresponding variant of GMP seems excellent and is usually more efficient than DFP (see Sargan and Sylwestrowicz, 1976b). Thus instead of successively solving equations of the DFP form

$$\psi_{i+1} = \psi_i - \lambda_i K_i q(\psi_i) = \psi_i - \lambda_i \psi_i^c, \qquad i = 1, 2, \ldots, \tag{14.14}$$

where i denotes the iteration number, λ_i is a scalar chosen to $\max_{\lambda_i} L(\psi_i - \lambda_i \psi_i^c)$ and K_i is recursively updated to converge to $Q(\cdot)^{-1}$, GMP solves

$$P_i \psi_i^c = q(\psi_i) \quad \text{with} \quad P_i = G_i \Lambda_i G_i', \tag{14.15}$$

where Λ_i is diagonal and G_i is lower triangular with a unit diagonal. The solution to (14.15) is obtained by first solving for ϕ_i from $G_i \phi_i = q_i$ and then obtaining ψ_i^c

from $G_i' \psi_i^c = \Lambda_i^{-1} \phi_i$ where both sets of equations involve simple recursive formulae; P_i is then updated to ensure that P_{i+1} is positive definite as in conventional variable-metric rules. Clearly, the EGE expression plays a central role in this class of algorithm.

3 If $Q(\cdot)$ has been programmed, modified Newton–Raphson seems to be efficient (see, for example, Hendry and Tremayne, 1976) as does the equivalent GMP algorithm, both being faster than routines using only $q(\cdot)$. Most of the optimization routines currently attached by AUTOREG are from the NAG (1977) implementation.

Special features of any given problem handsomely repay exploitation: for example, concentrating $L(\cdot)$ with respect to any set of parameters which reduces the dimensionality of the parameter space without creating a more complex function (as can be done for seasonal dummies which occur in every equation); or if $L(\cdot)$ can be reduced to a sum of squares of non-linear functions or is decomposable into a stepwise optimization form and so on. So far as possible, such features are incorporated into AUTOREG programs and this is a major reason for having a range of programs for special cases.

4 Method Evaluation

The *asymptotic* distributions of most of the estimators derivable from (14.5) are known for *correctly specified* models. Very little is known about estimator behaviour in a wide range of mis-specified situations (either asymptotic or finite sample results) and relatively little is known about the finite sample distributions of many of the estimators even when the model specification is correct. Although analytic research into these areas is in progress, the role of stochastic simulation experiments is likely to remain large for some time to come. For iterative estimators, the cost of replicated trials and intensive experimentation can be prohibitive and hence to achieve general and precise results requires efficient Monte Carlo techniques such as antithetic variates or control variables (denoted CV) or an unlimited budget! To ensure efficiency gains, a CV needs to have the same large-sample distribution as the estimator under study yet have known small-sample properties. These two statements suggest seeking CVs from the relevant EGE, and in particular making the choice to maximize analytical tractability. To illustrate the procedure involved, consider deriving the CV for θ for the FIML class based on (14.13), noting that $\mathscr{E}[Q(\theta)] = -T(\Omega^{-1} \otimes HM^*H')^u$ where $M^* = \mathscr{E}(T^{-1}X^{*\prime}X^*)$, and $(\ )^u$ denotes selecting elements corresponding to unrestricted coefficients in A. The optimization technique known as 'scoring' is based on

$$\theta_{i+1} = \theta_i - \{ \mathscr{E}[Q(\theta)] \}^{-1} q(\theta) |_{\theta=\theta_i} \qquad i = 1, 2, \ldots, \tag{14.16}$$

and, from EGE theory, one step of (14.16) from consistent initial values yields an asymptotic equivalent to FIML (see, for example, Rothenberg and Leenders, 1964). But θ is consistent for θ (!) and hence

$$\theta^* = \theta - \{ \mathscr{E}[Q(\theta)] \}^{-1} q(\theta) \tag{14.17}$$

is such that plim $T^{1/2}(\hat{\theta} - \theta^*) = 0$ whereas $\mathscr{E}(\theta)^* = \theta$ and $\mathscr{E}(\theta^* - \theta)(\theta^* - \theta)' =$

$\{\mathscr{L}[Q(\theta)]\}^{-1}$ since $\mathscr{L}[q(\theta)] = 0$ and $\mathscr{L}[q(\theta)q(\theta)'] = -\mathscr{L}[Q(\theta)]$. Thus θ^* is an appropriate CV for $\hat{\theta}$ (but is manifestly non-operational outside of the Monte Carlo context). In particular, for FIML and 3SLS, (14.17) yields [4]

$$\theta^* = \theta + [T(\Omega^{-1} \otimes HM^*H')^{\mathrm{u}}]^{-1}(\Omega^{-1} \otimes HX^{*\prime})^{\mathrm{u}}(AX')^{\rho}, \tag{14.18}$$

remembering that $Ax_t = e_t$ (compare Mikhail, 1972). Alternative derivations of CVs in dynamic systems using expansions based on Nagar (1959) are discussed in Hendry and Harrison (1974). The method of scoring also underlies the Lagrange multiplier class of tests – see, for example, Breusch and Pagan (1980).

To summarize the above results, the EGE defines the relevant class of estimator, with approximate non-iterative solutions and exact iterative solutions obtainable by a range of numerical optimization techniques, the choice of which can influence the statistical properties of the estimator, while one algorithm (i.e. scoring) applied to the true parameter values yields the CV required for efficient simulation study of the finite sample behaviour of the various estimators in the class. Note that θ^* differs from $\hat{\theta}$ by $O(1/T)$, and if the model were static then θ^* in (14.18) would be normally distributed (for a more extended discussion see Hendry and Srba, 1977). *Analysis* of CV expressions like (14.18) frequently yields more insight into an estimator's properties than extensive *simulation* of the estimator itself.

The construction of θ^* requires the population second moments of the data, and these are available from (14.11) and (14.12). For mis-specified models, appropriate CVs can be obtained in an analogous manner once the model has been reparameterized so that the relevant estimator automatically yields consistent estimates of the new parameters. For example, in an ordinary least squares (OLS) context considered in detail in Hendry (1979b), where [5]

$$y = X\beta + \varepsilon \quad \text{but} \quad \mathscr{L}(X'\varepsilon/T) = \alpha \neq 0, \tag{14.19}$$

let

$$\beta_l = \beta + [\mathscr{L}(X'X)]^{-1}\mathscr{L}(X'\varepsilon)$$

and let

$$\omega = y - X\beta_l.$$

Then for

$$\tilde{\beta} = (X'X)^{-1}X'y$$

$$\text{plim } \tilde{\beta} = \beta_l \qquad \mathscr{L}(X'\omega) = 0.$$

The reparameterized model is

$$y = X\beta_l + \omega, \tag{14.20}$$

and so $\tilde{\beta}$ is 'really' estimating β_l from the EGE $(X'\omega) = 0$ and the CV for $\tilde{\beta}$ is

$$\beta^* = \beta_l + [\mathscr{L}(X'X)]^{-1}X'\omega \tag{14.21}$$

As before, β_l, $\mathscr{L}(X'X)$ etc. only depend on M_0 and M_1. If the mis-specification is at all serious, the difference between β and β_l will dominate any discrepancy between β_i and $\mathscr{E}(\tilde{\beta})$ (assuming that the moment exists) and between $\mathscr{E}(\tilde{\beta})$ and $\tilde{\beta}$ on any one trial, so that simply conducting the (inexpensive) numerical asymptotic analysis will often answer a mis-specification question to adequate accuracy without resorting to simulation experiments which will be expensive even if well controlled. Similar procedures are available for existing higher moments. Finally, as noted by Hendry and Srba (1977), inefficient CVs can be obtained for some problems by applying inefficient numerical optimization methods to the EGE (e.g. inappropriate stepwise techniques) highlighting the interconnection between efficient optimization, efficient estimation and efficient simulation. Even so, the issue of capital/labour substitution again lurks in the background – e.g. if the asymptotic analysis itself requires a major labour input, then a crude simulation will be the 'cheaper' solution at present relative prices – and hence there remains a definite role for 'naive' stochastic simulation experiments. This applies forcefully to investigating issues associated with non-stationarity where theory tends to be especially intractable.

5 Structure of the Library

AUTOREG comprises nine main computer programs: *GIVE*, *RALS*, *FIML*, *ARFIML*, *ARRF*, *GENRAM*, *NAIVE*, *CONVAR* and *DAGER*. Programs are denoted in italic capitals: thus *FIML* is the program which computes (*inter alia*) FIML. The first six programs are for the estimation, testing and analysis of empirical models, the next two are for Monte Carlo investigations of the finite sample distributions and asymptotic behaviour of four of the estimation methods provided in *GIVE*, and *DAGER* provides a general data generation and asymptotic moment calculation routine.

The programs operate on the University of London CDC7600 according to a relatively standardized input procedure including their job control cards and the program instruction cards. Thus, for example, a card deck for *GIVE* will run unaltered on *RALS* (but produce more general – and more expensive – output), and a *FIML* deck needs no alteration to function on *ARFIML* or *RAML* (*RAML* is the special case of *GENRAM* where there are no non-linear parameter restrictions). Output is printed in a similar style and is reasonably well documented. Detailed manuals are available for every program (in some cases, both technical manuals and simplified users' guides) although these assume that the user is familiar with the econometric principles of the programs being used.

A relatively complete picture of AUTOREG can be constructed by categorizing as follows: (i) possible program choices for different model specifications; and (ii) the range of estimators computed by each program and the optimization algorithms available. For (i), the taxonomy used in chapter 2 is adopted with different classes of model being defined by the values of p, r and $\kappa - k$ (assuming that n and m are greater than zero). For example, $p = 1$ defines a single equation, $r = 0$ entails no autocorrelation and $\kappa = k$ implies no (non-linear) restrictions on the parameters (linear restrictions are ignored in the taxonomy) so that $(1, 0, 0)$ yields OLS and so on. All these estimators are derived by maximizing the relevant specialization of (14.5) (or by approximating this via the appropriate EGE) and the associated section number from Hendry (1976a) is noted in parentheses to define each method unambiguously.

5.1 Possible Program Choices Categorized by $(p, r, \kappa - k)$

(a) $(1, 0, 0)$ This yields a simple linear equation estimable by OLS (3.8) (*GIVE*).

(b) $(1, r, 0)$ An (iterative) autoregressive least squares (ALS) estimator (7.1) is required for consistent asymptotically efficient estimates (*GIVE, RALS*).

(c) $(1, 0, \kappa - k)$ Non-linear least squares problems up to cubic functions of parameters can be solved (*GENRAM*), but –

(d) $(1, r, \kappa - k)$ this program would be more appropriate computationally when allowing for autocorrelation as well.

(e) $(p, 0, 0)$ If $B_0 \neq I$, an interdependent system occurs, which is estimable one equation at a time by instrumental variables (3.4) or 2SLS (3.2) (*GIVE, RALS*), or for a complete system by 2SLS (3.2), the limited information instrumental variables estimator (LIVE) (3.5) or (inefficiently in *numerical* terms) LIML (3.1) (using *FIML*), or simultaneously by FIML (2.1), 3SLS (2.2) or FIVE (2.5) (again using *FIML*).

       If $B_0 = I$, reduced form estimation occurs, only requiring multivariate least squares (MLS) (2.7) if the coefficients are unrestricted (*FIML*, autoregressive reduced form (*ARRF*)) or a specialization of 3SLS if there are exclusion restrictions.

(f) $(p, r, 0)$ If $B_0 \neq I$ but all of the R_i matrices are diagonal, autoregressive instrumental variables (AIV) methods (6.4) are viable (*GIVE, RALS*). If the R_i are non-diagonal but $B_0 = I$ then we have the vector generalization of (b) denoted ARF (5.7) (*ARRF*).

       If $B_0 \neq I$ and the R_i are non-diagonal, then a system method such as autoregressive FIML (5.1) or autoregressive 3SLS (5.2) is required (*ARFIML, RAML*).

(g) $(p, r, \kappa - k)$ Including the possibility that $r = 0$, this is the general model (14.1) + (14.2), estimable by maximizing (14.5) subject to (14.6) (*GENRAM*).

In the converse categorization 5.2, the individual estimation programs are listed in approximately decreasing frequency and increasing cost of use (note that a range of data transformations, graphing etc. is possible in all the programs).

5.2 Possible Estimators Categorized by Program and Optimization Method

(i) *GIVE*   Provides OLS, IV, ALS and AIV estimators, the latter two being for simple scalar error schemes of the form $u_t = R_i u_{t-i} + e_t$. Unrestricted distributed lags, Almon polynomials, simple and partial correlograms of data and residuals, various tests of dynamic specification, forecast accuracy etc. are also computed as are latent roots of data moment matrices; the COMFAC and

WALD routines developed by Sargan (1980a) can be attached as can Lagrange multiplier tests for residual autocorrelation (see Godfrey, 1977; Breusch and Pagan, 1980). *GIVE* is mainly designed to aid single-equation 'model building' in situations where the dynamic specification is uncertain. ALS and AIV are found by a grid search over $R_i = -0.92$ (0.1) 0.98 followed by stepwise optimization.

(ii) *RALS* This is the generalization of *GIVE* to scalar error processes of the form $u_t = \Sigma^r_{i=1} R_i u_{t-i} + e_t$ using the method of Powell (1965) to minimize Σe_t^2. Function minimization allows flexibility in implementing interesting cases – see, for example, Wallis (1972a) – and IV estimation is allowed.

(iii) *FIML*[6] In addition to providing structural and solved estimates, standard errors etc. for any of 2SLS, 3SLS, LIVE, FIVE, FIML and MLS, output includes tests of structural restrictions, forecast tests, seasonal shift intercepts, the simulation behaviour of estimated models, long-run and dynamic multipliers and latent roots of the dynamics. The analytical first derivative version of GMP (3.2) is recommended, although the Powell (1964) algorithm is also available.

(iv) *ARFIML* This generalizes FIML for (simple) non-diagonal vector autoregressive error schemes and outputs comparable information to *FIML*, although at present the EGE only includes one other estimator (namely, a variant of A3SLS). The optimization procedure is also the same as *FIML*.

(v) *ARRF* This provides the unrestricted reduced form equivalent of *ARFIML* and outputs system tests of dynamic specification as well as appropriate point estimates etc. Stepwise optimization, modified Gauss–Newton (recommended; see Hendry and Tremayne, 1976) and analytical second derivative GMP (3.3) are all available. Because of the very large dimensionality of the parameter space even with small systems, *ARRF* is a convenient test program for evaluating alternative optimization methods.

(vi) *RAML* This is simply the special case of *GENRAM* which generalizes *ARFIML* to unrestricted error processes like (14.2); optimization choices include the Powell (1964) method and either of the numerical or analytical derivative versions of GMP (3.1, 3.2), the last being recommended.

(vii) *GENRAM* Finally we reach the general case, where the coefficients of the B_i and C_i matrices can be written as combinations of up to cubic functions of θs (see Williams, 1972) with, if required, general vector autoregressive error processes of the form (14.2), allowing for various possible dependences of Ω on θ also, to encompass 'latent variables' structures. To obtain a high degree of flexibility for developing further capabilities *jointly* within *GENRAM* (e.g. 'switching of causality' models as in Richard (1980), only function optimization is used (either Powell or GMP (3.1)).

6 The Monte Carlo Programs

NAIVE and *CONVAR* were developed to investigate OLS, IV, ALS and AIV applied to various specifications of the system (14.1)–(14.4).[7] The effects of a vast range of mis-specifications on estimators and tests can be studied using crude simulation in NAIVE (the acronym for numerical analysis of instrumental variables estimators). In *CONVAR*, all the theoretical asymptotic first and second moments of the data and the estimators are calculated and CVs are used to produce efficient and precise simulation estimates of the finite sample moments of the econometric estimators (which has its major application in investigating the accuracy of asymptotic approximations). Both programs enforce $n \leqslant 1$, $l = 0$, $p \leqslant 2$, $m \leqslant 4$, $r \leqslant 1$, $T \leqslant 80$ but *CONVAR* also restricts B_1 and R_1 to be zero except for their (1, 1) elements. We are currently undertaking studies of the sizes and powers of a number of test statistics using both these programs and *DAGER*, which computes (14.11) and (14.12) and generates data from systems like (14.7) in order to calculate asymptotic power approximations such as those discussed in Sims (1977a, pp. 186–92).

7 Program Validation and Development Stage

All the AUTOREG programs have been carefully tested at several stages in their development as follows:

1 against published results (e.g. FIML, 2SLS, OLS);
2 against special cases of each other (e.g. RALS against *GIVE* for $r = 1$; *ARFIML* against *GIVE* for $p = 1$, $r = 1$; *RAML* against *RALS* for $p = 1$, $r = 2$, against *FIML* for $p = 8$, $r = 0$, and against *ARFIML* for $p = 2$, $r = 1$; *ARRF* against *ARFIML* for $p = 3$, $r = 1$);
3 by Monte Carlo simulation (OLS, ALS, IV, AIV, in *GIVE* by *NAIVE* and *CONVAR*; in turn, the coherence between asymptotic results and the CVs' behaviour applies a strong check on the validity of *CONVAR* which was also tested in comparable cases against *NAIVE*);
4 by single runs on artificial data generated by *DAGER* from known parameters.

Nevertheless, satisfying all these tests in no way implies that the programs are 'correct' and 'bugs' are regularly noted and corrected since additions and alterations are frequently made and these can inadvertently invalidate previously correct calculations (we regularly re-estimate the model in chapter 2 to check on this). However, changes to the operating system of the computer, or the compiler, and especially changes to other computers can reveal errors in operations which previously appeared to function correctly.

Four development stages can be distinguished: (i) for personal research only: (ii) usable by other researchers; (iii) adequately documented and tested for general use; (iv) thoroughly checked, simplified and 'foolproofed' to a sufficient extent for use in teaching. In such terms:

GENRAM, RAML and *DAGER*	are at stage (ii)
ARRF, RALS and *CONVAR*	are at stage (iii)
GIVE, NAIVE, FIML and *ARFIML*	are at stage (iv)

8 Computing Costs

The following are approximate CPU requirements from recent representative runs
of the various programs on the CDC7600 in seconds:

GIVE   About 0.1 s per ten-variable equation with autocorrelation estimated

RALS   8.2 s for re-estimating the model in chapter 2 (six equations each
            estimated with every order of autoregressive error process up to fifth)

FIML   1.7 s for the same model (six equations with 18 parameters in the
            concentrated likelihood function) including 2SLS, 3SLS and FIML
            (using GMP (3.2))

ARFIML   6.2 s for the building societies model of O'Herlihy and Spencer (1972)
            (six equations, 22 unrestricted parameters from 2SLS initial values)
            by GMP (3.2)

ARRF   18 s for the building societies model reduced form (78 'structural'
            parameters, 24 seasonals and 36 autoregressive coefficients, from MLS
            initial values) by Gauss–Newton

RAML   15 s for FIML by GMP (3.1) for the building societies model from 2SLS

NAIVE   The times for these are, of course, totally dependent on the number of
and   experiments and replications and the sample size chosen; for four
CONVAR   estimators for 40 models with 25 replications and variable sample sizes
            (i.e. the experiments conducted by Hendry and Srba, 1977). 60 s were
            required on CONVAR. By comparison, for two estimators, two
            models, 100 replications and sample size 60, 3.5 s were required on
            NAIVE.

Thus GIVE and FIML are usually exceedingly fast, RALS and ARFIML are
somewhat slower, NAIVE and CONVAR are completely problem dependent and
only RAML, and hence GENRAM and ARRF, consume really 'substantial' amounts
of CPU time per run.

GIVE, NAIVE and FIML have proved to be successful teaching programs in
both theory and applied econometrics courses at LSE at undergraduate and graduate
levels.

9 Future Developments

The most radical changes to AUTOREG are likely to arise from successful functioning of the distributed array processor (DAP) being installed in London University.
The DAP is a 64 × 64 array of microprocessors capable of parallel processing and,
as it is based on outer product formulations, the computing time for operations
like matrix multiplication and inversion increases only linearly with the size of
the problem up to 64 × 64 (after which partitioning must be used). Since these two
operations constitute the main cost of most second-derivative iterative algorithms,
the DAP will radically alter the efficiency ranking of many methods as well as
the scale of problem which can be routinely tackled (e.g. the modified Gauss–Newton

method proposed by Berndt et al. (1974) seems well suited to DAP implementation for estimating systems non-linear in both variables and parameters, as does the non-linear algorithm of Sargan and Sylwestrowicz (1976b)).

A further important development is the implementation of an overall model/data handling program which will flexibly attach the existing programs as if they were subroutines to ease usage of the library by non-specialists. Finally, minor additions to AUTOREG occur very regularly as the need arises in the authors' empirical and theoretical researches, such that every two or three years a new version of AUTOREG is defined (the present one is Mark IV). All requests for further information and/or enquiries relating to updating or obtaining AUTOREG or any of the programs therein for purposes of academic study, teaching or personal research should be directed to the first author.

Notes

1 Exact equations (identities) are easily incorporated in the analysis and are allowed for in all the relevant programs.

2 This formulation is intended to include the possibility that Ω depends on θ.

3 Within the preset limits of desired, or attainable, computational accuracy.

4 For an analysis of Monte Carlo when moments do not exist, see Sargan (1981).

5 The set of assumptions on which the data generation process (14.9) is based are sufficient to ensure that $\lim \mathscr{E}(X'X)/T = \text{plim}(X'X)/T$ and $\lim \mathscr{E}(X'\varepsilon)/T = \text{plim}(X'\varepsilon)/T$ in (14.19) as discussed in, for example, Hannan (1970, ch. 4).

6 The programs *FIML, ARFIML, RAML* and *GENRAM* in fact maximize concentrated likelihood functions, having analytically maximized with respect to all possible parameters: for example, for *RAML* these comprise $R_1, \ldots, R_r, \Omega$, coefficients of constants and seasonal adjustment dummy variables and/or trends. Early versions of these programs were used in Hendry (1971) and chapter 2.

7 In fact *NAIVE* also allows the 'observed' data to differ from that actually generated by the system due to measurement errors, and is not restricted to stationary systems. An early version of *NAIVE* was used in Hendry and Trivedi (1972), and an early version of *CONVAR* by Hendry and Harrison (1974).

15

Exogeneity

with Robert F. Engle and Jean-François Richard

Preamble

The direct antecedent to 'Exogeneity' was a paper which Jean-François Richard presented to the Vienna meeting of the Econometric Society in 1977 (eventually published as Richard, 1980). Although that paper was a *tour de force*, even its author would not have claimed that the original presentation was instantly transparent! This derived from its attempts to span the rather different 'traditions' of CORE and LSE, to cover a wide range of issues and to do so in a general framework: the discussion of exogeneity is at most a third of the paper, and its full set of implications is not explicitly stated. Rob Engle, when visiting LSE in 1979, proposed clarifying and if necessary extending the concept of weak exogeneity and relating it to other notions in the literature, so we set to work – incidentally precipitating what have proved for me to be two productive and continuing collaborations. In the summer of 1979, Ken Wallis hosted a three-week Econometrics Workshop at Warwick University, funded in part by the UK Social Science Research Council (now Economic and Social Research Council). This meeting was attended by researchers from all over the world and witnessed lengthy, stimulating and occasionally vigorous discussions about exogeneity, especially with Christopher Sims who had offered an alternative view in Sims (1972b, 1977b). Such interchanges helped to clarify our thinking and are another example of the invaluable role of funding agencies in fostering research.

Exogenous variables play a crucial role in econometrics, yet the concept of exogeneity is treated with remarkable imprecision and brevity in most textbooks. Moreover, specific claims about exogeneity have in the past provoked considerable controversy (see, for example, Orcutt, 1952). The general idea of *exogenous* connotes 'being determined outside of (the

Reprinted from *Econometrica*, 51(2) (March 1983) 277–304. This paper is an abbreviated and substantially rewritten version of CORE Discussion Paper 80–38 (and UCSD Discussion Paper 81–1). This was itself an extensive revision of Warwick Discussion Paper No. 162, which was initially prepared during the 1979 Warwick Summer Workshop, with support from the Social Science Research Council. We are indebted to participants in the workshop for useful discussions on several of the ideas developed in the paper and to Mary Morgan for historical references. We also greatly benefited from discussions with A.S. Deaton, J.P. Florens, S. Goldfeld, A. Holly, M. Mouchart, R. Quandt, C. Sims and A. Ullah. Three anonymous referees made many constructive comments. Financial support from the Ford Foundation, the National Science Foundation and the International Centre for Economics and Related Disciplines at the London School of Economics is gratefully acknowledged.

model under analysis)', and yet researchers frequently attempt to ascribe the status of 'exogenous' to a variable *per se* (as with, say, the sun's energy) and then deduce certain inferences therefrom (e.g. the variable is a valid instrument for estimation). As shown in this chapter, such notions are ambiguous and can deliver misleading conclusions, as with the construct of *strict exogeneity* in Sims (1977b). Instead, we argue for analysing exogeneity in the framework of model reduction, addressing the issue of when inferences about parameters of interest (denoted ψ) based on a complete analysis of the joint density function of all the observable variables $x'_t = (y'_t, z'_t)$ coincide with inferences based on only the conditional density of one subset of variables (y_t say) given another subset z_t. If there is no loss of information about ψ from only analysing the conditional submodel, then z_t is said to be *weakly exogenous* for ψ. The approach builds on both Koopmans (1950a) and Barndorff-Nielsen (1978).

Thus, weak exogeneity is a relationship linking certain variables to parameters of interest and is precisely the condition needed to sustain valid inferences about those parameters in models which condition on contemporaneous variables. The formulation of exogeneity in the following chapter is in terms of a 'sequential cut' from which ψ is 'recoverable', and at first sight looks rather artificial, but there is a sound intuitive basis: if all information about ψ can be recovered from the conditional model of y_t given z_t, then the marginal process determining z_t is irrelevant, and hence z_t is in practice determined outside of the (conditional) model under study. Conversely, if the marginal model of z_t contains information about ψ, a complete analysis must involve modelling z_t, so that z_t is determined within the model and hence it is not exogenous.

The resulting construct is not specific to a particular class of models and it highlights interesting aspects of previously studied problems. For example, weak exogeneity throws light on the old issue of 'the direction of regression': in a bivariate case, should one regress y_t on z_t or vice versa? As shown below, only one direction can deliver the parameters of interest and, in worlds of parameter change, at most one direction will yield constant parameters (see Engle and Hendry, 1989). Moreover, when applied to models involving unobservable expectations, weak exogeneity highlights potential internal contradictions and clarifies precisely which inferences can be sustained even when conditioning is invalid (see Hendry and Neale, 1988). As sketched in Richard (1980) and more extensively analysed in chapter 17, weak exogeneity is also intimately linked to economic theories in which agents form plans and act contingently on the available information.

A final benefit was the resulting formalization of a lacuna in DHSY, who had treated income as if it were weakly exogenous (but without that concept) on the pragmatic grounds that the resulting model adequately characterized all the available evidence. The examples in the present chapter seek to illustrate these points, revealing *en route* that weak exogeneity is neither necessary nor sufficient for strict exogeneity, that there is no necessary relationship between the presence of weak exogeneity and the validity of any particular estimation method (other than the relevant maximum likelihood estimator in sufficiently large samples), and that tests of weak exogeneity in dynamic systems are usually only of sufficient (and not of necessary) conditions for its presence.

Econometricians engage in many activities other than just within-sample inference, and so it is natural to enquire about the exogeneity conditions needed to sustain, say, conditional forecasting and conditional policy analysis. Since these last two must both commence from empirical models, weak exogeneity is necessary for the conditioning variables – but is not sufficient. Thus, to forecast more than one period ahead, conditional on fixed values of the zs, the additional requirement of no feedback from y onto z is needed (i.e. Granger non-causality: see Granger, 1969) leading to the concept of *strong exogeneity*. Similarly, to justify a policy analysis which involves changing the marginal model determining z_t while holding

$\not\psi$ constant, a condition of parameter invariance is required, leading to *super exogeneity*. However, Granger non-causality is neither necessary nor sufficient for super exogeneity.

This final construct of super exogeneity has a central role in the methodology. On the one hand, looking back, it both formalizes the intuitive ideas of chapter 11 above and clarifies the implicit link between parameter constancy and valid conditioning assumed in DHSY, allowing later empirical studies to be grounded on a more rigorous basis. Moreover, it links together a long sequence of important contributions to the analysis of autonomy and exogeneity from Frisch (1938), Haavelmo (1944) and Koopmans (1950a) through Bentzel and Hansen (1955), Strotz and Wold (1960) and Hurwicz (1962) to Lucas (1976) and Sargent (1981). On the other hand, looking forward, super exogeneity sets a limit to the reduction of models by conditioning if parameters of interest are to remain constant and be invariant to changes in marginal processes. This leads naturally to an even greater emphasis on testing constancy and invariance (see Engle and Hendry, 1989), focusing on periods when policy variables or expectations mechanisms are known (or believed) to have altered (an issue examined in Hendry, 1988b), necessarily exploiting recursive testing procedures (see Hendry and Neale, 1987).

Although the chapter does not consider any integrated processes, weak exogeneity seems as relevant to cointegrated systems as it is to stationary or changing worlds. Johansen (1992) shows that under weak exogeneity single-equation estimation remains efficient in a cointegrated system, whereas if weak exogeneity fails, then system modelling is needed despite the super consistency of estimators in I(1) processes (see Stock, 1987; Phillips, 1990; Phillips and Loretan, 1991; also see Granger (1986) for a survey of cointegration and Engle and Granger (1987) for the initiating analysis;[1] Johansen (1988) proposes a maximum likelihood estimator for the dimension of the cointegrating space). In some cases, the failure of weak exogeneity due to the presence of a cointegrating vector in several equations can lead to a large loss of efficiency (see Hendry and Mizon (1991) for an example). Thus, testing for weak exogeneity is as important in non-stationary cointegrated systems as it is in stationary cases (see Ericsson, 1992).

Note

1 Other authors also suffer from having papers appear in the reverse order to their writing!

1 Introduction

Since 'Exogeneity' is fundamental to most empirical econometric modelling, its conceptualization, its role in inference and the testing of its validity have been the subject of extensive discussion (see *inter alia* Koopmans, 1950a; Orcutt, 1952; Marschak, 1953; Phillips, 1956; Sims, 1972b, 1977b; Geweke, 1978, 1984; Richard 1980). Nevertheless, as perusal of the literature (and especially econometrics textbooks) quickly reveals, precise definitions of 'exogeneity' are elusive, and consequently it is unclear exactly what is entailed for inference by the discovery that a certain variable is 'exogenous' on any given definition. Moreover, the motivation underlying various 'exogeneity' concepts has not always been stated explicitly so that their relationships to alternative notions of 'causality' (see Wiener, 1956; Strotz and Wold, 1960; Granger, 1969; Zellner, 1979b) remain ambiguous. This results in part because some definitions have been formulated for limited classes of models so that appropriate generalizations such as to non-linear or non-Gaussian situations are not straightforward, while others are formulated in terms involving unobservable disturbances from relationships which contain unknown parameters. Whether or not such disturbances satisfy orthogonality conditions with certain observables may be a matter of construction or may be a testable hypothesis and a clear distinction between these situations is essential.

In this chapter, definitions are proposed for *weak* and *strong* exogeneity in terms of the distributions of observable variables,[1] thereby explicitly relating these concepts to the likelihood function and hence efficient estimation:[2] essentially, a variable z_t in a model is defined to be weakly exogenous for estimating a set of parameters λ if inference on λ conditional on z_t involves no loss of information. Heuristically, given that the joint density of random variables (y_t, z_t) can always be written as the product of y_t conditional on z_t times the marginal of z_t, the weak exogeneity of z_t entails that the precise specification of the latter density is irrelevant to the analysis and, in particular, that all parameters which appear in this marginal density are nuisance parameters. Such an approach builds on the important paper by Koopmans (1950a) using recently developed concepts of statistical inference (see, for example, Barndorff-Nielsen, 1978; Florens and Mouchart, 1980a). If, in addition to being weakly exogenous, z_t is *not caused* in the sense of Granger (1969) by any of the endogenous variables in the system, then z_t is defined to be strongly exogenous.

The concept of exogeneity is then extended to the class of models where the mechanism generating z_t changes. Such changes could come about for a variety of reasons; one of the most interesting is the attempt by one agent to control the behaviour of another. If all the parameters λ of the conditional model are invariant to any change in the marginal density of z_t, and z_t is weakly exogenous for λ, then z_t is said to be *super* exogenous. That is, changes in the values of z_t or its generating function will not affect the conditional relation between y_t and z_t. This aspect builds on the work of Frisch (1938), Marschak (1953), Hurwicz (1962), Sims (1977b) and Richard (1980).

The chapter is organized as follows: formal definitions of weak, strong and super exogeneity are introduced in section 2, and, to ensure an unambiguous discussion, the familiar notions of predeterminedness, strict exogeneity and Granger non-causality are also defined. These are then discussed in the light of several examples in section 3. The examples illustrate the relations between the concepts in familiar models showing the importance of each part of the new definitions and showing the incompleteness of the more conventional notions. Special attention is paid to the impact of serial correlation. The analysis is then applied to potentially incomplete dynamic simultaneous equations systems in section 4. The conclusion restates the main themes and implications of the chapter.

1.1 Notation

Let $x_t \in \mathbb{R}^n$ be a vector of *observable* random variables generated at time t, on which observations ($t = 1, \ldots, T$) are available. Let X_t^1 denote the $t \times n$ matrix

$$X_t^1 = (x_1, \ldots, x_t)' \tag{15.1}$$

and let X_0 represent the (possibly infinite) matrix of initial conditions. The analysis is conducted conditionally on X_0. For a discussion of marginalization with respect to initial conditions, see Engle et al. (1980), hereafter EHR. The information available at time t is given by

$$X_{t-1} = \begin{bmatrix} X_0 \\ X_{t-1}^1 \end{bmatrix}. \tag{15.2}$$

The process generating the T observations is assumed to be continuous with respect to some appropriate measure and is represented by the joint data density function $D(X_T^1 | X_0, \theta)$ where θ, in the interior of Θ, is an (identified) vector of unknown parameters. The likelihood function of θ, given the initial conditions X_0, is denoted by $L^0(\theta; X_T^1)$.

Below, $f_N^n(\cdot | \mu, \Sigma)$ denotes the n-dimensional normal density function with mean vector μ and covariance matrix Σ. The notation $x_t \sim IN(\mu, \Sigma)$ reads as 'the vectors $x_1, \ldots, x_T$ are identically independently normally distributed with common mean vector μ and covariance matrix Σ'. C_n denotes the set of symmetric positive definite matrices.

The vector x_t is partitioned into

$$x_t = \begin{bmatrix} y_t \\ z_t \end{bmatrix} \qquad y_t \in \mathbb{R}^p \qquad z_t \in \mathbb{R}^q \qquad p + q = n. \tag{15.3}$$

The matrices X_0, X_t^1 and X_t are partitioned conformably:

$$X_0 = (Y_0 \, Z_0) \qquad X_t^1 = (Y_t^1 \, Z_t^1) \qquad X_t = (Y_t \, Z_t). \tag{15.4}$$

The expressions '$x_t \| y_t$' and '$x_t \| y_t | w_t$' read respectively as 'x_t and y_t are independent (in probability)' and 'conditionally on w_t, x_t and y_t are independent'. In our framework it is implicit that all such independence statements are conditional on θ. The operator Σ denotes a summation which starts at $i = 1$ and is over all relevant lags.

2 Definitions

Often the objective of empirical econometrics is to model how the observation x_t is generated conditionally on the past, and so we factorize the joint data density as

$$D(X_T^1 | X_0, \theta) = \prod_{t=1}^{T} D(x_t | X_{t-1}, \theta) \tag{15.5}$$

and focus attention on the conditional density functions $D(x_t | X_{t-1}, \theta)$. These are assumed to have a common functional form with a *finite*[3] dimensional parameter space Θ.

The following formal definitions must be introduced immediately to ensure an unambiguous discussion, but the examples presented below attempt to elucidate their content; the reader wishing a general view of the paper could proceed fairly rapidly to section 3 and return to this section later.

2.1 Granger Non-causality

For the class of models defined by (15.5), conditioned throughout on X_0, Granger (1969) provides a definition of non-causality which can be restated as follows.

Definition 15.1 Y^1_{t-1} does not Granger-cause z_t with respect to X_{t-1} if and only if

$$D(z_t|X_{t-1}, \theta) = D(z_t|Z_{t-1}, Y_0, \theta), \tag{15.6}$$

i.e. if and only if

$$z_t \| Y^1_{t-1} | Z_{t-1}, Y_0. \tag{15.7}$$

If condition (15.6) holds over the sample period, then the joint data density $D(X^1_T|X_0, \theta)$ factorizes as

$$D(X^1_T|X_0, \theta) = \left[\prod_{t=1}^{T} D(y_t|z_t, X_{t-1}, \theta) \right] \left[\prod_{t=1}^{T} D(z_t|Z_{t-1}, Y_0, \theta) \right] \tag{15.8}$$

where the last term is $D(Z^1_T|X_0, \theta)$ and the middle term is therefore $D(Y^1_T| Z^1_T, X_0, \theta)$.

Where no ambiguity is likely, condition (15.6) is stated below as 'y does not Granger-cause z'. Note that the definition in Chamberlain (1982) is the same as definition 15.1.

2.2 Predeterminedness and Strict Exogeneity

Consider a set of $g \leqslant n$ behavioural relationships (whose exact interpretation is discussed in section 4 below):

$$B^* x_t + \sum C^*(i) x_{t-i} = u_t \tag{15.9}$$

where B^* and $\{C^*(i)\}$ are $g \times n$ matrix functions of θ, with rank $B^* = g$ almost everywhere in Θ and u_t is the corresponding 'disturbance'.

The following definitions are adapted from Koopmans and Hood (1953) – see also Christ (1966, chs IV.4, VI.4) and Sims (1977b).

Definition 15.2 z_t is *predetermined* in (15.9) if and only if

$$z_t \| u_{t+i} \quad \text{for all } i \geqslant 0. \tag{15.10}$$

Definition 15.3 z_t is *strictly exogenous*[4] in (15.9) if and only if

$$z_t \| u_{t+i} \quad \text{for all } i. \tag{15.11}$$

The connections between strict exogeneity and Granger non-causality have been discussed by several authors – and in particular by Sims (1977b) and Geweke

(1978) – for complete dynamic simultaneous equations models. This issue is reconsidered in section 4. See also the discussion in Chamberlain (1982) and Florens and Mouchart (1982).

2.3 Parameters of Interest

Often a model user is not interested in all the parameters in θ, so that his (implicit) loss function depends only on some functions of θ, say

$$f: \Theta \to \Psi; \qquad \theta \to \psi = f(\theta). \tag{15.12}$$

These functions are called *parameters of interest*. Parameters may be of interest, for example, because they are directly related to theories the model user wishes to test concerning the structure of the economy. Equally, in seeking empirical econometric relationships which are constant over the sample period and hopefully over the forecast period, parameters which are *structurally invariant* (see section 2.6) are typically of interest.

Since models can be parameterized in infinitely many ways, parameters of interest need not coincide with those which are chosen to characterize the data density (e.g. the mean vector and the covariance matrix in a normal framework). Consider, therefore, an arbitrary one-to-one transformation or reparameterization

$$h: \Theta \to \Lambda; \qquad \theta \to \lambda = h(\theta) \tag{15.13}$$

together with a partition of λ into (λ_1, λ_2). Let Λ_i denote the set of admissible values of λ_i. The question of whether or not the parameters of interest are *functions* of λ_1 plays an essential role in our analysis: that is, whether there exists a function ϕ,

$$\phi: \Lambda_1 \to \Psi; \qquad \lambda_1 \to \psi = \phi(\lambda_1), \tag{15.14}$$

such that

$$\forall \lambda \in \Lambda \qquad \psi = f[h^{-1}(\lambda)] \equiv \phi(\lambda_1). \tag{15.15}$$

When (15.15) holds, λ_2 is often called a *nuisance* parameter.[5]

2.4 Sequential Cuts

Let $x_t \in \mathbb{R}^n$ be partitioned as in (15.3) and let $\lambda = (\lambda_1, \lambda_2)$ be a reparameterization as in (15.13). The following definition is adapted from Florens and Mouchart (1980a) who generalized the notion of cut discussed (for example) by Barndorff-Nielsen (1978) to dynamic models.

Definition 15.4 $[(y_t|z_t; \lambda_1), (z_t; \lambda_2)]$ operates a (classical) *sequential cut* on $D(x_t|X_{t-1}, \lambda)$ if and only if

$$D(x_t|X_{t-1}, \lambda) = D(y_t|z_t, X_{t-1}, \lambda_1) D(z_t|X_{t-1}, \lambda_2) \tag{15.16}$$

where λ_1 and λ_2 are *variation free*, i.e.

$$(\lambda_1, \lambda_2) \in \Lambda_1 \times \Lambda_2. \tag{15.17}$$

Since Λ_i denotes the set of admissible values of λ_i, condition (15.17) requires in effect that λ_1 and λ_2 should not be subject to 'cross-restrictions', whether exact or inequality restrictions, since then the range of admissible values for λ_i would vary with λ_j ($i, j = 1, 2; j \neq i$).

2.5 Weak and Strong Exogeneity

The following definitions are adapted from Richard (1980). As in (15.12), ψ denotes the parameter of interest.

Definition 15.5 z_t is *weakly exogenous* over the sample period for ψ if and only if there exists a reparameterization with $\lambda = (\lambda_1, \lambda_2)$ such that

(i) ψ is a function of λ_1 (as in (15.15)).
(ii) $[(y_t | z_t; \lambda_1), (z_t; \lambda_2)]$ operates a sequential cut.

Definition 15.6 z_t is *strongly exogenous* over the sample period for ψ if and only if it is weakly exogenous for ψ and in addition

(iii) y does not Granger-cause z.

When (ii) holds, $L^0(\lambda; X_T^1)$ factorizes as in

$$L^0(\lambda; X_T^1) = L_1^0(\lambda_1; X_T^1) L_2^0(\lambda_2; X_T^1), \tag{15.18}$$

where

$$L_1^0(\lambda_1; X_T^1) = \prod_{t=1}^{T} D(y_t | z_t, X_{t-1}, \lambda_1), \tag{15.19}$$

$$L_2^0(\lambda_2; X_T^1) = \prod_{t=1}^{T} D(z_t | X_{t-1}, \lambda_2), \tag{15.20}$$

and the two factors in (15.18) can be analysed independently of each other (which, irrespective of whether or not (i) holds, may considerably reduce the computational burden). If in addition (i) holds, then all the sample information concerning the parameter of interest ψ can be obtained from the partial likelihood function $L_1^0(\lambda_1; X_T^1)$. If it were known (or assumed a *priori*) that z_t was weakly exogenous for ψ, then the marginal process $D(z_t | X_{t-1}, \lambda_2)$ would not even need to be specified. However, tests of the weak exogeneity of z_t for ψ, as described in section 6.1 of EHR and Engle (1982b), evidently require that the *joint* model $D(x_t | X_{t-1}, \lambda)$ be specified.

The factorization (15.18)–(15.20) does not entail that the conditional process generating $\{y_t | z_t\}$ and the marginal process generating $\{z_t\}$ can be separated from each other, i.e. for example, that z_t can be treated as 'fixed' in the conditional model $D(y_t | z_t, X_{t-1}, \lambda_1)$, since lagged values of y_t may still affect the process generating z_t.[6] Factorizing the joint data density $D(X_T^1 | X_0, \lambda)$ requires an additional assumption and this is precisely the object of Granger non-causality. When both (ii) and (iii) hold we can factorize $D(X_T^1|X_0, \lambda)$ as in

$$D(X_T^1|X_0, \lambda) = D(Y_T^1|Z_T^1, X_0, \lambda_1)D(Z_T^1|X_0, \lambda_2), \tag{15.21}$$

where

$$D(Y_T^1|Z_T^1, X_0, \lambda_1) = \prod_{t=1}^{T} D(y_t|z_t, X_{t-1}, \lambda_1), \tag{15.22}$$

$$D(Z_T^1|X_0, \lambda_2) = \prod_{t=1}^{T} D(z_t|Z_{t-1}, Y_0, \lambda_2). \tag{15.23}$$

It must be stressed that the definition of Granger non-causality as given in (15.6) and (15.8) includes *no* assumption about the *parameters*. This is precisely why it must be completed by an assumption of weak exogeneity in order to entail a complete separation of the processes generating respectively $\{y_t|z_t\}$ and $\{z_t\}$.

2.6 Structural Invariance and Super Exogeneity

A closely related issue of statistical inference is parameter constancy. Over time, it is possible that some of the parameters of the joint distribution may change perhaps through changing tastes, technology or institutions such as government policy making. For some classes of parameter change or 'interventions' there may be parameters which remain constant and which can be estimated without difficulty even though interventions occur over the sample period. This is a familiar assumption about parameters in econometrics which is here called invariance. Just as weak exogeneity sustains conditional inference within a regime, we develop the relevant exogeneity concept for models subject to a particular class of regime changes.

Definition 15.7 A parameter is *invariant* for a class of interventions if it remains constant under these interventions. A model is invariant for such interventions if all its parameters are.

Definition 15.8 A conditional model is *structurally invariant* if all its parameters are invariant for any change in the distribution of the conditioning variables.[7]

Since weak exogeneity guarantees that the parameters of the conditional model and those of the marginal model are variation free, it offers a natural framework for analysing the structural invariance of parameters of conditional models. However, by itself, weak exogeneity is neither necessary nor sufficient for structural invariance of a conditional model. Note, first, that the conditional model may be structurally invariant without its parameters providing an estimate of the parameters of interest. Conversely, weak exogeneity of the conditioning variables does not rule out the possibility that economic agents change their behaviour in relation to interventions. That is, even though the parameters of interest and the nuisance parameters are variation free over any given regime, where a regime is characterized by a fixed distribution of the conditioning variables, their variations between regimes may be related. This will become clear in the examples.

The concept of structurally invariant conditional models characterizes the conditions which guarantee the appropriateness of 'policy simulations' or other control exercises, since any change in the distribution of the conditioning variables has no effect on the conditional submodel and therefore on the conditional forecasts of the endogenous variables. This requirement is clearly very strong and its untested assumption has been criticized in conventional practice by Lucas (1976) and Sargent (1981).

To sustain conditional inference in processes subject to interventions, we define the concept of *super exogeneity*.

Definition 15.9 z_t is *super exogenous* for ψ if z_t is weakly exogenous for ψ and the conditional model $D(y_t|z_t, X_{t-1}, \lambda_1)$ is structurally invariant.

Note that definition 15.9 relates to *conditional* submodels: since estimable models with invariant parameters but no weakly exogenous variables are easily formulated (see example 15.2 below), super exogeneity is a sufficient but not a necessary condition for valid inference under interventions (see, for example, the discussion of feasible policy analyses under rational expectations in Wallis (1980) and the formulation in Sargent (1981)).

It is clear that any assertion concerning super exogeneity is refutable in the data for past changes in $D(z_t|X_{t-1}, \lambda_2)$ by examining the behaviour of the conditional model for invariance when the parameters of the exogenous process changed. For an example of this see chapter 11. However, super exogeneity for all changes in the distribution of z_t must remain a conjecture until refuted, both because nothing precludes agents from simply changing their behaviour at a certain instant and because only a limited range of interventions will have occurred in any given sample period (compare the notion of non-excitation in Salmon and Wallis, 1982). Such an approach is, of course, standard scientific practice. When derived from a well-articulated theory, a conditional submodel with z_t super exogenous seems to satisfy the requirement for Zellner causality of 'predictability according to a law' (see Zellner, 1979b).

2.7 Comments

The motivation for introducing the concept of weak exogeneity is that it provides a sufficient[8] condition for conducting inference conditionally on z_t without loss of relevant sample information. Our concept is a direct extension of Koopmans' (1950a) discussion of exogeneity. He shows that an implicit static simultaneous equations system which has the properties (a) that the variables of the first block of equations do not enter the second block, (b) that the disturbances between the two blocks are independent and (c) that the Jacobian of the transformation from the disturbances to the observables is nowhere zero, will have a likelihood function which factors into two components as in (15.18), a conditional and a marginal. The variables in the second block are labelled exogenous. Implicit in his analysis is the notion that the parameters of interest are all located in the first block and that this parameterization operates a cut. The failure to state precisely these components of the definition leads to a lack of force in the definition as is illustrated in several of the examples in this chapter. Koopmans then analyses dynamic systems in the same framework, leading to a notion of exogeneity which corresponds to our strong exogeneity and predeterminedness corresponding to that concept as defined above.

Koopmans presents sufficient conditions for the factorization of the likelihood but does not discuss the case where the factorization holds but his sufficient conditions do not. Our work therefore extends Koopmans' by making precise the assumptions about the parameters of interest and by putting the definitions squarely on the appropriate factorization of the likelihood. More recent literature has in fact stepped back from Koopmans' approach, employing definitions such as that of strict exogeneity in section 2.2. As shown in section 4, strict exogeneity, when applied to dynamic simultaneous equations models, includes condition (iii) of definition 15.6 together with predeterminedness; condition (ii) of definition 15.5 is not required explicitly but, at least for just identified models, is often satisfied by construction; condition (i) of definition 15.5 is certainly absent which, in our view, is a major lacuna[9] since, unless it holds, strict exogeneity of z_t does not ensure that there is no loss of relevant sample information when conducting inference conditionally on z_t. On the other hand, if (i) and (ii) hold, then (iii) becomes irrelevant[10] since it no longer affects inference on the parameters of interest. This does not mean that condition (iii) has no merit on its own – a model user might express specific interest in detecting causal orderings and ψ should then be defined accordingly – but simply that it is misleading to emphasize Granger non-causality when discussing exogeneity. The two concepts serve different purposes: weak exogeneity validates conducting *inference* conditional on z_t while Granger non-causality validates *forecasting* z and then forecasting y *conditional* on the future zs. As is well known, the condition that y does not Granger-cause z is neither necessary nor sufficient for the weak exogeneity of z. Obviously, if estimation is required before conditional predictions are made, then strong exogeneity which covers both Granger non-causality *and* weak exogeneity becomes the relevant concept.

Note that if $[\,(y_t|z_t;\lambda_1),(z_t;\lambda_2)\,]$ operates a sequential cut, then the information matrix, if it exists, is block-diagonal between λ_1 and λ_2. In fact for most of the examples discussed in this chapter and in EHR the condition that the information matrix be block-diagonal appears to be equivalent to the condition that the parameterization should operate a sequential cut. However, at a more general level, the finding that the information matrix is block-diagonal between two sets of parameters, one of which contains all the parameters of interest, does not entail that the likelihood function factorize as in (15.18). Block-diagonality of the information matrix may reflect other features of the likelihood function. Therefore, it seems difficult to discuss exogeneity by means of information matrices without explicitly referring to reparameterizations in terms of conditional and marginal submodels. Further, information matrices are often difficult to obtain analytically especially in the presence of lagged endogenous variables.

Note also that some definitions seem designed to validate specific estimation methods such as ordinary least squares within a single-equation framework. For example, Phillips (1956, section IV) presents conditions justifying least squares estimation in dynamic systems, which if fulfilled would allow regressors to be treated as 'given', despite the presence of Granger causal feedbacks. The concept of weak exogeneity is *not directly* related to validating specific estimation methods but concerns instead the conditions under which attention may be restricted to conditional submodels without loss of relevant sample information. Later selection of an *inappropriate* estimator may produce inefficiency (and inconsistency) even when weak exogeneity conditions are fulfilled.

Many existing definitions of exogeneity have been formulated in terms of orthogonality conditions between observed variables and (unobservable) disturbances in linear relationships within processes which are usually required to be Gaussian. Definitions 15.5 and 15.6 apply equally well to any joint density function and therefore encompass non-linear and non-Gaussian processes and truncated or otherwise limited dependent variables. As such non-classical models come into more use it is particularly important to have definitions of exogeneity which can be directly applied. See, for example, Gourieroux et al. (1980) or Maddala and Lee (1976). For a formulation tantamount to weak exogeneity in the context of conditional logit models, see McFadden (1979, section 5.1). Exogeneity has also been discussed from the Bayesian point of view by Florens and Mouchart (1980a). The issue then becomes whether or not the posterior density of the parameters of interest as derived from a conditional submodel coincides with that derived from the complete model. Such is the case if z_t is weakly exogenous and in addition λ_1 and λ_2 in definition 15.5 are *a priori* independent. However, the conditions are not necessary and it may be the case that, in the absence of a sequential cut, the prior density is such that the desired result is still achieved.

3 Examples

Many of the points made in the previous section can be illustrated with the simplest of all multivariate models, the bivariate normal. Because this is a static model, the concepts of weak and strong exogeneity coincide as do the concepts of predeterminedness and strict exogeneity. The central role of the choice of parameters of interest is seen directly.

Example 15.1 Let the data on y_t and z_t be generated by

$$\begin{bmatrix} y_t \\ z_t \end{bmatrix} \sim \text{IN}(\mu, \Omega) \qquad \mu = (\mu_i) \qquad \Omega = (\omega_{ij}) \qquad i,j = 1,2, \tag{15.24}$$

with the conditional distribution of y_t given z_t

$$y_t | z_t \sim \text{IN}(\alpha + \beta z_t, \sigma^2) \tag{15.25}$$

where $\beta = \omega_{12}/\omega_{22}, \alpha = \mu_1 - \beta\mu_2$ and $\sigma^2 = \omega_{11} - \omega_{12}^2/\omega_{22}$. Letting

$$u_{1t} = y_t - \mathscr{E}(y_t | z_t) \qquad v_{2t} = z_t - \mathscr{E}(z_t), \tag{15.26}$$

the model is correspondingly reformulated as

$$y_t = \alpha + \beta z_t + u_{1t} \qquad u_{1t} \sim \text{IN}(0, \sigma^2), \tag{15.27}$$

$$z_t = \mu_2 + v_{2t} \qquad v_{2t} \sim \text{IN}(0, \omega_{22}), \tag{15.28}$$

where $\text{cov}(z_t, u_{1t}) = \text{cov}(v_{2t}, u_{1t}) = 0$ by construction. The parameters of the conditional model (15.27) are $(\alpha, \beta, \sigma^2)$ and those of the marginal model (15.28) are (μ_2, ω_{22}). They are in one-to-one correspondence with (μ, Ω) and are variation free since, for arbitrary choices of $(\alpha, \beta, \sigma^2)$ and (μ_2, ω_{22}) in their sets of admissible values which are respectively $\mathbb{R}^2 \times \mathbb{R}_+$ and $\mathbb{R} \times \mathbb{R}_+$, μ and Ω are given by

$$\mu = \begin{bmatrix} \alpha + \beta\mu_2 \\ \mu_2 \end{bmatrix} \qquad \Omega = \begin{bmatrix} \sigma^2 + \beta^2\omega_{22} & \beta\omega_{22} \\ \beta\omega_{22} & \omega_{22} \end{bmatrix}, \tag{15.29}$$

and the constraint that Ω be positive definite is automatically satisfied (see lemma 5.1 in Drèze and Richard (1984), for a generalization of this result to multivariate regression models). It follows that z_t is weakly exogenous for $(\alpha, \beta, \sigma^2)$ or for any well-defined function thereof.

However, similar reasoning applies by symmetry to the factorization

$$z_t = \gamma + \delta y_t + u_{2t} \qquad u_{2t} \sim \text{IN}(0, \tau^2), \tag{15.30}$$

$$y_t = \mu_1 + v_{1t} \qquad v_{1t} \sim \text{IN}(0, \omega_{11}), \tag{15.31}$$

where $\delta = \omega_{12}/\omega_{11}$, $\gamma = \mu_2 - \delta\mu_1$, $\tau^2 = \omega_{22} - \omega_{12}^2/\omega_{11}$, and $\text{cov}(y_t, u_{2t}) = \text{cov}(v_{1t}, u_{2t}) = 0$ by construction. Therefore, y_t is weakly exogenous for (γ, δ, τ^2) or for any well-defined function thereof. In this example the choice of parameters of interest is the sole determinant of weak exogeneity which is therefore not directly testable.

Next, consider the concept of predeterminedness which is here equivalent to that of strict exogeneity. Regardless of the parameters of interest, z_t is predetermined in (15.27) by construction and so is y_t in (15.30). Which variable is predetermined depends upon the form of the equation, not upon the properties of the joint density function. Until some of the parameters are assumed to be more fundamental or structural (i.e. parameters of interest), the notion of predeterminedness has no force. When δ is the parameter of interest, z_t is predetermined in equation (15.27) but not weakly exogenous while y_t is weakly exogenous but not predetermined. Similar results hold in more complex models where the assumptions of exogeneity can be tested.

This example also illustrates the ambiguity in Koopmans' sufficient conditions as discussed in section 2.7 since their application leads to the conclusion that z_t is exogenous in (15.27) and (15.28) while y_t is exogenous in (15.30) and (15.31), a conclusion which seems to misrepresent Koopmans' views about exogeneity.

Now consider the concepts of structural invariance and super exogeneity. Will the parameter β in (15.27) be invariant to an intervention which changes the variance of z? The answer depends upon the structure of the process. If β is truly a constant parameter (because, for example, (15.27) is an autonomous behavioural equation) then σ_{12} will vary with σ_{22} since, given (15.26), $\sigma_{12} = \beta\sigma_{22}$. Alternatively it might be σ_{12} which is the fixed constant of nature in (15.24) and in this case β will not be invariant to changes in σ_{22}; z_t can be weakly exogenous for β within one regime with β a derived parameter which changes between regimes. By making β the parameter of interest, most investigators are implicitly assuming that it will remain constant when the distribution of the exogenous variables changes; however, this is an assumption which may not be acceptable in the light of the Lucas (1976) critique. Similar arguments apply to α or σ^2. Therefore, if $(\alpha, \beta, \sigma^2)$ are invariant to any changes in the distribution of z_t or, more specifically in this restricted framework, to changes in μ_2 and ω_{22}, then z_t is super exogenous for $(\alpha, \beta, \sigma^2)$. If, on the other hand, β is invariant to such changes while α and σ^2 are not, for example because μ_1 and ω_{11} are invariant, then z_t might be weakly exogenous for β within each regime but it is not super exogenous for β since the marginal process (15.28) now contains valuable information on the shifts of α and σ^2 between regimes.[11] It is clear from the above argument that weak exogeneity does not imply structural invariance. It is also clear that, even if β is invariant to changes in the distribution of z or in fact the conditional model (15.27) is structurally invariant, the parameter of interest could be γ and therefore z_t would not be weakly exogenous, and thus not super exogenous either.

Finally, since weak exogeneity explicitly requires that all relevant sample information be processed, over-identifying restrictions are bound to play an essential role in a discussion of weak exogeneity assumptions.[12] This will be discussed further in section 4 within the framework of dynamic simultaneous equations models. Example 15.2 illustrates the role of over-identifying restrictions in a simple structure.

Example 15.2 Consider the following two-equation over-identified model:

$$y_t = z_t\beta + \varepsilon_{1t}, \tag{15.32}$$

$$z_t = z_{t-1}\delta_1 + y_{t-1}\delta_2 + \varepsilon_{2t}, \tag{15.33}$$

$$\begin{bmatrix} \varepsilon_{1t} \\ \varepsilon_{2t} \end{bmatrix} \sim IN(0, \Sigma) \qquad \Sigma = \begin{bmatrix} \sigma_{11} & \sigma_{12} \\ \sigma_{12} & \sigma_{22} \end{bmatrix}. \tag{15.34}$$

Equation (15.33) is a typical control rule for an agent attempting to control y. For example, this could be a governmental policy reaction function or a farmer's supply decision or a worker's rule for deciding whether to undertake training. These cobweb models have a long history in econometrics. The parameter of interest is assumed to be β.

The reduced form consists of (15.33) and

$$y_t = \beta\delta_1 z_{t-1} + \beta\delta_2 y_{t-1} + v_t \tag{15.35}$$

$$\begin{bmatrix} v_t \\ \varepsilon_{2t} \end{bmatrix} \sim IN(0, \Omega) \qquad \Omega = \begin{bmatrix} \sigma_{11} + 2\beta\sigma_{12} + \beta^2\sigma_{22} & \sigma_{12} + \beta\sigma_{22} \\ \sigma_{12} + \beta\sigma_{22} & \sigma_{22} \end{bmatrix}, \tag{15.36}$$

and the conditional density of y_t given z_t is

$$D(y_t|z_t, X_{t-1}, \theta) = N(bz_t + c_1 z_{t-1} + c_2 y_{t-1}, \sigma^2) \tag{15.37}$$

where

$$b = \beta + \frac{\sigma_{12}}{\sigma_{22}} \qquad c_i = -\delta_i\frac{\sigma_{12}}{\sigma_{22}} \qquad \sigma^2 = \left(\sigma_{11} - \frac{\sigma_{12}^2}{\sigma_{22}}\right), \tag{15.38}$$

which can be written as the regression

$$y_t = bz_t + c_1 z_{t-1} + c_2 y_{t-1} + u_t \qquad u_t \sim \text{IN}(0, \sigma^2). \tag{15.39}$$

The condition which is of first concern is the value of the parameter σ_{12}. If $\sigma_{12} = 0$, then z_t is predetermined in (15.32) and is weakly exogenous for β since (β, σ_{11}) and $(\delta_1, \delta_2, \sigma_{22})$ operates a cut. Even so, for $\delta_2 \neq 0$, y Granger-causes z and therefore z is not strongly exogenous, nor is it strictly exogenous. However, the important criterion for efficient estimation is weak exogeneity, not strong exogeneity, and tests for Granger causality have no bearing on either the estimability of (15.32) or the choice of estimator.

If σ_{12} is not zero, then z_t is not weakly exogenous for β because this parameter cannot be recovered from only the parameters b, c_1, c_2, σ^2 of the conditional distribution (15.37). In (15.32) z_t is also not predetermined; however, in (15.39) it is, again showing the ambiguities in this concept. Whether or not a variable is predetermined depends on which equation is checked, and is not an intrinsic property of a variable.

The preceding results remain unchanged if $\delta_2 = 0$, in which case y does not Granger-cause z, yet z_t is still not weakly exogenous for β when $\sigma_{12} \neq 0$. Granger non-causality is neither necessary nor sufficient for weak exogeneity or, for that matter, for predeterminedness.

Suppose instead that b is the parameter of interest and $\delta_2 \neq 0$. Then ordinary least squares on (15.39) will give a consistent estimate. This will not be an efficient estimate, however, since the parameters should satisfy the restriction

$$\delta_1 c_2 = \delta_2 c_1 \tag{15.40}$$

and consequently joint estimation of (15.39) and (15.33) would be more efficient. The parameterization (b, c_1, c_2, σ^2), $(\delta_1, \delta_2, \sigma_{22})$ does not operate a cut because the parameter sets are not variation free and so z_t is not weakly exogenous for b. If, however, $\delta_2 = 0$ so that the system becomes just identified then z_t will be weakly exogenous for b as (b, c_1, σ^2), (δ_1, σ_{22}) operates a cut. In both cases, z_t is still predetermined in (15.39).

Which parameter 'ought' to be the parameter of interest requires further information about the behaviour of the system and its possible invariants. Usually, it seems desirable to choose as parameters of interest those parameters which are invariant to changes in the distribution of the weakly exogenous variables. Returning to the first case where β is the parameter of interest and $\sigma_{12} = 0$, the investigator might assume that (β, σ_{11}) would be invariant to changes in the distribution of z. If this were valid, z_t would be super exogenous, even though it is still Granger-caused by y and so it is not strongly exogenous nor strictly exogenous. Changes in the parameters of (15.33) or even of the distribution of z_t will not affect estimation of β nor will control of z affect the conditional relation between y_t and z_t given in (15.32). Conversely, if $\delta_2 = 0$ but $\sigma_{12} \neq 0$, then (b, c_1, σ^2) and (δ_1, σ_{22}) operates a cut, and z is strictly exogenous in (15.39) and strongly exogenous for b, yet that regression is by hypothesis not invariant to changes in either δ_1 or σ_{22}, cautioning against constructing cuts which do not isolate invariants.

The assumption of super exogeneity is testable if it is known that the parameters of the marginal distribution have changed over the sample period. A test for changes in β could be interpreted as a test for super exogeneity with respect to the particular interventions observed.

To clarify the question of structural invariance in this example, consider a derivation of the behavioural equation (15.32) based on the assumption that the agent chooses y to maximize his expected utility conditional on the information available to him. Let the utility function be

$$U(y, z; \beta) = -(y - z\beta)^2 \tag{15.41}$$

where β is a parameter which is by hypothesis completely unrelated to the distribution of z and hence is invariant to any changes in the δs in equation (15.33). Allowing for a possible random error v_t, arising from optimization, the decision rule is

$$y_t = \beta z_t^e + v_t \tag{15.42}$$

where z_t^e represents the agent's expectation of z_t conditionally on his information set I_t. In the perfect information case where z_t is contained in I_t, $z_t^e = z_t$ and (15.32) follows directly from (15.42). Hence β is structurally invariant and the assumption that $\sigma_{12} = \text{cov}(v_t, \varepsilon_{2t}) = 0$ is sufficient for the weak exogeneity of β and, consequently, for its super exogeneity. The imperfect information case raises more subtle issues since, as argued in, for example, chapter 17, z_t^e may not coincide with the expectation of z_t as derived from (15.33). In this example, however, we discuss only the rational expectations formulation originally proposed by Muth (1961) whereby it is assumed that z_t^e and $\mathcal{E}(z_t | \cdot)$ in (15.33) coincide. Hence (15.32) follows from (15.42) and

$$\varepsilon_{1t} = v_t - \beta \varepsilon_{2t} \tag{15.43}$$

so that $\sigma_{12} = \text{cov}(v_t, \varepsilon_{2t}) - \beta \sigma_{22}$. Therefore, the conventional assumption that $\text{cov}(v_t, \varepsilon_{2t}) = 0$ entails that $\sigma_{12} = -\beta \sigma_{22} \neq 0$ in which case z_t is neither weakly exogenous nor super exogenous for β even though β is invariant. On the other hand, rational expectations *per se* does not exclude the possibility that $\sigma_{12} = 0$ (so that z_t remains weakly exogenous for β) since, for example,

$$\text{cov}(v_t, \varepsilon_{2t}) = \sigma_{22}\beta \tag{15.44}$$

suffices.

Under the familiar assumptions $\text{cov}(v_t, \varepsilon_{2t}) = 0$, the conditional expectation (15.37) and the reduced form (15.35) coincide. No current value of z belongs in the conditional expectation of y_t given (z_t, I_t). Nevertheless, z_t is not weakly exogenous for β because the parameter β cannot be recovered from the reduced form coefficients c_1 and c_2 alone. This illustrates that, even when the current value fails to enter the conditional expectation, weak exogeneity need not hold.

If the c_i were the parameters of interest, then z_t would be weakly exogenous, but these reduced form parameters are not structurally invariant to changes in the δs. The Lucas (1976) criticism applies directly to this equation regardless of whether y Granger-causes z. The derivation and the non-invariance of these parameters suggests why they should not be the parameters of interest. Once again, testing for

Granger causality has little to do with the Lucas criticism or the estimability or formulation of the parameters of interest. It is still possible to estimate β efficiently, for example by estimating (15.32) and (15.33) jointly as suggested by Wallis (1980), but this requires specifying and estimating both equations.[13] If there is a structural shift in the parameters of the second equation, this must also be allowed for in the joint estimation. This example shows the close relationship between weak exogeneity and structural invariance and points out how models derived from rational expectations behaviour may or may not have weak exogeneity and structural invariance.

Example 15.3 This final example shows that with a slight extension of the linear Gaussian structure to include serial correlation the concept of predeterminedness becomes even less useful.

Consider the model

$$y_t = \beta z_t + u_t, \tag{15.45}$$

$$u_t = \rho u_{t-1} + \varepsilon_{1t}, \tag{15.46}$$

$$z_t = \gamma y_{t-1} + \varepsilon_{2t}, \tag{15.47}$$

$$\begin{bmatrix} \varepsilon_{1t} \\ \varepsilon_{2t} \end{bmatrix} \sim IN(0, \Sigma) \qquad \Sigma = \begin{bmatrix} \sigma_{11} & \sigma_{12} \\ \sigma_{12} & \sigma_{22} \end{bmatrix}. \tag{15.48}$$

Although this model is unidentified in a rather subtle sense, this need not concern us here as all the special cases to be discussed will be identified. The issue is dealt with more fully in EHR.

The conditional expectation of y_t given z_t and X_{t-1} implies the regression

$$y_t = bz_t + cy_{t-1} + dz_{t-1} + \eta_t \qquad \eta_t \sim IN(0, \sigma^2), \tag{15.49}$$

where

$$b = \beta + \frac{\sigma_{12}}{\sigma_{22}} \qquad c = \rho - \frac{\gamma\sigma_{12}}{\sigma_{22}} \qquad d = -\beta\rho \qquad \sigma^2 = \sigma_{11} - \frac{\sigma_{12}^2}{\sigma_{22}}. \tag{15.50}$$

The covariance between z_t and u_t is given by

$$cov(z_t, u_t) = \left(\sigma_{12} + \sigma_{11} \frac{\gamma\rho}{1 - \rho^2} \right) (1 - \gamma\rho\beta)^{-1}. \tag{15.51}$$

Note first that, as indicated by (15.51), the condition $\sigma_{12} = 0$ is *not* sufficient for the predeterminedness of z_t in (15.45). However, $\sigma_{12} = 0$ is sufficient for the weak exogeneity of z_t for the parameters β and ρ, as can be seen directly from (15.50) where the parameters of the conditional model (15.49) are subject to a common factor restriction but are variation free with those of the marginal model (15.47). Thus, the parameters of (15.49) could be estimated by imposing the restrictions through some form of autoregressive maximum likelihood method. Ordinary least squares estimation of β in (15.45) will be inconsistent whereas autoregressive least squares will be both consistent and asymptotically efficient. This example shows the advantages of formulating definitions in terms of expectations conditional on the past.

A second interesting property of this model occurs when $\sigma_{12} \neq 0$ but $\gamma = 0$. Again (15.51) shows that z_t is not predetermined in (15.45) but, surprisingly, it is weakly exogenous for β and ρ. The three regression coefficients in (15.49) are now a non-singular transformation of the three unknown parameters $(\beta, \rho, \sigma_{12}/\sigma_{22})$ and these operate a cut with respect to the remaining nuisance parameter σ_{22}. *Ordinary least squares estimation of (15.49) provides efficient estimates of its parameters* and the maximum likelihood estimate of β is $-d/c$. Both ordinary least squares and autoregressive least squares estimation of (15.45) would yield inconsistent estimates of β.

The case where

$$(1 - \rho^2)\sigma_{12} + \gamma\rho\sigma_{11} = 0 \tag{15.52}$$

raises several important issues which are discussed in detail in EHR. In short, the condition (15.52) identifies the model but violates both condition (i) and condition (ii) in definition 15.5 so that z_t is not weakly exogenous for (β, ρ), neither is it for (b, c, d) in (15.49). In particular, the autoregressive least squares estimator of β in (15.45) and (15.46) is inconsistent even though, as a consequence of the predeterminedness of z_t in (15.45), the first-step ordinary least squares estimators of β in (15.45) and ρ in (15.46) are consistent (but not efficient).

This concludes the discussion of the examples. It is hoped that these have shown the usefulness of the concepts of weak and strong exogeneity, structural invariance and super exogeneity in analysing familiar and possibly some unfamiliar situations. Further examples can be found in EHR including a truncated latent variable model based upon Maddala and Lee (1976).

4 Application to Dynamic Simultaneous Equations Models

In this section we shall apply our analysis to dynamic simultaneous equations models (DSEMs). As this is the arena in which notions of exogeneity are most heavily used and tested, it is important to relate our concepts to conventional wisdom. It will be shown that the conventional definitions must be supplemented with several conditions for the concepts to have force. However, when these conditions are added, then in standard textbook models predeterminedness becomes equivalent to weak exogeneity and strict exogeneity becomes equivalent to strong exogeneity. Finally, our framework helps clarify the connections between such (modified) concepts and the notions of Wold causal orderings (see Strotz and Wold, 1960), 'block recursive structures' (see Fisher, 1966b) and 'exogeneity tests' as in Wu (1973).

Following Richard (1979, 1980) the system of equations need not be complete and thus the analysis is directly a generalization of the conventional DSEM. Assuming normality and linearity of the conditional expectations $\phi_t = \mathscr{E}(x_t | X_{t-1}, \theta)$, let [14]

$$D(x_t | X_{t-1}, \theta) = f_N^n\left(x_t \,\Big|\, \sum \Pi(i)x_{t-i}, \Omega\right) \tag{15.53}$$

where $\{\Pi(i)\}$ and Ω are functions of a vector of unknown parameters $\theta \in \Theta$. *Define* the 'innovations' or 'reduced form disturbances' v_t by

$$v_t = x_t - \phi_t = x_t - \sum \Pi(i)x_{t-i}. \tag{15.54}$$

Then, ϕ_t being conditional on X_{t-1},

$$\text{cov}(v_t, x_{t-i}) = 0 \qquad \text{for all } i > 0 \tag{15.55}$$

and hence

$$\text{cov}(v_t, v_{t-i}) = 0 \qquad \text{for all } i > 0. \tag{15.56}$$

We define the dynamic multipliers $Q(i)$ by the recursion

$$Q(0) = I_n$$

and

$$Q(i) = \sum_{j=1}^{i} \Pi(j)Q(i-j) \qquad \text{for all } i \geqslant 1, \tag{15.57}$$

and note that

$$\text{cov}(v_t, x_{t+i}) = Q(i)\Omega \qquad \text{for all } i \geqslant 0. \tag{15.58}$$

Often the specification of θ is (partially) achieved by considering sets of behavioural relationships. Such relationships can correspond to optimizing behaviour given expectations about future events, allow for adaptive responses and include mechanisms for correcting previous mistakes. In our framework, where attention is focused on the conditional densities $D(x_t | X_{t-1}, \theta)$ it is natural to specify these relationships in terms of the conditional expectations ϕ_t. Consider, therefore, a set of $g \leqslant n$ linear behavioural relationships of the form

$$B\phi_t + \sum C(i)x_{t-i} = 0 \tag{15.59}$$

where B and $\{C(i)\}$ are $g \times n$ matrix functions of a vector of 'structural' coefficients $\delta \in \Delta$, with rank $B = g$ almost everywhere in Δ. The δs are typically parameters of interest. We can also define a g-dimensional vector of unobservable 'structural disturbances':

$$\epsilon_t = Bx_t + \sum C(i)x_{t-i} \tag{15.60}$$

which also satisfy, by construction, the properties (15.55) and (15.56).

Let Σ denote the covariance matrix of ϵ_t. In all generality Σ is also treated as a function of δ. From (15.53), (15.54), (15.59) and (15.60) we must have $\epsilon_t = Bv_t$ and

$$B\Pi(i) + C(i) \equiv 0 \qquad \text{for all } i \geqslant 0$$

$$\Sigma = B\Omega B'. \tag{15.61}$$

The identities (15.61) define a correspondence between Δ and Θ or, equivalently, a function h from Δ to $P(\Theta)$, the set of all subsets of Θ. To any given $\delta \in \Delta$, h associates a subset of Θ which we denote by $h(\delta)$. In the rest of the chapter it is assumed that (i) δ is *identified* in the sense that

$$\forall \delta, \delta^* \in \Delta \qquad \delta \neq \delta^* \rightarrow h(\delta) \cap h(\delta^*) = \varnothing, \tag{15.62}$$

and (ii) all values in Θ are compatible with (15.61),

$$\Theta = \bigcup_{\delta \in \Delta} h(\delta), \tag{15.63}$$

so that $\{h(\delta)\}$ is a partition of Θ.

Let s denote the number of non-zero columns in $\{\Pi(i)\}$ and C_n the set of $n \times n$ symmetric positive definite matrices. If $\Theta = \mathbb{R}^{sn} \times C_n$ except for the set of zero Lebesgue measure, then the model (15.53) is *just identified*. It is *over-identified* if Θ is a strict subset of $\mathbb{R}^{sn} \times C_n$.

When $g < n$, it often proves convenient to define an auxiliary parameter vector, say $\bar{\theta} \in \bar{\Theta}$ of the form $\bar{\theta} = (\delta, \theta_2)$ where θ_2 is a subvector of θ defined in such a way that $\bar{\Theta}$ and Θ are in one-to-one correspondence. If, in particular, $\{\Pi(i)\}$ and Ω are subject to no other constraints than those derived from the identities (15.61) as implicitly assumed in this section, then we can select for θ_2 the coefficients of $n - g$ unconstrained 'reduced form' equations,[15] whereby

$$\bar{\Theta} = \Delta \times \Theta_2, \quad \text{with} \quad \Theta_2 = \mathbb{R}^{s(n-g)} \times C_{n-g}. \tag{15.64}$$

The specification of many econometric models 'allows for' serial correlation of the residuals, i.e. incorporates linear relationships of the form

$$B^* x_t + \sum C^*(i) x_{t-i} = u_t \sim \mathrm{N}(0, \Phi) \tag{15.65}$$

where B^* and $\{C^*(i)\}$ are claimed to be parameters of interest (or well-defined functions thereof) and u_t is seen as a g-dimensional 'autonomous' process, subject to serial correlation. Note that if (15.65) is to be used to *derive* the distribution of x_t from that of u_t, then the system must be 'complete', i.e. $g = n$.

Provided that u_t has an autoregressive representation,

$$u_t = \sum R_i u_{t-i} + e_t \tag{15.66}$$

where $e_t \sim \mathrm{IN}(0, \Sigma)$, then (15.65) can be transformed to have serially uncorrelated 'errors' (the new parameterization being subject to common factor restrictions as in Sargan, 1980a) in which case the transformed model can be reinterpreted in terms of conditional expectations as in (15.53). More general specifications of u_t are not ruled out in principle, but might seriously complicate the analysis.

We can now unambiguously characterize and interrelate the concepts of Granger non-causality, predeterminedness and strict exogeneity, as given in definitions 15.1–15.3, for potentially over-identified and incomplete DSEMs which have been transformed to have serially uncorrelated residuals. Since these concepts may apply only to a subset of the equation system (15.59), this is accordingly partitioned into the first $g_1 \leqslant p$ equations and the remaining $g_2 = g - g_1 \leqslant q$ equations – see, for example, Fisher (1966b) on the notion of block recursive structures. We partition the Πs, Qs and Ω conformably with the variables $x'_t = (y'_t z'_t)$, B conformably with the variables and the equations and the Cs and Σ conformably with the equations as

$$\Pi(i) = \begin{bmatrix} \Pi_1(i) \\ \Pi_2(i) \end{bmatrix} = \begin{bmatrix} \Pi_{11}(i) & \Pi_{12}(i) \\ \Pi_{21}(i) & \Pi_{22}(i) \end{bmatrix},$$

$$Q(i) = \begin{bmatrix} Q_1(i) \\ Q_2(i) \end{bmatrix} = \begin{bmatrix} Q_{11}(i) & Q_{12}(i) \\ Q_{21}(i) & Q_{22}(i) \end{bmatrix},$$

(15.67)

$$\Omega = (\Omega_1 \Omega_2) = \begin{bmatrix} \Omega_{11} & \Omega_{12} \\ \Omega_{21} & \Omega_{22} \end{bmatrix} \qquad B = \begin{bmatrix} B_1 \\ B_2 \end{bmatrix} = \begin{bmatrix} B_{11} & B_{12} \\ B_{21} & B_{22} \end{bmatrix},$$

$$C(i) = \begin{bmatrix} C_1(i) \\ C_2(i) \end{bmatrix} \qquad \Sigma = \begin{bmatrix} \Sigma_{11} & \Sigma_{12} \\ \Sigma_{21} & \Sigma_{22} \end{bmatrix}.$$

Theorem 15.1 For the class of models defined by (15.53) plus (15.59):

(i) y does not Granger-cause z if and only if

$\quad Q_{21}(i) = 0 \qquad$ for all $i \geqslant 1$;

(ii) z_t is predetermined in the first g_1 equations of (15.59) if and only if

$\quad B_1 \Omega_2 = 0$;

(iii) z_t is strictly exogenous in the first g_1 equations of (15.59) if and only if

$\quad B_1 \Omega Q'_2(i) = 0 \qquad$ for all $i \geqslant 0$.

(iv)   Conditions (i) and (ii) are sufficient for (iii). If $g_1 = p$, they are also necessary for (iii).

(v)   If $B_{21} = 0$, $\Sigma_{12} = 0$ and rank $B_{22} = q \, (= g_2)$, then z_t is predetermined in the first g_1 equations of (15.59).

Proof: The proof follows from the definitions 15.1–15.3 together with (15.57), wherefrom it can be shown by recurrence that $(\Pi_{21}(i) = 0; \, i \geqslant 1)$ is equivalent to $(Q_{21}(i) = 0; \, i \geqslant 1)$. See EHR for more details.

In order to discuss weak exogeneity the parameters of interest must be defined. In the theorems below it will be assumed that the parameters of interest are all grouped together in the first g_1 equations. Thus it is not a cavalier matter which equations are put in the first group. For example, in a control problem, the first g_1 equations might describe the behaviour of the economic agents given the controlled values of z_t, while the remaining g_2 equations describe the control rules which have been operative.

Factorizing the joint density (15.53) also requires the introduction of an appropriate reparameterization. This is the object of lemma 15.1 which translates into our notation results which are otherwise well known.

Lemma 15.1 The joint density (15.53) factorizes into the product of the conditional density

$$D(y_t|z_t, X_{t-1}, \lambda_1) = f_N^p\left(y_t|\Delta_{12}z_t + \sum \Pi_{1.2}(i)x_{t-i}, \Omega_{11.2}\right) \tag{15.68}$$

and the marginal density

$$D(z_t|X_{t-1}, \lambda_2) = f_N^q\left(z_t\left|\sum \Pi_2(i)x_{t-i}, \Omega_{22}\right.\right) \tag{15.69}$$

with $\lambda_1 = (\Delta_{12}, \{\Pi_{1.2}(i)\}, \Omega_{11.2})$, $\lambda_2 = (\{\Pi_2(i)\}, \Omega_{22})$,

$$\Delta_{12} = \Omega_{12}\Omega_{22}^{-1} \qquad \Omega_{11.2} = \Omega_{11} - \Omega_{12}\Omega_{22}^{-1}\Omega_{21} \qquad \Pi_{1.2}(i) = \Pi_1(i) - \Delta_{12}\Pi_2(i). \tag{15.70}$$

Proof: See, for example, Press (1972, sections 3.4 and 3.5).

If the model (15.53) is *just identified*, then λ_1 and λ_2 are variation free with respective domains of variation $\Lambda_1 = \mathbb{R}^{p\times q} \times \{\mathbb{R}^{p\times n}\} \times C_p$ and $\Lambda_2 = \{\mathbb{R}^{q\times n}\} \times C_q$ and z_t is weakly exogenous for ψ if and only if ψ is a function of λ_1 only. However, in order to be operational within the framework of DSEMs, such a condition should be expressed in terms of the structural coefficients δ since these are themselves typically parameters of interest. Also, most applications involve over-identified models for which λ_1 and λ_2 are no longer variation free unless some additional conditions are satisfied. Thus, the object of theorem 15.2 is to derive *general* conditions on δ for the weak exogeneity of z_t for ψ. By their nature, these conditions are *sufficient* and, as in section 3, it is easy to construct examples in which they are *not necessary*. Consequently, in so far as so-called 'exogeneity tests' are typically tests for such conditions, rejection on such a test does not necessarily entail that the weak exogeneity assumption is invalid (see, for example, example 15.3 when $\sigma_{12} \neq 0$ and $\gamma = 0$).

Theorem 15.2 For the DSEM in (15.53) plus (15.59) consider the following conditions:

(i) $B_1\Omega_2 = 0$,
(ii) $B_{21} = 0$,
(iii) $(B_1, \{C_1(i)\}, \Sigma_{11})$ and $(B_2, \{C_2(i)\}, \Sigma_{22})$ are variation free,
(iv) ψ is a function of $(B_1, \{C_1(i)\}, \Sigma_{11})$,
(v) $\Sigma_{12} = 0$,
(vi)   rank $B_{22} = q$,
(vii) $(B_2, \{C_2(i)\}, \Sigma_{22})$ are just identified parameters.

The following sets of conditions are sufficient for the weak exogeneity of z_t for ψ:

(a) (i) (ii) (iii) (iv),
(b) (ii) (iii) (iv) (v) (vi),
(c) (i) (iii) (iv) (vii).

Proof: The basic result (a) generalizes theorem 3.1 in Richard (1980) in that it also covers cases where restrictions are imposed on Σ. The proof in Richard extends to the more general case since, under (i) and (ii), the identity $\Sigma = B\Omega B'$ separates into the two identities $\Sigma_{11} = B_{11}\Omega_{11.2}B'_{11}$ and $\Sigma_{22} = B_{22}\Omega_{22}B'_{22}$. Result (b) follows from (a) together with condition (ii) and (v) in theorem 15.1. Result (c) follows by applying (a) to a system consisting of the first g_1 behavioural relationships and g_2 *unrestricted* reduced form equations whose parameters are in one-to-one correspondence with $(B_2, \{C_2(i)\}, \Sigma_{22})$ and variation free with $(B_1, \{C_1(i)\}, \Sigma_{11})$ following conditions (vii) and (iii).

The major differences in the sufficient conditions for weak exogeneity and for predeterminedness are conditions (iii) and (iv) of theorem 15.2, which assure the model builder that there are no cross-equation restrictions to the second block of equations and that there are no interesting parameters in that block.

To show the importance of these conditions in any definition, consider a set of $g \leqslant p < n$ just identified behavioural relationships, as given by (15.59), such that $B\Omega_2 \neq 0$. As is well known (see, for example, Strotz and Wold, 1960) the system (15.59) can be replaced by an observationally equivalent one in which z_t is predetermined and hence is strictly exogenous if y does not Granger-cause z. For example let

$$\bar{B} = \Phi(I_g : -\Omega_{12}\Omega_{22}^{-1}),$$ (15.71)

$$\bar{C}(i) = -\bar{B}\Pi(i) \qquad i \geqslant 1,$$ (15.72)

where Φ is an arbitrary but known $g \times g$ non-singular matrix so that $(\bar{B}, \{\bar{C}(i)\})$ are just identified by construction. Such transformations, with $\Phi = I_2$, have been implicitly used in examples 15.1–15.2. Replacing (15.59) by

$$\bar{B}\phi_t + \sum \bar{C}(i)x_{t-i} = 0$$ (15.73)

leaves (15.53) unaffected, but now $\bar{B}\Omega_2 = 0$. Consequently, $(\bar{B}, \{\bar{C}(i)\})$ can be estimated consistently from the conditional model $D(y_t|z_t, X_{t-1}, \cdot)$ together with (15.73). These estimates would be efficient provided that (15.59) were just identified. However, it is essential to realize that, since $g \leqslant p < n$, the parameters $(B, \{C(i)\})$ are typically not functions of $(\bar{B}, \{\bar{C}(i)\})$ alone and, if the former are of interest, transforming (15.59) to (15.73) does not allow valid inference conditionally on z_t.

Thus, although at first sight, in normal DSEMs weak exogeneity appears to be close to the notion of a Wold causal ordering, without the concept of parameters of interest the latter lacks force since there may be no cut which separates the parameters of interest and the nuisance parameters. Nevertheless, it must be stressed that Wold and Jureen (1955, p. 14) *explicitly* include the condition that 'each equation in the system expresses a unilateral causal dependence' which, in the spirit of our use of sequential cuts, seems designed to exclude arbitrary transformations of the system (15.59); see also the distinction in Bentzel and Hansen (1955) between basic and derived models.

·In Wu's (1973) analysis, where $g_1 = 1$, it is implicit that conditions (iii) and (vii) of theorem 15.2 are satisfied in which case the condition for predeterminedness $(B_1 \Omega_2 = 0)$ is indeed sufficient for the weak exogeneity of z_t for the parameters of the first behavioural equation (but not necessarily for other parameters of interest). It must be stressed, however, that if the remaining behavioural equations in the model under consideration are over-identified, then predeterminedness might no longer be sufficient on its own for the weak exogeneity of z_t. Therefore, even if the conditions (iii) and (iv) of theorem 15.2 are incorporated in the definition of predeterminedness as is sometimes implicitly done, there would remain many situations where weak exogeneity and predeterminedness would still differ. Cases (a) and (b) in theorem 15.2 provide *sufficient* conditions which are applicable to more general cases than the one considered in Wu. Note, however, that condition (ii) in particular is not necessary and that case (c) could be made more general at the cost of some tedious notation as hinted by the following example. [16]

Example 15.4 Consider a (complete) DSEM with $n = 3$, $p = g_1 = 1$, $q = g_2 = 2$ and

$$B = \begin{bmatrix} 1 & b_1 & 0 \\ b_2 & 1 & 0 \\ 0 & b_3 & 1 \end{bmatrix} \qquad C(1) = \begin{bmatrix} c_1 & 0 & 0 \\ 0 & c_2 & c_3 \\ 0 & c_4 & 0 \end{bmatrix} \qquad C(i) = 0 \qquad i > 1.$$

The bs and cs are assumed to be variation free. The condition $B_1 \Omega_2 = 0$, which is equivalent to $\sigma_{12} = b_2 \sigma_{11}$ and $\sigma_{13} = 0$, is sufficient for the weak exogeneity of (y_{2t}, y_{3t}) for (b_1, c_1, σ_{11}) even though $B'_{21} = (b_2, 0) \neq 0$ and the third behavioural relationship is over-identified (but does not contain y_{1t}!). Note that the predeterminedness of y_{2t} in the first behavioural relationship ($\sigma_{12} = b_2 \sigma_{11}$) is sufficient for the consistency of ordinary least squares estimation of (b_1, c_1, σ_{11}) in that relationship but not for the weak exogeneity of (y_{2t}, y_{3t}) – or y_{2t} alone – for (b_1, c_1, σ_{11}). In the absence of additional restrictions such as $\sigma_{13} = 0$ a more *efficient* estimator of (b_1, c_1, σ_{11}) is obtained by, for example full information maximum likelihood estimation of the complete DSEM.

Note finally from theorem 15.1(v) and 15.2(b) that the standard block-recursive model is sufficient for both (block) predeterminedness and (block) weak exogeneity (again assuming the parameterization satisfies (iii) and (iv)); this may help explain its importance in the development of the theory of simultaneous equations models.

5 Summary and Conclusions

Given the pervasive role of the concept of 'exogeneity' in econometrics, it is essential to characterize uniquely the implications of claims that certain variables are 'exogenous' according to particular definitions. Also, it is useful to have definitions which require minimal conditions and yet are applicable to as wide a class of relevant models as possible. Consequently, general and unambiguous definitions are proposed for *weak*, *strong* and *super* exogeneity in terms of the joint densities of observable variables and the parameters of interest in given models, thus extending and formalizing the approach in Koopmans (1950a). 'Exogeneity' assertions are usually intended to allow the analysis of one set of variables without having to specify exactly how a second related set is determined and such an analysis could comprise any or all of inference, forecasting or policy. In each case, the conclusions are conditional on the validity of the relevant 'exogeneity' claims (a comment germane to theoretical models also, although we only consider observable variables) and, since different conditioning statements are required in these three cases, three distinct but interrelated concepts of exogeneity are necessary.

The joint density of the observed variables $x_t = (y_t'\ z_t')'$, conditional on their past, can always be factorized as the conditional density of y_t given z_t times the marginal density of z_t. If (i) the parameters λ_1 and λ_2 of these conditional and marginal densities are not subject to cross-restrictions (i.e there is a cut) and (ii) the parameters of interest (denoted by ψ) can be uniquely determined from the parameters of the conditional model alone (i.e. $\psi = f(\lambda_1)$), then inference concerning ψ from the joint density will be equivalent to that from the conditional density so that the latter may be used without loss of relevant information. Under such conditions, z_t is *weakly exogenous* for ψ and, for purposes of *inference* about ψ, z_t may be treated 'as if' it were determined outside the (conditional) model under study, making the analysis simpler and more robust.

Conditions (i) and (ii) clearly are not sufficient to treat z_t as if it were fixed in repeated samples, since the definition of weak exogeneity is unspecific about relationships between z_t and y_{t-i} for $i \geqslant 1$. However, if (iii) y does not Granger-cause z, then the data density of $X_t^1 = (x_1, \ldots x_t)'$ factorizes into the conditional density of Y_t^1 given Z_t^1 times the marginal of Z_t^1 and hence $\{z_t\}$ may be treated as if it were fixed. If (i), (ii) and (iii) are satisfied, then z_t is *strongly exogenous* for ψ and forecasts could be made conditional on fixed future zs.

Nevertheless strong exogeneity is insufficient to sustain conditional policy analysis since (i) does not preclude the possibility that, while λ_1 and λ_2 are variation free within any *given* 'regime', λ_1 might vary in response to a change in λ_2 between 'regimes'. The additional condition that (iv) λ_1 is invariant to changes in λ_2 (or more generally the conditional distribution is invariant to any change in the marginal distribution) is required to sustain conditional *policy* experiments for fixed λ_1, and z_t is *super exogenous* for ψ if (i), (ii) and (iv) are satisfied (so that (iii) is not necessary either).

In fact, if the generating process of the conditioning variables is susceptible to changes over either sample or forecast periods, then the failure of (iv) will invalidate inference and predictions based on the assertion that λ_1 is a constant parameter, whether or not z_t includes 'policy variables'. In worlds where policy parameters change, false super exogeneity assumptions are liable to produce predictive failures in conditional models (see Lucas, 1976). Control experiments which involve changes in λ_2 must first establish the super exogeneity of z_t for ψ under the class of interventions considered; we know of no sufficient conditions for establishing such results, but a necessary condition is that the conditional model does not experience predictive failure within sample (see chapter 11).

Even in constant-parameter worlds (and certainly in worlds of parameter change), the new concepts are distinct from the more familiar notions of predeterminedness and strict exogeneity. Following precise definitions of these two concepts, it is shown through examples that their formulation in terms of *unobservable* disturbances entails ambiguous implications for inference and that strict exogeneity is neither necessary nor sufficient for inference in conditional models without loss of relevant information. Moreover, models in which predeterminedness is obtained by construction need not have invariant parameters and, since predeterminedness is necessary for strict exogeneity, establishing only the latter does not provide a valid basis for conditional prediction or conditional policy. The various concepts are compared and contrasted in detail in closed linear dynamic simultaneous equations systems, and the usefulness of (i) and (ii) in clarifying the debate about Wold causal orderings is demonstrated.

It is natural to enquire about the testable implications of alternative exogeneity assumptions. Condition (iv) is indirectly testable (as noted) via tests for parameter constancy, although as with all test procedures. Rejection of the null does not indicate what alternative is relevant and non-rejection may simply reflect low power (so that there are advantages in specifying the regime shift process as in Richard, 1980). Condition (iii) is common to both strong and strict exogeneity notions and may be testable in the conditional model (see Sims, 1972b; Geweke, 1984) but may also require specification of the marginal density of z_t as in Granger (1969). Also, predeterminedness tests have been the subject of a large literature (see *inter alia* Wu, 1973).

To test weak exogeneity, the conditional and marginal densities could be embedded in a joint density function, although the choice of the latter may or may not generate testable implications. It is somewhat paradoxical to estimate the parameters of a (potentially very complicated) marginal model just to test whether or not one needed to specify that model. Moreover, mis-specifications in the marginal model may induce false rejection of the null of weak exogeneity. Nevertheless, Engle (1982b, 1984) considers various weak exogeneity tests based on the Lagrange multiplier principle. Also, on a positive note, while both weak exogeneity and parameter constancy are conjectural features in a conditional modelling exercise, if the data generating process of z_t has changed but the conditional model has not, then some credibility must attach to the latter since it was hazarded to potential rejection and survived.

Finally, we believe that the new concepts are not only general (being based explicitly on density functions and encompassing worlds of parameter change) and unambiguously characterized (thus clarifying a vital concept in econometrics) but also highlight interesting and novel aspects of familiar problems (as shown in the examples in section 3).

Notes

1 The emphasis on observables does not preclude formulating theories in terms of unobservables (e.g. 'permanent' components, expectations, disturbances etc.), but these should be integrated out first in order to obtain an operational model to which our concepts may be applied.

2 Throughout the chapter, the term 'efficient estimation' is used as a shorthand for 'conducting inference without loss of relevant information', and does not entail any claims as to, for example, the efficiency of particular estimators in small samples.

3 It is assumed that the dimensionality of Θ is sufficiently small relative to nT that it makes sense to discuss, 'efficient' estimation.

4 We use the term 'strictly exogenous' where some authors use 'exogenous' to distinguish this concept from that introduced below.

5 The concept of nuisance parameter, however, is ambiguous. Whether or not a parameter is a nuisance parameter critically depends on which (re)parameterization is used. If, for example, $\theta = (\alpha, \beta)$ and β is the sole parameter of interest, then α is a nuisance parameter. In contrast, a reparameterization using (α, γ) where $\gamma = \beta/\alpha$ entails that β is not a function of γ alone, and so α is not a nuisance parameter.

6 It follows that, unless y does not Granger-cause z, $L_1^0(\lambda_1; X_T^1)$ is not *sensu stricto* a likelihood function, although it is often implicitly treated as such in the econometric literature, but it is a valid basis for inferences about ψ, *provided that* z_t is weakly exogenous for ψ.

7 The definition can always be restricted to a specific class of distribution changes. This will implicitly be the case in the examples which are discussed in section 3.

8 It is also necessary for most purposes. However, since in (15.14) ψ need not depend on all the elements in λ_1 it might happen that ψ and λ_2 are variation free even though λ_1 and λ_2 are not in which case neglecting the restrictions between λ_1 and λ_2 *might* entail no loss of efficiency for inference on ψ. More subtly, whether or not cuts are necessary to conduct inference based on partial models without loss of information obviously very much depends on how sample information is measured. See in particular the concepts of G- and M-ancillarity in Barndorff-Nielsen (1978).

9 This criticism is hardly specific to the concept of exogeneity. For example, unless there are parameters of interest, it is meaningless to require that an estimator should be consistent since it is always possible to redefine the 'parameters' such that any chosen convergent estimation method yields consistent estimates thereof (see for example, Hendry, 1979b).

10 Evidently if one wished to test the conditions under which (ii) held then over-identifying restrictions such as the ones typically implied by Granger non-causality would affect the properties of the test.

11 This illustrates the importance of incorporating in definition 15.9 the requirement that the conditional model $D(y_t | z_t, X_{t-1}, \lambda_1)$ be structurally invariant even though ψ may depend only on a subvector of λ_1.

12 An interesting example of the complexities arising from over-identification occurs if $\omega_{11} = 1$ in (15.24) *a priori*. Then the factorization (15.27) and (15.28) no longer operates a cut as a result of the over-identifying constraint $\sigma^2 + \beta^2 \omega_{22} = 1$, while the factorization (15.30) and (15.31) still does. Further, β and σ^2 are well-defined functions of (γ, δ, τ^2) since $\beta = \delta/(\delta^2 + \tau^2)$ and $\sigma^2 = \tau^2/(\delta^2 + \tau^2)$, while α is not. Therefore, z_t is no longer weakly exogenous for (β, σ^2) while y_t now is! Neither of these two variables is weakly exogenous for α.

13 Depending on the model formulation, instrumental variables estimation of (say) (15.32) alone is sometimes fully efficient.

14 Our framework explicitly requires that the distribution of the endogenous variables be completely specified. Normality (and linearity) assumptions are introduced here because they prove algebraically convenient. Other distributional assumptions could be considered at the cost of complicating the algebra. Furthermore, there exist distributions, such as the multivariate Student distribution, for which there exist no cuts. Evidently weak exogeneity can always be achieved by construction, simply by specifying independently of each other a conditional and a marginal model, but is then no longer testable. More interestingly, conditions such as the ones which are derived below could be viewed as 'approximate' or 'local' exogeneity conditions under more general specifications. Given the recent upsurge of non-linear non-Gaussian models in econometrics this is clearly an area which deserves further investigation.

15 This is current practice in the literature on so-called limited information procedures. Non-Bayesian inference procedures based on likelihood principles are invariant with respect to the choice of these $n - g$ reduced form equations, provided they form a non-singular set of equations together with the g structural relationships (15.59). Also, in a Bayesian framework there exist prior densities on θ such that the corresponding posterior densities on δ have similar invariance properties. For details see for example Drèze and Richard (1984) for $g = 1$, or Richard (1979) for $g > 1$.

16 We are grateful to A. Holly for providing us with this example and, more generally, for pointing out several shortcomings in earlier drafts of this section.

16

On the Formulation of Empirical
Models in Dynamic Econometrics

with Jean-François Richard

Preamble

The next two chapters were written more or less contemporaneously with 'Exogeneity' (as was chapter 4) and each drew on, and influenced, the others. I spent an exceptionally fruitful six months at CORE with Jean-François Richard in 1980 (writing this chapter), immediately followed by six months in San Diego with Rob Engle (when much of chapter 17 was written). The complementarity of the CORE and LSE approaches to modelling now led Jean-François and I to seek a merger which integrated and hence extended both. Retrospectively, the developments seem quite natural but at the time were far from obvious (to me at least!). The theory of reduction discussed in Florens et al. (1974, 1976), Richard (1980) and Florens and Mouchart (1980a, b) fitted hand-in-glove with general-to-simple modelling strategies as described in chapter 3, Mizon (1977a), chapters 6, 7 and 11 and Sargan (1980a) and precisely matched what occurred in Monte Carlo (see Hendry and Harrison, 1974; Hendry, 1979b, 1984a). As noted in the preamble to the previous chapter, exogeneity formalized important aspects of both DHSY and chapter 11, whereas common factor ideas clarified the analysis in Richard (1980) for autoregressive error processes. Importantly for me, the concepts in reduction theory brought previously diverse ideas into a common framework and resolved a number of earlier methodological puzzles. These were distinct benefits, but since more seemed possible, chapter 16 sought to analyse the framework and thereby extend the manual of 'good empirical practice' through delineating more rigorous quality-control procedures.

The crucial concept was that all empirical models were implicitly derived from the data generation process by *reduction operations* (such as marginalizing and conditioning) rather than inheriting the properties of the theoretical model from which their formulation arose. Reductions induced transformed parameters, and corresponding disturbance terms, which together determined the quality of the empirical model. For example, excessive reduction of

Reprinted from *Journal of Econometrics*, 20 (1982) 3–33. The authors are greatly indebted to Frank Srba for undertaking the computations reported below, and to Jean-Pierre Florens, Knud Munk and Aris Spanos for many stimulating discussions on this topic, but do not hold them responsible for the views expressed herein. Financial support from the International Centre for Economics and Related Disciplines and from the Social Science Research Council to the Methodology, Inference and Modelling programme at the London School of Economics is gratefully acknowledged.

the lag length in a dynamic model could induce residual autocorrelation. The reduction idea simultaneously explained why residuals may not have the properties assumed for error terms and why such residuals could be 'redesigned' to satisfy some criterion, such as Durbin–Watson statistics of about 2.0 achieved by 'autocorrelation corrections'. I had earlier characterized this issue as problem 'camouflage'. Moreover, invalid reductions could generate non-constant parameterizations or non-encompassing models (e.g. omitting inflation from the consumption function) but it might not be possible to camouflage such mis-specifications by mechanistic corrections, unlike residual autocorrelation, since the relevant 'redesign' strategy was not obvious. An analysis of *model design* concepts had become essential.

Despite the lesson learned when writing 'Exogeneity' that the categorical imperative was 'be precise', and notwithstanding the overall framework of reduction, it was unclear *how* one formalized model formulation. We defined many of the concepts in an early draft of this chapter and investigated their implications and relationships, but even by mid-1981 the approach lacked a *Gestalt*. The key was a 'taxonomy of information sets' developed partly in response to a challenge by Larry Boland during a seminar at Simon Fraser University. The universe of available information was conceptually partitioned into the six disjoint sets of the (relative) past, present and future of the investigator's own data, evidence from rival models, and theory and measurement information (although later partitions have been finer, as noted in chapter 12). To each of the six elements in that partition there corresponded specific concepts from the modelling literature for which we could prove various properties and links. Consequently, six information sets characterized model selection criteria and hence null hypotheses, against which tests of different alternatives could be developed: the proliferation of tests was due to the potentially infinite range of alternatives, not to a large number of criteria. This provided the overall framework within which formal relationships between concepts could be established as well as offering new interpretations of existing ideas.

The chapter begins by distinguishing between theory models, which are free creations, and empirical models which must be reductions of the data generation process. As earlier, the Monte Carlo analogy is invoked as an obvious exemplar. An empirical illustration highlights the problems of empirical model formulation and the issues to be analysed. The main empirical model concepts considered relate to the following.

1 *Past data*: white noise and innovation processes; their mutual connections; their relationships to Granger causality and common factors; data coherency; parsimony and variance dominance leading on to model selection criteria.
2 *Contemporaneous data*: exogeneity, both weak and strong; and the distinction between exogeneity at the levels of the process and of the model.
3 *Future data*: parameter constancy and invariance; super exogeneity; and the consequent inadequacy of any model selection criterion based only on full-sample parsimonious non-dominance.
4 *Rival models*: encompassing, and its basis in model reduction, hence including 'non-nested' models as in Cox (1961) since all models are nested in the process; the necessity but insufficiency of variance dominance for model selection in linear models; and hence the anti-symmetry and obvious reflexivity of encompassing; the transitivity of encompassing is claimed, inducing an important potential role for encompassing to sustain a progressive research strategy; and parsimonious and minimal encompassing are introduced.
5 *Theory information*: theory consistency and parameters of interest, as well as the possibility of a feedback from economic theory to the actual data generation process.
6 *Measurement system*: data admissibility; identities; and functional form specification.

Drawing these concepts together leads to the definition of an empirical model being a tentatively adequate conditional data characterization (TACD), renamed *congruent* by Chris

Allsopp (see chapter 12 above). The earlier empirical illustration is then re-analysed in the light of the formal structure to interrelate the concepts with test statistics. In fact, Aart de Vos has pointed out to me that the selected model has a number of drawbacks and is not a good illustration. The chapter ends by demonstrating the inadequacy of dynamic simulation as a model evaluation criterion, in stark contrast to encompassing.

I can no longer remember why the proof that encompassing is transitive was dropped from the original paper – which is a pity because it was not correct! Consider three rival linear regression models, each of which claims to be a congruent representation against the *overall* information set, so that all the models are in a common probability space:

$$M_1: y = X\beta + \nu \qquad \text{with } \nu \sim N(0, \sigma_\nu^2 I) \tag{1}$$

$$M_2: y = Z\gamma + \varepsilon \qquad \text{with } \varepsilon \sim N(0, \sigma_\varepsilon^2 I) \tag{2}$$

$$M_3: y = W\delta + e \qquad \text{with } e \sim N(0, \sigma_e^2 I). \tag{3}$$

Denote encompassing by E and let the two hypotheses under test be $H_1: M_1 E M_2$ and $H_2: M_2 E M_3$. If encompassing were transitive, then $H_1 + H_2$ should imply that $M_1 E M_3$. Care is required in formulating such an idea. In the chapter, we implicitly employ the following argument: to 'complete' the specifications for testing H_1 and H_2, we need the two mappings of X onto Z and of Z onto W. Suppose that, historically, H_2 is first tested and accepted and then an investigator seeks to test H_1. To derive (3) from (2), a projection of Z onto W will suffice:

$$Z' = \Psi W' + U', \tag{4}$$

so that using (4), M_2 implies that

$$y = W\Psi'\gamma + \{\varepsilon + U\gamma\} \tag{5}$$

and hence $M_2 E M_3 \Rightarrow \delta = \Psi'\gamma$. Given M_2 *only*, then to test H_1 let

$$X' = \Pi Z' + V'. \tag{6}$$

Thus, $M_1 E M_2 \Rightarrow \gamma = \Pi'\beta$ from which it follows that $\delta = \Psi'\Pi'\beta$. Unfortunately, this argument does not prove *direct* transitivity. Certainly the proprietor of M_1 can derive the parameters of M_3 from M_1 but only by using M_2 as an *intermediary*. If (6) is interpreted as the projection of X onto Z and W, so that W is orthogonal to X given Z, then no problem arises. However, forgetting to retain W in the information set for testing encompassing can lead to problems. In a direct confrontation, M_1 need not encompass M_3 since if

$$X' = \Phi_1 Z' + \Phi_2 W' + E' \tag{7}$$

but we only project X onto W with a coefficient Γ, it will not be the case that $\Gamma = \Pi\Psi$ if $\Phi_2 \neq 0$.

The absence of direct transitivity is a result of changing the probability model during the analysis and is essentially the consequence of proceeding from the simple to the general *between studies*. At the end of testing H_2, we have ascertained that

$$\mathscr{E}(y|Z,W) = Z\gamma. \tag{8}$$

The explicit claim underlying M_1 is that

$$\mathscr{E}(y|X,Z,W) = X\beta. \tag{9}$$

However, if (6) rather than (7) is used to derive M_2, then implicitly M_1 becomes M_1^*:

$$\mathscr{E}(y|X,Z) = X\beta. \tag{10}$$

Equations (8) and (10) could *both* hold without (9) being true. In the projection framework, if M_1 is correctly stated as in (9), and (7) holds, then

$$y = X\beta + \nu = Z\Phi_1'\beta + W\Phi_2'\beta + \{\nu + E\beta\} \tag{11}$$

and H_1 will be valid only if $\Phi_1'\beta = \gamma$ and $\Phi_2'\beta = 0$. Although M_2 E M_3 and hence M_3 is redundant relative to M_2, the information set must not be curtailed to Z alone when testing M_1 against M_2, *interpreted as the claim that* $\mathscr{E}(y\,|\,X, Z, W) = Z\gamma$.

Alternatively, it can also occur that M_1 E M_2 and M_1 E M_3 but M_1 does not encompass the union of M_2 and M_3 (i.e. M_2 does not encompass M_3). This is due to the same problem of curtailing the information set, namely to (y, X, Z) for testing M_1 E M_2 and to (y, X, W) for testing M_1 E M_3. A very practical example was inadvertently discovered by DHSY, as noted above, who separately tested their model with a unit income elasticity (M_1) against one with an additional income term (M_2) and, on not rejecting that hypothesis, tested M_1 against a model with liquid assets (M_3), again not rejecting. Nevertheless, HUS rejected M_1 against a model with both a non-unit income elasticity and liquid assets. This problem was noted in chapter 12 and Ericsson and Hendry (1989) offer a more extensive analysis with the implication that, although the single occurrence of either of two items of evidence can corroborate a theory or model, their joint occurrence can refute it! The conundrum disappears if the converse route of general to simple is adopted. The analysis then commences with the joint density of (y, X, Z, W) and evaluates reductions towards one of the M_i. Consequently, if M_1 were to be selected, it would be because y, conditional on X, was independent of Z and W. Thus M_1 would be a valid reduction of M^m,

$$M^m: y = X\lambda_1 + Z\lambda_2 + W\lambda_3 + \eta, \tag{12}$$

and hence would encompass both submodels M_2 and M_3.

This approach leads to the notion of *parsimonious encompassing* (E_p) where the simple or small model is asked to account for the results of the larger or more general model within which it is nested. Since M_1 is nested within M^m, then M^m E M_1 automatically. However, it is an altogether different issue as to whether or not M_1 E_p M^m and it can do so only if M_1 is a valid reduction of M^m; i.e. given X, then Z and W are indeed irrelevant. M_1 will encompass M_2 and M_3 in such a situation since Z and W contain no information about y not already provided by X. Hendry and Richard (1989) provide a recent survey which clarifies the properties of E and E_p. In fact, what the above analysis establishes is that if M_1 $E_p M^m$ and M_2 is nested in M^m, then M_1 E M_2 (similarly for M_3 and the union of M_2 and M_3). It can also be shown that if we introduce an M_2^*,

$$M_2^*: y = X\mu_1 + Z\mu_2 + \xi, \tag{13}$$

then M_1 E_p M_2^* and M_2^* $E_p M^m$ together imply that M_1 $E_p M^m$. Moreover, if M^m is a valid reduction of a yet more general model M so that M^m E_pM, then M_1 E_pM. This follows since M_1 is a valid reduction of a valid reduction (note that we are concerned with concepts here: in finite samples, changes in degrees of freedom imply that reversals could occur).[1] Thus, parsimonious encompassing is transitive; and, closing the circle of the theory of reduction which brought it into being, parsimonious encompassing defines the limits to model reduction.

Finally, formal test statistics for encompassing have since been developed in Mizon (1984) and Mizon and Richard (1986). Chapter 19 updates the analysis.

Note

1 I wonder whether not including formal proofs of these transitivity claims will likewise be problematic in retrospect . . . (see Hendry, 1992, for details).

1 Introduction

Notwithstanding the emphasis on 'model building' in econometrics, there does not seem to exist a formal analysis of 'models' and/or of concepts relevant to empirical models in particular. This chapter is offered as a step towards developing such an analysis. While it is clearly feasible to undertake a completely formal treatment – corresponding to that of, say, Florens and Mouchart (1980a) for the theory of reduction – initially it seemed most useful and comprehensible to consider the problem more heuristically (and primarily in the context of linear processes).

The framework of the chapter is as follows. Available information is conceived of as being partitioned into disjoint sets: past, present and future observations, other data relevant to contending hypotheses, and theory information. For each item, specific concepts are relevant: 'white noise' for lagged data, 'exogeneity' for present, 'parameter constancy' for future, and 'encompassing' for contending models are some examples. For each concept, various properties are established (e.g. 'encompassing' is asymmetric and transitive and so defines an ordering) and relationships between concepts are developed (e.g. if model A has a larger residual variance than Model B, then it cannot encompass model B).

Many widely used concepts arise naturally in the present framework, although the insufficiency of certain of these as a basis for empirical modelling does not seem well known. For example, it is inappropriate to select models by the *sole* criterion that they have white noise residuals (or that combined with a parsimony condition) as this does not necessarily preclude better fitting models being developed from the same basic information. Indeed, these could even be more parsimonious than the initial model if the model building strategy does not ensure that the white noise process is in addition an innovation process relative to the available information. Similarly, simply selecting 'best fitting' models (again with or without parsimony conditions) does not by itself ensure encompassing. Perhaps less well known, and yet of great practical importance, selecting models by the goodness of their 'dynamic simulation tracking performance' is invalid in general and tells more about the structure of the models than about their correspondence to 'reality'.

It must be stressed that the purpose of the chapter is the formulation and preliminary analysis of a number of concepts relevant to the empirical econometric analysis of time-series observations. In such a framework, economic theory plays a relatively neutral role in the sense that the concepts apply irrespective of the models being based on inadequate (or naive) theories or on sophisticated, general and/or well-established theories (see for example the approach in Sargent, 1981). The relationship between theory models and empirical models is discussed in section 2, which is followed by an empirical illustration chosen to 'set the scene' for the analysis of section 4 in which the main concepts and their interrelationships are discussed.

The empirical example is reconsidered in section 5, and section 6 evaluates the role of dynamic simulation in model selection. Concluding comments are provided in section 7.

2 Theory Models and Empirical Models

A model of any set of phenomena is a formal representation thereof in which certain features are abstracted while others are ignored with the intent of providing a simpler description of the salient aspects of the chosen phenomena: 'a model always represents only some but not all the features of the original' (Hayek, 1963, p. 14). Models comprise sets of structures each of which is a well-defined characterization of that which is to be explained. Two classes of model are important: theory models and empirical models. Despite their common aim of seeking an 'accurate' representation of perceived 'reality' and their close interdependence in practice, it is essential to maintain a clear distinction between the two classes in what follows.

Theory models consist of the logically valid implications of sets of initial assertions and qualifying conditions (i.e. *ceteris paribus* clauses) so that, in principle, they are 'free creations of the human mind' (see for example Einstein, 1950). Succinctly, theory models postulate theory relationships between latent variables which are defined in the context of the theory using theory connectives such as 'causal dependence' (see for example Simon, 1953) and contextual concepts such as 'equilibrium' (see for example Spanos and Taylor, 1984). The empirical relevance or otherwise of the theory follows from the correspondence conditions (or measurement equations) mapping latent onto observable variables (for example Losee, 1980). However, since any given theory may not correctly and completely characterize the perceived world, the perceptibility of *necessary* connections among observed events is open to doubt (following Hume, 1758). Consequently, the unqualified term 'causality' will refer below only to an asymmetric relationship defined in the context of a theory model (for recent discussions of 'causality' in econometrics see *inter alia* Zellner, 1979b; Granger, 1980; Florens and Mouchart, 1981). Of course a major function of any economic theory model in econometrics is to sustain inferences from observed 'empirical regularities' to conjectured 'causal dependences'. In modern treatments, the anticipated presence or absence of certain data correlations is deduced from the causal structure of the theory model, and the outcome is used to 'corroborate or refute' the theory model. This obviates the need to try and infer 'causes from correlations', but only by focusing attention on the problem of 'testing' theory models.

Most theories form part of a sequence of formulations all of which are conditional on the empirical validity of many lower level theories (even if this is usually left implicit in our procedures) and are testable, if at all, only in conjunction with such theories, the *ceteris paribus* clauses and a particular model implementation. If observed data and theory implications are inconsistent, there is both latitude concerning to which features the inconsistency is attributed, and ample scope for introducing *ad hoc* assumptions to neutralize any anomalies (see Lakatos, 1974). However, an agglomeration of test failures against a background of well-established lower level theories may lead to the discarding of the sequence of theories in question as 'degenerating' in favour of less suspect alternatives (when such exist) until such time as that theory sequence can account successfully for previous anomalies. Generally, this last step will require explanations to have excess empirical content, some of which is corroborated. Blaug (1980) provides an excellent discussion of such issues in economics using Lakatos's concept of Scientific Research Programmes (see Worrall and Currie, 1978). Since this last notion evolved precisely because of the impossibility of 'proving' theories combined with the enormous difficulties of 'refuting' them, a primary construct used below is that of a 'progressive' research programme in which novel 'facts' are anticipated by the theory sequence and are later corroborated empirically.

The process of testing a theory model is generally undertaken via an empirical model which comprises relationships between *measured* variables. However, whereas the former may have been a 'free creation' and although it delineates the structure of the latter (which will generally use the same names for the observable counterparts of the latent variables), nevertheless the use of observed data creates a fundamental distinction between the two classes since an empirical model must, by default, be simply a *recombination of whatever process generated the data*. Which particular recombination is obtained depends on the constraints imposed by the theory and the properties of the underlying data generation process. In a Monte Carlo context, this analysis is trivially obvious: the data generation process determines the properties of the data set which determines whatever results are obtained on estimating any given relationship by a well-specified method. The implications of this viewpoint for empirical research will be discussed below, following a brief consideration of the role of statistical-theory models in econometrics.

The theory of statistical inference proceeds by postulating various stochastic processes, deducing implications of their behaviour and using the resulting analysis to interpret observed outcomes: the archetypal example is a coin-tossing 'model' as a Bernoulli trial. Being concerned with the logical study of a hypothetical data generation process (denoted by DGP below) in statistical theory the maintained theory model is never questioned, and issues of interest concern whether specific structures are identifiable, how 'best' to estimate the parameters of such as are etc. As expressed by Malinvaud (1966, p. 64), inference concerns narrowing the scope of the model in the light of the data. However, conflating the DGP and the model in empirical research provides an unsound basis for inference *until the model in some sense adequately characterizes the data*. The data directly convey information about the DGP (although we may not know how to interpret that information without an appropriate theory) and many features of most models are open to evaluation against the data to investigate how well the model describes that data. But even in the best formulated instances, the complexity of economic DGPs and the inherent simplicity of econometric models ensure that the axiom of correct specification (see Leamer, 1978, p. 4) is not a sufficient basis for inference. Should that axiom be valid in any particular case, the model simply coincides with the DGP and the potential recombination is an identity mapping, but this seems an unlikely eventuality.

Many of the concepts and issues described above are most easily clarified by examining an empirical illustration which is deliberately formulated to highlight the relevant points and is not claimed to represent in any way how econometricians actually conduct empirical research.

3 An Illustration: the Repayment of Mortgage Principal

The theory model is a static-equilibrium world in which all stocks and flows are constant so that in every period a constant proportion ($\mathscr{N}^{-1}$) of the outstanding stock of mortgage loans ($\mathscr{M}$) is repaid each period ($\mathscr{R}$),

$$\mathscr{R} = \mathscr{N}^{-1}\mathscr{M}. \tag{16.1}$$

Note that the repayment profile for any individual loan is nonetheless non-linear and dependent on the rate of interest ($\mathscr{I}$) even in such a world. Also, (16.1) is typical of many theory models in economics – it seems logically correct given the assumptions and provides the useful information that $\mathscr{R}/\mathscr{M}$ is independent of $\mathscr{M}$. Next, script letters denote latent variables defined in a static-equilibrium context in which (16.1) holds in both real and nominal terms, and indeed in various equivalent transformations such as linear-in-logs, first (or, $\forall j < \infty$, jth-order) differences etc., as stressed below. Finally, comparing between equilibria, an increase in $\mathscr{M}$ causes an increase in $\mathscr{R}$ (whereas, for example, an increase in repayments dynamically lowers the remaining mortgage stock *ceteris paribus*).

In the United Kingdom, most mortgages have been provided by building societies (see chapter 3 and Mayes, 1979), and for these institutions excellent quarterly time-series data (R_t, M_t) exist with negligibly small (pure) measurement errors (italic capitals denote the measured 'equivalent' of script variables, lower-case letters denote $\log_e$ of the corresponding capital and $\Delta_j x_t = x_t - x_{t-j}$). However, equivalent theory models do not necessarily yield equivalent empirical models: let $\mathscr{K} = \mathscr{N}^{-1}$ and then consider

$$\mathscr{R} = \mathscr{K}\mathscr{M} = \mathscr{K}\mathscr{M}_{-1},$$

$$\mathscr{R}/\mathscr{M}_{-1} = \mathscr{K},$$

$$\frac{\mathscr{R}}{\mathscr{P}} = \mathscr{K}\left(\frac{\mathscr{M}}{\mathscr{P}}\right) = \mathscr{K}\left(\frac{\mathscr{M}}{\mathscr{P}}\right)_{-1},$$

where $\mathscr{P}$ denotes an appropriate price index. Without wishing to belabour the point, log-linear equivalents exist of each of these, as do variants in (any order of) differences and so on. Unfortunately, all these theory-consistent models (and many more possibilities) can have distinctly different empirical properties in terms of (say) residual variance, heteroscedasticity, autocorrelation etc. Since almost no repayments of new loans occur within one quarter, for quarterly data lagged M seems preferable to current and logarithms seem preferable to original units as entailing positivity and a constant percentage residual variance. This suggests estimating

$$r_t = a_0 + a_1 m_{t-1} + S_t + \varepsilon_t \qquad t = 1, \ldots, T, \tag{16.2}$$

where S_t denotes three seasonal dummy variables (to allow for known seasonal activity in the housing market), and $a_0 = -\log_e N$ and $a_1 = 1$ are anticipated. Parenthetically, equations like (16.2) have occurred in many large estimated macroeconometric systems (see for example Waelbroeck, 1976) and, since m_{t-1} is 'predetermined', are usually estimated by ordinary least squares (OLS) on the auxiliary assumption that $\varepsilon_t \sim IN(0, \sigma_\varepsilon^2)$. For UK data from 1958(i) to 1979(iii) OLS estimation yields

$$\hat{r}_t = -3.2 + 0.97\, m_{t-1} + \hat{S}_t \qquad R^2 = 0.98 \qquad \hat{\sigma} = 0.097 \qquad DW = 0.49,$$
$$\quad\;\; (0.1)\;\; (0.02) \tag{16.3}$$

where the estimated standard errors are given in parentheses, $\hat{\sigma}$ is the residual standard error and DW is the Durbin–Watson statistic. Figure 16.1 shows the time-series graph of $(r_t, \hat{r}_t)$.

Certainly, $\hat{a}_1 \approx 1$ and $\hat{a}_0$ implies $N \approx 6$ years (close to the mean time between household moves in the United Kingdom), but DW rejects the assumption of serial independence in the residuals (and so the quoted standard errors are downward biased), although this is easily 'rectified'. However, while the R^2 is 'high', it is only 0.33 when $r_t - m_{t-1}$ is the regressand – and would be zero for that variable on seasonally adjusted data! Figure 16.2 highlights this lack of fit, despite being essentially a replot of figure 16.1. Granger and Newbold (1974) would describe (16.3) as a 'classic' spurious regression ($R^2 > DW$), and so 'refitting' in first differences to remove the trend and autocorrelation,

$$\Delta_1 \hat{r}_t = 0.83 \Delta_1 m_{t-1} + \hat{S}_t \qquad R^2 = 0.65 \qquad \hat{\sigma} = 0.067 \qquad DW = 1.80.$$
$$\quad\;\; (0.23) \tag{16.4}$$

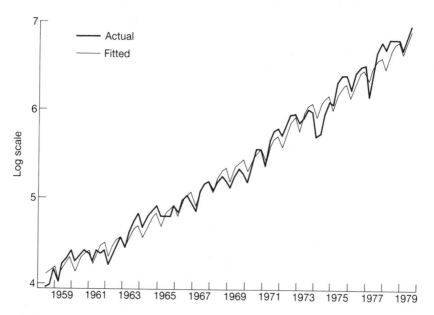

Figure 16.1 r_t.

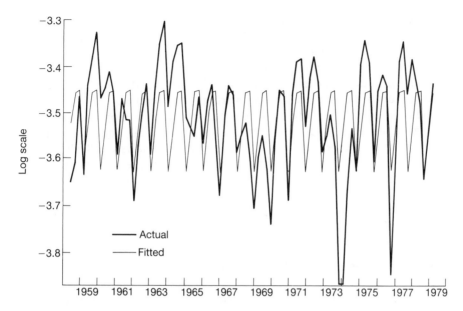

Figure 16.2 $r_t - m_{t-1}$.

The null of serially uncorrelated residuals can no longer be rejected against the alternative of first-order autocorrelation, (16.4) implements another of the theory-model equivalents, $\hat{\sigma}$ has fallen considerably, and $\hat{a}_1$ is not 'significantly different from unity'. On such criteria, (16.4) seems to provide an adequate model.

Appearances can be deceptive, however: if the error on (16.4) really were an autonomous white noise process, then $r_t - m_{t-1}$ would be a random walk, and so could assume any value, rendering (16.1) a useless theory (see chapter 8). Further, DW has been used as a selection criterion and, if the only equations reported are those with DW $\approx$ 2, it hardly provides useful 'test' information. Moreover, the claim that the residuals in (16.4) are white noise (even if it were true) does not entail that the equation is an 'adequate description of the data', since, for example, the unit common factor assumption in (16.4) could be invalid and hence either or both r_{t-1} and m_{t-2} could be significant if added as regressors (see Sargan, 1980a, and chapter 6). According to (16.1), we 'know' that $a_1 = 1$, yet after fitting (16.4) all that can be said is that [0.37, 1.29] provides a 95 per cent confidence interval for a_1!

It seems clear that a formal analysis of the various concepts involved in formulating empirical models, and of their interrelationships, is necessary in order to clarify the problems encountered above. Relating back to section 2, a crucial issue is that some unknown mechanism generated (r_t, m_t) from which (16.2) is a derived representation such that ε_t *must* contain everything affecting r_t not explicitly included in (16.2): the assertion that $\varepsilon_t \sim \text{IN}(0, \sigma_\varepsilon^2)$ is tantamount to the claim that (16.2) *is* the DGP even though (16.3) immediately contradicts that by its obvious failure to describe many salient data features. Thus, (a_0, a_1) is a (reduced) reparameterization of the parameters (θ) of the (unknown) underlying DGP induced by the method of estimation and so is defined implicitly by the auxiliary claims that $\mathscr{E}(\varepsilon_t) = 0$, and $\mathscr{E}(\varepsilon_t m_{t-1}) = 0$. The constancy of θ and the reduction necessary to obtain (16.2) determine the constancy (or otherwise) of $(\hat{a}_0, \hat{a}_1)$ as T varies, the properties of the residuals and so on (for a general analysis of the theory of reduction – in a Bayesian framework – see Florens and Mouchart, 1980a).

Relating forward to section 4, issues meriting consideration are the predictability of white noise errors, their use as an equation selection criterion and their relationship to goodness of fit, the theory consistency of empirical models, the validity of data transformations and so on. We hope that our analysis will allow a useful framework to be developed for formulating and selecting empirical models which do not coincide one-to-one with the actual DGP. Also, while (16.1) is obviously a very rudimentary starting point (to highlight specific issues), similar potential difficulties lurk behind any empirical study, however good its initial theory, the difference being a matter of degree not of kind.

4 An Analysis of Empirical-model Concepts

For notational convenience, the mechanism generating the outcome $X_T^1 = (x_1 \ldots x_T)$ of a k-dimensional time-sequential economic process is assumed continuous with respect to an appropriate measure as in, for example, chapter 15, and is therefore described by the density function

$$D(X_T^1 | X_0, \theta) = \prod_{t=1}^{T} D(x_t | X_{t-1}, \theta_0, \theta_t), \tag{16.5}$$

where $\theta = (\theta_0, \{\theta_t\}) \in \Theta$ is a finite-dimensional, identifiable, sufficient parameterization (see, for example, Madansky, 1976, ch. 2). Also, θ_0 denotes parameters which are fixed throughout the time horizon T, while θ_t regroups transient parameters (as in, say, Crowder, 1976). X_0 is the matrix of initial conditions and $X_{t-1} = (X_0 \ X_{t-1}^1)$. To aid the exposition and simplify proofs, the analysis is implicitly restricted to the linear framework, although we conjecture that many of the results apply more generally. If $\{x_t\}$ is assumed to be strongly mixing and (16.5) involves a finite lag dependence, then the results in Domowitz and White (1982) seem to provide an adequate basis for a valid asymptotic distribution theory for least squares approximations to a wide range of models. Below, T is assumed sufficiently large that large-sample theory is applicable.

The analysis is based on a partition of the available information (described in section 1 above) into past (or lagged) data, current data, future data, the separate data of contending hypotheses, and theory information. This ordering is chosen for analytical convenience so that the elements of the partition can be considered cumulatively.

4.1 Past Information

Definition 16.1 $\{e_t\}$ is a (mean) white noise process if $\mathscr{E}(e_t | E_{t-1}) = \mathscr{E}(e_t)$, $\forall t$, where $E_{t-1} = (E_0 \ E_{t-1}^1)$. Thus $\{e_t\}$ is not predictable linearly from its past (see Granger, 1983) beyond its unconditional mean (taken to be zero).

Note that $\{e_t\}$ may be predictable either fully or in part given an extended information set and indeed may have a temporal structure (see chapter 10). Also, $\{e_t\}$ need not be homoscedastic and in particular could follow an autoregressive conditional heteroscedastic (ARCH) scheme (see Engle, 1982a). If $\mathscr{E}(e_t) = 0$, $\forall t$, given definition 16.1, then $\{e_t\}$ is a (vector) martingale difference sequence (see Whittle, 1970, ch. 9). Since from any stochastic process with a rational spectrum a white noise component can be extracted by an appropriate filter, having a white noise residual is a *minimal* criterion for an empirical model to satisfy rather than an 'adequate' stopping point in a modelling exercise.

To minimize repetition, it is convenient to allow for the possibility that contemporaneous information might be available even though this section is explicitly concerned only with past data.

Definition 16.2 (i)$\{v_t\}$ is a mean innovation process (MIP) with respect to an information set $\mathscr{F}_t$ if $\mathscr{E}(v_t | \mathscr{F}_t) = 0$, $\forall t$; and (ii) $\{v_t\}$ is an innovation process with respect to $\mathscr{F}_t$ if it is an MIP and $D(v_t | \mathscr{F}_t) = D(v_t)$, $\forall t$.

Whether or not $\{e_t\}$ is an innovation process critically depends on the information set under consideration. White noise is certainly an MIP relative to its own history and if $\mathscr{F}_t$ contains $\mathscr{V}_{t-1}$, then innovations are also white noise. However, if $\mathscr{F}_t = (E_{t-1}, \mathscr{A}_{t-1})$ where $\mathscr{A}_{t-1}$ describes the past of an additional set of variables η_t, then $\{e_t\}$ is an MIP with respect to $\mathscr{F}_t$ only if η does not Granger-cause e (see Granger, 1969; and chapter 15).

As an example, let y_t be a subvector of x_t, let $v_t = x_t - \mathscr{E}(x_t | Y_{t-1})$ and let $\alpha(L)v_t = \varepsilon_t$ where $\alpha(L)$ is a rational polynomial matrix in the lag operator L such that $\{\varepsilon_t\}$ is vector white noise; then these conditions are not sufficient to ensure that $\{\varepsilon_t\}$ is an MIP with respect to X_{t-1}. Models with invalid common factors in lag polynomials are an instance of non-innovation white noise. Thus, for any given time series of data, a multiplicity of empirical models can be constructed which have disturbances that are not detectably different from white noise.

Econometric models typically consist of a hypothetical description of the (conditional) process generating a subset of the observable variables, say y_t. Let z_t denote the conditioning ('exogenous') observable variables and let w_t consist of all the other variables in x_t (whether latent or observable) so that x_t is now partitioned into (w_t, y_t, z_t). Let $S_{t-1} = (Y_{t-1}, Z_{t-1})$.

Definition 16.3 (i) A statistical model of $\{y_t | z_t; t = 1, \ldots, T\}$ is any parametric stochastic representation $\{P(y_t | z_t, S_{t-1}, \psi_0, \psi_t); t = 1, \ldots, T\}$ where $P(\cdot)$ is a probability density function and $\psi = (\psi_0, \{\psi_t\})$ is the corresponding parameterization. (ii) An empirical model of $\{y_t | z_t\}$ is any complete numerical specification of a statistical model thereof.

When no ambiguity arises, the generic 'model' is used as a shorthand below for whichever of these two concepts applies. However, the hypothesized density functions $\{P(y_t | z_t, S_{t-1}, \cdot)\}$ should not be confused with the genuine data density functions $\{D(y_t | z_t, S_{t-1}, \cdot)\}$ which they are designed to mimic. The latter can be derived, conceptually at least, from the DGP (16.5) by marginalizing with respect to W_T^1 and sequentially conditioning with respect to $\{z_t\}$ (see Florens and Mouchart, 1980a, b; and chapter 17). In the linear case, such reductions could be conducted analytically, as in chapter 15, so that, for example, under the axiom of correct specification, ψ would be an explicit function of θ. More generally, the properties of the pseudo-partial likelihood function

$$\mathscr{L}(\psi; S_T^1) = \prod_{t=1}^{T} P(y_t | z_t, S_{t-1}, \psi_0, \psi_t) \tag{16.6}$$

depend on the underlying DGP, as does the behaviour of estimators of ψ. Which ever interpretations model builders accord to ψ, such 'parameters' are *de facto* those functions of θ which happen to be consistently estimated by the 'estimators' that have been selected on the basis of the statistical model under consideration (see Hendry, 1979b; Domowitz and White, 1981).

Let $\mathscr{E}$ and $\mathscr{E}_p$ denote expectations operators with respect to the density functions $D(\cdot)$ and $P(\cdot)$ respectively. The 'errors' $e_t = y_t - \mathscr{E}_p(y_t | z_t, S_{t-1})$ receive considerable attention in econometric modelling, and correctly so since under the axiom of correct specification $\{e_t\}$ should be an MIP relative to (z_t, S_{t-1}) and even relative to (z_t, X_{t-1}) if W_{t-1} does not Granger-cause $(y_t z_t)$. In practice, however, $\{e_t\}$ often is not even white noise. Hence we define the following.

Definition 16.4 A model is data coherent if the error process $\{e_t\}$ is (at least) white noise.

Thus, the actual and fitted values differ 'randomly' in a data-coherent model: this is the notion used, for example in chapter 8. In effect, the Δ operator in (16.4) was an adequate filter for achieving residuals that were not first-order autocorrelated. However, DW ≈ 2.0 does not imply that the residuals are white noise: a 'portmanteau' test for a flat spectrum would be required to throw light on that issue (i.e. non-rejection achieved by low power[1] tests is hardly persuasive). Further, white noise need not be an MIP. Note that one important aspect of working with a model based on a mean innovation process (even if this is heteroscedastic) is that valid inference about ψ can proceed on the basis of results in Domowitz and White (1981, 1982) for a useful range of stochastic processes relevant to economics data.

Since simply possessing a white noise error process does not characterize a unique choice of model, let $g(\cdot)$ denote a (scalar) criterion function defined on $\mathscr{A}$, the class of models under consideration (for example, $g(\cdot)$ could denote the negative of the log-likelihood value, or that corrected for the number of estimated parameters or $\{-R^2\}$ or σ^2 or generalized variance for a system etc.). Then we have definition 16.5.

Definition 16.5 The model A_1 g-dominates the model A_2 if and only if $g(A_1) < g(A_2)$ (A_1 and A_2 are g-equivalent if $g(A_1) = g(A_2)$).

Variance dominance is a major selection criterion in actual empirical research, in part because of the proposition that 'true models' dominate 'false' when the 'model' contains the DGP as a special case (see for example Theil, 1971, p. 543; Leamer, 1978, p. 75). It remains to be discussed precisely how useful variance dominance is when $\mathscr{A}$ does not contain the DGP.

It follows from definition 16.5 that g-dominance is an asymmetric relationship and is transitive, both of which are important attributes of a selection criterion. However, *by itself* dominance is not necessarily a decisive criterion since a model based on the union of the regressors of all submodels (less redundant variables) cannot be variance- or likelihood-dominated in its class, or, as noted by Poirier (1981), a nesting model in a class of false models has the highest (large-sample) posterior odds. Nevertheless, we state theorem 16.1.

Theorem 16.1 Models without mean innovation error processes can be variance-dominated by a model with a mean innovation error on the same data.

This is a well-known result, based on the fact that $\mathscr{E}(y_t | z_t, S_{t-1})$ is the minimum mean square error predictor of y_t given (z_t, S_{t-1}) and that $\varepsilon_t = y_t - \mathscr{E}(y_t | z_t, S_{t-1})$ is an MIP relative to (z_t, S_{t-1}). Theorem 16.1 provides a partial answer to the question raised above about the usefulness of variance dominance when $\mathscr{A}$ does not contain the DGP. Moreover, if the set of conditioning variables in A_1 is a subset of those in A_2, then A_1 cannot variance-dominate A_2, thus inducing one variant of a progressive research strategy (see section 2 above). Indeed, this notion appears to lead naturally to model building strategies which focus (at some stage) on relatively 'unrestricted' models (in terms of choice of regressor variables and lag lengths) to calibrate the MIP error variance. Parsimony considerations may then induce a simplification search procedure (on these issues, see Sims, 1980; Leamer, 1978; and chapter 11). Thus we have definition 16.6.

Definition 16.6 The model A is g-parsimonious if $\dim(\psi) < \dim(\psi_i)$ for all models A_i which are g-equivalent to A or g-dominated by A.

Much of the so-called 'model selection' literature, in which model choice is based on the Akaike information criterion, the final prediction error or the Schwartz criterion etc. (see Amemiya, 1980; Chow, 1981; Sawyer, 1983), is concerned with selecting 'parsimoniously undominated' models for various choices of $g(\cdot)$, usually subject to a restriction that the residual process be white noise.

As will be seen below, it is unclear that model selection should emphasize 'parsimonious non-dominance' to the exclusion of other important features (such as invariance, encompassing and so on).

4.2 Contemporaneous Information

It is conventional in econometrics to condition analyses on current-dated information and this possibility was allowed for above with models being conditional on z_t.

The validity of such conditioning for purposes of inference, prediction and/or policy has long been a subject of debate in econometrics concerning alternative notions of exogeneity. That important topic is the subject of a separate recent paper (see chapter 15) and therefore will not be re-analysed herein beyond noting that we adopt the definitions and formulations of that chapter. However, in order to make the present chapter essentially self-contained, we briefly restate the definitions of weak and strong exogeneity as well as (in section 4.3 below) that of super exogeneity. Also, since we have already emphasized the distinction between the DGP and models, it is useful to distinguish explicitly between, say, D-exogeneity and P-exogeneity depending on whether we are discussing exogeneity at the level of the DGP (which is typically unknown but fundamentally determines the empirical findings) or exogeneity at the level of models thereof. The definition of D-exogeneity is based on the factorization

$$D(y_t, z_t | S_{t-1}, \cdot) = D(y_t | z_t, S_{t-1}, \cdot) D(z_t | S_{t-1}, \cdot),$$ (16.7)

where $D(y_t, z_t | S_{t-1}, \cdot)$ is derived from the DGP (16.5) by marginalizing with respect to W_T^1.

Definition 16.7 z_t is D-weakly-exogenous for a set of 'parameters of interest' if these are functions of those of the conditional DGP $D(y_t | z_t, S_{t-1}, \cdot)$ only, the latter being 'variation free' with the parameters of the marginal DGP $D(z_t | S_{t-1}, \cdot)$. Also, z_t is D-strongly-exogenous if, in addition, y does not Granger-cause z.

P-exogeneity is defined in a similar way with reference to a hypothetical density function $P(y_t, z_t | S_{t-1}, \cdot)$ which typically requires 'completing' the statistical model under consideration by an auxiliary model $P(z_t | S_{t-1}, \cdot)$, at least for the purpose of constructing parametric tests of P-exogeneity.

D-weak-exogeneity validates conducting inference on any function of the parameters of the conditional DGP $D(y_t | z_t, S_{t-1}, \cdot)$, possibly including some parameters of a mis-specified model thereof, without loss of relevant sample information. However, P-exogeneity is the concept which is *de facto* the object of any modelling exercise and, in particular, specification errors (including errors affecting the auxiliary marginal model for z_t) may lead to a rejection of P-exogeneity even though z_t is D-weakly-exogenous.

4.3 Future observations

The slightly unfortunate terminology 'future observations' is meant to denote that, if x_t is the current-dated variable, then $\{x_{t+1} \ldots\}$ comprises future information (even if such values are already known).

Definition 16.8 A statistical model A has constant parameters if $(\psi_0, \psi_t) = \psi$ for $t = 1, \ldots, T$.

A standard statistic for evaluating parameter constancy is the Chow test (see Chow, 1960) although there exists a large literature on investigating potential parameter variations related to the Kalman filter (for an exposition, see Harvey, 1981b). The important issue here, however, is that there is no necessary connection between parameter constancy and the criteria previously discussed. Since constant parameters are of interest for most modelling purposes, the inadequacy of (say) 'parsimonious non-dominance' as the sole selection criterion is clear.

Note that constancy of the parameters of the DGP entails constancy of the parameters of statistical models thereof, however mis-specified they may be, in so far as the latter are functions of the former. However, it is a common empirical finding that DGPs are subject to interventions affecting some of their parameters. A typical example is that of control variables which are subject to policy interventions. A critical issue for prediction or policy simulation experiments is the constancy of the parameters of the corresponding conditional DGP (or model thereof) under interventions affecting the DGP of the control variables.

Definition 16.9 (i) A statistical model has invariant parameters under a class of interventions if its parameters remain constant under such interventions. (ii) z_t is D-super-exogenous if it is D-weakly-exogenous and the conditional model has invariant parameters.

Parameter invariance is a more demanding requirement than just constancy since the latter may simply be the result of chance DGP constancy over the sample period or of invariance with respect to a limited class of interventions (covering those which occurred over the sample period), while the former typically requires parameter constancy under hypothetical interventions and is therefore conjectural (see for example Lucas, 1976; Sargent, 1981). However, within-sample parameter change is sufficient to reject that conjecture.

Finally, to use an invariant empirical model of $\{y_t | z_t, S_{t-1}\}$ (where z_t is weakly exogenous for the parameters of the conditional model) for prediction of Y_T^{t+1} conditional on Z_T^{t+1} requires that z_t be strongly exogenous over the period $]t+1, T]$. Otherwise, an auxiliary empirical model of $\{z_t | S_{t-1}\}$ is required in order to exploit the feedback of Y_{t-1} on z_t. Likewise, *conditional* simulation experiments (on which see section 6 below) require strong exogeneity.

4.4 Data Relevant to Contending Models

It is rare in economics to obtain a unanimous view on the precise determination of any economic variable and usually there is a proliferation of rival empirical models. In our framework, these all constitute recombinations of the DGP and hence are not 'independent representations', a point made in the context of time-series versus econometric models by Wallis (1977). Thus, while the underlying theory models may be separate or non-nested, in that none is a special case of any other, the empirical models are all nested within the DGP. This is manifest on attempting Monte Carlo analysis of 'non-nested' models – enough of the DGP must be specified to generate all the observables, whence the outcome depends on how the DGP was constructed (as well as on which separate hypotheses are postulated).

If the complete DGP were known (as in the Monte Carlo context since 'real' DGPs may be unknowable), then one could deduce what results would obtain on estimating a given set of models, irrespective of whether these were mutually separate or not. Consequently, one can ask of any specific model whether it mimics this property of the DGP in that it can account for the results obtained by other models; if so, then the first model is said to be encompassing.

Encompassing could be defined at a high level of generality where contending models may differ by:

1 their choices of endogenous variables;
2 their functional forms;
3 their choices of conditioning variables.

In view of the scope of the present chapter, we shall formulate definitions which cover only (2) and (3) and illustrate them with reference to *linear* models which differ solely in their choices of 'regressors'.

Let r_{1t} and r_{2t} be two different subsets of the variables in (z_t, Y_{t-1}, Z_{t-1}) (r_{1t} and r_{2t} may have variables in common, see for example Mizon and Richard (1986, section 4.4), in which case some of the density functions we introduce below are singular and degrees of freedom for test statistics have to be adjusted conformably). Let $A_1 = \{P_1(y_t|r_{1t}, \psi_{1t}); t = 1, \ldots, T\}$ and $A_2 = \{P_2(y_t|r_{2t}, \psi_{2t}); t = 1, \ldots, T\}$ be rival models. It is assumed that the model-builders had access to a common set of data and, accordingly, that

$$P_i(y_t|r_{it}, \psi_{it}) \equiv P_i(y_t|z_t, Y_{t-1}, Z_{t-1}, \psi_{it}) \qquad i = 1, 2, \qquad t = 1, \ldots, T,$$

(16.8)

which entails that

$$P_1(y_t|r_{1t}, \psi_{1t}) \equiv P_1(y_t|r_{1t}, r_{2t}, \psi_{1t}),$$ (16.9a)

$$P_2(y_t|r_{2t}, \psi_{2t}) \equiv P_2(y_t|r_{1t}, r_{2t}, \psi_{2t}).$$ (16.9b)

Definition 16.10 A_1 least squares encompasses A_2 if and only if ψ_{2t} can be derived from ψ_{1t} and the least squares description of the (data) relationship linking r_{1t} and r_{2t}.

To link A_1 and A_2 essentially requires specifying a set of mutually compatible auxiliary density functions $\{P_1(r_{1t}|r_{2t}, \lambda_t); t = 1, \ldots, T\}$ — and carrying out the following marginalization:

$$P_1(y_t|r_{2t}, \psi_{1t}, \lambda_t) = \int P_1(y_t|r_{1t}, \psi_{1t}) P_1(r_{1t}|r_{2t}, \lambda_t) dr_{1t}.$$ (16.10)

However, the weaker form of encompassing in definition 16.10 only requires considering least squares approximations of r_{1t} by r_{2t}.

Note that the validity of (16.10) requires that of formula (16.9a). (If (16.9a) did not hold, then A_1 should first be completed to form a model of y_t conditional on r_{1t} *and* r_{2t}.) Provided that $P_1(y_t|r_{2t}, \psi_{1t}, \lambda_t)$ and $P_2(y_t|r_{2t}, \psi_{2t})$ belong to a common class of parametric density functions, their reconciliation induces a mapping between parameter spaces, say,

$$\psi_{2t} = h(\psi_{1t}, \lambda_t) \qquad t = 1, \ldots, T.$$ (16.11)

The application of definition 16.10 at the level of empirical models requires checking whether or not (16.11) holds for the numerical values under consideration (see for example chapter 10). Alternatively, replacing the unknown parameters in (16.11) by appropriate estimators may provide the basis of an encompassing test statistic, using a Wald formulation. Mizon and Richard (1986) use another version of encompassing which builds on the pioneering work of Cox (1961). Let $\hat{\psi}_{2t}$ denote the maximum likelihood estimator of ψ_{2t} (under A_2) and let $g_T^1(\psi_{1t}) = \mathscr{E}_{p_1}(\hat{\psi}_{2t}|r_{1t})$ denote the expectation of $\hat{\psi}_{2t}$ with respect to Y_T^1 under the working assumption that A_1 is the relevant DGP, taking into account (16.9a).

Definition 16.11 A_1 Cox-encompasses A_2 if and only if

$$\psi_{2t} = g_T^1(\psi_{1t}) \qquad t = 1, \ldots, T.$$

It is easily shown that the two versions of encompassing coincide in linear worlds where the rival models differ only by their choices of regressors and, furthermore, that in a single-equation framework the conventional F test statistic can be interpreted as an encompassing test statistic (compare chapter 17, section 6, and Mizon and Richard, 1986, section 4.3). This interpretation offers the advantage that, in contrast with the conventional Neyman–Pearson framework, the validity of the 'nesting' model based on the union of the two sets of regressors is irrelevant within an encompassing framework.

It can also be shown that, in linear worlds, encompassing entails variance dominance. Let Σ_t be the covariance matrix of (y_t, r_{1t}, r_{2t}). Dropping the time subscript (as irrelevant to the essence of the argument) partition Σ conformably with (y, r_1, r_2):

$$\Sigma = \begin{pmatrix} \Sigma_{yy} & & \\ \Sigma_{1y} & \Sigma_{11} & \\ \Sigma_{2y} & \Sigma_{21} & \Sigma_{22} \end{pmatrix}$$

Let

$$\Sigma_{yy \cdot i} = \Sigma_{yy} - \Sigma_{yi} \Sigma_{ii}^{-1} \Sigma_{iy} \qquad i = 1, 2,$$

where $\Sigma_{yy \cdot i}$ is the covariance matrix of the residuals of the least squares approximation of y by r_i. We can establish the following lemma.

Lemma. If $\Sigma_{2y} = \Sigma_{21} \Sigma_{11}^{-1} \Sigma_{1y}$, then $\Sigma_{yy \cdot 2} \geq \Sigma_{yy \cdot 1}$.

Proof. $\alpha'(\Sigma_{yy.2} - \Sigma_{yy.1})\alpha$
$$= \alpha'(\Sigma_{y1}\Sigma_{11}^{-1}\Sigma_{1y} - \Sigma_{y2}\Sigma_{22}^{-1}\Sigma_{2y})\alpha$$
$$= \alpha'(\Sigma_{y1}\Sigma_{11}^{-1}\Sigma_{1y} - \Sigma_{y1}\Sigma_{11}^{-1}\Sigma_{12}\Sigma_{22}^{-1}\Sigma_{21}\Sigma_{11}^{-1}\Sigma_{1y})\alpha$$
$$= (\Sigma_{11}^{-1/2}\Sigma_{1y}\alpha)'[I - (\Sigma_{11}^{-1/2}\Sigma_{12}\Sigma_{22}^{-1/2})(\Sigma_{22}^{-1/2}\Sigma_{21}\Sigma_{11}^{-1/2})](\Sigma_{11}^{-1/2}\Sigma_{1y}\alpha)$$
$$\geq 0.$$

Since the assumption that $\Sigma_{2y} = \Sigma_{21}\Sigma_{11}^{-1}\Sigma_{1y}$ is the least squares counterpart of assumption (16.9a), the lemma establishes that, in a least squares framework, encompassing entails variance dominance. Since in addition encompassing is transitive, the concept is close to that of a 'sufficient model' in a theory of reduction in that, knowing the encompassing model, one can forget about other models, deriving them as the need arises (compare the notion of sufficient statistics). If A_1 encompasses A_2 when both models are linear least squares approximations the converse is false, and if A_2 in turn encompasses A_3 then A_1 encompasses A_3. Thus, encompassing is a central concept in any progressive research strategy especially in view of the lemma that variance dominance is necessary but not sufficient: an encompassing model will variance-dominate but a variance-dominating model need not encompass.

Two further consequences follow from this result: first, the emphasis on selecting variance-dominating models is somewhat misplaced and should follow automatically from a selection procedure which seeks an encompassing model, rather than being an 'independent' criterion; and second, since Cox-type non-nested hypothesis tests simply test for variance-encompassing (see Cox, 1961; Mizon and Richard, 1986), if tests of the dominated model against the dominating do not reject the former, the power of the test is revealed as low. Other intriguing implications can be derived. Let A_1 and A_2 be two rival models with claimed constant parameters. If A_1 encompasses A_2 and it is known that the relationship of r_{1t} to r_{2t} has altered over the sample period (a common occurrence in empirical work), the modeller knowing A_1 can deduce by using (16.11) over different subperiods what parameter change A_2 should exhibit (even though neither investigator has directly tested for such a contingency in A_2!). Similarly for residual autocorrelation: an encompassing model should allow one to predict the magnitude of this in contending models, and so on.

Accounting for all the salient features of rival models may seem at first sight an overly demanding criterion: strictly speaking the DGP is the only model that could encompass *all* its rivals while, at the same time, it is essentially unknowable given limited sample evidence. It is obvious that any model, however good an approximation to the DGP, could be rejected against a rival model expressly designed for that purpose. However, this is a vacuous exercise if it does not lead to the formulation of 'better' models and so encompassing seems bound to be an essential component of a progressive modelling strategy. In particular, in a subject with many separate models all being advocated as a basis for policy, encompassing seems a reasonable requirement which remains impressive when obtained from a parsimonious specification. Clearly, concepts such as minimal encompassing (with minimal dimension ψ) can be developed, and the notion can be generalized to systems in which endogenous regressors occur and/or hypotheses differ as to what variables are weakly or strongly exogenous etc.

4.5 Theory Information

Theory information plays an essential role in econometric analysis and it is doubtful if one could even define parameters of interest in the absence of an adequately articulated theory. Indeed, the DGP itself may be dependent on currently popular economic theory. In certain theories, ψ is highly constrained as in, say, rational expectations formulations; see Lucas and Sargent (1981). A weak condition is the following.

Definition 16.12 An empirical model is theory consistent if it reproduces the theory model under the conditions assumed by the theory.

Lest it be thought that this is vacuous, note that, for example, in section 2 above, (16.4) was not consistent with the static solution (16.1), from which it was ostensibly derived. As a further example, changes in assumptions about error autocorrelation can alter the consistency of a model with a given dynamic behavioural theory (see for example chapter 4).

Generally, theories incorporate measurement structures and hence models need to be consistent with whatever data constraints are automatically binding (e.g. identities, positivity, lying between zero and unity etc.).

Definition 16.13 An empirical model is data admissible if its predictions satisfy all data constraints with probability unity.

For example, $0 \leqslant \mathscr{R}/\mathscr{M} \leqslant 1$ holds for the variables in section 2, so neither (16.3) nor (16.4) are data admissible. Attempting to specify a functional form which is data admissible often leads to a model specification in which approximate normality of the error process is reasonable. Unfortunately, tractability and admissibility may conflict and/or no function can be found which jointly satisfies two data constraints (e.g. a linear identity and a positivity constraint).

As with admissible estimators, many investigators work with data-inadmissible models or achieve admissibility by artefact (see Brainard and Tobin, 1968), usually for convenience or because the probability of violating constraints is believed to be negligible.

4.6 Representing the DGP

Definition 16.14. A model is a tentatively adequate conditional data characterization (TACD) if:

1 it encompasses all rival models;
2 its error process is an MIP relative to the selected database;
3 its parameters of interest are constant;
4 it is data admissible;
5 its current conditioning variables are weakly exogenous for the parameters of interest.

A number of points need to be made about the concept of a TACD. First, such a model is not claimed to be the DGP, simply to adequately represent it. Thus, in a Monte Carlo, data generated from the TACD should reproduce all the investigated features of the original data. This does not preclude the development of 'better' TACDs using more information, such that these successively encompass previous results with MIPs having ever smaller variances. Second, we have not included 'theory consistency' as a criterion because of the well-known rationalization problem: there always exists some theory consistent with the observed results unless these are mutually contradictory (which hopefully (4) excludes). In any case, definition 16.14

is applicable however naive or sophisticated the initial theory may have been.[2] Next, weak exogeneity assertions often are only indirectly testable but are partially checked by (1) and (3) holding for worlds in which some elements of θ are transients which induce data correlation changes. Fourth, a sequence of TACDs would seem to characterize a useful research strategy, which would be progressive if the theoretical framework enabled successive improvements to be predicted in advance (rather than as responses to observed anomalies). Further, we believe it is possible to develop TACDs and would cite chapter 8 as a potential example. In practice, successively encompassing TACDs also can be generated (for example chapter 10). Parenthetically, we note that UK government policy has been based on a model which uses a version of the equation in chapter 8 (see HM Treasury, 1980) so that on this measure the approach is of some use. Finally, if the explanatory variables are all strongly exogenous, definition 16.11 can be modified to a tentatively adequate conditional DGP and, if the model is closed, to a tentatively adequate DGP (note that (2) subsumes data coherency).

Two more related issues remain to be discussed: the use of tests as selection criteria, and data mining. Concerning the former, a model would not be advanced as a TACD (by an investigator who intended to develop such a representation) unless appropriate test statistic values were obtained. Thus diagnostic tests employed in model selection are satisfied by design and do not constitute 'independent checks' on the validity of the model, although new statistics, later data and/or further rival models can provide genuine tests in so far as the TACD is hazarded to potential rejection. Next, data mining has been used in both dismissive and positive senses, but the latter connotation applies to any methodology aimed at developing TACDs since such an activity involves 'judgement and purpose' (see Leamer, 1978, ch. 1). The former sense is justified when the modelling is structureless through lack of either a theory context or a search strategy. But we wish to stress that despite estimating several variants prior to selecting any specific model, *conditional* on its being a TACD, then for example the quoted parameter standard errors (estimated as in, say, Domowitz and White, 1982) are consistent estimates of the sampling standard deviations of parameters estimated from such a DGP. Such conditional statements seem less than convincing if models are not even TACDs.

4.7 Parameters of Interest

While a given theory defines what 'parameters' are of general interest, usually it leaves latitude concerning precisely which features are basic and/or constant (e.g. propensities or elasticities etc.). Thus, additional considerations must be invoked in designing models and 'orthogonality' and 'parsimony' enter at this stage. By the former is meant a reparameterization based on *prior* considerations such that the associated variables are not highly intercorrelated; data-dependent transformations (such as principal components) are deliberately excluded from our notion. The parameters should have clear-cut interpretations (see for example Rothenberg, 1973) and near-orthogonal parameterizations often arise naturally in modelling economic behaviour (see chapter 8). Our practical experience is that such parameters tend to be robust to changes in both model specification and data correlations (which of course would follow trivially if 'included' and 'excluded' variables were, and remained, orthogonal).

The latter topic arises again here (see section 4.1 above) through its link with reparameterizations designed to enhance robustness and facilitate model selection when prior specification is uncertain: it seems a reasonable objective to try and achieve the maximum of explanation with the minimum of factors. Indeed, a data-admissible econometric model with a *parsimonious* specification of constant interpretable parameters related to a well-formulated theory which still succeeded in encompassing alternative (commensurable) hypotheses must deserve serious consideration in any scientific research strategy. Later models almost certainly will be developed which are in turn encompassing and based on 'sounder' theory, but this does not vitiate adopting the currently best available model. Note that our analysis does not exclude the possibility that an entire sequence of models is wholly misconceived and, after a long progression, is duly replaced by a (perhaps incommensurable) alternative sequence based on a totally different conceptual framework (as occurred, for example, with Cartesian and Newtonian theories of planetary motion).

5 The Empirical Illustration Reconsidered

The concepts discussed in section 4 are applicable to the empirical models in section 3, but it is readily established empirically that these equations fail on almost every criterion. Rather than criticize such simple formulations, however, the purpose of this section is to describe a TACD consistent with (16.1) which helps exposit our ideas constructively.

The underlying theory is one of dynamic adjustment around a steady state *defined by* (16.1). The model allows for activity changes in the housing market (most UK mortgages must be repaid on selling the associated house), the consequentially varying age profile of loans (for actuarial reasons, a larger percentage is repaid on longer-standing loans), changes in interest rates (total monthly payments are usually announced so that as I varies the proportion of repayments may alter) and premature repayments out of deposits (presumably from balances excess to liquidity requirements). The statistical model is an autoregressive–distributed lag of

$$q_t = \log \left\{ \frac{R_t/M_{t-1}}{1 - R_t/M_{t-1}} \right\}$$

on $\Delta_1 p_{t-1}, \Delta_1 I_{t-1}, \Delta_1 m_{t-1}, \Delta_1 d_{t-1}$ with four lags on each variable, plus constant, S_t, m_{t-1}, I_{t-1} and $V\Delta_1 I_{t-2}$, where P denotes an index of house prices and V is a dummy variable equal to unity until 1974(ii) and zero thereafter, and D denotes building society deposits. Thus, the specification is

$$q_t = \sum_{j=1}^{4} (\alpha_j q_{t-j} + \beta_j \Delta_1 p_{t-j} + \gamma_j \Delta_1 I_{t-j} + \lambda_j \Delta_1 m_{t-j} + \phi_j \Delta_1 d_{t-j}) + \delta_2 I_{t-1}$$
$$+ \gamma_0 V\Delta_1 I_{t-2} + S_t + \delta_0 + \delta_1 m_{t-1} + \varepsilon_t, \tag{16.13}$$

where $\{\varepsilon_t\}$ is to be an MIP relative to the available information. The logistic form for the dependent variable ensures data admissibility for the constraints

$0 \leqslant R/M \leqslant 1$, although R_t/M_{t-1} is so small that only positivity is relevant in practice. Also, P is included to reflect housing market activity, since demand changes rapidly result in house price changes given the essentially fixed stock. Initially estimated models implicitly set γ_0 at zero and experienced substantial predictive failure when $\Delta_1 I_{t-2}$ was included as a regressor, posing a conflict between goodness of fit and parameter constancy. However, this was diagnosed as due to a change in institutional arrangements in 1974 when continuously rising interest rates forced building societies to demand increases in total monthly payments to maintain positive repayments of principal (note the nadir of q_t in 1974 in figure 16.3). Thus, $\gamma_0 V$ is an example of a transient parameter.

The OLS estimates of (16.13) are not interesting *per se*, but it should be recorded that $\hat{\sigma} = 0.0419$ and that both the Chow (1960) test for parameter constancy (for several periods) and Harvey's (1981a) F version of the Lagrange multiplier test for sixth-order autocorrelation (see Godfrey, 1978) were not significant at the 0.05 level (these tests are denoted $\eta_1(\cdot)$ and $\eta_2(\cdot)$ below, with degrees of freedom in parentheses). This evidence is consistent with $\{\varepsilon_t\}$ being white noise and an MIP on the present information. Next, (16.13) was simplified by imposing restrictions consistent with (16.1), reparameterizing any short distributed lags and deleting inessential variables such that the overall F test of all the restrictions was not significant at the 0.05 level ($\eta_3(\cdot)$ below). Kiviet (1985) presents evidence about the independence of some of the above tests of specification and mis-specification (adopting the dichotomy in Mizon (1977b)); see also Kiviet (1986a).

The simplified equation thus selected for the period 1958(ii)–1981(iii) is

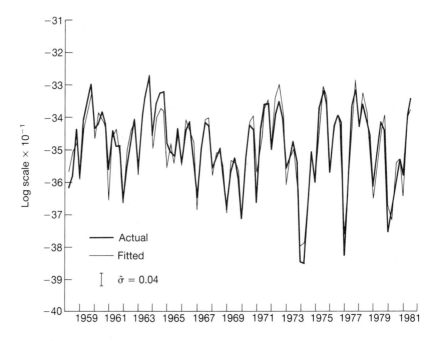

Figure 16.3 q_t.

$$\hat{q}_t = -1.34 + 0.60q_{t-1} - 0.058\Delta_1 I_{t-1} + 0.65\Delta_1 p_{t-1} - 0.78\Delta_4 m_{t-1}$$
$$(0.16)\ (0.04)\qquad (0.010)\qquad\quad (0.20)\qquad\quad (0.14)$$

$$-0.090V\Delta_1 I_{t-2} + 2.3\Delta_1 d_{t-1} + \hat{S}_t \qquad\qquad\qquad (16.14)$$
$$(0.027)\qquad\quad (0.4)$$

$$T = 94 \qquad R^2 = 0.90 \qquad \hat{\sigma} = 0.0405$$

$$\eta_1(20, 64) = 1.36 \qquad \eta_2(6, 78) = 0.51 \qquad \eta_3(17, 68) = 0.69 \qquad \eta_4(1) = 5.1,$$

where the heteroscedasticity-consistent standard errors are given in parentheses (see White, 1980b; Domowitz and White, 1982), and $\eta_4(1)$ is the test for first-order ARCH (see Engle, 1982a), asymptotically distributed as χ_1^2 on the null of no ARCH effect. It may be noted that the conventionally calculated standard errors are similar to those reported above.

Descriptive statistics relevant to the scaled residuals $\{\hat{\varepsilon}_t/\hat{\sigma}\}$ are maximum, 2.10; minimum, -2.34; skewness, -0.20; excess kurtosis, -0.53. There are no evident outlier problems, and the first four moments are similar to those of a normal distribution, perhaps being somewhat 'flatter'. Figure 16.3 shows the graph of $\{q_t\}$ and the corresponding fit.

Equation (16.14) appears to satisfy our criteria for being a TACD. The residual is white noise (on $\eta_2(\cdot)$) and not significantly different from the residual of (16.13) (on $\eta_3(\cdot)$), and so it is unlikely that this model could be significantly dominated on the present information set although there is evidence of autoregressive conditional heteroscedasticity ($\eta_4(\cdot)$). All the regressors are lagged or non-stochastic, and so $\hat{\sigma}$ measures the actual one-step-ahead forecast standard error, which is under 4 per cent of $\bar{R}$, and $\eta_1(\cdot)$ is consistent with constant parameters (in fact, for several horizons). It can be shown that the selected model encompasses both (16.3) and (16.4) above (although these are not 'special cases') and the other R_t equations considered in chapter 3, as well as variance-dominating the equation in Mayes (1979) (we have been unable to conduct a formal encompassing test against this last model, which has a standard error of 7.6 per cent of $\bar{R}$, but four lagged values of personal disposable income were insignificant at the 0.05 level if added to (16.13)). By construction, (16.14) is both data admissible, in that all values of $\hat{q}_t$ yield $0 \le R_t/M_{t-1} \le 1$, and consistent with (16.1). The static equilibrium solution yields $N = 7.3$ years, with substantial seasonal variation between 11.3 years and 6.9 years. The parameters are fairly well determined, with anticipated signs and sensible magnitudes, and have clear interpretations, almost all the squared correlations between regressors being negligible (the largest is 0.30 between q_{t-1} and a seasonal dummy). Five variables explain most of the non-seasonal variation in q_t since 1974, over which period the largest quarter-on-quarter change in $r_t - m_{t-1}$ was 0.40 (about $10\hat{\sigma}$), with the observed variance having increased markedly since 1973. However, an important caveat before regarding the estimated parameters as measures of invariants of housing market behaviour is that we have not included any factors to account for long-run changes in the propensity to move house (e.g. household formation rates, job mobility determinants etc.); hopefully (16.14) may provide a useful basis for developing a more general encompassing formulation in due course.

6 Dynamic Simulation

Most large-scale estimated dynamic econometric models have been studied by simulation techniques at some time. Indeed, simulation tracking performance is often viewed as a major aspect of 'validating' such models, i.e. of checking their overall correspondence to 'reality' at least as revealed by the observed historical data – see for example Sowey (1973) and McNees (1982). Judging by the frequency with which root mean square errors (RMSEs) based on dynamic simulations are quoted and by the fact that small RMSEs seem to be viewed as 'good', it is worthwhile specifically investigating the use of n-step MSEs (denoted by $M(n)$ below) as a dominance criterion for model selection.

Of course, $M(1)$ is the previously considered variance-dominance criterion, but the concern here is with $M(n)$ when n is 'large', to highlight the issues involved. The analysis builds on the work of Haavelmo (1940), but focuses on different aspects of model evaluation than 'spuriously significant' variables. Rather, our concern is with the choice of information set underlying different 'types' of simulation and the bearing that the results of deterministic simulation exercises may have on assessing the usefulness of a model for alternative purposes. The analysis proceeds by means of a simple example which incorporates all the required features; additional complications like non-linearities, omitted variables and unknown/non-constant parameters seem liable to exacerbate the problem.

Consider the linear stationary two-equation process in (16.15) and (16.16) where the parameters are *known* and constant and the latent roots lie within the unit circle:

$$y_t = \alpha z_t + \beta y_{t-1} + \varepsilon_t, \qquad \begin{pmatrix} \varepsilon_t \\ v_t \end{pmatrix} \sim \text{IN} \left[\begin{pmatrix} 0 \\ 0 \end{pmatrix}, \begin{pmatrix} \sigma_\varepsilon^2 & 0 \\ 0 & \sigma_v^2 \end{pmatrix} \right], \tag{16.5}$$

$$z_t = \lambda z_{t-1} + \gamma y_{t-1} + v_t, \qquad \begin{array}{l} 0 \leqslant \beta < 1, 0 \leqslant \lambda < 1, \\ 1 \geqslant \alpha \geqslant 0, -1 < \gamma \leqslant 0. \end{array} \tag{16.16}$$

The one-step-ahead system predictions are computed from

$$\begin{pmatrix} \hat{y}_t \\ \hat{z}_t \end{pmatrix} = \begin{bmatrix} \beta + \alpha\gamma & \alpha\lambda \\ \gamma & \lambda \end{bmatrix} \begin{pmatrix} y_{t-1} \\ z_{t-1} \end{pmatrix} \tag{16.17}$$

and so have error variances

$$\begin{pmatrix} \sigma_\varepsilon^2 + \alpha^2 \sigma_v^2 \\ \sigma_v^2 \end{pmatrix} = \begin{pmatrix} \text{var}(y_t \mid Y_{t-1}, Z_{t-1}) \\ \text{var}(z_t \mid Y_{t-1}, Z_{t-1}) \end{pmatrix}. \tag{16.18}$$

By way of contrast,

$$\text{var}(y_t \mid Y_{t-1}, Z_t) = \sigma_\varepsilon^2$$

from (16.15).

There are two alternative means of computing the deterministic dynamic simulation path for y_t: treating the model as 'open' (so the analysis is conditional on $\{z_t\}$) or as 'closed' (so (y_t, z_t) are jointly simulated), and we denote these by a tilde and an overbar respectively. Then

$$\tilde{y}_t = \alpha z_t + \beta \tilde{y}_{t-1} = \alpha \sum_{j=0}^{t-1} \beta^j z_{t-j} + \beta^t y_0 \qquad t = 1, \ldots, T, \qquad \tilde{y}_0 = y_0. \quad (16.19)$$

For simplicity in what follows, initial conditions are ignored when this clarifies the analysis without misleading the logic. From (16.19) and (16.15),

$$y_t - \tilde{y}_t = \sum_{i=0}^{t-1} \beta^i \varepsilon_{t-i}, \quad (16.20)$$

and hence

$$\operatorname{var}(y_t - \tilde{y}_t) = \sigma_u^2 (1 - \beta^{2t}) = \operatorname{var}(y_t \mid Z_t, Y_0) \quad (16.21)$$

where $\sigma_u^2 = \sigma_\varepsilon^2 / (1 - \beta^2)$.

Note from (16.20) that $y_t - \tilde{y}_t$ is autocorrelated and heteroscedastic, although $\{\varepsilon_t\}$ is neither. Also, as $M_y(n)$ is the average of (16.21) over $t = 1, \ldots, n$, for large n it is approximately equal to σ_u^2 or, more generally,

$$M_y(n) = \sigma_u^2 \left[1 - \frac{\beta^2 (1 - \beta^{2n})}{n(1 - \beta^2)} \right]. \quad (16.22)$$

This notation is not fully informative compared with (16.21), but (16.22) is the expected value of the usual deterministic simulation MSE *treating z as strongly exogenous*. Of course, if $\gamma \neq 0$ then z is not in fact strongly exogenous, but it is important to realize that (16.22) does not depend on the actual value of γ, but only on the assumption that the model is open.

Next, consider the closed model simulation

$$\begin{pmatrix} \bar{y}_t \\ \bar{z}_t \end{pmatrix} = \begin{pmatrix} \beta + \alpha \gamma & \alpha \lambda \\ \gamma & \lambda \end{pmatrix} \begin{pmatrix} \bar{y}_{t-1} \\ \bar{z}_{t-1} \end{pmatrix} \text{ with } \begin{pmatrix} \bar{y}_0 \\ \bar{z}_0 \end{pmatrix} = \begin{pmatrix} y_0 \\ z_0 \end{pmatrix}. \quad (16.23)$$

Thus

$$\begin{pmatrix} \operatorname{var}(y_t - \bar{y}_t) \\ \operatorname{var}(z_t - \bar{z}_t) \end{pmatrix} = \begin{pmatrix} \operatorname{var}(y_t \mid Y_0, Z_0) \\ \operatorname{var}(z_t \mid Y_0, Z_0) \end{pmatrix}, \quad (16.24)$$

which yields, for sufficiently large t, the unconditional variances of y_t and z_t given by (derived as in Hendry (1979b) for example)

$$\sigma_y^2 = \frac{\sigma_\varepsilon^2 (1 - \beta \lambda) + \alpha^2 (1 + \beta \lambda) \sigma_z^2}{(1 - \beta \lambda)(1 - \beta^2) - 2\alpha \beta \gamma},$$

$$\sigma_z^2 = \frac{\sigma_v^2 (1 - \beta \lambda) + \gamma^2 (1 + \beta \lambda) \sigma_y^2}{(1 - \beta \lambda)(1 - \lambda^2) - 2\alpha \gamma \lambda}. \quad (16.25)$$

In the special case that $\gamma = 0$, the unconditional variance of y is

$$\sigma_y^2 = \sigma_u^2 + \left\{ \frac{\alpha^2(1 + \beta\lambda)\sigma_v^2}{(1 - \beta\lambda)(1 - \beta^2)(1 - \lambda^2)} \right\} \tag{16.26}$$

Now, it is an inherent property of closed linear stationary models (which are at least TACDs) that their n-step simulation error variance is close to the unconditional data variance for large n or, alternatively expressed, that their deterministic simulation track converges on the unconditional data mean. Consequently, such models appear to track 'very badly' even when they are valid. Conversely, comparing (16.22) and (16.26) when $\{z_t\}$ is strongly exogenous, how well the model appears to simulate depends on the extent to which the variance of $\{y_t\}$ is due to $\{z_t\}$ (the term $\{\cdot\}$ in (16.26)). The crucial difficulty, however, is that (16.22) is unaffected by the value of γ, so that the 'accuracy' of the simulation track is primarily dependent on the extent to which the selected model attributes data variance to factors which are 'outside the model', *irrespective of whether or not such factors really are strongly exogenous in practice*. Nothing in the analysis of simulating $\{y_t\}$ conditional on Z_T^1 depended on z *being* strongly exogenous (except, of course, the meaningfulness of the procedure!), provided that the investigator acted *as if it were*, as is clear from the choice of conditioning sets in (16.21) and (16.24). Consequently, the validity of a model cannot be assessed by its n-step tracking performance alone.

Rather, $1 - M(n)/\sigma_y^2$ measures the extent to which the 'explanation' of $\{y_t\}$ is attributed to variables which are treated as if they are strongly exogenous: the validity of the *simulation* is better assessed by tests of all the strong exogeneity claims, and the validity of the *model* by the criteria discussed in section 4. This adds a caveat to the analysis in McNees (1982) since it is not appropriate to define exogenous as 'outside the scope of the model', and also points towards techniques for resolving his 'dilemma of model comparisons' by investigating, for example, encompassing and the one-step system predictions like (16.17).

It must be stressed that valid inter-model comparisons cannot be based simply on an agreement between modellers as to which variables may be taken as strongly exogenous for computing $M(n)$: even if a unique set is agreed and no other is used by any modeller, the model with the lowest $M(n)$ value $(n > 1)$ may have nothing to commend it. For example, consider a comparison between (16.15) and

$$y_t = \sum_{i=0}^{k} \phi_i z_{t-i} + e_t, \tag{16.27}$$

with the assertion that $\mathscr{E}(z_{t-i}e_t) = 0$, $\forall i > 0$, where (16.15) and (16.27) constitute 'rival hypotheses', when the DGP is (16.15) + (16.16) with $\gamma \neq 0$. By construction, (16.15) must therefore encompass and $M(1)$ dominate (16.27) although, if $\sigma_v^2/\sigma_\varepsilon^2$ happens to be small, σ_e^2 will be similar in magnitude to σ_ε^2 so that there will be little to choose between the models in terms of $M(1)$. But if both modellers agree to treat z as strongly exogenous, (16.27) will have a much better simulation track than (16.15) with error variance still equal to σ_e^2! Yet if (y_t, z_t) are jointly simulated, (16.15) should perform better, with both having far larger error variances than their equivalent conditional simulations (compare (16.21) and (16.24)).

For practical *ex ante* forecasting, the future values of non-deterministic 'exogenous' variables are unknown and have to be projected by auxiliary equations, often of a surprisingly *ad hoc* nature given that the resulting predictions of the endogenous variables will be conditional thereon. Thus, $\text{var}(y_{T+n} \mid Y_T, Z_T)$ is the relevant *n*-step forecast error variance and this varies from (16.18) for $n = 1$ to (16.25) for very large *n*, but never coincides with (16.21). It follows that conditional simulations of the form (16.19) do not help select models which will be best for *n*-step *ex ante* forecasts either.

There are several important implications of this analysis worth summarizing

1 Ranking models by $M(n)$ as a dominance criterion reflects how much of the explanation is attributed to variables not generated in the simulation; and hence
2 it is not necessarily a criticism of *closed* 'time-series models' that their values of $M(n)$ exceed those of open 'econometric' models for $n > 1$ (nor a virtue for the latter), especially if the former have the smaller $M(1)$ values in post-sample forecast tests.
3 $M(n)$ values calculated from simulations conditional on assumed known 'strongly exogenous' variables z need reflect neither the operational (*ex ante*) forecasting characteristics of the model (since z_{T+i} are unknown) nor the 'goodness' of the underlying model as a characterization of the DGP (if the z variables are not actually strongly exogenous). It is also worth adding that
4 stocks will usually appear to simulate 'badly' even when changes in stocks are quite well determined because of the additional dynamic latent root close to unity.

These conclusions are demonstrable by computer experiments in which the DGP is known and alternative models are simulated under valid and invalid strong exogeneity assumptions. It must be stressed, however, that the only point at issue here is the assessment of model validity by dynamic simulation, using $M(n)$ as a *selection criterion*. Comparative simulations – with the model fixed and the inputs perturbed as a numerical method for calculating multipliers – have not been criticized, although it is well known that such counterfactuals depend on assumptions about super exogeneity instead (see Lucas, 1976; and chapter 15).

7 Conclusion

An analysis of empirical-model concepts suggests that there are pertinent considerations affecting how such models should be designed when available theory is not a complete quantitative characterization of the world. Many of the notions investigated above are well known, but have previously been justified by arguments whose relevance is unclear when the model does not include the DGP as a special case. Moreover, the relationships between widely used criteria for model selection do not seem to have been the subject of much previous analysis.

Data modelling advances beyond mere description only if sustained by an associated theory, and so we have assumed throughout that the best available theory is adopted. Nevertheless, no economic theory is likely to explain all observed phenomena comprehensively and some means of ordering empirical models remains desirable. The main ordering discussed above is based on encompassing both because it offers a more stringent check on model adequacy than that conventionally used (e.g. variance dominance combined with white noise errors is only necessary and is not sufficient to ensure encompassing) and because it provides one possible operational implementation of a progressive research strategy.[3] By way of comparison, it does not seem valid to base an ordering on dynamic simulation n-step mean square errors (for large n) alone.

Our practical experience, despite the turbulence of the 1970s, is that theory-consistent data-coherent, parsimonious encompassing models can be developed. Further, those that have been proposed tend to manifest relatively constant parameters of interest for quite extensive time periods, despite changes in data correlations (for a recent appraisal of UK consumption functions, see Davis, 1982). The simple empirical example presented to illustrate the analysis is consistent with this view.

Notes

1   Or, of course, incorrectly sized.
2   Naturally, one anticipates that 'better' theories will lead to better TACDs or to more rapid development of these.
3   Even so, we regrettably concur with Blaug (1980) that empirical investigators in economics are unlikely to progress beyond being mere handmaidens to theorists.

17

The Econometric Analysis of Economic Time Series

with Jean-François Richard

Preamble

This chapter proposes a general framework for interpreting recent developments in time-series econometrics, emphasizing the problems of linking economics and statistics. There are six main expository themes: models are viewed as (reduced) reparameterizations of data processes through marginalizing and conditioning; the latter operation is related to the economic notion of contingent plans based on weakly exogenous variables; a typology of dynamic equations clarifies the properties of conditional models; estimation of unknown parameters is treated using estimator generating equations; tests are interrelated in terms of the efficient score statistic; and the concept of encompassing rival hypotheses (separate or nested) provides an 'overview' criterion for evaluating empirical estimates which have been selected to satisfy conventional criteria. The discussion is illustrated by an estimated model of the demand for money.

As noted above, chapters 4 and 14–16 were written more or less contemporaneously and draw upon (and reiterate) points from each other. Ole Barndorff-Nielsen invited myself and Jean-François Richard to do a survey of econometrics for a series in the *International Statistical Review*. Since such a task was manifestly infeasible, we reduced the topic to time-series econometrics and the *Review* deemed that acceptable. Instead of just summarizing what the main results in the field were, we decided to try and integrate our approach into an overall framework which also sought to explain the role of economic analysis within the statistical methodology. This decision involved discussing parameter change, expectations and plans, their mutual links to conditioning, and both long-run economic theory and dynamic adjustment (see section 2). One useful outcome was an explicit link between weak exogeneity and contingent plans. The original section 3, which presented the model typology for the first time, has been omitted here since chapters 4 and 19 provide more comprehensive treatments. The renumbered section 3 is an extension of the approach in chapter 13 to 'incomplete' systems,

Reprinted from *International Statistical Review*, 51 (1983) 111–63. We are grateful to Gordon Anderson, James Davidson, Clive Granger, Andrew Harvey, Louis Phlips, Aris Spanos and two anonymous referees of this journal for helpful comments on the material herein, to Mary Morgan for historical perspective, and to Frank Srba for undertaking the estimation reported above. Financial support from the National Science Foundation to the University of California at San Diego, the Social Science Research Council to the London School of Economics and the Ford Foundation is gratefully acknowledged.

and sections 4 and 5 respectively discuss testing and model selection. The empirical example in the old section 7 is included as an annex to chapter 11, and so the retained sections of this chapter are almost exclusively concerned with summarizing the formalization.

The outcome of our efforts was a rather extensive paper, especially as the published version was followed by discussions from Manfred Deistler, Rob Engle, Clive Granger, Teun Kloek, Grayham Mizon and Paul Newbold. Some of the issues our discussants raised are still the subject of lively research (especially cointegration).

Since completing this paper, I have attempted an update and clarification in Hendry (1987) which focuses more formally on the stages of the reduction process, and is the basis for the analysis in chapter 19.

1 Introduction

Most empirical econometric studies are an attempt to interpret and summarize economic data in the light of both statistical theory and economic analysis, while simultaneously seeking to evaluate the very legitimacy of these bodies of knowledge for the task at hand. Three important difficulties hamper progress.

First, it is essential to take due account of the nature of economic activity which derives from the transacting behaviour of large numbers of separate yet interdependent agents (such as producers and consumers) all striving to achieve their disparate, self-selected (and generally opposed) objectives, given their initial endowments, the available information about an uncertain future and the constraints imposed by the environment in which they operate. Since the plans of such agents are not necessarily mutually consistent *ab initio*, outcomes generally differ from plans and certain magnitudes must adjust to reconcile the various conflicting aims, in turn inducing different future behaviour. Consequently, an economy is an inherently dynamic, stochastic, multidimensional, interdependent, non-linear and evolving entity of considerable complexity, the overall functioning of which is only partly understood.

Second, and most unfortunately in view of the first problem, observations on economic quantities are usually imprecise, samples are small and are not derived from controlled experimentation, and the observed data relate to the final outcomes rather than the original plans and expectations. Finally, economic analysis, while providing the essential conceptual framework and yielding many useful insights, often provides only a first approximation to how such systems function in idealized states, such as (timeless) static equilibria in which all change has ceased or steady states in which only constant growth occurs. Succinctly, the data generation process is complicated, data are scarce and of uncertain relevance, experimentation is uncontrolled and available theories are highly abstract and rarely uncontroversial.

Empirical macroeconomic models constitute the econometrician's attempt to characterize such economies quantitatively, by summarizing economic time-series data using existing economic theories embodied in statistically estimated parametric relationships. Even if we assume that the difficulties described above did not lead one to regard econometrics as hopeless – which some have done, but we most certainly do not (see chapter 1) – it would be astonishing if the statistical formulation of existing empirical models was not easily criticized, and, indeed, this has provided one source of improvement, the other major contributors being developments in economic analysis and in econometric technique; for a recent discussion, see Malinvaud (1981).

To clarify the basis for further constructive criticism, we present a framework for interpreting some recent developments in time-series econometrics, which may be useful to statisticians in other subject areas. While our overview is perforce idiosyncratic – and in effect comprises our own 'theory' of econometrics – nevertheless, offering a framework seemed more helpful than adding to the already substantial set of surveys recording the subject-matter content of econometrics; for good recent reviews, see, *inter alia*, Zellner (1979a) and the texts by Judge et al. (1980) and Harvey (1981a), together with the many references therein for fuller bibliographic perspective. Although Bayesian procedures can be applied fruitfully to all the models considered below, we have analysed only non-Bayesian approaches given the scale of our topic; useful references for the interested reader are Zellner (1971), Leamer (1978), Florens and Mouchart (1980b) and Drèze and Richard (1984). Finally, Cox (1981) surveys recent developments in time-series analysis and Harvey (1981c) presents an exposition.

The chapter uses six main pedagogical devices to review the field described in the title. First, for simplicity, attention is restricted to linear normal data processes so that *models can be construed as reparameterizations* of such processes by marginalizing and/or conditioning (section 2.1). Next, the concept of *weak exogeneity*, which sustains inference in conditional submodels, also allows the statistical formulation of the data generating mechanism to be related to the economic notion of *contingent plans* on which economic agents are assumed to base their behaviour (section 2.3). Third, a *typology of dynamic equations* (presented in chapter 4 to exposit their properties) interrelates the many 'types' of model extant in empirical research. Fourth, the concept of an *equation for generating different estimators* summarizes and integrates a vast literature on alternative estimation methods in econometrics (section 3). Next, a large range of tests can be summarized in terms of the *efficient score statistic*, again providing coherence to a diverse and voluminous literature (section 4). Lastly, the notion of *encompassing* is used to characterize an important aspect of the model selection problem (section 5). In many respects, by emphasizing statistical considerations, the resulting approach is complementary to that of Sargent (1981), who characterizes the data process in terms of the decision rules of optimizing economic agents.

To motivate our framework, an empirical illustration first highlights several of the difficulties typically encountered in econometrics, albeit in a deliberately accentuated form. The example draws on our own research generally; this also allows testing the previously published model on new data. However, equation (17.3), estimated below, does not represent a level of naivity unknown in econometrics (as perusal of 'empirical' journals will reveal): many economists believe strongly in the validity of their theories, and use data evidence primarily to determine the orders of magnitude of a small number of unknown coefficients relevant to their theories.

A well-known theory of the demand for money by private individuals for transacting (exchanging money for goods and services) is that money holdings (denoted by M) are proportional (other things being equal) to nominal income PI, where P is an index of the price level and I is constant-price ('real') income:

$$M = H_1 PI, \tag{17.1}$$

for some constant H_1. The content of (17.1) is that economic agents demand 'real' money, M/P, as a function of 'real' income (and would not be fooled by a simple change in the *units* of a currency, e.g. dollars to marks), and that the velocity of circulation of money $V = PI/M$ will be constant, *ceteris paribus* (other things being equal), *independently* of the values of P and I. Here, the infamous '*ceteris paribus* clause' includes (implicitly) the restriction to a static equilibrium world, i.e. a state in which all change has ceased. More generally, if a dynamic (or steady-state) equilibrium is allowed with non-zero (but constant) inflation $\dot{p}$ and one wished to compare across states with different levels of $\dot{p}$ (and hence of interest rates R), since agents tend to economize on their money holdings as inflation and/or interest rates increase

$$M = H_2 PI R^{\alpha_1} (1 + \dot{p})^{\alpha_2} \qquad (\alpha_1, \alpha_2 \leqslant 0), \tag{17.2}$$

where a multiplicative function has been assumed consistent with the positivity of M and V.

The status of (17.2) is a dynamic equilibrium relationship and strictly all the variables involved are the latent constructs of the theory; for a clear statement about equilibrium economic theory, see Weintraub (1979). Often, such unobservables are mapped one-to-one onto observed data 'equivalents'. Here, the series are quarterly seasonally adjusted time series for the United Kingdom over the period 1963(i)–1980(ii), defined as follows:

M notes and coins in circulation plus sight deposits in Commercial Banks (M1 from *Financial Statistics*: see for example 1981, p. 232, section 7)
I constant-price total final expenditure (from *Economic Trends*, Annual Supplement, 1980, table 10: current values deflated by P in 1975 prices)
P implicit deflator of I (*Economic Trends*, 1980, tables 10–12)
R local government three-month interest rate (*Financial Statistics*, e.g. 1981, p. 232, sections 13, 15)

Given UK financial institutions, it is reasonable to assume that individuals can obtain the quantity of transactions money they desire (by substitution from other liquid assets) and that the banking system determines short-term interest rates. The time-series behaviour of velocity shown in figure 17.1 reveals a substantial increase over the sample period (from 1.36 to 2.32) and while this is not inconsistent with a unit response of M to PI in a theory such as (17.2), it does disconfirm (17.1) prior to 'estimation'.

Let $\dot{p} = \Delta_1 \log_e P$, with lower-case letters denoting logarithms of corresponding capitals and $\Delta_j q_t = (q_t - q_{t-j})$. Then, if we use this typical mapping, take logs in (17.2) and allow for a disturbance e_t:

$$(m_t - p_t - i_t) = h_2 + \alpha_1 r_t + \alpha_2 \Delta_1 p_t + e_t. \tag{17.3}$$

If we assume $e_t \sim \text{IN}(0, \sigma^2)$, with i_t, r_t and p_t being 'determined outside the model'

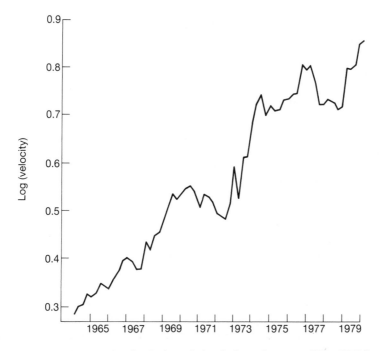

Figure 17.1   Time-series graph of velocity of circulation of money ($V = PI/M$).

independently of e_t, maximum likelihood estimation is simply ordinary least squares regression, which yields

$$(\widehat{m - p - i})_t = -0.01 - 0.21r_t - 4.0\Delta_1 p_t, \tag{17.4}$$

$$T = 65 \qquad R^2 = 0.63 \qquad \hat{\sigma} = 0.098 \qquad \text{DW} = 0.29 \qquad \eta_1(20, 42) = 5.7$$

$$\eta_2(6, 56) = 25.6,$$

where the coefficients on the right-hand side of (17.4) have standard errors 0.08, 0.05 and 1.1 respectively.

In equation (17.4), T is the sample size, R^2 the squared multiple correlation coefficient, $\hat{\sigma}$ the residual standard deviation (here, 9.8 per cent of M) and DW the Durbin–Watson statistic (which rejects the hypothesis of serially uncorrelated residuals). Also, $\eta_1(J, T - K - J)$ denotes the Chow (1960) test of parameter constancy for J periods and K regressors, approximately distributed as F(J, $T - K - J$) on the null of no parameter change for the last J observations, and $\eta_2(L, T - K - L)$ is the Lagrange multiplier based test for Lth-order residual autocorrelation, approximately distributed as F($L, T - K - L$) under the null of serial independence; see Godfrey (1978), Harvey (1981a) and section 4.

Although $(\hat{\alpha}_1, \hat{\alpha}_2)$ have the anticipated signs and 'reasonable' orders of magnitude, the results are uninterpretable: the standard errors are downward biased because of the positive residual autocorrelation, which in turn indicates a systematic departure of the model from the data, and parameter constancy is rejected. Even worse, including p_t and i_t as additional regressors, to test the proportionality in

(17.1) and (17.2), reduces $\hat{\sigma}$ to 0.039, but has DW = 0.34 casting grave doubt on the mainstay of the theory. In fact, the data standard deviation of $\Delta_1 m_t$ is only 0.025, and so the fit of (17.4) is worse than useless for explaining money holdings! Finally, the naive 'time-series model' that v_t ($= -m_t + p_t + i_t$) is a first-order autoregressive process has a residual standard error of 0.029, with $\eta_1(20, 44) = 0.9$ and $\eta_2(6, 58) = 0.5$, thus fitting and predicting better than these 'econometric equations'.

Fortunately, it is possible to explain the above findings and to develop an approach which avoids many of the problems. The primary objective of the chapter is to exposit the requisite concepts and a model based on (17.2) which is nevertheless considerably more useful than (17.4) is reported in chapter 11. Among the various issues that must be examined are the following:

1   the status of the explanatory variables i_t, r_t, p_t, $\Delta_1 p_t$ supposed to be 'determined outside the model' (see section 2.1);
2   the assumption of constant parameters (section 2.2);
3   the mapping from the latent variables of the theory to the observed data series (section 2.3);
4   the assumptions about e_t, made independently of (1) even though by definition e_t must contain everything not elsewhere specified (sections 2.2, 2.3);
5   the status of (17.2), given its equilibrium derivation and its dependence on *ceteris paribus* (section 2.4);
6   the role of time-series models and their relationships to econometric equations (section 2.3 and chapter 4);
7   the estimation of unknown parameters (section 3);
8   hypothesis and diagnostic tests (section 4);
9   model selection when specification is uncertain (section 5).

The general econometric problem of linking economics and statistics in data analysis is considered in the next section, together with the issues of stationarity and 'causality' as well as (1)–(6). For simplicity, statistical formulations in constant-parameter worlds are first considered in section 2.1, but results which depend critically on the constancy assumption are remarked on parenthetically, and that problem is then discussed in section 2.2. Economic formulations in terms of plans and expectations are analysed in section 2.3 in relation to the statistical framework, and the role of 'equilibrium' theory is evaluated in section 2.4.

2   An Econometric Framework

2.1   The Statistical Process under Stationarity

To establish notation and terminology, it is convenient to commence with the statistical formulation of the process postulated to generate the data in a stationary stochastic world. The observed data, denoted by the column vectors $\{x_t\}$, are a sample of T observations on K variables from the joint density function $D(x_1, \ldots, x_T | X_0, \theta)$ parameterized by an identifiable finite-dimensional vector of unknown parameters $\theta \in \Theta$ (a parameter space of non-zero Lebesgue measure), where X_0 is the matrix of initial conditions and $D(\cdot)$ is assumed continuous with respect to an appropriate measure. Let $X_t^1 = (x_1, \ldots, x_t)'$ and $X_t' = (X_0' X_t^{1\prime})$. Since economists conceive of the economy as an inherently sequential process, $D(\cdot)$ is automatically factorized as

$$D(X_T^1 | X_0, \theta) = \prod_{t=1}^{T} D(x_t | X_{t-1}, \theta).$$
(17.5)

The conditional densities on the right-hand side of (17.5) are assumed to be sufficiently constant over time for the objectives of the study, an issue we return to in section 2.2 below. Throughout, we refer to parameter 'constancy', reserving 'stability' for the property of the dynamic process being convergent. To achieve such a formulation may require transformations of the original data. While many of the concepts introduced below apply to a wide range of processes, for expository purposes $\{x_t\}$ is taken to be the outcome of such appropriate transformations that a normal linear equations system is an adequate approximation to the data generating process. Thus, conditional on θ and X_0, the resulting process can be expressed as

$$x_t | X_{t-1}, \theta \sim N(\mu_t, \Sigma) \qquad (t = 1, \ldots, T),$$
(17.6)

where

$$\mu_t = \mathscr{E}(x_t | X_{t-1}, \theta) = \sum_{i=1}^{n} \Pi_i x_{t-i},$$
(17.7)

$$\mathscr{E}[(x_t - \mu_t)(x_t - \mu_t)' | X_{t-1}, \theta] = \Sigma,$$
(17.8)

with $\{\Pi_i\}$ and Σ being functions of θ.

Since the lag length is invariably unknown, n requires selection with other features of the model, and hence a small value has to be imposed in practice given available sample sizes. If we set $\varepsilon_t = (x_t - \mu_t)$, which is a white noise innovation relative to X_{t-1} by construction, (17.7) yields the dynamic system

$$x_t = \sum_{i=1}^{n} \Pi_i x_{t-i} + \varepsilon_t.$$
(17.9)

Although there are interesting models of time-series heteroscedasticity of practical relevance (Engle, 1982a) it is convenient to assume that the data transformations also induce constant Σ in order to focus attention on (17.6) and (17.7).

While θ could consist of the elements of $(\{\Pi_i\}, \Sigma)$, parsimony typically leads to the latter being restricted, usually as explicit functions of a smaller set of invariants which are our original vector θ; in a Bayesian approach, such explicit expressions are necessary to avoid conditioning paradoxes in the assessment of a prior density on θ. Given that (17.6) and (17.7) characterize the data generating process and that $\{\Pi_i\}$, Σ are constant functions of θ, stationarity only requires that all the roots ξ_i of

$$\det\left(I - \sum_{i=1}^{n} \Pi_i \lambda^i\right) = 0$$

satisfy $|\xi_i| > 1$, in which case the dynamic process (17.9) is both stable and ergodic; see for example Hannan (1970, p. 204).

Crudely expressed, the statistical content lies in (17.6), and the economics content in appropriate specification of (17.7). Econometric modelling involves developing a parsimonious yet relatively complete description of a relevant part of (17.6) and (17.7) which in turn has constant parameters over historically useful time horizons and is specified in an economically meaningful structure. The associated economic theory formulation is discussed in section 2.3 below, but it is important to note that economists tend to analyse issues in terms of relationships which are claimed to characterize the structure of decision taking by agents, called *structural* relationships, rather than in terms of processes like (17.9) which are viewed as *derived* equations. Often, their models of the data generation process can be written in the form

$$A_0 \mu_t + \sum_{i=1}^{n} A_i x_{t-i} = 0, \tag{17.10}$$

where the $\{A_i\}$ are well-defined functions of θ, $A_0(\theta)$ is of full row rank for θ almost everywhere in Θ (Richard, 1979) and compatibility with (17.7) requires that, almost everywhere in Θ,

$$A_0 \Pi_i + A_i = 0 \qquad (i = 1, \ldots, n). \tag{17.11}$$

Restrictions imposed on the $\{A_i\}$ by economic theories generally induce restrictions on $\{\Pi_i\}$ and certain of the elements in $\{A_i\}$ may be parameters of interest themselves and hence be included in θ. If different values of θ are associated with a common value of $(\{\Pi_i\}, \Sigma)$ then there is a lack of identification: loosely speaking, a parameter λ is identified if it is a well-defined function of $(\{\Pi_i\}, \Sigma)$.

Data sets in economics typically consist of a relatively small sample of observations on a large number of variables. Therefore, to be manageable, the analysis must focus on a subset of the variables and, provided that the model user is not interested in all the parameters of θ, that subset sometimes can be analysed without loss of relevant sample information. Let ψ denote the parameters which are of direct interest because of their relevance either to policy or to testing economic theories (or because of their constancy for forecasting and/or invariance to particular policy 'interventions'). In so far as econometricians model in terms of parameters of interest, ψ may be a subvector of θ, but more generally, ψ is a vector function of θ: $\psi = f(\theta)$.

In our framework, 'models' are inherently reduced reparameterizations of the data generation process and, from the process (17.6) and (17.7), models may be derived by marginalizing, by conditioning or by doing both. These operations are rarely discussed explicitly by economists, as models tend to be formulated on the basis of *a priori* theories which are believed to characterize economic behaviour adequately so that the notions of processes and models are conflated as in (17.3). Such an approach requires the axiom of correct specification (Leamer, 1978, p. 4) that all the assumptions of the model are valid, and leads to a model building methodology in which violated assumptions are viewed as 'problems' to be 'corrected'. As an example of this approach in (17.4), since $\{e_t\}$ is autocorrelated, the serial correlation should be 'removed' and using the typical first-order autoregressive error assumption yields $\hat{\sigma} = 0.025$, significantly improving the fit. However, a test of the validity of the autoregressive error assumption (see Sargan, 1980a), denoted $\eta_3(h)$, approximately distributed as χ_h^2 when the error is autoregressive yields $\eta_3(2) = 17.1$, strongly rejecting the attempted reformulation. Thus, further 'problems' remain if this route is chosen.

Most estimation theory in econometric textbooks is predicated on knowing the 'correct' model, while simultaneously most practitioners are well aware that their models are inevitably inadequate in many respects. Consequently, it seems more useful to try and *design* empirical models such that their residuals are white noise *innovations* relative to the available information, thus using for example autocorrelation tests as *selection* criteria (that innovations like $\{\varepsilon_t\}$ in (17.9) are a martingale difference sequence then provides a feasible basis for developing large-sample distributional theory for estimators and test statistics; see for example Hall and Heyde (1980), Hannan et al. (1980) and Crowder (1976)). In terms of (17.4), we do not consider that model to be useful even with autocorrelation 'removed' since (among other flaws) the absence of autocorrelation is necessary but is not sufficient to ensure that the residuals are innovations.

Returning to the general case, let $x_t' = (w_t', y_t', z_t')$, where $\{w_t\}$ denotes a (very large) vector of variables to be integrated out (i.e. with respect to which the analysis is marginalized), $\{z_t\}$ is a vector to be treated as 'given' or 'exogenous' for the purposes of the analysis (i.e. on which the analysis is conditional) and $\{y_t\}$ is the vector of variables which are to be modelled. Generally, econometric models are first (implicitly) expressed in marginal form and then conditioning is considered, and so we follow that practice here and factorize the data densities (17.5) as

$$D(x_t|X_{t-1}, \theta) = D(w_t|y_t, z_t, X_{t-1}, \phi_1)D(y_t, z_t|X_{t-1}, \phi_2), \qquad (17.12)$$

where (ϕ_1, ϕ_2) is an appropriate reparameterization of θ. Loosely speaking, valid marginalization with respect to w_t requires that ψ be a function of ϕ_2 alone (which mapping remains constant over the relevant period) and that ϕ_1 and ϕ_2 are variation free (i.e. are not constrained by cross-restrictions, so that $(\phi_1, \phi_2) \in \Phi_1 \times \Phi_2$, where Φ_i denotes the set of admissible values of ϕ_i), whence there is a classical sequential cut in (17.12); see for example Florens and Mouchart (1980a) and Barndorff-Nielsen (1978). In practice, one may be willing to suffer some loss of efficiency to achieve a tractable model when ϕ_1 and ϕ_2 are not variation free, but it must be stressed that omitting variables from an analysis automatically enforces marginalization and an associated reparameterization (non-constant parameterizations will result from marginalizing with respect to important variates whose relationships with retained variables alter). Note that aggregation over time, space, agents, commodities etc. is equivalent to a combination of appropriately reparameterizing and then marginalizing with respect to the remaining disaggregated variables.

Often, models are also marginalized with respect to W_{t-1} and to be valid this requires that W_{t-1} does not influence (y_t, z_t). In economics, this is usually referred to as Wiener–Granger non-causality (Wiener, 1956; Granger, 1969, 1980) defined as: W_{t-1} does not Granger-cause $s_t = (y_t', z_t')'$ with respect to X_{t-1} if and only if

$$D(s_t|X_{t-1}, \phi_2) \equiv D(s_t|S_{t-1}, \phi_2). \qquad (17.13)$$

When (17.13) holds for $t = 1, \ldots, T$ it is often expressed as 'w does not Granger-cause s' in which case the analysis can be restricted to S_T^1 without loss of relevant sample information about ϕ_2 (and also about ψ provided that the conditions discussed above apply). Otherwise, integrating out lagged ws which do influence s_t alters the parameterization and hence jeopardizes parameter constancy, and frequently introduces moving-average errors into models. Note that Granger causality is defined with respect to a specific set of variables and its presence or absence can alter as the selected set of variables is changed.

Assuming that (17.13) holds and that $\psi = g(\phi_2)$, we next consider *conditioning* on z_t using the factorization

$$D(s_t | S_{t-1}, \phi_2) = D(y_t | z_t, S_{t-1}, \lambda_1) D(z_t | S_{t-1}, \lambda_2), \tag{17.14}$$

where (λ_1, λ_2) is an appropriate reparameterization of ϕ_2, and if $\mathscr{L}(\phi_2; S_T^1 | S_0)$ denotes the likelihood function then

$$\mathscr{L}(\cdot) = \prod_{t=1}^{T} \mathscr{L}_1(\lambda_1; y_t | z_t, S_{t-1}) \prod_{t=1}^{T} \mathscr{L}_2(\lambda_2; z_t | S_{t-1}). \tag{17.15}$$

If ψ is a function of λ_1 alone, and λ_1 and λ_2 are variation free (as discussed above for the ϕ_i), then z_t is said to be *weakly exogenous* for ψ, and inference about ψ from the partial likelihood $\mathscr{L}_1(\cdot)$ can be conducted without loss of relevant information; this concept derives from Koopmans (1950a) and is discussed in greater detail by Richard (1980) and in chapter 15. Consequently, the model for z_t does not need to be specified, provided that one does not wish to test the conditions for weak exogeneity. The importance of this is that the analysis is not only less costly, more comprehensible and more robust, but also that model selection is facilitated in the standard situation that the precise specification of the data generation process is not given *a priori*. In practice, many econometric studies simply specify $\mathscr{L}_1(\cdot)$ alone, leaving implicit whatever weak exogeneity assertions are necessary to complete $\mathscr{L}(\cdot)$ in (17.15).

While we have restricted the analysis to a sampling approach, Florens and Mouchart (1980a) discuss the concept of reduction (conditioning and marginalizing) within a Bayesian framework where weak exogeneity is no longer necessary for valid conditioning (conceptually at least) since, under an appropriate prior density, the absence of a cut may not affect inference on ψ. Also, these authors discuss the relationship between exogeneity and ancillarity.

If in addition to z_t being weakly exogenous for ψ, y does not Granger-cause z, then $D(z_t | S_{t-1}, \lambda_2)$ can be written as $D(z_t | Z_{t-1}, \lambda_2)$ in which case z_t is said to be *strongly exogenous* for ψ. This condition is required to justify conditionally forecasting $(y_{t+1}, \ldots, y_{t+m})$ given $(z_{t+1}, \ldots, z_{t+m})$. However, Granger non-causality of y for z is neither necessary nor sufficient for conducting inference conditionally on z_t without loss of relevant information.

The concepts introduced above may be illustrated using the following two-equation system:

$$\Delta_1 y_t = \beta_0 + \beta_1 \Delta_1 z_t + (1 - \beta_3)(z - y)_{t-1} + \varepsilon_{1t} \qquad (0 \leqslant \beta_1 < 1, 0 \leqslant \beta_3 < 1), \tag{17.16}$$

$$z_t = \gamma_0 + \gamma_2 z_{t-1} + \gamma_3 y_{t-1} + \varepsilon_{2t} \qquad (0 < \gamma_2 < 1, 0 \leqslant -\gamma_3 < 1), \qquad (17.17)$$

$$\begin{bmatrix} \varepsilon_{1t} \\ \varepsilon_{2t} \end{bmatrix} \sim IN(0, \Sigma), \qquad \Sigma = (\sigma_{ij}). \tag{17.18}$$

Equation (17.16) describes an error correction mechanism whereby an economic agent adjusts y, in response to changes in z and the previous disequilibrium, towards the equilibrium solution that $y = a + z$, where $a = \beta_0/(1 - \beta_3)$. Equation (17.17) is a typical control rule for another economic agent attempting to influence y by means of the (policy) variable z. For example, this could be a governmental policy reaction function or a farmer's supply decision so that the exclusion of y_t is very natural. The parameters of the system are exactly identifiable, and the process is stable under the conditions shown. If $\gamma_3 = 0$, y does not Granger-cause z, and yet z_t is not weakly exogenous for $\beta = (\beta_0, \beta_1, \beta_3)$ when $\sigma_{12} \neq 0$. If $\sigma_{12} = 0$, then $cov(z_t, \varepsilon_{1t}) = 0$ which, given that y_t is excluded from (17.17), is sufficient for the weak exogeneity of z_t for β. If $\sigma_{12} = \gamma_3 = 0$ then z_t is strongly exogenous for β.

Note the importance of the concept of parameters of interest in our definitions of weak and strong exogeneity. Obviously, there exist many nine-parameter models which are observationally equivalent to the original model (17.16)–(17.18) but have different 'behavioural' interpretations. One such model is obtained by replacing (17.16) and (17.18) respectively by

$$y_t = b_0 + b_1 z_t + b_3 y_{t-1} + e_{1t}, \tag{17.16'}$$

$$\begin{bmatrix} e_{1t} \\ \varepsilon_{2t} \end{bmatrix} \sim IN(0, \Omega) \qquad \Omega = (\omega_{ij}). \tag{17.18'}$$

Equation (17.16') now describes a partial adjustment process. The parameters $(\beta_0, \beta_1, \beta_3, \sigma_{12})$ and $(b_0, b_1, b_3, \omega_{12})$ are related by

$$\begin{aligned} b_0 - \beta_0 &= -\gamma_0(b_1 - \beta_1) & b_1 - \beta_1 &= \gamma_2^{-1}(1 - \beta_1 - \beta_3), \\ b_3 - \beta_3 &= -\gamma_3(b_1 - \beta_1) & \sigma_{12} - \omega_{12} &= \sigma_{22}(b_1 - \beta_1). \end{aligned} \tag{17.19}$$

Therefore, if $\sigma_{12} = 0$, z_t is *not* weakly exogenous for $b = (b_0, b_1, b_3)'$ unless $\beta_1 + \beta_3 = 1$ in which case the two models coincide. If instead $\sigma_{12} = \sigma_{22}\gamma_2^{-1}(1 - \beta_1 - \beta_3)$, then z_t is weakly exogenous for b but no longer for β.

Whether one is interested in β or in b may be simply a matter of preference among the corresponding economic theories. This would be the case in stationary worlds since no sample evidence could ever discriminate between these two theories. In contrast the choice between (17.16) and (17.16') is bound to become critical as soon as the economy under consideration is subject to interventions affecting the control equation (17.17). Worlds of parameter change are discussed in section 2.2 but it is obvious from (17.19) that β and b cannot *both* be invariant with respect to changes in (γ_2, γ_3), so that choosing the 'wrong' theory may entail parameter non-constancy or predictive failure.

In fact, the concept of exogeneity has been the subject of very extensive discussion in econometrics; see, *inter alia*, Koopmans (1950a), Orcutt (1952), Marschak (1953),

Phillips (1956), Sims (1972b, 1977a), Geweke (1978, 1984), Richard (1980) and chapter 15. As discussed above, the notion of weak exogeneity builds on the important paper by Koopmans (1950a) using recently developed concepts of statistical inference; see for example Barndorff-Nielsen (1978) and Florens and Mouchart (1980a). However, other concepts of exogeneity are also currently used in econometrics and in particular that of 'strict exogeneity'. Let u_t be the 'disturbance' associated with the (structural) relationships

$$u_t = \sum_{i=0}^{n} A_i x_{t-i} = A_0 \varepsilon_t; \tag{17.20}$$

then (Koopmans and Hood, 1953; Christ, 1966, chs IV.4, VI.4; Sims, 1977a) z_t is strictly exogenous in (17.20) if and only if it is uncorrelated with past, present and future us. Sims (1977a) and Geweke (1978) discuss the connections between strict exogeneity and Granger non-causality, and in chapter 15 it is shown that the strict exogeneity of z_t in (17.20) is neither necessary nor sufficient for the weak exogeneity of z_t for ψ. In particular, the strict exogeneity of z in (17.20) is uninteresting if it is achieved by a reparameterization from which ψ either cannot be derived or is not an invariant. Also note that, if distributional assumptions are made about $\{u_t\}$ in (17.20), then A_0 has to be square if $D(y_t|z_t, X_{t-1})$ is to be derived; in our framework, the distribution of the observables is characterized by (17.6) and (17.7) while (17.10) serves to induce restrictions on $\{\Pi_i\}$.

In summary, successively achieving valid marginalization and conditioning with respect to W_t and z_t respectively requires introducing a reparameterization of θ into $(\phi_1, \lambda_1, \lambda_2)$ such that (i) ϕ_1, λ_1 and λ_2 are all variation free and (ii) ψ is a function of λ_1 alone. Note that (i) is not necessary for validly analysing the submodel $D(y_t|z_t, S_{t-1}, \lambda_1)$ in that the weaker condition, (i') λ_1 and (ϕ_1, λ_2) are variation free, also supports jointly marginalizing and conditioning. However, while a joint analysis may appear conceptually attractive, it does not seem of great practical relevance, is often complicated and in any case rarely occurs in econometric practice where marginalization is not usually formally investigated (with the notable exceptions of integrating out unobservable variables and analysing the consequences of aggregation).

2.2 Parameter Change

A standard basis for time-series analysis is the assumption that $\{x_t\}$ is a weakly or wide-sense stationary process with constant *unconditional* first and second moments:

$$\mathscr{E}(x_t) = \gamma \qquad \mathscr{E}(x_t - \gamma)(x_{t-s} - \gamma)' = \Gamma(s).$$

Many important technical and data analytical advances have followed from this assumption, including the concepts discussed above. Nevertheless, γ and $\Gamma(\cdot)$ do not seem reasonable invariants for economic data, a point made by for example Koopmans (1937), even when the $\{x_t\}$ are transformations of the raw data series such as logarithmic differences, since stationarity requires far more than the absence of trends. Indeed, if γ and $\Gamma(s)$ were constants, all least squares approximations of components of x_t by any other subsets of current and lagged xs (including for example univariate autoregressive integrated moving average representations) would have constant coefficients, independently of their economic relevance. Consequently, predictive failure would not be a problem and data intercorrelations would be constant apart from sampling fluctuations: yet neither phenomenon is characteristic of empirical econometrics; see for example the $\eta_1(\cdot)$ test of (17.4).

In part, of course, this may be due to using inappropriate data transformations such that (say) the moments of $\{x_t^*\}$ are not time independent even though those of $\{x_t\}$ are. While this emphasizes the important role of functional form, it remains true that many major changes have perturbed Western economies in the last 15 years including the creation of OPEC and the consequent change in energy prices, the switch from 'fixed' to 'floating' exchange rates, the enlargement of the European Economic Community, and a vast increase in the scale and volatility of government intervention in economic affairs. These events in turn may well have altered how economic agents react to any given circumstances.

There are many ways in which such 'shocks' could be handled, but in essence all require isolating the changes to highlight the remaining constancies. Parameters which are invariant to interventions are obviously of interest and behavioural models which involve only such invariants provide a useful basis for forecasting and policy analysis. *A major objective of econometric modelling is the development of structural submodels with invariant parameters*, which entails both that the underlying part of the data generation process has a constant parameterization and that a correctly specified variant thereof is estimated. Conversely, the greatest drawback from invalid marginalizing and/or conditioning is that the derived parameters may depend on non-invariants and hence all may appear to be non-constant even though only a few elements of θ have changed; e.g. consider basing the data analysis on (17.1) rather than (17.2). Of course, in some hyperparameterization (almost certainly only specifiable *post hoc*), θ can be considered as constant but this simply creates problems in specifying the components of x_t; conversely, treating everything as variable precludes the use of economic theory. Consequently, we allow for some structurally invariant parameters with other elements of θ being relevant only over certain subperiods, the timing of which is not necessarily known *a priori* by the econometrician.

Since weak exogeneity requires that the parameters of interest and those of the exogenous process are variation free, it offers a useful framework within which to analyse the invariance of the former under interventions affecting the latter. However, weak exogeneity is not sufficient for structural invariance since economic agents can always modify their behaviour in retaliation to interventions if they so choose. For example, they can increase their responsiveness to interest rate changes if governments reduce the rate of monetary growth; see, *inter alia*, Lucas (1976) and chapter 15. Moreover, as stressed by Salmon and Wallis (1982), estimating the invariants of the data generation process also requires adequate 'excitation' of the observations in the absence of additional information (e.g. one cannot estimate an interest elasticity if interest rates never vary). In the light of these considerations, it is useful to introduce one further exogeneity concept to generalize that notion to worlds where regimes can change, namely that z_t is *super exogenous* for ψ if it is weakly exogenous and ψ is invariant to interventions which change λ_2.

Reconsider the models (17.16)–(17.18) and (17.16′)–(17.18′). If $\sigma_{12} = 0$, then z_t is super exogenous for β provided that this vector is invariant to changes in (γ_2, γ_3). Ordinary least squares estimation of (17.16) would then lead to the valid conclusion that (17.16) is a constant behavioural relationship and, equally importantly, would help isolate the source of parameter non-constancy in competing models. If $\sigma_{12} \neq 0$, full information maximum likelihood estimation of β would be required since ordinary least squares estimated coefficients of (17.16) would now also depend on (γ_2, γ_3). In contrast, full information maximum likelihood estimation of b in (17.16′)–(17.18′), and *a fortiori* ordinary least squares estimation of b in (17.16′), could lead one to the invalid conclusion that the economy under consideration had modified its behaviour in response to the policy change. Also, in the absence of policy changes over the observation period, (17.16′) would still be inappropriate for prediction or simulation under *new* control policies. Obviously the argument could be reversed in favour of b.

However, in contrast with the constant-parameter case, sample evidence is bound to discriminate between (17.16) and (17.16′) as soon as (17.17) has changed over the observation period. The possibility that neither (17.16) nor (17.16′) are invariant, or will continue to be invariant, cannot be ruled out. Our experience suggests, however, that there exist 'simple' behavioural equations which are remarkably constant over periods of considerable change; see chapter 8 for example and the 'follow-up' in chapter 10 as well as the results in chapter 11 (see equation (11.21)).

Since we have introduced the notion of policy interventions, it must be stressed that in such worlds, since policy depends on the past performance of the economy, usually it would be unrealistic to assume that y does not Granger-cause z, while the weak exogeneity of z for ψ continues to play an essential role in the analysis. For example, in terms of (17.3), if $\psi' = (\alpha_1, \alpha_2)$ and $\{e_t\}$ were white noise, then r_t could be weakly exogenous even if its current value was determined by the authorities in the light of the behaviour of m_{t-1}, i_{t-1} and p_{t-1}. More generally, consider an economy described by the conditional submodel $D(y_t | z_t, S_{t-1}, \lambda_1)$ which is subject to interventions from a government whose behaviour is described by the marginal submodel $D(z_t | S_{t-1}, \lambda_2)$. One would anticipate that government interventions would be fundamentally influenced by the past behaviour of the economy (Y_{t-1}) and that the control policies would be difficult to model; provided that z_t is super exogenous for ψ, neither difficulty impinges on inference about ψ. Moreover, when elements of λ_2 are operative at different times, if λ_1 is an invariant, the conditional model nevertheless allows valid prediction under policy changes, even though (say) a model of y_t marginalized with respect to z_t (or Z_t) would not; whether λ_1 can be an invariant when the agents' behaviour depends on what they *expect* policy to be is considered in section 2.3.

For the remainder of the chapter, we assume that the choice of $\{s_t\}$ is such as to allow valid marginalization with respect to w_t ($t = 1, \ldots, T$). To economize on notation and equations, it is then convenient to reinterpret (17.6)–(17.11) as holding *after* marginalization so that $x_t = s_t = (y_t', z_t')'$ and $\theta = \phi_2$; alternatively, imagine that no w variates are relevant to the formulation, although note that the $\{A_i\}$ may represent different functions of θ if marginalization is required. Also, ψ must remain a well-defined function of λ_1.

Now partition μ_t, Σ and $\{\Pi_i\}$ conformably with $(y_t', z_t')'$ such that, for example, $\mu_{1t} = \mathscr{E}(y_t|X_{t-1})$, $\mu_{2t} = \mathscr{E}(z_t|X_{t-1})$ etc. By properties of the normal density, from (17.7),

$$\mathscr{E}(y_t|z_t, X_{t-1}, \lambda_1) = D_0 z_t + \sum_{i=1}^{n} P_i x_{t-i}, \qquad (17.21)$$

where $P_0 = (Q_0 : D_0)$ say, and $\{P_i, i = 0, \ldots, n\}$ depend only on λ_1 as in (17.14). All the exogeneity concepts discussed above can be characterized directly for the changed notation; for example z_t is weakly exogenous for $\psi = g(\lambda_1)$ if $(\lambda_1, \lambda_2) \in \Lambda_1 \times \Lambda_2$ and is super exogenous if also λ_1 does not vary with λ_2. It is worth stressing that the economic distinction between 'variables explained by the model' and those 'determined outside the scope of the model' should not be confused with the statistical concepts of 'endogenous' and 'exogenous' and it is precisely the purpose of the concept of weak exogeneity to clarify when z_t can be treated as being determined outside the conditional submodel under analysis for purposes of inference on ψ. However, for other purposes, such as dynamic simulations of models conditional on a fixed set Z_T^1, strong exogeneity is required, although for n-step ahead predictions if y_t depends on z_{t-k} for $k \leqslant n - 1$ then $D(z_t|X_{t-1}, \lambda_2)$ must be modelled anyway; and for comparative model simulation studies (often called scenario studies) then super exogeneity of the perturbed variables is required. By itself, strict exogeneity, perhaps obtained by construction, is not sufficient for any of these purposes, and unless the equation in which strict exogeneity is claimed to occur happens to isolate invariants, predictive failure will result following major interventions.

The objective of the following subsection is to provide economic flesh for this statistical skeleton, complementing the statistical concepts with economic interpretations. Also, the main ideas in the remainder of the chapter are as follows. First, agents are assumed to formulate 'plans' for the variables whose values they seek to determine, contingent on the available information; these variables are taken to be the subset y_t and the planned magnitudes (y_t^p) are identified with either $\mathscr{E}(y_t|X_{t-1})$ or $\mathscr{E}(y_t|z_t, X_{t-1})$ depending on the information set. Next, the behavioural relationships may be either the result of optimization (forward looking) or simply servomechanistic rules (feedback) depending on the decision problem. For the former, the expectation held about z_t *by the agent* (denoted by z_t^e) must be modelled and considerable debate surrounds the assertion that $z_t^e = \mathscr{E}(z_t|X_{t-1})$ which conflates the economic with the statistical interpretation of the 'expectations' involved. Third, while economic theories are often developed without reference to any specific data phenomena, nevertheless such theories generally specify the variables comprising x_t, the parameters of interest ψ and their mapping to the $\{A_i\}$ in (17.10), likely invariances, possible exogeneity assertions and (on occasion) potential values of n. In addition, the relevant theory may constrain the class of admissible dynamic equations, often by specifying the form of the equilibrium solution as in section 2.4. While this may suggest the estimation method (section 3) models are rarely adequately articulated to encompass all the main features of the data generating process. Consequently, data modelling and post-data model evaluation remain important (sections 4, 5).

Finally, when $\{x_t\}$ satisfies certain data constraints (e.g. identities or positivity etc.), it is highly desirable that the model also automatically satisfies the same constraints, which necessitates a careful consideration of functional forms.

2.3 The Economic Model: Plans and Expectations

We postulate that agents in the economy base their decisions on contingent plans (Bentzel and Hansen, 1955) which implement optimizing behaviour given limited information (since information has costs of collection, processing etc.). Such plans are the *behavioural relationships* noted above, and involve expectations about future events, adaptive responses to changes in the environment and mechanisms for correcting past mistakes. Moreover, systems of such relationships must account for how outcomes are determined and how disequilibria between plans and realizations are reconciled by changes in prices, in quantities and/or in the extent of rationing. Finally, empirical relevance requires the specification of mappings between the many latent variables of the theory and the observables of the data analysis. However, a complete discussion of all the interactions between economic analysis and statistical modelling is well beyond the scope of our chapter, and so we focus on the interpretation of conditional submodels as formulated above.

Let $y_t \in \mathbb{R}^p$, $z_t \in \mathbb{R}^q$ respectively denote those variables to be explained by the economic model and those determined outside the scope of the theory, with y_t^p and z_t^e being respectively the economic agents' contingent plans for y_t and their expectations for z_t. On the one hand, it is often natural to assume that y_t^p coincides with the statistical expectation of y_t on the grounds that rational agents would notice and correct systematic departures from their plans, although whether that expectation is $\mathscr{E}(y_t|X_{t-1}, \cdot)$ or $\mathscr{E}(y_t|z_t, X_{t-1}, \cdot)$ obviously depends on the agents' information sets at the time their plans are finalized. Economists often phrase such statements with y_t^p determining $\mathscr{E}(y_t|X_{t-1})$ since the data generation process is the economy and so $\mathscr{E}(y_t|\cdot)$ takes whatever values it does because of economic behaviour. However, as discussed above, a careful distinction is required between the data process and any postulated *model* thereof, since the assumed and actual determinants of y_t^p need not coincide. On the other hand, failures of market clearing such as rationing could necessitate more complicated mappings of y_t^p to y_t than simply deviating by white noise errors and there is a large literature on this particular problem, which is loosely called 'disequilibrium econometrics': see, *inter alia*, Goldfeld and Quandt (1976), Bowden (1978) and Quandt (1982), and for an application to planned economies, Portes and Winter (1980). Moreover, in the system as a whole, agents' plans may be inconsistent and as a consequence some participants may find their plans thwarted.

If the process which generates z_t is beyond the agent's control, as we hypothesize, z_t^e might differ from the statistical expectation of z_t, and hence an auxiliary model of 'expectations formation' is required, potentially (and usually) different from the data generation process of z_t. Moreover, the current plan frequently depends on expectations about future values of z_t and all such unobservables must be eliminated to produce an estimable model; however, we restrict the analysis to current expectations to simplify the algebra since no new issues of principle arise in addition to those already present when $z_t^e \neq z_t$. Data about anticipations and expectations can be obtained from surveys, a well-known study being Katona and Mueller (1968). However, to date use of this source has yielded equivocal results in macroeconomic time-series studies; see for example Carlson and Parkin (1975). In any case prediction often necessitates auxiliary equations to forecast the expectations data. Marget (1929) provides an early discussion of how economic forecasts may affect the way agents behave.

To clarify the framework, all the ingredients of the economic model intended to represent the data generation process of x_t in (17.6) and (17.7) are restated together as follows.

First, a specification of the behavioural plan (with parameters denoted by *) is

$$y_t^p = D_0^* z_t^e + \sum_{i=1}^{n^*} P_i^* x_{t-i}, \tag{17.22}$$

where D_0^*, $\{P_i^*\}$ are well-defined functions of $\theta_1 \in \Theta_1$, or in terms of structural relationships analogous to (17.10)

$$B_0^* y_t^p + C_0^* z_t^e + \sum_{i=1}^{n^*} A_i^* x_{t-i} = 0, \tag{17.23}$$

where $A_0^* = (B_0^*, C_0^*)$ and $\{A_i^*\}$ are well-defined functions of θ_1 and $B_0^*(\theta_1)$ is of full row rank for θ_1 almost everywhere in Θ_1. Compatibility of (17.22) and (17.23) requires that, almost everywhere in Θ_1,

$$B_0^* D_0^* + C_0^* = 0 \qquad B_0^* P_i^* + A_i^* = 0 \qquad (i = 1, \dots, n^*). \tag{17.24}$$

Second, we give a postulate concerning the formation of z_t^e. If there is *perfect information*, $z_t^e = z_t$; otherwise, it is assumed that

$$z_t^e = \sum_{i=1}^{m} G_i x_{t-i} \qquad (m \leqslant n^*), \tag{17.25}$$

where $\{G_i\}$ are well-defined functions of θ_1. Important special cases of (17.25) are noted below.

Third, we give a description of the actual process determining $\mu_{2t} = \mathscr{E}(z_t | X_{t-1})$, which from (17.6) and (17.7) is

$$\mu_{2t} = \sum_{i=1}^{n} F_i x_{t-i}, \tag{17.26}$$

where $\{F_i\}$ are well-defined functions of $\theta_2 \in \Theta_2$. As considered below, whether or not the parameters of (17.25) and (17.26) are related depends on the weak exogeneity of z_t for ψ. If z_t is weakly exogenous for the parameters of interest, then (17.26) is irrelevant, whereas (17.25) remains relevant unless z_t^e is observed.

Fourth, a mapping of the unobservables (y_t^p, μ_{2t}) to the observables (y_t, z_t) is, for example, in the case that $y_t - y_t^p$ is white noise,

$$y_t = y_t^p + u_{1t} \qquad z_t = \mu_{2t} + u_{2t}, \tag{17.27}$$

and conditionally on X_{t-1}

$$\begin{bmatrix} u_{1t} \\ u_{2t} \end{bmatrix} \sim N(0, \Omega) \qquad \Omega = \begin{bmatrix} \Omega_{11} & \Omega_{12} \\ \Omega_{21} & \Omega_{22} \end{bmatrix}. \tag{17.28}$$

However, this specification not only assumes agents are 'rational', it also short-circuits the steps from plans to realizations to measured outcomes, and excludes (for example) rationing. Since deterministic variables (such as seasonal dummies) and identities raise no substantive problems, it is convenient to assume that Ω is symmetric and positive definite. In terms of the four specifications above, the illustration in (17.3) comprises the assumptions of a plan which is independent of both past mistakes and anticipations, with perfect information about all the elements of z_t, where $\Omega_{12} = 0$ and $u_{1t} = e_t$ is white noise.

Generally, the parameters of the model (17.22)–(17.28) have to be related unambiguously to those of the data generating process (17.6) and (17.7). First, consider the perfect information case when $z_t^c = z_t$ and $n^* = n$ (for expositional purposes). From the properties of the multivariate normal density, if we let

$$H^* = \begin{bmatrix} I_p & D_0^* \\ 0 & I_q \end{bmatrix}, \tag{17.29}$$

then for (17.22), compared with (17.7),

$$H^* \begin{bmatrix} P_i^* \\ F_i \end{bmatrix} = \Pi_i \qquad H^* \Omega H^{*\prime} = \Sigma; \tag{17.30}$$

whereas for (17.23), compared with (17.10), $A_i^* = A_i$. Moreover, $\mathscr{E}(y_t | z_t, X_{t-1})$ from (17.21) requires that

$$D_0^* + \Omega_{12} \Omega_{22}^{-1} = D_0 \qquad P_i^* - \Omega_{12} \Omega_{22}^{-1} F_i = P_i \qquad (i = 1, \ldots, n). \tag{17.31}$$

Consequently, if $\Omega_{12} = 0$ and θ_1, θ_2 are variation free, then z_t is weakly exogenous for θ_1; see chapter 15. Therefore the condition that $\Omega_{12} = 0$ is equivalent (in this perfect information case) to requiring that the contingent plan y_t^p is the conditional expectation $\mathscr{E}(y_t | z_t, X_{t-1})$.

Next, under imperfect information as represented by (17.25), z_t^c can be eliminated from (17.22) or (17.23) to yield, if we take (17.22) as an example, with $n^* = n$ again,

$$y_t^p = \sum_{i=1}^{n} (P_i^* + D_0^* G_i) x_{t-i}. \tag{17.32}$$

Using this derived equation raises problems concerning the identifiability of the original parameters and makes the invariance of the coefficients in (17.32) dependent on the constancy of both (17.22) and (17.25). Formulae (17.30) and (17.31) must be replaced by

$$\begin{bmatrix} P_i^* + D_0^* G_i \\ F_i \end{bmatrix} = \Pi_i \qquad \Omega = \Sigma, \tag{17.33}$$

$$A_0^* = A_0 \qquad A_i^* + C_0^* (F_i - G_i) = A_i, \tag{17.34}$$

$$\Omega_{12} \Omega_{22}^{-1} = D_0 \qquad P_i^* + D_0^* G_i = P_i + D_0 F_i. \tag{17.35}$$

Note that (17.25) nests, *inter alia*, univariate time-series models, vector autoregressions, leading indicator forecasts etc.; see for example Wallis (1977) for a discussion of these interconnections and compare Wall (1980). Moreover, the assertion that $G_i = F_i$ ($i = 1, \ldots, n$) is known as 'rational expectations' (Muth, 1961; Sargent, 1979; Wallis, 1980; Lucas and Sargent, 1981; Wickens, 1982), in which case $\Omega_{12} = 0$ (an assumption often introduced in this literature) generally precludes the weak exogeneity of z_t for θ_1. Conversely, if policy is totally unpredictable (or G_i and F_i are unrelated) then z_t can be weakly exogenous for θ_1 when $\Omega_{12} = 0$; alternatively, if $\Omega_{12} \neq 0$ and $F_i = G_i$ then $D_0^* = D_0 = \Omega_{12} \Omega_{22}^{-1}$ is sufficient for the weak exogeneity of z_t for θ_1. In such a case, not only are agents 'perfect' forecasters, but their behaviour would not be affected by knowledge of the exact values of z_t prior to carrying out their plans (since D_0^* now coincides with the regression coefficients of y_t on z_t). Thus, even if z_t did not suit them, agents would act as if they saw no possibilities of 'renegotiating' with the control authority. Finally, if $\Omega_{12} \neq 0$, poor forecasting of z_t results in a loss of weak exogeneity since knowledge of z_t leads agents to revise their plans.

Clearly, care is required in formulating models involving expectations and joint analysis of y_t and z_t is usually necessary. Since most dynamic economic theories based on intertemporal optimization yield decision rules in which expectations about future events play a major role, this is likely to remain a very active research area; see for example Nickell (1981) and Muellbauer (1979).

Also, the choice of n^* is important since the formulae in (17.30)–(17.35) are invalid for $n^* < n$; marginalizing with respect to relevant lagged variables raises difficult issues of dynamic specification some of which are considered in chapter 4.

2.4 Equilibrium Economic Theories

In essence, section 2.3 dealt with behavioural rules for out-of-equilibrium states and the question arises what role static or long-run theories such as (17.1) or (17.2) might play in data analysis based on such rules. Two criticisms need to be rebutted, and doing so provides a convenient way of introducing more positive aspects: (i) that the 'long run' is irrelevant; and the obverse, (ii) that economic data are so informative about long-run trends that this is the one aspect for which theory is *not* required. The former is not necessarily true even if economies are *never* in equilibrium. If agents took appropriate account of past disequilibria in formulating their plans, then the system invariably would be tending towards some equilibrium and it becomes an empirical matter how important 'long-run' factors are. Note that equilibrium is a hypothetical state in this analysis, and derives its meaning from the context in which it is used as with (17.1). Indeed, if (17.1) is *defined* to be an equilibrium relationship then its main role in an analysis of non-equilibrium data is to characterize conjointly the solution which the estimated model should reproduce in an equilibrium environment and an associated measure of disequilibrium. For example, consider the special case of (17.22) given by (for the monetary data)

$$\Delta_1 m_t^p = \beta_0 + \beta_1 \Delta_1 p_t + \beta_2 \Delta_1 i_i + \beta_3 (m - p - i)_{t-1}. \tag{17.36}$$

For $\beta_3 \neq 0$, in a static equilibrium *defined by* $\Delta_1 m = \Delta_1 p = \Delta_1 i = 0$, (17.36) solves to

$$(m - p - i) = -\beta_0/\beta_3 \text{ or } M = H_1 PI, \tag{17.37}$$

where $H_1 = \exp(-\beta_0/\beta_3)$. Thus (17.37) reproduces (17.1); and correspondingly, $(m - p - i)_{t-1}$ is the associated measure of disequilibrium (apart from the constant β_0/β_3). Consequently, in addition to suggesting a list of potential regressors, static equilibrium theories often restrict the *class* of models implementing (17.22), which can be important for efficiency of estimation, although this begs the answer to (ii)! However, as suggested in section 1, static theories need not perform well when simply 'fitted to data' not allowing for lag reactions, as in (17.4).

Point (ii) above seems to be a data-based inference which may derive from noting both that the levels of many economic time series are growing over time and that these are highly intercorrelated so that their 'typical spectral shapes' show spectral power mainly concentrated at low frequencies (Granger, 1966). While this finding may be suggestive of trend-like or 'long-run' information, it entails nothing about the relevance of equilibrium theory to the data analysis of *relationships* since it pertains to univariate information only (e.g. near random walks with drift have 'typical spectral shapes' yet are uninformative about long-run trends). Moreover, it is well known that variables with typical spectral shapes will be highly intercorrelated in small samples *independently* of any 'true' relationships existing; this 'spurious regressions' problem follows from the analysis of Yule (1926) and is discussed by for example Granger and Newbold (1974), thus cutting the ground from under the other comment ostensibly supporting (ii). Again it appears that equilibrium theories might be useful, and in practice this seems to be the case; see for example chapter 8. Of course, well-articulated dynamic adjustment theories could be even more helpful but there is a distinct lack of these as yet; see for example the comments of Nerlove (1972) and Sims (1974a) and compare Sargent (1981).

In passing, note that economists are aware of the fallacy of *inferring* 'causes' from correlations even if some may do so inadvertently on occasion; rather, the former are treated as a property of *theoretical* models (usually under the phrasing 'y is a function of, or depends on, z' as with, say, (17.2) above), whereas the latter are necessarily all that can be observed. Thus, they deduce from theory what connections should be observable in practice, claiming to test their deductions from the presence or absence of various (partial) correlations; for a recent discussion of causality in economics, see Zellner (1979b). 'Best practice' applications of Granger causality tests use the approach just described, although there remains the difficulty that no assumptions are made about the parameters in, say, (17.13) (see chapter 15).

3 Estimation

Methods of estimating values of unknown parameters in otherwise known model specifications have constituted a major research area of econometrics. We include under this heading the derivations of estimators and their properties such as limiting, approximate and exact (finite sample) distributions, as well as issues of numerical accuracy, non-linear optimization and efficient Monte Carlo simulation. Even a brief survey and bibliography would exceed the present chapter, but some useful recent references for each topic respectively are Maddala (1977), Hausman (1975), Sargan (1976), Phillips (1980), Dent (1980), Berndt et al. (1974), Hendry and Srba (1977). Also, the close link between econometric estimation and the Kalman filter is well exposited by Harvey (1981b); note that the model in (17.22)–(17.28) above can be rewritten in state-space form for the latent variables (y_t^p, z_t^e).

The proliferation of estimators in econometrics appears to have bemused many statisticians; see, for example, the discussion following Anderson (1976). However, for the class of models describing (17.6) and (17.7) a concept is available which helps clarify the interrelationships between almost all the known methods, namely the notion of an *estimator generating equation*, referred to in chapter 13. Moreover, although appropriate notation must be established first, the formula for the estimator generating equation is remarkably simple and is closely related to the well-known score, i.e. the vector of first derivatives of the likelihood function. Here we present the estimator generating equation for the coefficients of the structural submodel (17.23) when z_t is weakly exogenous for the coefficients $A_i^* = A_i$.

Noting that (17.6) and (17.7) remain the data process, re-express (17.21) as

$$\mathcal{L}(y_t \mid z_t, X_{t-1}, \lambda_1) = \Pi \xi_t,$$

say, where $\Pi = (D_0 P_1 \dots P_n)$ and $\xi_t' = (z_t' x_{t-1}' \dots x_{t-n}')$. Now if we let $B = B_0$ and $C = (C_0 A_1 \dots A_n)$, the constraints in (17.24) can be written as

$$B\Pi + C = 0 \tag{17.38}$$

for all $\lambda_1 \in \Lambda_1$. We consider the case where $A = (B : C)$ is subject to only zero and normalization restrictions so that the parameters of interest ψ are the unconstrained elements of B and C and conversely A is linear in ψ. Let $Y = Y_T^1$, $\Xi = (\xi_1 \dots \xi_T)'$, $X = (Y : \Xi)$. If we assume known initial conditions for simplicity, then since $y_t \mid \xi_t \sim N(\Pi \xi_t, \Sigma)$ the log-likelihood function (up to an additive constant) is given by

$$L(\Pi, \Sigma, \psi \mid X) = -\tfrac{1}{2} \{ T \log |\Sigma| + \operatorname{tr}[\Sigma^{-1}(Y - \Xi \Pi')'(Y - \Xi \Pi')] \}. \tag{17.39}$$

Current econometric terminology distinguishes between full information maximum likelihood (FIML) estimators and limited information maximum likelihood (LIML) estimators. The former estimators are the maximum likelihood estimators of a 'complete' system of equations (B square non-singular almost everywhere) whereby prior restrictions are fully exploited. Limited information maximum likelihood estimators are the maximum likelihood estimators of an 'incomplete' system of equations (B rectangular with full row rank). The latter also applies to complete systems when, e.g. for numerical tractability, over-identifying prior restrictions on some of the equations under consideration are neglected. The following formulae are applicable to either case with appropriate interpretations of the symbols. Maximizing (17.39) with respect to (Π, Σ) when Σ is unrestricted (other than symmetric positive definite) but Π is subject to (17.38), we obtain (Richard, 1979)

$$\tilde{\Pi} = \hat{\Pi} - \hat{\Sigma}\tilde{B}'(\tilde{B}\hat{\Sigma}\tilde{B}')^{-1}(\tilde{B}\hat{\Pi} + \tilde{C}) \qquad \tilde{\Sigma} = \hat{\Sigma} + T^{-1}(\tilde{\Pi} - \hat{\Pi})\Xi'\Xi(\tilde{\Pi} - \hat{\Pi})',$$
(17.40)

where the tilde denotes a restricted maximum likelihood estimator,

$$\hat{\Pi} = Y'\Xi(\Xi'\Xi)^{-1} \qquad \hat{\Sigma} = T^{-1}Y'MY \qquad M = I_T - \Xi(\Xi'\Xi)^{-1}\Xi'.$$

Naturally, $\tilde{\Pi}$ is such that $\tilde{B}\tilde{\Pi} + \tilde{C} = 0$ from the left-hand equation (17.40) and so from the right-hand equation (17.40)

$$\tilde{B}\tilde{\Sigma}\tilde{B}' = T^{-1}\tilde{A}X'X\tilde{A}' = \tilde{V},$$
(17.41)

say. Note that

$$\underset{T \to \infty}{\text{plim}} \, \tilde{\Sigma} = \underset{T \to \infty}{\text{plim}} \, \hat{\Sigma} = \Sigma.$$
(17.42)

The concentrated log-likelihood function $L^*(\cdot)$ is given by

$$L^*(\psi|X) = -\tfrac{1}{2}T\log|(BY'MYB')^{-1}(YB' + \Xi C')'(YB' + \Xi C')|.$$
(17.43)

The score is

$$q(\psi) = \frac{\partial L^*(\cdot)}{\partial \psi},$$
(17.44)

where $\mathscr{E}_{Y|\psi}[q(\psi)] = 0$ and $\mathscr{I}$, the information matrix, is

$$\mathscr{I} = \mathscr{E}_{Y|\psi}[q(\psi)q(\psi)'].$$
(17.45)

When $Q(\psi) = \partial q(\cdot)/\partial \psi'$, since (17.23) is a valid representation by assumption, $-\mathscr{E}_{Y|\psi}[Q(\psi)] = \mathscr{I}$ also. Further, because A is linear in ψ, $\partial A/\partial \psi_j = R_j = (R_{1j} : R_{2j})$ is a matrix of known constants and hence the jth element of $q(\cdot)$ obtained from differentiating (17.43) with respect to ψ_j is

$$\text{tr}[(\tilde{B}Y'MY\tilde{B}')^{-1}\tilde{B}Y'MYR'_{1j} - (\tilde{A}X'X\tilde{A}')^{-1}\tilde{A}X'XR'_j] = 0$$
$$(j = 1, \ldots, J), \qquad (17.46)$$

or

$$\text{tr}\left[(\tilde{B}\hat{\Sigma}\tilde{B}')^{-1}\tilde{B}\hat{\Sigma}R'_{1j} - (\tilde{B}\tilde{\Sigma}\tilde{B}')^{-1}\tilde{A}\left(\frac{X'X}{T}\right)R'_j\right] = 0.$$
(17.47)

Equation (17.46) could be used, as it stands, for computation of maximum likelihood estimates $\tilde{\psi}$ of ψ and hence of $\tilde{A} = (\tilde{B}, \tilde{C})$, $\tilde{\Pi}$ and $\tilde{\Sigma}$. However, an asymptotically equivalent but much simpler form can be obtained by using (17.42) and

$$[\tilde{B}Y'MYR'_{1j} - \tilde{A}X'XR'_j] = -\tilde{A}X'\Xi(\hat{\Pi}':I)R'_j,$$
(17.48)

so that (17.47) is reformulated as

$$\text{tr}(\tilde{V}^{-1}\tilde{A}X'\Xi\hat{F}'R_j') = 0 \qquad (j = 1, \ldots, J), \tag{17.49}$$

where $F' = (\Pi' : I)$.

This is an intuitively reasonable, and relatively simple, expression for computing $\tilde{\psi}$. Since $\mathcal{E}(x_t | \xi_t) = F\xi_t$, $\Xi F'$ is the 'systematic component' of X, and AX' is orthogonal to this component with plim $T^{-1}AX'\Xi = 0$. Also, plim $T^{-1}\tilde{A}X'\Xi\hat{F}' = 0$ and R_j' serves to select the unrestricted coefficients. Consequently, it is natural to estimate ψ_j by setting to zero the finite sample equivalent weighted by the inverse covariance matrix $\tilde{V}^{-1}$. However, from (17.41), $\tilde{V}$ depends on $\tilde{A}$ so that (17.49) is non-linear in $\tilde{\psi}$ and maximum likelihood estimation necessitates solution of (17.49) by an iterative rule such as

$$\psi_{(k+1)} = \psi_{(k)} + \lambda_k G_k g_k \qquad (k = 1, \ldots, K), \tag{17.50}$$

where $\psi_{(1)}$ is a *vector* of initial values, K is the number of iterations (which could be predetermined or depend on a convergence criterion), g_k is a vector of search directions, G_k a modifying matrix to define the metric and λ_k a scalar step length. The log-likelihood function $L^*(\cdot)$ can be used as the objective function to ensure that each step increases the likelihood until an optimum is located; standard choices for g_k and G_k are $q(\psi_{(k)})$ and $Q(\psi_{(k)})^{-1}$ respectively, or sometimes $\mathcal{I}(\psi_{(k)})^{-1}$ for G_k: other choices are discussed in chapter 13 and in various papers in Dent (1980). On convergence, the maximum likelihood estimator of ψ is obtained, whatever numerical optimization algorithm is adopted, at least to the accuracy of the termination criterion.

This concept of alternative *optimization rules* for implementing maximum likelihood must be distinguished from alternative *approximations* to solving

$$\text{tr}(V^{-1}AX'\Xi F'R_j') = 0 \qquad (j = 1, \ldots, J), \tag{17.51}$$

where

$$V = A\left(\frac{X'X}{T}\right)A' \qquad F' = (\Pi' : I), \tag{17.52}$$

with

$$\Pi = \hat{\Pi} - \hat{\Sigma}B'(B\hat{\Sigma}B')^{-1}(B\hat{\Pi} + C). \tag{17.53}$$

Given V and F, equation (17.51) is *linear* in A and so is easily solved; moreover, given A, it is trivial to recompute Π and V. Thus, one can construe (17.51) as a method for *generating* estimators of A, conditional on estimators of V and F. Moreover, because plim $T^{-1}\bar{A}X'\Xi = 0$ for all consistent estimators $\bar{A}$ of A, $\mathcal{I}(\psi)$ is the same for all estimators of ψ based on consistent estimators of V and F, i.e. irrespective of their efficiency. Consequently, we refer to (17.51) as the estimator generating equation with the following properties.

1 Every solution is an approximation to the maximum likelihood estimator obtained by variations in the 'initial values' selected for V and F and in the number of steps taken through the cycle (17.51)–(17.53), including not iterating.

2 All known econometric estimators for linear dynamic systems can be obtained in this way, which provides a systematic approach to estimation theory in an area where a very large number of methods has been proposed.

3 Equation (17.51) classifies methods immediately into distinct groups of varying asymptotic efficiency as follows:

(a) as efficient asymptotically as the maximum likelihood $\tilde{A}$ if (V, F) are estimated consistently;

(b) consistent for A if any convergent estimator is used for (V, F);

(c) asymptotically as efficient as can be obtained for a single equation out of a system if $V = I$ but F is consistently estimated.

Other efficiency classes also exist but are of less interest. A comprehensive analysis of conventional econometric estimators is presented in chapter 13, and Lubrano (1979) considers 'incomplete' models (where B is non-square).

Given the structure of (17.51) it is unsurprising that there exist very large numbers of known distinct members of (a), (b) and (c), and other classes of even less interest, and the estimator generating equation highlights further methods which can be obtained with ease as well as clarifying into which asymptotic efficiency class they fall. Within efficiency classes, choices can be made on the criteria of computational ease, robustness in finite samples, the entailed value of $\mathcal{L}^*(\cdot)$ and so on. Moreover, the estimator generating equation approach applies to other situations in which the asymptotic distributions of estimators of parameters of interest (above, B, C) depend on 'auxiliary parameters' (above, Π, V) only through the latter's probability limits (even though, for example, Π, V are functions of B, C). Important examples are some errors-in-variables models, systems with vector autoregressive errors (i.e. valid common factors) and models with rational expectations; also Espasa (1977) applies the estimator generating equation concept to a wide range of spectral and related methods. Overall, (17.51) summarizes a vast literature, and offers the flexibility of generating new methods with known asymptotic properties as the need arises.

Nevertheless, the specification of econometric models is far less certain than the only unknowns being simply the values of some well-defined parameters. Thus, other considerations than 'optimal estimation' are important and, in practice, diagnostic testing and selection methods play a major role in modelling; see section 4 and 5. Indeed, 'mis-specification' of the model for the data generating process is certainly endemic in empirical research, although this is a somewhat unhelpful comment in our framework where a model is always viewed as a reparameterization of the data process. In an important range of cases, with $\delta = g(\psi)$, say, then a maximum likelihood estimator $\hat{\delta}$ of δ maximizing $\mathcal{L}^*(\delta)$ (or an estimator generating equation approximation thereto) will have

$$\operatorname*{plim}_{T \to \infty} \hat{\delta} = \delta = g(\psi) \neq \psi,$$

because of the incorrectly formulated likelihood function $\mathcal{L}^*(\cdot) \neq \mathcal{L}(\cdot)$, with a limiting variance matrix around δ given by $\Phi = \mathcal{J}^{-1}\mathcal{G}(q^*q^{*\prime})\mathcal{J}^{-1}$, where $q^* = \partial L^*(\cdot)/\partial \delta$, and not by $\mathcal{J}^{-1} = -\{\mathcal{G}[Q^*(\delta)]\}^{-1}$. In certain important cases, Φ

can be estimated consistently despite the model mis-specification; see, *inter alia*, White (1980a) and Hansen (1982). These results, related to earlier developments by Cox (1961), seem reasonably general and should provide a valuable approach to robust inference about δ when model specification is uncertain. White (1980c) uses the difference between $\mathscr{E}(q^*q^{*\prime})$ and $-\mathscr{I}$ for a diagnostic test of functional form mis-specification; although not explicit in our notation, $\Phi, \mathscr{I}$ etc. generally vary with T as discussed by Domowitz and White (1982).

Finally, the availability of many choices of asymptotically equivalent estimators combined with relatively small sample sizes puts a premium on results concerning the analytical derivations of exact and approximate finite sample distributions; Phillips (1980) provides an excellent review and bibliography. Although empirical researchers cannot yet compute exact distributions for even widely used estimators in typical economic data generation processes, useful approximate results have been established and could be calculated; see for example Sargan (1976).

4 Testing

As with estimation, the score $q(\theta)$ plays a central role in hypothesis and diagnostic testing, and has been used in a similar way to the estimator generating function to bring cohesion to a voluminous, diverse and often *ad hoc* literature; see, for example, Breusch and Pagan (1980). Establishing terminology first, econometricians distinguish the three standard testing principles (see for example Cox and Hinkley, 1974; Berndt and Savin, 1977):

1 Wald tests, denoted by W (Wald, 1943);
2 maximized likelihood ratio tests (see for example Cox and Hinkley, 1974, ch. 9);
3 Lagrange multiplier or efficient score tests (Aitchison and Silvey, 1960; Rao, 1973).

Consider testing the hypothesis that $H_0: f(\theta) = 0$, where $\hat{\theta}$ is given by $q(\hat{\theta}) = 0$ and, asymptotically,

$$T^{1/2}(\hat{\theta} - \theta) \sim N(0, V_\theta), \tag{17.54}$$

where

$$V_\theta = -\plim_{T \to \infty} [T^{-1}Q(\hat{\theta})]^{-1}. \tag{17.55}$$

If $\hat{\theta}$ is easily computed, the Wald form, which applies to the maintained model, is most convenient and, for example, provides a basis for common factor restriction tests (Sargan, 1980a) even though $f(\theta)$ is awkward to derive explicitly in such a case. Maximized likelihood ratio tests are also very well known, but require estimation of both unrestricted and constrained models (although this is anyway often required given the outcome of Wald or Lagrange multiplier tests). However, econometricians have only recently appreciated both that most diagnostic tests can be derived from the Lagrange multiplier principle and that, suitably constructed, such tests can have the same limiting distributions as Wald and maximized likelihood ratio equivalents under both null hypotheses and sequences of local alternatives (see for example

Breusch and Pagan, 1980). Let $\tilde{\theta}$ denote the restricted estimator of θ subject to $f(\theta) = 0$ obtained from the Lagrangian

$$L(\theta) + \mu'f(\theta), \tag{17.56}$$

using $q(\theta) + J\mu = 0$, where μ is a vector of undetermined multipliers and $J = \partial f(\cdot)/\partial\theta'$ is of rank N, when $f(\theta) = 0$ imposes N restrictions, and is continuously differentiable at θ. Then on H_0

$$\eta_M(N) = \tilde{\mu}'\tilde{J}'\mathcal{I}(\tilde{\theta})^{-1}\tilde{J}\tilde{\mu} = q(\tilde{\theta})'\mathcal{I}(\tilde{\theta})^{-1}q(\tilde{\theta}) \sim \chi^2(N), \tag{17.57}$$

asymptotically, where $\mathcal{L}[q(\theta)q(\theta)'] = \mathcal{I}(\theta)$, and the second expression in (17.57), which follows from (17.56), relates Lagrange multiplier to efficient score. Engle (1982b) presents a range of useful residual diagnostic tests based on the limiting distribution of $q(\cdot)$, as well as their relation to the C_α class of Neyman (1959) and the mis-specification tests of Hausman (1978).

By way of comparison with $\eta_M(\cdot)$ the Wald and maximized likelihood ratio tests of H_0: $f(\theta) = 0$ are given by

$$\eta_W(N) = Tf(\hat{\theta})'(\hat{J}\hat{V}_\theta\hat{J}')^{-1}f(\hat{\theta}) \qquad \eta_L(N) = 2[L(\hat{\theta}) - L(\tilde{\theta})]. \tag{17.58}$$

All three forms coincide for linear hypotheses in linear models, i.e. when $L(\theta)$ is quadratic, as, for example, with the $\eta_1(\cdot)$ test above in regression equations. Implicit in the left-hand equation (17.58) is the result that asymptotically

$$T^{1/2}[f(\hat{\theta}) - f(\theta)] \sim N(0, JV_\theta J'). \tag{17.59}$$

Given $\hat{\theta}$ and $\hat{V}_\theta$, $f(\hat{\theta})$ and $\hat{J}$ can usually be calculated numerically, which provides a convenient means of calculating standard errors of derived parameter estimates, an overall test being provided by the left-hand equation (17.58). Note that the $\eta_3(\cdot)$ test reported above is based on the maximized likelihood ratio principle whereas $\eta_2(\cdot)$ is a Lagrange multiplier test. Domowitz and White (1982) present mis-specification robust generalizations.

In general cases, not much is known as yet about the relative finite sample merits of the three types of test for economic time series; however, see Evans and Savin (1982). Also for some simulation evidence on common factor and residual autocorrelation tests, see chapter 7. It is worth noting that deriving (17.57) for a specific alternative may reveal why other tests of that alternative do not function appropriately; see, for example, Durbin (1970). Note also that many well-known diagnostic tests are indeed Lagrange multiplier based (e.g. the Durbin–Watson test).

Finally, there is considerable interest in the class of 'non-nested' hypothesis tests proposed by Cox (1961, 1962) and applications are now widespread; see, among many others, Pereira (1977), Pesaran and Deaton (1978) and Bean (1981), and for a recent summary MacKinnon (1983). However, these tests are most conveniently analysed in section 5.

5 Model Selection

Again, this has been an area of very active research in recent years covering problems of pre-test biases (Judge and Bock, 1978), model selection criteria (Sawa, 1978;

Amemiya, 1980), specification search strategies, in particular the important contribution by Leamer (1978), as well as posterior odds ratios; see for example Zellner (1971, ch. 10.5). Here, we explore the more obvious notion of checking whether the fitted model describes all the relevant data features that could be accounted for by knowing the data generation process; see for example chapter 8 and chapter 11.

If one *knew* the data generating process, then it would be possible to *deduce* in advance what results should be obtained by estimating various 'false' models from the same data set. Consequently, one can ask of any estimated equation or system which claimed to represent the data generation process whether it can account for all other models of the same process (which by hypothesis are 'false') either by nesting them as in chapter 8 or by providing a baseline against which they can be rejected as in Bean (1981). This is the property referred to as *encompassing*. It is important to realize that 'separate' hypotheses are susceptible to an encompassing investigation, and this notion helps clarify the role in model selection of 'non-nested' tests, a point most easily illustrated as follows (see Cox (1961) and Mizon and Richard (1986) for a more comprehensive analysis).

Consider two 'competing' single-equation hypotheses with claimed strongly exogenous regressors and parameters estimated by least squares, denoted by a circumflex: with the assertion $\varepsilon_{1t} \sim \mathrm{IN}(0, \sigma_{11})$,

$$y_t = \sum_{i=1}^{k_1} \beta_i z_{it} + \varepsilon_{1t}; \tag{17.60}$$

and, with the assertion $\varepsilon_{2t} \sim \mathrm{IN}(0, \sigma_{22})$,

$$y_t = \sum_{i=1}^{k_2} \gamma_i x_{it} + \varepsilon_{2t}. \tag{17.61}$$

We have also the 'auxiliary' data description

$$z_t = \Pi x_t + v_t, \tag{17.62}$$

where $\mathscr{E}(x_t v_t') = 0$ and $\mathscr{E}(v_t v_t') = \Omega$. If $x_t \subset z_t$, $\hat{\gamma}$ can be derived *exactly* from $\hat{\beta}$, $\hat{\Pi}$ and so we ignore this case.

An investigator accepting (17.60) and (17.62) proceeds to note

$$y_t = z_t' \beta + \varepsilon_{1t} = x_t' \Pi' \beta + \varepsilon_{1t} + v_t' \beta = x_t' \gamma_\beta + \varepsilon_{2t}^* \tag{17.63}$$

so that if his model is correct

$$\gamma = \gamma_\beta = \Pi' \beta \qquad \sigma_{22} = \sigma_{22}^* = \sigma_{11} + \beta' \Omega \beta. \tag{17.64}$$

Consequently, he should be able to deduce from (17.60) and (17.62) what is obtained on estimating (17.61). This yields as testable hypotheses

$$\mathrm{H_a}: \delta = \gamma - \Pi' \beta = 0 \qquad \mathrm{H_b}: \sigma_{22} - \sigma_{11} - \beta' \Omega \beta = 0. \tag{17.65}$$

The former is most easily tested using the Wald principle, estimating γ from (17.61) and Π, β from (17.62) and (17.60) and computing

$$W = \hat{\delta}' [\mathrm{var}\,(\hat{\delta})]^{-1} \hat{\delta}. \tag{17.66}$$

When H_a holds, $W \sim \chi^2(k_2)$ in large samples.

However, a simple transformation of W yields the 'classical' F test of $\delta = 0$ in the 'nesting model'

$$y_t = z_t' \beta + x_t' \delta + \varepsilon_{1t}^* \tag{17.67}$$

since $\gamma = \Pi' \beta$ if and only if $\delta = 0$ in (17.67). Thus, the encompassing and embedding approaches yield the same answer when exact test sizes are used. Moreover, $\gamma = \Pi' \beta$ implies $\sigma_{22} = \sigma_{11} + \beta' \Omega \beta$ and so H_b does not need separate testing. However, the converse is false, since the scalar equality cannot necessarily ensure the k_2-vector equality (unless $k_2 = 1$). The 'non-nested' tests prevalent in econometrics all seem to be testing the scalar hypothesis H_b (hence their one degree of freedom, yet the same non-centrality parameter as the F test when H_b is false) which could be called variance encompassing. Failure to reject H_b only weakly supports encompassing, since H_a could remain false, although rejection of H_b certainly entails rejection of H_a.

Like all inferential information, encompassing 'non-nested' test results should be interpreted carefully. This comment applies especially for equations which already satisfy all the criteria discussed earlier in this chapter. Summarizing these, we suggest selecting models which are

1 data coherent (fit deviates from data by an innovation), with
2 weakly exogenous regressors (valid conditioning on contemporaneous variables), and
3 constant parameters (especially over periods in which data correlations alter) having
4 data-admissible functional forms and
5 theory-consistent formulations, which
6 encompass a wide range of contending models.

Models with these properties appear to offer a useful approximation to the unknown data generation process enhanced if individual parameters are of direct interest, i.e. interpretable given the relevant theory, preferably are parsimoniously chosen and correspond to nearly orthogonal decision variables. Equation (17.4) fails on at least (1), (3) and (6).

6 Conclusion

The general properties of economic time series arising from the transacting behaviour of separate yet interdependent agents are discussed for a stationary world. The stochastic mechanism generating the observed data $\{x_1 \ldots x_t\} = X_t^1$, appropriately transformed so that linearity is reasonable, is formulated as the sequential process

$$x_t | X_{t-1} \sim N(\mu_t, \Sigma), \tag{17.68}$$

where

$$\mu_t = \sum_{i=1}^{n} \Pi_i x_{t-i} \qquad (t = 1, \ldots, T). \tag{17.69}$$

A statistical submodel characterizing aspects of this process is construed as resulting from

1   marginalizing with respect to a very large number of variables w_t and their lags W_{t-1} believed to be irrelevant when $x_t = (w_t', y_t', z_t')'$, and
2   conditioning on a subset of variables z_t.

The associated concepts are those of reparameterization, Granger non-causality (absence of feedback) and weak exogeneity of z_t for the parameters of interest, denoted by ψ, if $\psi = f(\lambda_1)$ can be estimated fully efficiently from the conditional submodel $D(y_t | z_t, Y_{t-1}, Z_{t-1}, \lambda_1)$.

In a stationary world, even if (1) and (2) were invalidly implemented, the parameters of the resulting submodel would be constant. Since parameter constancy is not characteristic of empirical econometric models, the chapter considers worlds of parameter change where only some of the parameters are structural invariants of agents' behaviour, and a primary objective of econometric modelling is to isolate such invariants. To achieve this aim, economists formulate theoretical models of agents' behaviour in terms of their making contingent plans for y_t, denoted by y_t^p, dependent on expected outcomes for z_t (z_t^e) and adapting to past realizations (X_{t-1}):

$$y_t^p = A_0 z_t^e + \sum_{i=1}^{n^*} A_i x_{t-i}. \tag{17.70}$$

A model of the expectational formation process is required unless z_t^e is observed or z_t is weakly exogenous for the $\{A_i\}$. The assumed correspondence between the economic model variables (y_t^p, z_t^e) and their counterparts in the statistical process (17.68) and (17.69) is important and various assumptions above expectations formation are noted.

In the original publication a range of distinct special cases of single-equation dynamic models is exposited, together with an outline of their respective properties and their relationships to equilibrium economic theories. This highlights the joint links of dynamic to stochastic specification, and of economic theories to empirical models. For correctly specified models, parameter estimation is considered by noting that the score $q(\psi)$ (the vector of first derivatives of $\log D(\cdot | \cdot, \lambda_1)$ with respect to ψ) provides an estimator generating equation the myriad solutions of which include most known econometric estimators for the class of model in (17.68) and (17.69). A similar concept summarizes diagnostic testing theory. The methodology of model selection is only briefly considered although the concept of encompassing tests helps relate 'classical' and 'non-nested' procedures and provides a strong check on model specification.

Throughout, many of the concepts and the problems inherent in econometric modelling are illustrated by empirical results on the demand for money for transactions purposes in the United Kingdom, reported in chapter 11.

Part IV
Retrospect and Prospect

The final part includes two chapters: a retrospective on the sequence of models for aggregate consumers' expenditure, and a postscript which seeks to report on developments between the time of the latest included paper and the completion of the preambles.

The theme of the methodology is one of progressive discovery of empirically and theoretically substantiated information about how economies function. The methodology itself has also progressed and gradually has been able both to explain more of what we observe to occur in empirical econometrics and to predict the general consequences of certain research strategies. It has been, and must remain, only a facilitatory tool, neither necessary nor sufficient for discovering valid structures. Nevertheless, any approach which enhances research productivity must be a valuable adjunct to progress by more rapidly disposing of false avenues. Conversely, to be useful, an approach must be fully understood and itself subject to critical appraisal.

The aim of part IV is to exposit the main ideas and methodology from two perspectives:

1 in terms of empirical research to relate the concepts to practical procedures;
2 in terms of an overview of the theoretical concepts and their interrelationships.

Chapter 18 was written for the 1983 meeting of the Scottish Economic Society as a response to difficulties which colleagues and students had experienced in understanding chapters 15–17. As usual, the attempt to explain the approach forced me to think more clearly; as usual, the result was far from being the final word on either consumers' expenditure or econometric methodology.

The concluding chapter is heavily based on chapter 1 of Hendry (1989). It was written almost five years later than any other chapter, and embodies the benefits of my having programmed the approach as well as having applied it to other problems (UK housing markets, US money demand and French consumers' expenditure *inter alia*).

The struggle to escape from previous modes of thinking and fully explore the reduction approach has had its costs. Most of the expositions I have written during the 1980s (including chapter 19) only focus on the statistical and empirical aspects of modelling, and by benign neglect appear to downplay the role of economic theory in the econometric enterprise. This emphasis was partly due to a desire to argue that reduction interpretations were fruitful whatever the pre-existing state of economic theory, and hence were not merely an adjunct of a specific economic analysis (e.g. Keynesian). But it was also partly because the then dominant paradigms of economic theory used to sustain empirical models (e.g. rational expectations and omniscient economic agents) did not seem to offer a useful starting point for discovering new knowledge. At the time that chapter 18 was written I was working on the last step of the cycle, namely how empirical evidence which was summarized in congruent models could be consolidated in theories of agent behaviour, but without much success (for example, Hendry and Spanos (1980) remains incomplete). Nevertheless, the divergence from the mode of 'theory claim, model assertion, hypothesis test, accept/reject' which led to the attempt to embody a progressive research strategy in a theory of reduction, began from and continues with the desire for a more empirically substantiated body of economic theory than is currently extant (see chapter 3 for example). Exciting developments await the creator of the tools for building theoretical summaries of empirical evidence which encapsulate the autonomous aspects of economic behaviour in terms of interpretable structures.

18

Econometric Modelling: the 'Consumption Function' in Retrospect

Preamble

The penultimate reprint is my alternative attempt at expositing the methodology using the well-known empirical illustration of the consumption function. The three primary objectives were to explain the overall framework briefly, to relate each theoretical concept in the information taxonomy to the relevant empirical counterpart and to evaluate the earlier research on the consumption function in chapters 8–10 by testing the model forms on UK data for the interwar period. Three secondary aims were to exposit the formalization in part III, which post-dated DHSY, to reinterpret some of their intuitive notions, and to show how the formalization could clarify problems experienced with the 'conventional' approach.

The paper commences almost exactly where chapter 10 ended, but its author (at least) believed he now had a far clearer picture of the structure of modelling. The discovery/evaluation dichotomy and the necessity but insufficiency of evaluation criteria to determine validity are stressed. Nevertheless, because modelling is essentially an exercise in design to achieve certain predetermined selection criteria, rigorous evaluation will eliminate poor designs. The tension between the valid, but destructive, use of econometrics as a device for critical evaluation, and its invalid, but constructive, use in model discovery has permeated this volume. Its resolution in the present chapter revolves around the idea in Popper (1963) that the validity of a theory (or model) is independent of how it is discovered: the apocryphal tale of Archimedes' discovery of the principle of buoyancy by spilling water from his bath is the best-known illustration of that theme, but other examples abound in the history of science (see

Reprinted from *Scottish Journal of Political Economy*, 30, 3 (November 1983) 193–220. Eighteenth Annual Lecture of the Scottish Economic Society delivered at the University of Stirling on 5 February 1983. The Society acknowledges with gratitude the financial support provided by Shell International for the Annual Lecture.

This research was supported in part by grants from the Social Science Research Council to the MIME Programme at the London School of Economics and by HR8789 to Nuffield College. I am indebted to Frank Srba and Neil Ericsson for the calculations reported below. The paper was prepared at the invitation of the Scottish Economic Society, the concluding section then being modified to clarify issues arising in discussion. Helpful discussions with Neil Ericsson, Robert Marshall and John Muellbauer are gratefully acknowledged.

for example Mason, 1977, or Losee, 1980). Thus, both discovery and evaluation procedures become issues of *research efficiency*: no approach is bound to succeed or is certain to fail, but some ways are much faster on average than others in developing models which will pass evaluation tests. Models which regularly fail evaluation tests are certainly invalid in some aspect.

Thus, section 1 sketches the theory of reduction as an explanation for the derivation of empirical models and consequently for their susceptibility to design. That view leads naturally to an analysis of design criteria, and both conventional criteria and the information taxonomy of chapters 16 and 17 are considered. Genuine *testing* can therefore only occur after the design process is complete and new evidence has accrued against which to test. Because new data had been collected since chapter 8 was published, the validity of the model could be investigated on the basis of Neyman–Pearson (1933) 'quality control' tests. Thus, in sections 3–8, the six information sets are taken in turn; for each I discuss the associated criteria, relate them to well-known test statistics (for which each criterion constitutes the null) and apply the resulting tests to DHSY on an extended sample. Both quarterly and annual data frequencies are used and the interwar and postwar UK data are compared, stressing the progressive research strategy that follows from an encompassing approach to econometrics. The conjecture about using nominal values is discussed in Harnett (1984). Finally, the discussion of encompassing only applies to parsimonious encompassing, as noted in the preamble to chapter 16.

I had moved from LSE to Oxford shortly before writing chapter 18 (which was the last empirical study I carried out on a mainframe computer) and Neil Ericsson was helping with the burden of computer programming and computing, thus starting another long and fruitful collaboration. John Muellbauer had become a colleague at Nuffield and it fell to him to detect – and persuade me to remove – the more egregious errors from such attempted expositions! Finally, my study in the history of econometric thought with Mary Morgan was throwing increasing light on methodology from an embryological viewpoint (see Morgan, 1990; Hendry and Morgan, 1991). The poem by Denis H. Robertson from 1952 encapsulates many of the concerns that have remained pertinent for postwar econometrics despite the Haavelmo revolution (see Morgan, 1987).

The non-econometrician's lament

As soon as I could safely toddle
My parents handed me a *model*.
My brisk and energetic pater
Provided the accelerator.
My mother, with her kindly gumption,
The *function* guiding my *consumption*;
And every week I had from her
A lovely new *parameter*,
With lots of little *leads* and *lags*
In pretty parabolic bags.

With optimistic *expectations*
I started on my *explorations*,
And swore to move without a swerve
Along my sinusoidal curve.
Alas! I knew how it would end:

I've mixed the cycle and the trend,
And fear that, growing daily skinnier,
I have at length become *non-linear*.
I wander glumly round the house
As though I were *exogenous*,
And hardly capable of feeling
The difference 'tween floor and ceiling.

I scarcely now, a pallid ghost,
Can tell *ex ante* from *ex post*:
My thoughts are sadly *inelastic*,
My acts incurably *stochastic*.

D. H. Robertson
3 September 1952
(italics added)

(from *The Business Cycle in the Post-War World*, ed. E. Lundberg, Macmillan, 1955)

1 Introduction

The main aim of this chapter is to exposit a number of concepts relevant to econometric modelling of economic time-series data by reappraising the model developed in chapter 8 (denoted DHSY below). On the one hand, this should help to clarify their investigation, which was conducted on a rather intuitive basis as a 'detective story', without formal analyses of several important notions and model types. Such analyses have appeared only recently. On the other hand, the relatively widespread use of the DHSY model (see the comprehensive study by Davis, 1984) suggests using it to illustrate the ensuing developments in econometric 'method' and so to generate a greater understanding of both the terminology and the conceptual basis of many recent modelling ideas. As the preceding poem reveals, however, the language itself is not recent; *plus ça change.* . . . The technical basis for the present discussion is presented in chapters 16 and 17.

A distinction of importance in what follows is between *evaluating* and *obtaining* empirical econometric relationships. These two aspects are certainly linked in so far as evaluation techniques help to exclude some potential models and may even comprise the main basis of various methods aimed at locating useful data descriptions. Nevertheless, a satisfactory evaluation outcome cannot be sufficient by *itself* for establishing a useful empirical equation, and at best is only necessary.

Precisely how one should or even could obtain useful empirical models is not obvious. As Haavelmo (1944, p. 10) expressed the matter, 'It is almost impossible, it seems, to describe exactly how a scientist goes about constructing a model. It is a creative process, an art . . .'. Thus, important elements include inspiration in the formulation of both relevant theory-models and their data analogues, as well as serendipity. Whereas formal evaluation is mechanistic, obtaining is almost the antithesis. To quote a well-known illustration, rejecting a null hypothesis against an alternative does not entail the validity of the latter. As stressed by Cross (1984) – citing Duhem – evidence can at most falsify conjunctions of hypotheses. A complete rethink of the problem may be necessary, perhaps leading to the adoption of a wholly different framework which could require considerable insight on the part of the investigator. A test may be mechanistic and can dispose but revision cannot be mechanistic if something of permanent value is to be proposed. This is just Popper's (1969) dichotomy between conjectures and refutations writ small: the only excuse for reiteration is to help avoid possible misunderstanding below.

Much of the following analysis concerns the role of evaluation in model building. Specifically, the DHSY approach used a number of selection criteria which a model had to satisfy to be acceptable and so we shall explore the notion of designing the model to fulfil those criteria. It transpires that most of the data-related criteria are relatively easily satisfied and so only weakly restrict the model choice. Thus, since they are merely necessary conditions, one cannot recommend a model *solely* because it 'passes' tests based on data criteria. Nevertheless, many published equations fail to satisfy all the criteria described later: 'badly designed' models have little in their favour if 'good design' is not too difficult to achieve.

Here, a model is viewed as a simplified representation intended to capture the salient features of certain observed phenomena. Theory models are freely created edifices in which latent constructs are manipulated according to well-defined rules and consistent assumptions to yield implications hopefully germane to interpreting observed outcomes. Most such models in OECD-area economies are based on an approach of decentralized optimization subject to environmental/institutional constraints (generally conditional on stringent '*ceteris paribus*' clauses). Anticipated correlations (or the absence thereof) are deduced from the asserted causal structure of the theory and the theory-model is 'tested' by checking the coherency of its implications with the data, usually by fitting a corresponding empirical model.

Nevertheless, the empirical model is anything but a free creation: its properties are determined by the actual process which generated the data. Often, the mismatch of fitted model and the anticipated outcome is viewed as a set of 'problems' to be solved or removed, leading to such notions as 'wrong signs', 'omitted variables biases', 'residual autocorrelations' and so on. I prefer to view this issue differently, and enquire instead what operations were conducted to reduce the data generation process to the model and hence whether the resulting parameters are of any interest for the desired purpose. Thus, there are 'wrong interpretations' (rather than 'wrong signs'), new parameters induced by marginalization with respect to relevant variables (instead of 'omitted variables bias'), sequential conditioning and so on.

More generally, it is postulated that there exists a stochastic process generating all the variables (denoted by w_i) which are, and/or are believed to be, relevant (allowing for whatever measurement methods are involved). This vast complex is called the data generation process (abbreviated to DGP). In practice, the DGP may well be unknowable to our limited intellect, important variables may be unobservable, and/or the stochastic mechanism need not be constant over time. Nevertheless, I assume that there does exist a 'meta-parameterization', denoted by θ, which characterizes what is relatively constant in the process. Less restrictively, the mechanism is assumed to generate outcomes sequentially over time. Empirical models result from reparameterizing the process, through eliminating (marginalizing with respect to) all but a small subset of variables (those remaining being denoted by x_i)

and conditioning one subvector y_t (called endogenous) of that remaining subset on another z_t (called 'exogenous' because it is not determined within the model). Here the basic statistical operations of conditioning and marginalizing are used in their conventional senses: given any two continuous random variables a and b then their joint probability distribution $D(a, b)$ can be expressed as

$$D(a, b) = D(a|b)D(b) \qquad (\text{or } D(b|a)D(a)) \qquad (18.1)$$

where $D(a|b)$ is the conditional distribution of a given b and $D(b)$ is the marginal distribution of b (see for example Whittle, 1970).

Thus, the conceptual framework[1] is that there exists some joint density denoted $D(w_1 \ldots w_T|\theta)$ which by repeated application of (18.1) corresponding to the notion of sequentially generating data yields the DGP:

$$D(w_1 \ldots w_T|\theta) = \prod_{t=1}^{T} D(w_t|w_{t-1} \ldots w_1; \theta). \qquad (18.2)$$

However, the model only involves the tiny subset x_t of the potential variables w_t and so both current and lagged values of all other variables must be eliminated. Doing this generates the model:

$$\prod_{t=1}^{T} F(x_t|x_{t-1} \ldots x_1; \lambda_t). \qquad (18.3)$$

Economic theory hopefully offers guidance on sensible selections of x, and the associated choice of $F(\cdot)$ etc. Note that λ_t will be a constant λ if θ is constant over $t = 1, \ldots, T$ and all excluded effects are, and remain, orthogonal to included influences. Finally, letting $x_t' = (y_t' z_t')$ where z_t is deemed 'exogenous' then (again using (18.1))

$$F(x_1 \ldots x_T|\lambda) = \prod_{t=1}^{T} F(y_t|z_t, x_{t-1}, \ldots, x_1; \alpha_1) \prod_{t=1}^{T} F(z_t|x_{t-1}, \ldots, x_1; \alpha_2). \qquad (18.4)$$

The first factor on the right in (18.4) is the conditional model for $\{y_t\}$ and the second is the marginal model for $\{z_t\}$. For simplicity, λ is assumed constant in (18.4) (see section 5 below) and α is the transformation of λ needed to sustain the factorization. Precisely how α is partitioned into α_1 and α_2 is very important for the legitimacy of the claim that z_t is exogenous (as discussed in section 4).

As an example, aggregation involves a data transformation from micro observations to a mixture of micro and macro data (with a corresponding transformation in the parameters) followed by elimination of the micro data, and a resulting greatly reduced set of variables and parameters. Whether or not the finally derived parameters are of interest will depend on their relationship to the underlying parameters θ, including such features as constancy, interpretability and so on. Finally, practicality necessitates restricting the lag length in the conditioning set, usually to a fixed finite value.

If we restrict ourselves to linear approximations (after suitable data transformations such as are briefly discussed in section 6 below) then the generic result ends up 'looking like' that appearing in most econometrics textbooks: e.g.

$$y_t = \beta'x_t + \varepsilon_t \qquad t = 1, \ldots, T \tag{18.5}$$

where x_t now comprises all the regressor variables and β is a parameter vector asserted to be of interest and to be constant over the sample. By construction from (18.5), however, $\{\varepsilon_t\}$ is simply $\{y_t - \beta'x_t\}$ and hence the 'error' must contain everything which actually influences $\{y_t\}$ but is not explicitly included in the model. It is this notion of $\{\varepsilon_t\}$ being a derived, rather than an autonomous, process which prompts the consideration of trying to *design* the model such that β and $\{\varepsilon_t\}$ satisfy certain pre-specified criteria. For example, one obvious condition is to ensure that the model adequately describes the data: after all, model aircraft are designed to fly! Other criteria also are important, and so relevant design considerations are over-viewed in the next section, and investigated in greater detail in sections 3–8.

First, however, the joint assertions that β is constant, x_t is 'exogenous' and (say) $\varepsilon_t \sim \text{IN}(0, \sigma^2)$ (denoting an independent normally distributed process with a zero mean and a constant variance of σ^2) in effect imply that (18.5) is the conditional DGP since, given data on x_t together with a value of β and the process for $\{\varepsilon_t\}$, then y_t can be generated as $\beta'x_t + \varepsilon_t$. In practice, if based only on prior reasoning and without careful data analysis, such assertions tend to come unstuck when estimation reveals the sorts of 'problems' noted earlier. Moreover, camouflaging the disease by 'removing' the symptoms seems an unlikely route to success. Conversely, (18.5) could be viewed as simply decomposing the actually observed y_t into a part which at present can be explained using observed data (i.e. $\beta'x_t$) and a part which cannot: with the growth of knowledge, their relative shares could alter radically, hopefully that of $\{\varepsilon_t\}$ diminishing. This matches the earlier analysis since the operations reducing the DGP (18.2) to the model (18.4) entail that $\{\varepsilon_t\}$ comprises (*inter alia*) all errors of measurement, of marginalizing and of functional form approximation and/or parameter variations as well as sampling variability. Thus, being a derived process, $\{\varepsilon_t\}$ must alter as the model does and hence is a far cry from any presumed 'autonomous shock' to the original DGP. It is this view which DHSY adopt and which I wish to discuss further.

2 Design Criteria

An important feature of viewing modelling as an exercise in design is the choice of the criteria by which the success of the modelling exercise is to be judged. Even for model aircraft, there is more to it than just being able to fly: other relevant factors include stability to atmospheric shocks, reliability of the motive force and robustness in the face of its failure, cost of construction, running cost and so on. Evidently, these criteria can pull the design in conflicting directions. Analogously, many criteria figure in designing econometric models and conflicts between these criteria can occur in practice.

The main criteria conventionally reported in econometrics seem to be related to

1 goodness of fit,
2 absence of residual autocorrelation,
3 validity of exogeneity assertions,

4 accuracy of predictions and parameter constancy,
5 absence of residual heteroscedasticity,
6 signs, magnitudes, precisions and interpretations of estimated coefficients and
7 validity of *a priori* restrictions on parameters.

In many cases, information relevant to only a small subset of these is recorded, making evaluation especially difficult. More fundamentally, however, what specific statistics should be reported for each criterion and how should reported statistics be interpreted?

To analyse the separate but interrelated issues involved, it is convenient to switch to a different taxonomy more closely connected to that used by DHSY; where an overlap occurs with (1)–(7) it is noted parenthetically. Thus, the concepts which will be investigated explicitly are recorded in table 18.1 together with the type of information relevant to each criterion and the associated tests used below.

The discussion now focuses on the actual empirical model chosen by DHSY, in order to exposit these notions and their relationships. Here, it is important to remember that statistical analysis proceeds using an 'as if' strategy. Conditional on treating the model as if it were the DGP, various test statistics are derived which have known distributions when each hypothesis is valid;[2] if the test outcome is consistent with its distribution, the model is temporarily retained – if not it is 'revised'. Since a reject outcome does not have a unique implication, the revision process (i.e. obtaining the model) can be painful and slow, often relying on lucky or inspired guesses etc. Sometimes this procedure is referred to pejoratively as 'data mining'. However, 'from the fact that it is of no scientific or logical significance how a theory is arrived at it follows that no way is illegitimate' (Magee, 1982, p. 32).

Nevertheless, if a model satisfying all requisite criteria has been selected by data-based revision, it can be *tested* only on (genuinely) new data or against new criteria or new rival models. Thus, numerical values of test statistics reported alongside parameter estimates usually serve to demonstrate the appropriateness (or otherwise) of the *design* exercise (e.g. wind-tunnel performance is fine) and *not* of the

Table 18.1 Design criteria and associated test statistics

	Design criterion	Conventional taxonomy	Type of information	Section	Associated tests
(i)	Data coherency	(1); (2); (5)	'Past'	3	$(-; \xi_2, \eta_2, \eta_3; \xi_4, \eta_4)$
(ii)	Valid conditioning	(3)	'Present'	4	(ξ_5)
(iii)	Parameter constancy	(4)	'Future'	5	(ξ_1, η_1)
(iv)	Data admissibility		'Measurement'	6	
(v)	Theory consistency	(6); (7)	'A priori'	7	$(-; \eta_3, \xi_3)$
(vi)	Encompassing		'Rival models'	8	(η_3, ξ_6)

model itself (e.g. the model stalls on takeoff!). Consequently, until a model has been rigorously tested against new evidence, it seems hazardous to place much weight on its implications, no matter how 'pleasing' these seem.

The results actually obtained after much trial and error by DHSY using quarterly (seasonally unadjusted) data for 1958(i)–1975(ii) based on ordinary least squares (OLS) estimation are recorded for convenience:

$$\widehat{\Delta_4 c_t} = 0.48\Delta_4 i_t - 0.23\Delta_1 \Delta_4 i_t - 0.09(c - i)_{t-4} + 0.006\Delta_4 D_t$$
$$\quad (0.03) \qquad (0.04) \qquad (0.01) \qquad\qquad (0.002)$$

$$\quad - 0.12\Delta_4 p_t - 0.31\Delta_1 \Delta_4 p_t$$
$$\quad\quad (0.02) \qquad (0.10)$$

(18.6)

$$T = 71 \qquad R^2 = 0.85 \qquad \hat{\sigma} = 0.62\% \qquad \{\xi_1(20) = 21.8\}$$
$$\xi_2(12) = 23.$$

Here, lower-case letters denote logarithms of corresponding capitals and

C_t	consumers' expenditure on non-durables and services in constant 1970 prices
I_t	personal disposable income in 1970 prices
P_t	implicit deflator of C_t
D_t	dummy variable equal to zero except for $+1$, -1 in quarters (i) and (ii) of 1968 and 1973 (and later in 1979(ii) and (iii))
T	sample size (after creation of any necessary lags)
R^2	squared multiple correlation coefficient
$\hat{\sigma}$	standard deviation of residuals (adjusted for degrees of freedom)
$\xi_1(n)$	asymptotically valid test of parameter constancy for n periods ahead distributed as $\chi^2(n)$ on the null
$\xi_2(m)$	$T\Sigma_{i=1}^m r_i^2$ where r_i denotes the ith-order residual autocorrelation coefficient
$(\cdot)$	conventionally calculated coefficient standard errors
$\{\cdot\}$	statistic refers to equation over shorter sample period than that for which coefficient estimates are reported

Also, $\eta_i(k,j)$ denotes an (approximate) F statistic with (k,j) degrees of freedom ostensibly testing the same null as the associated ξ_i (e.g. ξ_2, η_2 both test for residual autocorrelation and ξ_4, η_4 both test for heteroscedasticity etc.).

In terms of the criteria in (1)–(6), how well designed is (18.6)?

3 Data Coherency

The notion that a model should adequately characterize the empirical evidence seems unexceptionable. Nevertheless, it is far from obvious precisely how to define 'data coherent' and how to evaluate its presence or absence. Two separate aspects are the closeness of the description and the absence of a systematic lack of fit. The former requires a scalar criterion for ranking models – many examples are known such as R^2, $\bar{R}^2$, $\hat{\sigma}^2$, the Akaike information criterion etc. (see for example Chow, 1981). The residual standard deviation as a percentage of the level of the behavioural variable being modelled ($\hat{\sigma}$ above) is one of the more useful descriptive statistics and also corresponds to a notion of variance dominance: for a given variable, model A variance dominates model B if $\hat{\sigma}_A^2 < \hat{\sigma}_B^2$. This is already widely used in econometrics for the sort of argument presented in Theil (1971, p. 543), that the 'true model' variance dominates false models (at least in large samples). An alternative justification for its use when all the models are approximations is noted below in section 8 and discussed more formally in chapter 16.

Next, residual autocorrelation clearly reveals a systematic lack of fit (where residual denotes the unexplained remainder) and so a necessary condition for a non-systematic residual is that it be *white noise*. As defined here, a white noise process is that which cannot be predicted linearly from its own past alone. The output of a computer pseudo-random number generator generally has this property. Since models are usually more easily estimated under a null hypothesis of no residual serial correlation, white noise is tested for by using the Lagrange multiplier approach (see for example Godfrey, 1978; Breusch and Pagan, 1980; Engle, 1982b; and, for a lucid exposition, Pagan, 1981). The resulting tests are generalized descendants of the well-known Durbin–Watson statistic, but are valid in dynamic models and can be constructed for any reasonable order of autocorrelation. Following Harvey (1981a, p. 173) and the simulation results in Kiviet (1985), these tests seem best expressed as approximate F statistics, denoted by $\eta_2(k, T - k - l)$ for testing kth-order residual autocorrelation in a model with T observations and l regressors (this effectively replaces $\xi_2(\cdot)$).

All the tests have been recalculated for DHSY based on the latest available data for 1964(i)–1982(ii) (*Economic Trends*, Annual Supplement, 1983 edition, no. 8), with the estimates shown below:

$$\widehat{\Delta_4 c_t} = 0.45\Delta_4 i_t - 0.16\Delta_1\Delta_4 i_t - 0.10(c - i)_{t-4} + 0.008\Delta_4 D_t$$
$$\quad\quad [0.026] \quad\quad [0.038] \quad\quad\quad [0.013] \quad\quad\quad\quad\quad [0.003]$$

$$- 0.12\Delta_4 p_t + 0.03\Delta_1\Delta_4 p_t \quad\quad\quad\quad\quad\quad\quad\quad (18.7)$$
$$\quad [0.020] \quad\quad [0.091]$$

$$T = 68 \quad\quad R^2 = 0.81 \quad\quad \hat{\sigma} = 0.89\% \quad\quad \eta_2(6, 57) = 1.9$$

Square brackets indicate standard errors calculated as in White (1980b). Figure 18.1 shows the graph of $\Delta_4 c_t$ against $\widehat{\Delta_4 c_t}$. Although $\eta_2(\cdot)$ is not significant at the 5 per cent level, its value suggests that some residual autocorrelation may persist.

It must be stressed that white noise can have 'structure' (e.g. a model can underpredict peaks and overpredict troughs) and can involve intertemporal connections as in

$$u_t = \varepsilon_{1t} + \delta\varepsilon_{2t-1} \quad\quad\quad\quad\quad\quad\quad\quad (18.8)$$

where the ε_{it} are unrelated white noise. Consequently, white noise may be predictable in part (or entirely) from other information (as from ε_{2t-1} in (18.8)): as an example, imagine knowing the formula of a random number generator. On all this, see for example Granger (1983), and chapter 10. Moreover, most economic variables can be 'filtered' to produce a white noise residual (this is the basis of Box–Jenkins methods – see their (1976) book – and is related to the use of Δ_4 above). Omitting from a model filtered variables which are nearly white noise will not produce residual

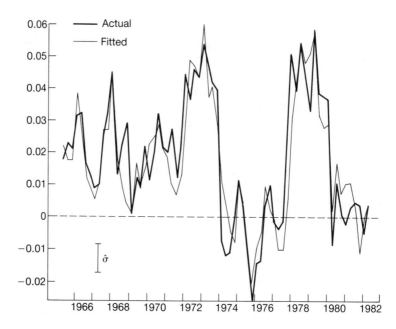

Figure 18.1   DHSY, equation (18.7).

autocorrelation, and yet such components of the white noise error will be predictable from the observed data. Worst of all, residuals which are apparently white noise may even be predictable using lagged functions of variables already included in a model! This can occur when residual autocorrelation is incorrectly viewed as being due to error autocorrelation and then 'removed' (as in a Cochrane–Orcutt transformation); the residual may become (nearly) white noise but, as an invalid common factor has been imposed, remains predictable from lagged variables already in the model (see for example chapter 6).

From this discussion, it should be clear that white noise residuals can be achieved by appropriately designing the model (e.g. removing autocorrelation or adding enough lagged variables) and hence constitute a very weak criterion of model adequacy – albeit one which many behavioural models fail to satisfy. A stronger condition is to require the residual to be an innovation, unpredictable both from its own past and from the past of other variables in the model. If a general model is estimated at the outset then its $\hat{\sigma}^2$ measures the innovation variance, and a test for a restricted model's error being an innovation is simply that it does not fit significantly worse than the initial equation (i.e. is not variance dominated by it). Conventionally, an F test is used; and against the alternative of a model explaining c_t by five lags of itself, of i_t and of p_t (plus $\Delta_4 D_t$), (18.7) yields $\eta_3(12, 51) = 1.0$. Thus, (18.7) is not variance dominated by the more general model. Nevertheless, a portmanteau test like $\eta_3(\cdot)$ will have little power against a specific alternative (such as one invalid restriction), and so again the criterion turns out to be weak. Note that $\eta_3 \leqslant 1$ as the error variance of the general model is less than or exceeds that of the restricted equation.

Returning to (18.7), the fit remains reasonably close (a residual standard deviation of under 0.9 per cent of expenditure), but is almost 50 per cent worse than (18.6); this could reflect invalid marginalization, less accurate data series or a 'noisier' world. Given the casual empiricism of the 1970s the last merits a brief investigation in terms of testing for residual heteroscedasticity. As shown by $\xi_1(\cdot)$ and $\eta_1(\cdot)$ in section 5 below, potential heteroscedasticity does not take the form of an increased residual variance pre- and post-1977(ii), nor from (18.6) did a shift occur between pre-1971 and the period 1971(i)–1975(iv): such evidence does not support the conjecture of a noisier world. Of the remaining possibilities, we tested for heteroscedasticity of an autoregressive conditional variety (ARCH – see Engle, 1982a), with $\xi_4(1) = 0.5$, and for functional form mis-specification (see White, 1980b), with $\eta_4(17, 46) = 0.4$. Neither statistic indicates any problems, but their powers may not be large (see for example Engle et al. (1985) for the former). In any case, the standard errors reported in (18.7) are heteroscedasticity consistent (see White 1980b; Domowitz and White, 1982). Finally, a simple indicator of residual outliers is to calculate their skewness (SK) and excess kurtosis (EK) after scaling to zero mean, unit variance: this yields $SK = 0.3$ and $EK = 0.2$, revealing a distribution whose first four moments are very similar to those of the standard normal. The data accuracy conjecture is briefly discussed in section 6.

On the basis of this evidence, the model seems to be reasonably data coherent. However, this is on the new observations and using new tests whereas the model was designed to satisfy only the earlier data-coherency tests on the previous data. While tests may be weak within the estimation sample, this stricture can hardly apply to outcomes obtained on new data.

4 Valid Conditioning

The legitimacy of treating current dated variables as 'givens' has generated substantial debate in econometrics as seen by the many references in chapter 15. Statistically, the precise conditions for treating z_t as weakly exogenous in the conditional model for y_t in (18.4) are that the parameters of interest can be obtained from α_1 alone and that no information about α_1 is lost by ignoring α_2. If so, then the model for z_t does not require estimation and a fully efficient analysis can be conducted just from the conditional model, and so the modelling exercise is both cheaper and more robust. Thus, the partition of α into α_1 and α_2 requires that the two subsets of parameters are 'unconnected'; it is not sufficient simply to choose not to model z_t.

Economically, if the behavioural model for y_t is a contingent plan with agents reacting to the actual values of z_t, rather than say the expected values, then z_t can often be treated as weakly exogenous (see chapter 17). Note that this allows for the possibility of feedback for y onto z (e.g. x_{t-1} includes y_{t-1} and occurs in the marginal model in (18.4)). However, z_t is strongly exogenous if it is weakly exogenous and no such feedback occurs. While this last concept may be closer to the textbook notion of 'exogeneity', it is often unrealistically strong and unnecessary for most inference purposes.

Even for quarterly observations, the assertion that agents form a contingent plan is strong, as it excludes both within-quarter feedbacks (e.g. from expenditure onto income) as well as expectations-based plans. Time aggregation is necessarily present and the substantive issue is how good any weak exogeneity approximation is. This is difficult to test directly, although an indirect evaluation is possible as part of investigating parameter constancy (see the next section). Empirically, some evidence may be gleaned by comparing (18.7) with an annual-data equivalent for consumers' non-durable expenditure (denoted by C_t^a etc.) for 1952–80 which yields the following estimates (a circumflex denotes OLS and a tilde two-stage least squares):

$$\widehat{\Delta_1 c_t^a} = 0.48\Delta_1 i_t^a - 0.12(c^a - i^a)_{t-1} - 0.16\Delta_1 p_t^a \tag{18.9}$$
$$[0.04] \qquad [0.02] \qquad\qquad [0.04]$$

$T = 27 \qquad R^2 = 0.90 \qquad \hat{\sigma} = 0.52\% \qquad \eta_1(4, 20) = 1.0$

$\eta_2(2, 22) = 0.2 \qquad \xi_4(1) = 3.6 \qquad \eta_4(5, 19) = 0.8 \qquad SK = 0.5$

$EK = -0.2$

$$\widetilde{\Delta_1 c_t^a} = 0.48\Delta_1 i_t^a - 0.13(c^a - i^a)_{t-1} - 0.19\Delta_1 p_t^a \tag{18.10}$$
$$(0.07) \qquad (0.03) \qquad\qquad (0.05)$$

$T = 27 \qquad \hat{\sigma} = 0.54\% \qquad \xi_1(4) = 4.7 \qquad \xi_2(4) = 1.9$

$\xi_5(5) = 5.2 \qquad SK = 0.6 \qquad EK = -0.5.$

The data are shown in figure 18.3: note that the largest change in successive values of $\Delta_1 c_t^a$ is about $10\hat{\sigma}$. The instrumental variables used in (18.10) were i_{t-1}^a, c_{t-1}^a, p_{t-1}^a, $\Delta_1 p_{t-1}^a$, 1, $\Delta_1 i_{t-1}^a$, $\Delta_1 c_{t-1}^a$, $\Delta_1 l_{t-1}$ where L denotes real liquid assets. Also $\xi_5(n)$ is Sargan's (1964a) test of the independence of the instruments from the error, distributed as $\chi^2(n)$ in large samples for n valid over-identifying instruments. Thus, even at the annual level, there is little direct evidence of simultaneity although quarterly feedback of c_{t-1} onto y_t has been established (see chapter 10).

Overall, despite the time aggregation to years, the results in (18.9) and (18.10) are very similar to those in (18.7), and seem equally data coherent (there is some evidence in (18.9) of an ARCH effect, however). The main difference is the apparent improved goodness of fit of (18.9) over (18.7), as $\hat{\sigma}$ is substantially lower in the former and indeed is smaller than in (18.6). However, calendar-year changes are smoothed relative to four-quarter changes, and it must be remembered that $\hat{\sigma}$ in (18.9) is a percentage of annual expenditure, whereas in (18.6) and (18.7) it is a percentage of quarterly expenditure. There may also be a problem of relative data accuracy: for example if there exists a within-year (seasonal allocation) error so that $\varepsilon_t = u_t + s_t$ where $\sum_{i=0}^{3} s_{4j-i} = 0 \ \forall j$, then s_t vanishes in a between-year analysis. This measurement accuracy issue is further considered in section 6. Note that EK indicates a distribution more concentrated than the normal for the residuals in (18.9) and (18.10) (rather than having fatter tails).

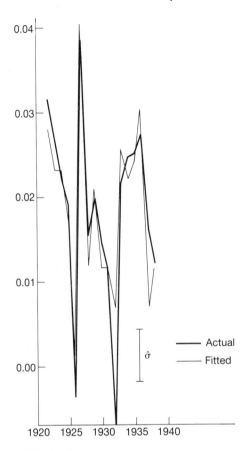

Figure 18.2 Equation (18.13), $\Delta_1 c_t^a$.

5 Parameter Constancy

Having covered the use of past and contemporaneous information, we turn to the 'relative future' (i.e. $t + j$ for $j > 0$, relative to t). Re-express (18.5) in matrix notation incorporating all the observations as

$$y = X\beta + \varepsilon \tag{18.11}$$

Partition the data into two subsamples $(y_1 X_1)$ and $(y_2 X_2)$ where it is found that

$$T_1^{-1} X_1' X_1 \neq T_2^{-1} X_2' X_2 \qquad T_1^{-1} X_1' y_1 \neq T_2^{-1} X_2' y_2 \tag{18.12}$$

yet $\hat{\beta}_1 \approx \hat{\beta}_2$ (the expressions in (18.12) are intended to convey 'substantial' differences between the subperiod data correlations). Excluding chance offsetting influences, that conjunction of evidence seems to require that y is and remains $X\beta$ plus an orthogonal disturbance. Note that $\hat{\beta}_1 \approx \hat{\beta}_2$ alone is not sufficient since the subperiod data moments may be very similar.

Comparison of (18.6) with (18.7) revealed remarkable constancy in the coefficients other than $\Delta_1\Delta_4p_t$ and for (18.7) the last 20 quarters yield $\xi_1(20) = 29$ and $\eta_1(20, 43) = 1.4$ (the Chow (1960) test), consistent with numerical and statistical parameter constancy, although $\hat{\sigma}$ is slightly larger over the later period. Table 18.2 reports the intercorrelations of the four main regressors and the regressand within successive fourths of the sample period (roughly 17 observations apiece) and over the entire sample as well as the partial correlations over the entire sample between the regressors and Δ_4c_t. Most combinations of change and constancy are apparent, with two of the correlations having a range of unity or more (e.g. -0.57 to $+0.43$ for Δ_4c_t with Δ_4p_t). Also, two of the partials have opposite signs to the full-sample simple correlations and are much larger in absolute value, consistent with a behavioural basis for the model and re-emphasizing the dangers in an inherently multivariate subject of drawing conclusions from simple correlations (a point stressed by Koopmans, 1937, p. 128). Finally, the parameter constancy is consistent with the assertion that i_t is weakly exogenous in DHSY, with the caveat that the correlation of Δ_4c_t with Δ_4i_t is relatively constant itself.

Despite its drawbacks as a statistical test (see Kiviet, 1986a), $\xi_1(\cdot)$ remains a helpful indicator of numerical parameter constancy and hence of the likely usefulness of the equation for *ex ante* forecasting. A large value of $\xi_1(\cdot)$ when $\eta_1(\cdot)$ is not significant means that forecasts would have been inaccurate although the underlying parameters had not altered.

An interesting test of the constancy of the DHSY model is to fit it unaltered to *interwar* data and (18.13) reports OLS estimates for 1920–38 (annual observations from Feinstein, 1972, in 1938 prices):

$$\widehat{\Delta_1c_t^a} = 0.50\Delta_1 i_t^a - 0.080(c^a - i^a)_{t-1} - 0.053\Delta_1 p_t^a \qquad (18.13)$$
$$[0.06] \qquad [0.026] \qquad\qquad\qquad [0.027]$$

Table 18.2 DHSY correlation structure

	1 Δ_4c_t	2 Δ_4i_t	3 $\Delta_1\Delta_4i_t$	4 $(c-i)_{t-4}$	1	2	3	4
			I				*II*	
2 Δ_4i_t	0.63				0.83			
3 $\Delta_1\Delta_4i_t$	0.12	0.57			-0.04	0.30		
4 $(c-i)_{t-4}$	0.27	0.26	0.14		-0.46	-0.16	0.30	
5 Δ_4p_t	-0.45	-0.47	-0.28	-0.25	0.43	0.08	-0.26	-0.48
			III				*IV*	
2	0.72				0.86			
3	0.10	0.45			0.17	0.38		
4	0.33	0.33	0.13		0.58	0.63	0.22	
5	-0.57	-0.31	-0.06	-0.21	-0.42	-0.34	-0.35	-0.46
			Overall				*Partials*	
2	0.84				0.88			
3	0.11	0.38			-0.39			
4	0.30	0.31	0.18		-0.61			
5	-0.53	-0.36	-0.14	-0.61	-0.48			

$T = 17$ $R^2 = 0.81$ $\hat{\sigma} = 0.53$ per cent $\{\xi_1(4) = 7.0\}$

$\eta_1(4, 10) = 1.1$ $\xi_2(4) = 2.6$ $\eta_2(2, 12) = 0.4$ $\eta_3(5, 9) = 0.7$

$\eta_4(4, 10) = 0.6$ $SK = -1.0$ $EK = 1.9$.

Figure 18.2 shows the graph of the actual and fitted time series. Given one's prior beliefs as to relative data accuracy, it is remarkable that the goodness of fit values of (18.9) and (18.13) are almost identical (yet the model was designed on postwar quarterly data). All of the within-period test statistics are satisfactory (except SK and EK both of which reflect one outlier of $-2.7\hat{\sigma}$ in 1932), but are rather weak

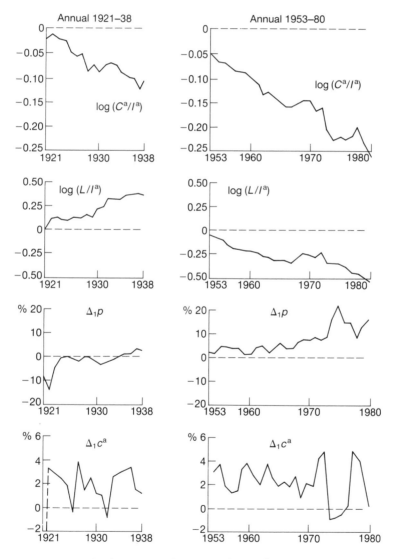

Figure 18.3   Comparative interwar and postwar time series.

evidence as the sample is only 17 observations (η_3 tests against c_t^a on c_{t-1}^a, c_{t-2}^a, i_t^a, i_{t-1}^a, i_{t-2}^a, 1, $\Delta_1 p_t^a$, $\Delta_1 p_{t-1}^a$). The pre-war/postwar parameters are recognizably similar, although the inflation effect is smaller pre-war and barely significant (see section 6). To interpret the overall outcome, consider the actual data series, which are shown in figure 18.3.

The downward trend in the average propensity to consume, the steady upward trend in inflation and the relative variance of $\Delta_1 c_t^a$ (until 1974) are remarkably similar. Against this, the liquid asset-to-income ratio is completely different, as is the *level* of inflation. The derived steady-state solutions from (18.9) and (18.13) respectively are

$$(C^a/I^a) = \exp(-4.4g - 1.3\dot{p})\,(\text{postwar}) \qquad \xi_3(2) = 283 \qquad (18.14)$$
$$(0.63)\ \ (0.11)$$

$$(C^a/I^a) = \exp(-6.2g - 0.66\dot{p})\,(\text{pre-war}) \qquad \xi_3(2) = 24 \qquad (18.15)$$
$$(1.3)\ \ (0.42)$$

where $\xi_3(n)$ is distributed as $\chi^2(n)$ on the null that the derived parameters are jointly zero, and g and $\dot{p}$ are the annual rates of growth of real income and of prices. At $\dot{p} = 0$, the pre-war ratio is lower than the postwar (0.88 versus 0.92 at $g = 2$ per cent) consistent with the observable evidence, but without offering any explanation as to why. One possibility is the value of the liquid asset-to-income ratio; another is noted in section 7. The concurrence of the falling C^a/I^a ratio and large-scale unemployment in parts of both periods also prompts many conjectures. The most obvious of these is the underconsumption hypothesis (see Keynes, 1936, ch. 23) although there is no evidence that shifts in the consumption function itself induced the depression. Downward price flexibility also seems possible in the British economy! While the coefficient of $\dot{p}$ in (18.14) is twice that in (18.15), the latter is badly determined and so it is unclear as yet whether there is any significant difference between the two periods in the postulated model.

Once the dynamics have been fully modelled, the power of parameter constancy tests to detect 'shifts' may actually be rather low. This occurs because, when a weight near unity is given to the previous value of the regressand, any permanent change in the level of a series is adjusted to in the next period so that only at the occurrence of the shift is a large discrepancy between anticipated and actual fit observed. Averaged over several periods of non-shift, the initial change may be undetectable. This suggests carefully examining the recursive residuals (see for example Harvey, 1981a, p. 150). Yet again, in isolation the criterion seems weak, although the prevalence of model predictive failure definitely confirms that it is not vacuous.

6 Data Admissibility

The next information set is that characterizing the measurement system and a model is data admissible if its fitted/predicted values automatically satisfy definitional and/or data constraints. Thus, in (18.6), (18.7) etc. the log transform ensures that $\hat{C}_t > 0$ although this is not the only transform guaranteeing positivity. A more useful property is that the errors from a logarithmic dependent variable model could have constant variance and generally seem closer to normality for inherently positive variables in economics. However, $C_t > 0$ is not the only pertinent restriction since there is the definition

$$I_t^a = C_t^a + S_t^a \tag{18.16}$$

(where S_t^a denotes 'broad savings' comprising durables plus financial asset accumulation).

Since one could equally well have modelled 'savings' rather than expenditure behaviour (but without constraining $\hat{S}_t^a$ to positivity, thus excluding a log transform for savings), data admissibility requires that $\hat{C}_t^a + \hat{S}_t^a = I_t^a$. Sometimes such a result is 'achieved' by constructing $\hat{S}_t^a$ from (18.16) but this leaves open the possibility that the implied savings model may be implausible (a point made in another context by Brainard and Tobin, 1968).

The alternative is to model both variables consistently with (18.16) and check that each is indeed data coherent etc. (see for example Deaton and Muellbauer, 1980, ch. 1.2). Here we do so for interwar data without cross-equation restrictions, using the rather natural choice of the savings ratio (S_t^a/I_t^a) in an error correction formulation, since $c^a - i^a = \log(C^a/I^a) = \log(1 - S^a/I^a) \approx -S^a/I^a$ where S^a denotes 'broad savings'. Taking the analogue of (18.13) but with an added intercept yields

$$\Delta_1\left(\frac{S^a}{I^a}\right)_t = \underset{[0.064]}{0.43}\Delta_1 i_t^a - \underset{[0.038]}{0.129}\left(\frac{S^a}{I^a}\right)_{t-1} + \underset{[0.020]}{0.071}\Delta_1 p_t^a + \underset{[0.004]}{0.0050} + \hat{u}_t \tag{18.17}$$

$$R^2 = 0.83 \qquad \hat{\sigma}_u = 0.0048.$$

The estimated companion equation for C_t^a corresponding to (18.17) is

$$\Delta_1 c_t^a = \underset{[0.071]}{0.53}\Delta_1 i_t^a - \underset{[0.042]}{0.125}(c^a - i^a)_{t-1} - \underset{[0.022]}{0.076}\Delta_1 p_t^a - \underset{[0.005]}{0.0046} + \hat{v}_t \tag{18.18}$$

$$R^2 = 0.82 \qquad \hat{\sigma}_v = 0.0053.$$

For the fitted values to satisfy (18.16), $\hat{u}_t + \hat{v}_t$ should be zero for all $t = 1, \ldots, T$, and, of course, must have a mean of zero. However, its standard deviation is only 0.00018 and it has a maximum of $0.08\hat{\sigma}_u$. Also, the coefficients of $\Delta_1 i_t^a$ add to almost unity, those of the error corrections are similar and the remaining coefficients have opposite signs as required in order for (18.16) to hold.[3] Indeed, even the derived steady-state solutions aggregate closely (using $\exp(x) \approx 1 + x$):

$$\hat{C}^a + \hat{S}^a = I^a[1 + 0.04(0.05 - 10g - \dot{p})].$$

Overall, therefore, data admissibility seems acceptable for the DHSY formulation given a savings-ratio companion equation. As emphasized by Spanos and Taylor (1984), since identities hold automatically by the design of the measurement system, they need not be imposed provided that consistent sets of relationships are formulated; conversely, a model need not be useful if identities are imposed but the entailed equations are invalid. Of course, since logical consistency and tractability of functional forms can conflict, admissibility may be abandoned deliberately, and this should be recorded if so.

The other major property of the measurement system in economics is its notorious inaccuracy (see for example Morgenstern, 1950). For the present, the main issue is the surprising robustness of the DHSY model in the face of the very large data revisions that have occurred over recent years. The entire series on the quarterly savings ratio was revised between 1981 and 1982; the largest change was from 10.6 to 7.6 per cent in 1974(iv), and the standard deviation of the revisions was 0.7 per cent – which is of the same order of magnitude as the standard error on the equation! Yet the coefficients of the DHSY equation changed relatively little and the residual variance increased only marginally when fitted to the second set of revised data.

A conjecture which might account for such an anomalous outcome arises from distinguishing *within*-revision errors from *between*-revision errors. If the entire informational basis for constructing C, I, S etc. is altered, they may all change in a 'coherent' way such that, within a consistently revised series, our estimates of uncertainty based on between-observation errors remain low. An analogy would be with a natural scientist's only estimate of the uncertainty of his calculations being based on between-reading variations which could be very small relative to a large – but unknown – error in the whole level of measurements provided by his instrument. Two conclusions would then follow: first, we would grossly underestimate the uncertainty in our models from error variances and parameter covariances alone; second, models which adequately characterized economic behaviour yet were robust to data inaccuracies would be invaluable (the results in Swann (1985) suggest a close link between the latter and near orthogonal parameterizations). Since DHSY can be reformulated almost exactly in nominal terms, and the nominal data are little revised, the increased error variances may be attributable to less accurate price indices: we hope to report on this conjecture shortly.

7 Theory Consistency

The importance of theory consistency is disproportionately large relative to its space in this chapter simply because I have little to add to the existing literature. On the one hand, sensible modelling cannot begin without some theoretical context and parameters are uninterpretable in the absence of a well-articulated theory. As repeatedly stressed in economics (for some references, see chapter 1), it is easy to generate garbage when measuring without theory. On the other hand, theory without measurement is in danger of straying from the non-operational to the irrelevant, and imposing theory-based models on data without testing is as unjustifiable as directionless data mining (for an excellent discussion, see Leamer (1978); Sargent (1981) emphasizes the role of economic theory in data analysis).

One interesting exercise is the use of the well-established life-cycle hypothesis (LCH) in interpreting (18.14) and (18.15).[4] If A_t denotes total assets in constant prices, then a logarithmic approximation to the LCH yields the following expression for the steady-state C/I ratio:

$$c - i = f\left(R, \frac{N}{I}\right) - \frac{A}{I}g - \frac{L}{I}\dot{p} \qquad (18.19)$$

where $f(\cdot)$ denotes a function of R (the real rate of interest) and N (non-financial assets). Since $A = N + L$, the coefficient of g should exceed that of $\dot{p}$ (as it does in both periods). Also, as shown in figure 18.3, L/I has a mean of about unity, and so the derived coefficients have interpretable orders of magnitude. Perhaps the main counter-indicator is that A/I would have to be larger pre-war than postwar whereas L/I must behave conversely, conflicting with figure 18.3. However, the standard errors are large in (18.15), and so those results might not differ significantly from (18.19) (using the expansion of $\exp(x) = 1 + x$ as before).

Next, the error correction mechanism (ECM) is consistent with static-equilibrium homogeneity postulates by construction, although care is required to ensure sensible behaviour in growth scenarios (see *inter alia* Currie, 1981; chapter 9; Salmon, 1982; Kloek, 1982; Patterson and Ryding, 1982; and chapter 17). Here 'equilibrium' is a contextual concept defined by 'all change ceasing', and is not an assertion about behaviour over a long run of real time (see Spanos and Taylor, 1984). Nevertheless, the target to which agents are postulated as adjusting importantly affects the meaning and interpretation of the estimated model. From (18.15), at $g = 0.02$ and $\dot{p} = 0$, $C^a/I^a = 0.88$, which is close to the *lowest* observed value (see figure 18.3). This suggests that the entire interwar period is one of disequilibrium, with consumers gradually adjusting C/I downwards, from the high value induced by the First World War, towards 0.88! The estimated mean lag of $6\frac{1}{4}$ years is consistent with such an interpretation of slow movement towards a distant 'equilibrium'.

More surprisingly, despite imposing a unit elasticity, the ECM can quite adequately 'track' the observed fall in $(C/I)_t$ without any modifying regressors:

$$(\widehat{c^a - i^a})_t = -0.45\Delta_1 i_t^a + 0.93(c^a - i^a)_{t-1} \qquad (18.20)$$
$$[0.06] \qquad [0.02]$$

$T = 17 \qquad R^2 = 0.96 \qquad \hat{\sigma} = 0.55 \text{ per cent} \qquad \xi_1(4) = 3.7$

$\eta_1(4, 11) = 0.7 \qquad \eta_2(1, 14) = 0.1 \qquad SK = -0.2 \qquad EK = 0.1$

$\eta_4(2, 13) = 1.2.$

Figure 18.4 shows the graph and fit of (18.20), although in this instance the R^2 value is a useful index of the goodness of the track. In several respects (namely SK, EK, ξ_1 and η_1), equation (18.20) may even be preferred to (18.13). However, the purpose of presenting the estimates in (18.20) is to illustrate how ECMs only enforce unit elasticity in a hypothetical equilibrium and can adequately characterize data which strongly violate a constant-ratio restriction but only by attributing the observed outcome to disequilibrium, with consequentially large mean lags.

Alternative interpretations are also sustainable, with far more rapid adjustment. These necessitate moving, or temporary, equilibria, with rapid adjustment thereto combined with a slow underlying drift towards some steady-state outcome. One simple example can be based on attributing the fall in C/I to the rise in I such that the income elasticity of expenditure is unity only in an equilibrium with very high

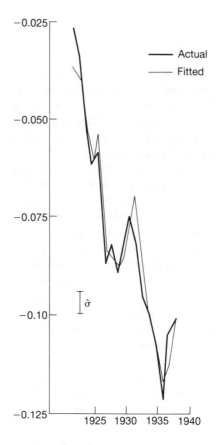

Figure 18.4 Equation (18.20), $c^a - i^a$.

income levels and otherwise is less than unity. Thus, adding $1000/I_t^a$ to (18.13), we have

$$\widehat{\Delta_1 c_t^a} = 0.63\Delta_1 i_t^a - 0.50(c^a - i^a)_{t-1} + 0.22/I_t^a - 0.13 - 0.07\Delta_1 p_t \qquad (18.21)$$
$$[0.10] \qquad [0.20] \qquad\qquad [0.12] \qquad [0.07] \; [0.02]$$

$$T = 17 \qquad R^2 = 0.87 \qquad \hat{\sigma} = 0.48 \text{ per cent} \qquad \eta_1(4, 8) = 2.2$$
$$\xi_2(4) = 1.5 \qquad SK = -0.2 \qquad EK = -0.4.$$

While an alternative parameterization would be desirable, and there may be some parameter non-constancy in (18.21), the illustration should suffice: the fit is 12 per cent better than (18.20), and now the mean lag is under one year, but the result as it stands is not consistent with a unit elasticity in equilibrium. Fitting the equivalent of (18.21) to postwar data yields $\hat{\sigma} = 0.46$ per cent (a similar improvement over (18.9)) while leaving the estimates of coefficients in common with (18.9) almost unchanged.

All the previous models are conditional on observed income, rather than modelling any income expectations process. The latter view, using rational expectations, has been the focus of a substantial literature leading to the concept of 'surprise' consumption functions. In these, the change in consumption (trend adjusted) is a white noise process, but is predictable if current income is known (see for example Hall (1978) and Wickens and Molana (1982) for UK data). However, the tests in chapter 10 not only reject the Hall model, but also show that it is encompassed by the DHSY specification (see section 8). Muellbauer (1983) also presents evidence rejecting the Hall model. Nevertheless, the two types of model are related both theoretically and empirically: for example, Nickell (1985) derives ECMs as the solution to a dynamic optimization problem and the parameterization in DHSY is close to using 'innovations' via the four-quarter-change specification.

Auxiliary criteria in econometric estimation have usually included the match of ~tual to anticipated signs and magnitudes of parameters and such features as lag ʼ ᴖn profiles. Precision of estimation (large t values) is also often stressed, ᴖᴗ the economic significance of the estimates (e.g. it would be odd to droᴗ from (18.6) even if its standard error exceeded the coefficient when one belıᴗ ʼᴖy) (18.14) was a valid theory). For behavioural models, near orthogonalıᴗᴗ ᴗs formulated according to sensible decision variables also seems desirable ᴗᴗ ? p. 202). If relevant but excluded influences would enter the model orthogᴗ ᴖmain orthogonal over time, then estimated parameters can stay constant desᴗ ᴗecification'. In the terminology of Domowitz and White (1982), the model wᴗ ᴗrrect to first order.

8 Encompassing

Encompassing is the notion of being able to accounᴗ ᴖsults obtained by rival models given one's own findings. A failure to achievᴗ ᴗassing indicates an incomplete model, but, again, how it should be revised is ıᴗ ᴖvious. In a linear least squares framework, encompassing is both transitive anɑ ᴗetric (if model A accounts for the results of B, and B encompasses C, then ᴗ encompasses C; whereas B cannot at the same time encompass A). Moreover, encompassing entails variance dominance (intuitively, it is unsurprising that a badly fitting model cannot explain the findings of a well fitting one). However, variance dominance need not entail encompassing: it is necessary but not sufficient – a strong argument for seeking an encompassing model building strategy which also reveals why just selecting a 'best fitting' model offers no necessary protection against picking a spurious relationship.

Of equal interest is the fact that 'non-nested' tests (which directly confront rival models), based on the Cox (1961) approach, are tests for variance encompassing in a regression context (i.e. they test whether σ_A^2 can account for σ_B^2 and/or vice versa): see, *inter alia*, Pagan (1981), Deaton (1982), Mizon and Richard (1986) and the discussion following MacKinnon (1983) who surveys the relevant literature. Note, therefore, that only one direction of testing is useful (hazarding the better model against the poorer); the other should follow automatically or else reveals low test power. Thus, variance dominance seems necessary to avoid rejection on such tests.

The drawbacks of a research strategy based on non-nested tests (denoted by ξ_6 in table 18.1) are that variance encompassing is necessary but not sufficient for parameter encompassing, and that it emphasizes a 'negative' rather than a 'positive' approach since all contending models could end being rejected. However, it fits well with a Popperian approach of learning by rejection (see for example Boland, 1982), in many cases may be the only feasible test (as for large systems when sample size is inadequate) and may have high power against interesting alternatives if model 'mis-specification' is reflected in increased residual variance.

Another slightly surprising aspect of encompassing is that a Wald-based test of parameter encompassing between regression models is a simple transformation of the classical F test for adding a subset of variables to a linear regression equation (see for example chapter 17 and Dastoor, 1983). This suggests that no clear demarcation can be drawn in linear worlds between embedding or nesting approaches (as for example DHSY used) or non-nested methods (as in, say, Pesaran, 1974). For example, the $\xi_5(\cdot)$ test is also a Wald test of the hypothesis that the structural form encompasses the reduced form parameters. Nevertheless, encompassing seems to correspond to a 'progressive research strategy' (see Lakatos, 1974; Worrall and Currie, 1978) in that encompassing models act like 'sufficient statistics' to summarize the pre-existing state of knowledge. This was the main theme of DHSY. Recently, Cross (1982, 1984) has argued persuasively for progressive research strategies in economics in general and encompassing seems to offer one econometric implementation of such a view (for a general discussion of 'scientific method' see Chalmers (1976), and for its role in economics see Blaug (1980)).

It must be stressed that a nesting model which formed the union of all other hypotheses would automatically, but rather vacuously, encompass and so a parsimony criterion remains pertinent. If the DGP is known to be $D(\cdot)$ in (18.2), say, then knowledge of θ is encompassing and is the minimal set of parameters which allows explanation of *all* submodels of $\{w_t\}$. However, if the DGP is not known, then no minimal-encompassing model need exist. Nevertheless, parsimonious encompassing formulations which accounted for most interesting rival hypotheses may be feasible, and would have to have innovation errors. Conversely, an encompassing model with an innovation error process can in turn be encompassed by other models using different information sets.

As an example, in chapter 9 Hendry and von Ungern-Sternberg (HUS) encompass DHSY by adding an integral correction term to ensure stock as well as flow equilibrium. Continuing this line, Pesaran and Evans (1984) argue that capital gains G should also be part of the information set and find 'corroborating' evidence for *total* consumers' expenditure on annual data (1952–80). Testing their hypothesis on non-durables data against the HUS model yields

$$\widehat{\Delta_1 c_t^a} = 0.43 \Delta_1 i_t^* - 0.21 (c^a - i^*)_{t-1} + 0.07 (l - i^*)_{t-1} + 0.005 G^a / I_t^* + 0.004$$
$$\qquad [0.02] \qquad [0.03] \qquad\qquad [0.01] \qquad\qquad [0.004] \qquad\quad [0.003]$$

$$(18.22)$$

$$R^2 = 0.94 \qquad \hat{\sigma} = 0.41 \text{ per cent} \qquad \eta_1(4, 18) = 1.3 \qquad \{\xi_1(4) = 17.5\}$$
$$\eta_2(2, 20) = 0.01 \qquad \eta_4(12, 10) = 0.04 \qquad SK = 0.3 \qquad EK = -0.4$$

where $I_t^* = I_t^a - \beta \dot{p} L_{t-1}$ with $\beta = 1$ and $\dot{p} = \frac{1}{2}\Delta_2 p_t^a$. This equation has a smaller innovation variance than (18.9) because of the integral correction, but G does not help explain $\Delta_1 c_t^a$. Thus, G must primarily affect durables expenditure, which is intuitively reasonable.

On quarterly data, there is some evidence that the real interest rate may influence consumers' expenditure/savings decisions (see for example Davis, 1984). Also, Bollerslev and Hylleberg (1985) reject the unit elasticity assumption and argue that a model with additional terms in income outperforms DHSY. Interestingly, if a DHSY type of formulation is retained for the income components of the relationship (but using the equivalent of i^*), then despite adding in changes in liquid assets, liquid assets/income, real interest rates, seasonal dummies and fourth-order error autocorrelation (to 'correct' for a change in the seasonal allocation of expenditure) the coefficients in common with (18.7) are virtually identical. This demonstrates both the robustness of that aspect and the predictability of an innovation process on an extended information set.

The concept of encompassing applies to models developed on a common data set and need not generalize across data sets. An unfortunate illustration of this is the dramatic failure of a model like (18.22) (but without G) on interwar data: $\hat{\sigma}$ is 0.8 per cent (compare (18.13)) and the proportionality of C^a to I^* and L can be rejected when $\beta = 1$. (This may be due to the very different behaviour of L/I pre-war and postwar: an encompassing explanation is not yet clear.) Even so, a progressive strategy remains feasible and, by accounting for both data sets, may yield greater insight into the behaviour of consumers' expenditure.

9 Summary and Conclusion

The chapter sought to exposit econometric modelling concepts while reappraising the consumers' expenditure equation in chapter 8 and some of its successors. Available information was viewed as being partitioned into six sets comprising (relative) past, contemporaneous and future observations, the measurement system, a priori theoretical information and the data information used in rival models. For each set, relevant concepts and associated statistics were discussed as aids in designing models to satisfy 'sensible' criteria. Results for interwar and postwar data were presented to illustrate the analysis and to explain the process of model evaluation. The emphasis was on the need to satisfy all the criteria, each of which may be weak in isolation, and especially on encompassing previous findings in a progressive research strategy. However, no analysis was offered as to how to obtain useful models, since issues of 'creativity' are inherently involved in selecting which of many potential revision routes to pursue when evaluation procedures highlight defects in a model.

As presaged in the introduction, this last topic has engendered some confusion, specifically concerning the role of 'sequential simplification' methods for model selection. Having experimented with a wide range of different model building methods, I believe there remain major difficulties with the uncritical and/or mechanical application of all approaches which are basically variants of expanding or contracting searches. When a sequence of hypotheses is ordered and nested and includes the DGP as a special case, sequential simplification has certain desirable large-sample properties (see Anderson, 1971, ch. 3.2; Mizon, 1977a). That there can be no imperative to adopt such a strategy when hypotheses are not uniquely ordered and/or are non-nested is clear from the well-known drawbacks of forward versus backward selection algorithms in regression. Additional difficulties (noted for example in chapter 11) include inadequate sample size, non-uniqueness of the chosen model and most importantly the potential inappropriateness of the initially specified 'unrestricted' formulation. Simplification *per se* merely provides an interpretation of the multidimensional evidence and is useful only if it creates a more plausible and robust data representation. Not only does one face the standard 'garbage-in, garbage-out' problem, the use of data-based restrictions in a single sample can endow the whole with a 'spurious' air of precision, although the earlier sections sought to elucidate the interpretation to be placed on data-instigated models. Specifically, since models can be designed to fulfil most data evaluation criteria on a given sample, satisfying such criteria cannot decisively determine the credibility of the model. Thus, one must distinguish between statistics which act as selection criteria and those which act as tests, with a consequential stress on the importance of investigating encompassing and hazarding models to potential rejection on new evidence.

Even if the hypotheses constituted an ordered nest, the *procedure* being used for simplification may not be justifiable and a very different model type may prove more useful (see for example chapter 7 where Mizon and Hendry investigated the COMFAC method but chose their model on other grounds). In non-ordered situations, substantive economic phenomena under debate may sometimes be either retained or discarded at choice by suitably modifying the order of testing.

None of the above counters the need to estimate the 'general' formulation at some stage of an empirical analysis: it defines the innovation variance on the given information choice, and is entailed by the given framework. Thus, it would seem very hazardous to accept any model which fitted significantly worse than such a baseline, in the absence of good reasons to the contrary (possible reasons might include a justification based on 'overfitting' if a large enough number of lagged variables could be shown to act like 'dummies', each partialling out what would otherwise be a few large residuals). Expanding searches which do not define a baseline, and terminate arbitrarily, have especially serious flaws in a multivariate discipline, a point made by Haavelmo (1944, ch. 4). Specifically, a failure to partial out dynamic reactions adequately seem both to camouflage underlying economic responses and to lead to subsequent predictive failure.

Econometrics offers considerable scope as a critical apparatus and this is precisely the role of stringent evaluation procedures (a theme more extensively explored in chapter 1). Offsetting this, models can be designed to satisfy most selection criteria by data-based revision. This in part may serve to short-circuit a more laborious learning process and in part puts the onus for testing on later evidence. Encompassing could be viewed as just one of the selection criteria, in which case it is more than averagely demanding: even though an embedding model automatically encompasses nested rivals, the resulting parameters may not have sensible interpretations, and parsimonious encompassing is a natural extension of the conceptual framework.

Conversely, encompassing could be viewed as an element in a progressive research strategy, in which case its role would be to stimulate useful conjectures concerning how to reconcile potentially anomalous and disparate evidence. 'Mechanistic procedures' like contracting searches can at best yield convenient data summaries within sample and must await genuine testing: their plausibility depends on their encompassing existing results and having interpretable parameters related to a coherent theory. But 'iterative model building' based on expanding searches likewise lacks credibility unless it satisfies the various selection criteria, including encompassing. By whatever means empirical models are obtained, and whatever criteria they satisfy, they can almost always be tested against other alternatives or re-evaluated at a later date; and they most certainly should be if advocated as a basis for policy.

Finally, a formulation which encompasses both pre-war and postwar data, annual and quarterly observations, the various rounds of data revisions and all the proposed information sets is not yet available; nor have inter-country tests been conducted. Thus, there is plenty of scope for further progression.

Notes

1   Initial conditions are ignored for simplicity of notation.
2   Joint tests are feasible and interesting results have been obtained by Kiviet (1986a) and Godfrey and Wickens (1982) *inter alia*.
3   The transform of (18.18) to the log-normal would add $\frac{1}{2}\hat{\sigma}_v^2$ to the intercept, but that term is negligible here (see for example Kennedy, 1983).
4   I am grateful to John Muellbauer for suggesting this link.

19

Postscript: the Econometrics of PC-GIVE

Preamble

A postscript should be short, pithy and distinctly worth appending: laudable but ambitious aims! The more limited objective of this final chapter is to relate some of the main ideas analysed above to recent developments as a guide to the prospects likely to materialize. The framework that has evolved through the above studies, and many of those on which I have drawn, is as follows:

1 data are generated by a complicated and evolving mechanism created, measured and changed by human actions;
2 empirical models, while suggested by theoretical reasoning and past evidence, actually arise by reduction operations on that mechanism with consequential transformations of the underlying parameters;
3 inappropriate marginalization influences parameter interpretability, constancy and invariance;
4 inappropriate sequential factorization potentially induces residual autocorrelation, *not* to be removed by arbitrarily asserting and imposing common factor restrictions;
5 inappropriate conditional factorization may invalidate exogeneity claims;
6 being created by reduction operations, models are susceptible to design, and a taxonomy of information sets delineates the relevant design criteria and hence the null hypotheses for valid model evaluation tests;
7 the 'problem' approach to econometric modelling is an implicit design process, founded on the *non sequitur* of adopting the alternative hypothesis when a test rejects the null;
8 explicit design procedures which mimic the reduction notion by progressing from the general to the specific have achieved some success in practice, although no sufficient conditions exist to justify any constructive methodology; and
9 parsimonious encompassing sustains a progressive research strategy and determines the limits to reduction; but checking the validity of any entailed reductions necessitates returning to the most general model whenever the information set is extended.

A large number of less central, but nevertheless important, issues in empirical modelling can also be analysed in the same framework, including collinearity as a function of the choice of parameterization; the links of theory models (which are cognitive entities) to empirical models (which are recombinations of observed data); functional form specification; the selection of test statistics; the accuracy of the underlying data series; testing of the Lucas (1976) critique; and encompassing a vector autoregressive representation (VAR) based on the modelling approach in Sims (1980) *inter alia*. To discuss all these topics would require a book in itself and is well beyond the objectives of this last chapter. In fact, since completing this volume in draft, I have written a companion book on *Econometric Methodology* (Hendry, 1992), completing a trilogy on the computational, developmental and methodological aspects of the approach. A fourth book on *Dynamic Econometrics* (Hendry et al.) is in progress, and a separate text on unit roots and cointegration is forthcoming (Banerjee et al., 1992). I hope their availability will allow a more thorough evaluation of the framework. However, the objective of the final chapter is the more limited one of trying to interlink the various strands and approaches in a short space. It has been edited to be more self-contained than in the original publication and, specifically, the typology which duplicates some of chapter 4 has been abbreviated and updated. Since the most time intensive of all my research activities has been computer programming, it seems fitting to end with a chapter based on the software.

1 An Overview

The philosophy underlying the computer program PC-GIVE which embodies the methodology is as follows. Economic time-series data are generated by a process of immense generality and complexity. The econometrician seeks to model the main features of the data generation process (DGP) in a simplified representation based on the observable data and related to prior economic theory. Since many important data features are inevitably assumed absent in any economic theory, empirical models have to be developed interactively to characterize the data adequately and be consistent with the theory. For example, a theory-model might assume white noise errors, whereas the lack of any precise mapping of decision periods to data observation periods may mean that the estimated model manifests substantial residual autocorrelation (perhaps of a seasonal form). Equally, the parameters of the theory may correspond to model coefficients which are not empirically constant over time. PC-GIVE is designed to reveal such 'problems', and more generally to test models destructively.

An important component of any modelling exercise is to estimate the most general model which it is reasonable to entertain *a priori* (see Pagan, 1987). PC-GIVE facilitates formulating general linear dynamic models while offering protection against the possibility that the initial generality is in fact too specific to characterize the available data adequately (see chapters 16 and 17 for greater detail), corresponding loosely to a constructive aspect of modelling. Both of these aspects are analysed below.

Most econometrics packages focus on the estimation of economic models of varying degrees of complexity assuming that their qualitative characteristics are known but the numerical values of the parameters need calibration. While estimation represents a necessary ingredient in econometrics research, it is far from sufficient for practical empirical modelling. PC-GIVE has been explicitly developed to aid the process of discovering 'good' models by offering a wide range of evaluation tools, some of which are sophisticated estimation methods re-oriented to highlight potential model weaknesses. There is no royal road to developing 'good' models, but some considerations which have proved helpful in related studies are discussed below, including an analysis of the criteria by which models might be judged.

In fact, there are many *necessary* but *no sufficient* conditions for model validity. Delineating these necessary conditions, and analysing the intimate links between them, the available information and statistics for evaluating model adequacy, forms the focus for the following discussion.

The class of dynamic linear systems analysed by PC-GIVE is described in section 2 in terms of a model typology. This is followed by discussions of model evaluation in section 3, an information taxonomy for model evaluation and design in section 4, and the types of test used in section 5. Section 6 then considers modelling strategies and the chapter concludes with a brief discussion of estimation techniques in section 7.

2 The Model Class

2.1 Single-equation Models

The class of models basic to PC-GIVE is that of linear dynamic systems. Dynamic linear equation analysis follows from the use of lag operators (denoted by L) such that $L'x_t = x_{t-r}$ for a variable x_t. Scalar polynomials in L are denoted by $a(L) = \sum_{i=m}^{n} a_i L^i$. Lag polynomials like $a(L)$ define either autoregressions when the equation is of the form

$$a(L)y_t = \varepsilon_t \tag{19.1}$$

with $m = 0$ and $a_0 = 1$ where ε_t is white noise (i.e. a serially uncorrelated process), or finite distributed lags if

$$y_t = b(L)x_t + \varepsilon_t. \tag{19.2}$$

The autoregressive–distributed lag (ADL) class is given by

$$a(L)y_t = b(L)x_t + \varepsilon_t. \tag{19.3}$$

Many different xs may be used conjointly if required in models like (19.3), in which case the equation is written in a more convenient notation as

$$b_0(L)y_t = \sum_{i=1}^{k} b_i(L)x_{it} + \varepsilon_t \tag{19.4}$$

if there are k 'explanatory' variables $(x_{1t}, \ldots, x_{kt})$.

Many important properties of the dynamic model (19.3) are determined by the polynomials $a(L)$ and $b(L)$. For example, the model is stable if all the roots λ_i of the polynomial $a(L) = 0$ satisfy $|\lambda_i| < 1$.[1] Further, (19.3) has common factors (denoted COMFAC) if some of the roots of $a(L)$ coincide with roots of $b(L)$, so that, for example, $a(L) = (1 - \rho L)a^*(L)$ and $b(L) = (1 - \rho L)b^*(L)$. In such a case

$$a^*(L)y_t = b^*(L)x_t + u_t \tag{19.5}$$

where $u_t = \rho u_{t-1} + \varepsilon_t$, generating the autoregressive error from a common factor in the structural lag polynomials (see Sargan, 1980a; chapter 6; and section 2.2 below). If (y_t, x_t) are jointly stationary, then

$$\mathscr{E}\left[y_t - \frac{b(1)}{a(1)}x_t\right] = \mathscr{E}(y_t - Kx_t) = 0 \tag{19.6}$$

is the long-run average solution to (19.3), which requires that $a(1) \neq 0$ (i.e. no $\lambda_i = 1$) in order to be well defined and $b(1) \neq 0$ to be non-trivial. If in (19.1) r roots are equal to unity in absolute value, then y_t is non-stationary and is said to be *integrated of order* r, denoted I(r). If $a(1) \neq 0$ and $b(1) \neq 0$ when y_t and x_t are both I(1), but $y_t - Kx_t$ is I(0), then y_t and x_t are said to be *cointegrated* (see Engle and Granger, 1987; Granger, 1986; Hendry, 1986b). The solution in (19.6) remains valid in the cointegrated case, perhaps with an intercept. Section 2.2 assumes that x_t is I(1) and that y_t and x_t are cointegrated.

2.2 A Typology of Simple Dynamic Models

Chapter 4 provides a detailed analysis of single-equation models like (19.4) and shows that most of the widely used empirical models are special cases of (19.4). There are *nine* distinct model types embedded in (19.4), a point most easily seen by considering the special case of $k = n = 1$ and $m = 0$, so that all of the polynomials are first order and only one x variable is involved:

$$y_t = \alpha_1 y_{t-1} + \beta_0 x_t + \beta_1 x_{t-1} + \varepsilon_t \tag{19.7}$$

where $\varepsilon_t \sim \text{IN}(0, \sigma_\varepsilon^2)$ ($\text{IN}(\mu, \sigma^2)$ denotes an independent normal random variable with mean μ and constant variance σ^2).

Equation (19.7) is a special case of a linear single-equation dynamic model, with the apparently restrictive assumption that $\{\varepsilon_t\}$ is a white noise process. Yet most widely used model types are indeed schematically represented in (19.7), and the typology highlights their distinct characteristics, strengths and weaknesses. If any member of the typology is believed to be the model which generated the data, then this belief entails accepting any less restricted but identifiable member, together with the restrictions needed to reduce the general model to the special one asserted. That statement has profound implications not only for the general methodology of modelling espoused herein but also for such major issues of current contention as the practice of 'allowing for residual autocorrelation', the validity of analysing over-identified simultaneous systems (the Sims critique: see Sims, 1980) and the imposition of restrictions based on prior theory, including the 'Lucas critique' (see Lucas, 1976).

To clarify the basis of our approach, table 19.1 lists the nine cases, deriving each via restrictions on the parameter vector $\theta' = (\alpha_1, \beta_0, \beta_1)$ of (19.7), noting that an intercept can be included without loss of generality in all models and is omitted for simplicity of exposition only. Four of the cases impose two restrictions on θ and five impose one, and these will be referred to respectively as one- and two-parameter models since σ^2 is common to all stochastic models (compare table 4.1).

Three important issues must be clarified: the status of $\{x_t\}$; the dependence of

Table 19.1 Typology of simple dynamic models

	Type of model	θ	Entailed restrictions on (19.7)	
(i)	Static regression	$(0, \beta_0, 0)$	$\alpha_1 = \beta_1 = 0$	(no dynamics)
(ii)	Univariate autoregressive process	$(\alpha_1, 0, 0)$	$\beta_0 = \beta_1 = 0$	(no covariates)
(iii)	Leading indicator	$(0, 0, \beta_1)$	$\alpha_1 = \beta_0 = 0$	(no contemporaneity)
(iv)	Growth rate	$(1, \beta_0, -\beta_0)$	$\alpha_1 = 1, \beta_1 = -\beta_0$	(no levels)
(v)	Distributed lag	$(0, \beta_0, \beta_1)$	$\alpha_1 = 0$	(finite lags)
(vi)	Partial adjustment	$(\alpha_1, \beta_0, 0)$	$\beta_1 = 0$	(no lagged x)
(vii)	Autoregressive error (COMFAC)	$(\alpha_1, \beta_0, -\alpha_1\beta_0)$	$\beta_1 = -\alpha_1\beta_0$	(one common factor)
(viii)	Long-run proportionality: error correction	$(\alpha_1, \beta_0, 1-\alpha_1-\beta_0)$	$\alpha_1 + \beta_0 + \beta_1 = 1$	(long-run unit response)
(ix)	Dead-start	$(\alpha_1, 0, \beta_1)$	$\beta_0 = 0$	(only lagged information)

the model's properties on the data properties; and whether each model type is being treated as correctly specified or as an approximation to a more general DGP such as (19.4). These three problems arise in part because the analysis has not commenced from the most general system needed to characterize the observed data adequately, and in part because the DGP is unknown in practice, and so we do not know which data properties to take as salient features in an analytical treatment (never mind the empirical study to follow!). The system formulation is offered in section 2.3, and so for the present we shall treat $\{x_t\}$ as if it were weakly exogenous for the parameters of interest in θ (see chapter 15 and section 4.2 below). As noted earlier, x_t is assumed I(1), and for convenience we will take Δx_t to be a stationary process. This determines the answer to the second issue; but since some economics time series seem I(0) (e.g. unemployment), the case $x_t \sim$ I(0) remains relevant. If x_t and y_t are cointegrated, then $u_t = y_t - Kx_t \sim$ I(0), but such a belief may be false and the case $u_t \sim$ I(1) $\forall K$ must be noted. The typology treats each case in turn as if it were the correct specification, but notes both the historical success of such an assumption and the likely consequences when it is incorrect.

Static Regression

Equations of the form $y_t = b_0 x_t + u_t$ (with b_0 and x_t vectors in general) have played a large role in many macroeconometrics systems as erstwhile 'structural equations'.

In practice, $\{u_t\}$ has usually been highly autocorrelated (reminiscent of nonsense correlations – see Yule, 1926) so that inference about b_0 is invalid (see for example Granger and Newbold, 1974; Phillips, 1986). Recently, however, static equations have reappeared as part of a two-stage strategy for investigating cointegration with the focus on testing whether or not $\{u_t\}$ is I(1) against the alternative that it is I(0) (see Engle and Granger, 1987). Then, b_0 would be a 'direct' estimator of K in (19.6). Even so, the success of such an estimator in finite samples has been questioned (see Banerjee et al., 1986) and must be dependent on the actual mean lag between y and x, noting that a static equation imposes that mean lag at zero. Alternatively, the strategy of removing the autocorrelation in $\{u_t\}$ by fitting an autoregressive process is considered in autoregressive errors (COMFAC models) below. Finally, viewed as a 'structural equation', all the restrictions on dynamics and covariates are testable against (19.4), as are the implicit restrictions highlighted in section 4 below.

Univariate Autoregressive Processes

The equation $y_t = a_1 y_{t-1} + e_t$ serves as our representative of univariate time-series models (see Box and Jenkins, 1976). If y_t is I(1), $a_1 = 1$, inducing a random walk when e_t is white noise. Autoregressive equations are widely used for *ex ante* forecasting and have proved a powerful challenger to econometrics systems in that domain.[2] In economics, the manifest interdependence of economic decisions (e.g. one person's income is another's expenditure) entails that univariate autoregressions *must* be derived and not autonomous processes. Here, the autoregression is obtained by eliminating, or marginalizing with respect to, x_t. For example, let $x_t = x_{t-1} + v_t$ where $v_t \sim \text{IN}(0, \sigma_t^2)$ when in fact $\alpha_1 = 1$ and $\beta_1 = -\beta_0$; then $y_t = y_{t-1} + \varepsilon_t + \beta_0 v_t$ and has a non-constant variance $\sigma_\varepsilon^2 + \beta_0^2 \sigma_t^2$. Consequently econometric models should both fit better than autoregressions (or else are at least dynamically misspecified) and forecast better (or else the econometric model must be highly suspect for policy).

That both these minimal requirements are sometimes not satisfied is due in part to the inappropriateness of some methodological practices. A major objective of PC-GIVE is to offer an alternative approach which circumvents such difficulties by commencing from a general dynamic specification which automatically embeds the relevant special cases.

Leading Indicator

Models of the form $y_t = c_1 x_{t-1} + v_t$ can be used in forecasting if x leads y with sufficient reliability (e.g. orders ahead of output). In the absence of a sound behavioural theory, however, c_1 need not be constant. If it is not, this will lead to poor forecasting, especially in periods of change when good forecasts are most needed. Moreover, there seems no good reason for excluding lagged ys, and if a general dynamic model is postulated then the econometric considerations in sections 3, 4, 5 and 6 apply.

Growth-rate Models

The evolutionary and trend-like behaviour of many economic time series led earlier investigators to recommend differencing data prior to statistical analysis. One example is Granger and Newbold (1977a), although, as argued in chapters 3 and 5, there are other transformations (such as ratios) which potentially could also remove trends. This leads on to the concept of cointegration discussed below. Growth-rate models are of the form

$$\Delta y_t = d_0 \Delta x_t + \eta_t.$$

Such models successfully avoid 'nonsense regressions' problems in I(1) data, and from the transformed dependent variable a useful measure of goodness of fit can be calculated. Nevertheless, if the variance of Δx_t is large relative to that of Δy_t, d_0 must be small even if y_t and x_t are cointegrated with $K = 1$ (this is the 'permanent income' issue in one guise: see chapter 8). Further, although $y_t = Kx_t$ implies $\Delta y_t = K\Delta x_t$, the converse is false in a stochastic world because of integrating the error.

Alternatively, there are no *a priori* grounds for excluding levels from economic relationships since initial disequilibria cannot be assumed to be irrelevant: i.e. the time path of Δy_t for a given sequence Δx_t will also depend in general on the relationship between y_0 and x_0. Two further insights into the drawbacks of growth-rate models are discussed below.

On the methodological level, an egregious mistake still being committed in applied economics is to begin with a linear approximation to a steady-state theory of the form $y_t = f(x_t)$, fit a static model thereto, discover severe residual autocorrelation and 'correct' that either by differencing or by using 'Cochrane–Orcutt' (but see their 1949 article) and finding an autoregressive parameter near unity. While the goodness of fit may not be greatly worsened by imposing differencing, dynamic responses can be substantially distorted and ignoring long-run feedbacks may seriously distort policy.

Distributed Lags

Although using only one lag makes the resulting model highly schematic, the equation $y_t = f_0 x_t + f_1 x_{t-1} + \xi_t$ is representative of the class of finite distributed lags. Such models remain open to the objections noted in static regression above, are highly dependent on whether x_t is weakly or strongly exogenous unless ξ_t is white noise (which in practice it rarely is in this class) and tend to suffer from 'collinearity' due to the inappropriate parameterization of including many levels of the regressor. Imposing so-called '*a priori* restrictions' on the lag coefficients to reduce the profligate parameterization has little to recommend it, although such restrictions are at least potentially testable. It is hard to see any theoretical grounds for completely excluding lagged ys, given that they are another way of representing a distributed lag relationship; and as shown below, considerable dangers exist in arbitrarily removing any residual autocorrelation from ξ_t.

Partial Adjustment

The equation $y_t = g_0 x_t + g_1 y_{t-1} + \zeta_t$ occurs regularly in empirical macroeconomics, and can be derived from assuming a long-run desired target of the form $y_t = K x_t$ subject to quadratic adjustment costs (see for example Eisner and Strotz, 1963; Nickell, 1985). While such a model type seems reasonable in principle, it does *not* entail that the y and x variables which agents use in their decision rules are precisely the levels variables under study by the economist. For example, agents may use the (log of the) consumption–income ratio as their y_t, and the growth rate of income as their x_t, rather than the levels of both.[3] The resulting econometric specification, however, is wholly different despite the common element of 'partial adjustment'.

Even when y_t and x_t are cointegrated in levels, the partial adjustment model has little to recommend it unless it happens to coincide with the DGP. The mean lag is $g_1/(1 - g_1)$ whereas the median lag (the number of periods to reach the half-way stage towards equilibrium) is $-\log 2 g_1/\log g_1$, so that a skewed distribution is imposed without consulting the data: when g_1 is near unity, both measures entail extremely slow adjustment, exacerbated by any untreated positive residual autocorrelation. Further, x_t and y_{t-1} are usually highly correlated and so again an unfortunate parameterization is being selected. Since there are no good arguments for *a priori* excluding all lagged xs and plenty of empirical evidence to show that they do matter in many cases, this model type again seems suspect.[4]

Autoregressive Errors or COMFAC Models

As noted in section 2.1, the roots of $a(L)$ and $b(L)$ in (19.3) may be equal at some lag lengths, allowing cancellation. In the case of (19.7) with $\beta_0 \neq 0$, we can write the equation as

$$(1 - \alpha_1 L)y_t = \beta_0 \left[1 + \frac{\beta_1}{\beta_0} L \right] x_t + \varepsilon_t.$$

Thus, if, and only if, $\alpha_1 = -\beta_1/\beta_0$ or $\beta_1 + \alpha_1\beta_0 = 0$, the equation can be rewritten as $y_t = \beta_0 x_t + \varepsilon_t/(1 - \rho L)$ or

$$y_t = \beta_0 x_t + u_t \tag{19.8}$$

where $u_t = \rho u_{t-1} + \varepsilon_t$ and $\rho = \alpha_1$, yielding a static model with an autoregressive error. The term $1 - \alpha_1 L$ is a factor (in this simple case, the only factor) of $a(L)$ and similarly $1 + (\beta_1/\beta_0)L$ is a factor of $b(L)$, so that when these are equal there is a factor in common in $a(L)$ and $b(L)$ (leading to the name COMFAC). The converse that (19.8) induces a common factor is obvious, and so there is an isomorphism between autoregressive errors and common factors in the lag polynomials: if you believe one, you must believe the other. Clearly, (19.8) imposes restrictions on (19.7), and so these are testable, and rejection entails discarding the supposed reduction to (19.8) (see chapter 6). Therefore the ADL class includes all models with autoregressive errors.

Perhaps the greatest *non sequitur* in the history of econometrics is the assumption that autocorrelated residuals imply autoregressive errors, as is entailed in 'correcting serial correlation using Cochrane–Orcutt'. Dozens of mis-specifications in time-series data will induce residual autocorrelation without corresponding to common factors in the lag polynomials of the underlying general model (19.3). Indeed, the entire order of testing is incorrect: to estimate any models like (19.8) first necessitates establishing the validity of (19.3), then showing that $a(L)$ and $b(L)$ have common factors and finally testing H_0: $\rho = 0$. Showing that $\rho \neq 0$ in equations like (19.8) does *not* prove that there are valid common factor restrictions. PC-GIVE offers algorithms for testing common factor restrictions in equations like (19.4) on the basis of the results in Sargan (1980a) and using his Wald approach. If such restrictions are accepted, generalizations of (19.8) are estimable using the RALS estimator described in Hendry (1989).

Two points of importance from (19.8) are that

1   it imposes a zero mean lag irrespective of the actual lag latencies since the short-run and long-run responses are forced to be equal by the choice of model type, and
2   growth-rate models can be interpreted as imposing a common factor and setting ρ to unity.

Error Correction Mechanisms

The issue of appropriate reparameterizations of θ has arisen on several occasions above and many alternatives are conceivable. One natural choice is as follows: from (19.7)

$$\Delta y_t = (\alpha_1 - 1)y_{t-1} + \beta_0 \Delta x_t + (\beta_1 + \beta_0)x_{t-1} + \varepsilon_t$$
$$= \beta_0 \Delta x_t + (\alpha_1 - 1)(y_{t-1} - Kx_{t-1}) + \varepsilon_t \tag{19.9}$$

where $K = (\beta_0 + \beta_1)/(1 - \alpha_1)$ is the long-run response in (19.6) above. The new parameters in $f(\theta) = \psi = (\beta_0, (1 - \alpha_1), K)'$ correspond to the impact effect, the feedback effect and the long-run response: note that no restrictions are imposed in this transformation. The term $(y - Kx)_{t-1}$ was called an error correction mechanism (ECM) in chapter 8 since it reflects the deviation from the long-run equilibrium outcome, with agents removing $1 - \alpha_1$ of the resulting disequilibrium each period. Sargan (1964a) provides a real-wage example and in chapter 3 some non-unit ECMs were considered. The special case $K = 1$ is of considerable interest in econometrics as it corresponds to long-run proportionality (or homogeneity in log-linear models), but ECMs are well defined for $K \neq 1$, although usually K will then need to be estimated. Indeed, as chapter 4 notes, logistic formulations or more general functions may be necessary to model agents' behaviour if they adjust more or less rapidly depending on the extent of disequilibrium (see Escribano, 1985).

Engle and Granger (1987) establish an isomorphism between ECMs and cointegrated processes: if y_t and x_t are each I(1) and are cointegrated, then there exists an ECM of the form $y - Kx$, and conversely. The former does not entail that the ECM necessarily enters the y_t equation rather than the x_t equation, and it may enter both which would violate weak exogeneity (see Hendry and Mizon (1991) for an example).

In our simple typology, the only ECM case to impose any restrictions on (19.9) is $K = 1$ or $\alpha_1 + \beta_0 + \beta_1 = 1$, revealing that all long-run proportionality theories can be reproduced in static equilibrium by an appropriate ECM. Here, this restriction yields

$$\Delta y = \gamma_0 \Delta x_t - \gamma_1 (y - x)_{t-1} + \omega_t. \tag{19.10}$$

Thus another interpretation of the growth-rate model is revealed, namely that it corresponds to imposing long-run homogeneity ($\alpha_1 + \beta_0 + \beta_1 = 1$) and the absence of feedback from the level $1 - \alpha_1 = 0$, which jointly entail a unit root. Consequently, small values of γ_0 are compatible with long-run proportionality. Further, partial adjustment (see above) now corresponds to imposing $\gamma_0 = -\gamma_1$.

The parameterization in (19.10) has several advantages beyond being more interpretable: the regressors Δx_t and $(y - x)_{t-1}$ will not usually be highly correlated, and proportionality is easily tested by adding x_{t-1} as a (relatively non-collinear) regressor. Further, a less strong lag shape is being imposed, since the mean lag is $(1 - \gamma_0)/\gamma_1$ which depends on both parameters and hence can be small even if $1 - \gamma_1$ is around 0.9, whereas the median lag is zero for $\gamma_0 \geqslant \frac{1}{2}$ and is $-\log[2(1 - \gamma_0)]/\log \gamma_1$ for $\gamma_0 < \frac{1}{2}$.

Note that $\beta_1 < 0$ in (19.7) need not entail any negative weights $\{w_i\}$ in the solved representation $y_t = \sum_{i=0}^{\infty} w_i x_{t-i} + u_t$. Thus, do not delete lagged xs because their coefficients appear to have 'wrong signs', since on a reparameterization they may have the correct sign.

Finally, ECMs can be confused with COMFAC models despite their very different implications for lag responses. This arises because COMFAC is an ECM with the restriction that long-run and short-run responses are equal, as can be seen by rewriting (19.8) in the form $y_t = \beta_0 x_t + \rho(y_{t-1} - \beta_0 x_{t-1}) + \varepsilon_t$ or

$$\Delta y_t = \beta_0 \Delta x_t + (\rho - 1)(y - \beta_0 x)_{t-1} + \varepsilon_t. \tag{19.11}$$

Thus, the degree of mis-specification of (19.11) for (19.9) depends on $(\alpha_1 - 1) \times (K - \beta_0) \neq 0$ which could be small even if $K = 1$ and, for example, $\beta_0 = 0.4$. Nevertheless, despite (19.9) and (19.11) having similar goodness of fit, the mean lag in (19.9) when $K = 1$ could be large at the same time as (19.11) imposes it at zero.

Dead-start Models

The main consideration arising for dead-start models is the exclusion of contemporaneous information. This could be because

$$y_t = \alpha_1 y_{t-1} + \beta_1 x_{t-1} + \varepsilon_t \tag{19.12}$$

is structural, and hence is a partial adjustment type. Alternatively, (19.12) could be a derived form, from which x_t has been eliminated, as with a VAR, in which case (19.12) is unlikely to be autonomous, and its parameters would be susceptible to alteration with changes in the behaviour of the x_t process. In this second case, the coefficients are not interpretable since they are (unknown) functions of the correlations between x_t and (y_{t-1}, x_{t-1}).

Care is obviously required in selecting an appropriate type of model to characterize both a given theory and the associated data: some of the methodological considerations discussed below help clarify that choice.

2.3 Dynamic Systems

When y_t and x_t are vectors, expressions like (19.3) constitute dynamic linear systems. More formally, the system can be written as

$$\pi_0(L)y_t = \pi_1(L)z_t + v_t \tag{19.13}$$

where $\pi_j(L) = \Sigma_{i=0}^{n_j}\pi_{ji}L^i$, $v_t \sim \text{IN}(0, \Omega)$, *and* z_t is weakly exogenous for the parameters of interest in the system.[5] Identity equations can be included, corresponding to singularities in Ω. In (19.13), it is assumed that $\pi_{00} = I$ (the unit matrix) and that $\pi_j(1) \neq 0$ $(j = 0, 1)$ so that y and z are cointegrated. In conventional parlance, (19.13) is a 'reduced form', but since no structural model has been specified from which it can have been reduced, we shall refer to (19.13) as the *system* (see Hendry et al., 1988). If z_t is deterministic, (19.13) is 'closed' and is a VAR. However, at least conceptually, one could imagine extending the system to endogenize z_t and make a bigger VAR, and so if $\pi_{10} = 0$ (19.13) is simply part of a VAR (cut across equations), and if $\pi_{10} \neq 0$ it is a VAR conditional on z_t.

A *model* of the system is created by pre-multiplying (19.13) by a matrix B_0 of full row rank:

$$B_0 y_t = \sum_{i=1}^{n_0} B_0 \pi_{0i} y_{t-i} + \sum_{j=0}^{n_1} B_0 \pi_{1j} z_{t-j} + B_0 v_t \tag{19.14}$$

or

$$B(L)y_t = C(L)z_t + \varepsilon_t \tag{19.15}$$

with $\varepsilon_t \sim \text{IN}(0, \Sigma)$. The system is said to be complete if B_0 is non-singular. Let A be the matrix of all the coefficients $(B_0, -B_1, \ldots, -B_{n_0}, -C_0, \ldots, -C_{n_1})$ and x_t the column vector of all the variables $(y_t, \ldots, y_{t-n_0}, z_t, \ldots, z_{t-n_1})$; then (19.15) can be written neatly as

$$Ax_t = \varepsilon_t \sim \text{IN}(0, \Sigma).$$

A must be restricted if the $\{B_i, C_i\}$ are to be unique: otherwise, a further non-singular multiplication of (19.14) would produce a different model, yet one which looked exactly like (19.15), thereby destroying uniqueness. The usual rank and order conditions apply, and both are fully implemented in PCFIML: consult, for example, Judge et al. (1980). All the model types of section 2.2 could occur within (19.15), and, if A is over-identified, the imposed restrictions are testable.

When developing a model of a system, it seems sensible to commence from the unrestricted representation (19.13), test its validity and then reduce the system to the model. All the attributes needed for congruency (see section 4) can be tested, but care is required in modelling integrated data. As a first step, cointegration tests can be conducted to establish the dimension of the cointegrating space, and the relevant set of cointegration restrictions and differences can be imposed to reduce the data to I(0). This order will facilitate later testing since conventional limiting distributions can be used: see Phillips (1990) and Hendry and Mizon (1991) for discussions of modelling cointegrated processes, Johansen (1988) and Johansen and Juselius (1990) for analyses of the maximum likelihood estimator, and Hendry et al. (1988) for an approach to structural system modelling in I(0) processes. Such a methodology implements the general-to-simple notion in the system context and contrasts with the alternative of specifying a structural model at the outset and testing its restrictions against the (derived) reduced form. Since the latter may be invalid, it provides an unreliable benchmark for any tests. Techniques for estimating systems and associated models, as well as general derivations of standard errors etc., are considered in section 7 below.

Since (19.13) is a model of itself, and there are likely to be valid parsimonious representations of the system (19.13), the critique in Sims (1980) lacks force. Specifying a model in structural form merely corresponds to imposing non-linear restrictions across functions of the πs in (19.13), and one cannot *a priori* exclude such restrictions being valid. For example, if the response of y to x in (19.7) is very rapid compared with that of x to y in a second equation, a structural model of their joint representation can impose valid restrictions on the VAR. The concept of encompassing discussed in section 4 will clarify this issue further.

3 Model Evaluation

While it is easy to specify and analyse (19.3), (19.4) or (19.15) (or any generalizations thereof) when they are regarded as mathematical formulations, it is far harder to develop useful empirical relationships for a given time series on a set of variables. In particular, the orders of the lag lengths of every polynomial ($a(L)$, $b(L)$ etc.) must be established, as must the presence or absence of any given x, the constancy of the entities called parameters, and the properties of the error term. Indeed, this description begs the very issue of what defines the 'usefulness' of an econometric relationship. At a general level, the utility of anything clearly depends on the purposes for which it is being developed. Hence if a completely specified loss function existed for judging a particular modelling exercise, it would seem natural to develop a model to optimize that criterion. Two problems arise, however, neither of which can be sidestepped. First, it is very rare in econometrics to be able to specify the loss function fully. Models are wanted for prediction, for scenario or policy analyses, for testing economics hypotheses and for understanding how the economy functions. Empirically, there often exist conflicts in criteria for selecting models to achieve such multiple objectives. For example, a model which predicts well historically may yield no insight into how a market will behave under some change in regulations, the implementation of which will cause the model to mispredict. Second, even assuming that a fully specified loss function did exist and that the optimal model could be selected, there remains the difficulty of establishing how 'good' that best model is. For example, the best model that could be found may still suffer from non-constant parameters and hence yield a low level of utility; worse still, by not knowing this weakness, serious losses may accrue in the future. Thus, whatever the basis on which a model has been formulated or developed, there is an issue of assessment or evaluation.

To use the program PC-GIVE easily and efficiently, it is essential that this aspect be understood. Since we do not know how the economy works, we do not know the best way of studying it. Consequently, any model might correspond to reality, however unlikely its mode of creation; or unfortunately it might transpire to be invalid, however clever and thorough its development. Nevertheless, conditional on taking a model as stated by its proprietor, a vast range of states of the world will be excluded by that model and thus it is open to evaluation against the available information (see Hendry (1987) for a more extensive analysis). For example, because its residual process is white noise, a particular model may claim to explain a given data set adequately; yet the residuals may not be an innovation process, and so testing the latter hypothesis might reveal an important model weakness (as in the COMFAC procedure discussed in section 2 above). This is the destructive testing aspect of PC-GIVE and accounts for its wide range of pre-programmed statistics for model evaluation.

Testing concentrates on the empirical validity of assertions about a given model. Tests are statistics with a known distribution under a null hypothesis and some power against a specific alternative. The tests below are designed to have central t, F or χ^2 distributions under the null, and corresponding non-central distributions against some alternative. Usually, they are invariant to the direction of the departure from the null for a given class of alternatives and only depend on the distance (this holds for t^2, F and χ^2 statistics). However, most tests also have some power to detect other alternatives, and so rejecting the null does *not* entail accepting the alternative, and in many instances accepting the alternative would be a *non sequitur*. Rejection reveals model invalidity, albeit with some chance of a type I error of incorrectly rejecting a valid null.

First, however, we need to delineate the relevant class of null hypotheses, and then derive associated test statistics for reasonable alternatives. The former task is considered in section 4 in terms of a taxonomy of available information and the latter in section 5 where the main test principles are briefly described.

4 An Information Taxonomy

In the case of (19.3), the data set of observations on $\{y_t\}$ and $\{x_t\}$ can be denoted by $W_t^1 = (w_1, \ldots w_t)$ where $w_t' = (y_t\, x_t)$. Thus, $W_T^1 = (W_{t-1}^1: w_t: W_T^{t+1})$ yields the trichotomy of the (past: present: future) relative to t. In addition, we must allow for theory information, measurement information and the information in rival models (see chapters 16 and 17 and Gilbert (1986) for expositions). Statistical tests can be constructed to evaluate a model against each element of this taxonomy. Such tests require both formulation of the appropriate null hypothesis for the relevant information set and devising of a reasonable class of alternatives against which the test should have power. The taxonomy clarifies the relevant null hypotheses, and generally points up interesting alternatives against which to test model validity. The six major information sets for model evaluation are discussed in the next six subsections and are drawn together in the theory of reduction in section 4.7.

4.1 The Relative Past

The residuals should be white noise (unpredictable from their own past) and hence should not be significantly autocorrelated. If they are autocorrelated, a better fitting model can be developed by 'removing' the autocorrelation (although this is *not* a recommended practice since it may impose invalid common factors). PC-GIVE provides valid tests and diagnostic information for residual autocorrelation, including Lagrange multiplier tests for a wide range of orders of autoregressive errors, as well as residual correlograms and autoregressions.

Further, the errors should not be explainable from the information set being used. Alternatively expressed, the errors should be an innovation process which is unpredictable from lagged functions of the available data; being white noise is a necessary, but *not* sufficient, condition for being an innovation. As noted, a good example arises when 'removing' autocorrelation by fitting, say, autoregressive error processes, since that automatically ensures the former but may impose invalid common factor restrictions and hence does not entail the latter (see Sargan, 1964a, 1980b). This problem can be avoided by beginning with a general specification like (19.4) and testing for valid common factors prior to imposing them. In PC-GIVE, the COMFAC tests to check such restrictions are based on Sargan's algorithms.

More formally, denote the process generating W_T^1 by $D(W_T^1|\theta_T^1, W_0)$ where W_0 are the initial conditions and θ_T^1 are the 'parameters' of the process, which may depend on the historical time (hence indexing by 1, ..., T). Since $W_T^1 = (w_1 \ldots w_T)$, the data density $D(\cdot)$ can be sequentially factorized as $\Pi_{t=1}^T D(w_t|W_{t-1}^1, \theta_t, W_0)$ which is the product of each time period's density.[6] Assume $\theta_t = \theta \; \forall t$ (constancy is the topic of section 4.3 to follow) and let W_{t-1} include the initial conditions so that $D(\cdot)$ at every t is $D(w_t|\theta, W_{t-1})$. Then

$$D(W_T^1|\theta, W_0) = \prod_{t=1}^T D(w_t|\theta, W_{t-1}).$$

If we let $\nu_t = w_t - \mathscr{E}(w_t|W_{t-1})$, then by construction $\{\nu_t\}$ is a mean innovation process precisely because $\mathscr{E}(\nu_t|W_{t-1}) = 0$. Moreover, since lagged νs can be derived from W_{t-1} (by lagging their definition), they are also white noise. Thus, the DGP can be expressed without loss in an innovation-error representation. A well-known example is provided by the stationary first-order autoregressive process $y_t = \mu y_{t-1} + e_t$, when $\{e_t\}$ is jointly normal and $\mathscr{E}(e_t e_s) = 0 \; \forall t \neq s$. Then, $D(y_1 \ldots y_T|\mu, \sigma_e^2, y_0)$ is the multivariate normal density $N(0, \sigma_e^2\Omega)$ where Ω is a $T \times T$ symmetric matrix with (i, j)th element $\mu^{|i-j|}/(1 - \mu^2)$. The factorization of the joint density of $(y_1 \ldots y_T)$ into $\Pi_{t=1}^T D(y_t|Y_{t-1}; \mu, \sigma_e^2)$ yields a product of individual densities involving terms like $N(\mu y_{t-1}, \sigma_e^2)$ and

$$\nu_t = y_t - \mathscr{E}(y_t|Y_{t-1}) = y_t - \mathscr{E}(y_t|y_{t-1}) = y_t - \mu y_{t-1} = e_t$$

is indeed the innovation (see for example Judge et al., 1980, ch. 8).

Neither white noise errors nor innovations need be homoscedastic, and so the standard errors of OLS estimators in PC-GIVE also allow for residual heteroscedasticity (see White, 1980b; MacKinnon and White, 1985). Tests of both ARCH

(Engle, 1982a) and unconditional heteroscedasticity are provided. Similarly, tests for normality are included to check on the distributional assumptions underlying finite sample inference.

To summarize these aspects relating to the (relative) past of the process, namely W_{t-1}^1, a reasonable null is that the unexplained component of a behavioural model should be a homoscedastic innovation.

4.2 The Relative Present

All current-dated regressors to be conditioned on should be at least weakly exogenous (see chapter 15) to sustain valid and efficient inferences. Using the factorization in section 4.1, if y_t is to be conditioned on x_t we need

$$D(w_t|\theta, W_{t-1}) = D(y_t|x_t, W_{t-1}, \phi_1)D(x_t|W_{t-1}, \phi_2),$$

where ϕ_1 and ϕ_2 are variation free (i.e. impose no restrictions on each other) and all of the parameters of interest can be obtained from ϕ_1 *alone*. If so, x_t is said to be weakly exogenous for those parameters of interest and only the conditional model $D(y_t|x_t, W_{t-1}, \phi_1)$ needs to be estimated, since the marginal model $D(x_t|W_{t-1}, \phi_2)$ contains no information about the parameters of interest.

While weak exogeneity is not easy to test directly, tests based on Engle (1984) can be calculated from stored regression predictions. However, valid conditioning in conjunction with other hypotheses may entail many testable hypotheses: for example, parameter constancy in a structural equation, despite non-constancy in a reduced form or marginal process, strongly supports weak exogeneity (see Favero and Hendry, 1989). Note that lagged variables are predetermined once the errors are innovations. Conversely, parameters of current endogenous variables (other than the dependent variable) should be estimated using instrumental variables or full information maximum likelihood techniques. Moreover, any instruments chosen must themselves be weakly exogenous for the parameters of interest.

Thus, for the (relative) present, namely w_t above, the crucial null hypothesis is that the conditioning variables (regressors or instruments) are valid.

4.3 The Relative Future

The 'parameters' should be constant over time, where such parameters are those entities which are anticipated on *a priori* grounds to be the basic invariants of the model. Here, an invariant is a parameter which remains constant over a range of interventions or regime shifts in policy or marginal variables. If x_t in (19.7) is weakly exogenous for θ, and θ is invariant to changes in the distribution of $\{x_t\}$, then x_t is super exogenous for θ. In this formulation, constancy is necessary for invariance.

Much of the power of PC-GIVE resides in its recursive procedures. These are a vital tool for investigating issues of invariance and super exogeneity by showing that the behaviour of the x_t process did actually alter without changing the parameters of interest. This is one way of testing assertions that parameters are liable to suffer from the Lucas critique (see Hendry, 1988b).

To understand the basis of recursive estimation, we adopt a notation similar to that in textbook treatments. Denote the specified equation by

$$y_t = \beta' x_t + u_t$$

where β is asserted to be constant, $\mathscr{E}(x_t u_t) = 0 \; \forall t$ and $\mathscr{E}(u_t u_s) = \delta_{ts} \sigma^2 \; \forall t, \; s$ ($\delta_{ts} = 1$ if $t = s$ and is zero otherwise). Let the complete sample period be $(1, \ldots, T)$ and consider the least squares outcome on a subsample up to t (for $t > k$ when there are k regressors in x_t): $\hat{\beta}_t = (X_t' X_t)^{-1} X_t' Y_t$ with $X_t = (x_1 \ldots x_t)'$ and $Y_t = (y_1 \ldots y_t)'$. If the sample were increased by one observation, then

$$X_{t+1}' X_{t+1} = X_t' X_t + x_{t+1} x_{t+1}' \quad \text{and} \quad X_{t+1}' Y_{t+1} = X_t' Y_t + x_{t+1} y_{t+1}.$$

However, given $(X_t' X_t)^{-1}$, one does not need to invert $(X_{t+1}' X_{t+1})$ to calculate $\hat{\beta}_{t+1}$. Rather

$$(X_{t+1}' X_{t+1})^{-1} = (X_t' X_t)^{-1} - \frac{\lambda_{t+1} \lambda_{t+1}'}{1 + \lambda_{t+1}' x_{t+1}}$$

where $\lambda_{t+1} = (X_t' X_t)^{-1} x_{t+1}$. Thus, the inverse can be sequentially updated and $\hat{\beta}_{t+1}$ follows directly. A similar updating formula is available for updating the residual sum of squares (RSS) from the innovations given by

$$\text{RSS}_{t+1} = \text{RSS}_t + \frac{v_{t+1}^2}{1 + \lambda_{t+1}' x_{t+1}}$$

where $v_t = y_t - x_t' \hat{\beta}_{t-1}$. Hence equation and parameter standard errors are readily calculated:

$$\hat{\sigma}_{t+1}^2 = \frac{\text{RSS}_{t+1}}{t - k + 1}$$

and

$$\text{var}(\hat{\beta}_{t+1}) = \hat{\sigma}_{t+1}^2 (X_{t+1}' X_{t+1})^{-1}.$$

Finally, from the sequence of $\{\text{RSS}_t\}$, sequences of tests (e.g. for parameter constancy) can be calculated, based on Chow (1960).

If instrumental variables estimators are used, the recursive formulae are similar but more cumbersome (see Hendry and Neale, 1987). For both types of recursive estimator, a large volume of output is generated which can be analysed graphically, e.g. plotting $\{\text{RSS}_t\}$ against t and so on. The systems estimator is again similar in structure except that y_t becomes a vector of endogenous variables at time t.

Thus, in this group of tests about the (relative) future, denoted above by W_T^{t+1}, the crucial null is parameter constancy.

4.4 Theory Information

Econometrics is essentially concerned with the mutual interplay of economic theory and empirical evidence. Neither has precedence, and both are essential. It is difficult to characterize this information source in the abstract, partly because it is so pervasive and partly because it is itself under scrutiny. The role which theory information plays depends on the precise context, as is easily seen by contrasting exercises modelling the demand for cheese with either modelling the supply of money or the determination of an international exchange rate. Through national income accounts concepts, economics affects the measurement of the data variables, and theory-models influence the choice of the data to examine and the classes of models and functional forms to use, as well as suggesting what parameterization is of interest. Conversely, a major objective of a study in economics may be to test the validity of some theoretical propositions.

Not all theories are equal, and indeed theories differ greatly in their 'level', some being very low level and well established (e.g. those concerned with measuring the output of apples or the volume of visible imports), some being medium level and widely used but potentially open to revision as knowledge improves (e.g. price indices or concepts of the capital stock) and yet others being high level and under test (e.g. a rational expectations intertemporal substitution theory of labour supply, or a surplus-rent theory of house price determination). Thus, that all observations are theory laden does not entail that data-based studies are impossible or even misguided; rather, the respective roles of evidence and theory will vary with the reliability of each in the given context (for a more extensive discussion, see Hendry, 1992).

To test any theory requires a baseline, and so first one must determine the extent to which that baseline satisfies the evaluation criteria. Thus, we are led to distinguish between the statistical model and the econometric model, where the former is the baseline and is judged on statistical criteria, and the latter is interpreted in the light of the economic theory but tested against the former (see for example Spanos, 1986). This distinction is at its clearest for the system and the model thereof in the PCFIML module, where a test of over-identifying restrictions is automatically calculated to check the coherence between the two.

Overall, one can do little better than state the need for an econometric model to be theory consistent.

4.5 Measurement Information

This too is not open to a general discussion, but relates to the issue of data admissibility: could a given model logically have generated the observed and future potential data? For example, the unemployment rate must lie between zero and unity; a logit transformation ensures that, but a linear model could generate negative unemployment (see White (1990) for a critique). The relevance of such considerations depends on the problem under study, but since (for example) cointegration between the logarithms of any given set of $I(1)$ variables need not entail cointegration between the levels, choosing the appropriate functional form can be vitally important.

4.6 Rival Models

The final necessary condition to ensure that a model is in the set of useful contenders is that it is not dominated (in some sense) by another model. More stringently, one might desire that no other model (M_2 say) explained features of the data which one's own model (M_1) could not. This idea is formalized in the notion of encompassing other models, to test whether they capture any specific information not embodied in a given model (see chapter 8; Mizon, 1984; Mizon and Richard, 1986; Hendry and Richard, 1989). Thus, any contending model should encompass (i.e. account for) previous empirical findings claimed to explain the given dependent variable(s). Encompassing is denoted by E; thus if the relevant models are M_1 and M_2, M_1 E M_2 reads as 'M_1 encompasses M_2'.

The ease of handling general models allows embedding approaches to be almost automatic in PC-GIVE. Encompassing and non-nested hypotheses tests are offered for OLS and instrumental variables, based on Cox (1961), Pesaran (1974) and Ericsson (1983), that allow pairs of single-equation models to be tested directly. As argued in Hendry and Richard (1989), encompassing essentially requires a simple model to explain a more general one within which it is nested (often the union of the simple model with its rivals); this notion is called parsimonious encompassing and is denoted by E_p.

A crucial property of parsimonious encompassing is its transitivity in the population (degrees of freedom changes in a sample, as always, can induce reversals). Let $\subset$ denote nesting and consider $M_1 \subset M_2 \subset M_3$. If $M_1 E_p M_2$ and $M_2 E_p M_3$, then $M_1 E_p M_3$. This follows because when $M_1 E_p M_2$ and $M_2 E M_1$ (by virtue of nesting it), then M_1 represents a limit to which M_2 can be validly reduced (although further reduction may be feasible as is entailed, for example, by the sequence $M_3 \rightarrow M_2 \rightarrow M_1$). Since M_2 is a valid reduction of M_3 by hypothesis, then M_1 must also be a valid reduction of M_3. Indeed, despite encompassing initially arising as a distinct concept in a different research area, it is an intimate component of the theory of reduction discussed in section 4.7 and a further major reason for adopting a general-to-specific methodology.

Let M^m be the minimal nesting model of two non-nested models M_1 and M_4 (so that neither M_1 nor M_4 is a special case of the other). M^m may be hard to synthesize, and may not be unique without arbitrary restrictions, but this difficulty actually reflects the inherent problems of any specific-to-general approach and is not a difficulty for encompassing *per se*: the relevant issue of interest here is when M_1 does or does not encompass M_4, not the route by which the problem arose. If $M_1 E_p M^m$, then M_4 can contain no specific information not already embodied in M_1 (since otherwise M^m would reflect that information and M_1 could not be a valid reduction). Conversely, if $M_1 E M_4$ then $M_1 E_p M^m$. Thus, it should not matter whether M_1 is tested against M_4, $M_1 \cup M_4 = M^m$ or any combination thereof (including the orthogonal complement of M^m relative to M_1). Tests which are invariant to such common variables consequently seem essential, and the F test has that property for linear models.

In the multi-equation context, the econometric model should encompass the statistical system (usually a VAR or unrestricted reduced form) and this is the test for over-identifying restrictions noted above (see Hendry and Mizon, 1991).

Consequently, the crucial null hypothesis in this information set is that the econometric model should parsimoniously encompass the statistical system.

4.7 The Theory of Reduction

We now draw together the elements of the taxonomy. The key concept underpinning the above analysis is that models are reductions of the DGP, obtained by transforming the initial variables to those which are to be investigated; marginalizing with respect to the many variables deemed irrelevant (but perhaps incorrectly treated as such); sequentially factorizing as in subsection (1); and conditioning on other variables deemed to be weakly exogenous (as in subsection (2)): see chapter 17 and Hendry (1987). Every reduction induces a transformation of the original parameters λ of the DGP; consequently, invalid reductions may result in the coefficients of the selected model not being constant or invariant or even interpretable (as in so-called 'wrong signs'). Thus, implicitly the analysis really begins with a far bigger set of variables U_T^1 (say) than the set W_T^1 considered by the current group of investigators, so for example U includes all the disaggregated variables which were eliminated when only aggregate time series were retained for analysis. The process of elimination or reduction then transforms λ into the θ_T^1 used above, although nothing guarantees that λ itself is constant.

The taxonomy of information sets (1)–(6) arises naturally when considering each possible reduction step, so that reduction theory is invaluable in the context of model evaluation for delineating null hypotheses and in the context of discovery for specifying the relevant design criteria. It also offers insights into many of the central concepts of econometrics in terms of whether a reduction does or does not involve a loss of information. Thus, we can consider the reverse of the taxonomy by relating extant concepts to associated reduction steps.

1   The theory of sufficient statistics concerns when reduction by marginalizing with respect to a subset of observations retains all the information relevant to the parameters of interest, which is of key interest in aggregation.

2   The concept of Granger non-causality concerns when there is no loss of information from marginalizing with respect to the entire history of a subset of variables (e.g. the elements of U_{t-1} which are not included in W_{t-1}): this concept is germane to marginalizing and not to conditioning (contrast Sims (1980) with chapter 15).

3   The concept of an innovation concerns when there is no information remaining in lagged data: as shown above, all models can be expressed with innovation errors via sequential factorization; thus, all forms of autocorrelated error representation are at best 'convenient simplifications'.

4   The concept of weak exogeneity concerns when there is no loss from ignoring information in the marginal distributions of the conditioning variables.

5   The concept of invariance or autonomy concerns when the reduction sequence has successfully isolated 'basic parameters' of the DGP.

6   The concept of encompassing concerns when alternative models contain no additional information about the variables being modelled, so that an encompassing model represents a limit (though not necessarily the final limit) to the set of feasible reductions.

The theory of reduction also clarifies and extends the theory of encompassing by revealing that all models are comparable via the DGP. Indeed, the concept of reduction points up that model design is endemic, but because all models must arise as reductions of the DGP the pertinent issue is their validity, not how they were designed. Some designs are inadvertent (as when 'residual autocorrelation is removed') whereas others are deliberate (as in general to specific). Thus, reduction theory even explains why the 'problems' approach to econometric modelling arises: overly reduced empirical representations of the DGP will usually manifest all sorts of symptoms of mis-specification. However, badly designed models will often result from sequentially 'correcting' these symptoms by adopting the alternative hypothesis corresponding to every null hypothesis that is rejected (see Hendry, 1979a).

Models that are satisfactory against all six of the above information sets are called congruent (with the available information). Succinctly, PC-GIVE is designed for efficiently developing congruent models and for evaluating existing models for potential departures from congruency.

5 Test Types

Various test principles are commonly used in econometrics and the three main ones are Wald, Lagrange multiplier (LM) and likelihood ratio (LR) tests (see Breusch and Pagan, 1980; Engle, 1984). For example, the Chow (1960) test for parameter constancy is derivable from all three principles, whereas the test of over-identifying restrictions is LR, the portmanteau tests for autocorrelation in OLS are based on LM and the COMFAC tests are Wald tests. In each instance, the choice of test type tends to reflect computational ease. Under the relevant null hypothesis and for local alternatives, the three test types are asymptotically equivalent; however, if equations are mis-specified in other ways than that under test, or the sample size is small, different inferences can result.

Although LM tests conventionally come in the form TR^2 where T is the sample size and R^2 is the squared multiple correlation (TR^2 is distributed as χ^2), recent research indicates that F forms have more appropriate significance levels and that χ^2 versions reject acceptable models too often (see Kiviet, 1986b).[7] Thus, PC-GIVE tends to report F forms when possible. Pagan (1984) exposits testing in terms of residual diagnostic procedures. Further details on econometric testing can be found in Harvey (1981a), Spanos (1986) or relevant chapters of *The Handbook of Econometrics* (Griliches and Intriligator, 1984).

While a basic feature of PC-GIVE is that most of the test statistics are calculated by a simple choice from a menu, others are inbuilt (e.g. parameter constancy tests are undertaken if the user initially specifies some post-sample observations). Similar considerations apply to tests for the validity of any given choice of instrumental variables, and to the significance of lagged variables in VAR or unrestricted reduced form representations, as well as tests of over-identifying restrictions in systems.

6 Modelling Strategies

Turning now to constructive aspects, since the DGP is unknown, any method of discovery might produce a Nobel-prize winning model, as illustrated by the apocryphal tale of Archimedes' 'Eureka' or Poincaré's memoirs. Nevertheless, different research strategies are likely to have different efficiencies. If one needs to estimate 'literally hundreds of regressions' to develop a single linear relationship between four or five variables, that strategy would seem to have a low level of efficiency relative to an approach which could locate at least as 'good' a model in a couple of steps. This is the second aspect of PC-GIVE, whereby it facilitates 'general-to-specific' model simplification approaches (see for example Mizon, 1977a; and chapter 6). Unsurprisingly, these mimic the theory of reduction in section 4.7. Thus, PC-GIVE provides easy ways of formulating polynomials like $a(L)$; solves for $a(1)$, $b(1)$ etc. (where n might be 8 for quarterly data) for both single equations and vector processes and provides associated standard errors; and tests for whether $(x_{t-m} \cdots x_{t-n})$ as a group contribute to the model's explanatory power. For single equations, common factor (COMFAC) simplifications are checked and long-run coefficients such as K in (19.6) are derived together with standard errors. Finally, all the necessary conditions for model validity which were discussed in section 4 above can be checked.

Naturally, a premium rests on a sensible specification of the initial general model and here is where both economic theory and previous studies (to be encompassed in due course) play a major guiding role. Economic theories are powerful at specifying long-run equilibria (such as (19.6) above) which delineate the menu of variables, and earlier work often indicates at least minimal lag length requirements. Once formulated, the general model should be tranformed to an interpretable (probably orthogonal) parameterization and then simplified before rigorous testing. More detailed discussions are provided in Hendry (1986a, 1987, 1992).

7 Model Estimation

Like many of the other aspects considered above, appropriate estimation is a necessary rather than a sufficient condition for developing useful models. Given a particular model form and a distributional assumption about the data, the log-likelihood function can be formulated and is denoted $L(\theta)$ where θ is the vector of unknown parameters of interest. Maximum likelihood estimators (MLEs) solve $\partial L/\partial \theta = 0$ for $\hat{\theta}$, although that system of first-order conditions may be non-linear and require iterative solution methods. In large samples, for correctly specified problems, MLEs have many excellent statistical properties. Moreover, for simultaneous equations models linear in both variables and parameters, almost all other estimation methods can be obtained as approximate solutions of $\partial L/\partial \theta = 0$, based on choosing different initial values θ_0 and selecting different numbers of iterative steps in alternative numerical methods. Thus, estimation within PC-GIVE is encapsulated in a simple formula called the estimator generating equation (EGE: see chapters 13 and 17 and Hendry et al., 1988). Here we note that OLS and instrumental variables estimation are special cases of the EGE when an individual equation is being studied (even if that equation is implicitly part of a system).

The standard errors of $\hat{\theta}$ are usually calculated from the inverse of the Hessian

$$H = -\frac{1}{T}\left(\frac{\partial^2 L}{\partial\theta\partial\theta'}\right),$$

although that formula assumes a correctly specified error (i.e. a homoscedastic innovation). In PC-GIVE, heteroscedastic consistent standard errors can be computed for OLS.

The distributional assumptions for $\hat{\theta}$ implicit in the inference of PC-GIVE are that, conditional on having a congruent representation,

$$T^{1/2}\,R(\hat{\theta} - \theta) \xrightarrow{\text{D}} N(0,\,I)$$

where T is the sample size, the probability limit of $\hat{\theta}$ is θ (the invariant parameter of interest) and $V = \text{plim } H^{-1}$ such that $V^{-1} = R'R$. This assumes that variables are transformed to I(0) and that all the components of congruency are valid. Naturally, these assumptions should be rigorously evaluated in order to sustain such a conditioning claim since 'the three golden rules of econometrics are test, test and test' (see chapter 1). If a function of θ is of interest, say $g(\theta) = \phi$, the standard errors of $\hat{\phi} = g(\hat{\theta})$ are derived from the Taylor series approximation

$$\hat{\phi} - \phi = J(\hat{\theta} - \theta) \tag{19.16}$$

where $J = \partial g(\theta)/\partial\theta'$ is the Jacobian of the transformation, and hence

$$T^{1/2}(\hat{\phi} - \phi) \xrightarrow{\text{D}} N(0,\,JVJ'). \tag{19.17}$$

J can usually be derived analytically for cases of interest, but otherwise can be calculated by numerical differentiation.

The preceding analysis of estimation (and implicitly also of testing) sidesteps an important issue which textbook notation also tends to camouflage, namely that estimation methods and associated tests are applied to the whole sample directly rather than recursively (adding observations one at a time). As stressed above, PC-GIVE incorporates a variety of recursive estimators including recursive least squares and recursive instrumental variables and the generalization of the former to a system of equations with common regressors. Such recursive estimators can yield evaluation information in a powerful way, yet for least squares are not computationally burdensome relative to direct methods (see Hendry and Neale, 1987).

8 Conclusion

We have completed our journey through the development of a methodology for empirical modelling of economic time series. The approach arose from my failures in applying pre-existing methods, described in part I, and the apparent lack of progressivity in empirical knowledge in the profession. It then gradually evolved through a series of applied studies which resolved some difficulties but at the cost of creating others. That aspect is traced in part II, which concluded at a stage where the various successful themes could be integrated into a formal structure. The process of formalization was described in part III which showed how each idea led to others in a mutually supporting sequence. Finally, part IV exposited the formalization in terms of the empirical problem which figured most prominently in the book and updated the analysis to the present. The primary aim of the book was to clarify the current status of the methodology by reviewing its evolution, since the reasons for excluding certain approaches help account for the adoption of others.

I also hope that the book has managed to capture the intellectual excitement engendered by developments wherein a clarification or new concept in one area resolves a major stumbling block in another, such that a comprehensive framework emerges from the shadows as an integrated network of ideas, concepts, tools and practices founded on successful empirical studies. If it has done so, it will have achieved its second main objective.

Notes

1   The actual roots of $a(L) = 0$ are the inverse of the $\{\lambda_i\}$, and the term root here is a shorthand for eigenroot, where $a(L)$ is viewed as a scalar matrix polynomial, for consistency with eigenroots of dynamic systems below.

2   See for example Nelson (1972) and more recently the vector analogues in Doan et al. (1984).

3   The latter anyway seems suspect since few consumers appear to suffer great adjustment costs in response to increases in their expenditure when income has risen.

4   Lags would arise naturally if y and x were not the levels the economist selects.

5   x_t in (19.3) may well be 'endogenous' in the sytem context (19.13) even though it is not jointly determined with y_t in (19.3). Also, n_j in (19.13) may differ between y_t and z_t as well as between variables within that partition.

6   This exploits the fact that if $P(a)$ denotes the probability of an event a, then $P(ab) = P(a|b)P(b)$, and this can be repeated starting at T, $T - 1$, $\ldots$, 1.

7   Incidentally, Kiviet's results also show that the Chow test and LM tests for autocorrelated residuals are approximately independently distributed.

References

Aigner, D.J. (1971) 'A compendium on estimation of the autoregressive moving average model from time series data', *International Economic Review*, **12**, 348–69.

Aitchison, J. (1962) 'Large sample restricted parameter tests', *Journal of the Royal Statistical Society*, B, **20**, 234–50.

Aitchison, J. and Silvey, S.D. (1960) 'Maximum likelihood estimation and associated tests of significance', *Journal of the Royal Statistical Society*, B, **22**, 154–71.

Allen, R.G.D. (1963) *Mathematical Economics*, 2nd edn, London: Macmillan.

Amemiya, T. (1966) 'Specification analysis in the estimation of parameters of a simultaneous equations model with autoregressive residuals', *Econometrica*, **34**, 283–306.

Amemiya, T. (1980) 'Selection of regressors', *International Economic Review*, **21**, 331–54.

Anderson, G.J. (1974) 'Building society behaviour', Unpublished M.Sc. Dissertation, London School of Economics.

Anderson, G.J. and Hendry, D.F. (1984) 'An econometric model of United Kingdom building societies', *Oxford Bulletin of Economics and Statistics*, **46**, 185–210.

Anderson, T.W. (1958) *An Introduction to Multivariate Statistical Analysis*, New York: Wiley.

Anderson, T.W. (1971) *The Statistical Analysis of Time Series*, New York: Wiley.

Anderson, T.W. (1976) 'Estimation of linear functional relationships: approximate distributions and connections with simultaneous equations in econometrics (with discussion), *Journal of the Royal Statistical Society*, B, **38**, 1–36.

Anderson, T.W. (1980) 'Maximum likelihood estimation for vector autoregressive moving average models', in D.R. Brillinger and G.C. Tiao (eds), *New Directions in Time Series*, New York: Institute of Mathematical Statistics, pp. 45–59.

Anderson, T.W. and Rubin, H. (1949) 'Estimation of the parameters of a single equation in a complete system of stochastic equations', *Annals of Mathematical Statistics*, **20**, 46–63.

Ando, A. and Modigliani, F. (1963) 'The "life cycle" hypothesis of saving: aggregate implications and tests', *American Economic Review*, **53**, 55–84.

Artis, M.J. and Lewis, M.K. (1976) 'The demand for money in the United Kingdom: 1963–1973', *The Manchester School*, **43**, 147–81.

Astrom, K.J. (1970) *Introduction to Stochastic Control Theory*, New York: Academic Press.

Baba, Y., Hendry, D.F. and Starr, R.M. (1992) 'The demand for M1 in the USA, 1960–1988', *Review of Economic Studies*, **59**, 25–60.

Ball, R.J. and Burns, T. (1968) 'An econometric approach to short run analysis of the UK economy, 1955–66', *Operational Research Quarterly*, **19**, 225–56.

Ball, R.J. and Drake, P.S. (1964) 'The relationship between aggregate consumption and wealth', *International Economic Review*, **5**, 63–81.

Ball, R.J., Boatwright, D.B., Burns, T., Lobban, P.W.M. and Miller, G.W. (1975) 'The London Business School quarterly econometric model of the UK economy', in G.A. Renton (ed.), *Modelling the Economy*, London: Heinemann Educational, ch. 1.

Banerjee, A., Dolado, J.J., Hendry, D.F. and Smith, G. (1986) 'Exploring equilibrium relationships in econometrics through static models: some Monte Carlo evidence', *Oxford Bulletin of Economics and Statistics*, **48**, 253–77.

Banerjee, A., Dolado, J.J., Galbraith, J.W. and Hendry, D.F. (1992) *Co-integration, Error Correction and the Econometric*, Analysis of Non-Stationary Data, Oxford: Oxford University Press.

Barndorff-Nielsen, O.E. (1978) *Information and Exponential Families in Statistical Theory*, New York: Wiley.

Barro, R.J. (1978) 'Unanticipated money, output and the price level in the United States', *Journal of Political Economy*, **86**, 549–80.

Basmann, R.L. (1957) 'A generalized classical method of linear estimation of coefficients in a structural equation', *Econometrica*, **25**, 77–83.

Basmann, R.L. (1960) 'On the asymptotic distribution of generalized linear estimates', *Econometrica*, **28**, 97–107.

Basmann, R.L. and Bakony, L.I. (1961) Letter to the editor, *Econometrica*, **29**, 249–50.

Basmann, R.L., Richardson, D.H. and Rohr, R.J. (1974) 'Finite sample distributions associated with stochastic difference equations – some experimental evidence', *Econometrica*, **42**, 825–40.

Bean, C.R. (1977) 'More Consumers' expenditure equations', Academic Panel Paper (77)35, London: HM Treasury.

Bean, C.R. (1978) 'The determination of consumers' expenditure in the UK', Government Economic Service Working Paper No. 4, London: HM Treasury.

Bean, C.R. (1981) 'An econometric model of investment in the United Kingdom', *Economic Journal*, **91**, 106–21.

Bentzel, R. and Hansen, B. (1955) 'On recursiveness and inter-dependency in economic models', *Review of Economic Studies*, **22**, 153–68.

Bergstrom, A.R. (1984) 'Continuous time stochastic models and issues of aggregation over time', in Z. Griliches and M.D. Intriligator (eds), *Handbook of Econometrics*, vol. II, Amsterdam: North-Holland, ch. 20.

Berndt, E.R. and Savin, N.E. (1977) 'Conflict among criteria for testing hypotheses in the multivariate linear regression model', *Econometrica*, **45**, 1263–78.

Berndt, E.R., Hall, B.H., Hall, R.E. and Hausman, J.A. (1974) 'Estimation and inference in nonlinear structural models', *Annals of Economic and Social Measurement*, **3**, 653–65.

Bewley, R. (1979) 'The direct estimation of the equilibrium response in a linear dynamic model', *Economic Letters*, **3**, 357–62.

Bispham, J.A. (1975) 'The NIESR model and its behaviour', in G.A. Renton (ed.), *Modelling the Economy*, London: Heinemann Educational, ch. 3, appendix.

Blalock, H.M., Jr (1961) *Causal Inferences in Nonexperimental Research*, Chapel Hill, NC: University of North Carolina Press.

Blaug, M. (1980) *The Methodology of Economics: How Economists Explain*, Cambridge: Cambridge University Press.

Bock, M.E., Yancey, T.A. and Judge, G.G. (1973) 'Statistical consequences of preliminary test estimators in regression', *Journal of the American Statistical Association*, **68**, 109–16.

Boland, L.A. (1982) *The Foundations of Economic Method*, London: Allen & Unwin.

Boland, L.A. (1989) *The Methodology of Economic Model Building*, London: Routledge.

Bollerslev, T. and Hylleberg, S. (1985) 'A note on the relation between consumers' expenditure and income in the UK', *Oxford Bulletin of Economics and Statistics,* **47**, 153-70.

Bowden, R.J. (1978) *The Econometrics of Disequilibrium*, Amsterdam: North-Holland.

Box, G.E.P. and Jenkins, G.M. (1976) *Time Series Analysis Forecasting and Control*, revised edn, San Francisco, CA: Holden-Day.

Box, G.E.P. and Pierce, D.A. (1970) 'Distribution of residual autocorrelations in autoregressive–integrated moving average time series models', *Journal of the American Statistical Association*, **65**, 1509-26.

Box, M.J., Davies, D. and Swann, W.H. (1969) *Non-linear Optimization Techniques*, ICI Monograph No. 5, Edinburgh: Oliver & Boyd.

Brainard, W.C. and Tobin, J. (1968) 'Pitfalls in financial model building', *American Economic Review*, 99-122.

Bray, J. (1979) 'New models of the future', *New Statesman*, 18 May, 710-14.

Brechling, F. (1973) *Investment and Employment Decisions*, Manchester: Manchester University Press.

Breusch, T.S. and Pagan, A.R. (1980) 'The Lagrange multiplier test and its applications to model specification in econometrics', *Review of Economic Studies*, **47**, 239-53.

Brissimis, S.N. and Gill, L. (1978) 'On the asymptotic distribution of impact and interim multipliers', *Econometrica*, **46**, 463-9.

Brown, R.L., Durbin, J. and Evans, J.M. (1975) 'Techniques for testing the constancy of regression relationships over time (with discussion)', *Journal of the Royal Statistical Society*, B, **37**, 149-92.

Brown, T.M. (1952) 'Habit persistence and lags in consumer behaviour', *Econometrica*, **20**, 355-71.

Brown, T.M. (1960) 'Simultaneous least squares: a distribution-free method of equation system structure estimation', *International Economic Review*, **1**, 173-91.

Brundy, J.M. and Jorgenson, D.W. (1971) 'Efficient estimation of simultaneous equations by instrumental variables', *Review of Economics and Statistics*, **53**, 207-24.

Buiter, W.H. (1980) 'Walras' law and all that: budget constraints and balance sheet constraints in period models and continuous time models', *International Economic Review*, **21**, 1-16.

Byron, R.P. (1970) 'Initial attempts in econometric model building at NIESR', in K. Hilton and D.F. Heathfield (eds), *The Econometric Study of the United Kingdom*, London: Macmillan, ch. 1.

Cagan, P. (1956) 'The monetary dynamics of hyperinflation', in M. Friedman (ed.), *Studies in the Quantity Theory of Money*, Chicago, IL: University of Chicago Press, ch. 2.

Carlson, J.A. and Parkin, M. (1975) 'Inflation expectations', *Economica*, **42**, 123-38.

Carruth, A. and Henley, A. (1990) 'Can existing consumption functions forecast consumer spending in the late 1980's?', *Oxford Bulletin of Economics and Statistics*, **52**, 211-22.

Chalmers, A.F. (1976) *What is This Thing Called Science?*, Queensland: University of Queensland Press.

Chamberlain, G. (1982) 'The general equivalence of Granger and Sims causality', *Econometrica*, **50**, 569-82.

Chatfield, C. and Prothero, D.L. (1973) 'Box–Jenkins forecasting: problems in a case study (with discussion)', *Journal of the Royal Statistical Society*, A, **136**, 295-352.

Chong, Y.Y. and Hendry, D.F. (1986) 'Econometric evaluation of linear macro-economic models', *Review of Economic Studies*, **53**, 671-90. Reprinted in C.W.J. Granger (ed.), *Modelling Economic Series*, Oxford: Clarendon Press, 1990, pp. 384-410.

Chow, G.C. (1960) 'Tests of equality between sets of coefficients in two linear regressions', *Econometrica*, **28**, 591–605.

Chow, G.C. (1964) 'A comparison of alternative estimators for simultaneous equations', *Econometrica*, **32**, 532–53.

Chow, G.C. (1975) *Analysis and Control of Dynamic Economic Systems*, New York: Wiley.

Chow, G.C. (1981) 'Selection of econometric models by the information criteria', in E.G. Charatsis (ed.), *Proceedings of the Econometric Society European Meeting 1979*, Amsterdam: North-Holland, ch. 8.

Christ, C.F. (1966) *Econometric Models and Methods*, New York: Wiley.

Clayton, G., Dodds, J.C., Driscoll, M.J. and Ford, J.L. (1974) 'The portfolio and debt behaviour of building societies in Britain', *S.S.R.C. Flow-of-Funds Conference*.

Cochran, W.G. and Cox, G.M. (1957) *Experimental Designs*, New York: Wiley.

Cochrane, D. and Orcutt, G.H. (1949) 'Application of least squares regression to relationships containing auto-correlated error terms', *Journal of the American Statistical Association*, **44**, 32–61.

Coghlan, R.T. (1978) 'A transactions demand for money', *Bank of England Quarterly Bulletin*, **18**, 48–60.

Congdon, T. (1983) 'Has Friedman got it wrong?', *The Banker*, 117–25.

Cooley, T. and LeRoy, S. (1981) 'Identification and estimation of money demand', *American Economic Review*, **71**, 825–44.

Cooper, R.L. (1972) 'The predictive performance of quarterly econometric models of the United States', in B. Hickman (ed.), *Econometric Models of Cyclical Behaviour*, National Bureau of Economic Research, Studies in Income and Wealth 36, New York: Columbia University Press, pp. 813–947.

Courakis, A.S. (1978) 'Serial correlation and the Bank of England's demand for money function: an exercise in measurement without theory', *Economic Journal*, **88**, 537–48.

Court, R.H. (1973) 'Efficient estimation of the reduced form from incomplete econometric models', *Review of Economic Studies*, **40**, 411–18.

Cox, D.R. (1961) 'Tests of separate families of hypotheses', *Proceedings of the Fourth Berkeley Symposium on Mathematical Statistics and Probability*, vol. I, Berkeley, CA: University of California Press, pp. 105–23.

Cox, D.R. (1962) 'Further results on tests of separate families of hypotheses', *Journal of the Royal Statistical Society*, B, **24**, 406–24.

Cox, D.R. (1970) *Analysis of Binary Data*, London: Chapman and Hall.

Cox, D.R. (1981) 'Statistical analysis of time series: some recent developments', *Scandinavian Journal of Statistics*, **8**, 93–115.

Cox, D.R. and Hinkley, D.V. (1974) *Theoretical Statistics*, London: Chapman and Hall.

Cragg, J.G. (1968) 'Some effects of incorrect specification on the small sample properties of several simultaneous equation estimators', *International Economic Review*, **9**, 63–86.

Cross, R. (1982) 'The Duhem-Quine thesis, Lakatos and the appraisal of theories in macroeconomics', *Economic Journal*, **92**, 320–40.

Cross, R. (1984) 'Monetarism and Duhem's thesis', in P.J. Wiles and G. Routh (eds.), *Economics in Disarray*, Oxford: Basil Blackwell, ch. 4, pp. 78–99.

Crowder, M.J. (1976) 'Maximum likelihood estimation for dependent observations', *Journal of the Royal Statistical Society*, B, **38**, 45–53.

Currie, D. (1981) 'Some long run features of dynamic time series models', *Economic Journal*, **91**, 704–15.

Cuthbertson, K. (1980) 'The determination of consumer durables expenditure: an exercise in applied econometric analysis', Unpublished paper, National Institute of Economic and Social Research, London.

Dastoor, N.K. (1983) 'Some aspects of testing non-nested hypotheses', *Journal of Econometrics*, **21**, 213-28.

Davidson, J.E.H. (1975) 'Studies of the measurement error problem with special reference to the specification and estimation of the consumption function', Unpublished M.Sc. Dissertation, London School of Economics.

Davidson, J.E.H. (1981) 'Problems with the estimation of moving average processes', *Journal of Econometrics*, **16**, 295-310.

Davidson, J.E.H. and Hendry, D.F. (1981) 'Interpreting econometric evidence: the consumption function in the United Kingdom', *European Economic Review*, **16**, 177-92. Reprinted in this volume as chapter 10.

Davidson, J.E.H., Hendry, D.F., Srba F. and Yeo, J.S. (1978) 'Econometric modelling of the aggregate time series relationship between consumers' expenditure and income in the United Kingdom', *Economic Journal*, **88**, 661-92. Reprinted in this volume as chapter 8.

Davies, G. (1979) 'The effects of government policy on the rise in unemployment', Centre for Labour Economics Discussion Paper 95/16, London School of Economics.

Davis, A.W. (1971) 'Percentile approximations for a class of likelihood ratio criteria', *Biometrika*, **58**, 349-56.

Davis, E.P. (1984) 'The consumption function in macroeconomic models: a comparative study', *Applied Economics*, **16**, 799-838.

Davis, N., Triggs, C.M. and Newbold, P. (1977) 'Significance levels of the Box–Pierce portmanteau statistic in finite samples', *Biometrika*, **64**, 517-22.

Day, R.H. (1967) 'Technological change and the sharecropper', *American Economic Review*, **57**, 427-49.

Deaton, A.S. (1972a) 'The estimation and testing of systems of demand equations', *European Economic Review*, **3**, 390-411.

Deaton, A.S. (1972b) 'Wealth effects on consumption in a modified life-cycle model', *Review of Economic Studies*, **39**, 443-53.

Deaton, A.S. (1976) 'Personal consumption', in T.S. Barker (ed.), *Economic Structure and Policy*, London: Chapman and Hall, ch. 4, pp. 89-103.

Deaton, A.S. (1977) 'Involuntary saving through unanticipated inflation', *American Economic Review*, **67**, 899-910.

Deaton, A.S. (1980) 'Savings and inflation: theory and British evidence', Paper presented to the International Economic Association Conference, Bergamo, Italy.

Deaton, A.S. (1982) 'Model selection procedures or, does the consumption function exist', in G.C. Chow and P. Corsi (eds), *Evaluating The Reliability of Macro-Economic Models*, New York: Wiley, ch. 5.

Deaton, A.S. and Muellbauer, J.N.J. (1980) *Economics and Consumer Behaviour*, Cambridge: Cambridge University Press.

Dent, W.T. (ed.) (1980) *Computation in Econometric Models*, Special Issue of *Journal of Econometrics*, **12**.

Desai, M.J. (1981a) 'Testing monetarism: an econometric analysis of Professor Stein's model of monetarism', *Journal of Economic Dynamics and Control*, **3**, 141-56.

Desai, M.J. (1981b) *Testing Monetarism*, London: Francis Pinter.

Dhrymes, P.J. (1971) *Distributed Lags: Problems of Estimation and Formulation*, San Francisco, CA: Holden-Day.

Dhrymes, P.J. (1972) 'Asymptotic properties of simultaneous least squares estimators', *International Economic Review*, **13**, 201-11.

Dhrymes, P.J. (1973) 'Small sample and asymptotic relations between maximum likelihood and three-stage least squares estimators', *Econometrica*, **41**, 357–64.

Dickey, D.A. and Fuller, W.A. (1979) 'Distribution of the estimators for autoregressive time series with a unit root', *Journal of American Statistical Association*, **74**, 427–31.

Dickey, D.A. and Fuller, W.A. (1981) 'Likelihood ratio statistics for autoregressive time series with a unit root', *Econometrica*, **49**, 1057–72.

Dixon, L.C.W. (1972) *Nonlinear Optimization*, London: English Universities Press.

Doan, T., Litterman, R. and Sims, C.A. (1984) 'Forecasting and conditional projection using realistic prior distributions', *Econometric Reviews*, **3**, 1–100.

Dolado, J.J., Jenkinson, T. and Sosvilla-Rivero, S. (1990) 'Cointegration and unit roots: a survey', *Journal of Economic Surveys*, **4**, 249–76.

Domowitz, I. and White, H. (1981) 'Nonlinear regression with dependent observations', Discussion Paper 81–32, University of California at San Diego.

Domowitz, I. and White, H. (1982) 'Mis-specified models with dependent observations', *Journal of Econometrics*, **20**, 35–58.

Doornik, J.A. and Hendry, D.F. (1992) *PCGIVE 7: An Interactive Econometric Modelling System*. Oxford: Institute of Economics and Statistics, University of Oxford.

Drettakis, E.G. (1973) 'Missing data in econometric estimation', *Review of Economic Studies*, **40**, 537–52.

Drèze, J.H. and Richard, J.-F. (1984) 'Bayesian analysis of simultaneous equation systems', in Z. Griliches and M.D. Intriligator (eds), *Handbook of Econometrics*, vol. I, Amsterdam: North-Holland, ch. 9.

Duesenberry, J.S. (1949) *Income, Saving and the Theory of Consumer Behaviour*, Cambridge, MA: Harvard University Press.

Durbin, J. (1970) 'Testing for serial correlation in least squares regression when some of the regressors are lagged dependent variables', *Econometrica*, **38**, 410–21.

Durbin, J. (1988) 'Maximum likelihood estimation of the parameters of a system of simultaneous regression equations', *Econometric Theory*, **4**, 159–70.

Durbin, J. and Watson, G.S. (1950, 1951, 1971) 'Testing for serial correlation in least squares regression, I, II and III', *Biometrika*, **37**, 409–28; **38**, 159–78; **58**, 1–19.

Edgerton, D.L. (1974) 'On the asymptotic equivalence of fix-point (FP) and iterated instrumental variables (IIV) estimators', unpublished paper, University of Lund.

Edwards, A.W.F. (1972) *Likelihood*, Cambridge: Cambridge University Press.

Effron, B. and Morris, C. (1975) 'Data analysis using Stein's estimator and its generalizations', *Journal of the American Statistical Association*, **70**, 311–19.

Einstein, A. (1950) *Out of My Later Years*, Jefferson City, MO: Scholastic Press.

Eisenpress, H. and Greenstadt, J. (1966) 'The estimation of non-linear econometric systems', *Econometrica*, **34**, 851–61.

Eisner, R. and Strotz, R.H. (1963) 'Determinants of business investment', in *Commission on Money and Credit: Impacts of Monetary Policy*, Englewood Cliffs, NJ: Prentice Hall, pp. 60–138.

Engle, R.F. (1976) 'Interpreting spectral analyses in terms of time-domain models', *Annals of Economic and Social Measurement*, **5**, 89–109.

Engle, R.F. (1982a) 'Autoregressive conditional heteroscedasticity, with estimates of the variance of United Kingdom inflation', *Econometrica*, **50**, 987–1007.

Engle, R.F. (1982b) 'A general approach to Lagrange multiplier model diagnostics', *Annals of Applied Econometrics*, **20**, 83–104.

Engle, R.F. (1984) 'Wald, likelihood ratio and Lagrange multiplier tests in econometrics', in Z. Griliches and M.D. Intriligator (eds), *Handbook of Econometrics*, vol. II, Amsterdam: North-Holland, ch. 13.

Engle, R.F. and Granger, C.W.J. (1987) 'Cointegration and error correction: representation, estimation and testing', *Econometrica*, **55**, 251-76. Reprinted in R.F. Engle and C.W.J. Granger (eds.), *Long-run Economic Relationships*, Oxford: Oxford University Press, 1991, pp. 81-111.

Engle, R.F. and Hendry, D.F. (1989) 'Testing super exogeneity and invariance', Discussion Paper 89-51, University of California at San Diego, forthcoming *Journal of Econometrics*.

Engle, R.F., Hendry, D.F. and Richard, J.-F. (1980) 'Exogeneity, causality and structural invariance in econometric modelling', CORE Discussion Paper 80-83; UCSD Discussion Paper 81-1.

Engle, R.F., Hendry, D.F. and Richard, J.-F. (1983) 'Exogeneity', *Econometrica*, **51**, 277-304. Reprinted in this volume as chapter 15.

Engle, R.F., Hendry, D.F. and Trumble, D. (1985) 'Small sample properties of ARCH estimators and tests', *Canadian Journal of Economics*, **18**, 66-93.

Ericsson, N.R. (1983) 'Asymptotic properties of instrumental variables statistics for testing non-nested hypotheses', *Review of Economic Studies*, **50**, 287-304.

Ericsson, N.R. (ed) (1992) *Cointegration, Exogeneity, and Policy Analysis*. Special issue of *Journal of Policy Modeling*, **14**, 3 and 4.

Ericsson, N.R. and Hendry, D.F. (1985) 'Conditional econometric modelling: an application to new house prices in the United Kingdom', in A.C. Atkinson and S. Fienberg (eds), *A Celebration of Statistics*, New York: Springer-Verlag, ch. 11.

Ericsson, N.R. and Hendry, D.F. (1989) 'Encompassing and rational expectations: how sequential corroboration can imply refutation', Discussion Paper 354, Board of Governors of the Federal Reserve System.

Escribano, A. (1985) 'Non-linear error correction: the case of money demand in the UK (1878-1970)', Mimeo, University of California at San Diego.

Espasa, A. (1977) *The Spectral Maximum Likelihood Estimation of Econometric Models with Stationary Errors*, vol. 3, Applied Statistics and Econometrics Series, Gottingen: Vanderhoeck & Ruprecht.

Espasa, A. and Sargan, J.D. (1977) 'The spectral estimation of simultaneous equation systems with lagged endogenous variables', *International Economic Review*, **18**, 583-605.

Evans, G.B.A. and Savin, N.E. (1981, 1984) 'Testing for unit roots: I and II', *Econometrica*, **49**, 753-79; **52**, 1241-70.

Evans, G.B.A. and Savin, N.E. (1982) 'Conflict among the criteria revisited: the W, LR and LM tests', *Econometrica*, **50**, 737-48.

Evans, M.K. (1969) *Macro-Economic Activity*, New York: Harper & Row.

Fair, R.C. (1970) 'The estimation of simultaneous equations models with lagged endogenous variables and first order serially correlated errors', *Econometrica*, **38**, 507-16.

Farebrother, R.W. (1974) 'The graphs of a *k*-class estimator', *Review of Economic Studies*, **41**, 533-8.

Favero, C. and Hendry, D.F. (1989) 'Testing the Lucas critique', A.W. Phillips Lecture at the 1989 Australasian Meeting of the Econometric Society (Discussion Paper 101, Oxford Institute of Economics and Statistics); forthcoming, *Econometric Reviews*.

Feinstein, C.H. (1972) *National Income, Expenditure and Output of the United Kingdom, 1855-1965*, Cambridge: Cambridge University Press.

Feldstein, M.S. (1970) 'Corporate taxation and dividend behaviour', *Review of Economic Studies*, **37**, 57-72.

Fisher, F.M. (1962) *A Priori Information and Time Series Analysis*, Amsterdam: North-Holland.

Fisher, F.M. (1965) 'Dynamic structure and estimation in economy-wide econometric models', in J.S. Duesenberry, L.R. Klein, G. Fromm and E. Kuh (eds), *Brookings*

Quarterly Econometric Model of the United States, Amsterdam: North-Holland, ch. 15, pp. 589–636.

Fisher, F.M. (1966a) 'The relative sensitivity to specification error of different k-class estimators', *Journal of the American Statistical Association*, **61**, 345–56.

Fisher, F.M. (1966b) *The Identification Problem in Econometrics*, New York: McGraw-Hill.

Fisher, F.M. (1970) 'Tests of equality between sets of coefficients in two linear regressions: an expository note', *Econometrica*, **38**, 361–6.

Fisher, W.D. and Wadycki, W.J. (1971) 'Estimating a structural equation in a large system', *Econometrica*, **39**, 461–5.

Fisk, P.R. (1967) *Stochastically Dependent Equations*, Statistical Monograph 21, London: Charles Griffin.

Flemming, J. (1973) 'The consumption function when capital markets are imperfect: the permanent income hypothesis reconsidered', *Oxford Economic Papers*, **25**, 160–72.

Florens, J.-P. and Mouchart, M. (1980a) 'Initial and sequential reduction of Bayesian experiments', CORE Discussion Paper 8015, Louvain-la-Neuve, Belgium.

Florens, J.-P. and Mouchart, M. (1980b) 'Conditioning in econometric models', CORE Discussion Paper 8042, Louvain-la-Neuve, Belgium.

Florens, J.-P. and Mouchart, M. (1981) 'A linear theory for non-causality', CORE unpublished paper, Louvain-la-Neuve, Belgium.

Florens, J.-P. and Mouchart, M. (1982) 'A note on non-causality', *Econometrica*, **50**, 583–92.

Florens, J.-P., Mouchart, M. and Richard, J.-F. (1974) 'Bayesian inference in errors-in-variables models', *Journal of Multivariate Analysis*, **4**.

Florens, J.-P., Mouchart, M. and Richard, J.-F. (1976) 'Likelihood analysis of linear models', CORE Discussion Paper 7619, Louvain-la-Neuve, Belgium.

Florens, J.-P., Mouchart, M. and Rolin, J.-F. (1990) *Elements of Bayesian Statistics*, New York: Marcel Dekker.

Frenkel, J. (1981) 'Flexible exchange rates, prices and the role of 'News': lessons from the 1970's', *Journal of Political Economy*, **89**, 665–705.

Friedman, B.M. (1976) 'Substitution and expectation effects on long-term borrowing behaviour and long-term interest rates', Discussion Paper 495, Harvard University.

Friedman, M. (1956) *Studies in the Quantity Theory of Money*, Chicago, IL: University of Chicago Press.

Friedman, M. (1957) *A Theory of the Consumption Function*, Princeton, NJ: Princeton University Press.

Friedman, M. and Schwartz, A.J. (1982) *Monetary Trends in the United States and the United Kingdom: Their Relation to Income, Prices and Interest Rates, 1867–1975*, Chicago, IL: University of Chicago Press.

Frisch, R. (1933) Editorial, *Econometrica*, **1**, 1–4.

Frisch, R. (1938) 'Statistical versus theoretical relations in economic macrodynamics', *League of Nations Memorandum* (reproduced by University of Oslo in 1948 with J. Tinbergen's comments).

Fuller, W.A. (1976) *Introduction to Statistical Time-Series*, New York: Wiley.

Garganas, N.C. (1975) 'An analysis of consumer credit and its effects on the purchases of consumer durables', in G.A. Renton (ed.), *Modelling the Economy*, London: Heinemann Educational, ch. 19.

Geweke, J. (1978) 'Testing the exogeneity specification in the complete dynamic simultaneous equations model', *Journal of Econometrics*, **7**, 163–85.

Geweke, J. (1984) 'Inference and causality in economic time series models', in Z. Griliches and M.D. Intriligator (eds), *Handbook of Econometrics*, vol. II, Amsterdam: North-Holland, ch. 19.

Ghosh, D. (1974) *The Economics of Building Societies*, London: Saxon House.

Ghosh, D. and Parkin, J.M. (1972) 'A theoretical and empirical analysis of the portfolio, debt and interest behaviour of building societies', *Manchester School*, **40**, 231–44.

Gilbert, C.L. (1986) 'Professor Hendry's econometric methodology', *Oxford Bulletin of Economics and Statistics*, **48**, 283–307. Reprinted in C.W.J. Granger (ed.), *Modelling Economic Series*, Oxford: Clarendon Press, 1990, pp. 279–303.

Gill, P.E., Murray, W. and Pitfield, R.A. (1972) 'The implementation of two revised quasi-Newton algorithms for unconstrained optimization', *Numerical Analysis and Computing Bulletin*, **11** (National Physical Laboratory).

Ginsburgh, V. and Waelbroeck, J. (1976) 'Computational experience with a large general equilibrium model', in J. Los and M.W. Los (eds), *Computing Equilibria: How and Why*, Amsterdam: North-Holland.

Godambe, V.P. (1976) 'Conditional likelihood and unconditional optimum estimating equations', *Biometrika*, **63**, 277–84.

Godambe, V.P. and Thomson, M.E. (1974) 'Estimating equations in the presence of a nuisance parameter', *Annals of Statistics*, **2**, 568–71.

Godfrey, L.G. (1977) 'Some tests for specification errors', Discussion Paper, University of York.

Godfrey, L.G. (1978) 'Testing against general autoregressive and moving average error models when the regressors include lagged dependent variables', *Econometrica*, **46**, 1293–1301.

Godfrey, L.G. and Poskitt, D.S. (1975) 'Testing the restrictions of the Almon lag technique', *Journal of the American Statistical Association*, **70**, 105–8.

Godfrey, L.G. and Wickens, M.R. (1982) 'Tests of misspecification using locally equivalent alternative models', in G.C. Chow and P. Corsi (eds), *Evaluating the Reliability of Macro-Economic Models*, New York: Wiley, ch. 6.

Godley, W.A.H. and Nordhaus, W.D. (1972) 'Pricing in the trade cycle', *Economic Journal*, **82**, 853–82.

Goldberger, A.S. (1959) *Impact Multipliers and Dynamic Properties of the Klein–Goldberger Model*, Amsterdam: North-Holland.

Goldberger, A.S., Nagar, A.L. and Odeh, H.S. (1961) 'The covariance matrices of reduced-form coefficients and of forecasts for a structural econometric model', *Econometrica*, **29**, 556–73.

Goldfeld, S.M. (1973) 'The demand for money revisited', *Brookings Papers in Economic Activity*, **3**, 577–646.

Goldfeld, S.M. and Quandt, R.E. (1972) *Non-Linear Methods in Econometrics*, Amsterdam: North-Holland.

Goldfeld, S.M. and Quandt, R.E. (1976) *Studies in Non-linear Estimation*, Cambridge, MA: Ballinger.

Goodhart, C.A.E. (1978) 'Problems of monetary management: the UK experience', in A.S. Courakis (ed.), *Inflation, Depression and Economic Policy in the West: Lessons from the 1970's*, Oxford: Basil Blackwell.

Goodhart, C.A.E. (1982) 'Monetary trends in the United States and the United Kingdom: a British review', *Journal of Economic Literature*, **20**, 1540–51.

Gourieroux, C., Laffont, J.-J. and Montfort, A. (1980) 'Disequilibrium econometrics in simultaneous equations systems', *Econometrica*, **48**, 75–96.

Granger, C.W.J. (1966) 'The typical spectral shape of an economic variable', *Econometrica*, **34**, 150–61.

Granger, C.W.J. (1969) 'Investigating causal relations by econometric models and cross-spectral methods', *Econometrica*, **37**, 424–38.

Granger, C.W.J. (1980) 'Testing for causality – a personal viewpoint', *Journal of Economic Dynamics and Control*, **2**, 329–52.

Granger, C.W.J. (1981) 'Some properties of time series data and their use in econometric model specification', *Journal of Econometrics*, **16**, 121–30.

Granger, C.W.J. (1983) 'Forecasting white noise', in A. Zellner (ed.), *Applied Time Series Analysis of Economic Data*, United States Bureau of the Census, 308–14.

Granger, C.W.J. (1986) 'Developments in the study of cointegrated economic variables', *Oxford Bulletin of Economics and Statistics*, **48**, 213–28.

Granger, C.W.J. (ed.) (1990) *Modelling Economic Series*, Oxford: Clarendon Press.

Granger, C.W.J. and Newbold, P. (1974) 'Spurious regressions in econometrics', *Journal of Econometrics*, **2**, 111–20.

Granger, C.W.J. and Newbold, P. (1977a) 'The time series approach to econometric model building', in C.A. Sims (ed.), *New Methods in Business Cycle Research*, Minneapolis, MN: Federal Reserve Bank of Minneapolis, ch. 1.

Granger, C.W.J. and Newbold, P. (1977b) *Forecasting Economic Time Series*, New York: Academic Press.

Granger, C.W.J. and Watson, M.W. (1984) 'Time series and spectral methods in econometrics', in Z. Griliches and M.D. Intriligator (eds), *Handbook of Econometrics*, vol. II, Amsterdam: North-Holland, ch. 17.

Granger, C.W.J. and Weiss, A.A. (1983) 'Time series analysis of error-correction models', in S. Karlin, T. Amemiya and L.A. Goodman (eds), *Studies in Econometrics, Time Series and Multivariate Statistics*, New York: Academic Press.

Grether, D.M. and Maddala, G.S. (1972) 'On the asymptotic properties of some two-step procedures for estimating distributed lag models', *International Economic Review*, **13**, 737–44.

Griliches, Z. (1961) 'A note on serial correlation bias in estimates of distributed lags', *Econometrica*, **29**, 65–73.

Griliches, Z. (1967) 'Distributed lags: a survey', *Econometrica*, **35**, 16–49.

Griliches, Z. (1974) 'Errors in variables and other unobservables', *Econometrica*, **42**, 971–98.

Griliches, Z. and Intriligator, M.D. (eds) (1984) *Handbook of Econometrics*, vol. II, Amsterdam: North-Holland.

Guilkey, D.K. (1974) 'Alternative tests for a first order vector autoregressive error specification', *Journal of Econometrics*, **2**, 95–104.

Gupta, Y.P. (1969) 'Least squares variants of the Dhrymes two-step estimation procedure of the distributed lag model', *International Economic Review*, **10**, 112–13.

Guthrie, R.S. (1976) 'A note on the Bayesian estimation of Solow's distributed lag model', *Journal of Econometrics*, **4**, 295–300.

Haavelmo, T. (1940) 'The inadequacy of testing dynamic theory by comparing theoretical solutions and observed cycles', *Econometrica*, **8**, 312–21.

Haavelmo, T. (1943) 'The statistical implications of a system of simultaneous equations', *Econometrica*, **11**, 1–12.

Haavelmo, T. (1944) 'The probability approach in econometrics', *Econometrica*, **12**, Supplement.

Hacche, G. (1974) 'The demand for money in the United Kingdom: experience since 1971', *Bank of England Quarterly Bulletin*, **14**, 284–305.

Hall, P. and Heyde, C.C. (1980) *Martingale Limit Theory and its Applications*, London: Academic Press.

Hall, R.E. (1978) 'Stochastic implications of the life cycle–permanent income hypothesis: theory and evidence', *Journal of Political Economy*, **86**, 971–87.

Hamburger, M.J. (1977) 'The demand for money in an open economy', *Journal of Monetary Economics*, **3**, 25–40.

Hannan, E.J. (1970) *Multiple Time Series*, New York: Wiley.

Hannan, E.J., Dunsmuir, W.T.M. and Deistler, M. (1980) 'Estimation of vector ARMAX models', *Journal of Multivariate Analysis*, **10**, 275–95.

Hansen, L.P. (1982) 'Large sample properties of generalized method of moments estimators', *Econometrica*, **50**, 1029–54.

Harnett, I. (1984) 'An econometric investigation into recent changes of UK personal sector consumption expenditure', Unpublished M. Phil. Thesis, University of Oxford.

Harvey, A.C. (1981a) *The Econometric Analysis of Time Series*, Oxford: Philip Allan.

Harvey, A.C. (1981b) 'The Kalman filter and its applications in econometrics and time-series analysis', Invited Paper, Symposium uber Operations Research, Augsburg.

Harvey, A.C. (1981c) *Time Series Models*, London: Philip Allen.

Harvey, A.C. and Phillips, G.D.A. (1979) 'The estimation of regression models with autoregressive-moving average disturbances', *Biometrika*, **66**, 49–58.

Hatanaka, M. (1974) 'An efficient two-step estimator for the dynamic adjustment model with autoregressive errors', *Journal of Econometrics*, **2**, 199–220.

Hausman, J.A. (1975) 'An instrumental variable approach to full-information estimators for linear and non-linear econometric models', *Econometrica*, **43**, 727–53.

Hausman, J.A. (1978) 'Specification tests in econometrics', *Econometrica*, **46**, 1251–71.

Hay, G.A. and Holt, C.C. (1975) 'A general solution for linear decision rules: an optimal dynamic strategy applicable under uncertainty', *Econometrica*, **43**, 231–59.

Hayek, F.A. (1963) *Studies in Philosophy, Politics and Economics*, London: Routledge & Kegan Paul.

Hendry, D.F. (1970) 'The estimation of economic models with autoregressive errors', Unpublished Ph.D. Thesis, London University.

Hendry, D.F. (1971) 'Maximum likelihood estimation of systems of simultaneous regression equations with errors generated by a vector autoregressive process', *International Economic Review*, **12**, 257–72. 'Correction' in **15**, 260.

Hendry, D.F. (1973) 'On asymptotic theory and finite sample experiments', *Economica*, **40**, 210–17.

Hendry, D.F. (1974) 'Stochastic specification in an aggregate demand model of the United Kingdom', *Econometrica*, **42**, 559–78. Reprinted in this volume as chapter 2.

Hendry, D.F. (1975a) 'The consequences of mis-specification of dynamic structure, auto-correlation and simultaneity in a simple model with an application to the demand for imports', in G.A. Renton (ed.), *Modelling the Economy*, London: Heinemann Educational, ch. 11.

Hendry, D.F. (1975b) 'Testing dynamic specification in a model of building society behaviour', *Association of University Teachers of Economics Conference*.

Hendry, D.F. (1975c) 'The limiting distribution of inconsistent instrumental variables estimators in a class of stationary stochastic systems', Cowles Foundation Discussion Paper **39**, Yale University.

Hendry, D.F. (1976a) 'The structure of simultaneous equations estimators', *Journal of Econometrics*, **4**, 51–88. Reprinted (abridged) in this volume as chapter 13.

Hendry, D.F. (1976b) 'Discussion of "Estimation of linear functional relationships: approximate distributions and connections with simultaneous equations in econometrics" by T.W. Anderson', *Journal of the Royal Statistical Society*, B, **38**, 24–5.

Hendry, D.F. (1977) 'On the time series approach to econometric model building', in C.A.

Sims (ed.), *New Methods in Business Cycle Research*, Minneapolis, MN: Federal Reserve Bank of Minneapolis, pp. 183–202. Reprinted (abridged) in this volume as chapter 5.

Hendry, D.F. (1979a) 'Predictive failure and econometric modelling in macro-economics: the transactions demand for money', in P. Ormerod (ed.), *Economic Modelling*, London: Heinemann, ch. 9. Reprinted in this volume as chapter 11.

Hendry, D.F. (1979b) 'The behaviour of inconsistent instrumental variables estimators in dynamic systems with autocorrelated errors', *Journal of Econometrics*, **9**, 295–314.

Hendry, D.F. (1980) 'Econometrics: alchemy or science?', *Economica*, **47**, 387–406. Reprinted in this volume as chapter 1.

Hendry, D.F. (1981) 'Econometric evidence in the appraisal of UK monetary policy', in *The Third Report of the Select Committee of the House of Commons on the Treasury and Civil Service*, vol. 3, London: HMSO, pp. 1–21.

Hendry, D.F. (1983) 'Econometric modelling: the "consumption function" in Retrospect', *Scottish Journal of Political Economy*, **30**, 193–220. Reprinted in this volume as chapter 18.

Hendry, D.F. (1984a) 'Monte Carlo experimentation in econometrics', in Z. Griliches and M.D. Intriligator (eds), *Handbook of Econometrics,* vol. II, Amsterdam: North-Holland, ch. 16.

Hendry, D.F. (1984b) 'Econometric modelling of house prices in the United Kingdom', in D.F. Hendry and K.F. Wallis (eds), *Econometrics and Quantitative Economics*, Oxford: Basil Blackwell, ch. 8.

Hendry, D.F. (1985) 'Monetary economic myth and econometric reality', *Oxford Review of Economic Policy*, **1**, 72–84. Reprinted in this volume as chapter 12.

Hendry, D.F. (1986a) 'Empirical modelling in dynamic econometrics: the new-construction sector', *Applied Mathematics and Computation*, **20**, 201–36.

Hendry, D.F. (1986b) 'Econometric modelling with cointegrated variables: an overview', *Oxford Bulletin of Economics and Statistics*, **48**, 201–12. Reprinted in R.F. Engle and C.W.J. Granger (eds), *Long-Run Economic Relationships*, Oxford: Oxford University Press, 1991, pp. 51–63.

Hendry, D.F. (1986c) 'Using PC-GIVE in econometrics teaching', *Oxford Bulletin of Economics and Statistics*, **48**, 87–98.

Hendry, D.F. (1987) 'Econometric methodology: a personal perspective', in T.F. Bewley (ed.), *Advances in Econometrics*, Cambridge: Cambridge University Press, ch. 10.

Hendry, D.F. (1988a) 'Econometrics in action', *Empirica*, 2/87, 135–56.

Hendry, D.F. (1988b) 'The encompassing implications of feedback versus feedforward mechanisms in econometrics', *Oxford Economic Papers*, **40**, 132–49.

Hendry, D.F. (1989) *PC-GIVE, An Interactive Econometric Modelling System*, Oxford: Institute of Economics and Statistics, University of Oxford.

Hendry, D.F. (1992) *Lectures on Econometric Methodology*, Oxford: Oxford University Press, to be published.

Hendry, D.F. and Anderson, G.J. (1977) 'Testing dynamic specification in small simultaneous systems: an application to a model of building society behaviour in the United Kingdom', in M.D. Intriligator (ed.), *Frontiers of Quantitative Economics*, vol. III, Amsterdam: North-Holland, ch. 8C. Reprinted in this volume as chapter 3.

Hendry, D.F. and Ericsson, N.R. (1991a), 'An econometric analysis of UK money demand in *Monetary Trends in the United States and the United Kingdom* by Milton Friedman and Anna J. Schwartz', *American Economic Review* (1991) **81**, 8–38.

Hendry, D.F. and Ericsson, N.R. (1991b) 'Modelling the demand for narrow money in the United Kingdom and the United States', *European Economic Review*, **35**, 833–86.

Hendry, D.F. and Harrison, R.W. (1974) 'Monte Carlo methodology and the small sample behaviour of ordinary and two-stage least squares', *Journal of Econometrics*, **2**, 151–74.

Hendry, D.F. and Mizon, G.E. (1978) 'Serial correlation as a convenient simplification, not a nuisance: a comment on a study of the demand for money by the Bank of England', *Economic Journal*, **88**, 549–63. Reprinted in this volume as chapter 6.

Hendry, D.F. and Mizon, G.E. (1990) 'Procrustean econometrics: or stretching and squeezing data', in C.W.J. Granger (ed.), *Modelling Economic Series*, Oxford: Clarendon Press, pp. 121–36.

Hendry, D.F. and Mizon, G.E. (1991) 'Evaluating dynamic econometric models by encompassing the VAR' in P.C.B. Phillips (ed.), *Models, Methods and Applications of Econometrics*, Oxford: Basil Blackwell, to be published.

Hendry, D.F. and Morgan, M.S. (1991) *Classic Readings in the Foundations of Econometric Analysis*, Cambridge: Cambridge University Press, to be published.

Hendry, D.F. and Neale, A.J. (1987) 'Monte Carlo experimentation using PC-NAIVE', in T. Fomby and G. Rhodes (eds), *Advances in Econometrics*, vol. **6**, Greenwich, CT: JAI Press, pp. 91–125.

Hendry, D.F. and Neale, A.J. (1988) 'Interpreting long-run equilibrium solutions in conventional macro models: a comment', *Economic Journal*, **98**, 132–49.

Hendry, D.F. and Richard, J.-F. (1982) 'On the formulation of empirical models in dynamic econometrics', *Journal of Econometrics*, **20**, 3–33. Reprinted in C.W.J. Granger (ed.), *Modelling Economic Series*, Oxford: Clarendon Press, 1990, pp. 304–34. Reprinted in this volume as chapter 16.

Hendry, D.F. and Richard, J.-F. (1983) 'The econometric analysis of economic time series', *International Statistical Review*, **51**, 111–63. Reprinted (abridged) in this volume as chapter 17.

Hendry, D.F. and Richard, J.-F. (1989) 'Recent developments in the theory of encompassing', in B. Cornet and H. Tulkens (eds), *Contributions to Operations Research and Econometrics. The XXth Anniversary of CORE*, Cambridge, MA: MIT Press, ch. 12.

Hendry, D.F. and Spanos, A. (1980) 'The treatment of unobservable variables in dynamic systems and disequilibrium econometrics', Unpublished paper, London School of Economics.

Hendry, D.F. and Srba, F. (1977) 'The properties of autoregressive instrumental variables estimators in dynamic systems', *Econometrica*, **45**, 969–90.

Hendry, D.F. and Srba, F. (1980) 'AUTOREG: a computer program library for dynamic econometric models with autoregressive errors', *Journal of Econometrics*, **12**, 85–102. Reprinted in this volume as chapter 14.

Hendry, D.F. and Tremayne, A.R. (1976) 'Estimating systems of dynamic reduced form equations with vector autoregressive errors', *International Economic Review*, **17**, 463–71.

Hendry, D.F. and Trivedi, P.K. (1972) 'Maximum likelihood estimation of difference equations with moving average errors: a simulation study', *Review of Economic Studies*, **39**, 117–45.

Hendry, D.F. and von Ungern-Sternberg, T. (1981) 'Liquidity and inflation effects on consumers' expenditure', in A.S. Deaton (ed.), *Essays in the Theory and Measurement of Consumers' Behaviour*, Cambridge: Cambridge University Press, ch. 9. Reprinted in this volume as chapter 9.

Hendry, D.F. and Wallis, K.F. (eds) (1984) *Econometrics and Quantitative Economics*, Oxford: Basil Blackwell.

Hendry, D.F., Leamer, E.E. and Poirier, D.J. (1990a) 'A conversation on econometric methodology', *Econometric Theory*, **6**, 171–261.

Hendry, D.F., Muellbauer, J.N.J. and Murphy, T.A. (1990b) 'The econometrics of DHSY', in J.D. Hey and D. Winch (eds), *A Century of Economics*, Oxford: Basil Blackwell, pp. 298–334.

Hendry, D.F., Neale, A.J. and Ericsson, N.R. (1991) *PC-NAIVE: An Interactive Program for Monte Carlo Experimentation in Econometrics*, Oxford: Institute of Economics and Statistics, University of Oxford.

Hendry, D.F., Neale, A.J. and Srba, F. (1988) 'Econometric analysis of small linear systems using PC-FIML', *Journal of Econometrics*, **38**, 203–66.

Hendry, D.F., Pagan, A.R. and Sargan, J.D. (1984) 'Dynamic specification', in Z. Griliches and M.D. Intriligator (eds), *Handbook of Econometrics,* vol. II, Amsterdam: North-Holland, ch. 18. Reprinted (abridged) in this volume as chapter 4.

Hendry, D.F., Richard, J.-F. and Marshall, R. (1987) *Dynamic Econometrics* (in preparation).

Hendry, D.F., Spanos, A. and Ericsson, N.R. (1989) 'The contributions to econometrics in Trygve Haavelmo's *The Probability Approach in Econometrics*', *Sosialøkonomen*, **11**, 12–17.

Henry, S.G.B., Sawyer, M.C. and Smith, P. (1976) 'Models of inflation in the United Kingdom', *National Institute Economic Review*, **76**, 60–71.

Herschel, J. (1830) *A Preliminary Discourse on the Study of Natural Philosophy*, London: Longman, Rees, Browne, Green & Taylor.

Hibbert, J. (1979) 'National and sectoral balance sheets in the United Kingdom', Paper presented to the Austrian Meeting of the International Association for Research in Income and Wealth, August 1979.

Hickman, B.G. (1972) *Econometric Models of Cyclical Behaviour*, National Bureau of Economic Research, Studies in Income and Wealth 36, New York: Columbia University Press.

Hicks, J.R. (1939) *Value and Capital: An Enquiry into Some Fundamental Principles of Economic Theory*, Oxford: Clarendon Press (2nd edn, 1950).

Hicks, J.R. (1979) *Causality in Economics*, Oxford: Clarendon Press.

Hildreth, C. and Lu, J.Y. (1960) 'Demand relations with autocorrelated disturbances', Technical Bulletin 276, Agricultural Experimental Station, Michigan State University.

Hilton, K. and Heathfield, D.F. (eds) (1970) *The Econometric Study of the United Kingdom*, London: Macmillan.

HM Treasury (1980) *Macroeconomic Model Technical Manual*, London: HM Treasury.

Holt, C., Modigliani, F., Muth, J. and Simon, H. (1960) *Planning Production, Inventories and Work Force*, Englewood Cliffs, NJ: Prentice Hall.

Hood, W.C. and Koopmans, T.C. (eds) (1953) *Studies in Econometric Method*, Cowles Commission Monograph 14, New York: Wiley.

Houthakker, H.S. (1956) 'The Pareto distribution and the Cobb–Douglas production function in activity analysis', *Review of Economic Studies*, **23**, 27–31.

Houthakker, H.S. and Taylor, L.D. (1970) *Consumer Demand in the United States, 1929–1970*, Harvard, MA: Harvard University Press.

Hsiao, C. (1984) 'Identification', in Z. Griliches and M.D. Intriligator (eds), *Handbook of Econometrics*, vol. I, Amsterdam: North-Holland, ch. 4.

Hume, D. (1758) *An Enquiry Concerning Human Understanding*, 1927 edn, Chicago, IL: Open Court.

Hurwicz, L. (1962) 'On the structural form of interdependent systems', in E. Nagel et al. (eds), *Logic, Methodology and the Philosophy of Science*, Palo Alto, CA: Stanford University Press.

Hylleberg, S. and Mizon, G.E. (1989) 'Cointegration and error correction mechanisms', *Economic Journal (Supplement)*, **99**, 113–25.

Johansen, S. (1988) 'Statistical analysis of cointegration vectors', *Journal of Economic Dynamics and Control*, **12**, 231–54. Reprinted in R.F. Engle and C.W.J. Granger (eds), *Long-run Economic Relationships*, Oxford: Oxford University Press, 1991, 131–52.

Johansen, S. (1992) 'Cointegration in Partial Systems and the Efficiency of single equation analysis', *Journal of Econometrics*, **52**, 389–402.

Johansen, S. and Juselius, K. (1990) 'Maximum likelihood estimation and inference on cointegration – with applications to the demand for money', *Oxford Bulletin of Economics and Statistics*, **52**, 169–210.

Johnson, H.G. (1971) *Macroeconomics and Monetary Theory*, London: Gray-Mills.

Johnston, J. (1972) *Econometric Methods*, 2nd edn, New York: McGraw-Hill (3rd edn, 1984).

Jonson, Ben (1612) *The Alchemist*, London: Thomas Snodham.

Jonson, P.D. (1976) 'Money, prices and output: an integrative essay', *Kredit und Kapital*, **84**, 979–1012.

Jorgenson, D.W. (1965) 'Anticipations and investment behavior', in J.S. Duesenberry, L.R. Klein, G. Fromm and E. Kuh (eds), *Brookings Quarterly Econometric Model of the United States*, Amsterdam: North-Holland.

Jorgenson, D.W. (1966) 'Rational distributed lag functions', *Econometrica*, **34**, 135–49.

Judd, J. and Scadding, J. (1982) 'The search for a stable money demand function: a survey of the post-1973 literature', *Journal of Economic Literature*, **20**, 993–1023.

Judge, G.G. and Bock, M.E. (1978) *The Statistical Implications of Pre-Test and Stein-Rule Estimators in Econometrics*, Amsterdam: North-Holland.

Judge, G.G., Griffiths, W.E., Hill, R.C., Lütkepohl, H. and Lee, T.-C. (1980) *The Theory and Practice of Econometrics*, New York: Wiley (2nd edn, 1985).

Kalman, R. (1979) 'System theoretic critique of dynamic economic models', Unpublished paper, University of Florida, Gainsville.

Katona, G. and Mueller, D. (1968) *Consumer Response to Income Increases*, Washington, DC: Brookings Institution.

Keller, W.J. (1975) 'A new class of limited-information estimators for simultaneous equations systems', *Journal of Econometrics*, **3**, 71–92.

Kendall, M.G. (1973) *Time-Series*, London: Charles Griffin.

Kendall, M.G. and Stuart, A. (1961) *The Advanced Theory of Statistics*, vol. 2, New York: Charles Griffen.

Kenkel, J.L. (1974) 'Some small sample properties of Durbin's tests for serial correlation in regression models containing lagged dependent variables', *Econometrica*, **42**, 763–9.

Kennan, J. (1979) 'The estimation of partial adjustment models with rational expectations', *Econometrica*, **47**, 1441–55.

Kennedy, P. (1983) 'Logarithmic dependent variables and prediction bias', *Oxford Bulletin of Economics and Statistics*, **45**, 389–92.

Keynes G. (1946) 'Newton, the man', Paper read at the Newton Tercentenary Celebrations at Trinity College, Cambridge; in Keynes, J.M. (1951) *Essays in Biography*, London: Rupert Hart-Davies.

Keynes, J.M. (1936) *The General Theory of Employment, Interest and Money*, London: Macmillan.

Keynes, J.M. (1939) 'Professor Tinbergen's method', *Economic Journal*, **49**, 558–68.

Keynes, J.M. (1940) 'Comment', *Economic Journal*, **50**, 154–6.

Keynes, J.N. (1890) *The Scope and Method of Political Economy*, London: Macmillan.

Kiviet, J.F. (1985) 'Model selection test procedures in a single linear equation of a dynamic simultaneous system and their defects in small samples', *Journal of Econometrics*, **28**, 327–62.

Kiviet, J.F. (1986a) 'On the rigor of some mis-specification tests for modelling dynamic relationships', *Review of Economic Studies*, **53**, 241–61.

Kiviet, J.F. (1986b) *Testing Linear Econometric Models*, Amsterdam: University of Amsterdam Press.

Klein, L.R. (1958) 'The estimation of distributed lags', *Econometrica*, **26**, 553–65.

Klein, L.R. (1969) 'Estimation of interdependent systems in macro-econometrics', *Econometrica*, **37**, 171–92.

Klein, L.R. (1974) *A Textbook of Econometrics*, 2nd edn, Englewood Cliffs, NJ: Prentice Hall.

Klein, L.R., Ball, R.J., Hazlewood, A. and Vandome, P. (1961) *An Econometric Model of the UK*, Oxford: Oxford University Press.

Kloek, T. (1982) 'Dynamic adjustment when the target is nonstationary', Unpublished paper, Erasmus University, Rotterdam (see *International Economic Review*, **25**, (1984) 315–26.

Kohn, R. (1979) 'Identification results for ARMAX structures', *Econometrica*, **47**, 1295–1304.

Koopmans, T.C. (1937) *Linear Regression Analysis of Economic Time Series*, Haarlem: Netherlands Economic Institute.

Koopmans, T.C. (1947) 'Measurement without theory', *Review of Economics and Statistics*, **29**, 161–72.

Koopmans, T.C. (1949) 'A reply', *Review of Economics and Statistics*, **31**, 86–91.

Koopmans, T.C. (1950a) 'When is an equation system complete for statistical purposes?', in T.C. Koopmans (ed.), *Statistical Inference in Dynamic Economic Models*, Cowles Commission Monograph 10, New York: Wiley, ch. 17.

Koopmans, T.C. (ed.) (1950b) *Statistical Inference in Dynamic Economic Models*, Cowles Commission Monograph 10, New York: Wiley.

Koopmans, T.C. (1957) *Three Essays on the State of Economic Science*, New York: McGraw-Hill.

Koopmans, T.C. (1979) 'Economics among the sciences', *American Economic Review*, **69**, 1–13.

Koopmans, T.C. and Hood, W.C. (1953) 'The estimation of simultaneous linear economic relationships', in W.C. Hood and T.C. Koopmans (eds), *Studies in Econometric Method*, Cowles Commission Monograph 14, New York: Wiley, ch. 6.

Koyck, L.M. (1954) *Distributed Lags and Investment Analysis*, Amsterdam: North-Holland.

Kremers, J.J.K., Dolado, J.J. and Ericsson, N.R. (1989) 'The power of cointegration tests', Unpublished paper, Board of Governors of the Federal Reserve System, Washington, DC. Forthcoming, *Oxford Bulletin of Economics and Statistics*.

Kuhn, T.S. (1970) *The Structure of Scientific Revolutions*, revised edn, Chicago, IL: Chicago University Press.

Laidler, D.E. (1982) 'Friedman and Schwartz on "Monetary trends" – a review article', *Journal of International Money and Finance*, **1**, 293–305.

Laidler, D.E. (1985) *The Demand for Money; Theories and Evidence*, New York: Harper & Row.

Laidler, D.E. and Cross, R. (1976) 'Inflation, excess demand in fixed exchange rate open economies', in M. Parkin and G. Zis (eds), *Inflation in the World Economy*, Manchester: Manchester University Press.

Lakatos, I. (1974) 'Falsification and the methodology of scientific research programmes', in I. Lakatos and A.E. Musgrave, *Criticism and the Growth of Knowledge*, Cambridge: Cambridge University Press, pp. 91–196.

Leamer, E.E. (1974) 'False models and post-data model construction', *Journal of the American Statistical Association*, **69**, 122–31.

Leamer, E.E. (1975) '"Explaining your results" as access biased memory', *Journal of the American Statistical Association*, **70**, 88–93.

Leamer, E.E. (1978) *Specification Searches: Ad-Hoc Inference with Non-Experimental Data*, New York: Wiley.

Leamer, E.E. (1983) 'Let's take the con out of econometrics', *American Economic Review*,

73, 31–43. Reprinted in C.W.J. Granger (ed.), *Modelling Economic Series*, Oxford: Clarendon Press, 1990, pp. 29–49.

Leamer, E.E. (1984) 'Model choice and specification analysis', in Z. Griliches and M.D. Intriligator (eds), *Handbook of Econometrics*, vol. I, Amsterdam: North-Holland, ch. 5.

Lee, Y.S. (1971) 'Asymptotic formulae for the distribution of a multivariate test statistic: power comparisons of certain multivariate tests', *Biometrika*, **58**, 647–51.

Lehmann, E.L. (1959) *Testing Statistical Hypotheses*, New York: Wiley.

Leontief, W. (1971) 'Theoretical assumptions and nonobserved facts', *American Economic Review*, **61**, 1–7.

L'Esperance, W.L. and Taylor, D. (1975) 'The power of four tests of autocorrelation in the linear regression model', *Journal of Econometrics*, **3**, 1–22.

Losee, J. (1980) *A Historical Introduction to the Philosophy of Science*, Oxford: Oxford University Press.

Lubrano, M. (1979) 'Consistent approximations of the maximum likelihood estimator in linear models', CORE Discussion Paper 7924, Louvain-la-Neuve, Belgium.

Lucas, R.E. (1976) 'Econometric policy evaluation: a critique', in K. Brunner and A.H. Meltzer (eds), *The Phillips Curve and Labor Markets*, Amsterdam: North-Holland (Carnegie-Rochester Conference Series on Public Policy, vol. 1, a supplementary series to the *Journal of Monetary Economics*).

Lucas, R.E. and Sargent, T. (eds), (1981) *Rational Expectations and Econometric Practice*, London: Allen & Unwin.

Lyttkens, E. (1973) 'The fix-point method for estimating inter-dependent systems with the underlying model specification' (with discussion), *Journal of the Royal Statistical Society*, *A*, **136**, 353–94.

Maasoumi, E. (ed) (1988), *Contributions to Econometrics: John Denis Sargan*, Cambridge: Cambridge University Press.

MacKinnon, J.G. (1983) 'Model specification tests against non-nested alternatives', *Econometric Reviews*, **2**, 85–110.

MacKinnon, J.G. and White, H. (1985) 'Some heteroscedastic covariance matrix estimators with improved finite sample properties', *Journal of Econometrics*, **29**, 305–25.

Madansky, A. (1964) 'On the efficiency of three-stage least squares estimation', *Econometrica*, **32**, 51–6.

Madansky, A. (1976) *Foundations of Econometrics*, Amsterdam: North-Holland.

Maddala, G.S. (1971a) 'Simultaneous estimation methods for large- and medium-size econometric models', *Review of Economic Studies*, **38**, 435–46.

Maddala, G.S. (1971b) 'Generalized least squares with an estimated covariance matrix', *Econometrica*, **39**, 23–34.

Maddala, G.S. (1977) *Econometrics*, New York: McGraw-Hill.

Maddala, G.S. and Lee, L.F. (1976) 'Recursive models with qualitative endogenous variables', *Annals of Economic and Social Measurement*, **5**, 525–45.

Maddala, G.S. and Rao, A.S. (1973) 'Tests for serial correlation in regression models with lagged dependent variables and serially correlated errors', *Econometrica*, **41**, 761–74.

Magee, B. (1982) *Popper*, Glasgow: William Collins, Fontana paperback.

Malinvaud, E. (1966) *Statistical Methods of Econometrics*, 1st edn, Amsterdam: North-Holland.

Malinvaud, E. (1970) *Statistical Methods of Econometrics*, 2nd edn, Amsterdam: North-Holland.

Malinvaud, E. (1981) 'Econometrics faced with the needs of macroeconomic policy', *Econometrica*, **49**, 1363–75.

Mann, H.B. and Wald, A. (1943) 'On the statistical treatment of linear stochastic difference equations', *Econometrica*, **11**, 173–220.

Marget, A.W. (1929) 'Morgenstern on the methodology of economic forecasting', *Journal of Political Economy*, **37**, 312–39.

Marquardt, D.W. (1963) 'An algorithm for least squares estimation of nonlinear parameters', *Journal of the Society for Industrial and Applied Mathematics*, **11**, 431–41.

Marschak, J. (1953) 'Economic measurements for policy and prediction', in W.C. Hood and T.C. Koopmans (eds), *Studies in Econometric Method*, Cowles Commission Monograph 14, New York: Wiley, pp. 1–26.

Marshall, A. (1926) *Official Papers*, London: Macmillan.

Mason, S.F. (1977) *A History of the Sciences*, 2nd edn, New York: Collier.

Mayer, Th. (1982) 'Monetary trends in the United States and the United Kingdom: a review article', *Journal of Economic Literature*, **20**, 1528–39.

Mayes, D.G. (1979) *The Property Boom*, Oxford: Martin Robertson.

McAleer, M., Pagan, A.R. and Volker, P.A. (1985) 'What will take the con out of econometrics?', *American Economic Review*, 293–301. Reprinted in C.W.J. Granger (ed.), *Modelling Economic Series*, Oxford: Clarendon Press, 1990, pp. 50–71.

McCarthy, M.D. (1972) 'The Wharton quarterly econometric forecasting model mark III', *Studies in Quantitative Economics*, **6**, Wharton School, University of Pennsylvania.

McFadden, D. (1979) 'Econometric analysis of discrete data', Fischer-Schultz Lecture, European Meeting of the Econometric Society, Athens.

McNees, S.K. (1982) 'The role of macroeconometric models in forecasting and policy analysis in the United States', *Journal of Forecasting*, **1**, 37–48.

Meek, R.L. (ed.) (1973) *Turgot on Progress, Sociology and Economics*, Cambridge: Cambridge University Press.

Middleton, K.W.E. (1965) *A History of the Theories of Rain (and other forms of Precipitation)*, London: Oldbourne.

Mikhail, W.M. (1972) 'Simulating the small sample properties of econometric estimators', *Journal of the American Statistical Association*, **67**, 620–4.

Mizon, G.E. (1974) 'The estimation of non-linear econometric equations: an application to the specification and estimation of an aggregate putty–clay relation for the UK', *Review of Economic Studies*, **41**, 253–70.

Mizon, G.E. (1977a) 'Model selection procedures', in M.J. Artis and A.R. Nobay (eds), *Studies in Modern Economic Analysis*, Oxford: Basil Blackwell, ch. 4.

Mizon, G.E. (1977b) 'Inferential procedures in nonlinear models: an application in a UK industrial cross section study of factor substitution and returns to scale', *Econometrica*, **45**, 1221–42.

Mizon, G.E. (1984) 'The encompassing approach in econometrics', in D.F. Hendry and K.F. Wallis (eds), *Econometrics and Quantitative Economics*, Oxford: Basil Blackwell, ch. 6.

Mizon, G.E. and Hendry, D.F. (1980) 'An empirical application and Monte Carlo analysis of tests of dynamic specification', *Review of Economic Studies*, **49**, 21–45. Reprinted in this volume as chapter 7.

Mizon, G.E. and Richard, J.-F. (1986) 'The encompassing principle and its application to testing non-nested hypotheses', *Econometrica*, **54**, 657–78.

Modigliani, F. (1975) 'The life cycle hypothesis of saving twenty years later', in M. Parkin and A.R. Nobay (eds), *Contemporary Issues in Economics*, Manchester: Manchester University Press.

Moore, B.J. (1983) 'Monetary trends in the United States and the United Kingdom, a review', *The Financial Review*, **18**, 146–66.

Morgan, M.S. (1987) 'Statistics without probability and Haavelmo's revolution in econometrics', in L. Kruger, G. Gigerenzer and M.S. Morgan (eds), *The Probabilistic Revolution*, vol. 2, Cambridge, MA: MIT Press, pp. 171–97.

Morgan, M.S. (1990) *The History of Econometric Ideas*, Cambridge: Cambridge University Press.

Morgenstern, O. (1950) *On the Accuracy of Economic Observations*, Princeton, NJ: Princeton University Press.

Mosbaek, E.J. and Wold, H.O. (1970) *Interdependent Systems*, Amsterdam: North-Holland.

Mouchart, M. and Orsi, R. (1976) 'Polynomial approximation of distributed lags and linear restrictions: a Bayesian approach', *Empirical Economics*, **1**, 129–52.

Muellbauer, J.N.J. (1979) 'Are employment decisions based on rational expectations?', Unpublished paper, Birkbeck College.

Muellbauer, J.N.J. (1983) 'Surprises in the consumption function', Conference paper supplement to *Economic Journal*, **93**, 34–49.

Muellbauer, J.N.J. and Winter, D. (1980) 'Unemployment, employment and exports in British manufacturing: a non-clearing markets approach', *European Economic Review*, **13**, 383–409.

Muth, J.F. (1961) 'Rational expectations and the theory of price movements', *Econometrica*, **29**, 315–35.

Nadiri, M.R. and Rosen, S. (1969) 'Interrelated factor demand functions', *American Economic Review*, **59**, 457–71.

Nagar, A.L. (1959) 'The bias and moment matrix of the general K-class estimators of the parameters in simultaneous equations', *Econometrica*, **27**, 575–95.

NAG Library of Computer Programs MK5 (1977), Oxford University Computing Laboratory.

Naylor, T.H., Seaks, T.G. and Wichern, D.W. (1972) 'Box–Jenkins methods: an alternative to econometric models', *International Statistical Review*, **40**, 123–37.

Neale, A.J. (1988) 'Recursivity in econometrics: an historical overview', Mimeo, Nuffield College, Oxford.

Nelson, C.R. (1972) 'The prediction performance of the FRB–MIT–PENN model of the US economy', *American Economic Review*, **62**, 902–17.

Nerlove, M. (1958) *The Dynamics of Supply*, Baltimore, MD: Johns Hopkins University Press.

Nerlove, M. (1972) 'On lags in economic behaviour', *Econometrica*, **40**, 221–51.

Nerlove, M. and Wallis, K.F. (1966) 'Use of the Durbin–Watson statistic in inappropriate situations', *Econometrica*, **34**, 235–8.

Neyman, J. (1959) 'Optimal asymptotic tests of composite statistical hypotheses', in U. Grenander (ed.), *Probability and Statistics*, New York: Wiley, pp. 213–34.

Neyman, J. and Pearson, E.S. (1933) 'On the problem of the most efficient tests of statistical hypotheses', *Philosophical Transactions of the Royal Society of London*, *A*, **231**, 289ff.

Nicholls, D.F., Pagan, A.R. and Terrell, R.D. (1975) 'The estimation and use of models with moving average disturbance terms: a survey', *International Economic Review*, **16**, 113–34.

Nickell, S.J. (1981) 'An investigation of the determinants of manufacturing employment in the United Kingdom', Discussion Paper 105, Centre for Labour Economics, London School of Economics.

Nickell, S.J. (1985) 'Error correction, partial adjustment and all that: an expository note', *Oxford Bulletin of Economics and Statistics*, **47**, 119–30.

O'Herlihy, C.St.J. and Spencer, J.E. (1972) 'Building societies behaviour, 1955–1970', *National Institute Economic Review*, **61**, 40–52.

Orcutt, G.H. (1952) 'Toward a partial redirection of econometrics', *Review of Economics and Statistics*, **34**, 195–213.

Orcutt, G.H. and Winokur, H.S. (1969) 'First order autoregression: inference, estimation and prediction', *Econometrica*, **37**, 1–14.

Osborn, D.R. (1976) 'Maximum likelihood estimation of moving average processes', *Annals of Economic and Social Measurement*, **5**, 75–87.

Osborn, D.R. (1977) 'Exact and approximate maximum likelihood estimators for vector moving average processes', *Journal of the Royal Statistical Society*, B, **39**, 114–18.

Oxford Bulletin of Economics and Statistics (1986), Special issue: *Econometric modelling with cointegrated variables*, **48**, 3.

Pagan, A.R. (1977) 'The stability of the demand for money re-examined', Discussion Paper 45, Australian National University.

Pagan, A.R. (1981) 'Reflections on Australian macro modelling', Unpublished paper, Australian National University.

Pagan, A.R. (1984) 'Model evaluation by variable addition', in D.F. Hendry and K.F. Wallis (eds), *Econometrics and Quantitative Economics*, Oxford: Basil Blackwell, pp. 103–5.

Pagan, A.R. (1985) 'Time series behaviour and dynamic specification', *Oxford Bulletin of Economics and Statistics*, **47**, 199–211.

Pagan, A.R. (1987) 'Three econometric methodologies: a critical appraisal', *Journal of Economic Surveys*, **1**, 3–24. Reprinted in C.W.J. Granger (ed.), *Modelling Economic Series*, Oxford: Clarendon Press, 1990, pp. 97–120.

Palm, F. and Zellner, A. (1980) 'Large sample estimation and testing procedures for dynamic equation systems', *Journal of Econometrics*, **12**, 251–84.

Patinkin, D. (1976) 'Keynes and econometrics: on the interaction between macroeconomic revolutions of the interwar period', *Econometrica*, **44**, 1091–1123.

Patterson, K.D. and Ryding, J. (1982) 'Deriving and testing rate of growth and higher order growth effects in dynamic economic models', Bank of England Discussion Paper 21.

Peck, J.K. (1975) 'The estimation of a dynamic equation following a preliminary test for autocorrelation', Cowles Foundation Discussion Paper 404, New Haven, CT: Yale University Press.

Pereira, B. de B. (1977) 'Discriminating among separate models: a bibliography', *International Statistical Review*, **45**, 163–72.

Persons, W.M. (1925) 'Statistics and economic theory', *Review of Economic Statistics*, **7**, 179–97.

Pesaran, M.H. (1974) 'On the general problem of model selection', *Review of Economic Studies*, **41**, 153–71.

Pesaran, M.H. (1981) 'Diagnostic testing and exact maximum likelihood estimation of dynamic models', in E.G. Charatsis (ed.), *Proceedings of the Econometric Society European Meeting 1979: Selected Econometric Papers in Memory of Stefan Valavanis*, Amsterdam: North-Holland, ch. 3.

Pesaran, M.H. and Deaton, A.S. (1978) 'Testing non-nested non-linear regression models', *Econometrica*, **46**, 677–94.

Pesaran, M.H. and Evans, R.A. (1982) 'An inflation-adjusted life-cycle explanation of UK personal savings: 1953–1980', Unpublished paper, University of Cambridge.

Pesaran, M.H. and Evans, R.A. (1984) 'Inflation, capital gains and UK personal savings: 1953–81', *Economic Journal*, **94**, 237–57.

Phelps Brown, E.H. (1972) 'The underdevelopment of economics', *Economic Journal*, **82**, 1–10.

Phillips, A.W. (1954) 'Stabilization policy in a closed economy', *Economic Journal*, **64**, 290–323.

Phillips, A.W. (1956) 'Some notes on the estimation of time-forms of reactions in inter-dependent dynamic systems', *Economica*, **23**, 99–113.

Phillips, A.W. (1957) 'Stabilization policy and the time form of lagged responses', *Economic Journal*, **67**, 265–77.

Phillips, A.W. (1966) 'Estimation of stochastic difference equations with moving average disturbances', Walras–Bowley Lecture of the Econometric Society, San Francisco, CA.

Phillips, P.C.B. (1977) 'Approximations to some finite sample distributions associated with a first order stochastic difference equation', *Econometrica*, **45**, 463–85.

Phillips, P.C.B. (1980) 'Finite sample theory and the distributions of alternative estimators of the marginal propensity to consume', *Review of Economic Studies*, **47**, 183–224.

Phillips, P.C.B. (1986) 'Understanding spurious regressions in econometrics', *Journal of Econometrics*, **33**, 311–40.

Phillips, P.C.B. (1991) 'Optimal inference in cointegrated systems', *Econometrica*, **59**, 283–306.

Phillips, P.C.B. and Loretan, M. (1991) 'Estimating long run economic equilibria', *Review of Economic Studies*, **58**, 407–36.

Phlips, L. (1978) *Applied Consumption Analysis*, Amsterdam: North-Holland.

Pierce, D.A. (1971) 'Distribution of residual autocorrelations in the regression model with autogressive-moving average errors', *Journal of the Royal Statistical Society*, B, **33**, 140–6.

Pierce, D.A. (1977) 'Relationships – and the lack thereof – between economic time series, with special reference to money and interest rates', *Journal of the American Statistical Association*, **72**, 11–22.

Pindyck, R.S. and Rubinfeld, D.L. (1976) *Econometric Models and Economic Forecasts*, New York: McGraw-Hill.

Pissarides, C.A. (1978) 'Liquidity considerations in the theory of consumption', *Quarterly Journal of Economics*, **82**, 279–96.

Poirier, D.J. (1981) 'Posterior odds analysis when all competing models are false', *Economics Letters*, **8**, 135–40.

Popper, K.R. (1959, 1968) *The Logic of Scientific Discovery*, London: Hutchinson.

Popper, K.R. (1961) *The Poverty of Historicism*, London: Routledge & Kegan Paul.

Popper, K.R. (1963, 1969) *Conjectures and Refutations*, London: Routledge & Kegan Paul.

Portes, R. and Winter, D. (1980) 'Disequilibrium estimates for consumption goods markets in centrally planned economies', *Review of Economic Studies*, **47**, 137–59.

Powell, M.J.D. (1964) 'An efficient method for finding the minimum of a function of several variables without calculating derivatives', *Computer Journal*, **7**, 155–62.

Powell, M.J.D. (1965) 'A method for minimising a sum of squares of non-linear functions without calculating derivatives', *Computer Journal*, **7**, 303–7.

Powell, M.J.D. (1972) 'Some properties of the variable metric algorithm', in F.A. Lootsma (ed.), *Numerical Methods for Non-Linear Optimization*, New York: Academic Press, ch. 1.

Prais, Z. (1975) 'Real money balances as a variable in the production function', *Review of Economics and Statistics*, **57**, 243–4.

Press, S.J. (1972) *Applied Multivariate Analysis*, New York: Holt, Rinehard & Winston.

Prothero, D.L. and Wallis, K.F. (1976) 'Modelling macro-economic time series' (with discussion), *Journal of the Royal Statistical Society*, A, **139**, 468–500.

Quandt, R.E. (1982) 'Econometric disequilibrium models', *Econometric Review*, **1**, 1–63.

Quandt, R.E. (1984) 'Computational problems and methods', in Z. Griliches and M.D. Intriligator (eds), *Handbook of Econometrics*, vol. I, Amsterdam: North-Holland, ch. 12.

Rao, C.R. (1973) *Linear Statistical Inference and its Applications*, 2nd edn, New York: Wiley.

Reid, D.J. (1977) 'Public sector debt', *Economic Trends*, May, 100–7.

Reinsel, G. (1979) 'Maximum likelihood estimation of stochastic linear difference equations with autoregressive moving average errors', *Econometrica*, **47**, 129–52.

Renton, G.A. (ed.) (1975) *Modelling the Economy*, London: Heinemann Educational.

Revell, J. (1973) 'UK building societies', Economics Research Paper 5, Bangor (also see *The British Financial System*, London: Macmillan).

Richard, J.-F. (1977) 'Bayesian analysis of the regression model when the disturbances are generated by an autoregressive process', in A. Aykac and C. Brumat (eds), *New Developments in the Applications of Bayesian Methods*, Amsterdam: North-Holland, pp. 185–209.

Richard, J.-F. (1979) 'Exogeneity, inference and prediction in so-called incomplete dynamic simultaneous equation models', CORE Discussion Paper 7922, Université Catholique de Louvain, Louvain-la-Neuve, Belgium.

Richard, J.-F. (1980) 'Models with several regimes and changes in exogeneity', *Review of Economic Studies*, **47**, 1–20.

Riley, C.J. (1974) 'A model of building society behaviour', *Association of University Teachers of Economics Conference*.

de Rola, S.K. (1973) *Alchemy: The Secret Art*, London: Thames & Hudson.

Rothenberg, T.J. (1973) *Efficient Estimation with a Priori Information*, Cowles Foundation Monograph 23, New Haven, CT: Yale University Press.

Rothenberg, T.J. and Leenders, C.T. (1964) 'Efficient estimation of simultaneous equations systems', *Econometrica*, **32**, 57–76.

Salmon, M. (1979a) 'Notes on modelling optimising behaviour in the absence of an "Optimal" theory', Unpublished paper, University of Warwick.

Salmon, M. (1979b) 'Recursive estimation, parameter variation and misspecification: an application to the UK consumption function', Working paper, Warwick University.

Salmon, M. (1982) 'Error correction mechanisms', *Economic Journal*, **92**, 615–29.

Salmon, M. and Wallis, K.F. (1982) 'Model validation and forecast comparisons: theoretical and practical considerations', in G.C. Chow and P. Corsi (eds), *Evaluating the Reliability of Macro-Economic Models*, New York: Wiley, ch. 12.

Salmon, M. and Young, P.C. (1978) 'Control methods for quantitative economic policy', in S. Holly, B. Rustem and M. Zarrop (eds), *Optimal Control for Econometric Models: An Approach to Economic Policy Formation*, London: Macmillan, ch. 6.

Samuelson, P.A. (1947) *Foundations of Economic Analysis*, Harvard, MA: Harvard University Press.

Sargan, J.D. (1958) 'The estimation of economic relationships using instrumental variables', *Econometrica*, **26**, 393–415. In E. Maasoumi (ed) *Contributions to Econometrics: John Denis Sargan*, Cambridge: Cambridge University Press, 1988. (Two volumes). Reprinted in E. Maasoumi (*op. cit.*) ch. 1.4.

Sargan, J.D. (1959) 'The estimation of relationships with autocorrelated residuals by the use of instrumental variables', *Journal of the Royal Statistical Society*, B, **21**, 91–105. In E. Maasoumi (ed) *Contributions to Econometrics: John Denis Sargan*, Cambridge: Cambridge University Press, 1988. (Two volumes). Reprinted in E. Maasoumi (*op. cit.*) ch. 1.5.

Sargan, J.D. (1961) 'The maximum likelihood estimation of economic relationships with autoregressive residuals', *Econometrica*, **29**, 414–26. In E. Maasoumi (ed) *Contributions to Econometrics: John Denis Sargan*, Cambridge: Cambridge University Press, 1988. (Two volumes). Reprinted in E. Maasoumi (*op. cit.*) ch. 1.6.

Sargan, J.D. (1964a) 'Wages and prices in the United Kingdom: a study in econometric methodology', in P.E. Hart, G. Mills and J.K. Whitaker (eds), *Econometric Analysis for National Economic Planning*, London: Butterworths, pp. 25–63. Reprinted in D.F. Hendry and K.F. Wallis (eds), *Econometrics and Quantitative Economics*, Oxford: Basil Blackwell, 1984.

Sargan, J.D. (1964b) 'Three-stage least-squares and full maximum likelihood estimates', *Econometrica*, **32**, 77–81. In E. Maasoumi (ed) *Contributions to Econometrics: John Denis Sargan*, Cambridge: Cambridge University Press, 1988. (Two volumes). Reprinted in E. Maasoumi (*op. cit.*) ch. 1.7.

Sargan, J.D. (1972) 'The identification and estimation of sets of simultaneous stochastic equations', Unpublished paper, London School of Economics. In E. Maasoumi (ed) *Contributions to Econometrics: John Denis Sargan*, Cambridge: Cambridge University Press, 1988. (Two volumes). (See E. Maasoumi (*op. cit.*) ch. 1.12.)

Sargan, J.D. (1976) 'Econometric estimators and the Edgeworth approximation', *Econometrica*, **44**, 421–48. In E. Maasoumi (ed) *Contributions to Econometrics: John Denis Sargan*, Cambridge: Cambridge University Press, 1988. (Two volumes). Reprinted in E. Maasoumi (*op. cit.*) ch. 2.5.

Sargan, J.D. (1978) 'Dynamic specification for models with autoregressive errors. Vector autoregressive case', LSE Econometrics Programme Working Paper.

Sargan, J.D. (1980a) 'Some tests of dynamic specification for a single equation', *Econometrica*, **48**, 879–97. In E. Maasoumi (ed) *Contributions to Econometrics: John Denis Sargan*, Cambridge: Cambridge University Press, 1988. (Two volumes). Reprinted in E. Maasoumi (*op. cit.*) ch. 1.10.

Sargan, J.D. (1980b) 'The consumer price equation in the post-war British economy. An exercise in equation specification testing', *Review of Economic Studies*, **47**, 113–35.

Sargan, J.D. (1981) 'On Monte-Carlo estimates of moments which are infinite', *Advances in Econometrics*, **1**, 267–99.

Sargan, J.D. (1983) 'Identification in models with autoregressive errors', in S. Karlin, T. Amemiya and L.A. Goodman (eds), *Studies in Econometrics, Time Series and Multivariate Statistics*, New York: Academic Press, ch. 4. In E. Maasoumi (ed) *Contributions to Econometrics: John Denis Sargan*, Cambridge: Cambridge University Press, 1988. (Two volumes). Reprinted in E. Maasoumi (*op. cit.*) ch. 1.14.

Sargan, J.D. and Drettakis, E.G. (1974) 'Missing data in an autoregressive model', *International Economic Review*, **15**, 39–58. In E. Maasoumi (ed) *Contributions to Econometrics: John Denis Sargan*, Cambridge: Cambridge University Press, 1988. (Two volumes). Reprinted in E. Maasoumi (*op. cit.*) ch. 2.10.

Sargan, J.D. and Mehta, F. (1983) 'A generalization of the Durbin significance test and its application to dynamic specification', *Econometrica*, **51**, 1551–67.

Sargan, J.D. and Sylwestrowicz, J.D. (1976a) 'COMFAC: algorithm for Wald tests of common factors in lag polynomials', *Users' Manual*, London School of Economics.

Sargan, J.D. and Sylwestrowicz, J.A. (1976b) 'A comparison of alternative methods of numerical optimization in estimating simultaneous equation econometric models', London School of Economics Discussion Paper A3.

Sargent, T.J. (1977) 'Observations on improper methods of simulating and teaching Friedman's time series consumption model', *International Economic Review*, **18**, 445–62.

Sargent, T.J. (1978) 'Rational expectations, econometric exogeneity and consumption', *Journal of Political Economy*, **86**, 673–700.

Sargent, T.J. (1979) *Macro-economic Theory*, New York: Academic Press.

Sargent, T.J. (1981) 'Interpreting economic time series', *Journal of Political Economy*, **89**, 213–48.

Sargent, T.J. and Sims, C.A. (1977) 'Business cycle modelling without pretending to have too much *a priori* economic theory' in C.A. Sims (ed.), *New Methods in Business Cycle Research*, Minneapolis, MN: Federal Reserve Bank of Minneapolis.

Savin, N.E. (1973) 'Systems *k*-class estimators', *Econometrica*, **41**, 1125–36.

Savin, N.E. (1984) 'Multiple hypothesis testing', in Z. Griliches and M.D. Intriligator (eds), *Handbook of Econometrics*, vol. II, Amsterdam: North-Holland, ch. 14.

Sawa, T. (1973) 'Almost unbiased estimators in simultaneous equations systems', *International Economic Review*, **14**, 97–106.

Sawa, T. (1978) 'Information criteria for discriminating among alternative regression models', *Econometrica*, **46**, 1273–91.

Sawyer, K.R. (1983) 'Testing separate families of hypotheses: an information criterion', *Journal of the Royal Statistical Society*, B, **45**, 89–99.

Schumpeter, J. (1933) 'The common sense of econometrics', *Econometrica*, **1**, 5–12.

Shepherd, J.R., Evans, H.P. and Riley, C.J. (1975) 'The Treasury short-term forecasting model', in G.A. Renton (ed.), *Modelling the Economy*, London: Heinemann Educational, ch. 2.

Siegel, J.J. (1979) 'Inflation induced distortions in government and private saving statistics', *Review of Economics and Statistics*, **6**, 83–90.

Silver, J.L. and Wallace, T.D. (1980) 'The lag relationship between wholesale and consumer prices: an application of the Hatanaka–Wallace procedure', *Journal of Econometrics*, **12**, 375–88.

Simon, H.A. (1953) 'Causal ordering and identifiability', in W.C. Hood and T.C. Koopmans (eds), *Studies in Econometric Method*, Cowles Commission Monograph 14, New York: Wiley, ch. 3.

Sims, C.A. (1972a) 'The role of approximate prior restrictions in distributed lag estimation', *Journal of the American Statistical Association*, **67**, 169–75.

Sims, C.A. (1972b) 'Money, income and causality', *American Economic Review*, **62**, 540–52.

Sims, C.A. (1974a) 'Distributed lags', in M.D. Intriligator and D.A. Kendrick (eds), *Frontiers of Quantitative Economics*, vol. 2, Amsterdam: North-Holland, ch. 5.

Sims, C.A. (1974b) 'Seasonality in regression', *Journal of the American Statistical Association*, **69**, 618–26.

Sims, C.A. (ed.) (1977a) *New Methods in Business Cycle Research*, Minneapolis, MN: Federal Reserve Bank of Minneapolis.

Sims, C.A. (1977b) 'Exogeneity and causal ordering in macroeconomic models', in C.A. Sims (ed.), *New Methods in Business Cycle Research*, Minneapolis, MN: Federal Reserve Bank of Minneapolis, ch. 2.

Sims, C.A. (1980) 'Macroeconomics and reality', *Econometrica*, **48**, 1–48. Reprinted in C.W.J. Granger (ed.), *Modelling Economic Series*, Oxford: Clarendon Press, 1990, pp. 137–89.

Sowey, E.R. (1973) 'Stochastic simulation of macroeconomic models: methodology and interpretation', in A.A. Powell and R.A. Williams (eds), *Econometric Studies of Macro and Monetary Relations*, Amsterdam: North-Holland, ch. 8.

Spanos, A. (1979) 'Latent variables and disequilibrium models', Unpublished paper, Birkbeck College, London.

Spanos, A. (1986) *Statistical Foundations of Econometric Modelling*, Cambridge: Cambridge University Press.

Spanos, A. and Taylor, M. (1984) 'The monetary approach to the balance of payments: a critical appraisal of the empirical evidence', *Oxford Bulletin of Economics and Statistics*, **46**, 329–40.

Srivastava, V.K. (1971) 'Three-stage least-squares and generalized double k-class estimators: a mathematical relationship', *International Economic Review*, **12**, 312–16.

Stock, J.H. (1987) 'Asymptotic properties of least-squares estimators of co-integrating vectors', *Econometrica*, **55**, 1035–56.

Stone, R. (1951) *The Role of Measurement in Economics*, Cambridge: Cambridge University Press.

Stone, R. (1966) 'Spending and saving in relation to income and wealth', *L'industria*, **4**, 471–99.

Stone, R. (1973) 'Personal spending and saving in postwar Britain', in H.C. Bos, H. Linneman and P. de Wolff (eds), *Economic Structure and Development (essays in honour of Jan Tinbergen)*, Amsterdam: North-Holland.

Strotz, R.H. and Wold, H.O.A. (1960) 'Recursive versus non-recursive systems: an attempt at a synthesis', *Econometrica*, **28**, 417–21.

Swann, G.M.P. (1985) 'Uncertainty in regression estimates: the relative importance of sampling and non-sampling uncertainty', *Oxford Bulletin of Economics and Statistics*, **47**, 303–10.

Taylor, C.T. and Threadgold, A.R. (1979) '"Real" national savings and its sectoral composition', Bank of England Discussion Paper 6.

Teräsvirta, T. (1976) 'Effect of feedback on the distribution of the portmanteau test statistic', Manuscript, London School of Economics.

Theil, H. (1961) *Economic Forecasts and Policy*, 2nd. edn, Amsterdam: North-Holland.

Theil, H. (1964) *Optimal Decision Rules for Government and Industry*, Amsterdam: North-Holland.

Theil, H. (1971) *Principles of Econometrics*, London: Wiley.

Theil, H. and Boot, J.C.G. (1962) 'The final form of econometric equation systems', *Review of International Statistical Institute*, **30**, 162–70.

Thomas, J.J. (1977) 'Some problems in the use of Almon's technique in the estimation of distributed lags', *Empirical Economics*, **2**, 175–93.

Thomas, J.J. and Wallis, K.F. (1971) 'Seasonal variation in regression analysis', *Journal of the Royal Statistical Society*, A, **134**, 57–72.

Tillman, J.A. (1975) 'The power of the Durbin–Watson test', *Econometrica*, **43**, 959–74.

Tinbergen, J. (1939) *A Method and its Application to Investment Activity*, Statistical Testing of Business-Cycle Theories I, Geneva: League of Nations.

Tobin, J. (1969) 'A general equilibrium approach to monetary theory', *Journal of Money, Credit and Banking*, **1**, 15–29.

Townend, J.C. (1976) 'The personal saving ratio', *Bank of England Quarterly Bulletin*, **16**, 53–61.

Trivedi, P.K. (1970) 'Inventory behaviour in UK manufacturing 1956–67', *Review of Economic Studies*, **37**, 517–36.

Trivedi, P.K. (1973) 'Retail inventory investment behaviour', *Journal of Econometrics*, **1**, 61–80.

Trivedi, P.K. (1975) 'Time series analysis versus structural models: a case study of Canadian manufacturing behavior', *International Economic Review*, **16**, 587–608.

Trivedi, P.K. (1982) 'Distributed lags, aggregation and compounding: a suggested interpretation', Unpublished paper, Australian National University.

Trivedi, P.K. (1984) 'Uncertain prior information and distributed lag analysis', in D.F. Hendry and K.F. Wallis (eds), *Econometrics and Quantitative Economics*, Oxford: Basil Blackwell, 173–210.

Trivedi, P.K. and Pagan, A.R. (1979) 'Polynomial distributed lags: a unified treatment', *Economic Studies Quarterly*, **30**, 37–49.

Trundle, J. (1982) 'The demand for M1 in the UK', Bank of England Discussion Paper.

von Ungern-Sternberg, T. (1978) 'Real balance effects and negative income: the rise in the savings ratio', Unpublished paper, University of Bonn.

Vining, R. (1949a) 'Methodological issues in quantitative economics', *Review of Economics and Statistics*, **31**, 77–86.

Vining, R. (1949b) 'A rejoinder', *Review of Economics and Statistics*, **31**, 91–4.

Waelbroeck, J.K. (ed.) (1976) *The Models of Project LINK*, Amsterdam: North-Holland.

Wald, A. (1943) 'Tests of statistical hypotheses concerning several parameters when the number of observations is large', *Transactions of the American Mathematical Society*, **54**, 426–82.

Wall, K.D. (1976) 'FIML estimation of rational distributed lag structural form models', *Annals of Economic and Social Measurement*, **5**, 53–63.

Wall, K.D. (1980) 'Generalized expectations modelling in macroeconometrics', *Journal of Economic Dynamics and Control*, **2**, 161–84.

Wall, K.D. and Westcott, J.H. (1974) 'Macroeconomic modelling for control', *IEEE Transactions on Automatic Control*, **19**, 862–73.

Wall, K.D., Preston, A.J., Bray, J.W. and Peston, M.H. (1975) 'Estimates of a simple control model of the UK economy', in G.A. Renton (ed.), *Modelling the Economy*, London: Heinemann Educational, ch. 14.

Wallis, K.F. (1967) 'Lagged dependent variables and serially correlated errors: a reappraisal of three pass least squares', *Review of Economics and Statistics*, **69**, 555–67.

Wallis, K.F. (1969) 'Some recent developments in applied econometrics: dynamic models and simultaneous equation systems', *Journal of Economic Literature*, **7**, 771–96.

Wallis, K.F. (1972a) 'Testing for fourth order autocorrelation in quarterly regression equations', *Econometrica*, **40**, 617–36.

Wallis, K.F. (1972b) 'The efficiency of the two-step estimator', *Econometrica*, **40**, 769–70.

Wallis, K.F. (1974) 'Seasonal adjustment and relations between variables', *Journal of the American Statistical Association*, **69**, 18–31.

Wallis, K.F. (1977) 'Multiple time series analysis and the final form of econometric models', *Econometrica*, **45**, 1481–97.

Wallis, K.F. (1980) 'Econometric implications of the rational expectations hypothesis', *Econometrica*, **48**, 49–73.

Weintraub, E.R. (1979) *Microfoundations*, Cambridge: Cambridge University Press.

White, H. (1980a) 'Non-linear regression on cross-section data', *Econometrica*, **48**, 721–46.

White, H. (1980b) 'A heteroscedastic-consistent covariance matrix estimator and a direct test for heteroscedasticity', *Econometrica*, **48**, 817–38.

White, H. (1980c) 'Using least squares to approximate unknown regression functions', *International Economic Review*, **21**, 149–70.

White, H. (1990) 'A consistent model selection procedure based on M-testing', in C.W.J. Granger (ed.), *Modelling Economic Series*, Oxford: Clarendon Press, pp. 369–83.

Whittle, P. (1970) *Probability*, Harmondsworth: Penguin Library of University Mathematics.

Wickens, M.R. (1969) 'The consistency and efficiency of generalized least squares in simultaneous equation systems with autocorrelated errors', *Econometrica*, **37**, 651–9.

Wickens, M.R. (1982) 'The efficient estimation of econometric models with rational expectations', *Review of Economic Studies*, **49**, 55–67.

Wickens, M.R. and Molana, H. (1982) 'Stochastic life cycle theory with varying interest rates and prices', Discussion Paper 8224, University of Southampton (see *Economic Journal* (*Supplement*), **94**, (1983) 133–47).

Wiener, N. (1956) 'The theory of prediction', in E.F. Beckenbach (ed.), *Modern Mathematics for Engineers*, Series 1, New York: McGraw-Hill, ch. 8.

Williams, R.A. (1972) 'Demand for consumer durables: stock adjustment models and alternative specifications of stock depletion', *Review of Economic Studies*, **39**, 281–95.

Wilson, K.G. (1979) 'Problems in physics with many scales of length', *Scientific American*, **241**, 140–57.

Wold, H.O. (1959) 'Ends and means in econometric model building', in U. Grenander (ed.), *Probability and Statistics*, New York: Wiley, pp. 355-64.

Wold, H.O. (1969) 'Econometrics as pioneering in non-experimental model building', *Econometrica*, **37**, 369-81.

Wold, H.O. and Jureen, L. (1955) *Demand Analysis: A Study in Econometrics*, 2nd edn, New York: Wiley.

Wolfe, M.A. (1978) *Numerical Methods for Unconstrained Optimization*, New York: Van Nostrand Reinhold.

Working, E.J. (1927) 'What do statistical demand curves show?', *Quarterly Journal of Economics*, **41**, 212-35.

Worrall, J. and Currie, G. (eds) (1978) *The Methodology of Scientific Research Programmes*, vol. 1, *Imre Lakatos*, Cambridge: Cambridge University Press.

Worswick, G.D.N. (1972) 'Is progress in economic science possible?', *Economic Journal*, **82**, 73-86.

Wu, D.M. (1973) 'Alternative tests of independence between stochastic regressors and disturbances', *Econometrica*, **41**, 733-50.

Yeo, J.S. (1978) 'Multicollinearity and distributed lags', Unpublished paper, London School of Economics.

Yule, G.U. (1926) 'Why do we sometimes get nonsense-correlations between time-series? A study in sampling and the nature of time series', *Journal of the Royal Statistical Society*, **89**, 1-64.

Zellner, A. (1962) 'An efficient method of estimating seemingly unrelated regressions and tests for aggregation bias', *Journal of the American Statistical Association*, **57**, 348-68.

Zellner, A. (1971) *An Introduction to Bayesian Inference in Econometrics*, New York: Wiley.

Zellner, A. (1979a) 'Statistical analysis of econometric models', *Journal of the American Statistical Association*, **74**, 628-43.

Zellner, A. (1979b) 'Causality and econometrics', in K. Brunner and A.H. Meltzer (eds), *Three Aspects of Policy and Policymaking*, Amsterdam: North-Holland, pp. 9-54.

Zellner, A. and Palm, F. (1974) 'Time series analysis and simultaneous equation econometric models', *Journal of Econometrics*, **2**, 17-54.

Zellner, A. and Theil, H. (1962) 'Three-stage least-squares: simultaneous estimation of simultaneous equations', *Econometrica*, **30**, 54-78.

Zellner, A., Huang, D.S. and Chau, L.C. (1965) 'Further analysis of the short-run consumption function with emphasis on the role of liquid assets', *Econometrica*, **33**, 571-81.

Bibliography

'Survey of student income and expenditure at Aberdeen University, 1963-64 and 1964-65', *Scottish Journal of Political Economy*, **13** (1966) 363-76.

'Maximum likelihood estimation of systems of simultaneous regression equations with errors generated by a vector autoregressive process', *International Economic Review*, **12** (1971) 257-72. 'Correction' in **15**, 260.

'Maximum likelihood estimation of difference equations with moving-average errors: a simulation study', *Review of Economic Studies*, **32** (1972) 117-45 (with P.K. Trivedi).

'On asymptotic theory and finite sample experiments', *Economica*, **40** (1973) 210-17.

'Monte Carlo methodology and the small sample behaviour of ordinary and two-stage least-squares', *Journal of Econometrics*, **2** (1974) 151-74 (with R.W. Harrison).

'Stochastic specification in an aggregate demand model of the United Kingdom', *Econometrica*, **42** (1974) 559-78.

'The consequences of mis-specification of dynamic structure, autocorrelation and simultaneity in a simple model with an application to the demand for imports', in G.A. Renton (ed.), *Modelling the Economy*, London: Heinemann, 1975, ch. 11.

'The structure of simultaneous equations estimators', *Journal of Econometrics*, **4** (1976) 51-88.

'Estimating systems of dynamic reduced form equations with vector autoregressive errors', *International Economic Review*, **17** (1976) 463-71 (with A.R. Tremayne).

'Testing dynamic specification in small simultaneous systems: an application to a model of building society behaviour in the United Kingdom', in M.D. Intriligator (ed.), *Frontiers of Quantitative Economics*, vol. III, Amsterdam: North-Holland, 1977, ch. 8c (with G.J. Anderson).

'On the time series approach to econometric model building', in C.A. Sims (ed.), *New Methods in Business Cycle Research*, Minneapolis, MN: Federal Reserve Bank of Minneapolis, 1977, pp. 183-202.

'The properties of autoregressive instrumental variables estimators in dynamic systems', *Econometrica*, **45** (1977) 969-90 (with F. Srba).

'Econometric modelling of the aggregate time series relationship between consumers' expenditure and income in the United Kingdom', *Economic Journal*, **88** (1978) 661-92 (with J.E.H. Davidson, F. Srba and S. Yeo).

'Serial correlation as a convenient simplification, not a nuisance: a comment on a study of the demand for money by the Bank of England', *Economic Journal*, **88** (1978) 549–63 (with G.E. Mizon).

'Predictive failure and econometric modelling in macroeconomics: the transactions demand for money', in P. Ormerod (ed.), *Economic Modelling*, London: Heinemann, 1979, ch. 9.

'The behaviour of inconsistent instrumental variables estimators in dynamic systems with autocorrelated errors', *Journal of Econometrics*, **9** (1979) 295–314.

'Econometrics: alchemy or science?', *Economica*, **47** (1980) 387–406.

'An empirical application and Monte Carlo analysis of tests of dynamic specification', *Review of Economic Studies*, **49** (1980) 21–45 (with G.E. Mizon).

'AUTOREG: a computer program library for dynamic econometric models with auto-regressive errors', *Journal of Econometrics*, **12** (1980) 85–102 (with F. Srba).

'Liquidity and inflation effects on consumers' expenditure', in A.S. Deaton (ed.), *Essays in the Theory and Measurement of Consumers' Behaviour*, Cambridge: Cambridge University Press, 1981, ch. 9 (with T. von Ungern-Sternberg).

'Interpreting econometric evidence: the consumption function in the United Kingdom', *European Economic Review*, **16** (1981) 177–92 (with J.E.H. Davidson).

'Econometric evidence in the appraisal of UK monetary policy', in *The Third Report of the Select Committee of the House of Commons on the Treasury and Civil Service*, vol. 3, London: HMSO, 1981, pp. 1–21.

'The role of econometrics in macroeconomic analysis', *UK Economic Prospect*, **3** (1982) 26–38.

'A comment on "Econometric disequilibrium models"', *Econometric Reviews*, **1**, 65–70.

'A reply to Professors Maasoumi and Phillips', *Journal of Econometrics*, **19** (1982) 203–13.

'On the formulation of empirical models in dynamic econometrics', *Journal of Econometrics*, **20** (1982) 3–33 (with J.-F. Richard). Reprinted in C.W.J. Granger (ed.), *Modelling Economic Series*, Oxford: Clarendon Press, 1990, pp. 304–34.

'Exogeneity', *Econometrica*, **51** (1983) 277–304 (with R.F. Engle and J.-F. Richard).

'The econometric analysis of economic time series', *International Statistical Review*, **51** (1983) 111–63 (with J.-F. Richard).

'A comment on "Model Specification Tests Against Non-Nested Alternatives"', *Econometric Reviews*, **2** (1983) 111–14.

'Econometric modelling: the consumption function in retrospect', *Scottish Journal of Political Economy*, **30** (1983) 193–220.

'On Keynesian model building and the rational expectations critique: a question of method-ology', *Cambridge Journal of Economics*, **7** (1983) 69–75.

'Assertion without empirical basis: an econometric appraisal of "Monetary trends in . . . the United Kingdom" by Milton Friedman and Anna Schwartz', Bank of England Academic Panel Paper 22, 1983 (with N.R. Ericsson).

'On High and Low R^2 Contributions', *Oxford Bulletin of Economics and Statistics*, **45** (1983) 313–16 (with R.C. Marshall).

'Dynamic specification', in Z. Griliches and M.D. Intriligator (eds), *The Handbook of Econometrics*, Amsterdam: North-Holland, 1984, ch. 18 (with A.R. Pagan and J.D. Sargan).

'Monte Carlo experimentation in econometrics', in Z. Griliches and M.D. Intriligator (eds), *The Handbook of Econometrics*, Amsterdam: North-Holland, 1984, ch. 16.

'An econometric model of United Kingdom building societies', *Oxford Bulletin of Economics and Statistics*, **46** (1984) 185–210 (with G.J. Anderson).

Econometrics and Quantitative Economics, Oxford: Basil Blackwell, 1984 (edited with K.F. Wallis).

'Econometric modelling of house prices in the United Kingdom', in D.F. Hendry and K.F.

Wallis (eds), *Econometrics and Quantitative Economics*, Oxford: Basil Blackwell 1984, ch. 8.

'Present position and potential developments: some personal views on time-series econometrics', *Journal of the Royal Statistical Society*, A, **147** (1984) 327–39.

'Conditional econometric modelling: an application to new house prices in the United Kingdom', in A.C. Atkinson and S. Fienberg (eds), *A Celebration of Statistics*, New York: Springer-Verlag, 1985, ch. 11 (with N.R. Ericsson).

'Small sample properties of ARCH estimators and tests', *Canadian Journal of Economics*, **18** (1985) 66–93 (with R.F. Engle and D. Trumble).

'Monetary economic myth and econometric reality', *Oxford Review of Economic Policy*, **1** (1985) 72–84.

'An Excursion into Conditional Variance land', *Econometric Reviews*, **5** (1986), 63–69.

'Using PC-GIVE in econometrics teaching', *Oxford Bulletin of Economics and Statistics*, **48**, 1 (1986) 87–98.

'The role of prediction in evaluating econometric models', *Proceedings of the Royal Society of London*, A, **407** (1986) 25–34.

'Econometric evaluation of linear macro-economic models', *Review of Economic Studies*, **53**, 4 (1986) 671–90 (with Y.Y. Chong). Reprinted in C.W.J. Granger (ed.), *Modelling Economic Series*, Oxford: Clarendon Press 1990, pp. 384–410.

'Econometric modelling with cointegrated variables: an overview', *Oxford Bulletin of Economics and Statistics*, Special Issue, **48**, 3 (1986) 201–12. Reprinted in R.F. Engle and C.W.J. Granger (eds), *Long-Run Economic Relationships*, Oxford: Oxford University Press, 1991, 51–63.

'Exploring equilibrium relationships in econometrics through static models: some Monte Carlo evidence', *Oxford Bulletin of Economics and Statistics*, Special Issue, **48**, 3 (1986) 253–77 (with A. Banerjee, J.J. Dolado and G.W. Smith).

'Empirical modelling in dynamic econometrics: the new-construction sector', *Applied Mathematics and Computation*, **20** (1986) 201–36.

'Econometric methodology: a personal perspective', in T.F. Bewley (ed.), *Advances in Econometrics*, Cambridge: Cambridge University Press, 1987, ch. 10.

'Monte Carlo experimentation using PC-NAIVE', in T. Fomby and G.F. Rhodes (eds), *Advances in Econometrics*, vol. 6, Greenwich, CT: JAI Press, 1987, pp. 91–125 (with A.J. Neale).

'Econometric analysis of small linear systems using PC-FIML', *Journal of Econometrics*, **38** (1988) 203–26 (with A.J. Neale and F. Srba).

'The encompassing implications of feedback versus feedforward mechanisms in econometrics', *Oxford Economic Papers*, **40** (1988) 132–49.

'Interpreting long-run equilibrium solutions in conventional macro models: a comment', *Economic Journal*, **98** (1988) 808–17 (with A.J. Neale).

'Some foreign observations on macro-economic model evaluation activities at INSEE', in *Groupes d'Etudes Macroeconometriques Concertées*, Paris: INSEE, 1988, pp. 71–106.

'Econometrics in action', *Empirica*, **2/87** (1988) 135–56.

'Discrete samples and moving sums in stationary stochastic processes: corrigendum', *Journal of the American Statistical Association*, **83** (1988) 581 (with J. Campos and N.R. Ericsson).

'Encompassing', *National Institute Economic Review*, **125** (1988) 88–92.

PC-GIVE: An Interactive Econometric Modelling System, Oxford: Institute of Economics and Statistics, University of Oxford, 1989.

'A re-analysis of confluence analysis', *Oxford Economic Papers*, **41** (1989) 35–52 (with M.S. Morgan). Reprinted in N. de Marchi and C.L. Gilbert (eds), *History and Methodology of Econometrics*, Oxford: Clarendon Press, 1989.

'Comment on "Intertemporal consumer behaviour under structural changes in income"', *Econometric Reviews*, **8** (1989) 111–21.

'The contributions to econometrics in Trygve Haavelmo's *The Probability Approach in Econometrics'*, *Sosialøkonomen*, **11** (1989) 12–17 (with N.R. Ericsson and A. Spanos).

'Procrustean econometrics', in C.W.J. Granger (ed.), *Modelling Economic Series*, Oxford: Clarendon Press, 1990, pp. 121–36 (with G.E. Mizon).

'Recent developments in the theory of encompassing', in B. Cornet and H. Tulkens (eds), *Contributions to Operations Research and Econometrics. The XXth Anniversary of CORE*. Cambridge, MA: MIT Press, 1989, ch. 12 (with J.-F. Richard).

'The ET dialogue: a conversation on econometric methodology'. *Econometric Theory*, **6** (1990), 171–261 (with E.E. Leamer and D.J. Poirier).

'An analogue model of phase-averaging procedures', *Journal of Econometrics*, **43** (1990), 275–92 (with J. Campos and N.R. Ericsson).

'The econometrics of DHSY', in D. Winch and J.D. Hey (eds), *A Century of Economics*, Oxford: Basil Blackwell, 1990, 298–334 (with J.N.J. Muellbauer and A. Murphy).

'An econometric analysis of UK money demand in *Monetary Trends in the United States and the United Kingdom* by Milton Friedman and Anna J. Schwartz'. *American Economic Review*, **81** (1991), 8–38 (with N.R. Ericsson).

'A Monte Carlo study of the effects of structural breaks on unit root tests' in P. Hackl and A.H. Westlund (eds), *Economic Structural Change: Analysis and Forecasting*, Berlin: Springer-Verlag, 1991, 95–119 (with A.J. Neale).

'Using PC-NAIVE in teaching econometrics', *Oxford Bulletin of Economics and Statistics*, **53** (1991), 199–223.

PC-NAIVE: An Interactive Program for Monte Carlo Experimentation in Econometrics, Oxford: Institute of Economics and Statistics, University of Oxford, 1991 (with A.J. Neale and N.R. Ericsson).

'Modeling the demand for narrow money in the United Kingdom and the United States', *European Economic Review*, **35** (1991), 833–881 (with N.R. Ericsson).

'Likelihood evaluation for dynamic latent variables models', in H.M. Amman, D.A. Belsley and L.F. Pau (eds), *Computational Economics and Econometrics*, Dordrecht: Kluwer, 1991, 3–17 (with J.-F. Richard).

'The demand for M1 in the USA, 1960–1988', *Review of Economic Studies*, **59** (1992), 25–61 (with Y. Baba and R.M. Starr).

'An econometric analysis of TV advertising expenditure in the United Kingdom', *Journal of Policy Modeling*, **14** (1992), 281–311.

Econometrics: Alchemy or Science? Essays in Econometric Methodology. Oxford: Blackwell Publishers, 1992.

Co-integration, Error Correction and the Econometric Analysis of Non-Stationary Data, Oxford: Oxford University Press, 1992 (with A. Banerjee, J.J. Dolado and J.W. Galbraith).

'Testing integration and cointegration: An overview', *Oxford Bulletin of Economics and Statistics*, **54** (1992), 225–255 (with A. Banerjee).

PcGive7: An Interactive Econometric Modelling System. Oxford: Institute of Economics and Statistics, University of Oxford, 1992 (with J.A. Doornik).

'Assessing empirical evidence in macro-econometrics with an application to consumers' expenditure in France', in A. Vercelli and N. Dimitri (eds), *Macroeconomics: A Survey of Research Strategies*, Oxford: Oxford University Press, forthcoming.

'Testing the Lucas' critique: A review', forthcoming *Econometric Reviews* (with C. Favero).

'Testing super exogeneity and invariance in regression equations', forthcoming *Journal of Econometrics* (with R.F. Engle).

'On the limitations of comparing mean square forecast errors', forthcoming *Journal of Forecasting* (with M.P. Clements).

'Evaluating dynamic econometric models by encompassing the VAR', in P.C.B. Philips (ed.), *Models, Methods and Applications of Econometrics*, Oxford: Blackwell Publishers, forthcoming (with G.E. Mizon).

Lectures on Econometric Methodology, Oxford: Oxford University Press, forthcoming.

Classic Readings in the Foundations of Econometric Analysis, Cambridge: Cambridge University Press, forthcoming (with M.S. Morgan).

Index

The index cross references both the present volume and the original article. The first (and sometimes only) page reference is to the present page; the reference in parentheses then records the chapter and page numbers of the original publication in the form (*a:b*), where *b* is the page of the paper now published as chapter *a*. '*t*' stands for table.